'The essays of this handbook dissect the trends towards ⟨...⟩ Asia. Even India, long a poster boy of "third world" dem⟨...⟩ with its neighbours in a "non-democratic regime converg⟨...⟩ confirming Huntington's deterministic pessimism rega⟨...⟩ jumping on to wide-eyed bushy-tailed advocacy, authors of this important volume⟨...⟩ third trajectory, based on fine-grained empirical analysis and empathy with their subject, within a comparative framework. This handbook should become an indispensable tool for the people of South Asia, as well as for outsiders looking in.'

Subrata Mitra, *Emeritus Professor of Political Science at Heidelberg University, and Adjunct Professor, Dublin City University.*

'Situating South Asia's democratic trends in a broad historical context, this wide-ranging volume addresses a crucial, timely and policy-relevant question: why is democracy faltering in the world's most populous region? While authoritarianism was the twentieth century's historical norm, recent democratic improvements have faltered and even reversed. Assembling the best regional experts, this book exposes the proximate cause of regional democratic backsliding – leaders invoking cultural identities to legitimate non-democratic behaviour – while underscoring its deeper and more enduring institutional roots. It will serve as indispensable reading for regional experts, democracy watchers and policymakers alike.'

Maya Tudor, *Associate Professor, Blavatnik School of Government, Fellow, St Hilda's College, Oxford University.*

'Studies of democratic decline in South Asia tend to focus on just one country. This excellent and timely volume brings together leading scholars of Indian, Pakistani, Sri Lankan and Bangladeshi politics and society to explore, across a range of issues, what's similar and what's different about recent democratic weakening in the region. Indispensable.'

Steven I. Wilkinson, *Henry R. Luce Director, MacMillan Center, Nilekani Professor of India and South Asian Studies, Department of Political Science, Yale University.*

ROUTLEDGE HANDBOOK OF AUTOCRATIZATION IN SOUTH ASIA

This handbook offers a comprehensive analysis of the processes and actors contributing to autocratization in South Asia. It provides an enhanced understanding of the interconnectedness of the different states in the region, and how that may be related to autocratization.

The book analyzes issues of state power, the support for political parties, questions relating to economic actors and sustainable economic development, the role of civil society, questions of equality and political culture, political mobilization, the role of education and the media, as well as topical issues such as the Covid pandemic, environmental issues, migration, and military and international security. Structured in five sections, contributions by international experts describe and explain outcomes at the national level in India, Pakistan, Bangladesh and Sri Lanka. The final section analyzes conditions for democracy and autocratization and how they are affected by the interplay of political forces at the international level in this region.

- India – building an ethnic state?
- Pakistan – the decline of civil liberties
- Bangladesh – towards one-party rule
- Sri Lanka – the resilience of the ethnic state
- How to comprehend autocratization in South Asia – three broad perspectives

This innovative handbook is the first to describe and to explain ongoing trends of autocratization in South Asia, demonstrating that drivers of political change also work across boundaries. It is an important reference work for students and researchers of South Asian Studies, Asian Studies, Area Studies and Political Science.

Sten Widmalm is Professor in Political Science at the Department of Government, Uppsala University, Sweden. He has carried out extensive research on crisis management, political tolerance, democracy and conflicts in a global comparative perspective. His recent publications include *Political Tolerance in the Global South – Images from India, Pakistan and Uganda* (Routledge, 2016).

ROUTLEDGE HANDBOOK OF AUTOCRATIZATION IN SOUTH ASIA

Edited by Sten Widmalm

Routledge
Taylor & Francis Group

LONDON AND NEW YORK

Cover image: Election campaign 1991, photo by Sten Widmalm

First published 2022
by Routledge
2 Park Square, Milton Park, Abingdon, Oxon OX14 4RN

and by Routledge
605 Third Avenue, New York, NY 10158

Routledge is an imprint of the Taylor & Francis Group, an informa business

British Library Cataloguing-in-Publication Data
A catalogue record for this book is available from the British Library

Library of Congress Cataloging-in-Publication Data
Names: Widmalm, Sten, editor.
Title: Routledge handbook of autocratization in South Asia / edited by Sten Widmalm.
Other titles: Handbook of autocratization in South Asia
Description: First Edition. | New York : Routledge, 2022. |
Includes bibliographical references and index.
Identifiers: LCCN 2021031304 | ISBN 9780367486747 (Hardback) |
ISBN 9781032151021 (Paperback) | ISBN 9781003042211 (eBook)
Subjects: LCSH: Authoritarianism–Asia, South.
Classification: LCC JC480 .R685 2022 | DDC 320.53–dc23/eng/20211012
LC record available at https://lccn.loc.gov/2021031304

ISBN: 978-0-367-48674-7 (hbk)
ISBN: 978-1-03-215102-1 (pbk)
ISBN: 978-1-00-304221-1 (ebk)

DOI: 10.4324/9781003042211

Typeset in Bembo
by Newgen Publishing UK

CONTENTS

ILLUSTRATIONS

Table

Figures

CONTRIBUTORS

Editor

Sten Widmalm is Professor in political science at the Department of Government, Uppsala University, Sweden. He has carried out extensive research on crisis management, political tolerance, democracy and conflicts in a global comparative perspective. Widmalm is one of the co-authors of 'Civil Protection in the European Union' (2019), and the author of *Political Tolerance in the Global South – Images from India, Pakistan and Uganda* (2016, Routledge), *Decentralisation, Corruption and Social Capital – from India to the West* (2008) and *Kashmir in Comparative Perspective – Democracy and Violent Separatism in India* (2006).

Editorial Board

Amrita Basu, Amherst College, USA
Atul Kohli, Princeton University, USA
Carolin Rapp, University of Copenhagen, Denmark
Arild Engelsen Ruud, University of Oslo, Norway
Ian Talbot, University of Southampton, UK

Contributors

Maren Aase is a research fellow at the Centre for Development and the Environment (SUM) at the University of Oslo and a political scientist by training. Aase's work focuses on the politics of disaster risk governance, crisis prevention and emergency response in the regional context of South Asia. She has recently published on the politics of cyclone relief and aid beneficiary lists in *Disasters* (2020).

Syed Khaled Ahsan is a senior public sector specialist at the World Bank. His research interests are in decentralization/local governance and political economy of public-sector reforms. His major publications are: 'Transition to Federalism in Nepal', *Case Studies in Business and*

Management (2020) and (with S. Hasan and N. N. Imran) 'Bangladesh: Political Economy of Right to Information' World Bank (2020).

Amrita Basu the Paino Professor of Political Science and Sexuality, Women's and Gender Studies, at Amherst College, studies women's activism, feminist movements and religious nationalism in South Asia. Her most recent book, *Violent Conjunctures in Democratic India* (2015), explores when and why Hindu nationalists engage in violence against religious minorities. She is the author of *Two Faces of Protest: Contrasting Modes of Women's Activism in India* (1992) and the editor or co-editor of a number of books, including *Women's Movements in the Global Era: The Power of Local Feminisms* (2010, 2016), *Beyond Exceptionalism: Violence, Religion, and Democracy in India* (2006), *Localizing Knowledge In a Globalizing World* (2002), *Appropriating Gender: Women's Activism and Politicized Religion in South Asia* (1998), *Community Conflicts and the State in India* (1997) and *Women, Gender and Religious Nationalism in India* (forthcoming).

Moeen Cheema is an associate professor and Australian Research Council DECRA Fellow at the ANU College of Law. He has extensive experience of research, teaching and consultancy in the fields of comparative public law, criminal justice reform and legal developments in Pakistan. He is especially interested in constitutional politics and judicial review, intersection of state and Islamic law, and post-conflict state-building. Moeen completed a PhD in Law from the ANU and has an LLM from Harvard.

Soundarya Chidambaram is an assistant professor of political science at Bucknell University. She specializes in comparative politics with a focus on India and South Asia. Her research interests include urban politics, governance, and civil society. Dr Chidambaram holds a PhD in political science from Ohio State University. Her major publications include: 'How do institutions and infrastructure affect mobilization around public toilets vs. piped water? Examining intra-slum patterns of collective action in Delhi, India', *World Development* (2020); 'Play in the States: the Indian Voter's 2014 Mandate', *Economic & Political Weekly* (2014) and 'The "Right" Kind of Welfare: Seva vs. Patronage in South India's Urban Slums', *Asian Survey* (2012).

Neil DeVotta is a professor in politics and international affairs at Wake Forest University. His research interests include Asian security and politics, ethnoreligious nationalism, ethnic conflict resolution, and democratic transition and consolidation. He is the author of *Blowback: Linguistic Nationalism, Institutional Decay, and Ethnic Conflict in Sri Lanka* and editor of *Understanding Contemporary India* (2004) and *An Introduction to South Asian Politics* (2015) in addition to authoring numerous articles. He has also consulted for a number of organizations, including the United States Agency for International Development, Freedom House, Bertelsmann Stiftung, and Global Center for Pluralism.

Anwesha Dutta is a senior researcher at the Chr. Michelsen Institute in Bergen, Norway. Using political ecology and conservation social sciences approaches, she works at the intersection between forest and biodiversity conservation and political violence in India. She is interested in processes of green militarization, local institutions, extraction and governance of natural resources and park–people relationships using a social-ecological lens. She is currently the principal investigator for a project that explores the displacement-environment nexus between refugees and their (socio) ecological environments. She has authored several articles on themes related to resource extraction, green militarization and biodiversity conservation.

Shelley Feldman is currently Senior Fellow, Max-Weber-Kolleg für kultur- und sozialwissenschaftliche Studien, Universität Erfurt, Germany. Previously she was International Professor (1987-2016) at Cornell University and Visiting Professor at Binghamton and Bochum University. A long-term scholar of Bangladesh, she is currently completing a manuscript on in-situ displacement and the challenges of plural social formations.

Øivind Fuglerud is Professor of Social Anthropology at the Museum of Cultural History, University of Oslo, where he is keeper of the South Asia ethnographic collections. He has for 35 years conducted research on South Asia with a particular focus on Sri Lanka. His research interests include nationalism, political violence, migration, and diaspora formations. He has published a number of works on the civil war in Sri Lanka and its consequences, including *Life on the Outside: The Tamil Diaspora and Long-Distance Nationalism* (1999).

Šumit Ganguly is a Distinguished Professor of Political Science and holds the Tagore Chair in Indian Cultures and Civilizations at Indiana University, Bloomington. A specialist on the contemporary domestic and international politics of South Asia, he is the author, co-author, editor, or co-editor of more than 20 books on the region. He is currently editing (with Eswaran Sridharan) *The Oxford Handbook of Indian Politics*. Professor Ganguly is a member of the Council on Foreign Relations and a Fellow of the American Academy of Arts and Sciences.

Sandra Grahn is an assistant researcher at the V-Dem Institute, Department of Political Science at the University of Gothenburg. She works primarily on issues of autocratization, polarization, and populism.

Asheque Haque has been a politics and security researcher covering the South Asian region for the past 15 years. In Bangladesh, he has worked as a countering violent extremism professional with state and non-state actors. He has also collaborated with several universities and institutes, and published research reports on violent extremism in South Asia. He holds a master's degree in South Asia and Global Security from King's College, London. His areas of interest include violent extremism, identity politics, human rights and digital spaces.

Zoya Hasan is Professor Emerita, Jawaharlal Nehru University and former Dean of the School of Social Sciences, JNU. She is the author/editor of 18 books, including most recently Congress *After Indira: Policy, Power Political Change (1984-2009); Politics of Inclusion: Caste, Minority and Affirmative Action; Agitation to Legislation: Negotiating Equity and Justice in India*. Her forthcoming book is titled: *Ideology and Organization in Indian Politics: Rising Polarisation and the Decline of the Congress Party (2009-2019)*.

Patrick Heller is Lyn Crost Professor of Social Sciences and Professor of Sociology and International Studies, Brown University. He is the author of *The Labor of Development: Workers in the Transformation of Capitalism in Kerala, India* (1999) and co-author of *Social Democracy and the Global Periphery* (2006), *Bootstrapping Democracy: Transforming Local Governance and Civil Society in Brazil* (2011) and co-edited with Vijayendra Rao, *Deliberation and Development: Rethinking the Role of Voice and Collective Action in Unequal Societies* (2015). He has published articles on urbanization, comparative democracy, social movements, development policy, racial segregation, civil society and state transformation. His most recent project, 'Cities of Delhi', conducted in collaboration with the Centre for Policy Research in India, explores the dynamics of governance and social exclusion in India's capital city.

Sandya Hewamanne is Professor of Sociology at the University of Essex. She is the author of *Stitching Identities in a Free Trade Zone: Gender and Politics in Sri Lanka* (2008), *Sri Lanka's Global Factory Workers: (Un)Disciplined Desires and Sexual Struggles in a Post-Colonial Society* (2016) and *Re-stitching Identities in Rural Sri Lanka: Neoliberalism, Gender and Politics of Contentment* (2020). She has published numerous journal articles on labour and human rights, gender, and economic anthropology. She is the Founder and Director of IMPACT-Global Work, a non-profit promoting positive policy outcomes for global workers.

Christophe Jaffrelot is senior research fellow at CERI-Sciences Po/CNRS, France, Professor of Indian Politics and Sociology at the King's India Institute (London), UK, Non-Resident Fellow at the Carnegie Endowment for International Peace, USA, and President of the French Political Science Association. Among his recent publications are (as a co-editor with A. Kohli and K. Murali) *Business and Politics in India* (2019), (as a co-editor with A. Chatterji and T. B. Hansen) *The Majoritarian State. How Hindu Nationalism is Changing India* (2019) and as co-author with Pratinav Anil, *India's First Dictatorship. The Emergency, 1975–77* (2020). His most recent book is *Modi's India. Hindu Nationalism and the Rise of Ethnic Democracy* (2021).

Devin K. Joshi is an associate professor of political science in the School of Social Sciences at Singapore Management University. His research interests include ideology, political representation, and human development in India and China. His recent articles have appeared in *International Studies Quarterly, Journal of Contemporary Asia*, and *World Development*.

Johan Lagerkvist is Professor of Chinese Language and Culture and Director of Stockholm Center for Global Asia at Stockholm University, Sweden. His research interests concern state–society relations in the People's Republic of China (PRC) and Chinese foreign policy, particularly China's relations with developing countries in the Global South.

Marc Lanteigne is an associate professor at UiT: The Arctic University of Norway (Tromsø), specializing in Chinese and East Asian politics and foreign policy. He has taught international relations and comparative politics in Canada, China, New Zealand and the United Kingdom. Among his books are *China and International Institutions: Alternate Paths to Global Power* and *Chinese Foreign Policy: An Introduction*. He is co-editor of books including *China's Evolving Approach to Peacekeeping*, and has written numerous articles on China's politics, economics, and security thinking, including cross-regional diplomacy and strategic cooperation.

David G. Lewis is Associate Professor in International Relations at the University of Exeter. He previously held posts at the Department of Peace Studies, the University of Bradford, and with the International Crisis Group in Central Asia and in Sri Lanka. His current research focuses on the rise of illiberalism in global politics and comparative authoritarianism. His most recent book is *Russia's New Authoritarianism: Putin and the Politics of Order* (2020).

Staffan I. Lindberg is Professor of Political Science and Director of the university-wide research infrastructure V-Dem Institute at the University of Gothenburg, founding Principal Investigator of *Varieties of Democracy* (V-Dem), founding director of the national research infrastructure DEMSCORE, Wallenberg Academy Fellow, author of *Democracy and Elections in*

Africa as well as other books and over 50 articles on issues such as democracy, elections, democratization, autocratization, accountability, clientelism, sequence analysis methods, women's representation, and voting behaviour. Lindberg also has extensive experience as consultant on development and democracy, and as advisor to international organizations.

Dinoo Anna Mathew is affiliated with the Department of Government, Uppsala University, Sweden. Her doctoral degree is in peace and conflict studies from the University for Peace, Costa Rica and her current research interests are intersections of gender, caste and class, inclusive peace building, democracy and governance. Her recent publication is titled 'Criticality of the Local in Evolving Peaceful and Inclusive Society in Kerala', *Social Action* (2019).

Farah Mihlar is a Sri Lankan/British academic and human rights activist. She lectures in conflict studies, human rights and transitional justice at the University of Exeter, UK. Her PhD was on religious changes among Sri Lanka's minority Muslim population, and her current research is on post-conflict justice for minority groups in Sri Lanka. Prior to becoming an academic she had a long-standing career in international human rights working for the UN and INGOs.

Kenneth Bo Nielsen is associate professor of social anthropology at the University of Oslo. He works on the political economy of development in India, and is particularly interested in land conflicts and dispossession, social movements, and popular politics. He is the author of *Land Dispossession and Everyday Politics in Rural Eastern India* (2018), and co-editor of numerous books on various aspects on Indian democracy and politics, including *Social Movements and the State in India: Deepening Democracy?* (2016) and *Indian Democracy: Origins, Trajectories, Contestations* (2019).

Alf Gunvald Nilsen is a professor of sociology at the University of Pretoria. His research focuses on social movements and the political economy of democracy and development in the global South, with a particular focus on India. He is the author of *Dispossession and Resistance in India: The River and the Rage* (2010) and *Adivasis and the State: Subalternity and Citizenship in India's Bhil Heartland* (2019). He is also the co-editor of numerous books, including *New Subaltern Politics: Reconceptualizing Hegemony and Resistance in Contemporary India* (2015), *Social Movements and the State in India: Deepening Democracy?* (2016), and *Indian Democracy: Origins, Trajectories, Contestations* (2019).

Ali Riaz is Distinguished Professor of Political Science at Illinois State University and a Nonresident Senior Fellow of Atlantic Council. He was the chair of the Department of Politics and Government (2007–2017), and Thomas E Eimermann Professor (2018–2020). Riaz previously taught at universities in Bangladesh, England, and South Carolina, worked as a Broadcast Journalist at the British Broadcasting Service (BBC) in London, and served as a public policy scholar at the Woodrow Wilson International Center for Scholars at Washington DC. His primary areas of interest are democratization, violent extremism, political Islam, South Asian politics, and Bangladeshi politics. Riaz's recent publications include *Election in A Hybrid Regime: Explaining the 2018 Bangladeshi Election* (2019). He has edited *Religion and Politics in South Asia* (second edition, 2021), and co-edited *Political Violence in South Asia* (2019) and *Routledge Handbook of Contemporary Bangladesh* (2016).

Arild Engelsen Ruud (PhD LSE) is Professor of South Asia Studies at the University of Oslo, Norway. He writes on issues of democracy and politics in South Asia, specifically West Bengal and Bangladesh. He is author of *Poetics of Village Politics* (2004) on West Bengal's rural communism, co-editor of *Power and Influence in India* (2013), *South Asian Sovereignty: The Conundrum of Worldly Power* (2019), *Outrage: The Rise of Religious Offence in Contemporary South Asia* (2019), and *Masks of Authoritarianism: Hegemony, power and public life in Bangladesh* (forthcoming), and co-author of *Mafia Raj: The Rule of Bosses in South Asia* (2018).

Rizvan Saeed is a social science researcher working on issues of masculinity, gender, minority rights and online violent extremism. He is associated with the South Asian Research and Resource Centre (SARRC) Pakistan as Senior Researcher.

Ahmad Salim is a prolific writer, archivist and co-founder of research institute 'South Asian Research and Resource Centre'. He has been honoured with Pakistan's Presidential Pride of Performance Award on his contributions to literature.

Ian Talbot graduated in 1976 from Royal Holloway College, University of London, and obtained a PhD in 1981. He has published extensively in the fields of Colonial Punjab History, the Partition of India, and the History of Pakistan. His works on Pakistan include *Pakistan: A Modern History* (2009), *Pakistan: A New History* (2012) and *The History of British Diplomacy in Pakistan* (2021). He is presently Emeritus Professor of Modern South Asian History at the University of Southampton, UK.

Aiysha Varraich is a research fellow jointly at Global Integrity Washington DC and University of Nottingham. She is also a PhD candidate at the Quality of Government Institute at Gothenburg University, Sweden. The focus of her dissertation is on how religion subverts contemporary theories of clientelism, specifically in Pakistan. She is the co-author (with Bo Rothstein) of *Making Sense of Corruption* (2017) and co-editor (with Ina Kubbe) of *Corruption and Informal Practices in the Middle East and North Africa* (2019).

Serdar Yilmaz is a lead public sector specialist at the World Bank. His research interests include fiscal decentralization, public expenditure management, subnational governance, and governmental accountability. His most recent publications include: (with M. S. Tosun and D. Huynh) "All-of-Government Response to the COVID-19 Pandemic: The Case of Vietnam", *Public Administration and Development* (2020), (with S. K. Ahsan, G. Dedu, and S. Rana) "Transition to Federalism in Nepal", *Case Studies in Business and Management* (2020) and (with Farah Zahir) *Intergovernmental Transfers in Federations* (2020).

FOREWORD

In the summer of 2019, the idea for this book project was formulated. The main concern motivating it was the rapid deterioration of democracy in India. However, the situation in Bangladesh, Pakistan and Sri Lanka was on a similar trajectory. It was decided, therefore, that a Handbook on Autocratization in South Asia was needed, in order to catch, describe, and to explain the ongoing trends. Six months later the Covid-19 pandemic broke out, turning the situation from bad to worse in so many ways. Autocratization was mainly reinforced. As this foreword is being written, it seems the Covid situation for affluent democracies is about to improve. Yet democracy has suffered in those countries too. As for most parts of South Asia, and for India in particular, the Covid death rate there is still pointing upwards. There is no way to predict the effects of all this. Some speculate that authoritarian leaders will eventually be removed from power as a consequence of the pandemic in South Asia. One thing, however, is clear: a sharp focus on democratization and autocratization is needed more now than at any other time since independence. Once the pandemic has subsided, it will become more evident we have a new world order. Authoritarian China is now the most important power – not only in South Asia, but arguably also in the world. This will also decide the chances for the states studied in this book to get back on the democratic path once again.

The most important thanks go to all the authors who have contributed to this book: Maren Aase, Syed Khaled Ahsan, Amrita Basu, Moeen Cheema, Soundarya Chidambaram, Neil DeVotta, Anwesha Dutta, Shelley Feldman, Øivind Fuglerud, Šumit Ganguly, Sandra Grahn, Asheque Haque, Zoya Hasan, Patrick Heller, Sandya Hewamanne, Christophe Jaffrelot, Devin Joshi, Johan Lagerkvist, Marc Lanteigne, David Lewis, Staffan Lindberg, Dinoo Anna Mathew, Farah Mihlar, Alf Gunvald Nilsen, Kenneth Bo Nielsen, Ali Riaz, Arild Engelsen Ruud, Rizvan Saeed, Ahmad Salim, Ian Talbot, Aiysha Varraich and Serdar Yilmaz. Several authors, moreover, have given helpful advice and support to other authors in this book. Valuable assistance has furthermore been provided by the very resourceful editorial board, consisting of Amrita Basu, Atul Kohli, Carolin Rapp, Arild Engelsen Ruud and Ian Talbot.

The Department of Government at Uppsala University has served as the base for this project, and I am greatly indebted to Prefekt Christina Bergqvist, Vice Prefekt Karl-Oskar Lindgren, acting Prefekt Sven Oskarsson, and all my colleagues there.

The ambition was embraced early on to make as much as possible of this book freely available via Open Access. What we have achieved in this regard has only been possible with the help of very generous grants from The Royal Society of Arts and Sciences of Uppsala. Valuable support has also been provided by Göran and Birgitta Atmer's Foundation; by the H2020 European Research Council [grant number 724191], PI: Staffan I. Lindberg; and by the Vice-Chancellor's office at the University of Gothenburg.

Dorothea Schaefter, Christopher Taylor and Alexandra de Brauw at Routledge, all their colleagues, and Sean Connolly and Thara Kanaga who helped us in the final phase, have been highly supportive of me and of the authors. Their professional advice and friendly encouragement have been crucial throughout the project.

Last but not least, thanks to Peter Mayers, Ashok Swain, Sverker Gustavsson, and anonymous advisors for all their help with this book.

Uppsala, 7 May 2021
Sten Widmalm

Introduction

Autocratization in South Asia

1

AUTOCRATIZATION IN SOUTH ASIA

Sandra Grahn, Staffan I. Lindberg and Sten Widmalm

A pronounced trend towards democracy in South Asia is now in reverse. Not long ago, the picture was different. India was on a steady climb in democracy ratings for decades. Economic liberalization, which was the hallmark of reforms led by finance minister Manmohan Singh in the 1990s under the premiership of Narasimha Rao, appeared to be compatible with giving more space for political competitors in a landscape which had long been dominated by the Congress party. India's neighbours were gradually taking steps to follow its lead towards greater democracy. In the early 1990s, Bangladesh showed great promise with political and substantial liberalization reforms as Khaleda Zia became the first female prime minister. A long spell of military rule in Pakistan came to an end late in 2007. The tragic assassination of Benazir Bhutto, just after she had returned from exile and taken the lead as the country's most popular civilian leader, marked the beginning of a first peaceful transition towards democracy. Pakistan then managed to pass Huntington's two-turnover test (Huntington 1991) with no fewer than three elections (2008, 2013, and 2018) leading to alternations in power. Two of the three largest parties formed successive governments completing full terms in office. After decades of war, Sri Lanka entered a more peaceful era after the Tamil Tigers were brutally defeated in 2009. Since then, Sri Lanka had three general elections and peaceful power transitions. During the last three decades, South Asia clearly became part of the "third wave of democratization" alongside many other countries around the world. Following the end of the Cold War, democracy seemed to be a natural gravitational point that states inevitably moved towards if unfettered. (In)famously, Francis Fukuyama proclaimed that in some respects history was coming to an end (Fukuyama 1992). This idea that liberal democracy was accepted as a supra-ideology seemed to find support in South Asia as well.

We now know that such perceptions were misguided for understanding democratic development in most parts of the world. According to Freedom House, the level of freedom in the world is now in decline for the fifteenth consecutive year (Repucci and Slipowitz 2020). The Varieties of Democracy (V-Dem) Institute traces the beginnings of the increase in "autocratizing" countries further back, starting even before 2000 (Lührmann et al. 2020: 15). South Asia is a part of this "third wave of autocratization" (Lührmann and Lindberg 2019). Over the last ten years, Prime Minister Sheikh Hasina has pushed Bangladesh towards becoming a one-party state. Freedom of speech is being muffled in Pakistan and minorities are at risk in Sri Lanka.

DOI: 10.4324/9781003042211-2

India is rapidly sinking in reports on democracy and liberal freedoms provided by Freedom House, Reporters Without Borders, Pen International and Amnesty International. The most recent release of indicators of democratic performance from V-Dem shows that India in 2020 moved from being an *electoral democracy* to becoming an *electoral autocracy* (Alizada et al. 2021). Although India's democracy has since independence been exposed to severe challenges, it did achieve "a sufficient level of institutional guarantees of democracy such as freedom of association, suffrage, clean elections, an elected executive, and freedom of expression". However, India now falls "short of democratic standards due to significant irregularities, limitations on party competition or other violations" (Lindberg, Lührmann, Tannenberg 2018: 61) which motivates the downgrading. Therefore, it is no exaggeration to claim that South Asia is going through a democratic crisis.

Nonetheless, this does not automatically translate into proof that the region called South Asia is irreversibly transitioning to authoritarian rule. These processes are rarely linear in either direction. All countries included in this book have traversed trajectories towards democracy that have been all but straightforward. Democracy has been interrupted, suspended, and seen such severe backlashes that made it seem implausible that it could recover, yet it did. So, the question is, how severe is the autocratization trend? What are its characteristics? How deep does it go? This book aims at providing answers to such questions, to enable realistic assessments of the chances for a democratic recovery in the foreseeable future.

A broader discussion on trends in South Asia is included in Chapter 30. However, the focus in this book is mainly on the four countries with the most significant impact on the region as a whole, which is also the four with the greatest variation in regime trajectories. All four countries – India, Pakistan, Bangladesh, and Sri Lanka – share the experience of some or even major democratic achievements since gaining independence from British colonial rule. But their paths differ greatly. Democratic take-offs have been interrupted quickly in some cases while India for a long time trod a more linear path towards democracy. Democracy survived or made comebacks in spite of severe constraints of economic resources as well as conflicts in and between countries, states, and provinces. Also, no sooner had the colonial rule come to an end, before the whole region became an important arena for the Cold War with adverse effects on both political stability and development. The paths towards democracy have always been rocky in South Asia. However, as Sheri Berman (2019) points out, this is more of a rule rather than an exception if we take a historical view on democratization in the world. Consequently, as analysts we must not overinterpret what could be temporary swings and keep in mind the democratic achievements of the past. This is to remind us that trajectories portrayed in this volume may defy the perspectives provided by various kinds of historical determinism that always awaits an endgame where civilizations will clash (Huntington 1993). Changes in developments may eventually transpire even if current trajectories – as we shall see – are disheartening.

The guiding motivation for this book is to complement previous contributions that have provided insights and knowledge on forces supporting democratization in South Asia. The focus in this volume is on the trends, factors, changes, and circumstances that support the opposite – autocratization. There is an urgent need to understand causes behind the reversal. For such a large region it is impossible to cover *all* relevant events and topics associated with autocratization. However, the authors offer their rich insights, perspectives, and knowledge on what they regard as central for understanding autocratization in the four countries that are represented in this book.

The natural starting point for an introductory chapter is to define more closely what the most central concept of concern here stands for. It is necessary to explain what is meant by studying, or saying that a country is experiencing, *autocratization*. Secondly, it provides a broad overview of the trajectories relating to democratic performance across all four countries, using data collected by V-Dem (Coppedge et al. 2021). This is followed by a look at the trends for the region as a whole. The final section of the chapter discusses the broader context in which India, Pakistan, Bangladesh, and Sri Lanka are located. In order to understand domestic trends, it is also necessary to have perspective on how the trend for South Asia fits in with the world at large.

The following chapters provide more detailed and in-depth knowledge on autocratization in each country. The participating authors provide their analyses and perspectives on the major forces of autocratization in the four countries. The chapters stand as individual contributions in their own right. There is no attempt to provide a single standpoint synthesizing all the insights provided by the participating authors. However, in the final analysis, the chapters of Part 5 ("How to comprehend autocratization in South Asia – three broad perspectives") draw on the contributions of this book and other research contributions to present commonalities in, and divergent patterns of, autocratization in South Asia. It contains discussions of the role played by the recent expansion of China and ideas relating to nationalism and liberalism that are being shaped and changed today. It is also argued that it is tempting to conclude that the observable patterns will be perpetual – as if South Asia is simply reverting to a trajectory that is common for most other parts of Asia where democracy has always had a bleak future. However, the chapters in this book point to an array of processes that cannot be reduced to an enduring path-dependency determined by economic, historical, and cultural factors. Even when deterministic patterns sometimes find empirical support, it is important to remember that such perspectives on causes may be palatable for political reasons. If it is concluded that forces of history for example led to autocratization in a country, or several countries, then this may function to absolve political leaders and the citizens voting for them, of their roles and responsibilities. In the trajectories described here, agency is visible and important.

Regime types and autocratization

Let us start by clarifying central regime-related concepts that have already been mentioned. The determination that India recently went from being an *electoral democracy* to becoming an *electoral autocracy,* was based on the "Regimes of the World" scale with four categories (Lührmann, Tannenberg, and Lindberg 2018). States which are de-facto multiparty carry out free and fair elections, and do so while also upholding the rule of law and liberal principles, are classified as liberal democracies. If the rule of law is somewhat in question and liberal principles are not fully guaranteed, a country slides down the scale and is classified as an electoral democracy. If the respect for democratic institutions is further in doubt, the country moves into the autocracy-sphere. If multiparty elections are still actually held but "rulers are not accountable to citizens", then the country is an electoral autocracy. If even multiparty elections for the chief executive or the legislature are absent, then the state reaches the regime-type end station of closed autocracy. A journey in the direction of this end-point but regardless of from what level it started, is referred to as *autocratization*.

Autocratization is the opposite to democratization, and both involve periods of substantial and sustained changes in levels of democracy, respectively (Lührmann and Lindberg 2019). Following the literature, we use the Electoral Democracy Index (EDI) to measure autocratization in South Asia. The EDI is based on Dahl's conceptualization of polyarchy (Dahl 1971, Teorell et al. 2019) as it goes beyond pure electoral contestation and participation, adding freedom of expression (freedom of speech and alternative sources of information combined) as well as conditions of a broad swathe of associational freedom (Coppedge et al. 2021). The third wave of autocratization sweeping across the globe is characterized by leaders who have come to power through free and fair elections but derail freedom of expression and associations once in power (Lührmann and Lindberg 2019). Among the ten most negatively affected indicators over the last ten years, nine are aspects of freedom of association and expression (Lührmann et al. 2021). This also applies to autocratization in South Asia.

Episodes of autocratization capture periods with a definitive start and end date during which substantial and sustained declines in democratic qualities take place (Edgell et al. 2020, Wilson et al. 2020). As discussed above, regime transformations are typically nonlinear, and such declines may result in democratic breakdown, further deterioration under non-democracy, or the regime could avert breakdown by reversing the trend and sustaining minimal levels of democracy necessary to be considered democratic. The new Episodes of Regime Transformation (ERT) dataset provides identification of episodes of both democratization and autocratization measured on V-Dem's latest version of the Electoral Democracy Index (Coppedge et al. 2021). It identifies the onset and end dates, as well as the outcome, of both democratization and autocratization episodes (Edgell et al. 2020). This will be the natural starting point presented in the beginning of the next section which provides a broad portrayal of autocratization in South Asia. As the analysis proceeds at country level, the figures will focus on measurements of freedom of association and expression, and on variables capturing the characteristics of elections.

Autocratization in India, Pakistan, Bangladesh, and Sri Lanka

Figure 1.1 depicts the overall level of democracy as measured by the EDI in Bangladesh, India, Pakistan and Sri Lanka from the end of the Cold War in 1989 to the present (2020). The recent period with episodes of autocratization in South Asia, based on the ERT, is marked. This bird's-eye view on democratic performance and autocratization over time in the four countries in focus in this book makes it clear that South Asia is currently going through a state of transformation characterized as autocratization. Since independence, the ongoing crisis is currently at least as severe as the situation was in the early and mid-1970s (this is discussed further in Chapter 28). Since the withdrawal of British colonial forces, Sri Lanka and India were the only countries to immediately achieve a successful democratic take-off. However, Indira Gandhi suspended democracy in 1975, and then also democracy started to decline in Sri Lanka. Nonetheless, India fairly quickly managed to get back on the democratic path in 1977. After three decades, democratic performance of the whole region appeared to be improving. Until recently.

While the onset of the global third wave of autocratization has been traced back to before 2000, the countries in South Asia seem to have joined later and Sri Lanka counters the trend. While much of the world including South Asia register significant democratic regression, Sri Lanka has democratized and qualifies to be classified as a relatively decent electoral democracy since 2015. There is however, a decline in 2018–2020, which corresponds to several worrying trends pointed out in the section on Sri Lanka later in this book. India's piecemeal, uneven, and protracted degeneration into what is today a questionable borderline-case of just barely keeping electoral democracy started in earnest around 2006 to 2007. Yet, the more definitive descent arrived along with Narendra Modi coming into power as the 14th Prime Minister of India in 2014. India's episode of autocratization is ongoing at present and transformed its regime type to an electoral autocracy.

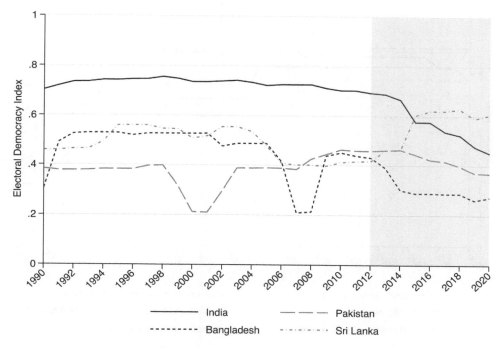

Figure 1.1 Electoral democracy (polyarchy), 1990–2020
Source: Varieties of democracy, version 11.1 (March 2021).

After the period from January 2007 to January 2009 under a military-backed caretaker government period, politics was somewhat democratic in Bangladesh for about five years until the current episode of autocratization started. The episode is ongoing with the outcome unknown just as in the case of India, with the difference that Bangladesh is clearly an electoral autocracy today. Finally, Pakistan experienced a military coup in 1999, which was followed by a politically violent decade. Some civil liberties were upheld, although General Musharraf reigned with support from the military up until early 2008. Although Pakistan then made a promising transition towards democracy and eventually even passed Huntington's two-turnover test, another decline of democracy set in around 2015. Pakistan is since then in an episode of autocratization just like much of the region (and many countries in the world). Our first deeper insights to this episode of autocratization are provided by looking at how freedom of expression is present in the media, in academia and in cultural life, by taking into account the freedom to organize groups and activities in civil society and to form political parties, and how well elections are handled or restricted by various political forces.

India

It makes sense to start the analysis with the most populated country, the largest economy, and the strongest political impact in the region. The direction which India takes typically has a great influence on its neighbours. The episode of autocratization in India under Prime Minister Modi affects all measurements included in EDI, except the extent of suffrage. According to V-Dem's *Democracy Report 2020*, India belongs to the top-ten group

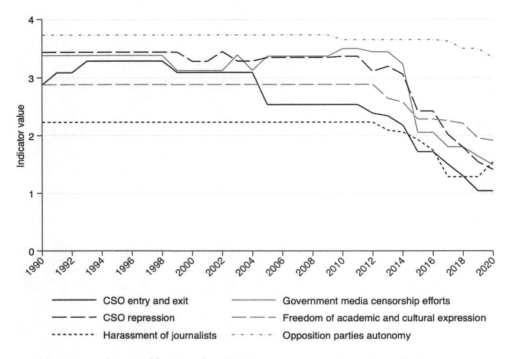

Figure 1.2 Key indicators of freedom of association, expression, and the media, India 1990–2020
Source: Varieties of democracy, version 11.1 (March 2021).

of countries in the world that have autocratized the most over the past ten years (Lührmann et al. 2020: 16). Figure 1.2 depicts that the areas affected negatively first and by far the most are freedom of expression, association, and the media. Here the indicators for associational freedom include measurements of repression directed towards Civil Society Organizations (CSOs), the way the state may regulate the entry or exit of CSOs "into public life", and also to what extent opposition parties are autonomous in relation to the regime in power (Coppedge et al. 2021). The measurements of freedom of expression consist of variables measuring the extent of harassment directed towards journalists, an assessment of efforts made by the government to censor print and broadcast media, and the amount of freedom granted to academia and culture.

Evidently, the government led by Manmohan Singh (2009–2014) had a negative impact on democratic governance to some degree. It was in fact corruption scandals that paved important parts of the way for the BJP leading up to the 2014 election. There was, however, a more significant and steep decline in almost all indicators when Modi and the BJP came into power, and this descent has continued since. Apparently, the Modi government has imposed severe *de facto* restrictions of liberal freedoms without directly attacking the autonomy of opposition parties. In fact, barriers to parties entering politics remain low, elections are fully multiparty, no significant parties have been banned, and opposition parties retain a high degree of autonomy from the government and the ruling BJP party.

However, the Modi-led government in India *has* used laws on sedition, defamation, and counterterrorism to silence critics (Human Rights Watch 2019). By far the most dramatic change is the almost close to eradication of freedom from government censorship of media in

India. Along with the dismal situation for journalists and civil liberties activists who actually write critically about the government and therefore get harassed, imprisoned, or subjected to abuse, this is a very concerning trajectory (Widmalm 2016: 211–212). The arbitrary arrests of the civil rights activists and journalists accused in the so called "Bhima Koregaon-case" are just one dramatic example (Jaffrelot 2020).

Independent civil society organizations are especially hard hit in the ongoing autocratization episode. As will be discussed later in this book, the pressure is mainly directed towards organizations that have supported civil rights – especially for minorities and women. Civil society organizations aligning themselves with the Hindutva movement have rather gained more freedom (Basu 2015). What is severely affected is the freedom of independent civil society organizations to exist, and to organize activities autonomously from government interference and direction. The two civil society indicators included in Figure 1.2 have taken a steep dive over especially the past six years or so after the BJP assumed power.

Furthermore, the quality and fairness of elections have also deteriorated significantly over the past five to six years (The Wire 2021). Figure 1.3 shows variables that are commonly used to indicate to what extent elections are clean. The variable "Election free and fair" is a broad measurement taking into account the whole election process and its quality. "Election government intimidation" measures more specifically to what extent opposition parties and their representatives were exposed to harassment or intimidation by the government. The freedom from government intervention in the Election Management Body (EMB) in the country is captured in "EMB autonomy". Finally, a kind of residual category is included in "Election other voting irregularities", which captures any kind of intervention in the elections and vote fraud. Figure 1.3 evinces a significant decline on all these indicators for India in the current period.

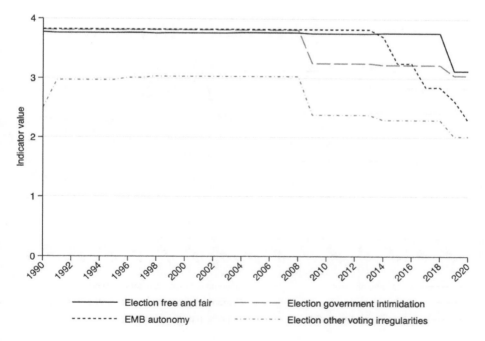

Figure 1.3 Key indicators of the quality of elections, India 1990–2020
Source: Varieties of democracy, version 11.1 (March 2021).

The autonomy of the election management body depreciates severely over the period since 2013 signalling perhaps the most concerning aspect of decline. Government intimidation of opposition declined already with the 2008 elections but has not worsened further much since. Voting irregularities have been somewhat of an issue in India for a long time but got worse again in 2008 and again deteriorated further in 2019. The overall freedom and fairness of elections, finally, took a hard hit with the last elections held under Prime Minister Modi's reign in 2019.

To sum up, the present episode of autocratization in India is affecting key areas of democracy, and it particularly concerns freedom of expression, association and the media. There is undoubtedly a decline in the quality of elections, but it is the media and civil society that are curbed in the most dramatic ways.

Pakistan

Pakistan is different from the other countries in the region in that it has never qualified as an electoral democracy. Even with multiparty elections and increases in various freedoms, Pakistan has fallen short of ever crossing the threshold (see Figure 1.1).

Figure 1.4 shows, in a very similar pattern to India, that the main deterioration of associational freedoms in the last ten years or so, is due to increasing control of independent civil society organizations. The Pakistani government has progressively tightened their control of which organizations are allowed to exist to an extent where there are few independent organizations left to exist and repression is active even if moderate.

The developments in Pakistan over the past decade are also similar to India's in the area of freedom of expression including alternative sources of information, but even more pronounced and to worse levels, as displayed in Figure 1.4.

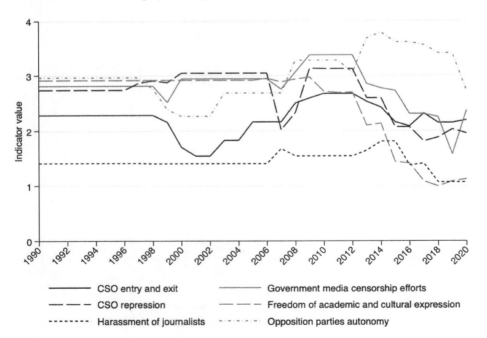

Figure 1.4 Key indicators of freedom of association, expression, and the media, Pakistan 1990–2020
Source: Varieties of democracy, version 11.1 (March 2021).

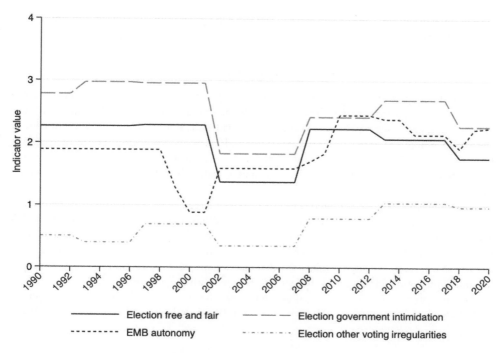

Figure 1.5 Key indicators of the quality of elections, Pakistan 1990–2020
Source: Varieties of democracy, version 11.1 (March 2021).

Academics' and cultural workers' freedom is also much worse in Pakistan than in India, and has fallen close to rock-bottom alongside journalists who now are almost always harassed if and when they dare to write critically about powerful actors in the country. It should be mentioned here also that Reporters Without Borders (RSF) warn that the Government of Pakistan may now even be persecuting journalists in exile (RSF 2020). Government censorship of the media has gone from largely absent as late as 2012, to frequent and severe in 2019. There are additional similarities to India. The restrictions of CSOs and the deterioration of freedom of expression in various forms have been possible without restricting the autonomy of the opposition parties. And the decline of freedom for organizations working for civil liberties is matched by the opposite trend for organizations that are religious and anti-democratic (Widmalm 2016: 212–216). Yet, the recent episode of further autocratization in Pakistan is driven primarily by a deterioration in the freedom of expression.

Figure 1.5 demonstrates that electoral autocracy in Pakistan has had rather unusual characteristics. The quality and integrity of elections has been for a long time, and still is, the chief issue.

Voting irregularities are a recurring problem. Some of these seem to have become slightly worse since 2008. There are declining levels of autonomy of the election management body, there is a general lack of freedom and fairness in the elections, as well as a worsening of government intimidation of the opposition in the last elections.

In sum, Pakistan went through an episode of very gradual and protracted liberalization of its electoral autocracy from 2007 to 2015 but never became a democracy. After that, the tide has turned into an episode of autocratization driven primarily by dramatic increases in government control of civil society as well as a sharp increase in the government's largely successful efforts to curb media freedom.

Bangladesh

Bangladesh's trajectory – depicted in Figure 1.6 – over the past decade is typical for the third wave of autocratization as depicted by Lührmann and Lindberg (2019) and Lührmann et al. (2020), with one particular exception. Bangladesh is one of the very few countries in the world where the integrity and fairness of multiparty elections are undermined almost from the outset. This happened in a dramatic fashion with the elections in 2014. The usual sequence is that media and civil society are suppressed before the formal institutions come under attack.

This somewhat unusual autocratization pattern is reflected in almost all indicators describing how elections are handled, shown in Figure 1.7. While the election management body's autonomy has long been limited in Bangladesh, it was constrained further in a dramatic fashion in 2011 and 2012, then gradually deteriorated further over the last few years to be almost non-existent. Meanwhile the large declines in other election qualities such as absence of government intimidation, voting irregularities, and violence, came with the elections in 2014.

The indicators of associational freedoms in Figure 1.6 have remained at relatively democratic levels much longer than the election-related ones in Bangladesh, as shown in Figure 1.7. While

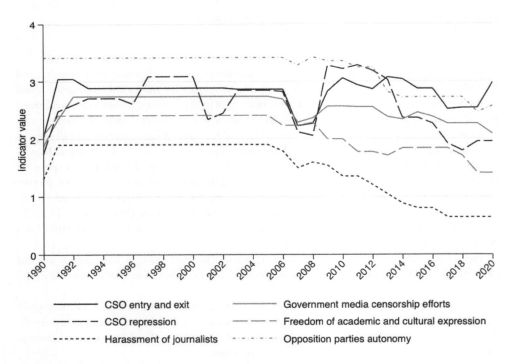

Figure 1.6 Key indicators of freedom of association, expression, and the media, Bangladesh 1990–2020
Source: Varieties of democracy, version 11.1 (March 2021).

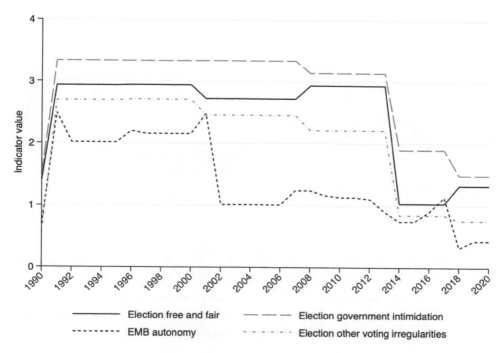

Figure 1.7 Key indicators of the quality of elections, Bangladesh 1990–2020
Source: Varieties of democracy, version 11.1 (March 2021).

the autonomy of opposition parties took a hit following the 2012 elections, civil society was not affected until around 2016 when also barriers to political parties forming were raised.

In comparison, freedom of expression displays a much more disparate picture in Figure 1.6, where some areas such as the level of harassment of journalists and media's self-censorship have been much worse than media's freedom to reflect varying perspectives and provide non-biased information, as well as the freedom of academics and cultural workers. But all aspects have been in a gradual and significant decline since 2012 in a pattern that is typical for the third wave of autocratization. The most dramatic change continuing to dominate the autocratization process in Bangladesh is a kind of breakdown of democracy in connection with the 2014 and 2018 elections (Riaz 2021). The Awami League government, guided by Prime Minister Sheik Hasina, pursued policies aimed at intimidating and harassing political opponents, which resulted in a massive boycott of the election then. Democracy has not recovered since.

Sri Lanka

In contrast to the other countries in this book, Sri Lanka's political trajectory has from 2014 to 2018 been in a democratic direction. Juxtaposed to India, which is in the top-ten of autocratizing countries in the world over the last ten years, Sri Lanka is in the top-four group of seeing the largest gains in democratic qualities among all democratizing countries (Lührmann et al. 2020: 23) and regained its status as an electoral democracy in this period.

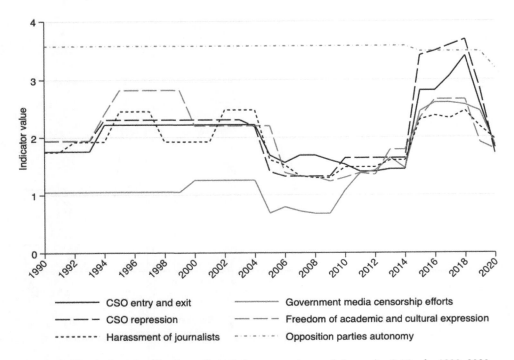

Figure 1.8 Key indicators of freedom of association, expression, and the media, Sri Lanka 1990–2020
Source: Varieties of democracy, version 11.1 (March 2021).

Figure 1.8 displays how the positive developments were spearheaded by improvements in freedom of expression and alternative sources of information already around 2010, followed by significant advances in the quality of elections and associational freedoms a few years later as shown in Figure 1.9.

Figure 1.8 demonstrates that the freedom of expression indicators follow a very similar pattern to the quality of elections but foreshadows those. From lows in the middle of the first decade of the 2000s, the pro-government bias in the media lessens significantly around 2008 along with smaller improvements in a series of other aspects of indicators. These advances continue in a gradual but steady fashion over the following years, portending the transition back to democracy a few years later.

As illustrated by the indicator of opposition parties' autonomy in Figure 1.8, most associational freedoms remained unaffected by the war and other dynamics that derailed many aspects of democracy in Sri Lanka off and on in the 1990s and 2000s. Just as in the other countries discussed above, more autocratic periods are associated with severe restrictions on, and repression of, independent civil society associations. With the end of the civil conflict, which was extremely brutal, there is an almost seismic shift in associational freedoms for this sector.

As shown in Figure 1.9, the improvements in the quality of elections are the results of almost across-the-board advances in all the indicators. Notably, the first change for the better comes for the autonomy of the election management board, a critical foundation for democratic elections. This is followed by a broad swathe of positive changes in the qualities of elections in 2014, and then again a dramatic set of improvements in 2019.

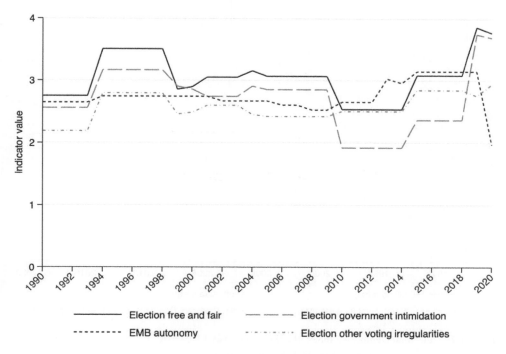

Figure 1.9 Key indicators of the quality of elections, Sri Lanka 1990–2020
Source: Varieties of democracy, version 11.1 (March 2021).

Consequently, the development for Sri Lanka is from a democratic perspective very impressive. Nonetheless, the contributions later in this book will show that the democratization process for Sri Lanka is to say the least fragile. The risk for backsliding is imminent. The decline in several indicators since 2018 that are included in Figure 1.8 suggests that such a downward turn may have already been initiated. The constitutional crisis in 2018, the fact that the previous prime minister refused to leave office after the election, and that afterwards, the president appointed his own brother as prime minister, and a dramatic increased militarization of the state and society, are causes for concern (DeVotta 2021).

Autocratization in South Asia in a comparative perspective

A *very* broad and comparative perspective on what has been described here – using the EDI for South Asia, including Bangladesh, Sri Lanka, India, Pakistan, Bhutan, Nepal, Maldives, and Afghanistan – may not appear to represent such a dramatic decline (Figure 1.10). Undoubtedly 2020 is worse than 2011, but it is still far better than 2007. In what way are these numbers telling us that there is an ongoing episode of autocratization covering the whole region?

The level of the EDI for South Asia rose quickly in 2007, then starts to sink slowly – struggling not to slip too much below the 0.5 mark. For a short while South Asia almost managed to reach the average EDI level of the world. Since then the EDI level in the world and South Asia have both been on a slight downward trajectory. If the trend is persistent,

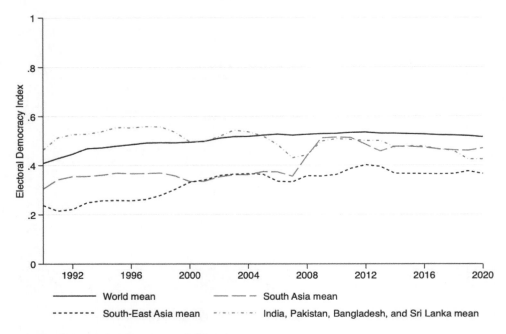

Figure 1.10 Electoral Democracy Index, the World and Asia 1990–2020
Source: Varieties of democracy, version 11.1 (March 2021).

South Asian countries will within two or three years pass the level of democracy of South-East Asia (Laos, Timor-Leste, Indonesia, Philippines, Cambodia, Myanmar, Thailand, Singapore, Malaysia, Vietnam) which seems to have stagnated in a non-democratic equilibrium. The reason for this is that the recent EDI for South Asia is propped up by small countries such as the Maldives, which saw a dramatic improvement in democratic performance 2017–2020. This masks a more general and continued downward trend for the region. It also needs to be repeated that when India moves downwards on the measurements provided here – when it moves closer to the democratic performance indicators of Pakistan as civil liberties are lost – it drags about three-quarters of the population in the whole region with it. When the government of India stops protecting essential democratic freedoms, a large part of the whole world become citizens of a backslider region. The weight of India should be taken into account. Consequently we need to shed light on this with an alternative way of presenting the changes in democratic performance in South Asia. The effect is illustrated by looking at a comparison provided based on V-Dem data showing how many countries in the world are democratizing and how many are autocratizing.

In Figure 1.11, the graph to the left depicts the number of countries in the whole South Asia region that are democratizing and how many are autocratizing. In the graph to the right the effect is weighted in relation to population. The sharp upward turn of autocratization there is mostly influenced by the democratic decline in India since it has a population of about 1.4 billion. Democratization in Sri Lanka is visibly affecting the trend for the whole of South Asia shown in Figure 1.10, while it completely disappears in Figure 1.11. So why not then only study India to describe autocratization in "South Asia"?

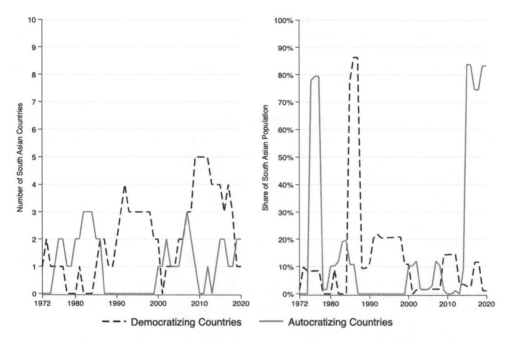

Figure 1.11 Electoral Democracy (Polyarchy), democratizing, and autocratizing countries 1972–2020 in South Asia

Source: Varieties of democracy, version 11.1 (March 2021).

The answer is that *comparisons* may reveal commonalities – including factors which may drive autocratization as well as democratization and that may have nothing to do with the size of a population. If we find factors that are steering both Sri Lanka and India towards less democracy, then this may suggest that such factors may be relevant threats to democracy in many other places in South Asia, and outside the region, as well. South Asia, even if we cannot fit all the countries in the region into the analysis here, undoubtedly provides what has inspired the name for the V-Dem project – varieties of both democracy, and autocratization. Some paths are very country-specific, and this will become evident when the four countries are discussed in their own sections.

Even if the impact of India is great in the region, the paths to and from democracy are interesting *per se*. Sometimes patterns are replicated so that an episode of autocratization appears to connect a whole region. However, even if several countries are moving in the same direction at the same time, they still may do so for different reasons. In this first chapter we have already seen here that the ongoing autocratization episode of South Asia is *characterized* by factors that all four countries have in common. Autocratization is observable in the areas of civic life, freedom of opinion, media, academia and cultural life. Nonetheless, this is the broader picture. As will be evident in the coming sections, all countries have unique traits too. Just as they in the past have taken different paths to democratization, they have individual features as well relating to the current autocratization episode. Here we need to add also that countries in South Asia are spurred by their unique relationships to neighbours in the region. And sometimes when one country gives up its support for democracy, a contagion effect is activated and neighbouring countries become encouraged to do the same. Therefore, the patterns we observe at the macro level can only be understood by going deeper into the country-specific cases. And when that is done, the more is learned about the varieties or uniformities in the processes leading to autocratization. For the future, this may provide insights and tools that can be used to employ counter measures to prevent a new autocratization episode – given that the will and power to do so is there.

Bibliography

Ali, Riaz. 2021. "The Pathway of Democratic Backsliding in Bangladesh." *Democratization* 28(1): 179–197.

Alizada, Nazifa, Rowan Cole, Lisa Gastaldi, Sandra Grahn, Sebastian Hellmeier, Palina Kolvani, Jean Lachapelle, Anna Lührmann, Seraphine F. Maerz, Shreeya Pillai, and Staffan I. Lindberg. 2021. *Autocratization Turns Viral: Democracy Report 2021.* Gothenburg: V-Dem Institute, University of Gothenburg.

Basu, Amrita. 2015. *Violent Conjunctures in Democratic India.* New York: Cambridge University Press.

Berman, Sheri. 2019. *Democracy and Dictatorship in Europe: From the Ancient Régime to the Present Day.* New York: Oxford University Press.

Coppedge, Michael, John Gerring, Carl Henrik Knutsen, Staffan I. Lindberg, Jan Teorell, David Altman, Michael Bernhard, Agnes Cornell, M. Steven Fish, Lisa Gastaldi, Haakon Gjerløw, Adam Glynn, Allen Hicken, Anna Lührmann, Seraphine F. Maerz, Kyle L. Marquardt, Kelly McMann, Valeriya Mechkova, Pamela Paxton, Daniel Pemstein, Johannes von Römer, Brigitte Seim, Rachel Sigman, Svend-Erik Skaaning, Jeffrey Staton, Aksel Sundtröm, Eitan Tzelgov, Luca Uberti, Yi-ting Wang, Tore Wig, and Daniel Ziblatt. 2021. "V-Dem Codebook v11" Varieties of Democracy (V-Dem) Project. https://v-dem.net.

Dahl, Robert A. 1971. *Polyarchy: Participation and Opposition.* New Haven: Yale University Press.

DeVotta, Neil. 2021. "Sri Lanka: The Return to Ethnocracy." *Journal of Democracy* 32(1): 96–110.

Edgell, Amanda B., Seraphine F. Maerz, Laura Maxwell, Richard Morgan, Juraj Medzihorsky, Matthew C. Wilson, Vanessa A. Boese, Sebastian Hellmeier, Jean Lachapelle, Patrik Lindenfors, Anna Lührmann, and Staffan I. Lindberg. 2020. Episodes of Regime Transformation Dataset, v1.0. https://github.com/vdeminstitute/vdemdata.

Fukuyama, Francis. 1992. *The End of History and the Last Man.* London: Hamish Hamilton.

Human Rights Watch. 2019. www.hrw.org/world-report/2019/country-chapters/india.

Huntington, S. P. 1991. *The Third Wave.* Norman, Oklahoma: University of Oklahoma Press.

Huntington, S. P. 1993. "The Clash of Civilizations." *Foreign Affairs* 72(3): 22–49.

Jaffrelot, Christophe. 2020. "Arrests in Bhima Koregaon Case Frame a Transformation in India's Polity and Police Force." *Indian Express.* October 21. https://indianexpress.com/article/opinion/columns/bhima-koregaon-case-stan-swamy-nia-chargesheet-naxals-6907744/ (accessed 5 April 2021).

Lührmann, Anna and Staffan I. Lindberg. 2019. "A Third Wave of Autocratization Is Here: What Is New About It?" *Democratization* 26(7): 1095–1113, open access: 10.1080/13510347.2019.1582029.

Lührmann, Anna, Marcus Tannenberg, and Staffan I. Lindberg. 2018. "Regimes of the World (RoW): Opening New Avenues for the Comparative Study of Political Regimes." *Politics and Governance* 6(1). doi: 10.17645/pag.v6i1.1214.

Maerz, Seraphine F., Amanda B. Edgell, Joshua Krusell, Laura Maxwell, Sebastian Hellmeier, and Nina Ilchenko. 2020. "Vdemdata – an R package to load, explore and work with the most recent V-Dem (Varieties of Democracy) dataset." https://github.com/vdeminstitute/vdemdata.

Repucci, Sarah and Amy Slipowitz. 2021. "Freedom in the World 2021: Democracy under Siege. Freedom House." https://freedomhouse.org/report/freedom-world/2021/democracy-under-siege (accessed 15 April 2021).

RSF. 2020. "RSF warns Pakistani authorities not to threaten journalists living abroad." https://rsf.org/en/news/rsf-warns-pakistani-authorities-not-to-threaten-journalists-living-abroad (accessed 31 August 2021).

Teorell, Jan, Michael Coppedge, Svend-Erik Skaaning, and Staffan I. Lindberg. 2019. "Measuring Polyarchy Across the Globe, 1900–2017." *Studies in Comparative International Development* 54(1): 71–95. Open access: https://doi.org/10.1007/s12116-018-9268-z.

Widmalm, Sten. 2016. *Political Tolerance in the Global South – Images from India, Pakistan and Uganda.* London: Routledge.

Wilson, Matthew C., Richard Morgan, Juraj Medzihorsky, Laura Maxwell, Seraphine F. Maerz, Anna Lührmann, Patrik Lindenfors, Amanda B. Edgell, Vanessa Boese, and Staffan I. Lindberg. 2020. *Successful and Failed Episodes of Democratization: Conceptualization, Identification, and Description.* Gothenburg, V-Dem Institute: V-Dem Working Papers, no. 97.

The Wire. Staff Reporter. 2021. "ECI's Conduct of 2019 Elections Raises 'Grave Doubts' About Its Fairness: Citizens' Report." In The Wire. 15 March 2021. https://thewire.in/rights/election-commission-bjp-polls-fairness-citizens-commission-on-elections-report (accessed 15 April 2021).

PART I

India

Building an ethnic state?

2

NEO-AUTHORITARIANISM IN INDIA UNDER NARENDRA MODI

Growing force or critical discourse?

Devin K. Joshi

As the world's largest electoral democracy in terms of population, India not only symbolizes the democratic potential of developing and post-colonial states, but also serves as a crucial test case for assessing the global influence of neo-authoritarianism. As India's current Prime Minister, Narendra Modi, has pointed out: "India is the largest democracy on earth. If you add up the next forty democratic countries you will just about reach the total of the electorate in India" (quoted in Price 2015: 14).

Within the Indian context, with its proud democratic heritage dating back to independence from British rule in the mid-twentieth century, the idea of authoritarianism is generally associated either with foreign countries, the pre-Independence colonial *raj* under which India was under the control of the British Empire, or the Emergency Decree of Prime Minister Indira Gandhi (1975–77). While the period of Congress Party dominance in Indian politics over much of the period from the 1950s to the mid-1990s was seen by its critics as a one-party monopoly (and even a one-family monopoly), the rise of the BJP (Bharatiya Janata Party) as the major opponent of Congress on the national stage since the 1990s has ushered in an era of increased political competition. However, the BJP itself has an ambivalent relationship with democracy. As Amrita Basu (2013: 81) notes, "the BJP's relationship to democracy has been double edged. While it has deepened democracy in some respects, it has also undermined it through its explicit commitment to Hindu majoritarianism, its periodic engagement in anti-minority violence, and its close ties to non-elected undemocratic civil society organizations." The leadership style of Narendra Modi has also been characterized as "authoritarian populism" which "seeks to harness popular discontent against elite corruption with majoritarianism to create an antagonism between the 'Hindu people' and a 'corrupt elite' that panders to minorities" (Chacko 2018: 1).

Addressing these claims, this chapter examines whether neo-authoritarianism is truly on the rise in India or whether this is merely a claim made by critics. This chapter proceeds as follows. After first exploring the concept of neo-authoritarianism, it then focuses on media coverage of Narendra Modi's centralizing leadership style, his control of other government institutions, relationship with civil society, and the transformation of state–media relations with attention

DOI: 10.4324/9781003042211-4

to his rule as Chief Minister of Gujarat state, the transition period in 2014 when Modi first became India's Prime Minister, and Modi's re-election to that post in 2019. Noting how a sizeable number of democratic deficits were already present under previous Indian governments, the study nevertheless concludes that since 2014 neo-authoritarianism has been not only a critical discourse but also a growing force in India.

Neo-authoritarianism

Although multi-party elections are still regularly held in India, critics have questioned the democratic credentials of a country whose governing practices look increasingly authoritarian. To take just one indicator, India's low ranking on the 2019 World Press Freedom Index (140th out of 180 nations) is hardly suggestive of a strong commitment to democratic flows of information and communication (Reporters Without Borders 2020). But does this reflect a more systematic shift towards neo-authoritarianism? Answering this question requires us to unpack the concept of neo-authoritarianism. While traditional authoritarianism has been around for centuries and has legitimated its rule via historical myths and traditions, *neo-authoritarian* regimes are marked by the following four elements.

Firstly, they seek public legitimacy through 'development' and 'nationalism' (Sahlin 1977). The concept of neo-authoritarianism itself first emerged alongside decolonization in the 1970s from analyses of dictatorial regimes in sub-Saharan Africa, but this idea soon became prominent during the 1980s and 1990s in post-Maoist China where neo-authoritarianism was conceptualized as a vehicle for modernization under which single-party rule and limits on political pluralism could accompany a focus on rapid economic growth and industrialization for an interim period of time in order to later set up a foundation for establishing a functioning democracy (Petracca and Xiong 1990; Perry 1993). By emphasizing state authority over society plus political stability while seeking to advance "the simultaneous construction of a free enterprise system and centralized state power" (Sautman 1992: 76), neo-authoritarianism is politically conservative on the one hand yet economically market-oriented on the other hand (Fu and Chu 1996).

A second component of neo-authoritarianism is the role of strong leadership. As Chinese scholar Wu Jiaxiang has argued, "neo-authoritarians do not stress political structure, but the political leader" who is an "authoritative," "brilliant," and "far-sighted" strongman who takes "resolute and decisive actions" to "enhance capital accumulation, dispose of resources effectively and provide the law and order necessary for commodity trade" (Sautman 1992: 79). Leaders of this ilk embrace scientific and technological modernization while simultaneously resisting intrusions of Western cultural norms by identifying with traditional values "as the foundation of national spirit" (Petracca and Xiong 1990: 1106). To achieve these goals, the leader works to strengthen the bureaucracy and military and the leader applies severely coercive means to suppress crime and corruption and to mute political opposition (Sautman 1992: 86).

Thirdly, while the advent of neo-authoritarianism is often associated with ex-totalitarian regimes softening their degree of authoritarianism as in post-Communist Russia (Becker 2004; Umland 2012), neo-authoritarianism can also emerge in reverse fashion when democratically elected leaders introduce creeping centralization and strong-armed measures to neutralize opponents (e.g., Levitsky and Ziblatt 2018). Either way, the primary legitimation of neo-authoritarian governance rests on prospective economic outcomes as opposed to a democratic procedural basis and it often appears to be driven by a *logic of late industrialization* since it is difficult for post-colonial states to enter the ranks of "first world" nations given intense international competition vis-à-vis a large number of already advanced economies (e.g., Kohli 2004). For example, Rodan's (1989) study of Singapore found its leaders were incentivized to adopt an economic strategy reliant upon high levels of state autonomy, civil servant loyalty, inducements to foreign capital, control over labour unions, and minimization of welfare expenditures. Yet, while economic objectives may be its primary drivers, a neo-authoritarian political state is compatible with either neo-liberal or developmental state approaches to capital accumulation.

A fourth significant feature of neo-authoritarianism is that the state's prioritization of rapid capital accumulation inhibits its commitment to competitive political pluralism. Thus, neo-authoritarian regimes allow some space for civil society associations to organize independently and occasionally critique the government but they also use an array of direct and indirect means to limit the political capacity of autonomous organizations from being able to dislodge or challenge the ruling clique or coalition (Petracca and Xiong 1990). This involves both muting domestic rivals and going after foreign-funded non-government organizations who are depicted as "agents of influence" and portrayed as interfering in domestic politics (Umland 2012: 30). When it comes to the media, neo-authoritarian states also tend to use drift-net laws, libel and defamation suits, denial of press credentials, intrusive auditing, and condoning or tolerating violence against opposition journalists and editors to bring about "self-censorship, the most common and important limit on journalistic activity" (Becker 2004: 150). Neo-authoritarians also usually place stronger controls over electronic and broadcast media than print media which may be independently owned as well as "relatively autonomous, accessible to the population and highly critical of the regime" (ibid.: 150).

To sum up, neo-authoritarianism is a system that combines media management and intimidation, civil society curtailment, centralization of state power, and prioritization of market-based economic growth over the promotion of social equality. Under this system, there is a limited degree of political pluralism combined with an unbalanced playing field as common under hybrid regimes featuring 'electoral authoritarianism' (Schedler 2006) or 'competitive authoritarianism' (Levitsky and Way 2010). The neo-authoritarian justification for this imbalance, however, is that a meaningful democracy requires "a high standard of living and experienced officials" and that neo-authoritarianism is a means to eventually achieving this state (Sautman 1992: 94).

Chief Minister Modi

We now begin to address the question of whether neo-authoritarianism is on the rise in India under Narendra Modi by examining his leadership style during his long tenure from 2001 to 2014 as the Chief Minister of the state of Gujarat. Modi, a career politician who earned correspondence Bachelor's and Master's degrees in political science from Delhi University and Gujarat University respectively, had been involved with the state's politics dating back to the 1970s. Formerly a full-time missionary (*pracharak*) for the Rashtriya Swayamsevak Sangh (RSS), which is one of the most important organizations promoting Hindu nationalism in India, Modi ended up developing a reputation as a formidable behind the scenes political organizer. For instance, during Indira Gandhi's 1975 Emergency decree, when

> Tens of thousands of opposition leaders and activists were imprisoned and the RSS was again banned. Modi narrowly avoided going to jail himself and took to wearing elaborate disguises as he travelled around distributing clandestine propaganda and helping to organize peaceful protests demanding the restoration of democracy.
>
> *(Price 2015: 33)*

> [Modi] set about compiling lists of contacts who could be trusted to carry out clandestine tasks and then used their knowledge of another wider circle of sympathizers and democrats to arrange accommodation for activists who needed places to hide. He also began raising money to pay living expenses of political refugees and activists, and arranged for disbursement of funds.
>
> *(Marino 2014: 42)*

Continuing his work as a key operative for the BJP, Modi developed a "growing reputation as a back-room genius" (Price 2015: 37) and in October 2001 was appointed interim chief minister of Gujarat. A few months later in early 2002, Gujarat became engulfed in massive rioting and violence after a train with Hindus aboard was set on fire resulting in about two thousand people (mostly Muslims) being killed in retaliatory communal violence across the state of Gujarat (see Yagnik and Sheth 2005). Modi was repeatedly blamed by NGOs, politicians, and the media for not taking swifter and more decisive action to stop the violence and prosecute the perpetrators. As a result, for the next 12 years he "was refused entry to the United States as a religious extremist and frozen out diplomatically by Britain, the European Union and many other western countries" (Price 2015: 1). Yet, despite heightened controversy over Modi's role during the carnage, a reputation for being anti-Muslim, and a perceived willingness to condone communal violence as a strategy to gain political popularity, Modi's charismatic leadership style brought him repeated electoral victories in 2002, 2007, and 2012 sustaining him in the position of chief minister.

Whereas a growing number of supporters viewed him as a champion of *vikas* (development) referring to improved standards of living, Modi was labelled an authoritarian ruler and schemer by critics who alleged that under his rule land was being "sold to industrialists at throwaway prices" with life "a daily struggle for many Muslims still living in closed, segregated communities twelve years after the riots" (Marino 2014: 210, 223). In response, Modi's supporters sought to reframe him not as a demon but as demonized. As one of his biographers noted,

> Modi is an uncomfortable example for the Congress and other 'secular' parties like the SP, BSP, JD(U), and the Left. His programme of empowerment is a challenge to their own model of entitlement and an alternative development path for India...Few Muslims had voted for him in December 2002. But in December 2013, 31 per cent did.
>
> *(ibid.: 118, 162)*

While not all agree on whether Modi was an authoritarian chief minister, he clearly ruled in a populist style and prioritized market-led and private investment-led economic growth over social equality and political pluralism (e.g., Joshi and McGrath 2015). As one biographer put it, "Modi operates with ruthless efficiency by appealing directly to the people over the heads of other politicians" and by transferring officials who did not work efficiently or in support of his plans (Marino 2014: xix). While reportedly taking a strong stand against corruption, "the criticism that Gujarat's administration was authoritarian remained. Critics said nothing moved without Modi's go-ahead. He held several ministerial portfolios and, despite the attempt at empowering bureaucrats, micromanaged all important decisions" (ibid.: 175).

In a nutshell, while serving as chief minister in Gujarat, Modi's apparent one-man dominance over the bureaucracy, extensive efforts at information management, promotion of private investment over political pluralism or social equality, and emphasis on native culture to the point of appearing to tolerate communalism and discrimination against foreigners and minorities (particularly Muslims) fuelled Modi's reputation of being neo-authoritarian.

Prime Minister Modi

In May 2014, India's Bharatiya Janata Party (BJP) and the New Democratic Alliance (NDA) coalition campaigning in the parliamentary election with Modi as its prime ministerial candidate won a landslide victory over the incumbent Congress Party-led United Progressive Alliance (UPA) government. The BJP was able to capture 282 of the 542 seats in the Lok Sabha (LS), the House of the People, while its broader coalition, the NDA got 336 seats. Congress won only 44 seats. Now holding an outright majority of LS seats, the BJP was able to form the first Indian government at the national level in nearly two decades without requiring the help of regional parties as coalition partners (Jaffrelot 2015). Yet, despite Modi's popularity and decisive win at the ballot box – no doubt facilitated by a colonial relic, namely, a first-past-the-post (FPTP) electoral system generating a manufactured majority since the BJP had only won 31% of the national vote – there were creeping accusations of Modi shifting India as a whole in the direction of neo-authoritarianism, depictions similar to those when he ruled in the state of Gujarat. Many feared Modi's goal was to make the BJP the "natural party of governance" and to stay in power for a long time (Marino 2014: 274).

In the aftermath of the 2014 election, news media likened Modi's leadership style to that of Indira Gandhi who famously pulled the plug on Indian democracy in 1975 with her "Emergency Decree" which ushered in two years of dictatorial rule as she was unwilling to let go of her position as prime minister. For instance, journalist Indrajit Hazra likened Modi's role in the 2002 Gujarat riots to Indira Gandhi's role in the 1984 attack on the Golden Temple in Amritsar.

> The irony of Modi being in the same political mold as Indira Gandhi…Both are intensely popular politicians transcending the political affiliations of most Indians. Both are authoritarian figures, one blooming from the Nehru–Gandhi gene pool while the other stemming from the RSS factory…And both are associated today with two calendar years – 1984 and 2002 – mentioned aloud only on the anniversaries of two respective carnages.
>
> *(Hazra 2014)*

Jairam Ramesh from the opposition Congress Party likewise described Modi in ways similar to many descriptions of Indira Gandhi.

> He is in complete command of both the administration and the party. His is the only voice that is heard and that counts. This may give an impression of cohesion and coherence in governance but it has already established an extreme centralization of power…He was cheered wildly by corporate India. But strangely, he has decided to choke its access both to himself and to his colleagues.
>
> *(Ramesh 2014)*

Even a senior member of Modi's own party, L. K. Advani, expressed similar views.

> 'Forces that can crush democracy are stronger today,' Mr Advani said in an interview with The Indian Express ahead of the 40th anniversary of the Emergency, which

was imposed on June 25, 1975. Congress and AAP leaders asserted that Mr Advani's observations were targeted against Mr Narendra Modi, who, according to them, was not following democratic norms while running the government.

(United News of India 2015a)

As these excerpts reveal, news media reported on Modi's style of ruling as concentrating power in himself while disempowering countervailing forces.

Modi was also portrayed as exercising a strong degree of control over parliament and the cabinet due to many BJP newcomers joining the Lok Sabha in 2014. This influx of "inexperienced candidates with little or no voter recognition" (Price 2015: 170) was seen by many as a deliberate tactical move to make the new MPs loyal only to Modi. Critics observed how legislative bills were not being assigned to parliamentary standing committees for scrutiny plus items were smuggled into bills at the last minute (Ramesh 2015). Modi also introduced proposed legislation to amend the constitution, to change how judicial appointments are made, and his government was accused of interfering with state governments by not following basic norms of federalism, for instance, in appointing Tathagata Roy as governor of Tripura.

> First, Mr Modi has undoubtedly centralized all authority and decision-making. In the process, he has reduced all but one or two ministers at most to non-entities. He operates directly with the top bureaucracy across ministries and departments, very often without the knowledge of the ministers concerned, and has now started direct interactions with top civil servants in the states as well.
>
> *(Ramesh 2015)*

Other seemingly neo-authoritarian actions included efforts to sideline the cabinet and parliament through executive orders called ordinances which bypass ordinary parliamentary voting procedures. Such ordinances were related to land acquisition, increasing FDI limits in insurance, opening up coal mining to private companies, and regularizing illegal colonies in Delhi (*Deccan Chronicle* 2014). Though only meant for extraordinary circumstances, Indian governments have issued about ten ordinances per year since Independence, whereas Modi's government passed nine ordinances alone in December 2014 (*United News of India* 2015b; see also Panda 2015). As one sympathetic biographer portrayed the situation:

> Sloth in the bureaucracy has been replaced by punctuality...In the Modi government, Ministers sort out inter-departmental queries promptly. Bureaucrats have specific timelines. Delivery and results are key. Once timelines and budgets are set by the PMO, strict adherence to both is monitored.
>
> *(Marino 2014: 283)*

Another aspect of neo-authoritarianism is restrictions on civil society and an increasingly shrinking space for civil society activities. Shortly after Modi's election, this became a prominent issue of concern as captured in the following criticism.

> Modi is a democratically elected authoritarian. Within a year of taking power, he is showing the same authoritarianism that marked his regime in Gujarat. His government has attacked Greenpeace, Action Aid, Amnesty International and other international NGOs as being "anti-development". Vociferous critics and campaign groups

are liable to go on a blacklist, and be blocked from receiving any foreign funding – even while their leader goes abroad touting for international investment.

(Chakraborty 2015)

Aside from intimidation and tighter regulations, others expressed alarm that civil society membership and discourses were being shaped by a government-led agenda. For example, the composition of the Indian Council of Historical Research and film censorship boards were altered by new appointees supposedly affiliated with the Hindu Right (*Deccan Chronicle* 2015). Meanwhile student groups such as the Ambedkar Periyar Study Circle (APSC) at IIT Madras experienced de-recognition supposedly for expressing critical views of Modi (*Press Trust of India* 2015). Such actions have led to a palpable fear that "civil society activities will not be tolerated if they question the official establishment line. Most of these institutions are now on the defensive and apprehensive" (Ramesh 2015).

There have also been suspicions that the Indian government has been intentionally creating or at least indirectly supporting divides within the civil society through communal mobilization (*Deccan Chronicle* 2015). As one observer has complained, "There is no question that the Prime Minister, for the most part, has resisted making incendiary and inflammatory statements, but then he has allowed his colleagues to do so as part of a deliberate strategy" (Ramesh 2015). Perhaps most irksome to his opponents has been Modi's unwillingness to condemn communalist behaviour attributed to the Hindu Right (such as lynching and other forms of violence) and efforts by his fellow partisans to convert or 'reconvert' Indians to Hinduism (Yechury 2014).

There have also been accusations of neo-authoritarian practices in state–media relations. Notably, freedom of expression in the mass media and the expression of views counter to that of Modi have reportedly come under threat as documented by Reporters Without Borders, an international NGO. In 2017, they found:

With Hindu nationalists trying to purge all manifestations of "anti-national" thought from the national debate, self-censorship is growing in the mainstream media. Journalists are increasingly the targets of online smear campaigns by the most radical nationalists, who vilify them and even threaten physical reprisals. Prosecutions are also used to gag journalists who are overly critical of the government, with some prosecutors invoking Section 124a of the penal code, under which "sedition" is punishable by life imprisonment. No journalist has so far been convicted of sedition but the threat encourages self-censorship. The government has also introduced new foreign funding regulations to limit international influence.

(https://rsf.org/en/india; accessed on April 1, 2018)

The threat of defamation suits has also provided the Modi government with a vehicle to intimidate and potentially retaliate against critics. As Liang (2015: 389) argues, there has been an increased use of tactics "by the religious right who has perfected the art of harassment by law" requiring those accused of defamation or incendiary speech to "incur extensive travel, time expenditure, harassment, and high legal fees to defend themselves". In addition to perceptions of widespread practices of censorship and self-censorship especially in film, broadcast media, and social media (e.g., *India Today* 2015), there has been growing fear that the public sphere is becoming saturated with messages favourable to the government while drowning out or muting competing/alternative voices. According to Jairam Ramesh of the Congress Party,

The Prime Minister has maintained an extraordinarily tight control on public communication. He has displayed a pronounced bias in favour of social media in conveying what he wishes to convey. His chief ministerial tenure had been marked by a conspicuous absence of occasions on which he could be questioned and this tradition of a monologue has continued.

(Ramesh 2014)

Meanwhile, journalist Ajaz Ashraf has commented about Modi that

He is an excellent communicator, boasting a philosophy of his own. Its principal thrust is to saturate the popular consciousness with his images, leaving no space for others… His twitter handle has 12.6 million followers, more than any newspaper in India boasts. He has a message out at every conceivable opportunity, communicating directly with people to tell them what he thinks is important, what his side of the story is.

(Ashraf 2015)

In similar fashion, the Aam Admi Party's Yogendra Yadav proclaimed that "Modi today symbolizes three things, authoritarian rule and development at any cost and rule of the majority community" (*Times of India* 2014). As these passages illustrate, critics had become convinced that Modi's government was overstepping the proper separation between the government and an autonomous civil society and media sphere while contributing to intimidation and harassment of dissidents and people belonging to certain minority communities.

Discussion

After becoming prime minister, news media reporting on the incoming Modi regime's treatment of parliament, civil society, and the media was clearly suggestive of neo-authoritarian practices exercised in multiple spheres of Indian governance. There were also quite a range of people depicting the Modi government as authoritarian although many of these figures were members of the political opposition especially from Leftist parties whom one might expect to be dissatisfied with an anti-secular right-wing government.

Against this background, it is worth considering whether the neo-authoritarian characteristics of Modi's government are all that different from the previous UPA government. After all, some aspects of democracy were deficient or in decline in India prior to Modi becoming prime minister. For instance, the Lok Sabha had experienced "a sharp decline in sitting days and duration of sitting hours" plus high rates of absenteeism, lost working hours due to disruption, parliamentary questions ignored by ministers, and a declining number of bills passed between 1952 and 2012 (Verma and Tripathi 2013: 157; see also Rubinoff 2013). Scholars had also documented various democratic deficits in India including governments' disregard for following proper parliamentary procedures (Verma and Tripathi 2013), intimidation and restrictions on civil society (Jaffrelot 2015), government influence over mass media and social media (Liang 2015), and severe underrepresentation in Indian politics of women, youth, and the working class (Joshi 2012, 2015; Kalra and Joshi 2020).

Relatedly, media commentators have pointed out how all governments in India (regardless of party composition) have exhibited authoritarian tendencies and that when given a chance whichever party is in control would try to suppress dissent in parliament and civil society (Chisti 2015). As for mass media, broadcast media in India has long been subjected to censorship and has functioned as a significant source of propaganda in favour of the ruling party especially during the period of Congress Party dominance from the 1950s through the 1980s. Others have also noted how the problem of "paid news" in India where "stories appearing in the media that appear to be independent but which have, in fact, been paid for" is "nothing new, and had been going on for years" (Price 2015: 161). However, as in other neo-authoritarian systems, Indian print media (unlike radio and television), is "not under the direct control of the government" and arguably "enjoys a fair share of political freedom" (Karan 2009: 199) though this has also come into question in recent years.

In this respect, the Modi government may be simply continuing a variety of pre-existing trends, but the influence of neighbouring China over the past two decades should perhaps not be underestimated in shaping Indian thinking on governance amidst a rising trend of authoritarianism globally (e.g., Joshi and Xu 2017). As Twinning (2014) notes, "with an eye on the threat posed by India's northern neighbour, Modi has increased defence spending by 15%. He has signalled his determination to revitalize India's economic growth, not only to advance domestic welfare, but to provide the resources to propel the country's military modernization."

Moreover, since getting elected, more and more people (not just opposition party politicians) have also been labelling Modi as authoritarian. For example, distinguished historian Gyan Prakash has noted how compared to the previous UPA government, power concentration has taken place within the ruling BJP party, among institutions of government, and additionally Narendra Modi's government has been able to deploy extremist Hindu nationalist forces "on the ground to intimidate the opposition" (IANS 2018). A federal minister who quit Modi's government wrote him in a letter that "the Union Cabinet has been reduced to a rubber stamp, simply endorsing your decisions without any deliberation. Ministers have become figureheads as virtually all decisions are taken by you, your office" (Reuters News 2018). The former head of India's state media has similarly noted the prime minister's office exercising strong control over all personnel appointments resulting in "board positions at more than 70 state enterprises… lying vacant for 2–3 years because of the backlog of files in Modi's office" (Reuters News 2018).

Reflecting a neo-authoritarian mould, intolerance has been on the rise and dissent (especially against Modi and his government) has been increasingly labelled as anti-national, defamatory or seditious with the "investigative agencies and security apparatus" seemingly deployed "to silence its critics" (Bhushan 2019). Moreover, government personnel working in or heading various public agencies such as the Reserve Bank of India and Central Bureau of Investigation have been apparently removed or prompted to resign for not being loyal to Modi (Reuters News 2018).

India's 2019 parliamentary elections and their aftermath seem to have only reinforced these neo-authoritarian tendencies. Getting 37% of the votes, the ruling BJP increased its LS seats to 303 (56% of LS seats) compared to only 52 (10% of LS seats) for the Congress Party who received 19% of the votes. That year, the central government's takeover of the Muslim-majority state of Kashmir, census registry in Assam state whereby nearly two million people (many of whom are Muslim) were not counted as citizens, and the Citizenship Amendment Act which would make Muslims (who cannot conclusively prove that they are already Indian citizens) ineligible to obtain Indian citizenship, not to mention police brutality against Muslim student protesters conveyed a strong impression of state-directed Islamophobia that is widely at odds with India's post-Independence secular tradition (e.g., Mody 2019).

Conclusion

This chapter has analyzed the public discourse associating Narendra Modi and his government with neo-authoritarianism, in particular how his government has approached parliament and the cabinet as well as concerns that there has been shrinking space for civil society and changes in government–media relations which have imperilled the free-flow of public information. As demonstrated here, during his tenures as both chief minister and prime minister, there is no question that opposition party leaders have regularly framed Modi as authoritarian, especially around the time of the 2014 and 2019 national elections.

Thus, on the one hand, the findings here suggest that the current Modi government reflects "the conventional Indian belief that once your party was in power, you could get away with whatever you liked: rules were now for other people" (Marino 2014: 166). As a former chief election commissioner stated in 1980: "Political parties make strong demands for the conduct of free and fair elections to legislative bodies, but choose to ignore the application of the same principles when it comes to the functioning of their own party organs" (*Kashmir Monitor* 2014). While the Modi government has demonstrated clear signs of neo-authoritarian behaviour, one must remember that Indian politics has long been beleaguered by corruption, cronyism, criminalization, nepotism, clientelism, caste-ism, sexism, and dynasticism, practices which many would view at odds with a well-functioning liberal democracy (e.g., Kohli 1990; Chhibber 2012; Chandra 2016).

On the other hand, as this study has observed, while India today is not (yet) as authoritarian as it was during the 1975–1977 Emergency Decree, India has clearly been moving in a neo-authoritarian direction under Narendra Modi. Thus, in the absence of strong and active resistance, neo-authoritarianism may increasingly become a mainstay of Indian politics if Modi or other rulers with authoritarian tendencies are able to successfully perpetuate a climate of fear, intimidate civil society, neutralize political opponents, and flood the public sphere with their own particular self-serving discourses to the relative exclusion of competing discourses. Yet, there is also potential for a democratic resurgence like India experienced in 1977, after Indira Gandhi's Emergency Rule ended and it is perhaps ultimately up to India's masses and its elites to decide whether such a turnaround will be occurring again soon.

Bibliography

Ashraf, Ajaz. 2015. "Four Great Leadership Qualities of Modi." *Kashmir Monitor*. June 5, 2015.

Basu, Amrita. 2013. "The Changing Fortunes of the Bharatiya Janata Party." In Atul Kohli and Prerna Singh, (eds.) *Routledge Handbook of Indian Politics*. New York: Routledge, pp. 81–90.

Becker, Jonathan. 2004. "Lessons from Russia: A Neo-Authoritarian Media System." *European Journal of Communication* 19(2): 139–163.

Bhushan, Bharat. 2019. "Is General Election a Referendum Where the Polls are about 'Modi vs Nobody.'" *Business Standard*. March 18, 2019.

Chacko, Priya. 2018. "The Right Turn in India: Authoritarianism, Populism and Neoliberalisation." *Journal of Contemporary Asia* 48(4): 541–565.

Chakraborty, Aditya. 2015. "Europe Carpets the Greeks but Rolls out the Red Carpet for Narendra Modi. How's That Right?" *The Guardian*. April 8, 2015.

Chandra, Kanchan (ed.). 2016. *Democratic Dynasties: State, Party and Family in Contemporary Indian Politics*. New York: Cambridge University Press.

Chhibber, Pradeep. 2012. "Dynastic Parties: Organization, Finance, and Impact." *Party Politics* 19(2): 277–295.

Chisti, Seema. 2015. "It is a Myth that you are More Efficient under an Emperor: Coomi Kapoor." *Indian Express*. June 13, 2015.

Deccan Chronicle. 2014. "Executive Order, Parliamentary Disorder." December 31, 2014.

Deccan Chronicle. 2015. "Slew of Ordinances shows Modi's Authoritarian Streak." January 9, 2015.

Fu, Hu and Yun-Han Chu. 1996. "Neo-Authoritarianism, Polarized Conflict and Populism in a Newly Democratizing Regime: Taiwan's Emerging Mass Politics." *Journal of Contemporary China* 5(11): 23–41.

Hazra, Indrajit. 2014. "The Sardar De-Congressed." *Economic Times*. November 3, 2014.

IANS (Indo-Asian News Service). 2018. "Today's Authoritarian Governance is Far More Ominous for Democracy: Author Gyan Prakash." November 23, 2018.

India Today. 2015. "Nirbhaya Film: US Expert Backs Ban, How American Papers Covered It." March 5, 2015.

Jaffrelot, Christophe. 2015. "The Modi-Centric BJP 2014 Election Campaign: New Techniques and Old Tactics." *Contemporary South Asia* 23(2): 151–166.

Joshi, Devin. 2012. "Who Gets Unequal Parliamentary Representation? A Comparison of India and Sri Lanka." *Contemporary South Asia* 20(3): 401–406.

Joshi, Devin. 2015. "The Inclusion of Excluded Majorities in South Asian Parliaments: Women, Youth, and the Working Class." *Journal of Asian and African Studies* 50(2): 223–238.

Joshi, Devin and Kathleen McGrath. 2015. "Political Ideology, Public Policy and Human Development in India: Explaining the Gap between Gujarat and Tamil Nadu." *Journal of Contemporary Asia* 45(3): 465–489.

Joshi, Devin and Yizhe Xu. 2017. "What Do Chinese Really Think of Democracy and India?" *Journal of Contemporary China* 26(105): 385–402.

Kalra, Sadhvi and Devin Joshi. 2020. "Gender and Parliamentary Representation in India: The Case of Violence against Women and Children." *Women's Studies International Forum* 82, DOI: 10.1016/j.wsif.2020.102402.

Karan, Kavita. 2009. "Political Communication in India." In Lars Wilnat and Annette Aw (eds.) *Political Communication in Asia*. New York: Routledge, pp. 191–215.

Kashmir Monitor. 2014. "Reviving Congress." August 17, 2014.

Kohli, Atul. 1990. *Democracy and Discontent: India's Growing Crisis of Governability*. New York: Cambridge University Press.

Kohli, Atul. 2004. *State-Directed Development: Political Power and Industrialization in the Global Periphery*. New York: Cambridge University Press.

Levitsky, Steven and Lucan A. Way. 2010. *Competitive Authoritarianism: Hybrid Regimes after the Cold War*. New York: Cambridge University Press.

Levitsky, Steven and Daniel Ziblatt. 2018. *How Democracies Die*. New York: Crown.

Liang, Lawrence. 2015. "Censorship and the Politics of Micro-Fascism." *Television & New Media* 16(4): 388–393.

Marino, Andy. 2014. *Narendra Modi: A Political Biography*. Noida: HarperCollins.

Mody, Anjali. 2019. "India Awakens to Fight for its Soul." *New York Times*. December 20, 2019.

Panda, Baijayant. 2015. "Order vs. Ordinance." *India Today*. February 2, 2015.

Perry, Elizabeth J. 1993. "China in 1992: An Experiment in Neo-Authoritarianism." *Asian Survey* 33(1): 12–21.

Petracca, Mark P. and Mong Xiong. 1990. "The Concept of Chinese Neo-Authoritarianism: An Exploration and Democratic Critique." *Asian Survey* 30(11): 1099–1117.

Press Trust of India. 2015. "Karunanidhi Slams 'Authoritarian' Irani for IIT-M Unrest." May 31, 2015.

Price, Lance. 2015. *The Modi Effect: Inside Narendra Modi's Campaign to Transform India*. London: Hodder & Stoughton.

Reporters Without Borders. 2020. World Press Freedom Index 2019. Available at: https://rsf.org/en/ranking/2019. (Accessed December 9, 2020.)

Ramesh, Jairam. 2014. "PM Must Establish Authority without Being Authoritarian." *The Mint*. August 31, 2014.

Ramesh, Jairam. 2015. "Opinion: The Namo 'Style'." *The Mint*. May 12, 2015.

Reuters News. 2018. "'Indira Gandhi 2.0': India Central Bank Coup a Sign of Modi's Authoritarian Ways." *Reuters News*. December 13, 2018.

Rodan, Garry. 1989. *The Political Economy of Singapore's Industrialization: National State and International Capital*. New York: St. Martin's Press.

Rubinoff, Arthur G. 2013/1999. "The Decline of India's Parliament." In Philip Norton and Nizam Ahmed (eds.) *Parliaments in Asia*. Abingdon: Routledge, pp. 13–33.

Sahlin, Michael. 1977. *Neo-Authoritarianism and the Problem of Legitimacy: A General Study and a Nigerian Example*. Stockholm: Raben & Sjogren.

Sautman, Barry. 1992. "Sirens of the Strongman: Neo-Authoritarianism in Recent Chinese Political Theory." *China Quarterly* 129: 72–102.

Schedler, Andreas (ed.) 2006. *Electoral Authoritarianism: The Dynamics of Unfree Competition*. Boulder: Lynne Rienner.

Times of India. 2014. "Modi against Basic Essence of Hindustan." November 4, 2014.

Twining, Daniel. 2014. "India, the Global Swing State for US and China." *Nikkei Report*. September 25, 2014.

Umland, Andreas. 2012. "Russia's New 'Special Path' after the Orange Revolution: Radical Anti-Westernism and Paratotalitarian Neo-Authoritarianism in 2005–8." *Russian Politics and Law* 50(6): 19–40.

United News of India. 2015a. "Advani Apprehends Emergency Imposition; Oppn Attacks PM." June 18, 2015.

United News of India. 2015b. "Cong will Oppose Ordinances Passed by BJP: Narayanasamy." January 11, 2015.

Verma, Rahul and Vikas Tripathi. 2013. "Making Sense of the House: Explaining the Decline of the Indian Parliament amidst Democratization." *Studies in Indian Politics* 1(2): 153–177.

Yagnik, Achyut and Suchitra Sheth. 2005. *The Shaping of Modern Gujarat: Plurality, Hindutva and Beyond*. New Delhi: Penguin.

Yechury, Sitaram. 2014. "New Year Ahead by No Acche Din." *Hindustan Times*. December 30, 2014.

3
PREFIGURING ALTERNATIVES TO AUTOCRATIZATION

Democratic dissent in contemporary India

Amrita Basu

A democracy that was once celebrated for its strong, autonomous institutions, vibrant civil society, and extensive civil rights and liberties, has sharply curtailed the peaceful expression of dissent. The Indian government has been censoring journalists and news outlets that criticize its repressive policies, disbanding progressive NGOs, and incarcerating critics without trial on baseless charges of sedition, defamation, and terrorism. Since assuming power in 2014, the Bharatiya Janata Party (BJP) government has decreed major policy changes, some of which violate federal and constitutional principles, with little deliberation and consultation. It has combined pro-poor populism and pro-corporate policies and promoted Hindu domination and minority subjugation. Two protests against these measures are especially significant: first, against the Citizenship Amendment Act (CAA) (2019–20), and second, against agrarian laws which render farmers more vulnerable to corporate exploitation (2020–present). An overview of the two protests will be followed by an exploration of how they challenge autocratization, through both their substantive demands and their democratic modes of organizing.

The most important of the many protests around the country opposing parliament's passage of the CAA occurred in Shaheen Bagh, southeast Delhi. On December 14, 2019, about a dozen women organized a sit-in at a highway, launching a 101-day nationwide movement; on some days it attracted 100,000 participants (Kumar and Abi-Habib 2020). The Shaheen Bagh protest persisted, despite record low temperatures, several court petitions seeking to evict the activists, and vicious rumours about them. The women vacated the protest site on March 24, 2020, when the government declared a lockdown to slow the spread of Covid-19.

The CAA provides an accelerated path to citizenship for non-Muslim immigrants who arrived in India before 2015 from neighbouring Muslim-majority countries. The Cabinet approved the creation of a National Population Register (NPR), which will document all Indian residents, citizens and non-citizens alike. The legislation empowers government functionaries to profile Muslims by requiring that they verify their citizenship. There is a clear link between the CAA and the government's publication of a version of the National Registry of Citizens (NRC) in Assam in August 2019, which excluded approximately two million people, including many Hindus who have lived in India for decades (BBC News 2019). The CAA enables Bengali Hindu migrants in Assam, whose names did not appear on the NRC, to

DOI: 10.4324/9781003042211-5

become citizens. If the government pursues the implementation of the NRC, as it has repeatedly stated it plans to do, it can revoke the citizenship of any Muslim who lacks documentation (Shankar 2020).

Several months after the anti-CAA protests, farmers organized a massive movement demanding that the government revoke three farm laws which eliminate guaranteed prices for certain crops and increase their vulnerability to corporate exploitation. The protests began in August, escalated in September, when parliament hurriedly passed the farm acts, and culminated on November 26th in a *Dilli Chalo* (Let's Go to Delhi) campaign; tens of thousands of farmers from Punjab and other north Indian states travelled to Delhi by foot, bicycle, and tractor to oppose what they called the black laws (Hollingsworth, Gupta, and Mitra 2020). The BJP-controlled Haryana government ordered police to dig trenches, create road blocks, and attack the farmers with water cannons, batons, tear gas, and rocks, to prevent them from entering the state. Undeterred, the farmers breached the barricades and blockaded roads, railway lines, and highways with tractors. They created makeshift camps at six entry points to Delhi; the largest were on the Singhu and Tikri borders. Carrying food, water, bedding, and other provisions that they claimed would last six months, they vowed to sit in until the government repealed the laws. Large numbers of women farmers joined the protest; 20,000–25,000 of them went to the Tikri border alone. By November 30, 2020, between 200,000 and 300,000 farmers had converged at border points on the way to Delhi (Mahajan 2020). To support the protesters, 250 million people across India – a global record – staged a 24-hour solidarity strike on November 26 (Pahwa 2020). Thousands of farmers entered the national capital on January 25 in anticipation of Republic Day celebrations and organized processions on government approved routes. Some protesters broke away, destroyed property, and injured hundreds of police officers. Movement leaders condemned this violence, which they believe was perpetrated by government supporters, and persuaded the farmers to return to the border sites. Relations between the government and the farmers' movement have become increasingly fraught. The government removed protesters' songs from YouTube, blocked their internet access, brought charges of sedition against journalists who have been covering the events, condemned international activists and celebrities who have supported the protests, and erected iron spikes on the entry points to Delhi. *Mahapanchayats* (congregations of village councils) in Haryana and Uttar Pradesh have organized huge gatherings to support the farmers' demands and condemn the government's actions. Participation in the sit-ins at the border sites subsequently grew. As of March 21, 2021, around 40,000 people were camping out at Singhu and Tikri.

Public investment in agriculture has long been declining, farmers' incomes and returns on investments have been falling, and indebtedness has been increasing (Ghosh 2020). North Indian farmers feel betrayed by Prime Minister Modi, who they voted for in the 2014 elections, because he promised to double their incomes in five years by increasing minimum support prices for agricultural produce. Instead, procurement prices under the current regime have been even lower relative to their costs than under the previous government (Himanshu 2019). Although the government claims that the reforms will free farmers from traditional wholesale *mandis* (markets), farmers allege that they will eliminate the safety net that minimum support prices provide. They oppose the weakening of regulated markets and public procurement and the vesting of authority to settle disputes in the central government and the bureaucracy rather than state governments and local panchayats. They also fear that private corporations, both domestic and global, will be able to determine what crops they grow and what prices they charge – which will increase landlessness, pauperization, and indebtedness.

The Shaheen Bagh and the farmers' protests have overcome the hurdles that single issue, grass roots movements typically encounter. Whereas distinctive cultural and political conditions confine most protests to the localities where they emerge, both of these broad-based national movements inspired similar protests in numerous places in Delhi and around the country. Those who could not visit or remain in Shaheen Bagh staged sit-ins wherever they lived. In one of our interviews[1], Ziya Us Salam, journalist and author, quoted a popular slogan, "every city, Shaheen Bagh". Punjabi Sikh farmers have been at the forefront of the protests because of the strength of their agricultural unions, their vital contributions to national food production, and their anger at the government's attempts to discredit them.[2] Many cities created their own "Nation for Farmers" campaigns. Protests in support of the farmers' movement have taken place across the world.

Notwithstanding several similarities between the two movements, the farmers' movement is larger and organizationally stronger. It is the culmination of a long history of mobilization by agrarian unions in Punjab and other states. Whereas the Shaheen Bagh movement lacked resources and organizational infrastructure, 40 farmers' unions created the Samyukta Kisan Morcha (Joint Farmers Front) to coordinate their efforts in November 2020. Compared to Shaheen Bagh, the farmers' movement enjoyed greater support from political parties, women's organizations, trade unions, and philanthropic groups. This is probably the result of several factors, including greater anti-Muslim than anti-Sikh sentiment. Farmers constitute a large voting bloc. Because 70 percent of the population derives its livelihood primarily from agriculture, farmers are considered indispensable to national wellbeing. For all of these reasons, the government was willing to negotiate with the famers, but not with the Shaheen Bagh protesters. However, the size and scale of the farmers' movement is both an asset and the source of potential internal division. For example, although Rakesh Tikait, a leader of the largest farmers' union, the Bharatiya Kisan Union (BKU), from Uttar Pradesh, had mobilized tens of thousands of people to participate in the farmers' protest since January 26, many activists distrust him because of his role in anti-Muslim violence in Muzaffarnagar in 2013.

Both movements challenged autocratization in four important ways, each of which will be analyzed in turn in this chapter. First, the Muslims who took the lead in anti-CAA protests and Punjabi Sikhs who spearheaded the farmers' protest, refuted allegations that as religious minorities, they were anti-national, and proudly affirmed both their faith and their secular commitments.

A second way that activists challenged autocratization, and in particular, the regime's hierarchical, secretive character, was by forging egalitarian, inclusive, communities. I describe this orientation as prefigurative, in that activists demonstrate through deliberative, inclusive processes, a commitment to democratic means and ends. The Shaheen Bagh and farmers' movements share the prefigurative orientations of many pro-democracy, anti-authoritarian movements that have emerged over the past decade in other parts of the world. Examples include feminist, square occupation, anti-globalization, and environmental movements (Berman 2019, Leach 2013, Yates 2020). Like prefigurative movements and orientations in other contexts, these two movements are moral, cultural, and expressive (Epstein 1991) and challenge dominant cultural codes (Melucci 1996). Although scholars tend to depict prefigurative as opposed to instrumentalist or strategic approaches as reflecting different priorities and world views (see Gorz 1968 and Boggs 1977), the two orientations need not be mutually exclusive. To the extent they diverge, this is related to differences in the movements' class, ethnic, and gender compositions, which influence in turn the resources they command.

Third, women in both movements challenged the government's populist claims to represent and protect them. Muslim women from Shaheen Bagh occupied public space and defied the narrow boundaries of identity politics to which Hindu nationalists have consigned them.

Women farmers spoke out against being rendered invisible by landlessness and the lack of social recognition of their labour (Quint 2020b).

Fourth, if the movements' democratic modes of activism challenge autocratization, so do their demands. Both movements have shown that the laws they oppose do not simply concern particular groups and issues but are relevant to all citizens because they erode democratic principles and privilege corporate over people's interests.

I. Linking secular and religious ideals

The BJP government conflates the Hindu majority with the "common people," while vilifying some religious minorities and seeking to assimilate others. On the one hand, it has sought to discredit and intimidate Muslims in Shaheen Bagh and Sikh farmers by describing Muslims as Pakistani terrorists and Sikhs as Khalistani separatists (in reference to the Sikh separatist movement in Punjab). Popular conspiracy theories claimed that the protesting farmers were actually Muslims, not Sikhs, and that Bilkis Bano, a renowned Shaheen Bagh activist, was paid to join the farmers' movement. (In fact, the police prevented Bilkis Bano from joining the sit-in.) (Jagga 2021, Pandey 2020). On the other hand, the government and right-wing social media have engaged in greater demonization of Muslims than of Sikhs. Hindu nationalists claim that Muslims are outsiders, whereas Sikhism is part of Hinduism. For example, on Gurpurab in November 2020, one of the holiest Sikh holidays and the birth anniversary of Guru Nanak, the founder of Sikhism, Prime Minister Modi tweeted, "I bow to Sri Guru Nanak Dev Ji on his Parkash Purab. May his thoughts keep motivating us to serve society and ensure a better planet"(Modi 2020).

Both protests have resisted the government's attempts to use religion to discredit and divide them. In opposing the CAA, Shaheen Bagh activists highlighted Muslims' daily experience of fear because of their clothing, names, and other markers of identity. In response to Modi's statement that you can identify those who engage in violence "by their clothes" (Quint 2019), women in burqas at Shaheen Bagh linked their faith to their democratic commitments. Ziya us Salam told us that many women felt that demanding constitutional rights was the will of Allah who believed, "…to fight for justice is the calling of every human being". As Hilal Ahmed (2020) argues, the protesters showed that far from turning them inward, their religious beliefs were tethered to their nationalist commitments.

The Shaheen Bagh protesters drew on early understandings of Indian secularism that promoted equality among people of all religions. They recited scriptures from the Gita, the Bible, the Quran, and the Guru Grant Sahib (Week 2020), as well as revolutionary poems by Pash, Habib Jalib, Muhammad Iqbal, and Ramdhari Singh Dinkar (PTI 2020). Challenging the BJP's allegations of their sectarianism, they demonstrated their support for another displaced group by organizing a meeting on January 19, 2020 in support of *pandits* (Brahmin Hindus) who were forced by militant groups to leave Kashmir in the 1990s (Ashraf 2020).

Sikh farmers resisted the government's misappropriation of their religion by organizing their own celebration of Gurpurab on the Singhu border where they prayed to Guru Nanak to make the government revoke the black laws (*Hindustan Times* 2020). Farmers at the sit-ins quote scriptures like 'sarbat da bhalla' (welfare for all) and invoke kar sewa (selfless service) to affirm Sikhs' commitment to the dignity of labour and opposition to the caste system. The camps on the border sites embody Sikh principles of *sewa* (service) and *langar* (a community kitchen in Sikh temples which serves free meals to all visitors, regardless of their religion, caste, class, and gender).

Sikhs also contest the government's attempt to discredit them as terrorists and Khalistani separatists (Arora 2020). One of their posters wryly proclaims, "When we save Hindus, we are angels; when we die to save the nation, we are martyrs; when we fight for our rights, we are Khalistani." They invoke memories of Punjabi revolutionaries and chant "Inquilab Zindabad" (Long Live Revolution). Posters of the young Sikh anti-colonial nationalist, Bhagat Singh, adorn the protest sites; young men wear tee shirts bearing his image, and women wear yellow scarves, the colour of his turban. Repudiating what they term the "godi" (lapdog or compliant) media, the farmers' movement has created its own YouTube channel, the Kisan Ekta Morcha, and the bi-weekly Trolley Times newspaper. According to Harinder Kaur Bindu, a leader of the BKU-Ekta Ugrahan, who we interviewed, the government's attempts to discredit the movement have backfired and revealed its own sectarianism.

Remarkable expressions of solidarity among opponents of the CAA and the farm laws attest to some of their shared experiences as religious minorities. The BKU organized a large delegation of Sikh farmers to travel from Malerkotla Punjab to join the protesters in Shaheen Bagh, in December 2019. The farmers brought posters which said in Urdu, "May brothers never fight again, may 1947 never be repeated" (Prabhu 2020). Recalling the horrific violence of Partition, but the ability of Sikhs and Muslims to prevent it in Malerkotla, they called for renewed unity in the face of the government's attempts to divide them (Rawat and Sanyal 2020). Sikh farmers brought rations and equipment to provide free meals to the surrounding community. A Delhi-based Sikh advocate, DS Bindra, reportedly sold a flat to set up a *langar* at Shaheen Bagh and other protest sites. As a result, he has been harassed by right-wing social media and the Delhi police (A. Menon 2020).

Muslims from Malerkotla reciprocated by travelling to the farmers' encampments at the Singhu border and preparing meals for them. Many women at the farmers' sit-ins said they were inspired by Shaheen Bagh women. Amandeep Kaur Deol of the Stree Jagriti Ekta Manch, who we interviewed, said that participating in anti-CAA protests gave her the confidence to become active in the farmers' movement. "We began to see that if women in Shaheen Bagh did not take the permission of their husbands, why should we?"

Both movements challenge autocratization by dispelling false characterizations of Islam and Sikhism, highlighting the way both religions promote equality, tolerance, and justice, and forging solidarities based on shared histories and aspirations.

II. Prefigurative movements

A hallmark of a prefigurative orientation is the creation of expressive, non-instrumental modes of communication. Both the Shaheen Bagh and the farmers' sit-ins became the sites of posters, murals, and art displays, that creatively challenged official narratives They were also the site of musical performances which forged composite cultural identities by drawing on diverse linguistic, regional, and religious traditions. The songs keep alive memories of resistance to repression in other times and places. The most popular songs at Shaheen Bagh included Aamir Aziz's *Sab Yaad Rakha Jayega* (We will remember everything, we will remember it all) and Faiz Ahmad Faiz's poem 'Hum Dekhenge', which was popularized in Lahore in 1986 to protest martial law in Pakistan under Zia-ul-Haq (Singh 2019) and was translated amidst the sit-in from Urdu into numerous regional languages.

Some 650 songs that the farmers' movement generated are inspired by rap, Sikh hymns, and folk melodies from Punjab and Haryana. They express the festivity associated with weddings, the faith evoked by religious hymns, and the revolutionary zeal associated with radical traditions. The songs of the Dalit poet Sant Ram Udasi (1939–1986) have become extremely popular.

Another hallmark of a prefigurative orientation is that it fuses a commitment to transforming both civil and political society. Contrary to Partha Chatterjee's view that there is a split in post-colonial societies between civil society, which is characterized by elitist, statist values, and political society, which is the realm of subaltern politics (Chatterjee 2004), both movements demand accountability from the state and civic responsibility for community welfare (food, housing, and shelter). People of different backgrounds and identities share responsibilities for cleaning, cooking, and childcare. The sites include health centres where doctors prescribe medications and health examinations. The camps the farmers have created on the border sites have gyms, salons, blood donation clinics, and libraries. Volunteers distribute refreshments and meals throughout the day to visitors and poor people from the neighbourhood.

The citizenship rights Shaheen Bagh women demanded were intimate and emotive. Intimate citizenship, Kenneth Plummer writes, does not "imply one voice, one way, or one model". On the contrary, it "…designates an array of stories and a multiplicity of voices, in which different lives, different communities, and different politics dwell" (Plummer 2003). Shaheen Bagh attracted people from a wide range of backgrounds and political affiliations. Strong bonds developed between older local residents and students from the neighbouring Jamia Milia Islamia University (hereafter Jamia). Punjabi farmers who joined the protest raised awareness about public policies that have contributed to the agrarian crisis. Trans activists joined the protest to oppose both the CAA and the new Transgender Persons (Protection of Rights) Bill, 2019, which requires proof of gender confirmation surgery for someone to be registered as trans-gender (Sarfaraz 2020). Even some BJP supporters, like Saksham Mishra from Kanpur, joined the protest because the new laws were, in Mishra's words, an "assault on the cultural fabric of the nation" (Mishra 2020).

The protesters at Shaheen Bagh promoted inclusive, pluralist citizenship. They exuberantly affirmed inclusive nationalism by reciting the national anthem at midnight on New Year's Eve, hoisting the tricolour on Republic Day, and inviting Modi to celebrate the festival of love on Valentine's Day. They distributed rose petals to the police. The most often read book at the site was the Constitution. Protesters read it aloud and displayed posters of its author, Dalit leader B. R. Ambedkar.

Compared to the Shaheen Bagh protest, the farmers' movement was less inclusive of the most vulnerable groups. The farmers' unions, which initially organized the protest, are dominated by Jat landowners in Punjab. They have not addressed questions that most con-cern landless labourers, like the recent passage of labour laws which extend the working day and dismantle workers' protections. Nonetheless, in early January, organizations of Dalit labourers, like the Punjab Khet Mazdoor Union and agricultural unions from Rajasthan and Maharashtra, which are more representative of landless and low caste labourers, refuted the government's charge that farmers were simply seeking to protect their class interests, and joined the sit-in at Tikri (Singh 2021). By participating, they reject the government's claims to champion Dalit rights, thereby demonstrating their opposition to autocratization. The Samyukta Kisan Morcha has welcomed their participation and called for broad class unity. Sikh gurdwaras (temples), which provide enormous support to the farmers' movement, emphasize equality across caste and class lines.

Prefigurative movements generally favour grass roots mobilization over electoral orientations. In this respect the two movements are similar. To maintain the movement's autonomy, the farmers' movement has not included even supportive party leaders in the negotiations with the government or allowed officials to speak on their platforms. To promote transparency and prevent dependence on any one leader, representatives from 31 farmers' unions alternate par-ticipating in these negotiations. Gurmeet Singh, vice-president of the BKU-Ekta Ugrahan, commented (Sethi 2020),

The pradhan (head) of the day chairs the meeting and later addresses the press about the decisions. No union leader should feel that because he is heading a smaller union he does not have the same say as the head of a larger union…This also makes it difficult for anyone to break the unity because in this kind of leadership everybody matters.

A comparison between the two movements suggests that a prefigurative orientation is born of both choice and necessity. The Shaheen Bagh movement defied instrumental logic in continuing the sit-in, despite the government's refusal to consider its demands, and prefigured democracy by enacting inclusive citizenship. The farmers' sit-ins were necessitated by the government's refusal to allow protesters into Delhi. However, despite growing public support and the government's increased willingness to negotiate, the movement refused to compromise. While engaging in a prefigurative approach, the farmers strategized, coordinated, mobilized, forged coalitions, marshalled resources, and determined how to frame their demands. The prefigurative orientation of both movements represented important challenges to autocratization.

III. Women's activism

Women in Shaheen Bagh and the farmers' protests have highlighted the detrimental impact of government laws and policies on their individual and societal roles. The government claims to promote women's empowerment and honour women's roles as wives and mothers while pursuing policies which undermine women's rights and the wellbeing of their families and communities. It paternalistically speaks for and about women while rendering them invisible as workers and citizens. Women in both movements have claimed voice and visibility as individuals, wives, mothers, and widows, thereby demonstrating their conjoined commitments to their communities and to their interests as victims of gender inequality.

In sharp contrast to the state's confrontational, aggressive, masculinist stance, the Shaheen Bagh sit-in reflected typically female values of nurturance, patience, and perseverance. Three local elderly women who are known as the Shaheen Bagh *dadis* (grandmothers) represent maternal strength, fortitude, and compassion. Nicholas Gill argues that those who experience temporary and shifting citizenship tend to value stillness in resisting exclusion (Gill 2009). The act of waiting patiently also offers a sharp contrast to the government's hurried and secretive decision-making style. Having experienced frequent displacement both before and after Partition, women resisted by refusing to be uprooted from their homes and communities. As Lucy Jackson (2016) theorizes, groups excluded from state-defined citizenry attach strong affective value to citizenship. They experience what she terms "emotive citizenship", that is "situated within their everyday intimate lives", and rooted in the here and now of home.

By anchoring motherhood within democratic values, Muslim women engage in what Werbner terms "political motherhood" (Werbner 1999, 221). They have opposed police violence against their husbands, sons, and grandsons who the state frames as anti-national terrorists and sexual predators. The catalyst to the Shaheen Bagh women's sit-in was their outrage at police attacks on students who were peacefully protesting against the CAA at Jamia. A video clip that went viral depicts four women surrounding a male student at Jamia to protect him from the police (Kuchay 2019). The protesters challenged Modi's claims to empower women through programmes like 'Beti Bachao, Beti Padhao' (Save the Daughter, Educate the Daughter), while disregarding the sufferings of women and girls who were sitting in the cold on the streets (NDTV 2020).

Several poems and songs challenge masculinist logic with symbols of feminine strength. Nabiya Khan's poem, that went viral, begins, "the revolution will come wearing bangles, bindis and hijabs". Darab Farooqui's poem, The Name is Shaheen Bagh, reflects the ways feminine modalities of protest imbue the movement with the warmth, love, and support that is commonly associated with home and community (*Quint* 2020a). A poster at Shaheen Bagh says: "Women's slogans will herald the uprising." A frequently heard refrain, drawn from South Asian women's movements, concerns *azaadi* (freedom). Its opening lines are: "My sisters demand freedom, freedom is our right, we will claim freedom, come what may." *Azaadi*, of course, refers to freedom from both patriarchal and state oppression (Menon 2020).

The Shaheen Bagh protest fostered what Farida Ayub called *bedari* (an awakening) about women's public roles. She told us: "People have understood that when women raise their voices, they strengthen communities and elevate them to new heights." Maya Bhagat said, "Men have always treated women as objects, as people who have to be told what to do. They think women can't have independent minds. This stereotype is so inbuilt that now we can't believe that women are standing up." Zaara Hashmi told us in an interview:

> People began to understand and listen to us. When we're in our homes, we can't be heard, but on the streets we can. Women were already aware, that is why they came out to protest. The movement made society realize that a woman's purpose is not just to have children and cook food. We can do a lot for this nation. We have capabilities that are suppressed, and (the protests) have created an atmosphere in which every woman can realize her potential.

Women have also played leading roles in the farmers' protests. More than 40,000 women joined the BKU-Ekta Ugrahan, and thousands of women joined 30 other farmers' unions in Punjab. The agrarian crisis has magnified gender inequalities and politicized women. The burdens on women have increased as a result of male migration to the cities rendering women increasingly responsible for what was traditionally considered men's work. Most of the women who joined *Dilli Chalo* were from the Malwa region, which has witnessed the highest rate of farmers' suicides in Punjab. Because more male than female farmers commit suicide as a result of indebtedness, the burdens of repaying debts at exorbitant interest rates fall largely on widows, who own little or no land. According to Kavitha Kuruganti of the All India Kisan Sangharsh Coordination Committee, although women conduct 75 percent of all farm work, they own only 12 percent of the land. She notes that the new laws will increase women's susceptibility to exploitation and make their labour even more invisible (Shergill 2020). Amandeep Kaur Deol commented in an interview, "As it is, we don't own land in our names and are paid half of what men earn. Unemployment is already so high. If we're forced to migrate to the cities, the only work we'll find will be as sex workers."

Fewer women have achieved leadership roles in the farmers' movement than in the Shaheen Bagh protests. Whereas Shaheen Bagh women organized within their own localities, female farmers must suspend their responsibilities to their families and cultivation and travel long distances to join the farmers' sit-ins. They have devised a partial solution by developing a rotation system whereby some women periodically return to their homes and other women from their villages replace them at the sit-in. Furthermore, some of the male leaders of the movement initially viewed women with suspicion and questioned why they were there (Kaur 2020). These women confronted the male leaders and persuaded them to allow more women to speak.

Farming women have been increasingly politicized over the course of the sit-in. They organized protests across the country to celebrate "Women Farmers Day" on January 18, 2021.

They were outraged when the Supreme Court Chief Justice SA Bobde urged women and the elderly to return home and implied that they were being "kept" at the protest (Newsclick 2021). Kavitha Kurungati commented, "One of the important points of concern is the paternalism and patriarchy reflected in observations with regard to women farmers. We urge the respected institution of the Supreme Court to recognise and appreciate the agency of women in this matter" (Bajwa 2021). Harinder Kaur Bindu who we interviewed travelled to the Tikri border on November 26 and has returned there intermittently. She said, "This was the first-time women travelled such long distances, often 300–400 kilometres. When there was no one to take care of our children and elderly relatives with us, we took them along. Men have come to realize that we have to join the movement for it to succeed." Men at the sit-ins have gained more respect for women's activism; they have signalled that sexual harassment will not be tolerated. Several women at the Tikri border commented that men did not assume that cooking and cleaning was primarily women's work.

Through their occupation of public space and their public voice and visibility, women in both movements have simultaneously challenged repressive laws and demanded an expanding bundle of citizenship rights.

IV. Challenges to neoliberalism and democratic erosion

Through their opposition to particular laws, both the Shaheen Bagh and farmers' movement engage in a broader critique of autocratization. Those who are excluded from citizenship rights are often at the forefront of struggles to achieve them. The Shaheen Bagh protesters are mindful, as Giorgio Agamben (2017) argues, that citizenship as a marker of political belonging supersedes social belonging in the nation-state. Agamben theorizes that the state's inclusion of citizens is premised on the exclusion of the non-citizen (what he calls bare life). For Agamben, the exclusion of non-citizens or stateless people ironically creates the foundations of citizenship.

For the Shaheen Bagh activists, demands for citizenship became a fulcrum for addressing a multitude of societal problems and state policies, including the threat of violent displacement, discrimination against Muslims, gender inequality, unemployment, poverty, and the lack of civic amenities in poor neighbourhoods. Amira Bashir told us that protesters criticized the government for investing millions of rupees in the NPR and NRC rather than funding programmes for women and the poor: "There is no budget for *tabdeeli* (progress or change), so poor people will suffer…The government should use funds to support migrant workers, and rape and child abuse victims. They should improve rural healthcare; even today poor people are dying because there are no doctors in their villages."

The Shaheen Bagh protesters show that, far from being empty abstractions, citizenship rights are crucial to the security and wellbeing of low income, marginalized communities. Their Citizens' Charter states: "Our struggle has been for an inclusive and participatory form of citizenship based on values of mutual empathy, care, and dignity. Now that we are called upon to show our commitment to these values, we shall rise to the occasion" (*India Legal* 2020). It emphasizes that "enshrined alongside their right to life and citizenship, is the inalienable right to a life of dignity, and these seemingly smaller issues are also an indicator of how (they) are treated as lesser citizens" (Shaheen Bagh Official 2020).

The pandemic has widened the chasm between the rich and poor and revealed the tensions between the government's populist and neoliberal policies. The farmers' unions have challenged three key features of autocratization: the growing centralization of power, the state's capitulation to business elites, and the violation of civil rights and liberties. In challenging the government's call for "One India, One Agriculture Market", farmers' unions uphold constitutional and federal principles that identify agriculture as the responsibility of state governments. This shows that the growing centralization of power undermines regional and local decision-making processes, while increasing corporate control (Singh 2020).

The farmers' movement claims that the state is catering to the interests of two of India's wealthiest families, Mukesh Ambani, the chair and managing director of Reliance Industries, and Gautam Adnani, chair of the Adnani multinational conglomerate. General secretary of the BKU-Ekta Dakaunda, Jagmohan Singh Patiala, commented, "We believe the newly enacted farm laws were passed to facilitate Reliance's entry into the farm sector. This is the only business which will never incur loss as everyone needs food, fruits, and vegetables" (Vishwadeepak 2020).

Union activists have called for the boycott of Reliance and Adnani products through social media, slogans, speeches, posters, and bumper stickers. Farmers have been switching their phone service from the Reliance-owned Jio to other mobile phone providers. In small towns and villages in Punjab, people have engaged in violent attacks on Reliance property. They have burned Reliance Jio SIM cards, destroyed cell phone towers, forced Adani's silos to close, disconnected power supplies to Jio mobile towers, and taken control of Reliance stores, petrol pumps, and a toll plaza (Bellman 2020). Leaders of the farmers' movement have supported the boycott but called for peaceful protest.

The farmers' unions have compared the government's high-handed passage of the farm laws with its decisions to demonetize currency in 2016 and abrogate Kashmir's special status in 2019. They charge that the government timed the passage of the farm laws amidst the pandemic lock-down to prevent protest. They have refused to co-operate with the committee the Supreme Court appointed to resolve the dispute because its four members have been vocal advocates of the farm laws. They have demanded that the government convene a special session of parliament where the farm laws can be openly reviewed.

Activists point out that one frequently ignored aspect of the reform is that it denies citizens legal recourse to dispute government actions. Section 13 of The Farmers' Produce Trade and Commerce (Promotion and Facilitation) Act, 2020, better known as the APMC Bypass Act, states that no legal proceedings, prosecutions or lawsuits can be brought against the central or state governments or their officers with "respect of anything which is in good faith done or intended to be done under this Act or of any rules or orders made thereunder". This provision prevents any citizen from pursuing public interest litigation against the government and big business (Sainath 2020).

The farmers' movement has taken a strong stand on the regime's violation of civil rights and liberties. On Human Rights Day, December 10, 2020, photographs of people who the government had incarcerated, adorned the podium on the Tikri border. The BKU Ekta-Ugrahan condemned the government for using draconian laws to imprison intellectuals, artists, activists, and anyone accused of challenging the regime. It released a statement which said, "The state wants people to remain confined to their narrow identities and narrow interests so that no one resists people being subjected to repression and torture." By demanding the release of political prisoners, the farmers' movement identified itself with a broader "people's struggle" (Brar 2020). In taking this stance, the farmers' movement not only opposed the incarceration of its own members but of everyone who challenges autocratization.

V. Conclusion

Judged solely by their political effectiveness, prefigurative movements have had mixed results. The Arab Spring generated hopes for democracy which were dashed by repression, coups, and civil wars. However, sit-ins must also be evaluated relative to alternative possibilities. Under prevailing political conditions, opportunities for expressing dissent are relatively limited; institutional channels are blocked and national political parties lack courage, power, and imagination. Although the activists at the sit-ins faced threats and harassment, their reliance on collective leadership and their sheer numbers, provided some protection from police violence and mass arrests. Unlike single acts of protest which by definition are of relatively short duration, prolonged sit-ins provide continual public reminders of popular discontent.

Regardless of their outcomes, prolonged-sits are often democratic acts. They educate the public about the dangers of government overreach and demonstrate the importance of active citizenship. They redefine who is a legitimate political actor and what is a legitimate form of political participation. They enable women to increase public awareness of the invisible labour they perform and to transgress the public–private divide (Sasson-Levy and Rapoport 2003, 399). As Asef Bayat notes, urban street occupations symbolically transcend "the physicality of the street, to convey collective sentiments of a nation or a community" (Bayat 2010, 212). Even when they fail to achieve their goals, they foster activism among other groups. The farmers' movement followed nation-wide protest against discriminatory citizenship laws. Other movements will surely follow.

The protests challenge the Indian state's attribution of political discontent to disaffected political elites who want to divide the country (the so-called "tukde-tukde gang). The sit-ins are not only the work of a broad swathe of society but their demands affirm broad-based nationalism and citizenship rights. People at Shaheen Bagh wore images of the flags on their bodies and continually read and posted passages from the Constitution. Punjabis expressed pride at serving in the army and feeding the nation. Popular slogans at the farmers' protest sites included "Hail the nation, Hail the farmer", and "No farmers, no food". Supporters of the protest refer to the farmers as India's "food soldiers". In reciting prayers as well as revolutionary slogans, both movements demonstrated the potential complementarity of faith, tolerance, and secularism. In cooking and eating together, participants rejected the caste and gender hierarchies that dietary practices create and sustain. In feeding police officers and the poor in neighbouring locales, they repudiated the discriminatory and opportunistic bases on which Hindu nationalists provide social services. Mothers and grandmothers showed that far from confining them to their homes, their domestic work and invisible labour fuelled their opposition to gender inequality.

In describing the historical memories that inspire occupations of public squares, Atef Said writes, "Spaces carry meanings that are constructed over time, redeployed and reconfigured in the present, and carried forward as inspiration for the future" (Said 2015). Both movements linked their attachment to the land to their identities, histories, and imagined futures. Older people shared stories about partition and anti-colonial nationalism while younger people described their experiences in students' and women's movements. Activists said that as important as their immediate goals were their legacies for future generations. Zaara Hashmi commented in an interview about Shaheen Bagh: "When our children ask us, 'where were you all when this was happening?' we can say, 'we were sitting on the streets fighting for you.' In this, we were successful: that we can look the next generation in the eye without shame and know that with whatever life we had in us, we fought." Amandeep Kaur asked, "What can we leave behind for our children other than a record of our struggle?"

Both the Shaheen Bagh and farmers' sit-ins draw on past memories to overcome fear and express hope for a more just future. By so doing they prefigure democratic alternatives to autocratization.

Notes

1 In addition to my own observations when I visited Shaheen Bagh in December 2019, Barkha Bhandari interviewed several students, activists, and journalists, in August 2020. And Ghazala Khan interviewed members of the farmer's union, women's organizations, and other activists in Malerkotla, Punjab in July–August 2020 and in February 2021. I use pseudonyms for many of the people who were interviewed. I'm grateful to Joan Cocks, Cynthia Enloe, Jayati Ghosh, Dipankar Gupta, Zoya Hasan, Mary Katzenstein, Mark Kesselman, Amna Pathan, Pritam Singh, Sten Widmalm, and Elisabeth Wood, for very helpful comments on this chapter.

2 For complex reasons that are beyond the scope of this chapter, farmers' unions in other parts of the country have had mixed responses to the protests; Maharashtrian unions have opposed it whereas unions in southern states have joined the sit-ins.

Bibliography

Agamben, Giorgio. 2017. *The Omnibus: Homo Sacer*. Redwood City, CA: Stanford University Press.

Ahmed, Hilal. 2020. "Who Represents India's Muslims? Thanks to CAA Protests, We now Know the Answer." *Print*, January 17, 2020. https://theprint.in/opinion/who-represents-indias-muslims-thanks-to-caa-protests-we-now-know-the-answer/350709/.

Arora, Kusum. 2020. "Farmers' Protest: Despite Rightwing Propaganda, 'Khalistani' Angle Finds Little Traction." *The Wire*, December 2, 2020. https://thewire.in/agriculture/farmers-protest-despite-rightwing-propaganda-khalistani-angle-finds-little-traction.

Ashraf, Asad. 2020. "Shaheen Bagh Protesters Express Solidarity with Kashmiri Pandits on Exodus Day." *India Today*, January 20, 2020. www.indiatoday.in/india/story/kashmiri-pandits-exodusday-migration-refugees-1638294-2020-01-19.

BBC News. 2019. "India Puts 1.9m People at Risk of Statelessness." August 31, 2019. www.bbc.com/news/world-asia-india-49520593.

Bajwa, Harpreet. 2021. "Farmers to Sit for Ninth Round of talks on Friday; Unions say Don't Have Much Expectations for Modi Government." *Indian Express*, January 15, 2021, www.newindianexpress.com/nation/2021/jan/15/farmers-to-sit-for-ninth-round-of-talks-on-friday-unions-say-dont-have-much-expectations-from-modi-government-2250367.html.

Bayat, Asef. 2010. *Life as Politics: How Ordinary People Change the Middle East*. Redwood City, CA: Stanford University Press.

Bellman, Eric 2020. "Protesting Farmers Target India's Largest Cell Company and its Billionaire Owner; More than 2,000 Cell Towers Operated by Mukesh Ambani's Reliance Industries have been Damaged Amid a Backlash Over Agriculture Deregulation." *Wall Street Journal (Online)*, January 6, 2021, *ProQuest*. Web. January 10, 2021.

Berman, Sheri. 2019. *Democracy and Dictatorship in Europe: from the Ancien Régime to the Present Day*. New York: Oxford University Press.

Boggs, Carl. 1977. "Revolutionary Process, Political Strategy, and the Dilemma of Power." *Theory & Society*, 4(3): 359.

Brar, Kamaldeep Singh. 2020. "BKU (Ugrahan) to Seek Release of 'Rights Activists', Delhi Riots Accused." *Indian Express*, December 10, 2020. https://indianexpress.com/article/india/bku-ugrahan-to-seek-release-of-rights-activists-delhi-riots-accused-7098812/.

Chatterjee, Partha. 2004. *The Politics of the Governed*. New York: Columbia University Press.

Epstein, Barbara 1991. *Political Protest and Cultural Revolution: Nonviolent Direct Action in the 1970s and 1980s*. Berkeley: University of California Press.

Ghosh, Jayati. 2020. "A Critique of the Indian Government's Response to the COVID-19 Pandemic." *Economia e Politica Industriale: Journal of Industrial and Business Economics*, 47(3–12), 519–530.

Gill, Nicholas. 2009. "Longing for Stillness: The Forced Movement of Asylum Seekers.' *M/C Journal*, 12(1).

Gorz, Andre. 1968. "The Way Forward." *New Left Review*, I, 47–66.

Himanshu. 2019. "What Happened to Poverty during the First Term of Modi?" *Mint*, August 15, 2019.

Hindustan Times. 2020. "Farmers Protesting at Delhi Border Offer Prayers on Guru Nanak Jayanti, Distribute 'Prasad'." November 30, 2020. www.hindustantimes.com/india-news/farmers-protesting-at-delhi-border-offer-prayers-on-guru-nanak-jayanti-distribute-prasad/story-guym76JB9Me7Wk3qN9pd8.

Hollingsworth, Julia, Swati Gupta, and Esha Mitra. 2020. "Tens of Thousands of Farmers Swarm India's Capital to Protest Deregulation Rules." *CNN*, December 6, 2020. www.cnn.com/2020/12/01/asia/delhi-farmers-india-protests-intl-hnk/index.html.

India Legal. 2020. "A Letter Addressed to the Judges of Supreme Court by 'the People of Shaheen Bagh'." March 26, 2020. www.indialegallive.com/top-news-of-the-day/news/letter-addressed-judges-supreme-court-people-shaheen-bagh/.

Jackson, Lucy. 2016. "Intimate Citizenship? Rethinking the Politics and Experience of Citizenship as Emotional in Wales and Singapore." *Gender, Place & Culture*, 23(6): 817–833. https://doi.org/10.1080/0966369X.2015.1073695.

Jagga, Raakhi. 2021. "Being Labelled Separatist, Khalistani Hurts the Most." *Indian Express*, February 13, 2021. https://indianexpress.com/article/cities/chandigarh/being-labelled-separatist-khalistani-hurts-the-most-7180722/.

Kaur, Mallika. 2020. "Unprecedented Farmers' Protests in India: Lest We Miss This Feminist Moment." *Ms. Magazine,* December 10, 2020. https://msmagazine.com/2020/12/10/india-farmer-protest-feminist-women/.

Kuchay, Bilal. 2019. "Meet India's Jamia Women who Took on Delhi Police in Viral Video." *Al Jazeera*, December 17, 2019. www.aljazeera.com/news/2019/12/17/meet-indias-jamia-women-who-took-on-delhi-police-in-viral-video/.

Kumar, Hari and Maria Abi-Habib. 2020. "Muslims Organize Huge Protests Across India, Challenging Modi." *New York Times*, January 4, 2020. www.nytimes.com/2020/01/04/world/asia/india-protests-modi-citizenship.html.

Leach, Darcy. 2013. "Prefigurative Politics" in *The Wiley-Blackwell Encyclopedia of Social and Political Movements*, edited by David A. Snow, Donatella Della Porta, Bert Klandermans, and Doug McAdam. Hoboken, New Jersey: Blackwell Publishing Ltd., pp. 1004–1006.

Mahajan, Anilesh S. 2020. "What Agitating Farmers Want, and Why the Centre may not Oblige." *India Today*. Retrieved December 6, 2020. www.indiatoday.in/india-today-insight/story/what-agitating-farmers-want-and-why-the-centre-may-not-oblige-1745475-2020-11-30.

Melucci, Alberto. 1996. *Challenging Codes: Collective Action in the Information Age*. Cambridge: Cambridge University Press.

Menon, Aditya. 2020. "United by Grief: Why Sikhs & Punjab Farmers are at Shaheen Bagh." *Quint*, February 20, 2020. www.thequint.com/news/politics/shaheen-bagh-sikh-farmers-punjab-langar-muslims-caa-nrc-protests.

Menon, Ritu. 2020. "Anti-CAA Protests by Muslim Women are about Where, How and Why You Belong." *Indian Express*, February 4, 2020. https://indianexpress.com/article/opinion/columns/shaheen-bagh-anti-caa-protest-mother-india-6249503/.

Mishra, Saksham. 2020. "'I am a BJP Supporter but I Oppose the CAA and I'm not Alone.' *Arré*, January 16, 2020. www.arre.co.in/pov/i-am-a-bjp-supporter-but-i-oppose-the-caa-nrc/.

Modi, N. @narendramodi. 2020, November 29, bow to Sri Guru Nanak Dev Ji on his Parkash Purab. May his thoughts keep motivating us to serve society and ensure a better planet. https://twitter.com/narendramodi/status/1333244471958355973?lang=en.

NDTV. 2020. "Shaheen Bagh Protesters vs Residents over Road Block." YouTube video, 13:49. January 13, 2020. www.youtube.com/watch?v=bPjiH_X2unE&t=618s.

Newsclick. 2021. "Don't Understand Why Children, Old People Kept in Protests." www.newsclick.in/%E2%80%98Don%E2%80%99t-Understand-Why-Old-People-Women-Kept-in-Protests%E2%80%99-CJI%E2%80%99s-Remarks-Spark-Outrage.

Pahwa, Nitish. 2020. "India Just Had the Biggest Protest in World History." *Slate*, December 9, 2020. https://slate.com/news-and-politics/2020/12/india-farmer-protests-modi.html.

Pandey, Neelam. 2020. "BJP Alleges Khalistani Agenda behind Farmer Protests, Says Congress Playing with Fire." *The Print*, February 13, 2021. https://theprint.in/politics/bjp-alleges-khalistani-agenda-behind-farmer-protests-says-congress-playing-with-fire/553292/Print.

Plummer, Ken. 2003. *Intimate Citizenship: Private Decisions and Public Dialogues*. Seattle: University of Washington Press.

Prabhu, Maya. 2020. "A Spirit of protest: How Indians are Uniting in Punjab." *Al Jazeera*, March 19, 2020. www.aljazeera.com/indepth/features/spirit-protest-indians-uniting-punjab-200310053308585.html.

PTI (Press Trust of India). 2020. "Anti-CAA Protest: Gita, Bible and Quran Recited at Shaheen Bagh, in Novel Inter-Faith Meet." 12 January. *The Week*. Accessed 24 June 2021. https://www.theweek.in/news/india/2020/01/12/anti-caa-protest-gita-bible-quran-recited-shaheen-bagh-in-novel-inter-faith-meet.html.

Quint. 2019. "'Those Creating Violence can be Identified by their Clothes': PM Narendra Modi on CAA Protests." December 15, 2019. www.thequint.com/news/india/can-be-identified-by-their-clothes-pm-narendra-modi-on-caa-protesters.

———. 2020a. "Naam Shaheen Bagh Hai: An Ode to Protesters who Sparked a Movement." February 24, 2020. www.thequint.com/news/india/naam-shaheen-bagh-hai-an-ode-to-protesters-who-sparked-a-movement.

———. 2020b. "What Women Farmers Protesting at Singhu and Tikri Borders Want." December 7, 2020. www.thequint.com/news/india/what-women-farmers-protesting-at-singhu-and-tikri-border-want.

Rawat, Gargi and Anindita Sanyal. 2020. "Sikh Farmers from Punjab Come to Cheer Shaheen Bagh Women, Cook Langar." *NDTV*, January 16, 2020. www.ndtv.com/india-news/sikh-farmers-from-punjab-come-to-cheer-shaheen-bagh-women-cook-langar-2164508.

Said, Atef. 2015. "We Ought to be Here: Historizing Space and Mobilization in Tahrir Square." *International Sociology*, 30(4): 348–366.

Sainath, P. 2020. "And You Thought It Was Only About Farmers." December 10, 2020. *The People's Archive of Rural India.* https://ruralindiaonline.org/articles/and-you-thought-its-only-about-farmers/

Sarfaraz, Kainat. 2020. "Transgender, Queer Groups March against CAA, NRC." *Hindustan Times*, January 4, 2020. www.hindustantimes.com/cities/transgender-queer-groups-march-against-caa-nrc/story-MU5PFAPVbhdLIUT4Q2y2lO.html.

Sasson-Levy, Orna and Tamar Rapoport. 2003. "Body, Gender, and Knowledge in Protest Movements: The Israeli Case.' *Gender and Society*, 17(3): 379–403.

Sethi, Chitleen K. 2020. "Five Reasons why Modi Govt. is Finding it Difficult to Tackle Protesting Farmers." *The Print*, December 8, 2020. https://theprint.in/india/5-reasons-why-modi-govt-is-finding-it-difficult-to-tackle-protesting-farmers/562291/.

Shaheen Bagh Official (@Shaheenbaghoff1). 2020. "The Shaheen Bagh Protest May Have Ended, but Our Movement Lives On." Twitter, March 24, 2020, 5:55 p.m. https://twitter.com/Shaheenbaghoff1/status/1242434958523760643.

Shankar, Soumya. 2020. "India's Citizenship Law, in Tandem with National Registry, could make BJP's Discriminatory Targeting of Muslims Easier.' *The Intercept*, January 30, 2020. https://theintercept.com/2020/01/30/india-citizenship-act-caa-nrc-assam/.

Shergill, Sunny. 2020. "Meet the Women Behind the Indian Farmers' Protest." *Aljazeera,* December 21, 2020. www.aljazeera.com/features/2020/12/21/meet-the-women-behind-the-indian-farmers-protests.

Singh, Pritam. 2020. "BJP's Farming Policies: Deepening Agrobusiness Capitalism and Centralisation." *Economic and Political Weekly*, 55(41), 14–17.

Singh, Sandeep. 2021. "'We Are One': Why Punjab's Landless Dalits are Standing with Protesting Farmers." *The Wire*, January 7, 2021. https://thewire.in/caste/punjab-landless-dalit-farmers-protest.

Singh, Sushant. 2019. "The Story of Faiz's Hum Dekhenge — From Pakistan to India, over 40 Years." *Indian Express*, December 27, 2019. https://indianexpress.com/article/explained/the-story-of-faizs-hum-dekhenge-from-pakistan-to-india-over-40-years-caa-protest-6186565/.

Week. 2020. "Anti-CAA Protest: Gita, Bible and Quran Recited at Shaheen Bagh, in Novel Inter-faith Meet." January 12, 2020. www.theweek.in/news/india/2020/01/12/anti-caa-protest-gita-bible-quran-recited-shaheen-bagh-in-novel-inter-faith-meet.html.

Vishwadeepak. 2020. "Protests against Farm Laws take Anti-Ambani, Anti-Adani Turn in Punjab." *National Herald,* October 12, 2020. www.nationalheraldindia.com/india/protests-against-farm-laws-take-anti-ambani-anti-adani-turn-in-punjab.

Werbner, Pnina. 1999. "Political Motherhood and the Feminization of Citizenship." In *Women, Citizenship and Difference*, edited by Nira Yuval Davis and Pnina Werbner. London: Zed Books, pp. 221–245.

Yates, Luke. 2020. "Prefigurative Politics and Social Movement Strategy: The Roles of Prefiguration in the Reproduction, Mobilisation and Coordination of Movements." *Political Studies,* 1–20.

4

AUTOCRATIZATION IN KASHMIR

Šumit Ganguly

This chapter will discuss the process of autocratization that has taken place in the Indian-controlled portion of the disputed state of Jammu and Kashmir since the early 1950s to the present day. The central argument of this chapter is that such an evolution has transpired largely because the Indian state, regardless of the government in office, has entertained deep misgivings about the irrevocable integration of the state into the Indian Union. As a consequence of these widely shared doubts a range of governments in New Delhi regardless of ideological disposition have tolerated political chicanery in the state, have given leeway to the use of undemocratic procedures and have, on occasion, resorted to questionable means to oust legitimate governments in the state. They have also passed draconian legislation that has substantially curtailed civil rights and personal liberties. Most recently, on August 5, 2019, the right-wing, Hindu nationalist Bharatiya Janata Party (BJP) abrogated the special status that the state had long enjoyed under the aegis of Article 370 of the Indian constitution. The writ of the Indian Central (national) government had been limited to defence, foreign affairs and communications. Furthermore, the state had its own constitution and its own flag. It had also enjoyed the right to forbid permanent settlement of non-residents in the state.

Background

Jammu and Kashmir had enjoyed these privileges owing to the particular circumstances of its integration into India. A brief discussion of the conditions under which it joined the Indian Union is in order. When the British Empire in India ended in 1947 it was divided into the two sovereign states of India and Pakistan. During colonial rule two classes of states had existed in the Indian Union. The states of British India were ruled directly from New Delhi, the capital of the Indian empire. Additionally, there were the "princely states" which were nominally independent but recognized the paramount status of the British. Under the terms of this arrangement the rulers of these states enjoyed a degree of autonomy but ceded control over defence, communications, and foreign affairs to the British (Ramusack, 2007).

As Independence approached, Lord Louis Mountbatten, the last Viceroy, decreed that these states had a choice: they could either join India or Pakistan but could not declare their independence when the British withdrew from their empire in India. Predominantly Muslim states that were contiguous would become parts of Pakistan while Hindu-majority states would

DOI: 10.4324/9781003042211-6

accede to India. Furthermore, he had argued that certain "geographic compulsions" would have to be taken into account as the monarchs chose to cast their lot with either India or Pakistan. A kingdom well within the borders of one of the two nascent states could not opt to join the other.

A unique situation confronted the state of Jammu and Kashmir. It was a princely state with a Hindu monarch, Maharaja Hari Singh, but with a Muslim-majority population. It also abutted the two emergent states. To complicate matters further, Maharaja Hari Singh had little interest in joining either India or Pakistan. As a Hindu monarch who was not especially well liked by his subjects, he had no desire to join a Muslim-majority state, Pakistan. By the same token, he was unwilling to join India because he feared that India's socialist-minded leader, Jawaharlal Nehru, would seize his vast estates.

Yet both countries were keen on merging the state into their respective domains. For India, which was founded on the principles of secular nationalism, integrating Kashmir was key to demonstrating that a predominantly Muslim region could thrive under the aegis of a secular state. Pakistan, in turn, was equally keen on acquiring the state because it saw an adjoining state with a mostly Muslim population as critical to the completion of its identity as the homeland for the Muslims of South Asia.

With the maharaja unwilling to accede to either country and in the wake of a tribal rebellion in the southwestern portion of the state, Pakistan's political leadership in connivance with the military launched a clandestine attack on the state. Maharaja Hari Singh, now in a state of complete panic, turned to India for military assistance as his forces proved to be completely powerless to stop the Pakistani onslaught (Whitehead, 2008). India agreed to provide assistance as long as two conditions were met: first, he would have to accede to India and second, the accession would need the imprimatur of Sheikh Mohammed Abdullah, the leader of the largest, secular and popular political organization in the state, the Jammu and Kashmir National Conference, which had played a vital role in opposing the rule of the Maharaja Hari Singh (Sisson and Rose, 1990). In the event, he agreed to both conditions and Indian forces were inducted into the state but not before the Pakistani intruders had seized as much as a third of the state.

The Delhi Agreement and after

Given the special circumstances of its accession to the Indian Union, Sheikh Mohammed Abdullah sought to forge a special relationship with the Indian state. This came to be codified in the agreement that he reached with Prime Minister Nehru in 1952. Under the terms of this agreement the state was allowed to have its own flag, draft its separate constitution, and also have a nominal head of state, known as the *Sadar-i-Riyasat*. Furthermore, the fundamental rights guaranteed under the Indian Constitution were abridged at the insistence of Sheikh Abdullah because their wholesale extension to the state would require it to compensate landowners whose properties had been subjected to land reform legislation (Das Gupta, 1968).

The autonomy that Abdullah had so zealously carved out would not prove to be long-lasting. In 1953, when Indian intelligence sources concluded that he was toying with the idea of declaring independence, he was deposed from office and incarcerated (Korbel, 2016). The same year a new constitution for Kashmir was adopted and under its terms Kashmir became an integral part of India. By 1960 the Indian Supreme Court assumed jurisdiction over the state (Brines, 1968).

Apart from these legal changes New Delhi had already chosen to overlook the questionable internal dynamics of Kashmir's politics. Despite Abdullah's extraordinary popularity, once in office he proved to be utterly high-handed in his ways and had displayed a strong streak of authoritarianism. As Jyoti Bhusan Das Gupta, a noted and early scholar of Kashmir's domestic politics, had astutely observed:

> Time has now come to pass judgment on Abdullah's government. Internally, it was hardly democratic. Opposition was suppressed, and civil liberties existed only in name and for those who shared his views. His economic views were radical but he combined them with a contempt for democratic practices in such a way as to invite comparison with the working of the like-minded totalitarian Governments elsewhere. He enjoyed tremendous popularity, yet resorted to questionable means to gain an electoral majority.
>
> *(Das Gupta, 1968, 209)*

It is evident from this description that the process of autocratization had started early in Kashmir and with the imprimatur of its principal leader. With this early resort to non-democratic practices and attendant norms it is hardly surprising that the National Conference would continue these measures even after Abdullah's removal from office. The formal reasons for his dismissal, however, were that he had lost the support of his Cabinet, that he had failed to mend differences within his Cabinet and that his policies had led to economic hardship in the state (Das Gupta, 1968, 208). His deputy, Bakshi Ghulam Mohammed, replaced him as the Prime Minister. Shortly after assuming office, Bakshi declared Kashmir's complete fealty to the Indian Union. Bakshi, who enjoyed the complete support of the government in New Delhi, proved to be equally disrespectful of democratic norms and principles. New Delhi, in turn, allowed him to act with impunity as long as he and his supporters did not raise the issue of secession.

Crucial choices and their consequences

For well over two decades, the Central (national) government in New Delhi had long overlooked the malfeasances of the National Conference governments in Srinagar. Electoral malfeasances in the state were rampant and the NC maintained a stranglehold on the politics of the state (Bhattacharjea, 1994). Political opposition in the state was anaemic and made little or no headway against the dominance of the NC. The NC steered clear of secessionist senti-ment and all Central governments proved willing to overlook any and all electoral shortcomings in the state. Furthermore, New Delhi, in turn, provided substantial amounts of economic assistance to the state to ensure political quiescence.

In 1975, after over a decade in political exile, one of Sheikh Mohammed Abdullah's key pol-itical acolytes, Mirza Afzal Beg, reached an accord with one of Prime Minister Indira Gandhi's principal political lieutenants, G. Parthasarathy. Under the terms of the Beg–Parthasarathy Accord the Sheikh was allowed to return to normal politics in the state with the understanding that he would not raise the secessionist bogey again. Shortly thereafter, Prime Minister Gandhi lost a national election and a coalition government under the banner of the Janata Dal assumed power with a former Congress leader, Morarji Desai, as the prime minister. In 1977 Desai committed himself to a free and fair election in Kashmir. Accordingly, the first election free of any electoral shortcomings since the 1950s took place in the state (Ganguly, 1997). Even though Sheikh Abdullah had suffered a heart attack three weeks before the election and was thereby unable to campaign, his party nevertheless won 47 out of a possible 76 seats in the state legislature.

Even as normal politics returned to the state, the process of autocratization that had long dogged the state continued apace. Even after Abdullah's return to power the state passed the Jammu and Kashmir Public Safety Act in 1978. It is ironic that the legislation did not originally have an explicit political intent. It was, instead, designed to curb timber smuggling, a rampant problem in the state (Ramachandran, 2019). Its underlying motivations had significant implications for civil liberties as it allowed detention without trial for up to a period of two years. With the onset of the 1989 insurgency, it has been used quite extensively to incarcerate political leaders (Duschinski and Ghosh, 2017). Most recently, in the wake of the abrogation of Article 370, it was also used to detain Farooq Abdullah.

In due course Abdullah anointed his son, Farooq Abdullah, as his chosen successor in 1981. In 1982, following his father's death, he became the Chief Minister of the State. In 1983, state-level elections were held and were also considered to be mostly free and fair. Within a year, however, factionalism within the National Congress led to the fall of the government. However, within two years, Farooq with the support of a Congress government in New Delhi was returned to office as the Chief Minister. Farooq's reliance on the Congress to return to office proved to be most consequential for his political fortunes. Many in the state and especially in the Kashmir Valley now saw him as an errand-boy of New Delhi.

Worse still, when the state went to the polls in 1987 the National Conference resorted to widespread electoral fraud. Earlier generations of Kashmiris may well have grudgingly accepted the outcome of the election. However, the generation of the 1980s who were far better educated, more politically conscious and better informed found the results to be unacceptable. Lacking a viable, alternative model of protest, substantial numbers of disaffected youth especially in the Kashmir Valley resorted to political violence.

The onset of the insurgency

The turning point, of course, came in December 1989 with the kidnapping of Rubiya Sayeed, the daughter of the Home Minister of the State, Mufti Mohammed Sayeed. To obtain her release the government caved in to the demands of the kidnappers. In its wake a full-scale insurgency erupted in the Valley.

Initially, a local, professedly-secular organization, the Jammu and Kashmir Liberation Front (JKLF) spearheaded the uprising. However, within months Pakistan quickly entered the fray, transforming a regional issue into an externally supported, religiously inspired extortion racket.

Fearing that it might lose effective control over significant parts of the state the central government in New Delhi unleashed a harsh, unyielding, and crude counter-insurgency strategy. It involved widespread cordon-and-search operations, the use of coercive interrogations of suspected insurgents and virtually unrestrained use of force. In considerable part this regime of repression took place under the governorship of a former civil servant and previous governor of the state, Jagmohan Malhotra. While he had proven to be a reasonably able administrator during his initial stint, in his second innings he proved utterly unsuited to the task.

Much of this approach was legally permissible because of the passage of suitable legislation. To begin with the Indian state was already armed with the sweeping powers embedded in the Terrorist and Disruptive Activities (Prevention) Act of 1987. This legislation had been passed largely to cope with the rise of terrorist activity in the adjoining state of Punjab. However, its provisions were extended to all of India. Under the terms of this act designated anti-terrorist courts could hold *in camera* proceedings, and the act protected the Central and state governments from any form of legal proceeding for actions taken in "good faith", permitted the use of the death penalty for terrorist acts and limited the rights of habeas corpus. Despite the existence of this legislation the government deemed it necessary to expand its legal writ. As a consequence, it resorted to more draconian measures especially designed to assuage the misgivings of the Indian Army about conducting counterinsurgency operations in the absence of a suitable legal shield (Ramchandran, 2015).

Among other matters it passed the Armed Forces Special Powers Act (Jammu and Kashmir) of 1990. Some of the provisions embedded in this act granted sweeping powers to the Indian Army as well as the paramilitary forces in the conduct of their operations in Kashmir. Once a region is declared to be a "disturbed area" the provisions of the act drastically limit civil liberties and personal rights.

It is important to underscore that this legislation which has been in effect in Jammu and Kashmir since shortly after the onset of the insurgency has its roots in India's colonial experience. It is based upon the Armed Forces (Special Powers) ordinance that the British colonial government had invoked in 1942 to crush the nationalist Quit India movement. And long before the AFSPA was applied to Kashmir it had first been promulgated in 1958 in India's northeast against the Naga rebels (Mathur, 2012).

To that end, certain features of this legislation, in particular, deserve discussion. As any number of activists and analysts have argued, the legislation grants considerable leeway to military and paramilitary personnel in the conduct of their operations. One or two features, in particular, deserve some discussion. First, as the following paragraph shows it virtually indemnifies any member of the armed forces from prosecution in the conduct of operations:

> If he is of the opinion that it is necessary so to do for the maintenance of public order, after giving such due warning as he may consider necessary, fire upon or otherwise use force, even to the causing of death, against any person who is acting in contravention of any law or order for the time being in force in the disturbed area prohibiting the assembly of five or more persons or the carrying of weapons or of things capable of being used as weapons or of fire-arms, ammunition of explosive substances.
> *(The Armed Forces Special Powers Act [Jammu and Kashmir] 1990)*

The act also permits members of the armed forces to arrest:

> Without warrant, any person who has committed a cognizable offence *or against whom a reasonable suspicion exists* [italics added] that he has committed or is about to commit a cognizable offence and may use such force as may be necessary to effect the arrest.
> *(The Armed Forces Special Powers Act [Jammu and Kashmir] 1990)*

Senior officials have defended these provisions on the grounds that they protect the armed forces from possible frivolous legal action in the routine conduct of their duties. However, in practical terms, the latitude that this act granted the armed forces led to extra-judicial killings, custodial deaths and fostered a culture of impunity in their ranks. Designed to cow the insurgents into submission this strategy proved to be almost entirely counterproductive. It successfully alienated segments of the population and especially Kashmiri youth who bore the brunt of these brutal tactics. If anything, the overall strategy only widened the scope of the insurgency as hapless individuals were caught in the counterinsurgency dragnet.

It was not until 1992, faced with a hardening and deepening of the insurgency, that the Indian state changed its strategy. The use of force remained under the legal aegis of the Armed Forces Special Powers Act (Jammu and Kashmir). However, the tactics that the armed forces adopted became far more calibrated and focused. Among other matters, the Indian Army created the

Rashtriya Rifles (RR), a dedicated counterinsurgency force which could be deployed without a long logistical tail. Furthermore, intelligence collection improved and better efforts were made to prevent infiltration from Pakistan. All these measures enabled the Indian state to restore a degree of order if not law in the state.

The evolution of the insurgency and beyond

Most importantly, the Indian state made arrangements to restore a semblance of political normalcy in the state through the conduct of reasonably free and fair elections. The first such election was held in 1996 and brought Farooq Abdullah of the NC back to power (Jones, 2008). Subsequently, a spate of other state level elections were held with the last one in 2014. All of these, for the most part, were deemed to be free of electoral taint. Despite the return of electoral democracy to the state the repressive machinery that had steadily been put in place over the years, and especially after the onset of the insurgency, remained largely intact. Accordingly, it is entirely possible to agree with the assessment of Paul Staniland that the situation in the state reflects the "paradox of normalcy". As he writes:

> The Indian state articulates a goal of normalcy that it does not allow to come to fruition. The official aspiration is a Kashmir where free elections, non-violent protest, and free speech replace the grim militarization of the 1990s. Yet, precisely as Kashmiris pushed forward such processes in the past half-decade, the Indian state cracked down on advocates because they articulated opposition to India's current relationship with Kashmir.
>
> *(Staniland, 2013)*

Of course, one of the most egregious strategies that elements of the Indian security forces have pursued even as legitimate governments have been in office is the practice of "fake encounters". This has involved the staging of incidents where suspected insurgents and terrorists have been killed with impunity. Segments of India's security forces have resorted to this egregious tactic largely because of the difficulties that they may have encountered in actually prosecuting these possible insurgents. Those capable of providing evidence against likely insurgents and terrorists may well have proven reluctant to serve as witnesses for fear of retaliation against themselves or their families. Under these circumstances, members of the security forces, on occasion, have resorted to this stratagem as a useful expedient. Despite the blatant illegality of this mechanism no member of the security forces has faced prosecution for these actions. Anthropologist Haley Duschinski has aptly referred to these extra-judicial killings as "regimes of impunity" (Duschinski, 2010).

Personnel drawn mostly from the paramilitary forces, most notably the Border Security Force (BSF) and the Central Reserve Police Force (CRPF) who constituted a Special Task Force (STF) and the Special Operations Group (SOG), have largely been responsible for these extra-judicial actions. In addition to these questionable methods various units of a range of paramilitary forces have been involved in "saturation tactics" that include the running of "checkpoints surveillance, cordon and search operations, human shields, prison detention, and torture" (Duschinski, 2009). These routine procedures have contributed to a widespread culture of repression and a significant constriction of civil liberties despite the persistence of electoral democracy in the state.

And it also needs to be highlighted that nationwide legislation, such as the Prevention of Terrorism Act (POTA) of 2002 passed in the aftermath of the terrorist attack on the Indian

Parliament in December 2001, which imposed severe penalties for involvement with terror, became applicable to Kashmir. Some of its key features underscore its anti-democratic ethos. It had an overly broad definition of what constituted terrorism, it allowed for detention without trial for 180 days and it allowed bail petitions to be postponed for an entire year. Faced with considerable opposition this act, however, was repealed in 2004. Nevertheless, a raft of other legislation which curtailed civil liberties both in Kashmir and elsewhere in India remained on the books (Roy and Singh, 2015; Ganguly, 2017).

The existence of this vast corpus of legislation aside, the military when frustrated with demonstrations that harried its routine operations but fell short of terror, again resorted to harsh (and potentially quite counter-productive) measures that showed scant regard for human rights. Specifically, in 2017, in the wake of a surge of popular protest including widespread stone pelting, the Indian Army picked up a Kashmiri man, Farooq Ahmed Dar, tied him to the bonnet of a jeep and paraded him through the locality as a warning to the protesters. By all accounts Dar had not participated in the protests and instead had been on his way to cast a vote in a national election. Not only was he subjected to this outrageous act but, worse still, the then Chief of Staff of the Indian Army, General Bipin Rawat, defended the action of the major who was responsible for using Dar as a human shield. To compound matters, he suggested that using Dar as a human shield amounted to an "innovation" and awarded him a medal (Rowlatt, 2017).

This culture of impunity, to some degree, has also been sustained because with rare and honourable exceptions the Indian press has not vigorously sought to expose and question the use of extra-legal tactics in pursuit of counterinsurgency operations in Kashmir. This failure to dispassionately probe the actions of Indian security forces in the state is an anomaly given that other lapses of policing in other parts of India are, for the most part, highlighted and commented upon at length. In this context, a careful quantitative examination of three major Indian metropolitan newspapers which enjoy a nationwide standing, *The Hindu*, *The Indian Express* and *The Times of India*, about the coverage of human rights in Kashmir arrived at some very revealing conclusions. Questioning official accounts of incidents in the state was deemed to be "anti-national" and the extent of civilian casualties was mostly overlooked. Worse still aspersions were cast about the reporting of human rights abuses on the part of global human rights organizations. Reports about the excessive or inappropriate use of force on the part of Indian security forces were treated as hostile propaganda. Most disturbingly, even an otherwise respected organization, the Press Council of India, appeared willing to accept the version of the armed forces when investigating allegations of a mass rape that apparently took place in 1991. In sum, it appears that much reportage of the state of human rights in Kashmir in the mainstream media has proven to be mostly state-centric in its orientation (Joseph, 2000). This willingness of a significant swathe of the Indian press to tacitly support the stance of the government in office has also enabled authorities to foster the culture of impunity that has long existed in Kashmir.

The end of Article 370 and its aftermath

On August 5, 2019, the Narendra Modi government passed legislation that formally abrogated Article 370 of the Indian Constitution (Ganguly, 2021). This move, of course, has been a long-standing demand of the BJP. Previous BJP governments had raised the prospect of its abrogation and had even included it in their election manifestos. However, in the end they had decided not to act. In considerable part, they had been inhibited from doing so because of the exigencies of coalitional politics as well as personal predilections of the Prime Minister. Modi, who had enjoyed a slender parliamentary majority in his first term (2014–2019) and had come to power on a mostly developmental platform, had also initially held off crossing the Rubicon.

However, within months of assuming office for a second term using his parliamentary majority he decided to revoke the special status of the state.

Doing so involved a legislative sleight of hand as he failed to follow through on a constitutional provision that required him to consult the state legislature before passing the legislation. Apologists for the government argued that it could not do so because the state legislature had been dissolved. That said, there is little or no question that the government was acutely aware that this move would be widely unpopular across much of the state and especially in the Kashmir Valley. It is reasonable to make this inference because prior to the revocation of its status the Central government had asked tourists to leave the region, it had blanketed the area with additional troops and issued a security alert claiming that militants were about to attack its troops (Jenkins, 2019).

The legislation bifurcated the state and created a legislature for the Kashmir Valley and Jammu but offered no such provision to the region of Ladakh. The two segments of the former state were now also made Union Territories under the control of the Central (federal) government. With this provision, along with Article 35 A, Kashmir will no longer have a separate constitution, its own flag, and all laws that Parliament passes will be applicable to the state and non-Kashmiris will now be able to purchase land in the state. The last issue is especially fraught because it raises the prospect of significant demographic changes. Even though this decision suborned constitutional norms and proprieties it was not entirely bereft of strategic logic. Having more firmly integrated the disputed areas into the Indian Union the government has undermined Pakistan's irredentist claim to the state. Quite predictably, Pakistan has lodged protests but the global community has paid scant heed to them (Ganguly and Tarapore, 2019).

Along with the abrogation of the article the government in New Delhi decided to incarcerate significant segments of the political leadership in the state under existing preventive detention laws. Only some of them were released in late December 2019 (Press Trust of India, 2019). Despite their release political activity in the state, for all practical purposes, remains at a standstill. While elections have been promised for the local legislature in Jammu and Kashmir the new constituencies have yet to be delineated and so the elections remain in abeyance.

The only elections that have been held thus are those for District Development Councils (DDCs). Organized and announced at very short notice they were conducted in late December 2020 against the backdrop of the Covid-19 pandemic. Non-BJP leaders vigorously argued that they had been given inadequate notice and thereby their ability to campaign had been severely hobbled. Their misgivings aside, the People's Alliance for Gupkar Declaration (PAGD), a conglomeration of six political parties including the two major local political parties, the People's Democratic Party (PDP) and the National Conference (NC), won a majority of the seats. The BJP, however, as a single party won the most seats. The Alliance performed best in the Valley and the BJP did well in Jammu. This outcome was hardly surprising given that Jammu is predominantly Hindu while the Valley is Muslim-dominated. Despite the success of the PAGD in the Valley and its hopes of restoring the statehood of Jammu and Kashmir, the likelihood of the BJP government resiling on its decision is all but slender to non-existent.

Conclusion

The exceptional terms under which the state of Jammu and Kashmir acceded to India explains a great deal about the Indian state's dealings with it. Virtually from the outset it tolerated a large degree of political chicanery in the state, granted leeway to a range of anti-democratic procedures and, over time, allowed the passage of legislation that curbed personal rights and civil liberties. It also tolerated a host of electoral malfeasances as long as local politicians did not raise the prospect of secession. All of these choices contributed to the erosion of democratic norms and procedures in the state.

Worse still, following the onset of the insurgency in 1989 and Pakistan's subsequent role in it, the Indian state contributed to the steady militarization of the state. It needs to be underscored that the Indian military presence in the state far exceeded previous deployments of its security forces to protect its borders from perceived threats from both the People's Republic of China and Pakistan. This process, in turn, led to a further denuding of civil rights and liberties even as the state saw the conducting of reasonably free and fair elections.

At this particular juncture it is hard to visualize a less autocratic dispensation for the bifurcated state in the foreseeable future. The National Democratic Alliance (NDA) government, which the BJP spearheads, has shown scant regard for the protection of personal rights and civil liberties within India (Ganguly, 2020). Given its propensity to shrink the scope of civil liberties across the country it is entirely reasonable to conclude that it will continue the repressive policies that have long been in place in the Indian-controlled portion of the disputed state.

Worse still, as long as Pakistan maintains its support for a range of terrorist organizations and they carry out random acts of terror, the BJP-led government will use them as a justification of maintaining the vast web of existing repressive legislation that curtails civil liberties. Furthermore, the present government recognizes that beyond the occasional criticism no foreign government is likely to sanction India in any meaningful fashion for its human rights record in the state. Given that most great powers are clearly willing to overlook far more egregious violations of human rights on a global basis the inference that the BJP-led government has made is hardly unreasonable. Consequently, the repressive apparatus that has existed in Kashmir for decades is likely to remain undisturbed.

Bibliography

Armed Forces Special Powers [Jammu and Kashmir] Act. 1990. Available at: www.mha.gov.in/sites/default/files/The%20Armed%20Forces%20%28Jammu%20and%20Kashmir%29%20Special%20Powers%20Act%2C%201990_0.pdf. Accessed on: January 17, 2021.

Bhattacharjea, A. *Kashmir, The Wounded Valley*. New Delhi: UBS Publishers, 1994.

Brines, R. *The Indo-Pakistani Conflict*. New York: Pall Mall, 1968.

Campbell-Johnson, A. *Mission with Mountbatten*. London: Penguin, 1985.

Das Gupta, J. B. *Jammu and Kashmir*. The Hague: Martinus Nijhoff, 1968.

Duschinski, H. "Destiny Effects: Militarization, State Power, and Punitive Containment in Kashmir Valley," *Anthropological Quarterly*, 82:3, 2009, 691–718.

Duschinski, H. "Reproducing Regimes of Impunity," *Cultural Studies*, 24:1, January 2010, 110–132.

Duschinski, H. and Shrimoyee Nandini Ghosh. "Constituting the Occupation: Preventive Detention and Permanent Emergency in Kashmir," *The Journal of Legal Pluralism and Unofficial Law*, 49:3, 2017, 314–337.

Ganguly, S. *The Crisis in Kashmir: Portents of War, Hopes of Peace*. New York: Cambridge University Press and Washington: Woodrow Wilson Center Press, 1997.

Ganguly, S. "India's Democracy at 70: The Troublesome Security State," *Journal of Democracy*, 28:3, July 2017, 117–126.

Ganguly, S. "Kashmir's Year of Hopelessness," *Foreign Policy.com*, August 5, 2020. Available at: https://foreignpolicy.com/2020/08/05/kashmirs-year-of-hopelessness/. Accessed on: January 13, 2021.

Ganguly, S and Tarapore, Arzan. "Kashmir A Casualty of India's Rising Power Status?" *The National Interest.com*, October 22, 2019. Available at: https://nationalinterest.org/feature/kashmir-casualty-indias-rising-power-status-90311. Accessed on: December 26, 2020.

Jenkins, L. "Thousands of Tourists Flee Kashmir After Security Alert," *The Guardian*, August 3, 2019. Available at: https://www.theguardian.com/world/2019/aug/03/thousands-of-tourists-flee-kashmir-after-security-alert. Accessed on: September 15, 2021.

Jones, S. "India, Pakistan, and Counterinsurgency Operations in Jammu and Kashmir," *Small Wars and Insurgencies*, 19:1, March 2008, 1–22.

Joseph, T. "Kashmir, Human Rights and the Indian Press," *Contemporary South Asia*, 9:1, 2000, 41–55.

Korbel, Joseph, *Danger In Kashmir*. Princeton: Princeton University Press, 2016.

Mathur, S. "Life and Death in the Borderlands: Indian Sovereignty and Military Impunity," *Race and Class*, 54:1, 2012, 33–34.

Press Trust of India. "5 Kashmiri Politicians Freed After 4 Months," *Kashmir Observer*, December 30, 2019. Available at: https://kashmirobserver.net/2019/12/30/5-kashmiri-politicians-freed-after-4-months/, 2017.

Ra, S. "India's Controversial Armed Forces (Special Powers) Act," *The Diplomat*, July 2, 2015. Available at:https://thediplomat.com/2015/07/indias-controversial-armed-forces-special-powers-act/. Accessed on: December 26, 2020.

Ramusack, B. *The Indian Princes and Their States*. Cambridge: Cambridge University Press, 2007.

Roy, A. and Kumar Singh, Ujjwal. "The Masculinist Security State and Anti-terror Law Regimes in India," *Asian Studies Review*, 39:2, 2015, 305–323.

Sisson, R. and Rose, Leo E. *War and Secession: Pakistan, India and the Creation of Bangladesh*. Berkeley: University of California Press, 1990.

Staniland, P. "Kashmir Since 2003: Counterterrorism and the Paradox of 'Normalcy'," *Asian Survey*, 53:5, October 2013, 931–957.

Rowlatt, J. "Why Indian Army Defended Kashmir 'Human Shield'," *BBC.com*, May 31, 2017.

Tunzelman, A. V. *Indian Summer: The Secret History of the End of an Empire*. London: Picador, 2008.

Whitehead, A. *A Mission in Kashmir*. New Delhi: Penguin, 2008.

5

RE-POSITING GENDER IN THE NEW NATIONALIST PARADIGM

Dinoo Anna Mathew

India in recent times has witnessed an expanding role of the national (union) government, with the dominant discourse revolving around military might, national security and a redefining of nationalism, the latter tilting heavily on majoritarianism as a plank for current political engagement and mileage. The increasing focus of the nation's development paradigm is centred on the concepts of 'oneness', 'one nation, one tax', 'one nation, one election' that are mooted by the national ruling party – the Bharatiya Janata Party (BJP). Nationalism and national security are major platforms on which the nation's progress and development are being charted. However these grand nationalist sentiments with a narrow ethnocentric focus obscure the everyday insecurities of local life and the chapter seeks to explain how. Three sets of issues viewed in the context of the current autocratization trends are especially highlighted here. The first relates to the narrow conception of security that has little worth for the rights and security of women and men especially among the marginalized groups. Their security as that of others is intertwined with their daily aspects of life and location in a particular caste, class or gender. The second relates to the various ways in which the space for autonomous functioning of local governments are shrinking due to the increasing centralizing trends by the union government and has the potential to hamper or even roll back the gender equality ideals envisaged and the gains on gender made through political decentralization. The third relates to how the insecurities and fault lines that already existed were magnified in the course of the pandemic.

Obscuring the local

The political vocabulary and its outreach in the past few years in the country have been dominated by the conceptions of military might, nationalism and national security, the core elements of the 2019 election manifesto of the BJP that sought to attract the electorate. This articulation of nationalism and the dominant narrative of safeguarding the nation from inimical neighbours found deep resonance with the voters in the past two elections to the lower house of parliament. However the question that looms large is: can the contours of national security that is advocated be divested of the core security concerns and wellbeing of its citizens?

DOI: 10.4324/9781003042211-7

The realist notion of security that is predominantly state centric has long been challenged by critical-security and feminist security studies (Steans 1998: 126, Tickner 2001: 43). Critical-security studies in broadening the conception of security from a traditional state centric and sovereignty analysis, have argued that security needs to be viewed from a bottom-up perspective, focusing on the individual with the goal of emancipation that frees people from social, physical, economic, and political constraints that restrain their free choice of doing what they want to do (Tickner 2001: 47). Deepening the debate, feminist security studies have overwhelmingly stressed the reassessment of notions of security to move beyond its traditional notions that privilege territorial integrity to viewing the manifold sources of insecurity that are immediate threats to women and specific groups according to their particular situations (Steans 1998: 126). Along with ecological concerns, feminist security studies therefore point out the insecurities posed to individuals and groups, especially women, by physical and structural violence (Terriff et al. 1999: 87). A broader understanding of security from a feminist perspective therefore entails locating women in their immediate environment, understanding the violations of their security while also assessing this from the standpoint of a patriarchal framework that promotes and sustains this violence (ibid. 86).

Viewed from this perspective, the insecurities faced by women in India are many and varied. Women continue to live in a society marked by patriarchal norms and attitudes and where there is a clear public–private distinction. According to the data from the National Crime Records Bureau, crimes against women have been steadily increasing over the years, with domestic violence against women the highest among them. This phenomenon of domestic violence which originates from and reifies the patriarchal norms in society denies women their fundamental security from violence. There is alarmingly high unemployment and abysmally low engagement of women in the labour market in India. The Economic Survey of India for the period 2019 to 2020 pointed out a decline in female labour force participation among the productive age group of 15 to 59 years, from 33.1 per cent in 2011 to 2012 to 25.3 per cent in 2017 to 2018, with a sharper decline evident in rural areas. The female worker population ratio also declined from 32.3 per cent in 2011 to 2012 to 23.8 per cent in 2017 to 2018 among the productive age groups. Unpaid domestic responsibilities and care work are disproportionately skewed towards women in India. In the last two decades there is an increasing proportion of working age women attending only to domestic duties and which in 2017 to 2018 was around 60 per cent (Economic Survey 2019 to 2020: 290). This is to a very large extent shaped by the prevailing social norms and unequal gender hierarchies that identify women's work with domestic responsibilities and care work and relegate them to a secondary status in the labour market. The devaluation of their contribution is compounded where their labour contribution is rendered invisible by viewing it as an extension of their domestic responsibilities or attributing to the essentialist notions of women's 'natural' care giving instincts. The critical aspects of their rights in terms of adequate wages and social protection are then not given their due importance. The agriculture sector, for instance, continues to be the main sector where women are employed, the nature of work is highly informal and women form the highest group of landless labourers (Chakraborty 2020: 289–290). It was only recently that women in the agricultural sector were recognized as farmers both by farmers' collectives and the state. With the decline in the agricultural sector, there has been an increased migration of men from rural to urban areas in search of work contributing to the high presence of female-headed households and feminization of agriculture. With limited access to land rights, to technical inputs and assets, and with restricted mobility, the challenges to women are many in such situations. Another instance is of community health workers known as accredited social health activists, mostly women, who are outside the ambit of any kind of livelihood security.

The same social and patriarchal norms extend to other arenas that depict women as needing to be controlled and incapable of making decisions on their own account. Some of these issues have been carried over from the past decades. Yet not only are these challenges progressively rising, currently there are disturbing trends that reflect a deepening of these concerns. Coupled with the interplay of caste and religion, an obvious manifestation of this phenomenon is the increasing incidence of honour killings and the calls to 'save' Hindu women from Muslim men through interfaith marriage or what the radical Hindu groups speciously call 'love jihad'. While some states in India already had legislation on freedom of religion, what is new is the increasing rhetoric around interfaith marriages with an overarching impulse to dictate women's choice regarding marriage, portraying them as defenceless and devoid of agency. To provide legal sanction, various states, especially those ruled by the ruling party at the national level, are rushing to bring in legislation regulating interfaith marriages focusing solely on religious grounds to decide the legality to the marriage. Other instances include the recent nonviolent protests, one led by women and formed against the backdrop of the amendments brought by the national government to the Citizenship Act. The other is the women farmers being one with their male counterparts protesting against the newly introduced farm laws by the national government. Both these agitations attracted participants across class, castes, and religious groups, lending a multihued articulation of their rights and insecurities. Despite the protracted nature of these protests, however, the state was and is found wanting in acknowledging and addressing their concerns and insecurities.

Since 1996 there have been multifaceted efforts by various governments to successfully pass the women's reservation bill providing for one third of the total number of seats in the lower house of parliament (Lok Sabha) for women. To date, the status quo on the women's reservation bill continues, even though its promise makes its way into political party manifestos, including that of the current political party. With the increasing impact of climate change and natural disasters, women suffer disproportionately through displacement, loss of livelihoods, lack of food, and gender-based violence. These environmental security issues and socio-structural security concerns of gendered violence, limited political and cultural autonomy, sexual division of labour, and increasing unemployment faced in their everyday lives are far more detrimental to women. Most of these gender insecurity concerns relate to the core issue of the sustainable development goal five: freedom from all forms of violence and discrimination and the promotion of gender equality and women's empowerment. Hence, where women continually face insecurities arising from direct gender-based violence, socio-structural violence and environment concerns among others, and where this does not come into the rhetoric of security that is being advanced, then the latter seeks to address only a partial notion of security. This narrow perspective of security that is foisted on citizens divests itself of addressing the lived realities of women and marginalized groups, the lived realities that matter to them most and shape their experience and idea of security.

Shrinking space of local governments

With the increasing linkages of global and local challenges of rapid urbanization, climate change, migration, displacement, growing inequalities and the drive against gender equality, various international bodies have been calling for a multi-level governance approach to address these issues. The United Nations, in setting the roadmap for the localization of sustainable development goals for instance, has underscored the significance of local governments as important partners in its achievement through promoting inclusion, diversity, and broad-based ownership (Global Taskforce of Local and Regional Governments 2016: 7). Further it calls for an approach for bringing together various government levels and different stakeholders to lead to a trans-formative change at the local level. Other organizations and networks, such as the United Cities for Local Government and the Global Parliament of Mayors, have been advocating the import-ance of cities engaging with global challenges and for multi-level governance frameworks that are inclusive. There is thus an increasing recognition of localization and local governments to design local actions involving local stakeholders and in ensuring the voice and decisions of women and marginalized groups to address global challenges.

Local governments, because of their proximity to people and the relevance of local ser-vices to their constituents, have the potential to advance women's participation and represen-tation in their decision-making processes. Internationally local and regional governments have been calling attention to the imperativeness of increased participation of women in local governments. The worldwide declaration on women in local government by the International Union of Local Authorities in 1998, which has since inspired many other calls for gender equality, stated: "Local government is an integral part of the national structures of governance and the level of government closest to the citizens. Therefore it is in the best position both to involve women in the making of decisions concerning their living conditions and to make use of their knowledge and capabilities in the promotion of sustainable development" (IULA 1998). Other significant initiatives included the European Charter for Equality of Women and Men in Local Life (2006), and the Paris Local and Regional Global Government Agenda for Equality of Women and Men in Local Life.

In India, given its size, vast population and the diversity of states that are held together in the federation, multi-level governance frameworks and localization assume even greater signifi-cance. However, it has been argued that while India adopted a federal structure, it conforms more to a 'quasi federal' structure and embodies both federal principles as well as strong cen-tralizing features (Singh N. 2016: 522, Singh M. 2016: 464). Autocratizing trends can therefore pose a clear and present danger. With regard to the legal constitution of local governments, even during the framing of the Indian Constitution, there were almost equal debates for and against inclusion of local governments as basic units of government with financial powers. Ultimately as a compromise formula, the provision for local governments was included in the Indian Constitution, under the Directive Principles of State Policy, which are non-enforceable recommendations for the governance of India (Sivaramakrishnan 2016: 562). It took another four decades for the passage of the 73rd and 74th constitutional amendment acts in 1992, man-dating the creation of rural and urban local self-governments respectively. The responsibility of devolving powers and responsibilities to local self-governments were left to the individual states of India. Hence the progress of decentralization varied across states, with many states making huge progress and others lagging behind. At the union government level, in the early 2000s there were systematic efforts towards facilitating the transfer of functions and functionaries by states to local governments through activity mapping (a process by which functions of local governments are delineated into activities and sub-activities to enable functional clarity for ser-vice delivery outcomes). Many states, in fact, progressed well in terms of activity mapping, yet the momentum kept varying.

The political decentralization process through the seventy-third and seventy-fourth con-stitutional amendment acts was a democratic mechanism that not only provided legal space for women's political leadership, but also a platform where the voices of women and men at the local level could be asserted, where they could stake a claim to democracy, and where the intersections of gender, caste, and class play out in the day-to-day lived realities. The acts provided 33 per cent reservation to women and proportional representation to scheduled castes and scheduled tribes in the rural and urban local governments. Various state governments moved further and provided 50 per cent reservation to women in local governments. This assumes enormous importance given that the proportion of women fielded as candidates for the lower house of parliament and the state legislative assemblies by political parties has been very low. However, at present there are discernible centralizing trends by the union government, leading to an incremental encroachment of the functional and financial space of the local governments. These put at risk the inclusive and equity issues sought to be addressed through the involvement of local governments.

The greatest trends are seen in the fiscal realm of local governments. It is evident that the presence of optimum amounts of funds at the discretion of the local government council is imperative to plan for locally relevant needs and priorities. In India, the revenue collected in the form of taxes and fees is a vital source for local governments with regard to funds at their disposal. However, this revenue has been declining over the years. Further, with the introduction of the goods and services taxes (GST) by the union government in 2017, the local governments in particular lost out on some of their rights of taxation especially with regard to entry tax, octroi, local body tax, and advertisement tax, which were a significant source of revenue. In the present arrangement, the proceeds from GST are divided only between the union and the states (ICRIER 2019: 6). The local government does not receive any proceeds even though three major taxes that they enjoyed earlier were absorbed into the GST. The other source of major revenue for local governments in India is the union finance commission grants. The recent Fifteenth Finance Commission has recommended rupees 90,000 crore as total grants for local governments for the 28 states for the period 2020 to 2021. However, out of this, 50 per cent of the funds for rural local bodies and for fifth and sixth schedule areas are tied in nature, meaning that they can be used only for the basic services of (a) sanitation and maintenance of open defecation-free status and (b) supply of drinking water, rainwater harvesting and water recycling (Fifteenth Finance Commission 2019: 49). Similarly for urban local bodies other than million-plus cities (cities with a population of one million or above), 50 per cent of the allocation is tied to drinking water (including rainwater harvesting and recycling) and solid-waste management. For the million-plus cities grants are allocated for the purpose of improving ambient air quality and for improving conservation, supply and management of water and efficient solid-waste management. With only 50 per cent of the allocation unconditional in nature, the local governments will have restricted funds at their disposal for planning efficiently for projects for their felt community needs.

The previous Fourteenth Finance Commission had specified 90 per cent and 80 per cent of its recommended allocation for rural and urban local governments respectively to be in the nature of basic grant and the remaining 10 per cent and 20 per cent as performance basic grants for rural and urban local governments respectively. The rationale was to provide unconditional support in the form of basic grants to the village *panchayats* and municipalities to improve the basic civic services including water supply, sanitation including septage management, sewerage and solid-waste management, storm water drainage, maintenance of community assets, maintenance of roads, footpaths and street lighting, and burial and cremation grounds (Fourteenth Finance Commission 2017: 123). To be eligible for performance grants, the Finance Commission laid the conditionality for local governments to submit audited annual accounts and to show an increase in own revenues over the preceding year. The commission also recommended that the union government accept their guidelines without imposing any further conditions. This, however, did not happen as pointed out by a study commissioned by the Fifteenth Finance Commission. The study highlighted that though the recommendations were accepted by the union government, in the course of time, further conditionalities were imposed by union ministries that sought to restrict the autonomy of local governments to spend the funds and by ascribing them to spend the resources on specific sectors determined by the union government (Accountability Initiative 2019: 17).

In other words, the union government brings out policies that require certain conditionalities which put the local governments at loggerheads with the conditions of the finance commission and that of the union government. This, coupled with the overall trend of low absorptive capacity of local governments that are unable to efficiently expend financial resources matching the needs or the priorities in their local development plans, leads to the situation where they are left in disarray. Low technical capacities and skills of local governments at financial and administrative levels has been a perennial problem which has not been given due and sustained importance. This impedes local innovation to address issues and challenges and to evolve alternative solutions.

Village *panchayats* are a microcosm of society in India. If viewed in that sense it is a platform where human interactions and frictions play out. Issues that have a direct impact on women (their freedom, independence, and safety) have a larger import in the local arena especially forums that are at the local level. Here the local councils are the immediate point of reference to articulate their issues. Where discretionary funds are limited, the scope for planning for women-specific needs and priorities diminishes. Issues of marital disputes, alcoholism, dowry, domestic violence, violence against women, gender impacts of declining agriculture, and rising unemployment among women then get lost or side-lined.

It was in 2005 to 2006 that a significant step towards including a gender budgeting statement in the Union budget was introduced. It was envisaged at that time that "the budget data will in due course be presented in a manner that the gender sensitivities of the budgetary allocations are clearly highlighted" (Gender Budgeting 2005 to 2006: 50). The budget statement has two parts which indicate budget provisions for schemes for the benefit of women: part A details schemes in which 100 per cent provision is for women and part B details schemes where 30 per cent provision has been earmarked for women. According to the gender budget statement of 2016 to 2017, "the purpose of gender budgeting is to monitor expenditure and public service delivery from a gender perspective, as a means of mainstreaming women's concerns in all activities and improving their access to public resources" (Ministry of Finance 2016 to 2017: 97). In examining the gender budget statements from 2005 to 2006 and 2020 to 2021, it is seen that the Ministry of *Panchayati Raj* (ministry responsible for rural local governments) furnished allocations under part B from 2008 to 2009 onwards until only 2016 to 2017. Thereafter there has been no reporting of allocation. The Ministry of Housing and Urban Poverty Alleviation has furnished allocations from 2006 to 2007 until 2016 to 2017 under part B, after which there has been an allocation only in 2020 to 2021 by the Ministry of Housing and Urban Affairs.

Another major centralizing trend is seen in the centralized provision of local services bypassing the functional and financial mandate of the local governments. As early as in 1993 the then Congress government had introduced a local area development scheme for members of parliament called the MPLADS. The scheme started with an annual allotment of one crore Indian rupees to each member of parliament to implement small works in his/her constituency. This was against the spirit of decentralization and federalism as the funds that were given to the members of parliament were actually funds that could have been at the disposal of the local governments. Further, by spending on local area development in their constituency, they were encroaching on the functional space of local governments who were and are still grappling with the ambiguities and overlap of their functions. The annual allotment was later increased to five crores of Indian rupees. Following this scheme various states' governments also initiated the local area development scheme for members of state legislative assemblies. The centrally sponsored schemes funded by the Union government with a matching grant from the state governments and which are tied to specific projects are yet another example of how national priorities get privileged over local needs and priorities. Over the years the scope of centrally sponsored schemes has been steadily increasing resulting in local governments being pressurized by imposed conditionalities, and a one-size-fits-all approach that goes against the grain of the 73rd and 74th constitutional amendment acts. The present BJP government had started yet another similar programme in 2014 called the *Saansad Adarsh Gram Yojana* (model village). It delegated responsibility to each member of parliament to adopt one village panchayat of his or her constituency and develop it into a model village by 2016, followed by two more village *panchayats* by 2019 and five more village *panchayats* by 2024. According to the performance review committee meeting of the *Saansad Adarsh Gram Yojana* in November 2017, 14 union ministries amended the guidelines or issued advisories with respect to 21 central schemes to enable priority for those *panchayats* that were identified under *Saansad Adarsh Gram Yojana* (Saansad Adarsh Gram Yojana 2017). All this points to how centralizing trends are autocratizing the spaces of local governments to function as de facto independent third tiers of government in the country.

There is enough evidence that argues for women to have an enabling environment in their homes so as to effectively exercise their responsibilities as locally elected members. However, critical aspects that still hamper women's prospects in political decentralization are the social norms and patriarchal environment in which women elected members have to function. Society continues to have deep-seated male-dominated attitudes that subordinate women. Data from the National Crime Records Bureau point to the increasing cases of crimes against women over the years. In 2019, the latest year for which data is available, there has been an increase of 7.3 per cent in cases of crimes against women (Crime in India 2019: xii). Evidently, it is domestic violence (cruelty by the husband or his relatives) that constitutes the majority of the cases registered under crimes against women.

Given the male-dominated political sphere, it is not surprising therefore that political representation of women in the parliament and state legislative assemblies has been very low. Political parties have for long restricted the number of women contestants to both the lower house of parliament and the state legislative assemblies. In fact, the percentage of women candidates contesting elections to the lower house of parliament was just 7 per cent in the period 2002 to 2019, some 4 per cent in 1977 to 2002 and 3 per cent in 1952 to 1977, even though women's winning strike rate is greater than men's (Roy and Sopariwala 2019: 242).

It is not that women are far removed from politics or are disinterested in the governance of the country. This is illustrated by the large numbers of women voters for all elections, which is highest for local government and state legislative assembly elections, followed by elections to the lower house of parliament. In fact, according to Roy and Sopariwala the greater turnout of voters, especially women in rural areas, has had an impact on the electoral strategies of major political parties (ibid. 49).

While arguing that the infringement of the financial and functional spaces of local governments is part of the current autocratization trends, this chapter also acknowledges the fact that just as other levels of governments, local governments too have their own challenges. However, this entails a separate discussion. Nonetheless, suffice to say that it cannot be assumed that local governments will be devoid of binding constraints and forces that negate the interests and rights of women and marginalized groups. What is required is for the national government and the states to provide the importance due to local governments as the primary sphere for local citizen engagement, a critical platform for realizing local aspirations and currently the only tier of government where mandated reservation is provided for women and marginalized groups. Local governments need to be nurtured and provided an enabling environment for them to work towards their potential of providing inclusive and accountable governance. It is true that local governments come under the ambit of the respective state governments and the latter in many states have shown reluctance to devolve functions and finances to local governments. However, the union government cannot shirk its responsibility towards enabling local governments to evolve as a self-governing third tier of the government in the federal structure. To date there have been no efforts by the present union government towards incentivizing state governments to devolve powers to local governments. On the other hand as the above discussion shows, there has been an incremental encroachment into the space of the local governments.

The Covid-19 pandemic

Societies are prone to shocks, both from within and those that are extraneous which are beyond their control. It is when they face these endogenous or exogenous shocks that they are really tested. The risks and vulnerabilities of women and marginalized groups are amplified during these times, especially where adequate attention and institutional measures to address these risks and vulnerabilities were minimal during 'normal' times. The pandemic took the form of such an extraneous shock that challenged and out-manoeuvred governments as the former ramped up its destructive scope. In India, the onset of the Covid-19 pandemic laid bare the lack of security and social protection for women and various social groups. Whereas such insecurities were rendered invisible during 'normal times' in the dominant narrative and discourses, it was only natural that they were exacerbated during the pandemic. The institutional measures to address these insecurities were severely lacking in their time-bound and sustained interventions. In April 2020 the United Nations Secretary-General called urgent attention to a "horrifying global surge in domestic violence" directed towards women and girls during the lockdown and importantly pointed out that violence is not just in the battlefield but "for many women and girls, the threat looms largest where they should be safest: in their homes" (United Nations 2020). In India, according to the National Commission for Women, there was an increased surge in the incidence of domestic violence. The Centre for Monitoring Indian Economy, a leading business information company and an independent think tank, had highlighted that women had a pronounced unequal share of job losses (13.9 per cent) as early as April 2020 and by November 2020 compared to men, a higher proportion of women were unable to re-enter the job market (Vyas 2020). Due to the prevailing gender inequalities and norms, girls are more likely to drop out of school than boys, severely affecting their educational and life outcomes. The pandemic has worsened the situation pushing them back reluctantly into domestic and informal jobs. The pandemic further exposed the weak and infrequent focus by the government on basic health care, especially primary health centres, impacting further the critical health care needs, especially of women in rural areas.

The above discussion reinforces the need for localized interventions that focus on better outcomes where factors of efficiency and equity are adequately addressed. The need for a sustained and enabling environment for local governments to be active and responsive in addressing these challenges cannot be overstated. However, during the pandemic, local governments were not considered as critical layers of government in responding to the overwhelming challenges thrown by the pandemic, challenges that at the same time were localized in nature and required localized approaches.

In response to the pandemic, the union government invoked the Disaster Management Act of 2005. While the act details the responsibilities of the union and state government, there is only a limited mention of the local governments. In India the lockdown came into force on 25

March 2020 and was lifted through varying phases by end of May 2020. For the implementation of the disaster management plan, local governments are the appropriate level of government, but they were never in the picture. In the initial stages as the lockdown eased, it was only the union government taking decisions. Later, the state governments were given directions within the overall framework set by the union government. The urban local governments came in last with the only exception being the Mumbai municipal corporation which took the responsibility for the *Dharavi* slum and to a large extent prevented the spread of the virus. Barring few state governments, like Kerala and Odisha that empowered local governments to work alongside them in addressing the pandemic, in many others there were hardly any formal powers that they enjoyed.

Conclusion

In India, since the overwhelming return of the BJP to power in the 2019 general elections, increasing trends towards undermining the power of states and a domineering stance of the centre has cast its shadow on the federal structure of the country. Politically this tension is manifest in the ways that the national government seeks to address issues without adequate deliberations and discussions. A recent case in point is the unilateral decision on critical farm law bills in parliament without reasonable discussion. Further, constraining the fiscal ability of states to spend on key priority areas, the national government's increasingly parochial attitude is steering the states into a bind.

The significance of multi-level governance and localized approaches to meet the diverse challenges facing the countries of the world cannot be emphasized enough. There is a need to realign priorities that take into account the lived realities of citizens especially those who are left behind in the overall growth and development of political discourse and practice. As the above discussion points out, this is particularly relevant for India, in a context where there has been a faltering of federal principles, a gradual concentration of powers and functions and its impact on issues relating to equality. The invisibility of the local and lived realities of people in security discourses resurfaces with the slow de-legitimization of the local governments, democratic institutions that are closest to the people. What is paramount is the urgent need to converse with people, especially women, the marginalized, the minorities, and those who feel left behind, building bridges with them and being responsive to their needs and securities; at the same time enriching and nourishing core democratic institutions such as the local governments that are invariably the first line of government that common citizens have access to. A divergent move that tends to centralize powers and functions fails to resonate with the needs of common citizens leaving them to deal with the insignificance of political rhetoric. This runs the risk of situations emerging that are more autocratic in nature sidestepping the essence of a democratic process. As is argued, for the 'real majority', that is, the poor, women, minorities, and marginalized groups, a negation of democracy and their rights is then a reality that they reluctantly have to live with.

Glossary

basic grant:	untied grant that may be used for core development activities of local governments
crore:	ten million
Dharavi:	one of Asia's largest slums and located in the Indian state of Maharashtra

fifth schedule area:	constitutionally designated tribal majority area in certain states of India
Lok Sabha:	lower house of parliament
panchayat:	village council
performance grant:	a targeted grant made based on specific goals achieved during a specified period
Saansad Adarsh Gram Yojana:	model villages
scheduled castes:	historically underprivileged groups of people recognized in the constitution of India
scheduled tribes:	tribes or tribal communities recognized in the constitution of India
sixth schedule area:	constitutionally designated tribal area in the north-eastern states of India

Bibliography

Accountability Initiative, Centre for Policy Research (2019) *Devolution of Union Finance Commission Grants to Panchayats. A Study for the Fifteenth Finance Commission*. Finance Commission, India (fincomindia.nic. in) (Accessed 16 October 2020).

Chakraborty, Shiney (2020) 'Covid-19 and Women Informal Sector Workers in India,' *Economic and Political Weekly*, 55(35), pp. 17–31

Council of European Municipalities and Regions (2006) *European Charter for Equality of Women and Men in Local Life*. www.charte_egalite_en.pdf (ccre.org) (Accessed 24 September 2020).

Government of India, *Saansad Adarsh Gram Yojana*. https://rural.nic.in/sites/default/files/SAGY_PRC_ 17Nov2017.pdf (Accessed 13 October 2020).

Government of India Disaster Management Act (2005) The Disaster Management Act, 2005.pdf (mha. gov.in) (Accessed 6 October 2020).

Government of India Ministry of Finance (2017) *Fourteenth Finance Commission*. New Delhi.

Government of India Ministry of Finance (2019) *Fifteenth Finance Commission*. New Delhi.

Government of India Ministry of Finance (2019–2020) *Economic Survey*. New Delhi.

Government of India Ministry of Finance (2005–2006 and 2020–2021) *Gender Budgeting*. New Delhi.

Government of India Ministry of Home Affairs (2019) *Crime in India*. New Delhi.

Global Taskforce of Local and Regional Governments. *Roadmap for Localizing the SDGs: Implementation and Monitoring at Sub-National Levels*. 818_11195_commitment_ROADMAP LOCALIZING SDGS. pdf (un.org). (Accessed 26 July 2020).

Indian Council for Research on International Economic Relations (2019) *Finances of Municipal Corporations in Metropolitan Cities of India. A Study for the Fifteenth Finance Commission*: Finance Commission, India (fincomindia.nic.in) (Accessed 16 October 2020).

International Union of Local Authorities (1998) *Worldwide Declaration on Women in Local Government*. Rat der Gemeinden und Regionen Europas: IULA Worldwide Declaration on Women in Local Governments (mittwaldserver.info) (Accessed 21 September 2020).

Roy, Prannoy and Dorab R. Sopariwala (2019) *The Verdict Decoding India's Elections*. India: Penguin Random House.

Seans, J. (1998) 'Feminist Perspectives on Security,' in *Gender and International Relations: An Introduction*. New Brunswick, NJ: Rutgers University Press.

Singh, Mahendra Pal (2016) 'The Federal Scheme,' in (eds.), Sujit Choudhry, Madhav Khosla, Pratap Bhanu Mehta, *The Oxford Handbook of The Indian Constitution*. New Delhi: Oxford University Press.

Singh, Nirvikar (2016) 'Fiscal Federalism,' in (eds.), Sujit Choudhry, Madhav Khosla, Pratap Bhanu Mehta, *The Oxford Handbook of The Indian Constitution*. New Delhi: Oxford University Press.

Sivaramakrishnan, K.C. (2016) 'Local Government,' in (eds.), Sujit Choudhry, Madhav Khosla, Pratap Bhanu Mehta, *The Oxford Handbook of The Indian Constitution*. New Delhi: Oxford University Press.

Terriff, Terry, Stuart Croft, Lucy James, and Patrick M. Morgan (1999) 'The Impact of Gender on Security,' in *Security Studies Today*. Cambridge: Polity Press.

Tickner, J.A. (2001) *Gendering World Politics*. New York: Columbia University Press.

United Nations (2020) *Amid Global Surge in Domestic Violence, Secretary General Urges Governments to Make Prevention, Redress Part of National Covid-19 Response Plans*, Meetings Coverage and Press Releases (un. org) (Accessed 28 October 2020).

Vyas, Mahesh (2020) *Female Workforce Shrinks in Economic Shocks*, Unemployment (cmie.com) (Accessed 18 December 2020).

6

AUTOCRATIC ENVIRONMENTAL GOVERNANCE IN INDIA

Anwesha Dutta and Kenneth Bo Nielsen

Introduction

In this chapter, we focus on the autocratization of environmental governance in India since the coming to power of Prime Minister Narendra Modi in 2014. If we broadly understand autocratization to mean "democratization in reverse" (Lührmann and Lindberg 2019), such a reversal has arguably occurred since 2014, as Modi's authoritarian populist regime has consolidated (Widmalm 2019). Like other such regimes, Modi's authoritarian populism is committed to the construction of a common sense that gravitates around a trope of economic growth and "development" that seeks to address frustrated subaltern aspirations in the context of rising unemployment while also opposing elitism and promulgating individual entrepreneurialism. This common sense is further wedded to a vitriolic rhetoric and politics of Hindu nationalism that expresses itself in autocratic forms through the policing of dissent, the targeting of "anti-national elements" both within and outside India, as well as communal and vigilante forms of violence targeting minorities (see Nielsen and Nilsen, this volume). This, in combination, pushes the Indian polity and public sphere in a majoritarian and authoritarian direction (Jakobsen et al. 2019; Nilsen et al. 2019) characterized by political unfreedom (Singh 2020).

In this chapter, we zoom in on the ways in which this autocratic turn has shaped environmental governance in fundamental ways. Earlier research on the linkages between political institutions and environmental policies tended to affirm that democratic institutions with robust legal systems that ensured freedom of speech, access to information, and enabled ecological lobbying generally improved environmental performance (Congleton 1992). While the opposite has been asserted for non-democracies, the relationship between political institutions and the state of the environment in fact varies across developing countries (Mak Arvin and Lew 2011). In a context in which we currently witness a rise in authoritarian populist regimes and a weakening of existing democratic institutions in many countries, we note that scholarly analyses of the relationship between these emergent regime types and environmental governance has only recently begun to emerge (McCarthy 2019). This chapter seeks to contribute to such emerging work by unpacking the linkages between authoritarianism, populism, and environmental governance in India under Modi. In doing so, we acknowledge the various positive environmental initiatives that have been undertaken by the Modi government. These include

DOI: 10.4324/9781003042211-8

important commitments to mitigate climate change and fight air and water pollution, and to invest in the transition to renewable energy. However, while such initiatives are undoubtedly important, we argue that Modi's broader agenda of prioritizing economic growth, enhancing the ease of doing business, and cracking down on so-called "anti-national" dissenters, has had decidedly negative consequences for India's environment and, indeed, for hundreds of millions of Indians.

The environmental stakes are high in India, a mega-biodiverse country that hosts about 10 per cent of the planet's biodiversity hotspots. The country's seventy million hectares of forests provide invaluable ecosystem services including biodiversity, water resources and climate change mitigation. They also provide direct livelihood support to more than 200 million people living in forests and fringe villages through the supply of fuelwood and non-timber forest produce (Lee and Wolf 2018). Yet, the high economic growth that has consistently been prioritized over other possible goals in the political economy over more than two decades – and which admittedly brought more than 250 million people out of poverty from 2005 to 2015, if only precariously so – has come about at the cost of significant degradation of natural resources and the environment. Indeed, in 2020, India ranked a lowly 168 out of 180 countries listed in the global Environmental Performance Index (EPI 2020). While the severe social and environmental challenges that arise from such "degradation-induced" development call for urgent interventions, we argue that what we witness under Modi's authoritarian populist regime is, rather, a relative disregard for key environmental challenges and a firm and growing commitment to economic growth, from which the regime derives legitimacy. As Palshikar (2019: 113–114) points out, Modi's authoritarian populism depends both on the support of corporate interests pushing an aggressive corporatized economy, *and* on the ordinary citizen being convinced that their economic wellbeing is a function of a strong nation – and therefore that the hurdles in becoming a strong nation (such as "anti-national activities") must be overcome. In the domain of environmental governance, this has manifested in the twin strategy of harnessing environmental policy and law to turn the environment into resources that can be incorporated into circuits of capital, while simultaneously intensifying policing and criminalizing environmental activists who are increasingly branded as anti-national enemies.

The chapter is structured as follows. We begin with a short historical overview of environmental governance in India. We then briefly discuss the autocratic turn under Modi, before turning to its impact on environmental governance. We subsequently single out two domains of environmental governance that we are particularly familiar with, namely forest governance and land governance. Although these two domains do not constitute an exhaustive account of the configuration of environmental governance in contemporary India (which would also include air, water, energy, etc.), we believe that the trends and processes we identify in these domains are diagnostic of a more general autocratic turn. The last section proceeds from the assumption that the ways in which a country responds to ruptures such as the Covid-19 pandemic can provide key insights into its governance context (Sareen et al. 2020). Against this backdrop, we analyze the autocratic undercurrent effecting significant changes to environmental governance during the pandemic. The conclusion summarizes our arguments about the autocratization of environmental governance under Modi.

A brief history of environmental governance in India

The first environment-related legislation in India was the *Forest Act* of 1865. The act consolidated state power to exercise exclusive control over designated forest areas, while the provision within the act towards accommodation of local communities' customary rights remained mostly on paper. A subsequent Forest Act 1878 demarcated forests into "reserved forests" and "protected forests". While protected forests were put under the sole control of the forest administration, within reserved forests, local populations were permitted limited usufruct access (Umashankar 2014). The Indian Forest Act 1927 eventually replaced the earlier Act of 1878, but the focus remained on the revenue-generating aspect of forests.

The early postcolonial decades were characterized by an overwhelming policy emphasis on nation-building through large-scale state investments in infrastructure, agriculture and industry. Environmental conservation received little attention, and only in 1966, when Indira Gandhi became Prime Minister, did environmental protection become *de rigueur* with strict implementation guidelines (Dutta 2020). Subsequently, the Wildlife Protection Act was passed in 1972, and in 1980 a committee was constituted which for the first time recommended the creation of a department of Environment in the Union government. Consequently, the Forest Conservation Act 1980 was passed, followed by the Environment (Protection) Act 1986. This act for the first time encompassed a comprehensive definition of environment as "water, air and land and the inter-relationship which exists along and between water, air, land and human beings, other living creatures, plants, micro-organisms and property" (section 2). Importantly, the act vested power in the central government to set environmental standards and grant environmental clearances for industries and activities.

While India thus expanded its legal framework for environmental protection from the 1980s, the liberalization of the economy simultaneously accelerated and led to increased industrialization, investments in modern intensive agriculture and growing commercial exploitation of resources (Williams and Mawdsley 2006). This brought to light the potential conflict between the environment and economic growth, with most Indian governments both then and now leaning more towards growth. This included the Congress-led United Progressive Alliance (UPA) government that preceded Modi, whose record on environmental governance was unimpressive. However, as we show below, this tilt towards economic growth at the expense of the environment has not only accelerated with the advent of the Modi government; it has also been pursued in a more autocratic manner than before.

Modi's new clearance raj

Modi brought the right-wing Hindu nationalist Bhartiya Janata Party (BJP) back from years of electoral decline to capture Parliament with a clear majority in 2014 (Jakobsen et al. 2019). The election campaign saw Indian capitalists rallying overwhelmingly behind Modi, including the likes of Mukesh and Anil Ambani, and Gautam Adani, who thrived under Modi's business-friendly regime (Jaffrelot 2019). A key means through which Modi – during his tenure as chief minister – sought to turn Gujarat into a favoured investment destination was the speed with which he ensured that all permits, licences, and environmental clearances could be obtained. Hence, a major target of his campaign rhetoric in 2014 was the ostensibly "policy-paralyzed" nature of the incumbent Congress Party that he alleged was caught up in what he spoke of as "the clearance raj", a euphemism for India's national wildlife, forest, and environmental laws that – according to Modi – acted as a slog on investments and national economic development.

As several chapters in this book note, Modi's style of governing is highly centralized. As Manor (2020: 109) argues, "most ministers in the central government learn what their policies are from their senior bureaucrats who transmit messages from the PMO". In the domain of environmental policy and governance, Modi's cabinet has worked to harness national policy to further the "ease of doing business" agenda, mostly by ensuring that permits and clearances – including environmental clearances – can be obtained swiftly by prospective investors. Within the first three months of assuming office in 2014, the Modi government issued environmental clearance to 33 out of 41 proposals diverting more than 7,000 hectares of forestland for the purpose of mining, construction, and special economic zones. A major share of the diverted land was allocated to private corporations. The environmental clearance process was also digitalized to enable "ease of application" (Anon. 2014); within two years, the average time for securing environmental permits had been reduced from 600 to 192 days (Aggarwal 2016). The government seeks to reduce this further to 100 days – and even less for specific growth sectors such as real estate, where the target is 60 days (Manohar 2019).

As Manor (2020: 97) reminds us, economic liberalizers need not be neoliberals by default. Nor are they by definition autocratic. However, we arguably detect an autocratic strand in Modi's efforts at economic restructuring at the expense of the environment. Notably, the dilution of the environmental clearance regime was implemented with very little preceding debate with key stakeholders, and without taking any steps to strengthen monitoring or other key environmental governance mechanisms, thus allowing the diversion of forestland for non-forestry purposes to proceed apace. Similarly, the National Board for Wildlife (NBW), which has the power to review all wildlife-related matters and approve projects in and around national parks and sanctuaries, has been significantly reconstituted. With Modi as the chairperson, the number of independent experts on the board has been reduced from 15 to three, and the board packed with "subservient officials" (Kaul 2017). But more significantly, its role as a deliberating and statutory policy-level body has been weakened. Thus, whereas the 47-member board used to have regular monthly meetings under the previous government, the NBW has reportedly not held a single meeting during Modi's prime ministership. All policy decisions and clearances have instead come from a much smaller standing committee (Kukreti 2020).

Comparably, a high-level committee established early on in Modi's first term to review and overhaul the gamut of laws on protection of wildlife, forests, and environment was severely criticized by the opposition, civil society, and environmental actors for being undemocratic and non-transparent, leading to its recommendations being struck down by a parliamentary committee. Nonetheless, several laws that have a direct bearing on environmental governance have been changed or diluted. This includes the Right to Fair Compensation and Transparency in Land Acquisition, Rehabilitation and Resettlement Act 2013, Wildlife Protection Act 1972, National Forest Policy 2018, Indian Forest Act 1927, and the Coastal Regulation Zone Act 2018. In addition to causing an overall weakening of environmental protection, the changes to these laws have also partially undermined legally enshrined rights of vulnerable groups in society, including the dispossessed, indigenous people, and forest-dwelling communities.

In addition to harnessing the legal and environmental policy framework to further the economic growth agenda, Modi's style of governance saw an increase in policing of environmental groups and activists. A confidential but "leaked" report by India's internal intelligence agency labelled Greenpeace India and other environmental organizations and activists as "anti-national" and accused them of negatively impacting India's GDP growth by several percent per year because of their opposition to environmentally damaging large-scale industrial projects. This was followed by what one observer called a "crackdown" on India's green NGOs (Bidwai 2015). The criminalization of environmental dissent under Modi entered the global spotlight when India entered the list of top contenders for the "deadliest countries for environmental activists" according to a Global Witness (2017) report, foregrounding India as one of three countries (alongside Colombia and the Democratic Republic of Congo) where the situation had considerably worsened. Killing of environmental activists had increased threefold from 2015 to 2016, "against a backdrop of heavy-handed policing and the repression of peaceful protests and civic activism", the report argues (Global Witness 2017: 6).

To summarize, the autocratic turn in environmental governance under Modi has combined "quick and decisive" and highly centralized action from above, mostly without popular deliberation, with increased policing of environmental activists. This has resulted in the dilution of environmental safeguards, violation of rights of vulnerable populations, and a much narrower space for popular participation and civil society engagement. In the following sections, we provide analyses of the authoritarian turn in environmental governance in the specific contexts of forests and land.

Forests

Since 2014, the Modi government has attempted to revise many of the existing forest and environment laws, while continuing to grant forest clearances in favour of development projects that adversely affect Adivasi, forest-dwelling populations and wildlife. The land rights granted to forest-dwelling communities via the Forest Rights Act 2006 – which, as stated in the Act, was introduced to undo the "historical injustice" caused by the seizing of forest areas by colonial and post-colonial regimes – have been particularly targeted. The government has refrained from amending this Act directly, instead working with other laws towards the same end. Thus, amendments proposed in 2019 to the Indian Forest Act 1927 sought to confer more power on forest authorities at the expense of forest-dwelling communities. According to observers, the amendments bordered on bestowing a "degree of veto power with the forest bureaucracy over the Forest Rights Act, 2006" (Sethi and Shrivastava 2019). The Modi government has also promoted forest conservation through large-scale afforestation and forest restoration for carbon sequestration. While forest conservation and restoration may be environmentally beneficent, new clauses specifying enhanced penalties on "violators" are likely to adversely affect marginalized forest-dwelling and tribal communities who have historically depended on protected areas for livelihood. Momentarily, these proposed amendments have been stalled by nationwide protests from environmental groups, who argue that their passage would undermine the hard-won rights of forest-dwelling and tribal communities who have historically been subjected to often violent repression by the forest department.

Other governmental efforts that in effect undermine legally enshrined rights to forests and land have been enabled by India's Nationally Determined Contribution under the Paris Agreement to creating an additional carbon sink of 2.5 to 3 billion tonnes through afforestation by 2030. India has sought to realize this goal through the Compensatory Afforestation Fund Act 2016 (CAFA) and Rules 2018. In short, CAFA seeks to offset the loss of forests cleared in one place for industrial, infrastructure, and other non-forest projects by acquiring an equal amount of land (including degraded forestland) elsewhere and creating new forests. In this context, the law considers "plantations" as forest cover, meaning that many newly afforested areas are actually plantations. Species prominent in these plantations are invariably non-indigenous and commercial species – including rubber, eucalyptus, teak, and pine – that come with massive social and ecological costs, often alienating local communities in and near new "forests". As in the other cases discussed above, these local communities are mostly tribal and forest-dwelling groups who are rarely considered stakeholders or consulted in the process.

Establishing afforestation and plantation activities under CAFA is usually done through fencing targeted sites, posting guards, installing CCTV cameras, and fixing signboards that restrict the entry of tribal and forest-dwelling communities (Saxena 2019). Such coercive and non-consensual forms of exclusion have met with criticism from civil society organizations, and with active resistance from local communities. Such resistance can arguably be read as a reaction to the increasing concentration of power in the hands of the forest bureaucracy. However, the fact that this bureaucracy is authorized by law to access the considerable afforestation funds that the state has been accruing for years, means that the state bureaucracy effectively wields a firm control over much forestland (Lele 2017). This recentralization of power in the hands of the state in effect undermines the rights of Adivasi and other forest dwellers under the Forest Rights Act.

Local opposition notwithstanding, the Modi government also promotes large plantation programmes under its Green India Mission, launched in 2014. The target is to raise 5 million hectares of new green cover by 2024 (Ghosh 2017), but as was the case with the afforestation initiatives discussed above, no distinction is made between forests and plantations. Aside from state-run plantation programmes, big private investors such as the Indian Tobacco Company and JK Paper Limited have acquired hundreds of thousands of hectares of agricultural lands under the Green India Mission in the states of Andhra Pradesh, Telangana, Odisha, and Chhattisgarh, for raising plantations of mainly eucalyptus.

Transitions in the field of forest governance under Modi have clearly followed a path of authoritarian populism. This has been realized through centralized, top-down processes of implementing new policies; further re-centralization of political and economic powers in the hands of the state and private investors; and erosion of social, political, and ecological rights of marginalized groups, for example, through forced and even violent evictions or exclusions from forestlands.

Land

Changes in the domain of land governance have primarily been designed to facilitate the commodification of land and making it available for investors (Levien 2018). From the mid-1990s, land emerged as a major factor in India's post-liberalization system of competitive federalism. In a context in which India's federal states have an increasingly free hand to attract private capital directly, the ability of state governments to offer affordable (or free) land to investors became an important component in inter-state competition. While a new Special Economic Zones Act 2005 ensured business-friendly conditions of operation, the colonial Land Acquisition Act 1894 – which enshrined the state's right of eminent domain – was used as a legal instrument by later governments to dispossess small farmers and Adivasi of their land, often for real estate (Searle 2016), mining, high-tech industries, or simply land speculation.

However, in many states such dispossessive practices were met with strong resistance as local communities refused to part with their land (Nielsen 2018). In response to the pressure of popular anti-dispossession movements, the incumbent UPA government in 2007 set in motion a process to introduce new legislation with enhanced rights for landowning and land-dependent communities. However, private developers in pursuit of land simultaneously pressed for legal changes that would make it *easier* to acquire land for private accumulation. The outcome of this tug of war was the Right to Fair Compensation and Transparency in Land Acquisition, Rehabilitation and Resettlement Act 2013, a compromise piece of legislation that was strong on guaranteeing rights to rehabilitation and resettlement for the dispossessed, but weak in terms of limiting the potential for overt misuse of eminent domain.

With neither side enthusiastic (Nielsen and Nilsen 2015; 2017), industry groups started to lobby for legal changes (Verma 2015). In response, and in a manoeuvre that was arguably in line with his business-friendly outlook, Modi sought to amend the 2013 Act shortly after being elected. This was done in autocratic fashion by bypassing parliament and introducing an ordinance (in December 2014) that modified key provisions in the said Act. Several so-called consent clauses that granted affected communities the right to block land dispossession for certain projects were removed. And, while the 2013 Act included mandatory social impact assessments – a key mechanism through which the negative local impacts of land dispossession are assessed, in consultation with local stakeholders – for all projects except irrigation, the ordinance did away with this provision for several types of projects. Several other clauses that bestowed rights and protection on affected communities were also eliminated. For example, the definition of public purpose for which the state can dispossess people of their land was expanded to enable land acquisition for private hospitals and educational institutions; and the stipulation that acquired land lying unused for five years must be returned to its original owner was removed (Ramesh and Khan 2015: 124–130).

In March 2015, the Modi government sought to turn the ordinance into law. In response, social movements and farmers' organizations protested the bill as an infringement on their hard-won legal rights to be treated as stakeholders, as well as to compensation and rehabilitation. The proposed bill ultimately foundered, leading Modi to repromulgate the ordinance by decree three times, until it finally lapsed for good in August 2015. Nonetheless, the Modi government would continue to dilute protective clauses related to the right to consent, compensation, and resettlement, by encouraging the individual states to bring about state-level amendments in line with the lapsed ordinance (Kohli and Gupta 2017). In theory, such state-level legislation cannot override national legislation unless it has received the assent of the President of India. However, Modi's Finance Minister in 2015 assured the states that such consent would be readily forthcoming. Modi's critics have likened this reduction of presidential assent to a mere formality to a "pernicious misuse of a constitutional provision" (Ramesh and Khan 2016).

As in the domain of forest governance, then, changes in the domain of land governance have followed a comparable autocratic modus operandi. Important legislations have been implemented via ordinances rather than through parliamentary procedure. The effect of the legal and policy changes discussed above has been to weaken a series of existing rights of land-dependent communities to enable the transfer of land to investors. Notably, efforts towards this end continue today. The government think-tank NITI Aayog continues to stress how land acquisition laws – that, as we argued above, ensure at least some measure of rights-based protection for small and marginal farmers and Adivasi – stand in the way of accelerated economic growth. Significantly, as Indian policy-makers and economists now debate how the economy can best recover from the damage inflicted on it by the Covid-19 pandemic, "simplifications" to the central land acquisition law remain high on the list of prioritized reforms (Pandey and Arnimesh 2020). In the final section, we analyze further select changes introduced during the pandemic and the associated lockdown that affect environmental governance.

Under cover of Covid

In late March 2020, as the Covid-19 pandemic spread worldwide, Modi introduced one of the strictest nationwide lockdowns in the world. It remained in place until 30 May, after which it was lifted in phases throughout 2020. Less than two weeks before the lockdown, the Modi government had put out a draft proposal to amend existing environmental impact assessment (EIA) norms. The draft proposal was roundly criticized by environmentalists and experts, with one scholar calling it "one of the most dangerous" of the many new laws and amendments introduced by Modi during the pandemic. The amendment, it was argued, would "deny citizens the social, legal and political forums available to protect the environment from bad government decisions" (Menon and Kohli 2020). More specifically, critics pointed out that the draft notification thinned out the regulatory requirements across most project sectors, and significantly curtailed or weakened existing appraisal, monitoring and compliance procedures, thus reducing the level of public scrutiny. Additionally, the notification enabled projects which had begun construction activities – or were simply operating without obtaining a clearance altogether – to apply for post-facto clearance. The notification also centralized decision-making by doing away with the requirement that committees be set up in consultation with state governments, thus giving the central government more control over the constitution of regulatory authorities and expert committees. Importantly, the draft considerably undermined the importance of social decisions and public consultation with project-affected communities: the time period for the public to submit responses to project-related public hearings was reduced from 30 days to 20, and the timeline for completing the public hearing process reduced from 45 to 40 days. This reduction of time is significant as it disproportionally affects marginal communities in remote areas where information is not easily accessible. Moreover, in the draft notification, many projects now fall entirely outside the purview of public consultations altogether (Menon and Kohli 2020; Kumar 2020; Gupta et al. 2020).

Due to the lockdown, the meetings of the different panels, boards, and committees involved in granting environmental clearances were cancelled. However, they resumed in April over videoconferencing to "help clear proposals for seamless economic growth", as the Ministry of Environment, Forest and Climate Change (MoEFCC) tweeted. During April and May, a full 191 projects were up for clearance through videoconferencing, sometimes leaving as little as ten minutes for a given panel to deliberate on each project (Gokhale 2020). Indeed, on a single day in April, more than 30 proposals affecting tiger reserves, sanctuaries, eco-sensitive zones, wildlife corridors, and other forest areas were cleared or discussed at virtual meetings (Ravi 2020). Among the many projects thus cleared were several big infrastructure projects and open cast coal mining in ecologically sensitive areas (Aggarwal and Ghosh 2020). This speeding-up of the clearance process in the context of a nationwide lockdown significantly reduced the scope for public deliberation insofar as affected communities could not send evidence or representations to the said panels, much less gather in public meetings to vent grievances or protest decisions. Nor could expert panellists do necessary field visits to verify facts independently.

This autocratic turn is further evident in how changes to environmental legislations and policies introduced under Covid-19 have further centralized decision-making, weakened public consultation and participation, and intensified the persecution of environmental activists under lockdown. In July 2020, the government ordered that the websites of three environmental advocacy groups – Fridays for Future (FFF), Let India Breathe, and There Is No Earth B – be blocked. The domain name owner of the FFF – the Indian chapter of the movement initiated by environmental activist Greta Thunberg – was served legal notice from the Delhi police under sections of the draconian anti-terror law, the Unlawful Activities (Prevention) Act 1967. The notice accused FFF's site of containing "objectionable contents and unlawful activities or terrorist act, which are dangerous for the peace, tranquillity and sovereignty of India" and ordered it blocked. The three groups thus targeted were spearheading a public awareness campaign and a petition against the changes introduced by the EIA draft notification discussed above (Huria 2020).

Conclusion

In this chapter, we have examined the autocratic turn in Indian environmental governance that has arguably occurred under Modi. This autocratic turn has been driven by the twin pillars of Modi's authoritarian populism, namely aggressive business-friendly growth-oriented economic policies, coupled with a centralization of power and a strong fist to hold dissenters down. In the domain of environmental governance, this had manifested in a policy approach that proactively works to enlist and weaken existing environmental laws and regulations to make natural resources available to investors: environmental clearances have been made easier to obtain, lands and forests made simpler to acquire, and monitoring mechanisms significantly weakened. The ways in which this has happened have had an evident autocratic undercurrent, as seen in recurring efforts to bypass parliament and the judiciary, weaken consultative forums, and dent existing legally enshrined rights to forests, lands, rehabilitation, and resettlement. Activists and civil society groups who have "come in the way" of this policy approach to protect environment and marginalized communities have been subject to increasing policing, criminalization and persecution over the past seven years. This has taken place in the context of widespread suppression of peaceful protests and a shrinking of democratic space for civic activism. The apparent intensification of autocratization under the Covid-19 pandemic does not, we believe, bode well for the future. Not only does it threaten to undo the advances made through years of post-colonial struggle by marginalized and tribal communities and environmental groups; it also brings to a standstill future courses of green activism and progressive environmental legislation.

Bibliography

Aggarwal, M. (2016). 'Steady rise in projects getting green clearance'. *Mint*. Available from: www.livemint.com/Politics/CSQ3OGRTsCIwVWaPBnQH4L/Steady-rise-in-projects-getting-green-clearance.html [27 January 2021].

Aggarwal, M. and Ghosh, S. (2020). 'Environment ministry unlocked many protected areas during the lockdown'. *Mongabay*, 12 June. Available from: https://india.mongabay.com/2020/06/environment-ministry-unlocked-many-protected-areas-during-the-lockdown [28 January 2021].

Anon. (2014). 'Environment clearances can now be sought online, says Prakash Javadekar'. *Firstpost*. Available from: www.firstpost.com/politics/environment-clearances-can-now-be-sought-online-says-prakash-javadekar-1558169.html [27 January 2021].

Bidwai, P. (2015). 'Modi government cracks down on green NGOs'. *Open Democracy*, 17. Available from: www.opendemocracy.net/en/openglobalrights-openpage/modi-government-cracks-down-on-green-ngos [27 January 2021].

Congleton, R.D. (1992). 'Political institutions and pollution control'. *The Review of Economics and Statistics*, 74(3), 412–421.

Dutta, A. (2020). 'Forest becomes frontline: Conservation and counter-insurgency in a space of violent conflict in Assam, Northeast India'. *Political Geography*, 77, 102–117.

EPI (2020). '2020 EPI Results'. Available from: Environmental Performance Index (yale.edu) [4 March 2021].

Ghosh, S. (2017). 'The green invasion: Promoting plantations in India'. *World Rainforest Movement Bulletin*, 233, 19–23.

Global Witness. (2017). *Defenders of the Earth: Global Killings of Land and Environmental Defenders in 2016*. London: Global Witness.

Gokhale, N. (2020). 'Despite COVID lockdown, environment ministry's expert panels race to clear projects'. *Mongabay*, 4 May. Available from: https://india.mongabay.com/2020/05/despite-covid-lockdown-environment-ministrys-expert-panels-race-to-clear-projects [28 January 2021].

Gupta, D., Nayak, S., Tanvani, K. and Viswanathan, V. (2020). *The Draft EIA Notification 2020: Reduced Regulations and Increased Exemptions*. New Delhi: Centre for Policy Research.

Huria, S. (2020). 'Criminalising ecological dissent in India'. *The Ecologist*, 10 August, Available from: https://theecologist.org/2020/aug/10/criminalising-ecological-dissent-india [28 January 2021].

Jaffrelot, C. (2019). 'Business-friendly Gujarat under Modi: The Implications of a New Political Economy' in Jaffrelot, C., Kohli, A. and Murali, K. (eds) *Business and Politics in India*. Delhi: Oxford University Press, 211–233.

Jakobsen, J., Nielsen, K.B., Nilsen, A.G. and Vaidya, A. (2019). 'Mapping the world's largest democracy (1947–2017)'. *Forum for Development Studies*, 46(1), 83–108.

Kaul, N. (2017). 'Rise of the political right in India: Hindutva-development mix, Modi myth, and dualities'. *Journal of Labor and Society*, 20(4), 523–548.

Kohli, K. and Gupta, D. (2017). *Mapping Dilutions in a Central Law*. Occasional Paper. New Delhi: Centre for Policy Research. Available from: www.cprindia.org/research/papers/mapping-dilutions-central-law-0 [28 January 2021].

Kukreti, I. (2020). 'National Board for Wildlife hasn't met even once since 2014'. *Down to Earth*, 10 April. Available from: www.downtoearth.org.in/news/wildlife-biodiversity/national-board-for-wildlife-hasn-t-met-even-once-since-2014-70374 [28 January 2021].

Kumar, A. (2020). 'Environment Ministry's Draft EIA Notification Pushes "Investment at Any Cost"'. *The Wire*, 25 March. Available from: https://science.thewire.in/environment/environment-ministry-draft-environment-impact-assessment-notification-investment-any-cost [28 January 2021].

Lee, J.I. and Wolf, S.A. (2018). 'Critical assessment of implementation of the Forest Rights Act of India'. *Land Use Policy*, 79, 834–844.

Lele, U.J. (ed.) (2017). *Managing a Global Resource: Challenges of Forest Conservation and Development*. London: Routledge.

Levien, M. (2018). *Dispossession without Development: Land Grabs in Neoliberal India*. Oxford: Oxford University Press.

Lührmann, A. and Lindberg, S.I. (2019). 'A third wave of autocratization is here: what is new about it?'. *Democratization*, 26(7), 1095–1113.

Mak Arvin, B. and Lew, B. (2011). 'Does democracy affect environmental quality in developing countries?' *Applied Economics*, 43(9), 1151–1160.

Manohar, A. (2019). 'Prakash Javedekar assures environmental clearance to real estate projects within 60 days'. *Zeebiz*, 19 August. Available from: www.zeebiz.com/india/news-prakash-javedekar-assures-environmental-clearance-to-real-estate-projects-within-60-days-108682 [28 January 2021].

Manor, J. (2020). 'India's political economy: Has something crucial recently changed?' in Chatterjee, E. and McCartney, M. (eds) *Class and Conflict: Revisiting Pranab Bardhan's Political Economy of India*. Delhi: Oxford University Press, 91–111.

McCarthy, J. (2019). 'Authoritarianism, populism, and the environment: Comparative experiences, insights, and perspectives'. *Annals of the American Association of Geographers*, 109(2), 301–313.

Menon, M. and Kohli, K. (2020). 'EIA legitimised environmental destruction: Now, govt "renovates" it for the worst'. *The Wire Science*. Available from: https://science.thewire.in/environment/eia-2020-environmental-degradation-draft [27 January 2021].

Nilsen, A.G., Nielsen, K.B. and Vaidya, A. (2019). *Indian Democracy: Origins, Trajectories, Contestations*. London: Pluto Press.

Nielsen, K.B. (2018). *Land Dispossession and Everyday Politics in Rural Eastern India*. London: Anthem Press.

Nielsen, K.B. and Nilsen, A.G. (2015). 'Law struggles and hegemonic processes in neoliberal India: Gramscian reflections on land acquisition legislation'. *Globalizations*, 12(2), 203–216.

Nielsen, K.B. and Nilsen, A.G. (2017). 'Law-struggles, law-making and the politics of hegemony in neoliberal India: Towards a critical perspective on the 2013 Land Acquisition Act' in D'Costa, A.P. and Chakraborty, A. (eds) *The Land Question in India: State, Dispossession, and Capitalist Transition*. Oxford: Oxford University Press, 129–150.

Palshikar, S. (2019). 'Toward hegemony: The BJP beyond electoral dominance' in Chatterji, A.P., Hansen, T.B. and Jaffrelot, C. (eds) *Majoritarian State*. Oxford: Oxford University Press, 101–116.

Pandey, N. and Arnimesh, S. (2020). 'Reduce cost of business, reform land acquisition – BJP suggests plan for post-Covid economy'. *The Wire*. Available from: https://theprint.in/economy/reduce-cost-of-business-reform-land-acquisition-bjp-suggests-plan-for-post-covid-economy/407426 [27 January 2021].

Ramesh, J. and Khan, M.A. (2015). *Legislating for Equity: The Making of the 2013 Land Acquisition Law*. New Delhi: Oxford University Press.

Ramesh, J. and Khan, M.A. (2016). 'Winking at the states'. *The Hindu*, 2 December. Available from: www.thehindu.com/opinion/lead/Winking-at-the-States/article16086906.ece [28 February 2021].

Ravi, R. (2020). 'While India focused on COVID-19, here's what govt did to the environment'. *The Logical Indian*, 5 June. Available from: https://thelogicalindian.com/environment/what-govt-did-to-environment-21499 [28 January 2021].

Sareen, S., Remme, D.V.A., Oskarsson, P. and Nielsen, K.B. (2020). *The Pandemic as a Rupture that Follows Rules: Comparing Governance Responses in India, Norway, Sweden and the USA*. Unpublished manuscript.

Saxena, K.B. (2019). 'Compensatory Afforestation Fund Act and rules: Deforestation, tribal displacement and an alibi for legalised land grabbing'. *Social Change*, 49(1), 23–40.

Searle, L.G. (2016). *Landscapes of Accumulation: Real Estate and the Neoliberal Imagination in Contemporary India*. Chicago: University of Chicago Press.

Sethi, N. and Shrivastava, K.S. (2019). 'Modi government plans more draconian version of colonial-era Indian Forest Act'. *The Wire*. Available from: https://thewire.in/rights/modi-government-plans-more-draconian-version-of-colonial-era-indian-forest-act [27 January 2021].

Singh, P. (2020). 'Alternatives: The economic consequences of Prime Minister Modi'. *Studies in Political Economy*, 101(2), 174–184.

Umashankar, S. (2014). *Evolution of Environmental Policy and Law in India*. Available from: SSRN: https://ssrn.com/abstract=2508852 [28 January 2021].

Verma, S. (2015). 'Subverting the land acquisition Act, 2013'. *Economic and Political Weekly*, 50(37), 18–21.

Widmalm, S. (2019). 'Under Modi govt, a two-pronged attack on India's democracy'. *The Wire*. Available from: https://thewire.in/politics/india-democracy-modi-government [27 January 2021].

Williams, G. and Mawdsley, E. (2006). 'Postcolonial environmental justice: Government and governance in India'. *Geoforum*, 37(5), 660–670.

7

LIVING DANGEROUSLY

The heartland heralds the new communal-authoritarian model of Indian democracy

Zoya Hasan

Indian democracy and its institutional structures face an unprecedented challenge. Elections in India are no doubt marked by high levels of political participation, political activity and voter turnout. But there's more to democracy than the holding of elections at regular intervals. The greatest contemporary challenge to India's democracy comes from majoritarian nationalism that seeks to reconfigure the Indian nation as one that belongs exclusively to the Hindu majority defined by a demographic trait. The landslide victory of the Bhartiya Janata Party (BJP) in 2019 reinforced the majoritarian trajectory India has embarked upon since the 2014 election. The conflation between nationalism and majoritarianism is the foundation of the new political dominance reflected in the increasing mainstreaming of Hindu nationalism in the public arena.

This project has worked through two processes – consolidation of Hindu dominance through authoritarian means and constant fear and objectifying of the other, defined in terms of religion, thus reminding people of a threat from an enemy within. This is the trope driving authoritarianism in Indian politics. More substantively, there is an attempt to redefine citizenship on the basis of religion, not civic equality that respects diversity and pluralism, and in the process transform the very meaning of democracy based on equal rights. Furthermore, the space for public deliberation and dissent has been narrowed. Politically, the suppression and criminalization of dissent, curbs on opposition, and crushing of protests pose a grave threat to democracy. This has contributed to democratic backsliding in India, noted by several international assessments, most notably, the V-Dem Institute's assessment which termed India an "electoral autocracy" (Lührmann et al. 2020). The political ecosystem has been vitiated by an erosion of public institutions which are meant to serve as checks and balances on the exercise of executive power. Although institutions have always had to negotiate with political rulers, and there have been periods in India's past when things came to a flash point, Emergency (1975–77) is an obvious example, never before have constitutional institutions had to function for political ends to this extent when there's no formal declaration of Emergency.

The two principal elements of this tectonic shift are embodied in the acceleration of authoritarian control and stepping up of communalism since the BJP came to power at the Centre in 2014. The coming together of both these elements has paved the way for the institution of a new right-wing authoritarian-communal regime. This regime has taken shape most strikingly in

DOI: 10.4324/9781003042211-9

states such as Uttar Pradesh – India's weightiest state and a political springboard for the national stage. Nine of the country's 14 prime ministers have been elected from constituencies in Uttar Pradesh. Narendra Modi, the current prime minister, is from Gujarat but chose to contest his first Lok Sabha election from the Varanasi constituency in Uttar Pradesh to underline the significance of the state and the eagerness of both the BJP and Rashtriya Swayamsevak Sangh (RSS) to signal its centrality to their strategy of establishing the dominance of Hindu nationalism. The BJP won a quarter of its 282 seats in 2014 from this state, helping it to an absolute majority in the Lok Sabha, and thus underlining the significance of the state in Indian politics.

Political developments in Uttar Pradesh fit into a more pronounced pattern of communal-authoritarian politics since the BJP was re-elected with a bigger majority in the 2019 general elections. Political shifts in this state are especially significant for what Pratap Bhanu Mehta describes as the wider process of creating "an irrevocably majoritarian state in all dimensions" (Mehta 2021). An examination of the working of the Uttar Pradesh regime and its politics would help to understand recent events that pose a challenge to Indian democracy and why it has increasingly become a host to aggressive communalism gradually morphing into an authoritarian order.

This chapter looks at the structural aspects of this project signified in the systematic attacks on dissent and the ways in which the checks and balances laid out in the Constitution for safeguarding fundamental rights have been compromised. This is attempted by looking at the state response to protests against the Citizenship Amendment Act (CAA). The government response encapsulates the problems of the communal-authoritarian model in a key state of the Union, where it has both a massive majority in the assembly and a chief minister who has demonstrated a penchant for extremism and vigilantism. By winning around 40 per cent of the popular vote in the assembly elections in 2017, the BJP mustered a huge legislative majority to go ahead with its political agenda virtually unopposed. In the rush to strengthen majoritarian consolidation, an authoritarian model of governing gained currency marked by erosion in civil and political rights and a wave of intolerance against dissenters and minorities.

Communal-authoritarian regime

The communal-authoritarian regime exercises power through majoritarian assertion, centralized control, curtailment of opposition, and suppression of individual freedom. The origins of this regime can be traced to the BJP's decisive victory in the assembly elections in 2017 in a campaign which openly pitted Hindus against Muslims with its top leaders insinuating that the majority community had not received a fair deal under previous governments. The appointment of Ajay Mohan Bisht, generally known as Yogi Adityanath, head of the Gorakhpur temple, as chief minister was a defining moment in this process. His entire politics revolved around a militant brand of Hindutva, an ideology of Hindu supremacy and fuelling antagonism against Muslims as public enemies.

From his first days in office, the BJP interpreted its landslide victory as a popular mandate for its project to construct a Hindu state. Yogi Adityanath used the instruments of governance to prioritize Hindu interests and used the police to target minorities (Verma and Mander 2020). The Citizenship Amendment Act (CAA), which offers pathways of citizenship to refugees aligned to religion (not limited to Uttar Pradesh), new laws regulating conversion as a way of deterring interfaith marriage, laws of cow protection, and also laws to empower vigilantes to take action on behalf of these laws are top priorities of the regime to reinforce Hindu supremacy. These are the various ways in which Hindu nationalism is inscribed in law. But not just laws. Hindu nationalism is the dominant tendency in politics and civil society in this state.

This shift is based on two long-term projects: the first cultural and the second political. This joint project set the stage for the dramatic expansion of the Hindu right. The origins of the cultural project can be traced to the promotion of Hindi which played a key role in producing a Hindi-Hindu socio-cultural construct in the politics of north India, and in particular the cultural development of Uttar Pradesh society. At the cultural level, the primacy given to Hindu identity is visible in the BJP–RSS's efforts to play up Hindu fairs, festivals, and icons, and turning these into opportunities for political mobilization. The political project was embodied in the campaign for a Ram Mandir in Ayodhya which kick-started the rise of the current identity politics around religion. The construction of a Ram temple at Ayodhya has redrawn the basic contours of state politics in favour of the BJP. Importantly, this movement laid the groundwork for a communal majority in Uttar Pradesh which, given its huge size, helps the Hindu right to establish a strong base to offset its weakness elsewhere in India. The mass support garnered by this movement entrenched Hindu nationalism in the heartland.

The ideology of Hindu nationalism has succeeded in popularizing the idea that it is the nation, as defined by Hindu identities, that matters and no other identities such as caste. The nation is defined by Hindus, mobilized around their religious identity (and frequently a common language), which leaves little room for other identities. The BJP has used this broad-based identity to co-opt backward castes and Dalits who have been keen to align themselves to the cultural world of Hindi-Hindu nationalism. The consolidation of this identity has gone beyond caste, but this consolidation relies heavily on the exclusion of Muslims to neutralize caste.

Communal politics combined with longstanding problems of bias in the criminal justice system have created a pervasive climate of impunity, where minority communities feel insecure, with no recourse when such crimes occurred. These fears have been compounded by targeted violence that takes a variety of forms, the most common being mass violence and mob lynchings. Several Muslims were lynched on allegations of eating beef or even just transporting cattle for slaughter. Most of those incidents were perpetrated by vigilante militias and were the direct result of the communal atmosphere that the Hindu right created with little scope for punishment of those who committed the crimes (Seema Chishti 2017).

Muslims in Uttar Pradesh have been marginalized and pushed out of the public sphere and from political institutions. The 2006 Sachar Committee Report had brought public attention to the backward socio-economic status of Indian Muslims, suggesting that in terms of such parameters as employment, education, and literacy, they were badly off, if not worse off, than the historically oppressed Scheduled Castes and Scheduled Tribes. Most available official data and research suggests that there has been no substantive improvement in the condition of the Muslim poor (every third Muslim is multi-dimensionally poor, according to a 2018 UNDP report) and nowhere is this truer than in Uttar Pradesh (Friese 2018).

The politics of polarization has reduced Muslim electoral representation to an extremely low level in the state assembly. Christophe Jaffrelot points out, "in general, when the BJP conquers a new state that was ruled by a regional party, the number of Muslim MLAs drops" (Jaffrelot 2019). This was dramatically demonstrated when the proportion of Muslim MLAs in Uttar Pradesh dropped from 17 per cent to 6 per cent in the 2017 assembly elections. The BJP didn't field a single Muslim candidate in Uttar Pradesh even though Muslims constitute one-fifth of the population of the state. The basic idea is to push them out of the system, first by rendering them irrelevant electorally, and then marginalizing them in the public sphere through their electoral inconsequentiality. As a result, the BJP says it has ended the veto that Muslims had over a number of issues in Indian politics. This resonated with the Hindu base of the party which believed that Congress pandered to minority communities for electoral gains and that BJP was rectifying this overkill (Daniyal 2017).

But the Uttar Pradesh regime is not only communal; it is also authoritarian in its attempts to exercise pervasive control. This regime brooks no dissent or protest. It targets anyone and everyone who dares to question the government, and this is not restricted to political Opposition alone. Public protests have been regularly stifled and a protest provides grounds for arrest and locking up protesters. The police can be sent anywhere to serve notice on citizens to stop them from participating in protests and journalists to stop them from covering them. More importantly, police have been given a free hand to detain and arrest people on any issue. On the whole, the politics of the BJP is both authoritarian and communal which tends to divide society by unleashing passions that relegate minorities to second class status. Communalism and authoritarianism are two sides of the same coin – the government was fomenting both processes (Mehta 2019). For this it creates the quintessential other, which communal politics continually needs to stoke hate and fear. Its aim is to corner minority groups by a constant focus on issues such as cow-protection, interfaith marriage, religious conversion, reconversion, and, most importantly, the CAA.

Citizenship Amendment Act

This brings us to the CAA and the public protests against it, the focal point of this chapter. In December 2019, Parliament adopted the Citizenship Amendment Act (CAA), which grants special access to Indian citizenship to non-Muslim immigrants and refugees from three neighbouring countries, Pakistan, Afghanistan, and Bangladesh, on grounds of religious perse-cution in these countries. The CAA seeks to fast track citizenship to non-Muslim minorities on grounds of religious persecution. It offers quick protection and citizenship by creating an exemption from the "illegal migrants" category for Hindus, Sikhs, Buddhists, Jains, Parsis, and Christians from these three countries, but discriminates against refugees and immigrants who happen to be Muslim. The government claims that the legislation applies to those who were "forced or compelled to seek shelter in India due to persecution on the ground of religion". The CAA is not, however, a stand-alone law. It is paired with a proposed National Register of Citizens (NRC) and the National Population Register (NPR). Many observers believe the national register's purpose is to disenfranchise Muslim voters by effectively classifying them as illegal immigrants. These suspicions gained ground as BJP leaders publicly used the CAA to assure Hindus in other parts of India that they would be protected in the citizenship verification process and conspicuously omitting Muslims from the list of protected religions.

The CAA is illogical as it singles out one particular religion for exclusionary treatment. The assumption that Muslims cannot be persecuted in Muslim-majority countries and where the state religion is Islam is unconvincing. This assumption is belied by the ill-treatment of Hazaras Shias in Afghanistan and Ahmadiyas in Pakistan. This narrative would be diluted if it is shown that Muslims also face persecution in Muslim majority countries. There can be only one reason why a government would exclude 'persecuted Hindu' such as the Tamils of Sri Lanka from the list. It is because their oppressors are not officially Muslim or official representatives of Islam. Clearly, the idea is not simply to help persecuted minorities, but to demonize and isolate one group. Their exclusion furthers a political narrative that suits the right-wing ideology – that Muslims persecute non-Muslims. This narrative will be diluted if it were shown that Muslims also face persecution in Muslim-majority countries. This leaves no room for doubt that the CAA advances the government's political agenda, which is to transform secular India into a majoritarian Hindu India. The CAA, in addition to making the naturalization of Muslim migrants from the neighbouring countries difficult, would, at an ideological level, establish the notion of India as a Hindu Homeland to which the BJP is doctrinally committed. The CAA signalled a move towards the assertion of Hindu supremacy vis-à-vis people of other faiths, especially Muslims.

The attempt to create a stratified citizenship provoked a massive opposition, by far the biggest since Independence. It was the most sustained popular protest since the BJP came to power in May 2014. Since then, no action of the regime had provoked this scale of opposition. The ground of protest is clear: India cannot be a Republic founded on discrimination and a pervasive sense of fear. It cannot exclude or target anyone simply on the basis of their religious identity. Many people feared that the government could force citizenship reviews on all Indians and that Hindus without proper papers would be allowed to stay in India under the CAA while Muslims without proper papers would be asked to leave. Government denied this, affirming that they were merely seeking to address illegal migration and help persecuted minorities from neighbouring countries. Failing to convince many people, the government resorted to attempts to curb these demonstrations through widespread internet shutdowns, arbitrary arrests and bans on assemblies. In states like Uttar Pradesh the government responded with brute force.

Vilifying protests

The BJP government at the Centre launched a countrywide campaign to defend the CAA and to generate public support for it. The Uttar Pradesh government did nothing of the kind; it did not bother to explain the merits of the CAA and disabuse people of their apprehensions regarding its implications for them. Far from responding to legitimate concerns regarding the discriminatory aspects of the CAA, the state government went about vilifying and punishing those who criticized the new law. Several BJP leaders resorted to strange language to describe those who were protesting against the CAA. The deputy chief minister, Keshav Prasad Maurya, claimed that "Those who are opposing the Citizenship (Amendment) Act are mentally affected. Such people should get medical treatment" (The New Indian Express 2020). Another BJP leader, Raghuraj Singh, said that people raising slogans against Prime Minister Narendra Modi and Uttar Pradesh chief minister Yogi Adityanath "will be buried alive" (Outlook India 2020).

Citizenship protests and regime response

Major protests broke out in Uttar Pradesh. In fact this state was the epicentre of protests against the changes in the citizenship regime. Protests against the CAA were held at 102 places across the state on 19 December (The Hindu 2019). The biggest demonstrations took place on the day of the all-India strike on 19 December called by various political parties and social organizations in the country under the common banner titled Hum Bharat Ke Log (We the People of India): National Action Against Citizenship Amendment (Clarionindia.net 2019). Protests occurred in Firozabad, Bhadohi, Bahraich, Farrukhabad, Gorakhpur, Sambhal, Rampur, Moradabad, Meerut, Varanasi, Kanpur, Bijnor, Hathras, Saharanpur, Bulandshahr, Mahoba, Hamirpur, Lucknow, Allahabad, and Agra among others.

The protests were organized by a mix of civil society, local community and youth groups, and often just spontaneously to express opposition to the CAA. Many protest marches planned merely to hand over a memorandum to the local authorities but even this was frowned upon as the government was averse to any opposition to the CAA. It refused to allow any opportunity for people to express their disagreement with the Act. This was confirmed by a fact-finding report, which observed that "The police systematically attempted to prevent protests, then, when protests went ahead anyway, they used disproportionate and violent means to subdue protesting citizens, including the suspension of emergency medical and legal services. In order to perpetuate the atmosphere of fear, with a longer view of breaking the economic spine of the Muslim community, the police destroyed and looted private residences" (Karwan-e-Mohabbat 2020a).

From the beginning the government adopted a confrontational approach using strong arm tactics to curb and restrict protest. Public protests were harshly dealt with by selectively using the law-enforcement machinery to prevent people from protesting (Citizens Against Hate 2020), including the massive deployment of police, internet blackouts, and the imposition of curfews. Around 3,305 persons were detained by the police (Citizens Against Hate 2020). Even when there was no formal protest call, police forces were positioned in Muslim neighbourhoods to prevent people from gathering in groups making it effectively impossible for them to protest. Section 144 was enforced all over the state ahead of protests on 19 December (Citizens Against Hate 2020). Section 144 of the Criminal Procedure Code (CrPC) of 1973 authorizes the District Magistrate to issue an order to prohibit the assembly of four or more people in an area. Section 144 is a serious restriction on the fundamental rights to expression, assembly and association and is expected to be invoked only in circumstances where concrete evidence is available of threats to public order (Yamunan 2019). It was later imposed in specific parts of cities, towns, and districts to prohibit people from gathering, especially in the western and central districts of the state which have a high concentration of Muslim population, and in the capital city of Lucknow, which also has a large population of Muslims.

The use of formidable new technologies for surveillance and control aided this process. These range from jamming the internet and cutting off mobile phone coverage, to using drones to closely monitor movement of people. Internet services were suspended in about a dozen districts. Public warnings, house arrests, and preventive detentions were then carried out against persons whom the authorities accused of coordinating protests, most often civil society notables and human rights defenders. Notices were issued to more than 3,000 people cautioning them not to participate or motivate others to participate in the protests (The Wire 2019).

Clamping down on dissent was manifest from the way the police were allowed to storm Aligarh Muslim University (AMU), a central, publicly funded university with a large number of Muslim students. State-wide restrictions against CAA protests had followed the initial protest moves by AMU students. Protest marches, sit-ins, and debates on the university grounds had regularly taken place in AMU (Khan 2020). Both students and teachers led protest marches with memoranda to authorities to withdraw the CAA (The Indian Express 2019a). There were reports of harsh police action inside the campus, including in hostels; at least six students were hospitalized with grievous injuries (Karwan-e-Mohabbat 2020b). The police reportedly used stun grenades and fired tear gas canisters into student hostels.

Police crackdown to shut down protests had the opposite effect. People, horrified and angry at the violence, poured into the streets as never before. Overall, the state witnessed the harshest crackdown, making it something akin to a 'war-zone'. Muslims were the main victims of state brutality and maximum casualties in the protests occurred in UP (Johari and Subramanian 2019). At least 23 people were killed. Most of the dead were Muslim daily wage earners. Most of the deaths were caused by police bullets (Citizens Against Hate 2020). The police registered a total of 498 cases, took 5,558 people into custody, and arrested 1,246 people in this regard (DNA India 2019). The state government blamed the protesters for the violence while reports and videos indicate that the police attacked peaceful crowds with lathis, tear-gas, and bullets (Karwan-e-Mohabbat 2020a). These denials did not tally with accounts of local residents recorded in the various reports (Ahmad 2019). In some cases, police officers were captured on video breaking into people's homes, roughing up the occupants, vandalizing private property, destroying private cars, two-wheelers, shops, and business establishments (Ahmad 2019).

No other state went this far in using punitive methods and encouragement of mobs to target legitimate protesters resulting in a widespread suppression of fundamental rights in the state during the anti-CAA protests (The Wire 2019). *The Indian Express* captured the adversarial character of the Uttar Pradesh regime in its editorial:

> The right to assemble and protest peacefully is guaranteed by India's Constitution. That thousands of people, particularly young people, belonging to diverse faiths, regions, ethnicity and language, have chosen to contest the CAA despite the tame response from political parties is a sign of the argumentativeness of Indian democracy. However, the state government was unmindful of democratic niceties. Its tone has been confrontational; it has refused to allow any outlet for people to express their disagreement with the controversial Act.
>
> (The Indian Express *2019b*)

The excessive use of force was encouraged by the chief minister who issued threats of exacting "revenge" against protesters (Sharma 2019). Police action came after the chief minister declared his plan to take revenge himself at a public rally (The Indian Express 2019c). As police violence in Uttar Pradesh made global headlines, his office posted a series of congratulatory tweets: "Every violent protestor will cry now because there is a Yogi government in Uttar Pradesh." These tweets posted from the account of the chief minister said: "Every rioter is shocked. Every demonstrator is stunned. Everyone has been silenced after seeing Yogi Adityanath government's strict actions. Do whatever now, compensation will be taken from anyone who damages public property. Every violent protester will cry now because there is a Yogi government in Uttar Pradesh" (Deccan Chronicle 2019). Under his watch, the Uttar Pradesh police have acted as a "uniformed vigilante force" which has fired upon demonstrators with impunity, and especially during the CAA protests "behaved as if it were wearing khaki half-pants instead of uniform trousers" (Kesavan 2019).

Two days later, the chief minister said that "the cost of damage to property during the citizenship protests would be avenged" with fines collected from those responsible. People across the state were served notices demanding monetary damages for alleged acts of vandalism of public property by arbitrarily confiscating people's properties. Banners were put up at busy intersections in Lucknow displaying photographs and addresses of people who had been served recovery notices. The administration began proceedings by identifying and sealing properties of the accused (India News 2019). The action was part of the state-wide campaign to punish those allegedly responsible for violence (Hindustan Times 2020). The move to confiscate property was illegal because it is not supported by any law and results in pre-judging people without a fair trial (Bhatnagar 2019). Confiscation of property normally occurs after a criminal trial. On 9 March, the Allahabad High Court ordered the Uttar Pradesh government to remove the posters and declared the action as "without having the authority of law". The apex Court held that there was no law to support the actions of the state government. Rather than obeying the order, the government challenged it in the Supreme Court.

Many of those arrested were not even allowed legal help. Some advocates who reached out to victims were also arrested. The police excesses were a form of overreach that can only be characterized as repression (Citizens Against Hate 2020). The *kambalchor* (blanket theft) incident (18 January 2020) exemplifies this approach. Several women were protesting around Ghanta Ghar in Lucknow on a winter night in December (Business-standard.com 2020). Video footage shows the police turned up and snatched blankets and food leaving the protesters crying "police chorhai" (police is a thief). Later the police put out a tweet claiming that this *kambalchori* was done "in a legal way" and after following "due process"(Mathur 2020). There is no "law" that permits blankets to be stolen by the police from peaceful assemblies but the police brazenly claimed due process and even reprimanded people for spreading misinformation. This incident raises serious questions regarding the conduct of the police and state administration, and the degree to which their actions contributed to the escalation in violence (India Today 2019). It also raises questions about the use of law for unlawful actions. Furthermore, it indicates the institutionalization of discrimination within the state apparatus itself (Mathur 2020). This has resulted in police colluding with and outsourcing law enforcement to vigilante groups which has serious implications for the life and security of citizens. The government response to the CAA protests is indicative of how the BJP in Uttar Pradesh has institutionalized political repression.

Apart from some rulings by the Allahabad High Court, none of the public institutions have been effective in checking the excesses of the Uttar Pradesh police and administration. Indeed, powerful sections of society ranging from legal professionals and the media to bureaucracy and state law enforcement agencies have been only too happy to agree with the government in seeing every act of democratic dissent as an anti-national conspiracy to undermine the government.

The BJP government in Uttar Pradesh was elected with a huge majority and could have dealt with the citizenship protests more humanely but it didn't because it lacks the democratic mindset to do so. The state government's response was harsh, focused on isolating and punishing protesters (Ahuja and Singh 2020). The government refused to recognize the legitimacy of the protests, leave alone talking to or assuaging the misgivings of the protesters. This state stands out because its agencies were active perpetrators of violence. No other state has used the state apparatus and state violence to such degree to serve an ideological purpose.

The ideological signal it wanted to send out to the public was clear: the state and the nation belong to the majority (Bhushan 2019). India is a Hindu country and Hindus must have supremacy over its polity and society. Muslims have been given too much power by the Constitution and by political parties, especially the Congress, which ruled India for most of the years since Independence. The CAA is an attempt to change this. It is a political project that seeks to redefine citizenship in such a way, albeit legally, that Muslims become second class citizens. The project's objective is the eventual disenfranchisement of Muslims, and the CAA and the state government's response to the citizenship protests is the clearest signal of this agenda. That this has found acceptance is an indication of the normalization of communalism at an ideological level and in political practice.

Divisive calculations and democratic backsliding

The authoritarian regime and its intolerance for dissent especially public protests have brought India's democratic standing into question. The V-Dem Institute in its 2020–21 report has faulted the performance of the Modi government on democracy and has said that India is no longer an "electoral democracy", classifying the country as an "electoral autocracy" (Lührmann et al. 2020). Much of the decline which occurred after the BJP's victory in 2014 was due to the restrictions on civil society and free speech and the crackdown against citizenship protests and government's intimidation of critics. Many institutions that are meant to uphold the rights of citizens and society at large have been co-opted or subverted. Modern democracies rely on institutions to remain democracies. Institutions of democracy have proven to be weak. While every previous government is guilty of similar abuses, it seems that the nature and scale of recent events are qualitatively different, as evidenced by India's plummeting performance on various democratic indices over the last few years noted above. The checks and balances of constitutional government have been weakened as the autonomy of major institutions has been seriously undermined. Institutions, which should be impartial, have been used in the service of the ruling party to stifle opposition.

Uttar Pradesh is the bastion of serious communal-authoritarian consolidation and penetration of civil and political society by the RSS which has changed the texture of civil society in that state. In consequence, Uttar Pradesh is well on its way to becoming a Hindu state. The regime's political calculations have focused on maximizing power and outweigh any consideration of how institutions should function in a democratic setup. An elected government is effective because of the moral authority it commands and the manner in which the government exercises power. Institutions provide a framework of rights and wrongs, and governments function by persuading voters that they are doing the right thing. But in Uttar Pradesh, the moral authority to do so has been eroded by leaders who continue to steamroll norms associated with democratic freedoms and political decency. The courts and most of the media that usually provide checks and balances in a democratic system have been restrained.

The full force and brutality of the authoritarian state was demonstrated in the government response to the anti-CAA protests. The official response to the citizenship protests indicates that this regime is simply incapable of tolerating any criticism or dissent. The attempts to change the storyline into one of "violent, anti-national, separatist movement" are an indication of the disregard of the democratic rights of people and follow a certain pattern of criminalizing protests. The communal axis has been used to divide society so that people cannot unite against the authoritarian state. To some extent the BJP has succeeded in consolidating a Hindu majority vote bank by co-opting lower castes into the saffron fold, based not on mobilization against the dominant castes but on the active subordination and subalternization of another population group; however, this cannot neutralize wider material and political discontents for too long. It is hard to imagine that there won't be opposition against the way this regime has functioned to consolidate Hindu power.

There cannot be a democracy without debate and dissent, and where minorities do not have equal citizenship. In India the rights and freedoms relating to the voice of dissent are currently under threat whereas the voice which is consistent with the prevailing viewpoint enjoys the protection of the state and the majority. This has serious consequences for democracy. But this can change as there's a growing reaction against authoritarian tendencies of the government and its policies and politics. The sizeable pushback from various groups and the numerous protests we have witnessed in the last few years indicate the limits of majority rule and the public resistance to redefining our democracy to make it majoritarian. Even if protests and dissent don't have an immediate electoral impact, they do open the door for a more gradual erosion of the authoritarian regime.

Bibliography

Ahmad, S. (2019). "CAA protests: Police denials at odds with horror accounts of locals in Uttar Pradesh." [online] *Outlook India*. Available at: <www.outlookindia.com/website/story/india-news-police-denials-at-odds-with-horror-accounts-of-locals-in-uttar-pradesh/344650> [Accessed 17 November 2021]

Ahuja, A. and Singh, R. (2020). "Why electorally secure Modi govt cracked down on CAA protesters so brutally." [online] *The Print*. Available at: <https://theprint.in/opinion/why-electorally-secure-modi-govt-cracked-down-on-caa-protesters-so-brutally/345543/> [Accessed 19 December 2020]

Bhatnagar, G. V. (2019). "No legal backing for UP govt's action against property of 'rioters': Lawyers." [online] *The Wire*. Available at: <https://thewire.in/law/uttar-pradesh-protest-property> [Accessed 5 March 2021]

Bhushan, B. (2019). "Citizenship Amendment Bill is a bid to fashion an ethnic democracy." [online] *Business-standard.com*. Available at: <www.business-standard.com/article/opinion/citizenship-amendment-bill-is-a-bid-to-fashion-an-ethnic-democracy-119120900104_1.html> [Accessed 17 November 2021]

Business-standard.com (2020). "Women's protest at Lucknow's clock tower against CAA, NRC, NPR enters fifth day." [online] Available at: <www.business-standard.com/article/news-ani/women-s-protest-at-lucknow-s-clock-tower-against-caa-nrc-npr-enters-fifth-day-120012100263_1.html> [Accessed 17 November 2021]

Citizens Against Hate (2017). *Lynching without end: Report of fact finding into religiously motivated vigilante violence in India.* [online] Available at: <www.misaal.ngo/wp-content/uploads/2017/09/FINAL-report-Lynching-without-End.pdf>. [Accessed 17 November 2021]

Citizens Against Hate (2020). *Everyone has been silenced: Police excesses against anti-CAA protesters in Uttar Pradesh, and the post-violence reprisal.* [online] Available at: <http://citizensagainsthate.org/wp-content/uploads/2020/03/Citizens-Against-Hate-Everyone-Has-Been-Silenced.pdf> [Accessed 31 December 2020]

Chishti, Seema (2017) "The cow test." [online] *The Indian Express.* Available at: <https://indianexpress.com/article/opinion/columns/the-cow-test-cow-vigilantism-gau-rakshaks-rajasthan-india-alwar-4604282> [Accessed 17 November 2021]

Clarionindia.net (2019). "Over 60 groups to start non-cooperation movement against CAA, NRC on 19 Dec." [online] Available at: <https://clarionindia.net/over-60-groups-to-start-non-cooperation-movement-against-caa-nrc-on-19-dec/> [Accessed 23 March 2021]

Daniyal, S. (2017). "Opinion: It's becoming increasingly dangerous in Uttar Pradesh to even look Muslim." [online] *Scroll.in.* Available at: <https://scroll.in/article/859333/opinion-its-becoming-increasingly-dangerous-in-uttar-pradesh-to-even-look-muslim> [Accessed 30 November 2017]

Deccan Chronicle (2019). "Yogi Adityanath justifies harsh police action in UP." [online] Available at: <www.deccanchronicle.com/nation/current-affairs/291219/yogi-adityanath-justifies-harsh-police-action-in-up.html> [Accessed 17 November 2021]

DNA India (2019). "With more than 5000 people in custody, Yogi says UP is 'outstanding example' of how violent protests should be handled." [online] Available at: <www.dnaindia.com/india/report-with-more-than-5000-people-in-custody-yogi-says-up-is-outstanding-example-of-how-violent-protests-should-be-handled-2807175> [Accessed 17 November 2021]

Express News Service (2021). "Euphoric endorsement Narendra Modi enjoyed in 2014 is missing: Pratap Bhanu Mehta." [online] *The Financial Express.* Available at: <www.financialexpress.com/elections/euphoric-endorsement-narendra-modi-enjoyed-in-2014-is-missing-pratap-bhanu-mehta/1560417/> [Accessed 31 January 2021]

Friese, K. (2018). "Silenced minority?". [online] *India Today.* Available at: <www.indiatoday.in/magazine/nation/story/20210208-silenced-minority-1763812-2021-01-30> [Accessed 7 February 2021]

The Hindu (2019). "Anti-Citizenship Act protests on Dec. 19 | One dies of alleged firearm injury in Lucknow; two die in police firing in Mangaluru." [online] Available at: <www.thehindu.com/news/national/anti-caa-protests-live-updates-december-19/article30345949.ece> [Accessed 17 November 2021]

Hindustan Times (2020). "UP announces cash reward for arrest of absconding anti-CAA, NRC protesters." [online] Available at: <www.hindustantimes.com/india-news/up-announces-cash-reward-for-arrest-of-absconding-anti-caa-nrc-protesters/story-mBsPGgIzu0q4kxSSKCLcZO.html> [Accessed 17 November 2021]

India News (2019). "CAA protests in Uttar Pradesh: 2 days after Yogi Adityanath's warning, UP seals assets of 'rioters' | India News." [online] *The Times of India.* Available at: <https://timesofindia.indiatimes.com/india/2-days-after-yogi-adityanaths-warning-up-seals-assets-of-rioters/articleshow/72920784.cms> [Accessed 17 November 2021]

India Today (2019). "Every assailant was policeman: Activists accuse UP Police of assaulting Muslims during CAA stir, release videos." [online] Available at: www.indiatoday.in/india/story/every-assailant-was-policeman-activists-accuse-up-police-of-assaulting-muslims-caa-stir-release-videos-1632361-2019-12-29 [Accessed 17 November 2021]

The Indian Express. (2019a). "Citizenship Amendment Bill: 20 AMU students booked for protest on campus, hunger strike begins." [online] Available at: https://indianexpress.com/article/india/citizenship-amendment-bill-20-amu-students-booked-for-protest-on-campus-hunger-strike-begins-6162675/ [Accessed 17 November 2021]

The Indian Express (2019b). "Don't protest in UP." [online] Available at: <https://indianexpress.com/article/opinion/editorials/caa-protests-citizenship-law-caa-amu-up-death-toll-6183364/> [Accessed 17 November 2021]

The Indian Express (2019c). "Will take 'badla' by auctioning your properties: Yogi Adityanath to those involved in violence." [online] Available at: <https://indianexpress.com/article/india/will-seize-sell-property-of-protesters-to-compensate-damage-yogi-adityanath-on-caa-protests-6175004/> [Accessed 17 November 2021]

Jaffrelot, C. (2019). "Muslim exclusion in Narendra Modi's de facto Hindu Rashtra." [online] *The Caravan.* Available at: <https://caravanmagazine.in/perspective/muslim-exclusion-modi-de-facto-hindu-rashtra> [Accessed 17 November 2021]

Johari, A. and Subramanian, N. (2019). "In Uttar Pradesh, mapping reports of violence and police brutality from 15 districts." [online] *Scroll.in.* Available at: https://scroll.in/article/947980/in-uttar-pradesh-reports-of-violence-and-police-brutality-from-15-districts [Accessed 31 December 2020]

Karwan-e-Mohabbat (2020a). "Is UP at war with its own people?: Fact finding report by Karwan-e-Mohabbat reveals administration's inefficiency and possible complicity." [online] CJP. Available at: <https://cjp.org.in/is-up-at-war-with-its-own-people/> [Accessed 1 November 2020]

Karwan-e-Mohabbat (2020b). "The siege of Aligarh Muslim University: A fact finding report." [online] *Karwan-e-Mohabbat and Indian Cultural Forum.* Available at: <http://karwanemohabbat.in/wp-content/uploads/2020/06/The-Siege-of-AMU-KeM-Jan2020.pdf> [Accessed 17 November 2021]

Kesavan, M. (2019). "The year ahead will be dominated by the rising edifice of a Hindu Rashtra." [online] *Business-standard.com.* Available at: <www.business-standard.com/article/politics/the-year-ahead-will-be-dominated-by-the-rising-edifice-of-a-hindu-rashtra-119122701053_1.html> [Accessed 17 November 2021]

Khan, A. (2020). "A timeline of protests at Aligarh Muslim University, as I saw it." [online] *The Quint.* Available at: <www.thequint.com/my-report/caa-protests-students-aligarh-muslim-university-violence-timeline> [Accessed 17 November 2021]

Lührmann, A., Maerz, S. F., Grahn, S., Alizada, N., Gastaldi, L., Hellmeier, S., Hindle, G., and Lindberg, S. I. (2020). *Autocratization Surges – Resistance Grows.* Democracy Report 2020. Varieties of Democracy Institute (V-Dem).

Mathur, N. (2020). "'Kambalchor sarkar': Why UP's crackdown on protesters is unparalleled." [online] *The Wire.* Available at: <https://thewire.in/rights/uttar-pradesh-caa-protest-crackdown-kambalchor-sarkar> [Accessed 5 March 2021]

Mehta, Pratap Banu (2019). "Discrimination, not justice: Hope this generation does a better job of navigating the struggle than the one that came before." [online] *The Indian Express.* Available at: <https://indianexpress.com/article/opinion/columns/discrimination-not-justice-6173881/#:~:text=Let%20us%20hope%20this%20generation,but%20especially%20inside%20the%20state> [Accessed 17 November 2021]

Mehta, Pratap Bhanu (2021). "Euphoric endorsement Narendra Modi enjoyed in 2014 is missing: Express News Service." [online] *The Financial Express.* Available at: <www.financialexpress.com/elections/euphoric-endorsement-narendra-modi-enjoyed-in-2014-is-missing-pratap-bhanu-mehta/1560417/> [Accessed 31 January 2021].

Moorthy, N. (2018). "Sri Lankan refugees: Why Lankan refugees are reluctant to go back home | Chennai News." [online] *The Times of India.* Available at: <https://timesofindia.indiatimes.com/city/chennai/why-lankan-refugees-are-reluctant-to-go-back-home/articleshow/65591130.cms> [Accessed 17 November 2021]

The New Indian Express (2020). "Those opposing CAA mentally affected, need treatment: UP deputy CM Keshav Prasad Maurya." [online] Available at:<www.newindianexpress.com/nation/2020/jan/20/those-opposing-caa-mentally-affected-need-treatment-up-deputy-cm-keshav-prasad-maurya-2091724.html> [Accessed 17 November 2021]

Outlook India (2020). "Those raising slogans against PM Modi, CM Yogi 'Will Be Buried Alive': BJP Leader Raghuraj Singh." [online] Available at:<www.outlookindia.com/website/story/those-raising-slogans-against-pm-modi-cm-yogi-will-be-buried-alive-bjp-leader-raghuraj-singh/345648> [Accessed 17 November 2021].

Sharma, S. (2019). "We knew Adityanath was hostile to Muslims. But did we expect his regime to be so savage?" [online] *Scroll.in.* Available at: <https://scroll.in/article/948194/we-knew-adityanath-was-hostile-to-muslims-but-did-we-expect-his-regime-to-be-so-savage> [Accessed 23 March 2021].

Verma, A. and Mander, H. (2020). "The creation of a vigilante state in UP." [online] *Article 14.com.* Available at: <www.article-14.com/post/the-creation-of-a-vigilante-state-in-uttar-pradesh> [Accessed 5 March 2021]

The Wire (2019). "'Reign of Terror': Fact-finding team returns from UP with accounts of targeted police violence." [online] Available at: <https://thewire.in/rights/uttar-pradesh-caa-protests-report> [Accessed 1 November 2020]

Yamunan, S. (2019). "Citizenship Act protests: Why sweeping bans on public meetings in entire states are illegal." [online] *Scroll.in.* Available at: <https://scroll.in/article/947275/citizenship-act-protests-imposing-ban-on-large-gatherings-on-entire-states-is-illegal-arbitrary> [Accessed 2 November 2020].

8

HINDU NATIONALIST STATECRAFT AND MODI'S AUTHORITARIAN POPULISM

Kenneth Bo Nielsen and Alf Gunvald Nilsen

Political scientists have rightly considered the government of the right-wing Hindu nationalist Bharatiya Janata Party (BJP) under Prime Minister Narendra Modi, which first came to power in the 2014 general election and then consolidated its position in the subsequent general election in 2019, as constituting a watershed in the political life of the Indian republic. Milan Vaishnav and Jamie Hintson (2019) argue that the 2019 elections ushered in India's fourth dominant *party* system, centred on the BJP and its politics. Christophe Jaffrelot and Gilles Verniers (2020: 143) go further, and argue that the 2019 elections brought about a new *political* system, as Modi 2.0 has "radically changed gears and used the legislative and executive route to transform India into a *de jure* ethnic democracy" (see also Nilsen, Nielsen and Vaidya 2022). "Indeed", Achin Vanaik (2017: 29) writes, "the scale of BJP hegemony today can bear comparison to that of the Indian National Congress party in the first decades after Independence, under Jawaharlal Nehru and his daughter, Indira Gandhi."

But how do we explain the politics of this new hegemonic order in India? In this chapter, we focus on how Modi's authoritarian populism has come, increasingly, to mobilize the law in order to align the nation with the core tenets of Hindu nationalism. We see Modi's authoritarian populism as a form of conservative politics that constructs a contradiction between common people and elites, and then uses this contradiction to justify the imposition of repressive measures by the state (Hall 1988). We also see it, crucially, as a populism that draws a line between "true Indians" and their "anti-national" enemies, and subjects the latter to coercion in order, supposedly, to protect the former (Müller 2016). In line with the core tenets of Hindu nationalism, this line is defined in large part by religion – the ominous Other that authoritarian populism depends on in order to frame a unitary conception of the nation and national culture is, in Modi's India, the Muslim (see Nilsen 2021a, 2021b). In this chapter, we analyze how this religiously defined dividing line is being codified into law in order to align the nation with the core tenets of Hindu nationalism. We refer to this particular enactment of the BJP's political agenda as Hindu nationalist statecraft – that is, as a strategy centred on legally locking in claims that India is and should be a *Hindu rashtra* in ways that make it exceedingly difficult to reverse such claims in the future (see Nilsen 2020). In the hegemonic project of the BJP and the wider Hindu nationalist movement, we argue, this strategy allows religious majoritarianism to dictate law-making and override the precepts of secular constitutional morality, as well as the general democratic principle of protecting minority rights. Always-already conjoined with majoritarian

DOI: 10.4324/9781003042211-10

violence, Hindu nationalist statecraft arguably poses the most serious threat that India's secular, constitutional democracy has faced since its inception at independence in 1947.

The BJP from Ayodhya to Modi

The BJP first entered the arena of Indian politics as a minor player in 1980, when former members of the Bharatiya Jana Sangh, the political arm of the Hindu nationalist movement from the early 1950s to the late 1970s, established the party in order, as Christophe Jaffrelot (1996: 315) puts it, "to inherit the mantle of the Janata party" that had ruled India from 1977 to 1980. Furthermore, this would require a relative side-lining of Hindu nationalism vis-à-vis socioeconomic interests, reliance on political leaders that could appeal to group and sectional interests rather than on ideologues, and a readiness to enter into electoral alliances with mainstream political parties (ibid.: 315). However, it was not moderation that would propel the BJP from the status of a minor player to a force to be reckoned with in Indian politics – it was, rather, spectacular collective violence that drove this process.

In 1990, India was on the cusp of a dramatic political convulsion that unsettled the caste-based power relations that had prevailed since independence in 1947. In response to increasingly militant demands from below, the central government – a coalition of non-Congress parties known as the National Front, with outside support from the BJP – introduced a comprehensive scheme of affirmative action, granting reservations of 27 per cent of all jobs in the public sector to lower caste groups, the so-called Other Backward Classes. This caused uproar among India's middle classes and upper castes – the very same groups who constituted the core constituency of the BJP (see Hansen 1999). Responding to these developments, the BJP president Lal Krishna Advani launched a *rath yatra* – a chariot procession – that was to make its way across India to Ayodhya to lay claim to the disputed site of the Babri Masjid, a sixteenth-century mosque that, according to Hindu nationalist claims, had been erected on the birthplace of the Hindu deity Lord Ram. In doing so, Advani and other prominent BJP politicians aligned themselves decisively with the Ram Janmabhoomi (literally, birthplace of Ram) movement of the Vishva Hindu Parishad (World Hindu Council) – a central node in the vast network of the Hindu nationalist movement – and its demand that the Babri Masjid should make way for a Ram temple. Advani's goal was obvious, namely to shore up and consolidate middle class and upper caste support for his party (Hansen 1999; Jaffrelot 1996: chapters 12 and 13).

Beginning in late September 1990, Advani's *yatra* mobilized thousands of volunteers – among them Narendra Modi, who at that point in time was a prominent Hindu nationalist activist – and crossed through hundreds of towns and villages. Deploying hard-line religious symbolism, the procession sparked violent communal riots, and Advani was finally arrested in late October as he attempted to cross into the state of Uttar Pradesh. Despite Advani's arrest, large numbers of Hindu nationalist activists – estimates range between 40,000 and 75,000 – made their way to Ayodhya and laid siege to the Babri Masjid until they were dispersed after three days of running battles with security forces (Nilsen 2019). This, however, was not the end of the movement for a Ram temple in Ayodhya. On the contrary, in early December 1992, the Rashtriya Swayamsevak Sangh (RSS) – the ideological backbone of the Hindu nationalist movement – organized a rally that attracted about 150,000 *kar sevaks* (activist volunteers) to the site of the Babri Masjid. After speeches by Advani and other central BJP politicians, the crowd attacked the mosque and demolished it. The destruction of the mosque sparked new rounds of communal violence, in which more than 2,000 people – the majority of whom were Muslims – were killed (see Hasan 2014: chapter 1).

Whereas the demolition was a tragedy for India's Muslim citizens, it was a successful strategic move on the part of the BJP, which had withdrawn its support from the National Front government after the violent end of the *rath yatra*. In the general elections that ensued in 1991, the party, which had now firmly established itself as a defender of Hindu values and interests in a changing nation, won 120 seats – up from 85 seats in the 1989 elections. And by the end of the 1990s – a decade that witnessed deepening communal polarization – the BJP found itself for the first time at the head of a national coalition government and decisively established as a force to be reckoned with in Indian politics (Hasan 2014: chapter 1). In other words, Advani's ploy to galvanize electoral support through religious mythology and violence paid off, and as such it constitutes a crucial prehistory to today's political scenario in India, in which the BJP under Modi rules supreme.

The Emergence of Modi's Authoritarian Populism

Modi's rise to first regional and later national power was similarly lubricated by the kind of majoritarian collective violence that characterized Hindu nationalist politics in the 1980s and 1990s. Modi's trajectory began at an early age in the Rashtriya Swayamsewak Sangh (RSS) and only shifted to the BJP in the late 1980s. In the BJP, he played an important organizational role in the series of marches that mobilized youth towards anti-Muslim violence, and which culminated in the demolition of the Babri Masjid. Indeed, Modi has been described as Advani's "navigator" in his 1990 yatra (Kanungo 2019).

A decade later, Modi was installed as Chief Minister of Gujarat in 2001 to stabilize the BJP at a time of crisis. He had an unremarkable and not particularly popular term until events provided him with another opportunity to further Hindu nationalist politics by deploying extra-legal violence against minorities. In February 2002, a number of Hindu pilgrims were killed in a fire inside the Sabarmati Express train at Godhra station in Gujarat. Shortly afterwards, highly organized Hindu nationalist mobs who blamed Muslims for setting the train on fire unleashed an unprecedented anti-Muslim pogrom and attacked Muslim homes, neighbourhoods and businesses, killing hundreds, if not thousands, of Muslims. After three days of silence during which violent Hindutva activists largely had a free run, Modi spoke only to apparently defend the perpetrators by calling the pogrom a *svabhavik patrikriya*, a natural reaction (Ghassem-Fachandi 2019). Modi's association with the violence allowed him to reap electoral gains in successive state elections, to increase his grip over the state machinery and civil society (Shani 2007; Basu 2015; Berenschot 2011), and even to establish a relatively independent position vis-à-vis the powerful RSS.

Between the anti-Muslim pogroms of 2002 and his ascension to the pinnacle of national political power in 2014, Modi was reinvented as a market-friendly technocrat and primary architect of Gujarat's supposed development miracle (see Bobbio 2012, 2013; Sud 2012, 2020). This was the image that was front and centre of the BJP's campaign for the 2014 general election: Modi was portrayed as *vikas purush* – a man of development who would extend the scope of the Gujarat miracle to the Indian nation (Nilsen 2021a, 2021b). However, although its articulation was more subdued, Hindu nationalism was never absent from the BJP campaign trail in 2013–2014, and after the elections it became more and more central to the party's agenda (Kaul 2017). A majoritarian cultural politics crystallized around issues such as cow protection, the communal policing of interreligious love and of women's sexuality, the rewriting of school textbooks to bring them in line with Hindutva historiography, and the promotion of religious reconversion among Muslims and Christians (see Flåten 2016; Basu 2015). Hate speech has proliferated, and majoritarian rhetoric is clearly linked to communal violence against

Muslims and other marginal groups, such as Dalits. In fact, it was recently estimated that more than 86 per cent of all vigilante attacks on Muslims and Dalits since 2009 had taken place under Modi's premiership (Abraham and Rao 2017).

Following the general election in 2019, this majoritarian violence has become intertwined with a systematic effort on the part of the government to write Hindu nationalist ideology into law in a way that is unprecedented in postcolonial India. Indeed, the 2019 election marks a point of transition in Hindutva politics under Modi. As argued in this section, during Modi's first term in power, the majoritarian cultural nationalism that draws a line between "true Indians" and their enemies, and seeks to rally popular support for a crackdown on those enemies, was predominantly pursued through the vigilante violence of Hindu nationalist mobs. However, with the onset of Modi's second term in power, we are witnessing an increased recourse to the law to further advance the project of turning India into a *Hindu rashtra*. It is this effort – the locking in of Hindu nationalist claims to the nation into law – that we refer to as Hindu nationalist statecraft, and to which we turn below.

The Politics of Hindu nationalist statecraft

In August 2019, the Modi government revoked Kashmir's special constitutional status, relegating what was then India's only Muslim-majority state to a union territory. The abolition of Kashmir's statehood was an act of territorial engineering designed to advance the idea of a *Hindu rashtra* in very tangible ways. Not only did it set the stage for an onslaught against insurgent citizens who are overwhelmingly Muslim, it also cleared the ground for changing the demography of the state. The revocation of Kashmir's special constitutional status means that Kashmiri authorities no longer have the right to define who is a permanent resident with a right to own land in the state. This created the possibility of changing the make-up of its population to such an extent that the aspiration among Kashmir's Muslim-majority population for genuine freedom – for *azaadi* – would be rendered completely impossible (Nilsen 2020). As journalist Haris Zargar (2020a, 2020b) has noted, the subsequent introduction of new domicile land laws that discriminate in multiple ways against Kashmiris goes a long way towards reducing Kashmir to a settler-colony of India and its Hindu majority. Indeed, as argued by Partha Chatterjee (2019), Kashmir may well be seen as the BJP's laboratory for "developing the constitutional rules of internal colonialism". The symbolic politics of these legislative moves is abundantly clear: the Hindu nation is to be built by purging India's territory of the Muslim enemy within (see Nilsen, Nielsen and Vaidya 2022). But it may not stop there. As Chatterjee (2019) warns, the thrust of the majoritarian logic of Hindu nationalist statecraft nationalism may hit every minority – whether based on language, religion, caste, or gender – that appears to stand in the way of a homogeneous nationhood.

Subsequently, in November 2019, India's Supreme Court passed its verdict in the Ayodhya dispute, in favour of Hindu plaintiffs who claimed the right to the land where the Babri Masjid stood until its demolition in December 1992. In doing so, the Supreme Court lent credence to Hindu nationalist mythology which claims that this land is the birthplace of Lord Ram, and therefore rightfully belongs to India's Hindu majority. The verdict is troubling in itself. But even more worrisome, the verdict signalled that the Supreme Court, which is supposed to be an independent guardian of India's secular constitutional democracy, and which had been hailed since the Emergency as the last resort of the oppressed and the bewildered (Baxi 1985), had now been rendered increasingly "timid, tentative, fragmented and vulnerable, wary of hurting the central executive" led by Modi – who, tellingly, was the key speaker at the temple's ground-breaking ceremony held less than a year later (see Sebastian 2019). In fact, the trend for the Supreme Court to align itself with the political agenda of the Modi regime has intensified both prior to and after the Ayodhya verdict. This can be seen, on the one hand, in its non-confrontational stance on consequential legal interventions, including the abrogation of Article 370, and the Citizen Amendment Act and National Registry of Citizens that we turn to below; and, on the other hand, in the growing tendency – also prevalent in the lower courts – of citing "the national interest" to legalize the violation of citizens' rights, thus tilting "the scales of justice...against those opposed to the Modi government" (Chhibber 2020). This, Jaffrelot (2020a) argued in late 2020, marks a striking departure from business as usual: "over the last four years, none of [the Supreme Court's] decisions has come as a major embarrassment for the government. For these two power centres to be on the same wavelength for such a long time is unprecedented." One expert on the Indian Supreme Court sees in this "the complete capitulation of the Supreme Court to the majoritarian rule of Prime Minister Narendra Modi", reducing it to "a cheerleader for the Modi government's agenda" (Bhuwania 2020).

The Ayodhya judgment, in turn, was followed in early December 2019 by the passing into law of the Citizenship Amendment Act (CAA), mentioned above. The CAA offers expedited citizenship for persecuted religious minorities from India's Muslim-majority neighbouring countries Afghanistan, Pakistan, and Bangladesh who can prove that they have been living in India since before 31 December 2014. However, the CAA only extends this right to Hindus, Christians, Sikhs, Buddhists, Jains, and Parsis, but not to persecuted Muslims in these countries, such as the Ahmadis in Pakistan or the Hazaras in Afghanistan. Similarly, persecuted religious minorities from other neighbouring countries such as Nepal, Sri Lanka or Myanmar cannot avail of the offer of expedited citizenship.

The CAA will work in tandem with a national population register and a National Registry of Citizens (NRC) under which the right to Indian citizenship is directly linked to whether or not individuals can prove that they were born in India between January 1950 and June 1987, or that they are children of bona fide Indian citizens. As people often do not have the kind of documents required by this process, many risk losing their citizenship. However, Hindus who find themselves in this situation can resort to the lifeline offered by the CAA. Given that this opportunity is not afforded to Muslims, the CAA – NRC couplet is likely to create a hierarchy of citizenship graded along religious lines, in which Indian Muslims end up as second-class citizens (Nilsen 2020).

While the politics of Hindu nationalist statecraft is crucially enacted by the national government, the division of legislative powers between the national parliament and the state assemblies means that Hindu nationalist statecraft increasingly also animates law-making at the level of the federal states – especially in states where the BJP is in power. One example of this is cow protection, which falls within states' competence, and the related laws that have been introduced towards this end in different states since Modi came to power in 2014. Cow protection as a tactic to assert Hindu identity has deep roots among Hindu reform groups from the latter half of the nineteenth century, and was one of the core issues of the BJP's predecessor, the BJS, immediately after independence. Under Modi, it has acquired a renewed urgency. Modi is known to favour a national ban on cow slaughter (Andersen and Damle 2019: 179), but has so far not initiated the constitutional changes that would enable a national government to legislate on this issue. Instead, state-level legislative changes have systematically made the slaughter of cows or even the sale and possession of cow beef illegal in ever-larger parts of the country under Modi's tenure (Jaffrelot 2019: 59). Modi's home state of Gujarat, for instance, in 2017, amended an act from 1954 that criminalized cow slaughter, transportation of cows for slaughter, and the possession of beef, to extend the maximum sentence for cow slaughter to life imprisonment. Other BJP-controlled states such as Maharashtra (where BJP was ousted from office in late

2019) and Haryana have also toughened cow protection legislation by criminalizing beef consumption in 2015. The former has imposed a total ban on the slaughter of all cattle (bulls and bullocks included) and has completely banned all transport of cattle out of the state (Ramdas 2017), while in the latter, the state police has set up a "cow task force" (Jaffrelot 2019: 62). And Uttar Pradesh, under the hard-line Hindu nationalist chief minister Yogi Adityanath, recently imposed unprecedentedly strict legal punishments for various offences ranging from cow slaughter to "endangering the life of cows" by, for example, not providing them food and water. The Adityanath government is also known to publish the name and photograph of people accused of breaking the state Cow Slaughter Act if they try to evade the law enforcement agencies (Lalchandani 2020). Uttar Pradesh, along with Gujarat and Rajasthan, also recently introduced legal amendments enabling the confiscation of vehicles alleged to be transporting cattle for slaughter (Ramdas 2020). The southern state of Karnataka – ruled by the BJP since 2019 – followed suit in 2020 by passing the Prevention of Slaughter and Preservation of Cattle Bill, 2020, a bill that not only bans the slaughter of all cows, bulls, bullocks and calves, but also outlaws the slaughter of buffaloes below the age of thirteen, makes smuggling and transporting animals for slaughter an offence and empowers the police to conduct searches based on suspicion (Daniyal 2020).

These laws advance the project of Hindu nationalist statecraft in three interrelated ways. Most immediately, they criminalize the activities of entire beef eating communities, particularly Muslims but also Dalits and Christians, and render everyday social, culinary and economic activities illegal. Second, this enhanced legal protection for the cow and higher sentences for offenders boosts Hindu nationalist cow protection vigilantes, who now feel that their violent actions are backed by the letter of the law and endorsed by the governments that passed them. Again, the victims of such violence are invariably Muslims (but also Dalits) accused of killing and eating cows or illegally transporting them for slaughter. Such violent "Islamophobic gastronomy", Raj Patel (2018) argues, is in effect a way of adjudicating over citizenship that is becoming increasingly widespread within authoritarian populist regimes. Lastly, the consequences of the legal crackdown on beef have, in economic terms, hit Muslims and Dalits the hardest (Jakobsen and Nielsen 2021).

Another example of how Hindu nationalist statecraft that animates law-making at the level of the federal states is the recent introduction of laws by the Yogi Adityanath government in the state of Uttar Pradesh to prevent so-called love jihad. "Love jihad" is an Islamophobic conspiracy theory centred on the false claim that Muslim men marry Hindu women in order to force them to convert to Islam (Zargar 2020c). The Uttar Pradesh Prohibition of Unlawful Conversion of Religion Ordinance, which was passed into law in late November 2020, effectively criminalizes interfaith marriages, and in doing so it extends Hindu nationalist statecraft into the intimate domain. Several other BJP-ruled states such as Madhya Pradesh and Haryana have signalled their intention to introduce similar legislation. Based on the ideological construct of the Muslim man as a malevolent predator and the Hindu woman as a passive victim in need of patriarchal protection – a construct that has historically been foundational to Hindutva politics – the law echoes the foundational logic of Modi's authoritarian populism, in which Muslims constitute an enemy within that must be defeated to guard the sanctity of the Hindu nation (Gupta 2021). Much like the case of cow protection laws, the Uttar Pradesh legislation against "love jihad" illustrates the proximity between Hindu nationalist statecraft and extra-legal majoritarian violence. The policing of interfaith relationships has been a staple activity among Hindu nationalist vigilante groups under Modi – indeed, as Jaffrelot (2020b) has commented, in promulgating this law, the BJP-controlled state apparatus is picking up the baton from these vigilante groups (see also Chowdhury 2020).

Concluding remarks

There can be little doubt that India today is in the throes of a dramatic process of autocratization. Key pillars of the secular democratic order that came into being in 1947 are being eroded, and the driving force of that erosion is the politics of the Modi regime.

In this chapter, we have focused on the role that law and law-making has come to play in advancing a hegemonic project of authoritarian populism centred on a distinction between "true Indians" and their "anti-national enemies" within, embodied by Indian Muslims along with dissenters. Since Modi's re-election in 2019, India's BJP-led government has pursued what we refer to as Hindu nationalist statecraft – that is, writing the foundational claims of Hindu nationalism into law, and in so doing entrenching religious majoritarianism in the structural workings of the state. This obviously militates in fundamental ways against the secular fabric of India's constitutional order, in particular by abrogating the democratic rights of minority citizens in the country.

The turn towards Hindu nationalist statecraft must be understood as an extension of the strategies that the BJP has resorted to since it first made an appearance in India's political arena in the 1980s, in which parliamentary politics is intrinsically related to extra-legal violence. Indeed, Hindu nationalist statecraft works to compound the vigilante violence that has proliferated in India since Modi first took power in India in 2014. The fact that democratic opposition to these developments – in particular the anti-CAA/NRC protests of 2019 and 2020 – has been curbed by coercive measures simply underscores the perilous nature of the conjuncture that the Indian polity and society are currently confronting.

Glossary

azaadi:	freedom
Hindu Rashtra:	Hindu state
Hindutva:	Hinduness; ideology of Hindu nationalism
kar sevak:	activist volunteer
rath yatra:	chariot procession
svabhavik patrikriya:	natural reaction
vikas purush:	man of development
yatra:	*see* rath yatra

Bibliography

Abraham, D. and Rao, O. (2017). 86% Killed in cow-related violence since 2010 are Muslim, 97% attacks after Modi govt came to power. *Hindustan Times* [online]. 16 July. [Viewed 10 October 2019.] Available from: www.hindustantimes.com/india-news/86-killed-in-cow-related-violence-since2010-are-muslims-97-attacks-after-modi-govt-came-to-power/storyw9CYOksvgk9joGSSaXgpLO.html.

Andersen, W. and Damle, S. (2019). *Messengers of Hindu Nationalism: How the RSS Reshaped India.* London: Hurst and Company.

Basu, A. (2015). *Violent Conjunctures in Democratic India.* New York: Cambridge University Press.

Baxi, U. (1985). "Taking Suffering Seriously: Social Action Litigation in the Supreme Court of India". *Third World Legal Studies* 4(6), 107–132.

Berenschot, W. (2011). *Riot Politics: Hindu-Muslim Violence and the Indian State.* London: Hurst and Company.

Bhuwania, A. (2020). The crisis of legitimacy plaguing the Supreme Court in Modi era is now hidden in plain sight. *Scroll* [online]. December 1. [Viewed 25 February 2021.] Available from: https://scroll.in/article/979818/the-crisis-of-legitimacy-plaguing-the-supreme-court-in-modi-era-is-now-hidden-in-plain-sight.

Bobbio, T. (2012). "Making Gujarat Vibrant: *Hindutva*, Development and the Rise of Subnationalism in India". *Third World Quarterly* 33(4), 657–672.

Bobbio, T. (2013). "Never-ending Modi: Hindutva and Gujarati Neoliberalism as Prelude to All-India Premiership?" *Focaal* 67, 123–134.

Chatterjee, P. (2019). Kashmir is the test bed for a new model of internal colonialism. *The Wire* [online]. 28 August. [Viewed 25 February 2021.] Available from: https://thewire.in/government/kashmir-is-the-test-bed-for-a-new-model-of-internal-colonialism.

Chhibber, M. (2020). Indian courts speak of 'national interest' but they order often in Modi govt's interest. *The Print* [online]. 12 February. [Viewed 25 February 2021.] Available from: https://theprint.in/opinion/indian-courts-speak-of-national-interest-but-they-order-often-in-modi-govts-interest/363859/.

Chowdhury, D. R. (2020). Laws against 'love jihad' are yet another serious attack on India's once secular democracy. *Time* [online]. November 30. [Viewed 25 February 2021.] Available from: https://time.com/5915872/love-jihad-india-democracy/.

Daniyal, S. (2020). At a time of acute farmer distress, Karnataka's bovine slaughter bill will make lives even worse. *The Scroll* [online]. 16 December. [Viewed 25 February 2021.] Available from: https://scroll.in/article/981255/at-a-time-of-acute-farmer-distress-karnataka-s-bovine-slaughter-bill-will-make-lives-even-worse.

Flåten, L. T. (2016). *Hindu Nationalism, History and Identity in India: Narrating a Hindu Past under the BJP*. London: Routledge.

Ghassem-Fachandi, P. (2019). "Reflections in the crowd: Delegation, verisimilitude, and the Modi mask". In A. P. Chatterji, T. B. Hansen and C. Jaffrelot, eds., *Majoritarian State: How Hindu Nationalism is Changing India*. Oxford: Oxford University Press, pp. 83–98.

Gupta, C. (2021). Love taboos: controlling Hindu-Muslim romances. *The India Forum* [online]. 8 January. [Viewed 25 February 2021.] Available from: www.theindiaforum.in/article/love-laws-making-hindu-muslim-romances-illegitimate.

Hall, S. (1988). *The Hard Road to Renewal: Thatcherism and The Crisis of the Left*. London: Verso Books.

Hansen, T. B. (1999). *The Saffron Wave: Democracy and Hindu Nationalism in Modern India*. Princeton: Princeton University Press.

Hasan, Z. (2014). *Congress After Indira: Policy, Power, Political Change (1984–2009)*. Delhi: Oxford University Press.

Jaffrelot, C. (1996). *The Hindu Nationalist Movement in India*. New York: Columbia University Press.

Jaffrelot, C. (2019). "*A de facto* ethnic democracy? Obliterating and targeting the other, Hindu vigilantes, and the ethno-state". In A. P. Chatterji, T. B. Hansen and C. Jaffrelot, eds. *Majoritarian State: How Hindu Nationalism is Changing India*. Oxford: Oxford University Press, pp. 41–68.

Jaffrelot, C. (2020a). Supreme Court's apparent reluctance to question government on consequential issues affects its moral authority. *Indian Express* [online]. 7 September. [Viewed 25 February 2021.] Available from: https://indianexpress.com/article/opinion/columns/supreme-court-narendra-modi-government-6585721/.

Jaffrelot, C. (2020b). On 'love jihad', BJP picks up baton from vigilante groups. Police, judicial apparatus have aided this move. *Indian Express* [online]. 26 November. [Viewed 25 February 2021.] Available from: https://indianexpress.com/article/opinion/columns/love-jihad-law-india-bjp-7067013/.

Jaffrelot, C., and Verniers, G. (2020). "A new party system or a new political system?" *Contemporary South Asia* 28(2), 141–154.

Jakobsen, J. and Nielsen, K. B. (2021). "Bovine Meat, Authoritarian Populism and State Contradictions in Modi's India". Under review.

Kanungo, P. (2019). "Sangh and sarkar: The RSS power centre shifts from Nagpur to New Delhi". In A. P. Chatterji, T. B. Hansen and C. Jaffrelot, eds. *Majoritarian State: How Hindu Nationalism is Changing India*, Delhi: Oxford University Press, pp. 133–150.

Kaul, N. (2017). "Rise of the political right in India: Hindutva development mix, Modi myth, and dualities". *Journal of Labour and Society* 20(4), 523–548.

Lalchandani, N. (2020). Up to 10-year jail for cow slaughter in UP. *Times of India* [online]. 10 June. [Viewed 25 February 2021.] Available from: https://timesofindia.indiatimes.com/india/up-to-10-year-jail-for-cow-slaughter-in-up/articleshow/76293141.cms.

Müller, J.-W. (2016). *What Is Populism?* Philadelphia: University of Pennsylvania Press.

Nilsen, A. G. (2019). Onward march of Hindu nationalism. *Mail and Guardian* [online]. 15 November. [Viewed 25 February 2021.] Available from: https://mg.co.za/article/2019-11-15-00-the-onward-march-of-hindu-nationalism/.

Nilsen, A. G. (2020). India's breaking point. *Polis Project* [online]. January 11. [Viewed 25 February 2021.] Available from: https://thepolisproject.com/indias-breaking-point/#.XzuxoElS_OQ.

Nilsen, A. G. (2021a). "From inclusive neoliberalism to authoritarian populism: Trajectories of change in the world's largest democracy". In M. Ray, ed. *State of Democracy: Essays on the Life and Politics of Contemporary India.* Delhi: Primus Books.

Nilsen, A. G. (2021b). "India's trajectories of change, 2004–2019". In V. Satgar and M. Williams, eds. *Democratic Marxism Volume 6 – Capitalism Against Democracy*, Johannesburg: Wits University Press.

Nilsen, A. G., Nielsen, K. B. and Vaidya, A. P. (2022). "Theorizing Law, Social Movements and State Formation in India", Comparative Studies in South Asia, Africa and the Middle East.

Patel, R. (2018). Islamophobia Gastronomica – on the food police, rural populism and killing. *OpenIndia* [online]. 26 February. [Viewed 25 February 2021.] Available from: www.opendemocracy.net/openIndia/raj-patel/islamophobia-gastronomica-on-food-police-rural-populism-and-killing.

Ramdas, S. (2017). The beef ban effect: Stray cattle, broken markets and boom time for buffaloes. *The Wire* [online]. 6 April. [Viewed 25 February 2021.] Available from: https://thewire.in/politics/beef-ban-cattle-market.

Ramdas, S. (2020). Will Karnataka's new bill sound the death knell for its cattle wealth? *The Leaflet* [online]. 15 December. [Viewed 25 February 2021.] Available from: www.theleaflet.in/will-karnatakas-new-bill-sound-the-death-knell-for-its-cattle-wealth/#.

Sebastian, M. (2019). How has the Supreme Court fared during the Modi years? *The Wire* [online]. 12 April. [Viewed 25 February 2021.] Available from: https://thewire.in/law/supreme-court-modi-years.

Shani, O. (2007). *Communalism, Caste and Hindu Nationalism: The Violence in Gujarat.* Cambridge: Cambridge University Press.

Sud, N. (2012). *Liberalization, Hindu Nationalism, and the State: A Biography of Gujarat.* New Delhi: Oxford University Press.

Sud, N. (2020). "The actual Gujarat model: Authoritarianism, capitalism, Hindu nationalism and populism in the time of Modi". *Journal of Contemporary Asia*, pp. 1–25. DOI: 10.1080/00472336.2020.1846205.

Vaishnav, M. and Hintson, J. (2019). The dawn of India's fourth party system. *Carnegie Endowment* [online]. September 5. [Viewed 25 February 2021.] Available from: https://carnegieendowment.org/2019/09/05/dawn-of-india-s-fourth-party-system-pub-79759.

Vanaik, A. (2017). *The Rise of Hindu Authoritarianism: Secular Claims, Communal Realities.* London: Verso Books.

Zargar, H. (2020a). Modi advances settler colonial project in Kashmir. *New Frame* [online]. 15 June. [Viewed 25 February 2021.] Available from: www.newframe.com/modi-advances-settler-colonial-project-in-kashmir/.

Zargar, H. (2020b). Modi regime moves to dispossess Kashmiris of land. *New Frame* [online]. 17 November. [Viewed 25 February 2021.] Available from: www.newframe.com/modi-regime-moves-to-dispossess-kashmiris-of-land/.

Zargar, H. (2020c). The 'love jihad' returns to haunt Muslims in India. *New Frame* [online]. 15 December. [Viewed 25 February 2021.] Available from: www.newframe.com/the-love-jihad-returns-to-haunt-muslims-in-india/.

9

INDIA'S INEXORABLE PATH TO AUTOCRATIZATION

Looking beyond Modi and the populist lens

Soundarya Chidambaram

Introduction

The unlikely election of Donald Trump in the United States followed by the Brexit vote, contra extensive public opinion and scholarly research, brought into stark focus the rising appeal of populist parties and leaders across the western world. With similar trends manifesting in Eastern and Central Europe, Latin America, and Asia, populism has changed not only the landscape of global politics but also its lexicon (Kyle and Gultchin, 2018). While some scholars tend to assert that populist parties are synonymous with autocratization (Mudde, 2007), there are naysayers who highlight the intrinsic democratic potential of populism by examining movements such as Occupy Wall Street or populist parties like Syriza and Podemos. There are also differing perspectives on the causes of populism ranging from economic disaffection due to rising economic inequalities, a backlash against neoliberal globalization, Euroscepticism, political disenchantment with corrupt elite, to anti-immigration sentiments, and fear of loss of cultural status. One undeniable correlation though is that the electoral success of populist parties has also coincided with a decline of democracy across the globe (Günther and Lührmann, 2018). The focal point in this regard is the rise of populist demagogues and authoritarian strongmen who have caused democratic decline by cracking down on political dissent and curbing the autonomy of the judiciary and the free press, thus creating the conditions for democratic backsliding and decline (Levitsky and Ziblatt, 2018).

The path of the Bhartiya Janata Party (BJP) in India since 2014 seems to fit this description. The BJP's hegemonic control of Indian politics has been coterminous with aggressive cultural nationalist rhetoric manifesting itself as routinized intimidation and killing of journalists and political critics, vigilante lynching of Muslims and general clampdown on dissent (Kesavan, 2017). Narendra Modi, the Prime Minister and leader of the BJP, epitomizes the populist strongman with his charismatic appeal, centralization of power (Vaishnav, 2019), and ability to connect with the masses through clever use of media (Martelli and Jaffrelot, 2017; Vaishnav, 2021). Not surprisingly, scholars and commentators looking at contemporary Indian politics converge on the idea that Modi's populist leadership of the BJP is the reason for the havoc being wreaked on democratic institutions in the country (Kinnvall, 2019; Chatterji et al., 2019; Basu, 2018; Chacko, 2018; Nilsen, 2018).

DOI: 10.4324/9781003042211-11

However, crediting populist parties and leaders as the exclusive progenitors of authoritarianism is to overlook the deeper societal churning that produces both authoritarianism and the rising appeal of populism. For instance in the US, Trump's brand of populism is underpinned by a steady process of polarization and creation of echo chambers helping to entrench ethnoracially constituted "us" vs. "them" categories (Williamson et al., 2011). Admittedly, Modi's unique hold over Indian politics and strongman style of politics has hastened India's democratic decline, but we need to contextualize this within the broader trajectory of autocratization, and the chauvinistic nationalism of the radical right in India. Though there is an observed association between the BJP's populist trajectory (the posited independent variable here, or the "IV") and autocratization (the dependent variable in this case, or the "DV"), I argue that grassroots mobilization by radical right organizations acts as a confounding variable that decides the relationship between these variables – that is, a third factor at play in the background that may affect the purported explanatory relationship between the IV and the DV. The Hindu rightwing movement's targeted mobilization through civil society activism embeds majoritarian nationalism in public discourse, thus creating the impetus for autocratization while also helping the BJP's political chances (See Figure 9.1).

This chapter thus provides a corrective to the predominant ways in which discussions about autocratization and radical right movements are often framed. The former is discussed as a consequence of a discrete event in time such as a populist win. The latter is perceived either through the lens of violent tactics or simplistically as a means to advance electoral goals. The chapter is organized thus. Section II defines key terms, reviews the literature, and provides the framework for understanding why and how civil society works as a transmission channel for majoritarianism and autocratization. Section III uses the case of Karnataka in south India to illustrate the central argument by looking at how grassroots mobilization is custom fitted to regional specificities in order to advance the cause of majoritarian nationalism. The chapter concludes by discussing the implications for the study of Hindu Right mobilization in India. The case study particularly illustrates the path forward to understanding why, despite the macro emphasis on welfare provision, we observe subnational variation in grassroots mobilization

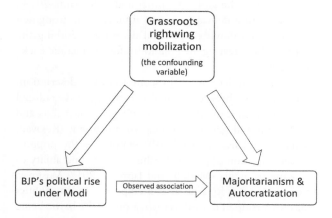

Figure 9.1 Theoretical framework specifying the main argument as compared to conventional explanations through identification of the confounding variable.

Source: author (Soundarya Chidambaram).

across regions and states. The chapter ends somewhat pessimistically by forecasting a trajectory of further autocratization once the populist moment passes.

Understanding the trajectory of autocratization in India through the civil society lens

India's path to democratic decline has come into stark relief recently. Varieties of Democracy now classifies India as an electoral autocracy (Alizada et al., 2021). Freedom House has downgraded India's ranking from Free to Partly Free "due to a multiyear pattern in which the Hindu nationalist government and its allies have presided over rising violence and discriminatory policies affecting the Muslim population and pursued a crackdown on expressions of dissent by the media, academics, civil society groups, and protesters" (Freedom House, 2021). In particular, these measures capture what the state does to hinder democratic foundations. However, autocratization is not merely the cumulative effect of state actions that erode macro-indicators of democratic functioning. Such a conceptualization would implicate political parties of all ideological persuasions in India, and certainly, Modi's rise to power in 2014 would not then constitute the flipping of the democracy/autocratization switch. I argue instead that autocratization should be understood as an incremental process of democratic erosion that, in India, has come about through the gradual mainstreaming of majoritarian ideas – a process mediated as much by grassroots radical right mobilization as it is by top-down political party actions. I use the term majoritarianism in this chapter, drawing upon Hansen's (2019) definition: "Majoritarianism commonly refers to the idea that pre-existing ethnic, racial or religious majorities have a natural right to dominate a certain political entity." In this sense, autocratization is as much a refl ection of people's acceptance of the reversal of democratic principles in favour of chauvinistic nationalism and a narrow conception of citizenship. Viewed thus, authoritarian politics in India has a much longer history that predates Modi's brand of populist politics.

This brings us to the radical right and the BJP's place in this universe vs. the conventional left–right spectrum. First, it is somewhat incongruous to equate the BJP with populist parties in the west. The latter, despite underlying nationalist and xenophobic elements, are essentially rooted in economic discontent and political disenchantment. In contrast, chauvinistic nationalism is at the core of the BJP's ideological agenda (Dreze, 2020; Jaffrelot, 2019), while its economic positioning changes on a need-to basis (Basu, 2018; Mukhopadhyay, 2019; Roychowdhury, 2017; Sen, 2019; Sircar, 2020). While comparisons could be made to "nativist populist radical right" parties in Europe that have sprung from exclusionary nationalist ideologies like Sweden Democrats or Golden Dawn in Greece (Mudde and Kaltwasser, 2017), two factors that set the BJP apart are i) its relative electoral strength, and ii) its unique advantage due to its embeddedness within a larger established movement.

To illustrate the first point, parties such as the Sweden Democrats, UK Independence Party, Alternative für Deutschland in Germany, and to some degree the National Front in France, were fringe/marginal parties that only recently gained traction due to a unique confluence of economic crisis coupled with increased immigration (Larsson, 2016). In contrast, the BJP's political trajectory has always been much more mainstream. Secondly, the BJP is one constituent of the organizationally streamlined, well resourced, radical right social movement in India that targets diverse grassroots constituencies through group-specific initiatives vernacularized to appeal within local contexts. In this chapter, the term radical right is used to characterize parties and movements rooted in an ethnic conception of nationhood and that use nationalist nostalgia and national pride to build support (Lubbers, 2019; Lubbers and Coenders, 2017).

For the radical Hindu right movement (referred to as Hindu Right in the text), the use of such chauvinist nationalist rhetoric is not merely a means to an end – an electoral strategy chosen for its political expediency – but rather the end itself in trying to bring its vision of the "*Hindu Rashtra*" to fruition. Modi himself is a product of the rightwing movement. He not only rose up the ranks of the Hindu Right but it was the latter that laid the groundwork for the appeal of Modi's rhetoric (NPR, 2019). This theoretical distinction between right populism and transformative radical right movements is important because while perhaps an electorally expedient populism can be resisted as we are seeing now in the US, the transformation of public consciousness using the civil society route is more insidious and much harder to displace (Vanaik, 2017). In India, what one may be witnessing is not just a temporary institutional decline of democracy but an ideological reckoning with democratic norms. For instance, Palshikar (2015) characterizes this phenomenon as the tilting of political culture in India towards *Hindutva*, while Harriss et al. (2017, p. 7) use the term "banal *Hindutva*" to describe this "steady spread of everyday forms of Hindu nationalism".

This brings us to the key explanatory variable, the radical right movement's civil society mobilization in India. For a long time, civil society was perceived to be an inherently pluralistic space that increases social capital (Fukuyama, 2001; Putnam et al., 1994). However, now there is empirical evidence highlighting the dark side of social capital (Berman, 1997; Bermeo and Nord, 2000; Carothers and Barndt, 1999; Diamond, 1994; Shirer, 1990; Whitehead, 1997). More broadly, it is no longer easy to dismiss the civil society sphere as a realm for non-state actors without political power or electoral impact. Civil society is neither epiphenomenal nor peripheral to national political developments. The Hindu Right's positioning as a social movement acting through civil society outside of formal political mechanisms is important particularly since it can mobilize various constituencies through strategies that are not available to the political party.

Studies that look at the Hindu Right's civil society activism often tend to focus narrowly on militant and provocative mobilization such as riots, religious processions, cow protection, or "love Jihad" as the route through which the rightwing primes its target audience and creates antagonistic narratives (Fuller, 2001; Kanungo, 2008; Spodek, 2010; Vijayan, 2018; Zavos, 2001). However, contentious polarization is not the only mode through which the Hindu Right lays the groundwork for the spread of majoritarian rhetoric. For instance, Islamist social movements provide a good point of comparison for how targeted welfare provision is used to advance movement goals rather than narrow electoral gains (Cammett and Issar, 2010; J. Clark, 2004; Clark, 2004; Wiktorowicz, 2000). In similar vein, the Hindu Right uses seemingly innocuous social service provision activities to create opportunities to connect with local communities in non-provocative ways that nonetheless come with socialization into the core agenda (Beckerlegge, 2016; Bhattacharjee, 2016; Chidambaram, 2012; Jaffrelot, 2008; Thachil, 2011). Beginning in the mid-1990s, the Hindu Right strategically invested in welfare provision to local communities across India (see Figure 9.2). This was partly due to the backlash against the nationwide violence following the rightwing-led movement that led to the demolition of a 500-year-old mosque in northern India in December 1992. Welfare was also perceived as a means to counter lower caste mobilization that would hamper the movement's vision of an undivided Hindu society (Jaffrelot, 2005).

However, many studies look at communities or regions in isolation (Baviskar, 2005; Dhar, 2004; Fuller, 2001; Hansen, 1996; Lobo, 2002; Longkumer, 2016; Teltumbde, 2020), or at aspects of welfare provision such as education without evaluating the broader connections that come about through these initiatives within local spaces (Chaudhary, 2017; Froerer, 2007; Sarkar, 1994). In contrast, this chapter takes a broader view of grassroots rightwing mobilization

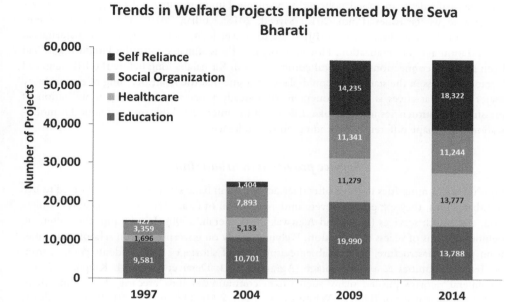

Trends in Welfare Projects Implemented by the Seva Bharati

Legend:
- Self Reliance
- Social Organization
- Healthcare
- Education

	1997	2004	2009	2014
Self Reliance	427	1,404	14,235	18,322
Social Organization	3,359	7,893	11,341	11,244
Healthcare	1,696	5,133	11,279	13,777
Education	9,581	10,701	19,990	13,788

Figure 9.2   Seva Bharati's expansion of welfare projects in India over two decades

Source: Data from various print and web editions of Rashtriya Swayamsevak Sangh's publications, Seva Disha and Sewa Sadhana, which provide detailed records of welfare initiatives launched by the grassroots organizations across Indian states. The web editions are available here: www.rashtriyasewabharati.org/sewa-disha.

to understand the concurrent mobilization of disparate sections within diverse spaces. First, I look at how education-focused welfare provision is utilized beyond just the target audience as a means of community-wide mobilization. Additionally, I look beyond welfare provision to focus on how heterogeneous segments of society simultaneously become primed to lean towards majoritarian ideas despite their very different socio-economic needs and characteristics. To do this, I draw on ethnographic fieldwork from the southern Indian state of Karnataka. I examine two varied sections of the urban population in Bengaluru, Karnataka's capital city – slum communities and young professionals in the IT/BPO sector – using fieldwork conducted in the city in 2009 along with secondary literature.

Karnataka: an empirical case study

Karnataka is an interesting case study for grassroots mobilization and autocratization. The Hindutva movement was traditionally an important influencer of politics in the northern part of India. In contrast, the south, with its history of social justice movements and anti-Brahminical politics, was seen as impervious to rightwing ideological mobilization. The emphasis on a Sanskritized homogeneous Hindu identity in particular did not often mesh with the religio-cultural traditions of the south. Yet, Karnataka is the one southern state where the BJP has consistently done well in the last two decades, both in national and in state elections. The state has also experienced intense polarization, anti-minority violence against Muslims and

Christians, incidents of moral policing by vigilante Hindu groups, and riling up controversies around wedge issues (Pinto, 2013; Sayeed, 2018; Kuthar, 2019). This ostensibly seems to confirm the hypothesis that the BJP's rise to power legitimates the space for majoritarian mobilization and autocratization. However, organizations affiliated with the Hindu Right had been building connections with local communities in Karnataka long before the BJP achieved electoral success in the state. One could plausibly argue that the mainstreaming of exclusionary majoritarian narratives is the denouement of a steady process of rightwing mobilization of grassroots constituencies in Karnataka. I flesh out the micro-level dynamics of how this mobilization takes shape differently depending on the audience.

Service provision in urban slums

Poor urban communities in India often face acute gaps in basic service provision. Forced to live in urban slums, they experience severe under-provision of basic services such as water, sanitation, and health services (Bapat and Agarwal, 2003; Zerah, 2000). In addition, they often lag behind in terms of access to education. Relying largely on government-run schools that suffer from poor infrastructure, teacher absenteeism, or staff shortages, puts students coming from poorer communities at a disadvantage (Agrawal, 2014; Desai et al., 2014; Kingdon, 2007). Neoliberal reforms pushed many such urban communities into precarity by forcing them into the informal sector (Harriss-White and Gooptu, 2001; Hensman, 2001; Roychowdhury, 2003), while exacerbating the gaps in public service provision. The absence of an organized union or civil society response leaves them without adequate representation or social safety nets. This was also the period when *Seva Bharati* (an RSS affiliate organization that caters specifically to urban slum communities) began investing significant resources in social services, particularly free educational services to children such as tutoring and/or offering alternatives to government-run schools across India (refer to Figure 9.2 above). The neoliberal economics of the 1990s provided the rightwing organizations a captive audience as it were for the uptake of this welfare strategy. This welfare provision trend was mirrored in Karnataka as well where there was a significant expansion in welfare provision by the Hindu Right (see Figure 9.3), and great emphasis on education initiatives in urban slums as revealed below.

My fieldwork revealed that *Rashtrothana Parishat* (RP), a rightwing affiliate organization which helped administer education-related welfare projects on behalf of the *Seva Bharati*, managed 150 non-formal tutoring centres in 109 urban slums in Bengaluru. The initiative employed 200 teachers, who were overseen by supervisors and provided monthly training sessions. I observed two such tutoring centres in two slums in the city to understand the dynamics and impact of community mobilization. First, these centres used education as the first step in the path towards more rigorous ideological immersion for schoolchildren (Sagar, 2020). This was done through the medium of curricular content but also participation in other activities. These centres were informal and were not forced to adhere to any approved models of coursework or monitored by any regulatory body. They developed their own curriculum using textbooks published by the RSS and the RP. The daily lesson plans helped disseminate majoritarian narratives through an emphasis on religio-cultural rituals and Hindu *samskara* (traditions) such as prayers and songs. Lessons about Hindu mythology were then seamlessly connected to historical events and patriotism, thus grounding nationalism in Hindu beliefs. My interview with a senior functionary of the Karnataka branch of Vidya Bharati (an RSS affiliate organization working in the field of education) provided interesting insights into the pedagogy and content at such centres as well as other formal schools run by RSS affiliates. He said:

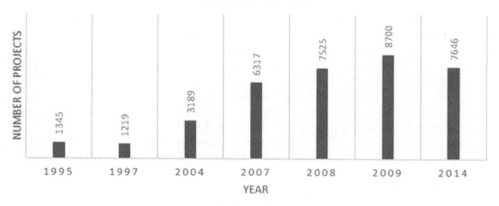

Figure 9.3   Seva Bharati's expansion of welfare projects in Karnataka over two decades

Source: Data from various print and web editions of Rashtriya Swayamsevak Sangh's publications, Seva Disha and Sewa Sadhana, which provide detailed records of welfare initiatives launched by the grassroots organizations across Indian states. The web editions are available here: www.rashtriyasewabharati.org/sewa-disha.

We insist on religious prayers, shlokas (Sanskrit religious chants), worship of Hindu gods at our educational centres and schools. Our philosophy is that teaching only school subjects is not enough. Emotional grounding is needed. We do not just teach geography, we emphasize religious geography. We want children not just to be able to mark the Ganges on the map of India, but truly understand why the Ganges is sacred to Hindus. We want to create amongst children an emotional attachment to the land. Some communist organizations and media people allege that what we are doing is "Saffronization" of education. To such skeptics, my answer is yes, we are providing religious education in the business, because we believe that education should be spiritually rooted and because this is giving us success.

(Interview with Assistant Organizational Secretary,
Vidya Bharati, 12 August 2009)

Teachers interviewed at the centres revealed that teenage boys good at sports and physical activity (the instructors were supposed to monitor this and report to the Parishat) were asked to attend weekly training camps at the Parishat premises on Sundays to learn martial arts, watch patriotic films and have conversations about nationalism and Hindu values. Periodically, trainees from all centres across the city would be invited to attend state RSS meets where prominent national and state level RSS leaders were invited to talk. For instance, during the course of the fieldwork, I was able attend one such public meeting in Bengaluru addressed by Mohan Bhagwat, the national leader of the RSS, on 22 November 2009. Newspapers estimated that around 15,000 RSS activists had gathered to hear the meeting. I was able to ride with a group of RSS workers and trainees from one such training centre. As we rode past a mosque or a church, the RSS workers started shouting slogans about Hindu unity, perhaps revealing the exclusionary and majoritarian way of thinking emphasized by these centres.

Second, the centres played a significant role in creating legitimacy for the Hindu Right within communities, paving the way for the uptake of other initiatives. The centres immersed themselves in the local social dynamics of the neighbourhood, and recruited instructors and volunteers from the local community, often providing much needed employment avenues as well as opportunities for upward social mobility, thus gaining acceptance and support within the communities. My interviews with the two instructors at the two centres revealed that both of them viewed their position with the Parishat as appealing long-term opportunities because of the lack of other channels of mobility/employment and the lack of linkages with local political patrons to advance their cause. One instructor specifically mentioned the apathy of the local councillor of the neighbourhood, responding to whether there had been any local political resistance to the setting up of a tutoring centre there, thus indicating why such service provision gains credibility quickly (interview with instructor, 1 December 2009). The other instructor told me that they had been promised a permanent teaching position (interview with instructor, 5 December 2009).

Third, the centres used their space for community celebration of Hindu festivals. This had two effects, both of which aligned with the Hindu Right's movement goals. Since these centres were often situated in religiously heterogeneous communities, the celebrations created local flashpoints used to drive a wedge between different religious groups, thus constructing ethnic antagonisms (this insight came from an interview with a professor of urban policy who had extensively studied Bengaluru's urban slum dynamics. The interview was conducted on 3 August 2009). Secondly, the celebrations served as platforms for political mobilization. It gave centres the opportunity to involve parents and the broader Hindu community in ongoing conversations about religion and culture, and building connections between communities and movement leaders who were periodically invited to speak at these occasions. Women, in particular, were incentivized to participate in Hindu religious rituals at temples and *bhajan mandalis* for religious prayers by employing games and competitions with cash prizes [interviews with centre instructor and two women in the neighbourhood, 5 December 2009]. I interviewed two journalists from two different newspapers who had reported about these centres and they corroborated this fairly standardized pattern of mobilization. "The first contact is through women and children. Free summer camps provide huge incentives for parents. Bhajan classes draw in the women. There is subtle inculcation of Hindu-centric rhetoric", reported one journalist (interview on 10 August 2009). "Educational manipulation has always been at the top of the RSS agenda. That is the way to promote cultural nationalism. Women are an untouched electorate and the RSS is cashing in on this advantage. The RSS has been operating clandestinely at the grassroots here for a long time", confirmed another journalist (interview on 12 August 2009).

On the one hand, the curriculum subtly created a synergy between Hindu religio-cultural traditions, patriotism and nationalism. Simultaneously, the centre mobilized the wider community beyond the intended audience of schoolchildren. They used the centres to create tangible rewards for the local community such as employment. They also mobilized women through activities that strategically straddle the middle ground between "traditional" and "modern", thus creating culturally/ideologically appropriate public spaces for women to serve within the local community without transgressing patriarchal boundaries. Thus, education became a means to a larger end – the incentivized incorporation of the broader Hindu community within the movement fold. Overall, it helped establish homogenized narratives and traditions of culture and religion and connected this back to themes of nationalism (Mohan, 2016; Pinto, 2013).

Modern-age shakhas *for young IT professionals*

At the time of the fieldwork, the RSS had also made a significant impact amongst young professionals that had become part of Bengaluru's IT success story. The IT/BPO sector was one that was traditionally ignored by trade unions for a long time. A Member of Parliament belonging to a left party told me that the left trade union movement had found it hard to unionize or mobilize IT professionals using traditional means. "The IT crowd is apolitical, and the trade union movement in Bengaluru has pretty much disappeared" (interview on 17 November 2009). Yet, the RSS had creatively reached out to them using welfare provision. My interviews with RP and an associate affiliate, Youth for Sewa, revealed that many people were initially attracted to volunteering opportunities for Parishat-sponsored activities such as blood donation drives, mobile health camps, or teaching children at the slum tutoring centres on a part-time basis (interview on 14 August 2009). This was then converted into broader politically themed meetings about religious conversion, terrorism, and nationalism among other themes (Lulla, 2010; Nanjappa, 2007). They were then recruited to attend IT *Milans* – a weekly adaptation of the traditional RSS daily *shakha* meetings. These allowed for IT professionals coming to the city from different parts of India to become part of a like-minded community. It was an initiative that began in 2000 that within a decade had grown to over 134 such meeting groups bringing together 6,000 professionals on a regular basis (Aravind, 2016). The RSS was able to woo young professionals to these meetings via offering Yoga lessons as a means of de-stressing and invoking Corporate Social Responsibility to get them involved in volunteer activities.

It would be erroneous to argue that all public discourse reflecting majoritarian and anti-democratic ideas can be traced back to these grassroots right organizations, or discount the fact that BJP's electoral wins helped reinforce these trends. However, one has to acknowledge that such civil society interventions definitely helped move the needle on how majoritarian ideas began to be perceived and debated and what kind of mainstream acceptance/support they have garnered over the years (Lankesh, 2008). In Karnataka, majoritarian notions about the protection of Hindu religious traditions and idealized revisionist historical narratives were reflected in macro-level policies, leading to several controversial bills. The Karnataka Prevention of Slaughter and Protection of Cow bill was passed in 2010 in what Rao (2011) calls silent communalism and religio-environmentalism. Similarly, a draconian anti-terrorism law, Karnataka Control of Organised Crimes (Amendment) Bill, perceived as targeting minority groups, was passed in 2009 (Sayeed, 2009). Rightwing affiliate organizations were accused of trying to "saffronize" school textbooks by introducing revisionist versions of history and culture (Chopra, 2012). Mass protests using ground-level volunteers were organized to rile up controversy around syncretic religious sites such as Bababudangiri (Menon, 2003). All these policies in a sense are a macro-aggregation of the kind of small-scale interventions initiated within local communities.

What the case study reveals markedly is the fact that these customized rightwing initiatives largely eschewed overtly negative, aggressive, or violent messaging in trying to draw two disparate segments into their network. Yet these actions were no less effective in how, over time, they changed broad attitudes towards minority rights and right-leaning policy agendas that were contrarian to secular democratic principles. Welfare provision allowed for inclusion of marginalized segments of society. Yet, as the outreach towards Bengaluru's IT sector demonstrates, the rightwing movement acts strategically by "vernacularizing" its initiatives in innovative ways to reach heretofore unmobilized constituencies. Overall, these civil society initiatives created spaces for inclusive participation from a broad cross-section of people in Bengaluru.

Concluding thoughts

The previous section established that the propagation of majoritarian nationalist discourse and the unfolding of autocratization is not simply a top-down process set in motion by populist strongmen. What the Karnataka case study demonstrates is how rightwing grassroots priming, the confounding variable identified in this study, works. The subtle nuances and impact of local mobilization initiatives are often overlooked because of the spotlight on aggressive tactics employed by right vigilante organizations. Everyday exposure to exclusionary and nativist ideas via innocuous community initiatives gradually mainstreams narratives that are polarizing, and over time leads to ethnic antagonisms. It is this slow entrenchment of majoritarianism that helps lay the groundwork for both autocratization of society and polity, and electoral victories for the BJP. This process could not be comprehended if one were to take a narrow view of autocratization and the rightwing in India. How the rightwing movement works at the grassroots through the civil society sphere is key to understanding how public culture has gradually transformed in favour of an ethnonational view of the nation.

The Karnataka case study reveals an additional important insight about the Hindu right's grassroots strategy. It is not surprising that the Hindu Right movement constructs exclusionary ethnonational "us" vs. "them" narratives by reinterpreting local cultural leitmotifs in various vernacular contexts. What this chapter uniquely illustrates is how these narratives are packaged and targeted at disparate constituencies using the rightwing's diverse network of specialized affiliate organizations. Moreover, grassroots mobilization is not monolithic. While there is a core emphasis on welfare, at the same time rightwing affiliate organizations are able to expand beyond this focus and customize strategies to appeal to various constituencies across different states/ regions. Locally relevant and resonant strategies of mobilization are a key part of the rightwing's arsenal. For instance, grassroots mobilization using aggressive "love jihad" or cow protection discourses is more evident in rural mofussil areas in north Indian states than in say urban parts of Karnataka. Even these more overtly aggressive forms of cultural policing vary in intensity temporally. Thus, from the perspective of future research, a fine-grained analysis is likely to reveal a significant degree of subnational variation in the kinds of themes and outreach activities that are used. It is also likely that there is significant variation in trajectories and timelines with respect to how quickly and deeply majoritarian discourses take hold and change political attitudes. For our current analysis, what appears then to be a macro trend that aligns with the global populist wave is essentially a cumulative process made up of smaller micro-level changes.

Historically, there has been a great ideological and strategic synergy between the rightwing movement and the party's agenda. However, with the populist approach yielding dividends, the fulcrum of decision-making seems to have shifted to the Prime Minister's office. However, there are also limits to constructing antagonistic ethnonational narratives for political mileage narratives and painting all political opponents as anti-national. Even with the decisive majorities in both 2014 and 2019, there are regions in the south and east that remain invulnerable to the righting mobilization that uses provocative cultural nationalistic messaging. Election losses in states such as West Bengal in the 2021 state legislative elections demonstrate this. The government's handling of the nationwide protests on the Citizenship (Amendment) Act, 2019 and farmers' agitations against new farm laws passed in 2020 to restructure the agriculture sector has drawn political criticism nationally and internationally, sometimes even from its own affiliate organizations, thus denting Modi's carefully crafted image. Similarly the downgrading of India's democratic ratings as well as attacks on academic freedom have drawn both national and international censure. What does this mean for BJP's brand of populism, the broader movement, and consequently autocratization of politics? When the populist moment inevitably runs out of steam, the party may have to go back to its organizational roots as it were, and act in synergy with the broader ideological movement agenda to refresh its image. This portends not an abatement but rather an exacerbation of the authoritarian trends that are already in motion across the country. A final pertinent question is can this process of autocratization (populist or not) be reversed? Can the deeply embedded discursive hegemony be effectively challenged? As the powers-that-be curb the space for meaningful dialogue and contemporary public discourse views even legitimate protests as seditious dissent, it is hard to imagine how these opposing forces can be reconciled.

Bibliography

Agrawal, T., 2014. Educational inequality in rural and urban India. *International Journal of Educational Development* 34, 11–19. https://doi.org/10.1016/j.ijedudev.2013.05.002

Alizada, Nazifa, Rowan Cole, Lisa Gastaldi, Sandra Grahn, Sebastian Hellmeier, Palina Kolvani, Jean Lachapelle, Anna Lührmann, Seraphine F. Maerz, Shreeya Pillai, and Staffan I. Lindberg. 2021. *Autocratization Turns Viral. Democracy Report 2021.* University of Gothenburg: V-Dem Institute.

Aravind, I., 2016. Devananda Gaddam: Meet the data architect who is taking technology to the RSS shakhas in Bengaluru – The Economic Times [WWW Document]. URL https://economictimes.indiatimes.com/news/politics-and-nation/devananda-gaddam-meet-the-data-architect-who-is-taking-technology-to-the-rss-shakhas-in-bengaluru/articleshow/54270280.cms?from=mdr (accessed 2.13.21).

Bapat, M., Agarwal, I., 2003. Our Needs, Our Priorities: Women and Men from the Slums in Mumbai and Pune Talk about their Needs for Water and Sanitation. *Environment and Urbanization* 15, 71–86. https://doi.org/10.1177/095624780301500221

Basu, A., 2018. Whither Democracy, Secularism, and Minority Rights in India? *The Review of Faith & International Affairs* 16, 34–46. https://doi.org/10.1080/15570274.2018.1535035

Baviskar, A., 2005. Adivasi Encounters with Hindu Nationalism in MP. *Economic and Political Weekly* 40, 5105–5113.

Beckerlegge, G., 2016. Sevā: The Focus of a Fragmented but Gradually Coalescing Field of Study. *Rosa* 9, 208–239.

Berman, S., 1997. Civil Society and the Collapse of the Weimar Republic. *World Pol.* 49, 401–429. https://doi.org/10.1353/wp.1997.0008

Bermeo, N., Nord, P., 2000. *Civil Society Before Democracy: Lessons from Nineteenth-Century Europe.* Rowman & Littlefield Publishers.

Bhattacharjee, M., 2016. Sevā, Hindutva, and the Politics of Post-Earthquake Relief and Reconstruction in Rural Kutch. *AE* 75. https://doi.org/10.18874/ae.75.1.04

Cammett, M., Issar, S., 2010. Bricks and Mortar Clientelism: Sectarianism and the Logics of Welfare Allocation in Lebanon. *World Pol.* 62, 381–421. https://doi.org/10.1017/S0043887110000080

Carothers, T., Barndt, W., 1999. Civil Society. *Foreign Policy* 18–29. https://doi.org/10.2307/1149558

Chacko, P., 2018. Authoritarian Populism in India. *Progress in Political Economy (PPE).* URL www.ppesydney.net/authoritarian-populism-in-india/ (accessed 1.13.21).

Chatterji, A.P., Hansen, T.B., Jaffrelot, C., 2019. *Majoritarian State: How Hindu Nationalism Is Changing India.* Oxford: Oxford University Press.

Chaudhary, N., 2017. RSS Textbook Visuals: Building a Hindu Rashtra through Bharat Mata and Gaumata Images. *Proceedings of the Indian History Congress* 78, 1155–1164.

Chidambaram, S., 2012. The "Right" Kind of Welfare in South India's Urban Slums: Seva vs. Patronage and the Success of Hindu Nationalist Organizations. *Asian Survey* 52, 298–320. https://doi.org/10.1525/as.2012.52.2.298

Chopra, R., 2012. NCERT probes into allegations of strong saffron slant in Karnataka textbooks by the BJP govt [WWW Document]. *India Today.* URL www.indiatoday.in/india/story/ncert-probes-into-bjp-allegations-of-saffronisation-of-karnataka-textbooks-124691-2012-12-19 (accessed 2.13.21).

Clark, J., 2004. Social Movement Theory and Patron-Clientelism: Islamic Social Institutions and the Middle Class in Egypt, Jordan, and Yemen. *Comparative Political Studies* 37, 941–968. https://doi.org/10.1177/0010414004267982

Clark, J.A., 2004. *Islam, Charity, and Activism.* Indiana University Press.

Desai, S., Barik, D., Agrawal, T., 2014. Poorly performing public services. *The Hindu*. URL www.thehindu.com/todays-paper/tp-opinion/poorly-performing-public-services/article5860718.ece (accessed 9.1.21).

Dhar, A., 2004. The Hindu: Making inroads into the tribal belt [WWW Document]. URL www.hinduonnet.com/thehindu/2004/03/18/stories/2004031803181300.htm (accessed 5.23.10).

Diamond, L., 1994. Rethinking Civil Society: Toward Democratic Consolidation. *Journal of Democracy* 5, 4–17. https://doi.org/10.1353/jod.1994.0041

Dreze, J., 2020. The Revolt of the Upper Castes [WWW Document]. *The India Forum*. URL www.theindiaforum.in/article/revolt-upper-castes (accessed 5.27.20).

Freedom House, 2021. India: Freedom in the World 2021 Country Report [WWW Document]. *Freedom House*. URL https://freedomhouse.org/country/india/freedom-world/2021 (accessed 3.16.21).

Froerer, P., 2007. Disciplining the Saffron Way: Moral Education and the Hindu Rashtra. *Modern Asian Studies* 41, 1033–1071.

Fukuyama, F., 2001. Social capital, civil society and development. *Third World Quarterly* 22, 7–20. https://doi.org/10.1080/713701144

Fuller, C.J., 2001. The "Vinayaka Chaturthi" Festival and Hindutva in Tamil Nadu. *Economic and Political Weekly* 36, 1607–1616.

Kuthar, G. 2019. How coastal Karnataka was saffronised: The story of the rise and rise of Hindu nationalism in syncretic South Kanara – India News, *Firstpost* [WWW Document]. URL www.firstpost.com/india/how-coastal-karnataka-was-saffronised-the-story-of-the-rise-and-rise-of-hindu-nationalism-in-syncretic-south-kanara-6363461.html (accessed 2.13.21).

Günther, L., Lührmann, A., 2018. *Populism and Autocratization. Populism and Autocratization* (No. 19), V-Dem Policy Brief. University of Gothenburg: V-Dem Institute.

Hansen, T.B., 1996. The vernacularisation of Hindutva: The BJP and Shiv Sena in rural Maharashtra. *Contributions to Indian Sociology* 30, 177–214. https://doi.org/10.1177/006996679603000201

Hansen, T.B., 2019. Democracy Against the Law: Reflections on India's Illiberal Democracy, in: *Majoritarian State*. Oxford University Press. https://doi.org/10.1093/oso/9780190078171.003.0002

Harriss, J., Corbridge, S., Jeffrey, C., 2017. Is India Becoming the 'Hindu Rashtra' Sought by Hindu Nationalists? (SWP 60).

Harriss-White, B., Gooptu, N., 2001. Mapping India's World of Unorganized Labour. *Socialist Register* 37.

Hensman, R., 2001. The Impact of Globalisation on Employment in India and Responses from the Formal and Informal Sectors. *International Institute for Asian Studies* (IIAS).

Jaffrelot, C. (Ed.), 2005. *The Sangh Parivar: A Reader, Critical issues in Indian politics*. Delhi: Oxford University Press.

Jaffrelot, C., 2008. Hindu Nationalism and the Social Welfare Strategy, in: Clarke, G., Jennings, M. (Eds.), *Development, Civil Society and Faith-Based Organizations: Bridging the Sacred and the Secular*, International Political Economy Series. London: Palgrave Macmillan UK, pp. 240–259. https://doi.org/10.1057/9780230371262_11

Jaffrelot, C., 2019. *A De Facto Ethnic Democracy?: Obliterating and Targeting the Other, Hindu Vigilantes, and the Ethno-State, Majoritarian State*. Oxford: Oxford University Press.

Kanungo, P., 2008. Hindutva's Fury against Christians in Orissa. *Economic and Political Weekly* 43, 16–19.

Kesavan, M., 2017. India: Assassinating Dissent [WWW Document]. *The New York Review of Books*. URL www.nybooks.com/daily/2017/09/15/india-assassinating-dissent/ (accessed 2.13.21).

Kingdon, G.G., 2007. The progress of school education in India. *Oxford Review of Economic Policy* 23, 168–195. https://doi.org/10.1093/oxrep/grm015

Kinnvall, C., 2019. Populism, ontological insecurity and Hindutva: Modi and the masculinization of Indian politics. *Cambridge Review of International Affairs* 32, 283–302. https://doi.org/10.1080/09557571.2019.1588851.

Kyle, J., Gultchin, L., 2018. *Populists in Power Around the World*. Tony Blair Institute for Global Change.

Lankesh, G., 2008. How Karnataka is becoming Gujarat of South [WWW Document]. URL https://churumuri.blog/2008/02/28/how-karnataka-is-becoming-gujarat-of-the-south/ (accessed 2.13.21).

Larsson, P., 2016. The Far Right Comes to Sweden [WWW Document]. URL https://jacobinmag.com/2016/01/sweden-democrats-jimmie-akesson-far-right-europe/ (accessed 3.16.21).

Levitsky, S., Ziblatt, D., 2018. *How Democracies Die*. Crown.

Lobo, L., 2002. Adivasis, Hindutva and Post-Godhra Riots in Gujarat. *Economic and Political Weekly* 37, 4844–4849.

Longkumer, A., 2016. The power of persuasion: Hindutva, Christianity, and the discourse of religion and culture in Northeast India. *Religion* 47, 1–25. https://doi.org/10.1080/0048721X.2016.1256845

Lubbers, M., 2019. What kind of nationalism sets the radical right and its electorate apart from the rest? Pride in the nation's history as part of nationalist nostalgia. *Nations and Nationalism* 25, 449–466. https://doi.org/10.1111/nana.12517

Lubbers, M., Coenders, M., 2017. Nationalistic attitudes and voting for the radical right in Europe. *European Union Politics* 18, 98–118. https://doi.org/10.1177/1465116516678932

Lulla, Anil, B., 2010. Sangh's e-Sevaks. *Open The Magazine.* URL https://openthemagazine.com/features/india/sanghs-e-sevaks/ (accessed 2.13.21).

Martelli, J.-T., Jaffrelot, C., 2017. Reading PM Modi, Through His Speeches [WWW Document]. *Carnegie Endowment for International Peace.* URL https://carnegieendowment.org/2017/08/15/reading-pm-modi-through-his-speeches-pub-72825 (accessed 2.14.21).

Menon, P., 2003. A communal campaign [WWW Document]. *Frontline.* URL https://frontline.thehindu.com/other/article30220299.ece (accessed 2.13.21).

Mohan, R., 2016. Indianise, nationalise, spiritualise: The RSS education project is in expansion mode [WWW Document]. *Scroll.in.* URL http://scroll.in/article/815049/indianise-nationalise-spiritualise-the-rss-education-project-is-in-for-the-long-haul (accessed 2.14.21).

Mudde, C., 2007. *Populist Radical Right Parties in Europe.* Cambridge: Cambridge University Press. https://doi.org/10.1017/CBO9780511492037

Mudde, C., Kaltwasser, C.R., 2017. *Populism: A Very Short Introduction.* Oxford, New York: Oxford University Press.

Mukhopadhyay, A., 2019. From "Sabka Saath, Sabka Vikas" to "Main Bhi Chowkidar": The forgotten macroeconomic flagships [WWW Document]. *ORF.* URL www.orfonline.org/expert-speak/from-sabka-saath-sabka-vikas-to-main-bhi-chowkidar-the-forgotten-macroeconomic-flagships-50640/ (accessed 4.26.20).

Nanjappa, V., 2007. Latest from RSS: The IT shakha [WWW Document]. URL www.rediff.com/news/2007/nov/12vicky.htm (accessed 2.13.21).

Nilsen, A.G., 2018. Authoritarian populism and popular struggles in Modi's India [WWW Document]. *OpenDemocracy.* URL www.opendemocracy.net/en/authoritarian-populism-and-popular-struggles-in-modi-s-india/ (accessed 1.13.21).

NPR, 2019. The Powerful Group Shaping The Rise Of Hindu Nationalism In India [WWW Document]. *NPR.org.* URL www.npr.org/2019/05/03/706808616/the-powerful-group-shaping-the-rise-of-hindu-nationalism-in-india (accessed 3.17.21).

Palshikar, S., 2015. The BJP and Hindu Nationalism: Centrist Politics and Majoritarian Impulses. *South Asia: Journal of South Asian Studies* 38, 719–735. https://doi.org/10.1080/00856401.2015.1089460

Pinto, A., 2013. *Five Years of Saffron Rule in Karnataka.* New Delhi: Manak Publications.

Putnam, R.D., Leonardi, R., Nanetti, R.Y., 1994. *Making Democracy Work: Civic Traditions in Modern Italy.* Princeton University Press.

Roychowdhury, A., 2017. What the Data Tells Us About "Sabka Saath, Sabka Vikas" [WWW Document]. *The Wire.* URL https://thewire.in/business/whatever-happened-to-modis-development (accessed 2.14.21).

Roychowdhury, S., 2003. Public Sector Restructuring and Democracy: The State, Labour and Trade Unions in India. *The Journal of Development Studies* 39, 29–50. https://doi.org/10.1080/00220380412331322811

Sagar, 2020. For the RSS, "sewa" is a means to achieve the Hindu Rashtra [WWW Document]. *The Caravan.* URL https://caravanmagazine.in/politics/rss-sewa-coronavirus-lockdown-brahmanical-hindu-rashtra (accessed 2.13.21).

Sarkar, T., 1994. Educating the Children of the Hindu Rashtra: Notes on RSS Schools. *Comparative Studies of South Asia, Africa and the Middle East* 14, 10–15. https://doi.org/10.1215/07323867-14-2-10

Sayeed, V.A., 2009. An Act in question [WWW Document]. *Frontline.* URL https://frontline.thehindu.com/the-nation/article30188460.ece (accessed 2.13.21).

Sayeed, V.A., 2018. A battlefront in the south [WWW Document]. *Frontline.* URL https://frontline.thehindu.com/the-nation/a-battlefront-in-the-south/article10074157.ece (accessed 2.13.21).

Sen, R., 2019. Everyone Thinks the Economy Is Issue No. 1 for India's Modi. It's Not – Foreign Policy [WWW Document]. URL https://foreignpolicy.com/2019/09/21/everyone-thinks-the-economy-is-issue-no-1-for-indias-modi-its-not/ (accessed 2.14.21).

Shirer, W.L., 1990. *Rise And Fall Of The Third Reich: A History of Nazi Germany*. New York: Simon and Schuster.

Sircar, N., 2020. Not vikas, Modi's 2019 election was built on politics of vishwas [WWW Document]. URL https://theprint.in/opinion/not-vikas-modis-2019-election-was-built-on-politics-of-vishwas/432487/ (accessed 3.21.21).

Spodek, H., 2010. In the Hindutva Laboratory: Pogroms and Politics in Gujarat, 2002. *Modern Asian Studies* 44, 349–399.

Teltumbde, A., 2020. *Hindutva and Dalits: Perspectives for Understanding Communal Praxis*. New Delhi: SAGE Publishing India.

Thachil, T., 2011. Embedded Mobilization: Nonstate Service Provision as Electoral Strategy in India. *World Politics* 63, 434–469. https://doi.org/10.1017/S0043887111000116

Vaishnav, M., 2019. Religious Nationalism and India's Future – The BJP in Power: Indian Democracy and Religious Nationalism [WWW Document]. *Carnegie Endowment for International Peace*. URL https://carnegieendowment.org/2019/04/04/religious-nationalism-and-india-s-future-pub-78703 (accessed 8.31.21).

Vaishnav, M., 2021. The Decay of Indian Democracy [WWW Document]. *Foreign Affairs*. URL www.foreignaffairs.com/articles/india/2021-03-18/decay-indian-democracy (accessed 3.21.21).

Vanaik, A., 2017. *The Rise of Hindu Authoritarianism: Secular Claims, Communal Realities*. Updated and expanded edition. London, New York: Verso.

Vijayan, M., 2018. The Ascent of Conservative Civil Society in India – The Mobilization of Conservative Civil Society. Washington, D.C.: Carnegie Endowment for International Peace.

Whitehead, L., 1997. Bowling in the bronx: The uncivil interstices between civil and political society. *Democratization* 4, 94–114. https://doi.org/10.1080/13510349708403504

Wiktorowicz, Q., 2000. Civil Society as Social Control: State Power in Jordan. *Comparative Politics* 33, 43–61. https://doi.org/10.2307/422423

Williamson, V., Skocpol, T., Coggin, J., 2011. The Tea Party and the Remaking of Republican Conservatism. *Perspect. polit.* 9, 25–43. https://doi.org/10.1017/S153759271000407X

Zavos, J., 2001. Conversion and the assertive margins: An analysis of Hindu nationalist discourse and the recent attacks on Indian Christians. *South Asia: Journal of South Asian Studies* 24, 73–89. https://doi.org/10.1080/00856400108723451

Zerah, M.-H., 2000. *Water: Unreliable Supply in Delhi*, 1st edition. New Delhi: Manohar Publications.

10

THE SOCIAL ROOTS OF THE AUTHORITARIAN TURN IN INDIA

Patrick Heller

Introduction

The debate on democracy today has rather suddenly taken a turn for the worse. At no point in post-World War II history have so many democracies flirted with authoritarianism. While definitions of backsliding proliferate (Przeworski 2019), few would question that in many democracies today the fundamental liberal pillars of democracy – the separation of powers, the protection of individual liberties and the autonomy of civil society – have been directly threatened. Cases range from older and supposedly more institutionalized democracies such as Trump's United States, to post-Soviet Eastern Europe (Orban's Hungary and the PiS in Poland), and the younger democracies of the post-colonial world including Bolsonaro's Brazil, Duterte's Philippines and Modi's India. In all these cases, democratically elected governments, riding a tide of some version of ethno-nationalist populism, have sometimes by stealth and sometimes more openly sought to weaken the basic legal and institutional conditions that support a constitutional democracy. As much as one might be tempted to identify a general phenomenon of reaction, closer examination reveals at least two types: those in which reaction has found a mass base in the disaffected ranks of lower socio-economic classes marginalized by globalization (the OECD cases), and others, such as India, that are clear instances of upper class revolts. It is certainly the case that across both types globalization is the common denominator, yet it has played out in very different ways, refracted by specific national histories and configurations of political forces. An increasingly rich literature in the OECD world has characterized these reactions as responses to the long-term effects of neo-liberal globalization that take the form of political closure, both by erecting new national boundaries of identity and belonging and repurposing liberal democracies, perceived to be increasingly ineffective, to be more decisive and representative of the "people". But though globalization has also played a role in the driving reaction in India, the configurational sequence and the outcomes have been quite different. In India more than anything else, the authoritarian turn has been driven by a middle class seeking to consolidate its economic position and hoard its social privileges.

If the causes are different, so are the outcomes and the degree to which democracy is threatened. As Ziblatt and Levitsky (2018) have argued, democracies today are being undermined through democratic means. Reactions across the board have been marked by three

DOI: 10.4324/9781003042211-12

specific regressions: an assertion of executive power that actively undermines the independent functions (checks and balances) of representative, bureaucratic and juridical institutions, a discursive assault on independent civil society (media, universities, NGOs and social movements) and discursive and sometimes legal efforts to redefine citizenship along narrow ethnic or nationalist lines. Trump's presidency and failed coup is the prototypical case, but right-wing movements in Western Europe are animated by a similar logic. India and other democracies in the Global South – notably Brazil, Turkey and the Philippines (Heller 2020) – have all these regressive features, but the assault on democratic institutions and practices is much more severe because they are not just a response to perceived failures of liberal democracy but also efforts to reassert traditional configurations of elite power. Thus, beyond assaults on the institutional pillars of democracy, reaction in Modi's India has extended to concerted efforts to marginalize and exclude Muslims and others defined as anti-nationalist. This has included open repression of civil society, efforts to de-certify specific socio-cultural groups and the use of state-sponsored vigilantism. Though Brazil, Turkey and the Philippines (Heller 2020) all fall into this category, the case of India stands out. There is arguably nowhere in the developing world where democracy made such progress, particularly in redefining social power, only to be subjected to such a sharp counter-reaction.

The authoritarian turn in India

Those who have followed the rise of the BJP and its alliance of civil society organizations – the Sangh Parivar – have long detected sharp authoritarian tendencies (Fernandes and Heller 2006; Corbridge and Harriss 2000). Since the BJP came to power in 2014 the signs of an authoritarian agenda have been clear and by 2021 even the staid international guardians of quantifiable democratic bona fides were sounding alarms (Freedom House annual reports and V-Dem scores). The erosion of democratic institutions and practices predates the BJP's rise to power. The last Congress-led United Progressive Alliance government (2009–2014) was marked by widespread corruption and a downturn in democratic indicators (V-dem). The BJP's rise to power however marks a critical juncture at two levels. The first (and the most discussed) is that a clear political realignment has taken place. Analysts have pointed to three distinct political developments: the increasing personal authority of Modi himself and a shift from the politics of accountability to the politics of trust (Sircar 2020), the rise of the BJP's distinct brand of ethno-national populism (Jaffrelot 2019) and sharp electoral realignments driven in large part by the implosion of the once hegemonic Congress Party (Jaffrelot and Verniers 2020). Beyond these conjunctural factors on the political plane, the focus of this chapter is on the deeper socio-cultural transformations at play. The authoritarian turn in India is only in part a story of institutional decline and the BJP's electoral fortunes. It must also be understood as a social reaction, driven primarily by a middle class reacting to the democratic empowerment of popular classes of the last several decades. The contours of that reaction have been significantly shaped by both the economic and social forces of globalization.

To the extent that populism is a style and strategy of politics marked by plebiscitarian and personalist forms of leadership (Weyland 2001: 5), then Modi is a classic incarnation. But this personalization of power (Sircar 2020) is itself the instantiation of the BJP's long-term Hindutva (making India into a Hindu nation) project of redefining the "people" in national-cultural terms. In government this has taken the form of marginalizing and demonizing Muslims as well as castigating and targeting rights activists (dubbed "urban Naxalites") as anti-national. And if Modi's persona was carefully cultivated at the sub-national level in the fertile terrain of Gujarat (a particularly fortuitous fusion of corporate business power and toxic communalization) and the BJP's Hindutva ideology has been long in the making, there can be no doubt that the BJP's electoral gains were made possible both by the collapse of the Congress and the BJP's own successes in broadening its appeal by building support among Other Backward Castes (OBC) and significant segments of the Dalit (previously referred to as "untouchable") and Adivasi (tribal) populations. But this convergence of an autocratic style of politics (populism), new cultural-political ideological framings (ethno-national) and broadened electoral alignments has to be understood as the political expressions of a deeper process of social transformation.

The effects of this reconfiguration of class and social power can be detected in three patterns of reaction that have marked the BJP's time in power. The first has been to redefine and to repurpose the welfare state from a right-based and universalistic logic to a logic of rationing and targeting welfare to those who "deserve" it. In an electoral context where being pro-poor is an electoral necessity, this is not a simple roll-back of the state, but rather a shift from public support and protection as a social right to benefits that are directly distributed by the central state (and often specifically in Modi's name). The BJP's language of moving from "entitle-ment" (associated with the normative goal of levelling inequalities) to "empowerment" reflects its direct appeals to an "aspirational" middle class. The second is muscular state support for a dominant identity built on the cultural exclusion of others. Though the Congress party itself has all too often compromised its secular and pluralist credentials for electoral expediency, the BJP's rise to political dominance has been forged largely on the strength of its efforts to redefine the nation in cultural-religious terms. This politics of cultural closure has been secured through state sanctioning of a dominant identity (especially curricular reforms in public educa-tion) and demonization of an "other", including the use of the police and vigilantes to enforce dominant cultural codes and contain the dangerous actors who threaten national values. The organizations of the Sangh Parivar (the group of voluntary associations that are the mass base of the BJP) have long aggressively promoted Hindu culture, but under the Modi govern-ment they have escalated their efforts, including sponsoring "cow protection" associations that have lynched accused beef eaters and launching a notorious campaign dubbed "Love Jihad" to combat the alleged scourge of Muslim boys seducing Hindu girls. These state-sponsored cultural practices of exclusion have now been legislated with the passage of the Citizenship Amendment Act (CAA) which recognizes all refugees from neighbouring countries as citizens if they are of any religion *except* Islam. The third prong of the reactionary project has been the valorization of traditional social relations and institutions, specifically the patriarchal family, the military, religion and the traditional caste order. The BJP itself is culturally and socially an expression of Brahminical authority and Modi has assiduously cultivated his image of religi-osity (Sircar 2020) and virile asceticism. Most notable, as in all hegemonic cultural projects, has been the BJP's educational policies which have not only focused on re-writing textbooks but have also included direct assaults on the autonomy of the university that have specifically taken the form of targeting liberal rights and secular values as corrosive of traditional social and cul-tural practices (Bhatty and Sundar 2020). Taking these three prongs together, we can say that to the social contract rooted in the constitutional rights and secularism once associated with the Congress, Hindutva counterposes an organic contract embedded in ethnic solidarity and traditional social structures.

Indian authoritarianism in global context

Much of the literature on democratic backsliding in OECD countries draws a direct line between increasing inequality and working class precarity associated with neo-liberal global-ization and the rise of right-wing populism (Przeworski 2019; Rodrik 2018). The relationship between globalization and reaction is more complicated and refracted through a very different socio-class configuration in the case of India. The most immediate trigger of reaction and the most distinct and politically exploited point of opposition to globalization in OECD democracies – immigration – is a marginal factor in India. Ethno-nationalism has been essentially inward looking. Second, there is no direct, mechanical link between the economic effects of globalization and reaction in India. Indeed, in the two decades that led up to reaction the Indian economy grew at a record pace and poverty declined significantly. Third, in contrast to Brexit and Trump, for example, Modi has not sought to leverage opposition to economic globalization and has in fact been closely aligned with domestic economic elites (professionals and corporates) that have a strong stake in globalization. Yet, having said this, globalization has played a role. The forces at work are however quite different from those highlighted in the OECD literature. As I hope to show, reaction has not been driven by working class discontent with shrinking economic opportunity and security as in the OECD world but rather by elite revolts that are tied both to the ways in which increased global economic integration has reshaped emergent middle class interests and by how previous left-reformist efforts to manage global integration by expanding social protection fundamentally challenged traditional social hierarchies and privilege.

The specificity of the Indian case is captured in an electoral analysis of the social base of reaction. Electoral data (presented below) from the 2019 election shows that even as the BJP broadened its electoral appeal, including among Dalits and Adivasis, the core of its support is rooted in the fractions of the dominant classes (proprietary and professional) and the emergent neo-middle class (Heller 2020). This is also reflected in educational patterns, with the more educated being more likely to support Modi (the obverse of OECD populism). As with all ethno-nationalist movements, appeals to religion have played an important role, especially in mobilizing the neo-middle class, as have appeals to strengthening the patriarchal family. There is also a clear regional pattern to reaction. Most striking is that the BJP has limited electoral traction in India's South, long a bastion of anti-Brahminism and the region of India that has made the most progress on social issues, notably challenging traditional caste power and expanding the welfare state.

These regional patterns become even more pointed when one considers global cities. The BJP in India has long been a mostly urban party, with roots in the urban trading classes (the *banias*). In the past decade it has made inroads into rural areas largely through targeted patronage and selective caste appeals (Thachil 2014) so much so that by the 2019 election its support was evenly balanced across rural and urban. But if one looks at how cities voted, a striking pattern emerges. All of India's most globalized and most cosmopolitan cities – New Delhi (the capital); Mumbai (home to Bollywood and finance) and Bangalore (IT) – voted overwhelmingly for the BJP. This is the exact opposite of the OECD pattern where global cities (London, New York, Seattle) continue to lean liberal-left, even as rural areas and more peripheral towns supported reaction.

I believe this difference reveals the particular nature of reaction in India. Upper-class groups who are concentrated in cities and especially those who have benefitted the most from globalization, that is professionals and those who occupy management or strategic organizational positions in global commodity chains along with ancillary white collar workers, feel threatened by the progress that subordinate groups made in the past two decades especially with respect to expanding the welfare state and gaining access to historically class-rationed institutions, most notably schools and health services. These elites are determined to hoard opportunities that they have historically monopolized, opportunities whose returns have been amplified by globalization. Those opportunities have been threatened not only by the expansion of the welfare state, but also increasingly vociferous subordinate groups demanding rights. The basis of elite privilege is narrow, fragile and predicated on blocking broader socio-economic inclusion. The huge inequalities that mark India, which, if anything, are amplified in its global cities through spatial segregation and the confinement of large swathes of the poor to slums, present an existential threat to the middle class and to the neo-middle class that, as explained below, has joined the reaction coalition.

From restricted democracy to democratic deepening

The transition to democracy in India was marked by limited ruptures with colonial-era social structures. Though India is unique in the democratic world of having moved directly to universal suffrage at the time of independence, political parties were monopolized by upper caste elites and the rural poor remained politically dependent on local dominant castes (Frankel and Rao 1989). Well into the 1980s, class/caste power continued to thwart genuine political, not to mention social, inclusion of the popular sectors (Heller 2019). Liberal and professional middle classes aligned with import substitution industrialization (ISI) interests (a nascent state-dependent bourgeoisie) to dominate politics all while protecting landed interests from threats from below. There were periods of popular mobilization throughout this period of restricted democracy, but dominant social and class interests prevailed and elite-led nationalist discourses of constitutionalism and modernity systematically misrecognized social hierarchy, suppressing the daily realities of class/caste exclusion. In retrospect, it is remarkable that outside of the southern states of Kerala and Tamil Nadu, lower caste mobilization in India remained episodic and did not disturb the political dominance of upper castes (Jaffrelot 2003). Second, limited mass incorporation underwrote a disarticulated developmental trajectory defined by a massive informal reserve army of labour sustaining a regime of labour squeezing accumulation.

The exclusionary pact began unravelling in the 1980s as India experienced an upsurge of lower caste mobilization that threatened the dominant pact. New political competitors emerged to challenge Congress party hegemony, expressing both regional and lower caste aspirations. As what Yadav (2000) has famously called the "second democratic uprising" saw lower castes and in particular other backward castes (OBCs) create their own political parties, the Congress lost its dominant position in a number of states and had to increasingly share power at the national level. The emergence of the BJP as a significant electoral force at precisely this time has been widely interpreted as an "elite revolt" and specifically an upper-caste response to mobilization from below (Corbridge and Harriss 2000). In an increasingly fragmented party system, the BJP and allies came to power in 1996. When a Congress-led coalition returned to power in 2004, the party was a shadow of its former self, more an assemblage of opportunistic rent-seekers and assorted political scions, than a party with a programme. A powerful faction of the party's leadership however was close to leading figures in civil society, which itself had increasingly coalesced around demands for rights-based social reforms. This faction, with support from coalition parties, pushed through a remarkable set of rights-based laws that included the right to information (RTI), but also legislation and policies designed to universalize access to education, food and work (Chiriyankandath et al. 2020). Most notably, the second Congress-led United Progressive Alliance (UPA) government pushed through the National Rural Employment Guarantee Act (NREGA), a rural right to work programme that guarantees government employment to all rural households. The programme has benefitted more than 100 million workers making it possibly the largest anti-poverty programme in history. A large body of research has clearly demonstrated not only that the programme has pushed up rural wages (Jenkins and Manor 2016), but that in some parts of India it has clearly disrupted traditional relations of labour domination (Veeraghavan 2017). Despite corruption scandals and a lack of party discipline, the Congress managed to get re-elected in 2008 in part on the popularity of NREGA (Heller 2017). Though the Indian state still suffers from significant deficits in capacity and accountability (Evans and Heller 2018) there is little doubt that the UPA period saw an unprecedented expansion of a rights-based welfare state and marked a rupture with the elite-dominated patronage politics that had long defined India's restricted democracy.

The reaction

The BJP's *Hindutva* project has deep historical roots, is ideologically cohesive, supported by a highly organized and disciplined party and movement, and is being, as we speak, ruthlessly advanced by deploying every tool in the arsenal of democratic authoritarianism.

The Hindu right has always had a project of building a Hindu nation, but it was not until the late 1980s that this project took political form. In building a viable electoral majority, the BJP faced two formidable challenges. On the one hand, it had to overcome its identification as a party of the forward castes. On the other hand, it had to marry its project of nationalism and social harmony with growing support among its most powerful class supporters for more market and globalization-friendly policies. Modi resolved both tensions as Chief Minister in the state of Gujarat (2001–2014) by completely communalizing the movement. He in effect unified the Hindu vote base by systematically demonizing Muslims and directly appealing to what he himself labelled the "neo-middle class" that is, aspiring and mostly rural other backward castes (OBCs) (Jaffrelot 2019; Chacko 2019: 400). At the same time he championed Gujarat as a pro-business state attracting large scale investments from Indian corporates and multinationals, providing a new ideological home for class interests that had supported the liberalization of the economy in the 1990s. As Chacko has argued, Modi in effect overcame the inherent tension between the market and the social by "marketizing *Hindutva* with the positioning of the state as a facilitator of the creation of a middle class of consumers and entrepreneurs who are also disciplined by *Hindutva* values" (2019: 398). The "Gujarat model", as it came to be known, produced high levels of growth but a dismal social development track record, with Muslims and Dalits largely excluded (Jaffrelot 2019). Building on his success in Gujarat and with the full-throated support of the business community, Modi rode to power at the national level in 2014 largely by portraying himself as Mr Development (*Vikas Purush*). As the 2019 election approached and it became clear the economy was sputtering, Modi reverted to the anti-Muslim playbook both by stepping up nationalist rhetoric against Pakistan and doubling down on traditional *Hindutva* issues (Varshney 2019). The electoral victory was resounding. During the first BJP government (2014–2019) Modi was cautious in pushing his ethno-nationalist agenda, franchising the Sangh Parivar's local cadres or sponsored vigilante groups to exert extra-legal power, but refraining from direct use of state power (Jaffrelot 2019). Since the BJP's return to power in May 2019 there is no longer any pretence. The state has been directly and quickly repurposed as an instrument of de-secularization. First, the government revoked Kashmir's special status and took direct control over India's only Muslim-majority state. Second, a supreme court widely seen as increasingly subservient to Modi then ruled that India's most disputed religious site where a mosque was torn down in 1991 was Hindu, all but sanctioning the violent tactics of *Hindutva* forces. A third and final blow to India's pluralist, secular and constitutional order was delivered in December 2019 with the passage of the CAA, which introduces "religion as a marker of citizenship" … and "creates categories of citizens with differing pathways to citizenship based on religious identity" (Aiyar 2019).

Explaining the reaction

Modi's election in 2014 and re-election in 2019 represents an elite response to democratic empowerment from below. In India, democratic deepening was led by the rise of lower castes and a range of new social movements that coalesced into a loose but effective coalition under the UPA. Class interests are not given and building electoral coalitions is a messy and indeterminate affair. When and how coalitions produce electoral majorities is highly contingent. As Gramsci (1971) emphasized, historic blocs are formed of dominant classes that can exert hegemony over allied groups by actively coordinating interests. In India the period of restricted democracy was supported by a class alliance in which the three dominant factions of the propertied classes – business, professional and landed – were each guaranteed a share of public resources, much to the exclusion of the masses (Bardhan 1999). That began to change with the UPA government (2004–2014). Though the government did continue to push the liberalization of the economy, business interests became increasingly frustrated with the government's determination to expand social programmes. NREGA in particular invited widespread attacks as a wasteful, anti-market policy, especially from landed elites who resented the government's interference in local labour markets they had long dominated (Veeraraghavan 2017). But the opposition of these dominant economic interests alone was hardly enough to build an electorally viable coalition and specifically to expand support from a growing middle class.

Sociologists have long argued that material interests are intertwined with cultural practices. The durable categories through which inequalities are reproduced are rooted in group practices that marshal cultural and social resources to protect privileges and hoard opportunities. This intertwining is sharply revealed in the ideological project of the BJP which has been framed by a new discourse of forming a reinvigorated nation based in an essentialist and singular identity, a nation of virtuous citizens standing in opposition to the undeserving poor, criminality/corruption and the coddling or "appeasement" of minorities. In this casteless meritocracy, the virtues of an achieving and aspiring middle class have displaced the language of universalism and social rights. Traditional institutions of temple, the military, the nation and the patriarchal family have been resurrected. National capital and businesses are celebrated as champions of progress and the *elan vital* of a renewed national spirit is held up against the corrosive effects of human rights and a vaguely defined "globalism" as carrier of anti-cultural materialism and secularism.

The discursive shift has been critical to redrawing the boundaries and the self-identity of the middle class. The upper middle class of professionals has always had a fickle relationship to democracy, but lent significant support to the Congress in its hegemonic decades (Fernandes and Heller 2006). The professional classes had – per Bardhan – a clear stake in the expansion of the developmental state and secular nationalism, most notably state funded higher education. If this class has defected, it is because the expansion of welfare policies to include the poor has threatened its privileged status position, especially with respect to educational institutions. In India upper middle class/Forward caste opposition to caste-based affirmative action has been fierce (Heller 2018) and the same class that owes in global economic success to public higher education, is now pushing for privatization of higher education (Subramanian 2015). Though upper-caste mobilization crystallized around opposition to affirmative action policies in the 1980s, the BJP has supported "reservations" since the 1990s as a pragmatic concession to incorporating OBCs (Chacko 2019). But practices in institutions dominated by upper castes remain resolutely exclusionary (Vithayathil 2018). Economically, the upper middle class has grown and has come to depend less on the state than on globalization for its economic well-being, hence the pattern of global cities supporting reaction. But the upper middle class can hardly sustain a winning electoral coalition. The pivotal shift has been the realignment of the neo-middle class.

The pattern of middle class reconfiguration in India has been dramatic, clearly delineated by caste boundaries. Historically, the electoral limits of the BJP were always its upper-caste identity. Yet by 2019 the BJP support base was resolutely and comprehensively Hindu, with every major caste category favouring the BJP over the Congress. The point spread went from a massive 41 percent for upper castes favouring the BJP over the Congress, to 29 percent for OBCs and 13 percent for Dalits with almost no Muslims (8 percent) voting for the BJP (Varshney 2019). In class terms, the income data is unreliable, but a survey that included occupational categories shows solid support for the BJP from white collar groups (services and professionals) and shop keepers and farmers. Unskilled rural and urban labourers aligned themselves with non-BJP parties (India Today 2019). In cultural terms, the BJP has mobilized the OBC neo-middle class by uniting Hindus against Muslims and by appealing to the social conservatism of a class that is "looking away from agriculture and towards the towns and cities" (Kaur 2014). In the northern states in particular, the BJP assiduously cultivated caste groups that aspired to forward caste status tapping into the deep aspirations of cultural distinction and upper caste/class emulation (sanskritization) that have always animated aspiring groups in deeply hierarchical societies (Bourdieu 1984). And it reconfigured the welfare state from universal entitlements such as the right to work (NREGA) to a series of discrete welfare programmes, often directly linked to Modi himself, that amount to the public provisioning of private goods (e.g., subsidized toilets and home cooking fuel). The BJP government has maintained NREGA because of its obvious populist appeal, a point Modi has made directly, but has also systematically reduced funding, centralized control and re-purposed the programme to appease landed interests (Narayan and Raja 2020). The government's focus instead had been to redirect support to the middle class. Arguing that the neo-middle class "needs proactive handholding" (as quoted in Chacko 2019: 401) new welfare programmes also included an array of micro loans, subsidies and labour deregulation to promote small business and reward entrepreneurship (Chacko 2019: 401). As Kaur (2014) has argued, this "emerging" middle class saw Modi's policies that emphasized economic growth over "entitlements" (coded as handouts for Dalits and Muslims) as opening the door to their aspirations, in contrast to the welfare policies of the UPA that largely benefitted the poor (and Dalits/Muslims). The reconfiguration of the welfare state was also clearly tied to a project of cultural transformation. As Chacko shows, a range of financialization schemes – including incentives for brothers to use a traditional religious ceremony as an occasion to open seed insurance schemes for their sisters – in effect marry neo-liberalism to Hindu nationalism by conjoining the family, the individual, and the state in the advancement of the nation (2019: 403).

So what's globalization got to do with it?

In explaining OECD reactions, commentators have pointed to how neo-liberalism has fuelled the politics of austerity, which in turn have triggered right-wing populism. But if anything, India defied neo-liberal globalization and witnessed an expansion of the welfare state in the run-up to reaction. The protagonist of the reaction has not been an ethnically and economically endangered working class but rather an urban middle class that in fact has benefitted most from economic globalization and an aspiring middle class hoping to ride its coattails.

On the economic front the impact of globalization has had much less to do with neo-liberalism and austerity than with the impact of a post-Fordist economy. The displacement of manufacturing by services and of nationally organized production by global value chains has fundamentally reconfigured class relations. Increased informalization and the decline of relatively stable occupational categories (including public-sector employment) has led to both fragmentation and precarization. This in turn has only increased the stakes of providing social protection and some compensation for job insecurity. The new services and information economy has also massively ratcheted up the returns to educational and organizational resources. The new premium on educational capital has fuelled new hoarding strategies, which has made global cities – where high-end educational institutions are concentrated – especially contested spaces. Simultaneously, and more directly linked to neo-liberalism, global commodification of urban land markets has driven up housing prices. The middle class's reproduction strategy is one of opportunity hoarding (Ferndandes and Heller 2006). When the welfare state is well developed and extensive the middle class has a stake in it, and is less inclined to ration social provisioning including access to education and health. Across Europe, resurgent ethno-nationalist parties have only pushed for denying welfare to immigrants and have not challenged the welfare state as such. Urban class compromises forged in the Fordist era have for the most part been preserved in the post-Fordist cities that have benefitted most from globalization. The pattern of reaction in India is reversed. In rapidly growing cities where access to good neighbourhoods and good institutions is the key to economic success in an increasingly information-driven and networked global economy, an upper middle class and its newly minted neo-middle class allies feel increasingly threatened by the encroachment of the poor (Muslims/lower castes). Hansen's description of the retrenchment zeitgeist of urban elites in the gated communities of India captures this politics of social status anxiety: "it is inside such upper-caste and middle-class colonies, carefully separated from the other parts of society, that one finds the deepest mistrust and resentment of popular politics, the government and democracy – generally denounced as the root of all corruption in the country and dominated by undeserving men and women who have risen above the station because of reservations [affirmative action] rather than talent and merit" (2015).

This sense of threat has been further heightened by the second dimension of globalization that has directly contributed to the destabilization of the traditional social order, namely the overlapping of domestic and global political fields (Paschel 2016; Evans 2020). Over the last three decades, international governance institutions, a new human rights eco-system and an expanding global public sphere have universalized the legitimacy of human rights and provided domestic groups with significant points of global leverage to advance their claims (Santos and Rodriguez 2005). In India, the democratic and rights-based normative and policy repertoires of Indian civil society – including women's groups, gay rights activists, right to the city movements, transparency movements, right to food campaigns and environmentalists – have strategically leveraged resonant global frames to make their demands on the Indian polity (Roychowdhury 2020; Mander 2018). In a world where communicative structures of traditional and social media are increasingly globalized these frames have become inescapable points of cultural and political reference that interrogate nation-based identities and social hierarchies. These frames are clearly perceived as existential threats by the BJP which has aggressively repressed CSOs with international ties as "anti-national" and has been especially hostile to international human rights and environmental movements (Mander 2018). In this respect, the BJP is, in Castell's sense, a quintessential "reactive movement" building "trenches of resistance on behalf of God, nation, ethnicity, family, locality, that is the fundamental categories of millennial existence now threatened under the combined, contradictory assault of techno-economic forces and transformative social movements" (1997: 2). Because Modi's government represents a social class that is by and large better educated, more globally oriented and celebrates itself as self-motivating and aspirational, it is clear that the cultural nationalism they cultivate has much less to do with "culture" in the sense of some deep primary identity, than with protecting accumulated privileges threatened by the destabilization of traditional social structures (Fernandes and Heller 2006). It is striking that while Modi has championed global technologies and global capital, Hindu nationalists are hostile to secularism and international human rights. When they denounce globalism, it is political liberalism, not capitalism, that they are attacking.

Democratic resilience

The BJP government – Sangh Parivar combine has shown itself willing to use any tools in the democratic toolkit to secure its power and push its exclusionary project. Most notably the combine has made concerted efforts to politicize independent institutions including the electoral commission and the judiciary, two institutions that displayed remarkable autonomy in the period of democratic deepening. But it has gone further than just violating norms or pushing the limits of democratic institutions. At the national as well as the state level where the BJP is in power, the combine has launched a broad-based assault on civil society including the media and universities, made concerted efforts to curtail the rights of those who do not fit their dominant national identity and outsourced intimidation and violence to surrogates.

But as dramatic and alarming as the current conjuncture might be, a full unravelling of democracy is highly unlikely. Electoral democracy will likely be preserved for four general reasons. First, Modi came to power through the ballot box and has invested his legitimacy in the expressed "will of the people". Second, unlike during the period of restricted democracy, the popular sectors have tasted the benefits of political participation and are unlikely to accept a full reversal. The massive mobilization of farmers to protest the BJP's ham-fisted efforts to neo-liberalize the agrarian sector are a sharp reminder that the popular sectors retain significant capacity for political action. Third, in highly diverse and pluralistic societies such as India, even elites understand that democratic contestation is necessary to preserving the social order. The middle class, to paraphrase Marx, will only be willing to go so far in giving up democratic rights for the right to maintain its privileges.

If there is unlikely to be a full reversal, what is at stake is the capacity of subordinate groups, both lower classes and historically marginalized racial/ethnic/caste identities, to effectively pursue their interests. The danger at hand is a contraction of the participatory and substantive spaces of democracy, that is a hollowing out that would return India to its past condition of restricted democracy and exclusionary development. What outcomes are possible depends less on institutions than on how always volatile and malleable historic blocs get organized and reorganized. And there are clearly limits to the project of authoritarian hegemony. The middle class has always been a fickle political actor, and the neo-middle class in particular has aligned itself with reaction on terms that are inherently precarious. At the economic level, the problem is that populists promise much to the people, but hubris is no substitute for programmatic and sustained coordination of class interests. The sharp decline of the Indian economy even before the Covid pandemic may prove politically insurmountable. And on the ideological level preserving right-wing populist blocs requires stitching together disparate identities and interests that are inherently unstable, especially in a rapidly changing economy. Finally, if India's democratic institutions are in a cycle of decline that predates but has been accelerated by the BJP's rise to power, the culture and practices of democracy, cultivated by decades of a wide range of identities and interests asserting their rights and pressing their claims, represent a formidable reservoir of resistance.

Bibliography

Aiyar, Y. (2019). In defense of Indian secularism, *The Hindustan Times*. December 18.

Bardhan, P. (1999). *The Political Economy of Development in India*. Oxford: Oxford University Press.

Bhatty, K. and Sundar, N. (2020). Sliding from majoritarianism toward fascism: Educating India under the Modi regime. *International Sociology*, 35(6): 632–650.

Bourdieu, P. (1984). *Distinction: A Social Critique of the Judgement of Taste*. Cambridge, MA: Harvard University Press.

Castells, M. (1997). *The Power of Identity*. Hoboken, NJ: John Wiley & Sons.

Chacko, P. (2019). Marketizing Hindutva: The state, society, and markets in Hindu nationalism. *Modern Asian Studies*, 53(2): 377–410.

Chiriyankandath, J., Maiorano, D., Manor, J. and Tillin, L. (2020). *The Politics of Poverty Reduction in India: The UPA Government, 2004 to 2014*. Hyderabad: Orient Black Swan.

Corbridge, S. and Harriss, J. (2000). *Reinventing India: Liberalization, Hindu Nationalism and Popular Democracy*. Cambridge: Polity Press.

Evans, P. (2020). Transnational social movements. In Janoski, T., De Leon, C., Misra, J. and William, Martin I. (eds) *The New Handbook of Political Sociology*. Cambridge: Cambridge University Press, pp. 1053–1077.

Evans, P. and Heller, P. (2018). *The State and Development*. Wider Working Paper 2018/12. United National University: UNU-Wider (available at www.patrickheller.com/uploads/1/5/3/7/15377686/evans-heller_state_and_development_wp2018-112.pdf)

Fernandes, L. and Heller, P. (2006). Hegemonic aspirations: New middle class politics and India's democracy in comparative perspective. *Critical Asian Studies*, 38(4): 495–522.

Frankel, F.R. and Rao, M.S.A. (1989). *Dominance and State Power in Modern India: Decline of a Social Order (Vol. 2)*. Oxford: Oxford University Press.

Gramsci, A. (1971). *Prison Notebooks*. New York: International Publishers.

Hansen, T.B. (2015). Communalism, democracy and Indian capitalism. *Seminar*, 674. www.india-seminar.com/semframe.html

Heller, P. (2020). The age of reaction: Retrenchment populism in India and Brazil. *International Sociology*, 35(6): 590–609.

Heller, P. (2019). Trajectories of democratic deepening: Brazil, India and South Africa compared. *Theory and Society*, 48(3): 351–382.

India Today. (2019). How India voted in 2019 election? Here is what India Today-Axis My India post-poll study tells us. May 31. www.indiatoday.in/diu/story/how-india-voted-2019-lok-sabha-election-india-today-axis-my-india-poll-1539617-2019-05-31

Jaffrelot, C. (2003). *India's Silent Revolution: The Rise of the Lower Castes in North India*. New York: Columbia University Press.

Jaffrelot, C. (2019). *L'Inde de Modi: National-Populisme et Democratie Ethnique*. Paris: Payard/CERI.

Jaffrelot, C. and Gilles, V. (2020). A new party system or a new political system? *Contemporary South Asia*, 29(2): 141–154.

Jenkins, R. and Manor, J. (2017). *Politics and the Right to Work: India's National Rural Employment Guarantee Act*. Oxford: Oxford University Press.

Kaur, R. (2014). The 'emerging' middle class: Role in the 2014 general elections. *Economic and Political Weekly*, 49: 26–27.

Levitsky, S. and Ziblatt, D. (2018). *How Democracies Die*. New York: Broadway Books.

Mander, H. (2018). India's Equivocal Engagement with Transnational Advocacy In Evans, P. and Rodríguez-Garavito, C. (eds) *Transnational Advocacy Networks: Reflecting on 15 Years of Evolving Theory and Practice*. Bogota, Colombia: Dejusticia, pp. 172–185.

Narayanan, R. and Annie, R. (2020). NREGA: A distress saviour or a saviour in distress? In Nikhil, D., Aruna, R., and Rakshita, S. (eds.) *We the People: Establishing Rights and Deepening Democracy*. New Delhi: Penguin Books Random House India Private Limited.

Paschel, T.S. (2016). *Becoming Black Political Subjects: Movements and Ethno-Racial Rights in Colombia and Brazil*. Princeton, NJ: Princeton University Press.

Przeworski, A. (2019). *Crises of Democracy*. Cambridge: Cambridge University Press.

Rodrik, D. (2018). Populism and the economics of globalization. *Journal of International Business Policy*, 1(1–2): 12–33.

Roychowdhury, P. (2020). *Capable Women, Incapable States: Negotiating Violence and Rights in India.* Oxford: Oxford University Press.

Santos, B. de Sousa and Rodríguez-Garavito, C. eds. (2005). *Law and Globalization from Below: Towards a Cosmopolitan Legality.* Cambridge University Press.

Sircar, N. (2020). The politics of vishwas: political mobilization in the 2019 national election. *Contemporary South Asia*, 28(2): 178–194.

Subramanian, A. (2015). Making merit: The Indian Institutes of Technology and the social life of caste. *Comparative Studies in Society and History*, 57(2), 291–322.

Thachil, T. (2014). *Elite Parties, Poor Voters: How Social Services Win Votes in India.* Cambridge University Press.

V-Dem. India is an Electoral Autocracy. P. 13, V-Dem DR 2021.

Varshney, A. (2019). Modi consolidates power: Electoral vibrancy, liberal deficits. *Journal of Democracy*, 30(4): 67–77.

Veeraraghavan, R. (2017). Strategies for synergy in a high modernist project: Two community responses to India's NREGA rural work program. *World Development*, 99: 203–313.

Vithayathil, T. (2018). Counting caste: Censuses, politics, and castelessness in India. *Politics & Society*, 46(4): 455–484.

Weyland, K. (2001). Clarifying a contested concept: Populism in the study of Latin American politics. *Comparative Politics*, 34(1): 1–22.

Yadav, Y. (2000). Understanding the second democratic upsurge. In Frankel F. (ed.) *Transforming India*, New Delhi: Oxford University Press, pp. 120–145.

11

FROM HINDU RASHTRA TO HINDU RAJ? A *DE FACTO* OR A *DE JURE* ETHNIC DEMOCRACY?

Christophe Jaffrelot

India was long considered a fine example of liberal parliamentary democracy among countries of the South. In addition to a strong legislature and judiciary, as well as a vibrant free press, political pluralism was nourished by federalism and cultural diversity, both linguistic and religious.

It is the erosion – even the obliteration – of the country's religious diversity that this chapter describes. This evolution calls into question India's secularism, a system for managing relations between state and religion that differs from what is known as *laïcité* in France, for instance. While in France the state is supposed to have no connection with religion, in India, the republic's institutions acknowledge that religion has a perfectly legitimate place in the public sphere. What secularism and *laïcité* have in common, however, is the rejection of the dominance of any *one* religion in that sphere.

It is this very principle that is being challenged by the Hindu nationalist movement, its matrix, the Rashtriya Swayamsevak Sangh (Association of National Volunteers – RSS) and its main political force, the Bharatiya Janata Party (Indian People's Party – BJP) which rose to power in 2014. Although this party was already at the helm of India's government from 1998 to 2004, this was the first time it enjoyed an absolute majority in the lower house of parliament, putting it in a position to implement its agenda.

This agenda derives directly from its ideology, Hindutva, which was codified nearly a century ago, in the footsteps of European ethnic nationalisms – even emulating them (Jaffrelot 1996). Like them, it accords a predominant role to the majority community, made up of so-called sons of the soil, over the minorities. For adherents of Hindutva, Hindus embody the Indian nation, and minorities whose religion originated abroad (Muslims and Christians) are mere outsiders who must assimilate by adopting the majority/majoritarian culture.

After the BJP victory in 2014, this programme was primarily implemented by civil-society-based organisations within the Hindutva movement that act as vigilante groups specialized in cultural policing. But since Narendra Modi's re-election to the prime ministership in 2019, the *de facto* ethnicization of India's democracy has taken on a new dimension. The BJP has in fact passed more and more laws at both the level of the states it governs and at the central government level, so that India is tending to become a *de jure* ethnocracy. India is thus in the process not only of building a Hindu Rashtra, a Hindu nation, but also a Hindu Raj, a Hindu state.

DOI: 10.4324/9781003042211-13

A *de facto* ethnic democracy or the rise of Hindu vigilantism (2014–2019)

If the notion of ethnic democracy, theorized by Sammy Smooha, sounds like a contradiction in terms – in that democracy is theoretically based on the values of individualism – it is because it describes the contradictions of the regime where it originated: the state of Israel. Certain pillars of democracy there have shown great resilience: rather free and fair elections are held at regular intervals, the judiciary's relative independence lends credibility to the rule of law, and a fairly free press provides a forum for criticism, all this in the context of a certain degree of pluralism. But not all citizens enjoy the same rights: as Israel is officially "the state of the Jews," this population imposes the symbols of its identity, lifestyle and social and political domination on the country's minorities. Smooha points out that even if this power relationship is enshrined in the law, it is augmented through practices, most discrimination being rather covert, arising from (sometimes) unwritten laws that have unintended effects, such as conditioning eligibility for Israeli state benefits on military service – which is performed mainly by Jews (Smooha 2002).

In India as well, during Narendra Modi's first term, the Hinduization of the public sphere developed to the detriment of champions of secularism and of minorities. The first victims of Hindu nationalists were none other than intellectuals, who were taken to task for their "liberalism" (which has become a derogatory term). The Hindu nationalists' preferred targets were highly regarded universities – such as Jawaharlal Nehru University in New Delhi – and progressive NGOs: Hindutva apologists were placed at the head of university administrations, and organizations were deprived of contributions from abroad (through the resurrection of a law that had been passed in 1976 during the Emergency (Jaffrelot and Anil 2021), the Foreign Contribution (Regulation) Act), forcing several of them to shut down operations.

This evolution has also resulted in calling into question the national narrative and especially the way the history of India had been taught in school. Textbooks have been rewritten so as to discard the idea of "Aryan invasions" (which deprived Hindus of their "sons of the soil" status), to depict the Muslim conquests and reign in a particularly violent light (ignoring the role of Sufism in mass conversions to Islam and a large degree of cultural syncretism) and, last, to tone down the role of great figures of contemporary history (starting with Nehru, and even Gandhi) and replace them with their own heroes, whose names have moreover been given to many avenues, universities, airports and so on.

Together with this Hinduization, which was also reflected in the noticeable presence of several Hindu dignitaries in the highest echelons of government – as can be seen in the choice of a priest, Yogi Adityanath, to head Uttar Pradesh following the BJP victory in the 2017 elections in that state – have been mounting discriminatory practices against Christian and Muslim minorities. Vigilante groups in charge of harassment campaigns sometimes only had very loose connections with the BJP – enabling it to preserve an aura of respectability – but they were nevertheless part of the Sangh Parivar which is the network that the RSS (known as the "Sangh") has created and that it coordinates as a "family" (parivar). Among these groups, the Bajrang Dal (BD), established in 1984, warrants special mention due to its involvement in heavy-handed operations such as, in 1992, the demolition of the Babri Masjid, the famous mosque built by Mughal emperor Babur in 1528 in Ayodhya that Hindu nationalists claim to have been erected on the birthplace of Lord Ram, where a Hindu temple allegedly stood and that they wished to rebuild. The Bajrang Dal had painstakingly recruited thousands of activists among a Hindu youth hard hit by unemployment, lacking self-esteem and for whom defence of Hinduism gave meaning to their lives, and even a job (Jaffrelot 2009).

This group, like so many others, became involved as of 2014 in campaigns targeting, by turn, mixed marriages, religious conversions and defence of the sacred cow. In the fall of 2014,

Table 11.1 Cow-related violence in India, 2012–18

Year	2012	2013	2014	2015	2016	2017	2018
Incidents	1	2	3	13	30	43	31
Victims	2	0	11	49	67	108	57
Deaths	0	0	0	11	9	13	13

Source: IndiaSpend.org, "Database on Bovine-Related Violence (from January 2010 to September 2, 2017)" (https://docs.google.com/spreadsheets/d/13REUhD4fW6olOy_ SjobWQRA1qQg3VY1pp87XMRJwJW4/pubhtml. Last accessed April 9, 2018). This online publication ceased to exist in 2017 but it set up another website dedicated to lynching victims in connection with sacred cows called "Hate Crime: Cow-related Violence in India" (http://lynch. factchecker.in). This publication also ceased to exist in 2018 when I could access it one last time.

in a campaign against so-called love jihad, BD members went on prowls to protect young Hindu women from Muslims supposedly out to woo them and trick them into marrying and converting. A remarkable example of investigative journalism by two news websites, *Cobrapost* and *Gulail.com*, bears testimony to the intimidation techniques used by Hindu nationalists (Cobrapost 2015). This strongarm intimidation campaign targeted Muslims as much as young Hindu women, even when they were of age and wanted to take a Muslim (or a Christian) for their husband.

Regarding conversions, the effort to fend off Muslim and even more so Christian proselytizing resulted not only in violence (churches desecrated, priests and nuns attacked, etc.), but also in reconversion operations called *ghar wapsi* (homecoming). The initiative for this campaign lies directly with the RSS, which gathered together 1,200 of its members and sympathizers in Nagpur on November 7 and 9, 2014 (a few weeks after the campaign against "Love Jihad" was launched). The Sangh branch responsible for carrying out the actual conversion operations was the Dharm Jagran Samiti (Religious Awakening Committee). The RSS assigned 58 *pracharak* (full-time cadres) to the task, a considerable number for such a campaign (Yadav 2018).

As for cow protection, which was actually extended to all bovines, it primarily took the form of inspecting trucks suspected of transporting cattle to the slaughterhouse. Many of the drivers intercepted on the roads of India were severely beaten by vigilantes armed with cricket bats or field hockey sticks and even knives and firearms. The use of firearms has developed considerably in recent years. The Gau Raksha Dal (cow protection movement) emblem is composed of two AK-4 type weapons wreathing the head of a calf. *IndiaSpend* estimates that in 2017 there were 43 bovine-related incidents, compared to 30 in 2016, 13 in 2015, 3 in 2014, 2 in 2013 and 1 in 2012. Twenty-four out of the 28 victims during the period between January and June 2017 were Muslim (Abraham and Rao 2017), probably the standard ratio.

Several dozen Muslims died of their injuries in lynchings, enough of them for the Supreme Court finally to turn its attention to the matter in 2018. The judges blamed mobs and social media (first and foremost WhatsApp) through which false information was spread to provoke and coordinate assaults (Ananthakrishnan 2018). By doing so, the Supreme Court shunned its responsibilities by not seeking the guilty parties, as Raheel Dhattiwala (2018) has pointed out, and played the game of the Hindu nationalists, who systematically legitimate anti-Muslim violence by referring to emotions and, more specifically, the "religious sentiment" that fuels champions of the faith who can quickly whip themselves up into a fury for a sacred cause.

The cultural policing carried out by Hindu vigilantes is a good illustration of the Hindu nationalist movement's modus operandi and in particular of its historical matrix, the RSS. The RSS in fact assigned itself the mission of extending its influence over the entire society, establishing its presence by setting up branches (*shakha*) in all of India's towns and villages. This long-term project, by which the RSS sought to conquer India from the bottom up via unrelenting social and ideological engineering to bring about a Hindu Rashtra (Hindu nation), moreover reflects a major characteristic of the Hindu tradition, which has never valued the state, but instead the social order born out of the caste system, an orthopraxy of which the upper castes were the custodians. RSS leaders, all of whom until fairly recently were of the Brahmin caste, had long adhered to this model that implied enforcing their order at a more societal than a political – or in any event bureaucratic – level. But recent developments indicated a certain evolution regarding this crucial element.

Towards a *de jure* ethnic democracy, or the triumph of state vigilantism (2019–)

The shift from a bottom-up strategy starting at the grassroots level to a top-down strategy involving the public authorities first became apparent in states governed by the BJP. In the mid-2010s, Maharashtra, Haryana and Gujarat all toughened their cow protection laws. In Maharashtra, it was now prohibited to slaughter not just cows but also many other bovines. Even possession of beef was outlawed (Daniyal 2015). The crime became punishable by up to a five-year prison sentence and a heavy fine. In Gujarat, even more drastic legislation in the matter was accompanied by similar decisions in major cities to prevent the religious mixing of populations: in some districts/neighbourhoods, the members of one religious community were permitted to sell or rent real estate only to people of the same religion (Jaffrelot and Laliwala 2018). Such regulations provided a legal basis for those who wanted to combat "land jihad," a new dimension in vigilante practices that aimed to dissuade Hindu landowners by force (or by intimidation) from renting or selling property to Muslims in mainly Hindu areas. These practices, together with new rules and the adverse effects of communal riots – which, in 2002, descended into a pogrom in Gujarat – have fostered the formation of veritable ghettos where Muslims both rich and poor are crammed together for lack of available housing elsewhere and for their own safety (Laliwala et al. 2021).

After the 2019 elections, several BJP-governed states announced the passing of laws officializing the practice of "love jihad" by making it virtually impossible for Hindu women to marry men of another faith. In Uttar Pradesh, the first state to go through with such legislation in 2020, marriages were impeded by the police on the pretext that the husband-to-be intended to convert his wife-to-be (a "crime" punishable by a ten-year prison term) (Rashid 2020). BJP leaders made no secret that they now wanted to impose their perception of what was good for society, not only by resorting to street vigilantism, but by the law, that is state vigilantism (Jaffrelot 2020). The home minister of Madhya Pradesh, another BJP-ruled state – along with Gujarat, which passed an "anti Love-Jihad" law – declared: "Any love that heads towards jihad, we will oppose it. Any love that offends our sentiments, we will oppose it" (Siddique 2021).

The most independent media outlets have reported on the growing unease among existing interfaith marriages in which the Muslim party seeks to conceal his/her given name or surname to mask his/her religious identity (an evolution also evidenced by the trend of Muslim couples to give their children non-Muslim-sounding names).

In enforcing this policy to prevent interfaith marriage, the police now play the role previously assumed by vigilante groups – further evidence of the shift from a bottom-up to a top-down strategy mentioned above, although the latter has not entirely replaced the former. This progression towards a Hindu Raj is not being accomplished solely through state-level legislation: it can also be noted at the national level.

In 2019, it was reflected in the passage of a constitutional amendment to article 370 and an amendment to the Citizenship Act (CAA). The former revoked the autonomy previously enjoyed by Jammu and Kashmir – which in the process lost its status as a state to become merely a Union Territory (UT) and wound up split in two when Ladakh was made another UT. This reform was justified by the government by the strength of Islamist separatism and the economic underdevelopment affecting the province – in spite of the empirical evidence which said otherwise (Dreze 2019). It was interpreted locally as an attempt to assimilate the only region with a Muslim majority into a Hindu-dominated Indian Union. Not only after the province became a Union Territory, its police now reported directly to the central government, but along with Art. 370, Art. 35A was also abolished. Under this article, the assembly of Jammu and Kashmir was empowered to define "permanent residents" of the state and to reserve for them certain rights, including the right to own land in the state and to have access to government jobs. Article 35A was one of the laws that was repealed after the abrogation of Art. 370 and then, in March 2020, the Modi government replaced "permanent residents" with domiciles of Jammu and Kashmir by a new provision: anyone who had lived in the region for 15 years, studied there for seven years or written school board examinations was eligible to own land and hold government jobs.

The Kashmiris' fear of losing their land was stoked by the fact that land had already started to be reserved for outside investors and the armed forces: 70% of the new mining contracts have gone to non-locals (Siddiq 2020) and two laws (The Control of Building Operations Act, 1988, and the Jammu and Kashmir Development Act, 1970) were amended in July 2020 to introduce some "special dispensation for carrying out construction activities in Strategic Areas" – in other words, some land could be easily confiscated and transferred to the army for its own use, a process that has started already (Zargar and Chakravarty 2020). Furthermore, in July 2020 as well, the government decided that army and paramilitary forces would not require a No Objection Certificate from its home department "for acquisition or requisition of land in favour of the Army, B[order] S[ecurity] F[orce], CRPF and other similar organizations" (Iqbal 2020).

These measures reflected the will of the BJP (which has never resigned itself to the federal structure of India's institutions) to transform India into a unitary nation-state (Aiyar and Tillin 2020) and to change the demographic balance in the only Muslim-dominated territory. Indeed, a few days after the abrogation of Art. 370, Narendra Modi declared during his August 15 address: "Today, as I address the nation from the Red Fort, I can proudly say that every Indian today can speak of One Nation, One Constitution ..." (Business Today 2019).

The Citizenship (Amendment) Act turned out to have also momentous consequences. The law, advertised as proof of the Indian government's concern for victims of religious persecution in the region, shows the selective nature of such concern. Indeed, only non-Muslim victims from Bangladesh, Afghanistan and Pakistan were eligible to become Indian citizens through this law – via an expedited six-year procedure. Rohingyas, Shias, Ahmadis and Hazaras could not claim refugee status, nor could the victims of religious persecution from Sri Lanka, Tibet, Myanmar or Nepal. The law sowed panic among many Indian Muslims who were afraid they would not be in a position to prove their Indian nationality for lack of documentation, something that is very hard to produce in a country that never had a systematic register of citizens. This fear was fuelled by the establishment of the National Register of Citizens in the state of Assam, where there was a large number of Muslim migrants from Bangladesh. The fact that CAA and NRC worked in tandem was made clear by Amit Shah himself when he said during a press conference in West Bengal – the video of which was posted on the BJP's YouTube page in April 2019: "Understand the chronology [...] First the Citizenship (Amendment) Bill will come, all the refugees will be given citizenship, and after that the NRC will be prepared" (ICF Team 2020). This meant that the non-Muslim undocumented migrants would gain access to some sort of naturalization procedure before the NRC was put in place and that this NRC could only affect Muslims. Moreover, in September 2019, the RSS chief, Mohan Bhagwat made it clear that "No Hindu will have to leave over NRC" (The Telegraph 2019).

Hindu militant WhatsApp groups gradually translated this message into their own idiom: the combination of the CAA and the NRC was a tool to "kick Muslims out of India." A journalist who had infiltrated these groups explains that "One major theme that a majority of the messages echo is that bringing the CAA and, then, the NRC, will automatically imply that India's Muslim population will be reduced. [...]" They list a 'four-step' process for India becoming a Hindu nation – starting with the CAA, followed by the NRC, then a law to control population, ultimately followed by a Uniform Civil Code.

In reaction to the CAA, thousands of demonstrators took to the streets in the fall of 2019. Most of them were Muslims who were afraid of becoming "doubtful citizens," but many students also took part in sit-ins, including in Shaheen Bagh, Delhi – by far the best-known place of protest where the Indian Constitution was eulogized in countless debates and speeches.

In reaction to this mobilisation, however, Uttar Pradesh was the state that saw the unleashing of maximum police violence in late 2019. The campus of Aligarh Muslim University, where the protest had gained momentum, was the first target. On December 15, the police and members of the Rapid Action Force (RAF) forcefully entered the university campus, breaking the iron gate at 10 p.m., and assaulted students. One student's hand had to be amputated (Srivastava 2012). The AMU vice chancellor claimed (The Hindu 2020), retrospectively, that he had invited the police to intervene, but why, in that case, did they break the main gate? Elsewhere in Uttar Pradesh, the police used real bullets to crack down on demonstrators, leaving 24 dead in the space of a few days (Pandey 2020) – out of the 31 casualties recorded throughout India (Sen and Singaravelu 2020). In addition, a large number of young Muslims, including minors, were arrested – and in many cases tortured (Indo-Asian News Service 2019).

But early in 2020 the epicentre of the crackdown was in Delhi, a state where the CAA was exploited by the BJP in the context of the election campaign that began in December 2019 and intensified in January 2020. There, too, the police – under the direct supervision of Narendra Modi's home minister, Amit Shah – conducted the crackdown. While Delhi is a state of the Indian Union, it does not enjoy the same autonomy as full-fledged states and, in particular, the police report directly to the central government's Home Ministry. First targeted was Jamia Milia University in December (The Economic Times 2019) where activists and the police joined forces. As the police habitually destroy CCTV cameras, their involvement in the clashes is attested primarily by amateur videos posted on social media.

The communal riots that took place in February 2020 in North-East Delhi – a very densely populated district where, according to the 2011 census, Muslims represented more than 29% of the population and Hindus, about 68% – were primarily due to the BJP's reaction to the anti-CAA movement in the context of the state elections. During the election campaign, BJP leaders targeted protesters against the CAA in Delhi – not only in Shaheen Bagh, but elsewhere in the city, including in the North-East, where many sit-ins were held – in order to polarize voters along communal lines. A member of the Modi government, Anurag Thakur, raised a slogan in an election rally that was to be repeated many times: "Desh ke ghaddaron ko, goli maaron saalon ko" (Shoot down the rascals/the traitors to the country) (Shamshad et al. 2020, p. 27).

On February 11, 2020, the BJP had a rude shock as only eight of its candidates, out of 70, could win a seat, against 62 for the Aam Aadmi Party of Arvind Kejriwal. BJP cadres wanted to take revenge (Mubayi 2020). Their post-election meetings were as aggressive as the pre-election ones. On February 23, 2020, Kapil Mishra, a BJP candidate who had lost the election in February 2020, led a provocative rally in North-East Delhi. Mishra addressed the gathering in the presence of the Deputy Commissioner of Police for North-East District, Ved Prakash Surya, who was standing right next to him *in full riot gear*. It projected an unexampled visual by associating an expert in communal provocation and a custodian of law and order. Thousands of assailants, led by Hindu nationalist cadres, including BJP former or sitting MLAs and municipal councillors (Singh 2020; Menon and Iyer 2020) forcibly entered houses to attack men and women (Shamshad et al. 2020, pp. 61–69); 600 houses were burnt (Alavi 2020) and shops looted with a remarkably accurate selectivity, as adjacent houses and shops were spared when they belonged to Hindus (Express News Service 2020); markets were razed to the ground as well (Shamshad et al. 2020); mosques were systematically targeted – they were looted, desecrated and burnt (Mody 2020). A businessman who happened to be a BJP cadre said that his factory had been burnt because he had a "Muslim name," suggesting that, like in Gujarat in 2002, the rioters were using lists of residents – maybe the voters lists (Express News Service 2020). In Tyre Market the fire brigade, which had rushed to the place, was attacked physically (Shamshad et al. 2020, p. 48). After four days, the official toll was 55 dead, including 13 persons with non-Muslim names (Shamshad et al. 2020, pp. 111–118).

While Hindu nationalists initiated the riots, the police played an important role in them. Not only did they not come to the rescue of the Muslims, but they took an active part in the violence on many occasions. In the complaints filed subsequently, victims declare that the police also incited the activists to attack them (Singh 2020). Police officers also took part in the looting and destruction of mosques, sometimes while chanting "Jai Shri Ram" (Shroff 2020a; 2020b). Possibly in reaction to the attitude of the police, two security personnel were killed during the riot: Ankit Sharma, an Intelligence Bureau staff member (Bhardwaj 2020), and Police Constable Ratan Lal. *The New York Times*, whose journalists emphasize that "Delhi's Police turned against Muslims," mentions the fact that not only one police officer was killed but that 80 others were injured, especially when Muslim protesters outnumbered the police (Gettleman et al. 2020). Seemingly as a result, the police directly assaulted Muslims even more brutally. One of these attacks, on February 24, 2020, was filmed and the videos went viral on social media. They showed five men beaten by the police in the Kardam Puri Pulia area and told to chant the national anthem. One of them, Faizan, died (Yadav 2020). In other places, the police were pelting stones at the Muslim mob along with Hindu rioters, or, as in Chand Bagh "the police were encouraging the mob to carry out the riots" (Shamshad et al. 2020, p. 74). The police also took part in the looting and destruction of mosques and madrasas – usually after destroying the CCTV cameras (Shamshad et al. 2020, pp. 40, 45). Not only could the victims not file a complaint, but they were accused of being responsible for the violence itself (Lalwani 2020) – whereas no FIR has been registered against Hindu activists who took part in the riots, BJP leaders who made provocative speeches or policemen who were seen attacking Muslims on videos. The detailed report filed by the fact-finding committee set up on March 9, 2020 by the Minorities Commission of the state of Delhi and from which much of the information above was drawn was not even used by the authorities. Not only that, but the chairman of the Delhi Minorities Commission, Zafarul-Islam Khan, was accused of sedition in April 2020 because of a Facebook post (Bedi 2020).

Instead, the narrative promoted after the Delhi riots by the police and the BJP government – both representing two sides of the same coin, that is, the state – consisted in exonerating the police and accusing the Muslims. On March 10, Amit Shah, the Home Minister to whom the Delhi police report directly, congratulated himself that the police succeeded in controlling the riots "within 36 hours," "not allowing the riots to spiral" (The Wire 2020). Shah concluded that these "riots were 'pre-planned' conspiracy" and that it "will be a lesson for the country on what befalls those who indulge in rioting" (The Wire 2020).

This enabled the police to resort to a stringent anti-terror law, the Unlawful Activities Prevention Act, 2019 (UAPA), under which a detainee may have to await trial for up to two years and not be released on bail or be apprised of the charges against him/her for six months. It is noteworthy that the Narendra Modi government had just amended the law to make it possible to label as "terrorists" isolated individuals and not solely men and women belonging to an organization.

Conclusion

The trajectory of India's democracy since 2014 has led it not only to renege on its traditional secularism by establishing a *de facto* ethnic democracy during Narendra Modi's first term, but also to embark on the path of a *de jure* ethnic democracy since 2019, the year in which the BJP, on the strength of its electoral success, set out to transform the law and the Constitution.

This evolution drew on greater recourse to the police, who have taken up the task of Hindu vigilante groups, transforming social violence into state violence. The officialization of this new power relationship came out in the open when the judge of the Delhi High Court, Justice Muralidhar, who was seeking to hold the police to account, was transferred to Chandigarh, removing the only remaining obstacle in the way of pursuing the violence (Sachdev 2020).

But in other circumstances, Indian judges have sided wholeheartedly with the authorities. The Supreme Court thus did not deem it worthwhile to examine the cases of either the abolition of article 370 of the Constitution or the CAA, despite the large number of petitions. It even reactivated implementation of the NRC in Assam and arbitrated in favour of building a Hindu temple in Ayodhya. Reinforced by the legalization of a plan that until then enjoyed popular legitimacy only, Narendra Modi officiated, as a priest, over the laying of the temple's cornerstone. If the *de jure* ethnic democracy that India is becoming actually increasingly resembles a theocracy, the attitude of the judges – compounded by the decline of other institutions including Parliament (Jaffrelot and Jumle 2020) and the Election Commission (Ostermann and Ahuja 2018) – calls into question the very qualifier "democracy." In just a few years, India has come to lengthen the list of countries whose authoritarianism dons a pluralist guise at election time, with several parties taking part, but the fairness of these elections is increasingly doubtful. In fact, Modi's India increasingly fulfils the criteria of ethnocracy. This concept introduced by Donald Horowitz (Horowitz 1985, 499–500) has been elaborated upon, once again, by Israeli social scientists. Oren Yiftachel applied it to his country in the late 1990s in an article that minimized the democratic side of the regime and emphasized, on the contrary, the domination of the state and the capture of its resources by a majority community at the expense of minorities (Yiftachel 1997; 2006).

If India can now be considered as an ethnocracy because of its democratic decline and the growing assertion of Hindu nationalism, it can be compared more easily to other South Asian countries, including Sri Lanka, Bangladesh and Pakistan. The parallel with the "country of the pures" is striking in more than one way. First, minorities are marginalized not only in all sites of power, but also physically, as evident from the ghettoization process experienced by Hindus, Christians and Ahmadis that runs parallel to what is now obvious in the case of Indian Muslims. Minorities should not mix either in terms of intermarriages. However, in Pakistan, minorities have separate electorates, whereas in India they vote with the Hindu majority. Secondly, red lines are crystallizing on both sides. In Pakistan, the anti-blasphemy law has become sacrosanct, whereas in India, to pay allegiance to the cow and to Lord Ram has not become part of the laws of the Republic (but some BJP-ruled states have passed acts in this direction already). Thirdly, the political leaders who do not defend the majority community are presented by the rulers as illegitimate and anti-national. In Pakistan, politicians are not supposed to express compassion for Ahmadis publicly and in India Modi has disqualified Sonia Gandhi because she was a Christian, according to him, and the Manmohan Singh government – which he called the "Delhi Sultanate" – because it allegedly was pro-Muslim (Jaffrelot 2013; 2016). In both countries, national-populist leaders, including Imran Khan and Narendra Modi, have exploited the fear and the anger of ethno-religious majorities in this context. Their mobilization techniques illustrate how, according to Arjun Appadurai, "predatory identities" exploit "the fear of small numbers," that comes from the "anxiety of incompleteness" that afflicts ethnic communities when they do not coincide with the nation-state (Appadurai 2018). Imran Khan and Narendra Modi brought their communities from fear to outrage and anger, a theme that all populists exploiting social frustration have played on in the early twenty-first century. In his book on the role of anger in the rise of nationalism, Pankaj Mishra draws examples as much from the nineteenth century as from the present (Mishra 2018): anger arises from fear itself because majorities are not supposed to feel vulnerable; and this anger can be turned towards the politicians who do not defend enough the majority community because of their cosmopolitanism or for other reasons.

Last but not least, India and Pakistan converge today towards similar forms of authoritarianism because of the role the "deep state" plays in both countries. While the army and the security apparatus at large have occupied the driver's seat for decades in Pakistan – even when civilians govern the country (but do not rule) – a similar scenario is unfolding itself in India: the Hindu nationalist movement is, indeed, infiltrating an increasingly large number of institutions, including the bureaucracy, the judiciary, the intelligence services and the army.

Nota Bene

This article draws on certain chapters of my book, *Modi's India. Hindu Nationalism and the Rise of Ethnic Democracy*, Princeton, Princeton University Press, and New Delhi, Westland, 2021, which the interested reader might refer to for further information. There are few footnotes for this reason.

Bibliography

Abraham, Delna and Ojaswi Rao, 2017, "86% killed in cow-related violence since 2010 are Muslim, 97% attacks after Modi govt came to power," *Hindustan Times*, July 16. URL: www.hindustantimes.com/india-news/86-killed-in-cow-relat...after-modi-govt-came-to-power/story-w9CYOksvgk9joGSSaXgpLO.html Last accessed March 26, 2018.

Aiyar, Yamini. and Louise Tillin, 2020, "'One nation,' BJP, and the future of Indian federalism," *India Review*, 19(2), March-April, pp. 117–135.

Alavi, Shams Ur Rehman, 2020, "Delhi Horror: Documenting the organised mob violence and killings in India's national capital," *NewsBits*, March 4. URL: www.newsbits.in/delhi-horror-documenting-the-organised-mob-violence-and-killings-in-indias-national-capital Last accessed September 1, 2020.

Ananthakrishnan, Gopalakirshnan, 2018, "Mobocracy can't be the new normal, get a law to punish lynching: SC to Govt," *The Indian Express*, July 3. URL: https://indianexpress.com/article/india/cji-condemns-lynchings-across-country-asks-parliament-to-make-new-law/ Last accessed September 28, 2020.

Appadurai, Arun, 2006, *Fear of Small Numbers. An Essay on the Geography of Anger*, Durham: Duke University Press, pp. 51–53.

Bedi, Aneesha, 2020, "Delhi Minorities Commission chief charged with sedition for 'provocative' social media post," *The Print*, May 2. URL: https://theprint.in/india/delhi-minorities-commission-chief-charged-with-sedition-for-provocative-social-media-post/413112/ Last accessed September 1, 2020.

Bhardwaj, Ananya, 2020, "IB staffer Ankit Sharma, killed in Delhi riots, was stabbed 12 times & had 33 blunt injuries," *The Print*, March 14. URL: https://theprint.in/india/ib-staffer-ankit-sharma-killed-in-delhi-riots-was-stabbed-12-times-and-not-400-times/380720/ Last accessed September 1, 2020.

Business Today, 2019, "Independence Day: Full text of PM Modi's address to nation," *Business Today*, August 15. URL: www.businesstoday.in/current/economy-politics/independence-day-pm-modi-address-nation-full-text-speech-15-august-red-fort/story/372903.html Last accessed September 3, 2020.

Cobrapost, 2015, "Operation Juliet: Busting the bogey of 'Love Jihad'," October 4. URL: http://cobrapost.com/blog/operation-juliet-busting-the-bogey-of-love-jihad-2/900 Last accessed April 9, 2018.

Daniyal, Shoaib, 2015, "Maharashtra's beef ban shows how politicians manipulate Hindu sentiments around cow slaughter," *Scroll.in*, March 3, 2015. URL: https://scroll.in/article/711064/maharashtras-beef-ban-shows-how-politicians-manipulate-hindu-sentiments-around-cow-slaughter Last accessed May 2, 2021.

Dhattiwala, Raheel, 2018, "'Blame It on the Mob' – How Governments Shun the Responsibility of Judicial Redress," *The Wire*, August 17. URL: https://thewire.in/communalism/mob-violence-lynching-government-legal-process Last accessed September 28, 2020.

Dreze, Jean, 2019, "Article 370 helped reducing poverty in Jammu and Kashmir," *National Herald*, August 9. URL: www.nationalheraldindia.com/india/economist-jean-dreze-jandk-more-developed-than-gujarat-special-status-helped-reducing-poverty Last accessed May 2, 2021.

Express News Service, 2020, "Factory burnt, BJP man says ignored by party because 'I have Muslim name'," *The Indian Express*, March 5. URL: https://indianexpress.com/article/cities/delhi/factory-burnt-bjp-man-says-ignored-by-party-6299749/ Last accessed September 1, 2020.

Gettleman, Jeffrey, Sameer Yasir, Suhasini Raj and Hari Kumar, 2020, "How Delhi's Police Turned Against Muslims," *The New York Times*, March 12. URL: www.nytimes.com/2020/03/12/world/asia/india-police-muslims.html Last accessed September 1, 2020.

Horowitz, Donald, 1985, *Ethnic Groups in Conflict*, Berkeley, University of California Press.

ICF Team, 2020, "Assam and CAA," *NewsClick*, March 12. URL: www.newsclick.in/Assam-CAA-Timeline-Assam-Accord-1985-Present Last accessed May 2, 2020.

IndiaSpend, 2018, "Hate Crime: Cow-related Violence in India." URL: http://lynch.factchecker.in Last accessed, March 26, 2018.

Indo-Asian News Service, 2019, "21,500 booked for violence in Kanpur," *India Today*, Dec. 24. URL: www.indiatoday.in/amp/india/story/21-500-booked-for-violence-in-kanpur-1631048-2019-12-24 Last accessed May 2, 2020.

Iqbal, Naveed, 2020, "J&K: Army, CRPF, BSF will no longer require NOC for land acquisition," *The Indian Express*, July 28. URL: https://indianexpress.com/article/india/jk-army-crpf-bsf-will-no-longer-require-noc-for-land-acquisition-6526708/ Last accessed September 3, 2020.

Jaffrelot, Christophe and Sharik Laliwala, 2018, "The segregated city," *Indian Express*, May 26. URL: https://indianexpress.com/article/opinion/columns/muslims-in-india-hindus-jains-gujarat-love-jihad-5191304/ Last accessed May 2, 2021.

Jaffrelot, Christophe and Pratinav Anil, 2020, *India's First Dictatorship – The Emergency, 1975–77*, London, Hurst; New York, Oxford University Press; New Delhi, HarperCollins.

Jaffrelot, Christophe and Vihang Jumle, 2020, "Bypassing parliament," *The Indian Express*, October 15. URL: https://indianexpress.com/article/opinion/columns/narendra-modi-government-parliament-lok-sabha-rajya-sabha-6725428/ Last accessed October 16, 2020.

Jaffrelot, Christophe and Pratinav Anil, 2021, *India's First Dictatorship: The Emergency, 1975–1977*, Oxford, Oxford University Press.

Jaffrelot, Christophe, 1996, *The Hindu Nationalist Movement and Indian Politics, 1925 to the 1990s*, New York, Columbia University Press; London, Hurst; New Delhi, Penguin India, p. 582 (updated edition in 1999).

Jaffrelot, Christophe, 2009, *The Militias of Hindutva: Communal Violence, Terrorism and Cultural Policing*, in L. Gayer and C. Jaffrelot (eds), *Armed Militias of South Asia. Fundamentalist, Maoists and*

Separatists, London, Hurst; New York, Columbia University Press; New Delhi, Foundation Books, pp. 199–236.

Jaffrelot, Christophe, 2013, "Gujarat Elections: The Sub-text of Modi's 'Hattrick' – High Tech Populism and the 'Neo-middle Class'," *Studies in Indian Politics*, 1(1), June, pp. 79–96.

Jaffrelot, Christophe, 2016, "Narendra Modi between Hindutva and subnationalism: The Gujarati *asmita* of a Hindu Hriday Samrat, *India Review*, 15(2), pp. 196 – 217.

Jaffrelot, Christophe, 2020, "On 'love jihad', BJP picks up baton from vigilante groups. Police, judicial apparatus have aided this move," *The Indian Express*, November 26. URL: https://indianexpress.com/article/opinion/columns/love-jihad-law-india-bjp-7067013/ Last accessed May 2, 2021.

Laliwala, Sharik, Christophe Jaffrelot, Priyal Thakkar and Abida Desai, 2020, "Paradoxes of Ghettoization: Juhapura 'in' Ahmedabad," *India Exclusion Report 2019–20*, February 16. URL: https://spire.sciencespo.fr/hdl:/2441/1ni56132699n1r9hm18of0urkr/resources/2021-jaffrelot-paradoxes-of-ghettoization-india-exclusion-report-2019-20.pdf Last accessed May 2, 2021.

Lalwani, Vijayta, 2020, "In Delhi violence investigation, a disturbing pattern: Victims end up being prosecuted by police," *Scroll.in*, May 23. URL: https://scroll.in/article/962526/in-delhi-violence-investigation-a-disturbing-pattern-victims-end-up-being-arrested-by-police Last accessed September 1, 2020.

Menon, Aditya and Aishwarya S. Iyer, "Delhi Riots Exclusive: BJP Councillor Led Mob, Claims 'Eyewitness'," *The Quint*, June 30. URL: www.thequint.com/news/politics/delhi-riots-bjp-councillor-kanhaiya-lal-kapil-mishra-jagdish-pradhan-muslims Last accessed September 1, 2020.

Mishra, Pankaj, 2018, *Age of Anger. A History of the Present*, London, Penguin.

Mody, Anjali, 2020, "In photos: fourteen Delhi mosques and a dargah that were burnt by Hindutva vigilantes in three days," *Scroll.in*, March 12. URL: https://scroll.in/article/955713/in-photos-fifteen-muslim-shrines-in-delhi-that-were-burnt-by-hindutva-vigilantes-in-three-days Last accessed September 1, 2020.

Mubayi, Vinod, 2020, "After Losing Delhi Election, BJP Wreaking Vengeance On City's Minorities," *Alternatives international*, Feb. 29. URL: www.alterinter.org/?After-Losing-Delhi-Election-BJP-Wreaking-Vengeance-On-City-s-Minorities Last accessed September 1, 2020.

Ostermann, Susan, and Amit Ahuja, 2018, "Institutional Tug of War: The Election Commission in a Time of Executive Resurgence," *CASI*, July 16. URL: https://casi.sas.upenn.edu/iit/ostermannahuja Last accessed May 2, 2020.

Rashid, Omar, 2020, "11 FIRs under U.P. ordinance so far," *The Hindu*, December 21. URL: www.thehindu.com/news/national/other-states/11-firs-under-up-ordinance-so-far/article33380361.ece? Last accessed May 2, 2021.

Sachdev, Vakasha, 2020, "Justice Muralidhar Will Not Continue Hearing Hate Speech FIR Case," *The Quint*, Feb. 26. URL: www.thequint.com/news/law/justice-muralidhar-delhi-violence-fir-case-hate-speech-transferred-chief-justice-high-court Last accessed May 2, 2021.

Sen, Sumant and Naresh Singaravelu, 2020, "Data | How many people died during anti-CAA protests? | How many people died during anti-CAA protests?" *The Hindu*, January 6, 2020. URL: www.thehindu.com/data/data-how-many-people-died-during-anti-caa-protests/article30494183.ece Last accessed August 27, 2020.

Shamshad, M.R., Gurminder Singh Matharu, Tehmina Arora, Tanvir Kazi, Haseena Hashia, Abu Bakr Sabbaq, Salem Baig, Devika Prasad, and Aditi Dutta, 2020, *Report of the DMC fact-finding Committee on North-East Delhi Riots of February 2020*, Delhi, Delhi Minorities Commission, Government of NCT of Delhi. URL: https://ia601906.us.archive.org/11/items/dmc-delhi-riot-fact-report-2020/-Delhi-riots-Fact-Finding-2020.pdf Last accessed August 31, 2020.

Shroff, Kaushal, 2020a, "Men in uniform torched Mustafabad's Farooqia Masjid, assaulted people inside: Locals," *The Caravan*, March 11. URL: https://caravanmagazine.in/conflict/men-in-uniform-torched-mustafabads-farooqia-masjid-assaulted-people-inside-locals Last accessed September 1, 2020.

Shroff, Kaushal, 2020b, "Delhi violence: Cops shouted 'Jai Shri Ram' with armed Hindu mob, charged at Muslims," *The Caravan*, Feb. 25. URL: https://caravanmagazine.in/conflict/delhi-violence-cops-shouted-jai-shri-ram-with-armed-hindu-mob-charged-at-muslims Last accessed October 3, 2020.

Siddique, Iram, 2021, "3 months of MP 'love jihad' law: 21 cases, couple knew each other in over half," *The Indian Express*, 20 March. URL: https://indianexpress.com/article/india/mp-love-jihad-law-7236429/ Last accessed May 2, 2021.

Sidiq, Nusrat, 2020, "Kashmir's mineral contracts largely handed to non-locals," *Asia Pacific*, July 27. URL: www.aa.com.tr/en/asia-pacific/kashmir-s-mineral-contracts-largely-handed-to-non-locals/1923634 Last accessed September 3, 2020.

Singh, Prabhijit, 2020, "Dead and buried," *The Caravan*, June 21. URL: https://caravanmagazine.in/politics/delhi-police-ignored-complaints-against-kapil-mishra-bjp-leaders-leading-mobs-delhi-violence Last accessed 2 May, 2020.

Smooha, Samy, 2002, "The model of ethnic democracy: Israel as a Jewish and democratic state," *Nations and Nationalism*, 8(4).

Srivastava, Piyush, 2019, "One student's hand had to be amputated, Bared: Police 'brutality' on AMU students," *The Telegraph*, Dec. 18. URL: www.telegraphindia.com/india/bared-police-brutality-on-amu-students/cid/1728324 Last accessed August 27, 2020.

The Economic Times, 2019, "Protests erupt across India over CAA, police action against Jamia students," *The Economic Times*, Dec. 16. URL: https://economictimes.indiatimes.com/news/politics-and-nation/from-lucknow-to-hyderabad-protests-across-campuses-against-police-crackdown-in-jamia/articleshow/72743549.cms?from=mdr Last accessed May 2, 2020.

The Hindu Special Correspondent, 2020, "At least 60 injured in police crackdown at Aligarh Muslim University," *The Hindu*, Dec. 15, 2019. URL: www.thehindu.com/news/national/students-injured-in-police-crackdown-at-aligarh-muslim-university/article30313968.ece Last accessed August 27, 2020.

The Telegraph Staff Reporter, 2019, "'No Hindu will have to leave over NRC'," *The Telegraph*, Sept. 22. URL: www.telegraphindia.com/west-bengal/no-hindu-will-have-to-leave-over-nrc/cid/1706854 Last accessed August 26, 2020.

The Wire Staff, 2020, "In LS Debate on Delhi Riots, Amit Shah Lauds Police for 'Controlling Violence in 36 Hours'," *The Wire*, March 11. URL: https://thewire.in/communalism/lok-sabha-delhi-riots-amit-shah Last accessed September 1, 2020.

Yadav, Anumeha, 2020, "Ground Report: Delhi Police Actions Caused Death Of Man In Infamous National Anthem Video," *Huffpost*, March 2. www.huffpost.com/archive/in/entry/delhi-riots-police-national-anthem-video-faizan_in_5e5bb8e1c5b6010221126276 Last accessed September 7, 2021.

Yadav, Shyamlal, 2018, "Agra a blip, RSS to step up 'ghar wapsi'," *The Indian Express*, December 11, 2014. URL: http://indianexpress.com/article/india/india-others/agra-a-blip-rss-to-step-up-ghar-wapsi/ Last accessed April 25, 2018.

Yiftachel, Oren, 1997, "'Israeli Society and Jewish-Palestinian Reconciliation': Ethnocracy and Its Territorial Contradictions'," *Middle East Journal* 51(4), pp. 505–519.

Yiftachel, Oren, 2006, *Ethnocracy: Land, and the Politics of Identity Israel/Palestine*, Philadelphia, Penn Press.

Zargar, Safwat and Ipsita Chakravarty, 2020, "A year of government policies that eroded hard-won land rights in Jammu and Kashmir," *Scroll.in*, August 4, 2020. URL: https://scroll.in/article/969275/a-year-of-government-policies-that-eroded-hard-won-land-rights-in-jammu-and-kashmir Last accessed September 3, 2020.

PART II

Pakistan

The decline of civil liberties

12

PAKISTAN'S HYBRID REGIME

Growing democratization, or increased authoritarianism?

Ian Talbot

Imran Khan presented his July 2018 election victory as ushering in a 'Naya Pakistan'. He galvanized urban youthful middle-class support around his 'modernizing agenda' to end 'dynastic politics', eliminate corruption, address environmental issues, reduce Pakistan's economic dependency, and bring back money that had been laundered overseas. Eight months later, he launched an ambitious poverty alleviation scheme which focused on the empowerment of women. On 20 July 2019, the first ever elections were held for seats for the merged tribal districts in the Khyber Pakhtunkhwa assembly. Attempts to establish a 'transformative' political regime followed a decade of gradual democratic consolidation in which governments had completed terms in office and power had been transferred following competitive multi-party elections. Does this evidence suggest that democracy is advancing in Pakistan, despite the army's continuing presence in public life? Is the country bucking the trend, elsewhere in South Asia, of democratic recession, a process which forms part of what has been termed the third wave of autocratization (Anna Lührmann and Staffan I. Lindberg, 2019)?

Autocratization can be understood as backsliding from a liberal or elective democracy to a more authoritarian regime type, or a reduction in the limited space for freedoms provided by authoritarian rulers (Bermeo, 2015; Diamond, 2015). Pakistan has been variously described as an electoral autocracy, 'partly free', or a hybrid regime. The latter term more accurately reflects Pakistan's heterogeneous elements when used by such scholars as Katharine Adeney (2017). Pakistan exists in a 'grey zone' in which multi-party elections coexist with reserved powers in the security and foreign policy areas for the powerful military (Shah, 2014).

The growing literature on autocratization recognizes that this global process is occurring simultaneously with some instances of democratization. A renewed interest in autocratization has come about because of the contemporary decline of liberal democracy in such countries as India, Hungary, Poland, and the United States. Pertinent for the Pakistan case study is the further finding that autocratization's contemporary manifestation is marked not by ceasing elections, but rather by the undermining of such democratic rights as freedom of expression, rule of law and freedom of association.

Claims of Pakistan's democratic advance can be focused too narrowly on the question whether elections in the past decade have been fair or free. The findings of international election observers superficially support claims of democratic advancement. Their reports have pointed out some deficiencies, but they generally give the election process a clean bill of

DOI: 10.4324/9781003042211-15

health (EU Election Observation Report, 2013; 2018). Within Pakistan, there has been fierce debate about the issue of pre-poll rigging and ballot fixing. Imran Khan campaigned vigorously on these issues following the 2013 polls (Mulla, 2017). Evidence regarding the most recent elections, however, points to his PTI party benefiting from the election engineering by the military. It did not want to see Nawaz Sharif returned to office. Intervention took the form of campaign restrictions, intimidation of Muslim League party workers and restrictions on media outlets that supported the Muslim League (Afzal, 2018). This chapter does not seek to go over this well-trodden ground. It argues instead that the examination of everyday experiences of infringements on political and human rights provides a more important means of assessing Pakistan's direction of travel with respect to democracy, rather than concentrating on the issue of electoral malpractice.

The chapter focuses on three areas that have been discussed with respect to global trends in autocratization. These are firstly restrictions on the print and electronic media. Secondly, the extent to which there are infringements of the rule of law and the independence of the judiciary. Finally, it examines the issue of freedom of association. It thus addresses the question that while elections have occurred on a more regular basis since 2008, are the rights and institutions that make the electoral process meaningful, being maintained or compromised? The study will utilize qualitative data drawn from civil society reports and newspaper accounts in support of its assessment. Before beginning this examination, it is necessary to briefly survey the historical context of processes of democratization and autocratization in Pakistan.

The historical context

The landscape which shapes autocratization in Pakistan is complex. Pakistan's political development cannot be understood simply in terms of the binary opposites of democratization and autocratization pursued respectively by civilian and military governments. Nor can its social development be similarly reduced to a straightforward clash between secular and Islamic visions for the future. Both Benazir Bhutto and Nawaz Sharif in the 1990s clashed with the judiciary and sought to undermine its independence (Talbot, 2005). They also harassed political opponents and attempted to control the media. Zulfiqar Ali Bhutto in the 1970s used the army to crush political opponents in Balochistan (Lieven, 2011). This enabled the army to restore its influence after the debacle of the 1971 Bangladesh war. Two decades later, civilian leaders conspired with the military in bids to undermine their elected rivals. These actions strengthened the influence in Pakistan's public and economic life, which the army had established during Zia-ul-Haq's rule (1977–88).

Nawaz Sharif during the 1990s also acceded to demands for Islamization to shore up his position. The linkages which the military had maintained with Islamic proxies were also maintained for strategic reasons, or even were established anew, with, for example, the creation of the Taliban in which Benazir Bhutto's interior minister Nasrullah Babar played a significant role (Talbot, 2002). Even the military's mainstreaming of militant groups in the 2018 elections is not without historical precedent, as Benazir Bhutto established ties with Islamist groups, despite her liberal pretentions.

The links between the military, Islamic groups, and political parties, further complicate the Pakistan landscape. It is well established that Islamic proxies were first used in the struggle for Kashmir shortly after independence (Swami, 2007). With the passage of time, what has been termed the mullah–military nexus came into existence (Haqqani, 2005). The Pakistan army assumed the role of the guardian of Pakistan's ideological as well as territorial integrity. The religious establishment in return lent the military legitimization. Nonetheless, this has taken different forms. Ayub Khan, Pakistan's first military ruler, favoured modernist Islam. Pervez Musharraf sought to draw on Sufi traditions in establishing a moderate Islamic regime image for western audiences. He also emphasized the dangers of Talibanization to encourage their governments to acquiesce with his regime, which as the 'war on terror' unfolded, adopted a Janus-like position with respect to Islamic militancy (Talbot, 2012)

The outset of the Zia regime marked the peak of Islamist groups' access to state power. It is from the period of the Soviet War in Afghanistan (1979–89) that Inter-Services Intelligence (ISI), the military security agency, cultivated close ties with militant groups (Kiessling, 2016). These ties have survived until the contemporary era with respect to groups either committed to fighting India, or who are regarded as providing leverage in Afghanistan. Some militant groups have however outgrown their state patronage and have directed firepower against the institutions of the Pakistan state itself. Such groups sometimes loosely referred to as the 'bad Taliban' have developed links with Al Qaeda or more recently Islamic State.

Three further elements complicate the landscape for contemporary autocratization. Firstly, the so-called religious establishment, although it was promoted to exclude liberal forces from power (Waseem, 2007), does not automatically support the military-run or -guided governments. Religious parties, such as Maulana Fazlur Rahman's Jamiat Ulema-e-Islam (F) have campaigned against them in the name of democracy. Secondly, the Pakistan state's long-term patronage of the religious establishment and of militant proxies has cumulatively limited the social as well as the political space for the expression of liberal and plural ideas. A social environment has emerged in parts of Pakistan that is hostile to attempts by civil society groups and political parties to address human rights issues facing religious minorities and women. Thirdly, since 1949, when the Public and Representative Office Disqualification Act (PRODA) came into existence, accountability relating to corruption and misuse of office has been open to political manipulation. Musharraf after his 1999 coup introduced tougher accountability processes that created a parallel corruption law system in the National Accountability Bureau (NAB). The Chairman has the power to hold the accused in investigative custody for 90 days (compared with 14 days under the ordinary laws), strip them of the right to bail and try them in a special court with a revised burden of proof and much tougher sentences than a provincial court would impose. Since 2018 NAB has become increasingly controversial as its investigations appear to be undermining leading opponents of Imran Khan. At the same time, it appears reluctant to investigate cases of those who are close to him.

The chapter focuses on the state's limitation of freedom of association and expression. But social pressure to conform to ideal Islamic norms reinforces autocratization trends. One example is the hostility, both on- and off-line, to the recent marches to celebrate International Women's Day that have been organized by the Aurat civil society organization. Others which lie beyond the scope of this study involve the restrictions on the Ahmadi community's freedom of religious expression, the barriers to reform of the Blasphemy Ordinance which has been used maliciously against the Ahmadi and Christian communities, the persistence of so-called honour killings and the suppression of female voting in parts of Khyber Pakhtunkhwa. NGOs and social movements working to address injustices in the above areas have faced both official and societal restrictions.

In sum, Pakistan's complex political and social landscape counsels against regarding any election as a breakthrough one for democratization. The high hopes vested in the youthful Benazir Bhutto's government in 1988 were quickly dashed. Conversely, autocratization is not necessarily accelerated by military rule or even by governments close to the army. The early years of the Musharraf regime (1999–2008) were, for example, marked by liberalization of the media. Military and civilian Pakistani governments alike have displayed democratizing and authoritarian tendencies. Pakistan's asymmetric social and political power relations and the entrenchment of the military are constant features regardless of regime type and the political affiliations of elected governments. This may explain why Pakistan's direction of travel either towards democratic consolidation or to autocratization is incremental. Pakistan's history provides evidence of its following trends elsewhere in South Asia, but usually more slowly and less obviously.

The media

The existence of more than 500 newspapers and periodicals in Pakistan points to a vibrant print media, despite the challenges of online competition. Both domestic and international analyses reveal a less favourable picture. The 2020 World Press Freedom index, produced by the Paris-based, *Reporters sans frontiers* (*Reporters Without Borders*), places Pakistan 145/180 countries (RSF, 2020). The drop of three places from 2019 reflects reports from within Pakistan, produced by *The Editors for Safety* and the *Council of Pakistan Newspaper Editors* that press freedom became more restricted in the lead-up to and aftermath of the July 2018 elections. Press freedom had in fact been restricted throughout the preceding decade, in the context of 'the war on terror' and ethnic insurgency in Balochistan.

Journalists' reporting was especially dangerous in Balochistan where they risked being both caught in the crossfire of insurgents and the military and of being harassed by the intelligence agencies. On 28 August 2020, the Balochistan Union of Journalists publicly observed the deaths of 45 journalists and media workers in the province since 2008 (*Dawn*, 29 August 2020). These threats have made Pakistan for some years one of the most dangerous countries for journalists to operate (Aslam, 2015). In July 2020, the outspoken journalist Matiallah Jan was kidnapped by unknown assailants in broad daylight outside the Government Girls School Islamabad. Fortunately, this was captured on CCTV footage which went viral on social media. The resulting furore led to him being released, rather than becoming one of the 'disappeared' (*Dawn*, 22 July 2020). Jan claimed that the security establishment was implicated in his abduction. Given the dangers involved, it is understandable that many journalists self-censor their work. A 2018 survey of Pakistani journalists found that 46 per cent of its respondents reported self-censoring because of fears for their safety.

The advent of the PTI Government which was on the 'same page' as the army led however to an increase in manipulation and harassment. Early in March 2020, Brad Adams, the Asia director of the *Human Rights Watch* organization, summed up the situation by declaring that, 'The space for dissent in Pakistan is shrinking fast and anyone who criticizes government actions can become a target' (*Dawn*, 14 March 2020). Media manipulation was revealed most clearly in news blackouts. There were also interruptions of the distribution of newspapers that printed anti-government and anti-military articles along with the withdrawal of government advertising. Journalists and media proprietors were arrested on anti-terrorism and accountability grounds. Finally, journalists suffered harassment from unknown assailants that were linked to the security agencies as well as to militant groups. The decades-long record of attacks, including murders being carried out with impunity, persisted with the advent of the PTI government. Seven journalists were killed in unsolved cases in 2019. In the past decade there have been sixteen unsolved murders and only three prosecutions in sixty assassinations. The Committee to Protect Journalists, an independent organization working to promote press freedom worldwide, in its 2019 Global Impunity Index ranked Pakistan as the eighth worst country for prosecuting murderers of journalists (Committee to Protect Journalists, 2019). The Ministry of Human Rights responded by introducing a draft Media Protection Bill early in 2020, but this initiative was quickly watered down by clubbing it together with other media legislation emanating from the Ministry of Information.

In the months prior to the 2018 polls, the military instigated a news blackout of the activities of the grassroots Pashtun civil roots movement, Pashtun Tahafuz Movement (PTM). It had been founded four years earlier and had demanded an investigation into extra-judicial killings in Waziristan as well as a removal of the landmines laid by the army during its operations in the tribal areas. Despite the peaceful nature of the PTM protests, the army saw the movement as a threat to its impunity. The clamp-down was justified on the grounds of national security. In January 2020, the PTM leader Manzoor Pashteen was arrested on charges of sedition. The Urdu language website of Voice of America was temporarily blocked, when it reported about the temporary detention of another leading PTM figure Mohsin Darwar who was elected to the National Assembly in 2018.

During its second year in office, the PTI government brazenly marked its displeasure at the Herald and the Jang media groups. Imran Khan publicly accused their flagship newspapers, *Dawn* and *Jang* of printing 'fake news'. In January 2020, the federal government withdrew all the advertisements which were traditionally placed in *Dawn*. This was a major economic blow for the paper which it attempted to overturn in legal cases in Sindh. Imran Khan's criticisms coincided with the army's displeasure at an interview in May 2018 between Nawaz Sharif and the paper's assistant editor Cyril Almeida (*Dawn*, 12 May 2018). The former prime minister complained about the existence of parallel governments in Pakistan and questioned the progress of the 2008 Mumbai terror attacks trial. Almeida had written extensively for *Dawn* on civil – military relations. Indeed, earlier in October 2016, he had published an insider piece which alleged rifts between the Sharif Government and the army, which the former denied.

The army's displeasure was revealed in an unofficial ban on the circulation of the paper in militarily controlled residential areas. The concerted campaign against Pakistan's oldest newspaper was also marked by protests outside its Karachi and Islamabad offices following its coverage of the November 2019 London Bridge terrorist attack. There were calls for *Dawn*'s editor to be hanged and the paper to be shut down. A crowd outside the Islamabad office chanted slogans in favour of the army's intelligence wing (Human Rights Commission of Pakistan, 2019). In January 2019, Almeida suspended his weekly column in *Dawn*.

The owner of the Jang media group was entangled in a case in which he was claimed to have illegally acquired seven acres of land, thirty-four years previously. Like political opponents of the government, Mir Shakilur Rehman faced prolonged detention without charge, while NAB probed the case in which he was referred. *Reporters Without Borders* unequivocally stated that the case was designed to intimidate the group's journalists who had been highly critical of the partisan actions of NAB (*Dawn*, 14 March 2020).

Rehman also owned Pakistan's largest private TV channel, Geo, which had fallen foul of the authorities. In the run-up to the 2018 polls, the channel was temporarily taken off air. On 1 July 2019, there was a furore involving its leading presenter Hamid Mir. Five years earlier he had been wounded by an assailant that Mir claimed had links with the security services. The broadcast of his live interview on 'Capital News' with the leading opposition politician and former President Asif Ali Zardari abruptly ended. The Pakistan Media Regulatory Authority (PEMRA) denied involvement. Hamid Mir in a BBC interview labelled Imran Khan's government as a 'civilian dictatorship' and claimed that censorship was daily increasing (BBC News, 2019a). Shortly afterwards, an interview with Maryam Nawaz Sharif, the former Prime Minister's daughter and vocal government critic, was also prematurely ended. These episodes became termed 'unannounced censorship'.

Taking TV channels off-air is not a new development of the PTI Government era. Cable operators blocked channels for example in November 2017, during the protests led by the Islamist group *Tehreek-e-Labbaik* (Mulla, 2017). There was also massive blocking of social media and content-sharing websites. Religious festivals which may provoke sectarian violence form other previous occasions when access has been blocked.

The case of the journalist Nasrullah Chaudhry can be seen, as not only an injustice to the individual, but part of a more general campaign to silence criticism of the government. In December 2019, an anti-terrorism court sentenced the veteran journalist, who worked for the Urdu daily *Nai Baat*, to five years in jail for alleged possession of banned material. This was the first case in which such a charge had been made in disregard of the need for sensitive sources for purely professional reasons. The Sindh High Court accepted this line of defence and acquitted Chaudhry (*Dawn*, 3 May 2020).

Citizen journalists and bloggers have also recently faced online restrictions and dangers. They have been threatened by mysterious individuals who it is claimed have links with the security services as well as by those connected with militant Islamic and ethnic groups. There was a spike of such cases in March 2019 in the wake of the visit of the Saudi Crown Prince Mohammad bin Salman, amidst the controversy of the murder of the journalist Jamal Khashoggi. In extreme cases, activists and investigative journalists faced assault and assassination attempts. In June 2019, the blogger and social media activist Muhammad Bilal Khan was murdered. He had been particularly vocal about the issue of enforced disappearances.

Reports released in 2019 by the Oxford Internet Institute (2019) and Freedom House (2019) painted a dismal picture of growing surveillance of the Internet and social media, and of large-scale attempts to manipulate opinion. Surveillance is assisted by the requirement that users link their internet and mobile connections to their national identity card. Cases have been brought against social media activists because of their online comments, as for example with the PMT activist Hayat Preyhel in July 2018. The PTI Government's proposals for increased regulation of online platforms were pushed back, but it revealed a commitment to closer control of content. The existing regulatory authority for online censorship has been accused of acting in a non-transparent and arbitrary manner. The increase in requests to Google to take down content further evidenced the PTI's restrictive approach. The Government sent 214 requests to Google to remove 3,125 pieces of content between July and December; 196 requests had been made in the previous six months. Taking all these key developments into consideration, Freedom House in its 2019 Report on the Net rated Pakistan as 'unfree'.

The judiciary

There is a well-established history of the judiciary lacking independence in Pakistan. Supreme Court judges from 1958 used the 'doctrine of necessity' to legitimize military coups (McGrath, 1999). The period after 2007 was however marked by judicial activism (Waseem, 2007) with growing talk of a 'clash of institutions'. There have been recent developments that could be interpreted as an attempt to undermine the judiciary's independence. Firstly, questions have been raised about the judgements that excluded Nawaz Sharif from office in advance of the 2020 polls. The continued legal pursuit of the Sharif family orchestrated by NAB has also been troubling. Maryam Nawaz Sharif early in July 2019 released a secretly recorded video that she claimed showed that her 69-years-old father had been wrongly convicted of corruption. The video revealed a conversation between Arshad Malik, the Accountability Court Islamabad Judge, and a PML-N supporter Nasir Butt. During the conversation, Malik stated that he had been blackmailed into convicting the former prime minister in the Al-Azizia Steel Mills case.

He subsequently rebutted the claim, saying that the video clip had been cut and edited and did not reflect what he said. He also said that the Sharif family had threatened him and tried to bribe him during the case. Judge Malik was suspended for misconduct. He was dismissed the service in July 2020 following a decision taken by a seven-member committee headed by the Lahore High Court Justice Muhammad Qasim Khan. This cast further doubt on the validity of Nawaz sharif's original conviction.

Another controversial case is that of Supreme Court Justice Qazi Faez Isa. President Arif Alvi accused him of misconduct over not declaring foreign assets and recommended that action be taken under Article 209 of the Constitution. His reference to the Supreme Court Judicial Council was intentionally leaked to the press. This encouraged a media campaign against Isa that tarnished his reputation and was also damaging to the prestige of the Supreme Court itself. The procedure for bringing the case against the Justice that he had 'undeclared assets' in Britain was based on flimsy grounds. Significantly, it was orchestrated by the newly formed Asset Recovery Unit (ARU) headed by Shahzad Akbar, the Special Assistant to Imran Khan on accountability. In June 2020, the Supreme Court dismissed the reference against Isa. His wife had testified that she was of independent financial means and that the properties were her own assets. The ARU's legal authorization to conduct the case was questionable. Its involvement indicated that Imran Khan was a party to the proceedings.

Justice Qazi Isa was highly regarded as an upright judge who could be a candidate for the role of Chief Justice in September 2023. He had however upset the military establishment with some notable rulings. This has led Zahid Hussain in an opinion piece to argue that the assets case was politically motivated (*Dawn*, 24 June 2020). There were two important cases in which Justice Isa had been critical of the security establishment. The first stemmed from the time in which he was a member of the Supreme Court Commission on the 2016 terrorist bombing in Quetta. The second involved the *suo motu* case into the 2017 Faizabad Dharna. Isa had shared a two-member bench with Mushir Alam, but he had individually authored the forty-three-page judgement. Just three months after it was delivered, President Ali made his accusations. Isa's judgement that the security services should be more accountable was common to both cases. This crossed a red line in public discourse.

Isa had formed a one-man judicial commission into state institutions' response to the bombing at Quetta General Hospital in which dozens had been killed on 8 August 2016. His report published four months later was highly critical of the role of Chaudhry Nisar Ali, the Minister for the Interior in the Nawaz Sharif Government. It also criticized the powerful army intelligence agency ISI's lack of transparency. 'The ISI does not have a website, address, email or telephone number', the report remarked, 'One can but commiserate with the poor citizens who may have to interact with them. If such nebulousness serves a purpose it could only be to remain aloof and unapproachable: unquestionable and unaccountable' (*The Express Tribune*, 16 December 2016).

The Justice returned to this theme in his judgement on the Faizabad Dharna. The Islamist *Tehreek-e-Labbaik* had paralyzed public life by its sit-in in Islamabad. The protests which called for the resignation of the Law Minister Zahid Hamid had been sparked by a change in the wording of the declaration related to the finality of the Prophet Muhammad enacted through the Elections Act of 2017. Controversy over the role of the military and security establishment in the protests was fuelled by video footage shot by a *Dawn* News TV reporter on his mobile phone that showed the Director-General of the Punjab Rangers Major-General Azhar Navid handing out money and encouraging protesters (BBC, 2019b).

Justice Isa's judgement provided a detailed assessment of the context for the dharna. Its sting was, firstly in the call for intelligence agencies not to exceed their mandate. This judgement was based on the large-scale interference with broadcasts that we have noted was designed to prevent coverage of the events. Secondly, Isa ruled that the Constitution emphatically prohibits members of the armed forces from engaging in any kind of political activity. 'The Government of Pakistan, the Ministry of Defence and the respective chiefs of the Army, the Navy and the Air Force are directed to initiate action against the personnel under their command who are found to have violated their oath' (*The Nation*, 10 February 2019).

Freedom of association

Autocratization has been globally associated not only with curbs on the media and the strengthening of the executive, but also limits on the freedom of association. In 2019, the Register of Trade Unions banned sixty-two labour unions in Balochistan. This action followed a judgement from the Balochistan High Court (Human Rights Commission Pakistan, *State of Human Rights in 2019*, p. 10). Labour unions are banned from mining and other activities in Balochistan, especially when the companies have non-Pakistani (i.e., Chinese) investment. From October 2015 there was also a stricter regulation of both the activities of International Non-Governmental Organizations (INGOs) and of the funding of domestic NGOs by foreign donors.

INGOs had to obtain permission from the Ministry of the Interior to be registered in Pakistan. Applications could be refused on the grounds of 'involvement in any activity inconsistent with Pakistan's interests, or contrary to Government policy'. These were sufficiently vague to enable the targeting of individuals and organizations deemed critical of government. All existing INGOs had to apply for registration. This was a cumbersome process. Only 74 out of 141 applications had been approved by 2019 (Human Rights Commission Pakistan, *State of Human Rights in 2019*, p. 225). Well-known organizations such as Action Aid and World Vision had to cease their activities in Pakistan. Registration went hand in hand with the requirement for No Objection Certificates from provincial governments to start relief work in specific geographical areas. Local NGOs were also restricted. They could only obtain foreign funding after a successful application for a Memorandum of Understanding with the Pakistan Government's Economic Affairs Division.

The restrictions were most marked in the tribal areas where the Pakistan army was conducting operations and in the province of Balochistan; the scene of a long running insurgency that was becoming increasingly strategically important as a result of the Chinese–Pakistan Economic Corridor (CPEC). Throughout Pakistan, however, NGO work on human rights issues is discouraged. There is scrutiny and what amounts to harassment even of those NGOs working in less contentious areas such as health and education. 'Intelligence personnel regularly visit offices and demand to see documents on staff and ongoing projects (Human Rights Commission Pakistan, *State of Human Rights in*, p. 181). Western diplomats as well as aid workers have criticized the restrictions. In December 2019, the Sindh Provincial Government cancelled the registration of over 7,000 NGOs (70 per cent of the total number) on the grounds that they had not shared their financial records (Human Rights Commission Pakistan, *State of Human Rights in 2019*, p. 92). The Covid-19 crisis, however, severely impacted on Pakistan's fragile public health provision. In late March 2020, Imran Khan's government eased for six months restrictions on NGOs and INGOs that sought to respond to the developing crisis.

The authorities have not just targeted NGOs that focus on human rights issues. Environmentalist groups have also been harassed. Their activities not only threaten vested interests with respect to land grabs, but they are viewed as 'anti-state' if they criticize activities associated with CPEC. This project is important to the military on strategic as well as economic grounds. The road building and power projects associated with CPEC have contributed respectively to deforestation in Khyber Pakhtunkhwa and pollution in the Thar desert area of Sindh. In 2016–17, 'The Friends of Thar' mobilized support in a campaign about the environmental impact of coal mining in the Gorano area of the desert. The authorities' response paralleled that towards the PTM. National press coverage was discouraged, although the Sindhi print and electronic media reported on the movement. Activists were charged before anti-terrorist courts, whilst others received threatening phone calls (Sibt-ul Hassan Turi, Usman Ashraf, 2018).

Conclusion

Even before the Covid-19 pandemic threatened Pakistan's fragile economy, it was clear that reality would not match up to the rhetoric of a Naya Pakistan. Increasingly technocrats, linked with previous military regimes, supplanted party loyalists in Imran Khan's inner circles. The 2018 election itself had seen some 'electables' replace long-time PTI members as party candidates. There was a dissipation of the tension in civil–military relations which had marked the third Nawaz Sharif government. However, this was not the result of further democratic consolidation, but rather because of the similarity of government and military viewpoints. This did not end speculation about a change of leadership, at the mid-term of the Imran Khan government. Despite his portrayal as the 'army's man', he remained under scrutiny with respect to poor governance and economic competence. Pakistan's political stability was no more guaranteed than at any previous time.

If there was little sign of democratization, what about autocratization? Here, there is evidence that space for freedom of expression was becoming more restricted. This was not as dramatic a trend as in other South Asian countries which had traditionally enjoyed greater freedoms than Pakistan. Freedom of association was also restricted, although political curbs on the activities of NGOs and social movements such as PTM predated Imran Khan's government. Societal pressures on those advocating minority rights were also the result of well-established trends. Contemporary developments thus consolidate pre-existing restrictions, injustices, and uneven power relations. Pakistan, for all its lack of freedom, thus provides incremental rather than dramatic evidence for a newly emerging third wave of autocratization in South Asia.

Bibliography

Adeney, Katharine, (2017), 'How to Understand Pakistan's Hybrid Regime: the importance of a multi-dimensional continuum', *Democratization*, vol. 24, no. 1, pp.119–37.

Afzal, Madhika, (2018), 'A Volatile Election Season in Pakistan', *Brookings*, Friday July 20.

Aslam, Rukhsana, (2015), 'Media, Politics and the Threats to Journalists in Pakistan', *Pacific Journalism Review*, vol. 21, no. 1, pp.177–94.

BBC News, (2019a), 'Pakistan Censorship: "Hovering above the Mute Button"', 28 July by Secunder Kermani. Available at www.bbc.co.uk/news/world-asia-49088653/ Accessed: 4 July 2020.

BBC News, (2019b), 'Why was Pakistani General Giving Money to Protestors?' 29 November by M. Ilyas Khan. Available at www.bbc.co.uk/news/world-asia-42149535/ Accessed: 4 July 2020.

Bermeo, Nancy, (2015), 'On democratic Backsliding', *Journal of Democracy*, vol. 27, no. 1, pp.5–19.

The Committee to Protect Journalists, 2019, cjp.org/reports/2019/10/getting-away-with-murder-killed-justice Accessed: 1 July 2020.

Diamond, Larry, (2015), 'Facing Up to Democratic Recession', *Journal of Democracy*, vol. 26, no. 1, pp.141–55.

European Union Election Observation Mission, (2013), Pakistan, Final Report General Elections, 11 May 2013. www.eods.eu/library/EUEOM%20FR%PAKISTAN%2010.07.2013_en.pdf Accessed: 1 March 2021.

European Union Election Observation Mission, (2018), Pakistan, Final Report General Elections, 25 July 2018. www.eods.eu/library/final_report_pakistan_2018_english.pdf Accessed: 2 March 2021.

Freedom House, (2019), Pakistan Freedom in the Net 2019. Available at www.freedomhouse.org/country/pakistan/2019/ Accessed: 2 July 2020.

Haqqani, Husain, (2005), *Pakistan: Between Mosque and Military*, Washington: Carnegie Endowment for International Peace.

Human Rights Commission of Pakistan, (2019) hrcp.web.org/hrcpub/wp-content/uploads/2020/04/KEY-ISSUES_State-of-Human-Rights-in-2019-20190503.pdf (page 11).

Kiessling, Hein, (2016), *Faith, Unity, Discipline: The Inter-Service-Intelligence (ISI) of Pakistan*, London: Hurst.

Lieven, Anatol, (2011), *Pakistan: A Hard Country*, London: Allen Lane.

McGrath, Allen, (1999), *The Destruction of Pakistan's Democracy*, Karachi: Oxford University Press.

Lührmann, Anna, and Staffan I. Lindberg, (2019), "A third wave of autocratization is here: what is new about it?", *Democratization*, vol. 26, no. 7, pp.1095–113.

Mulla, Ayesha, (2017), 'Broadcasting the Dharna: Mediating "Contained!" Populism in Contemporary Pakistan', *International Journal of Communication*, vol. 11, pp.4181–96.

Oxford Internet Institute, (2019), 'Use of Social media to Manipulate Public Opinion', Available at www.oci.ox.ac.uk/news/releases/use-of-social-media-to-manipulate-public-opinion-now-a-global-problem-says-new-report/ Accessed: 2 July 2020.

Reporters Without Borders, (2020), 'Pakistan Press Freedom Ranking', Available at www.rsf.org/en/ranking_table/ Accessed: 1 July 2020.

Shah, Aquil, (2014), 'Constraining Consolidation: Military Politics and Democracy in Pakistan (2007–2013), *Democratization,* vol. 21, no. 6, pp.1007–33.

Swami, Praveen, (2007), *India, Pakistan and the Secret Jihad: The Covert War in Kashmir, 1947–2004*, London: Routledge.

Talbot, Ian, (2002), 'Does the Army Shape Pakistan's Foreign Policy?' in Christophe Jaffrelot (ed.) *Pakistan: Nationalism without a Nation?* London: Zed, pp.311–37.

Talbot, Ian, (2005), *Pakistan: A Modern History*, London: Palgrave Macmillan.

Talbot, Ian, (2012), *Pakistan: A New History*, London: Hurst.

Turi, Sibt-ul Hassan, Usman Ashraf, (2018), 'Thar Coal Mining Project: The Oppression of Indigenous Hindu Community', *Ecologia Politica,* vol. 55, no. 1. Available at www.ecologiapolitica.info/?p=10762/ Accessed: 6 July 2020.

Waseem, Mohammad, (2007), 'Islam and the West: A Perspective from Pakistan' in James L. Peacock, M. Thornton and Patrick B. Inman (eds.) *Identity Matters: Ethnic and Sectarian Conflict*, New York: Berghahn Books, pp.190–205.

Waseem, Mohammad, (2007), 'Judging Democracy in Pakistan: Conflict between the Executive and the Judiciary', *Contemporary South Asia*, vol. 20, no. 1, pp.19–31.

13

RELIGIOUS CLIENTELISM AND DEMOCRATIC CHOICE

Clients of God

Aiysha Varraich

Introduction

One man, one vote is a central tenet of democracy. This, however, is regularly displaced in the context of developing democracies where various forms of inequalities permeate. The Indian Subcontinent is no exception. There are a number of power structures present in the region including but not limited to feudalism and clientelism. The former remains the perennial power structure undergirding much of the analyses of the democratic consolidation, or lack thereof, of Pakistan (Wilder 1997, Mohmand 2019). The latter, clientelism, is the main explanation that directly displaces the one man, one vote tenet and, as such, has the potential to not only hinder the democratic consolidation of developing countries, but also to contribute to democratic backsliding, that is, the autocratization of young democracies.

Much of the political science literature that examines vote choice in South Asia forwards the contemporary understanding of clientelism as a central explanation of voting behaviour, where clients sell their votes in exchange for a material good to the highest bidder (Kitschelt and Wilkinson 2007, Chandra 2007, Mohmand 2019). Effectively, citizens of the region are viewed through a marketized lens, where a cost–benefit analysis dominates as an explanation for their vote choice. What remains largely absent from the contemporary political science scholarship is a theory of clientelism that can explain why client-voters may be swayed by non-material incentives in casting their vote – that is, an understanding that goes beyond the economic lens of the material exchange, where instead what is witnessed is clientelism as politics, or a "total exchange" that is "at once economic, political, ritual and moral" (Piliavsky 2014: 11). This absence risks overlooking the role played by context and social identities that go beyond a quid pro quo understanding of the voter.

One such 'total exchange' is the power structure that permeates much of the rural expanse of Pakistan – the *pir-murid* relationship. Pir is the local term for living saints – the same term is used across the local languages. Murid is the term used for disciples/followers of pirs. Here the exchange takes place between voters and politicians both of whom play dual roles: patrons are both politician and living saint (*pir*) and clients are both voters and followers (*murids*) of these *pirs*. The exchange centres on non-material incentives, where voters cast their votes

DOI: 10.4324/9781003042211-16

for their saint-politicians in exchange for salvation. Unlike the marketized model of clientelism, *religious clientelism* allows the inclusion of context and social identities of the citizens as part of their calculus in casting their vote. This allows for a more holistic understanding of the *murid*-voter. It is important to note that material goods are also included in this calculus, but a *preference* and prioritization is given to non-material, religious goods, such as blessings, spiritual guidance and the ultimate – salvation. *Pir*-politicians have long formed part of the Pakistani political elite, with much attention devoted to their role as brokers able to deliver the vote (Talbot 2005, Wilder 1999, Gilmartin 1979, Malik and Malik 2017). Today, 16% of Pakistan's National Assembly are *pir*-politicians, with similar numbers, if not more, in the Provincial Assemblies. Despite this constant and growing presence of *pir*-politicians over the past seven decades, there remains a dearth of research on the actors that vote for them, specifically what drives the *murid*-client, and the role that this spiritual relationship plays in their political behaviour.

The purpose of this chapter is twofold. First it seeks to present a subtype of clientelism that takes into account *non-material* exchanges between patrons and clients, activated through the inclusion of the actors' social identity provided by religion. This can help further our understanding of how clientelism operates on the ground, and to provide a more nuanced and holistic analysis of the client-voter. Second, to examine how some functional aspects of this relationship, at the individual level, appear to hinder the self-determination of *murid*-voters when casting their votes. Because this effectively displaces the one man, one vote concept undergirding a core tenet of electoral democracy. This results in moving developing countries away from democratic consolidation and closer to authoritarianism.

I argue that in religious clientelism, religion as a social identity operates at two levels simultaneously – collective and individual. At the collective level, religion provides a social group identity to clients through which they relate to others in their spiritual community as well as their overall social life. As such the individual belongs to a community of likeminded people, all bound by the spiritual connection to a common leader and congregation – where the connection to the spiritual leader remains centre stage. At the individual level religion serves as belief system. By this I mean a private sphere through which the individual situates himself in relation to society, and makes sense of the world, but also relates to the supernatural, addressing questions pertaining to life after death, the meanings associated with different aspects of life and the like. It is this dual function of religion as both social identity and belief system in one that enables *non-material* goods to be part of the reciprocal exchange between client and patron. At the collective level it delivers the vote. At the individual level it allows for *individualized*, personal, private, non-material religious goods of salvation, spiritual guidance and blessings. I then explore how key aspects of this relationship may stymie the self-determination of *murid*-voters when casting their votes.

I draw on data that I have gathered through extensive fieldwork across Pakistan's Sindh and Punjab provinces (September–December 2015, and April–May 2019). This includes in-depth interviews with thirty-seven *murids*, twelve *pir*-politicians, and participant observation. I further draw on a database I created of *pir*-politicians across time in both national and provincial assemblies as well as secondary sources. The overarching contribution of the chapter is that it provides insights from the client-side of the relationship. Specifically, on a theoretical level, the chapter uses clientelism as a framework to analyze a religio-political bond, highlighting the importance of non-material aspects of the clientelistic relationship that can undermine how citizens vote. It is firmly grounded in original empirical data, reflective of how clientelism works on the ground, resulting in a theory derived through an inductive process accounting for the interplay of both social and political identities simultaneously in the analysis of citizens' voting behaviour.

At the empirical level, although *pir*-politicians and the power they wield has been the subject of much investigation (Ansari 1992, Talbot 2005, Wilder 1997, Malik and Mirza 2015), to my knowledge this is the first study to provide fine-grained, micro data on the *murid*-voter's preferences and how this relationship affects their voting decisions.

The remainder of the chapter is as follows: I first define clientelism, followed by a sketch of the five core elements of religious clientelism. I detail the actors, their resource base, affective ties of the relationship, its iterative nature and the presence of trust. The second part presents an analysis of key aspects of the relationship that can undermine a client-voter's self-determination. The chapter concludes with a discussion focused on whether this type of face-to-face clientelism is yet another factor contributing to the autocratization of Pakistan, or if it can help its democratic consolidation.

Delineating religious clientelism

Before sketching out religious clientelism, it is necessary to define the term. Clientelism is founded on the reciprocal relations between patrons and clients. By clientelism I mean a form of *personal, dyadic* exchange relationship often rooted in obligation between two parties of *unequal power* (whether this power be social, political, economic or religious), where the interchange is often of *non-comparable* goods and services. I have adapted James Scott's comparative framework to sketch out the five core characteristics of religious clientelism – (1) a dyadic relationship centred chiefly on a non-material exchange; (2) the resource base of the actors is personal; (3) the relationship is highly affective; (4) it is iterative; (5) the basis of religion fosters both trust and loyalty and finally the relationship is not purely of a quid pro quo nature (1972: 106).

First, religious clientelism is a dyadic relationship centred on two primary actors – the *pir*-politician (patron) and *murid*-voter (client). The *murid* swears allegiance to the *pir*-politician from whom he seeks spiritual enlightenment, and the ultimate, salvation – initiating a lifelong bond. This pledge reinforces the asymmetric character of the relationship, with the client in an inferior spiritual position to the *pir*-politician. The relationship centres on the iterative, and reciprocal, face-to-face interaction – cementing the personalized bond between the two actors. Typically, within larger clientelistic set-ups there may be a third actor involved, a broker, such as the *khalifa*, who acts as a representative of the *pir*-politician, found in the rural settings of Pakistan. Usually, a broker can play the role of patron too; however, I do not treat him as a patron in his own right because the *khalifa* normally has sworn allegiance to the *pir*-politician. More importantly he does not have access to either religious or political power. Effectively, the *khalifa* maintains no access to the goods that form part of the exchange relationship.

The patron is a *pir* (living saint) and a politician; he has both religious and socio-economic power. In the context of Pakistan, society is highly stratified, where people who exercise political power tend to belong to a higher socio-economic stratum, in terms of access and assets. Echoing this, most *pir*-politicians are also landlords in their own right – giving them immense social standing and large embedded networks (Ansari 1992). One apt example is the current Foreign Minister Makhdoom Shah Mehmood Querishi. He is considered a living saint because of his position as the spiritual head of the shrine of Baha'uddin Zakariya. He is also, according to the electoral register, a landlord in his own right. Another example is former Prime Minister Syed Yousaf Reza Gilani. He is the head of the shrine of Musa Pak, and has large landholdings, while serving as an active politician within the Pakistan People's Party. In effect, both are landlords, spiritual leaders and politicians.

The client in religious clientelism, *murid,* is a follower of a *pir*-politician and can be from a variety of socio-economic backgrounds; ranging from landlord (with access and ownership to land, contact networks, etc.), senior civil servant, middle-class banker, to the poor farmer that needs to work every day to put food on the table. Different permutations of these characteristics of the *murid* dictate the function that the clientelistic bond of *pir-murid* plays for them. For the poorer *murid,* the relationship functions as a coping mechanism – socially he or she may depend on his patron for access to the state machinery, including arbitration in land matters. On the religious plane the bond may help make sense of the material world, with the knowledge that this relationship provides access to salvation. For the *murid* who is a landlord, with hundreds of acres of land, the bond of *pir-murid* acts as an added layer of insurance. One example being mediation in cases of land squatting. This relationship creates expectations because both actors operate in an environment that reacts to the other.

Second, both actors' resource base is personal. This resource base ties in directly with the actions available to each actor. The *pir*-politician has a number of goods to offer their clients, which form part of his *ruhani* (spiritual) and *dunyawi* (worldly) duties towards the clients; both non-material and material goods. The religious non-material inducements that the *pir*-politician offers the *murid* are tied in with his personhood. Only someone descending from a lineage of *pirs* dating back to the original saint, is able to offer this. This legitimation factor functions as a barrier to entry for other politicians. The non-material religious inducements include but are not limited to spiritual guidance, making religion accessible and the promise of salvation. These are done by delivering sermons that highlight the access he provides to the other worldly – in the form of providing a condensed, easy access to day-to-day religion – such as reminders of what is sufficient as part of being a good believer. Other non-material goods include social wellbeing (including social standing, social identity as well as belonging), access (government office or to business/personal networks) and foremost impartial arbitration (in matters of land squatting, stealing of property, marriage breakdown, to name a few). The patron offers these through constant communication with his congregation via various nodes available to him. These include annual *urs* (death anniversary of the original saint), annual visits the *pir*-politician pays to his followers and on a regular basis through the extensive network of *khalifas.* This provision reinforces the *pir*-politician's social power (social standing as impartial arbitrator) and political power (through the *murid*'s political activity including votes). The material goods, normally provided as part of the *pir*'s worldly duties towards his *murids,* include building of schools, roads and getting jobs for the clients (whether in government or otherwise).

The *murid*'s resource base is also largely personal. The *murid* has a number of goods to offer the patron, including but not limited to allegiance, loyalty (religious, political and social), offerings (ranging from tithes, to land deeds, monetary donations), investment of time, and political support (this can range from showing up at political rallies, to casting their vote). The *murid* avails these non-material goods offered by the *pir*-politician through his position as a client, that is, through membership of the congregation. It is not an *active* good that is being exchanged, but one that requires investment of time and constant communication with the entirety of the informal institution associated with the *pir*-politician (the shrine, congregation, *khalifa* network). Importantly a client's access to non-material goods can only be removed if the client were to leave the relationship. Furthermore, the actors relate to each other on two levels, both religious and political, where both have duties towards each other, creating expectations, where there is a complex overlap of religious and social identities. It is crucial to point out that only if one's patron is running for office or has categorically expressed a political leaning towards a candidate, is the vote perceived as part of one's sworn spiritual allegiance, with the expectation of the *murid* is voting for their saint.

Third, the relationship is highly affective. Scott's framework is helpful here, which assesses the strength of a clientelistic bond in relation to how many linkages patron and client share. Many link reinforce the bond, resulting in a stronger bond, whereas fewer links between the actors are associated with a weaker bond (1972). In case of the *pir-murid*, the actors share multiple links, all in different spheres of life – social, political and religious. Each link reinforces the other. Some scholars argue the possibility of differentiating between these linkages being limited to the analytical level, where differentiation in practice is of little importance. One example is Jeremy Boissevain's study of Sicily, where patronage, friendship and kinship reinforce each other and exist as an amalgamation (1966: 29). I agree to a certain extent, where the linkages in practice indeed do exist as an amalgamation. However, I argue for a practical differentiation between the bonds of the *pir-murid*, because the religious bond appears to be driving the social and political linkages, and as such constitutes a differentiation both empirically and theoretically.

Fourth, the relationship is iterative. There is regular interaction between the actors. On a daily basis there is social interaction between *murids* of the same congregation, the *khalifa* of the *pir*-politician, and at least once-a-year interaction with the *pir* himself during the annual *urs* (death anniversary) at the *pir's* associated shrine. These face-to-face interactions with the entire system of religious clientelism are in stark contrast to today's vote-buying literature where interaction is limited to only election time (Mohmand 2011, Hicken 2011, Stokes et. al 2013).

Finally, in conjunction with these four attributes outlined above, religion as the basis of clientelism reinforces aspects of trust (Hosking 2014: 46) and loyalty. This is exercised at different levels and degrees. At the interpersonal level, the *murid* shares strong thick trust between himself and the *pir*-politician, where *murids* have committed valued resources (such as the oath of allegiance, tithes, investment of time and their vote) (Granovetter 1973). At the individual level, the *pir* serves as an authoritative figure, to whom *murids* look up as spiritual guide and intercessor, and in general, trust them more than ordinary human beings (Hosking 2014: 38). At the collective level, the myths associated with the *pir*-politician provide a narrative framework for trust. This trust, between patron and client, is reinforced by the iterative and reciprocal exchanges between both actors. Finally, at the institutional level the *murid* has trust in the shrine and the congregation – that is, generalized trust. This is a strong thin trust based not on knowing someone personally but is "based on first-hand knowledge of how society generally works". One example is the knowledge of what streets are safe to walk at night in the city one resides in, or what Bronislaw Malinowksi calls 'auto-pilot' trust which is based on one's cumulative experiences with said institution (Newton 2007).

Hindering self-determination?

Now that we have outlined and described the core characteristics of religious clientelism, we home in on the functional aspects of religious clientelism relationship which have the potential to subvert the political self-determination of the *murid*-voter's vote choice. For analytical purposes we divide these into three separate categories: (a) voting as a religious duty, (b) inability to change *pir*, and relatedly, (c) social sanctioning. It is important to note that in practice these three aspects are not entirely separable. In fact, they overlap considerably and operate in symbiosis in the process of the *murid* selecting how to cast their ballot.

Voting as a religious duty

The first functional aspect of the relationship that poses a potential threat to the self-determination of the *murid*-voter is when voting is understood as a religious duty. Most voters cast their vote for the *pir* as part of the expectations that exist between the actors. In this case what the *murids* believe is expected of them. As one disciple of the late politician and spiritual leader Amin Fahim puts it, "*Voting for Sain Sahib is not only our duty but it is also an expression of our love for him*" (interview, Karachi, November 2015). Although the act of voting is understood as a religious duty, this is not necessarily an active order from the *pir* – instead it appears to form part of the overall expectations held by both actors. The below quote highlights this expectation versus direct orders from the *pir*, where an explicit order would seal their choice in favour of the *pir*.

> Yes, I vote for him…He never tells us to, but if he were to tell us his opinions then we would be bound to do so…That is what a murid is, we are his disciples.
>
> *(Interview, Hala, November 2015)*

There is a mixed picture about whether or not direct orders coming from the *pir*-politician is the main modus operandi, indicated by a large majority pointing out "*We vote for whatever political party that the Sain [his Honour] tells us*", there seems to be a communication network at work, where "lists" are provided to the congregation through the *pir*'s substantial *khalifa* network. That voting is viewed as a religious duty is further reinforced by *murids* voting across party lines when their *pir*-politician switches party – across the political ideological left–right spectrum. One such example is the current Foreign Minister Shah Mehmood Querishi, who previously was with the left of centre Pakistan People's Party (PPP), and currently is part of the right of centre Pakistan Tehreek-e-Insaaf (PTI). One *murid* puts it bluntly, detailing *where* their political allegiance stems from and why they vote in a certain way.

> Our relationship is with Sain [His Honour], not with the party and not with anyone else. Listen, what is more important – this politics business or our faith? Imaan [faith] will be useful here and 'there' (pointing up to the sky, indicating heaven and afterlife).
>
> *(Interview, Multan, November 2015)*

The quote also highlights the religio-clientelistic relationship as the driving force behind the political choices of these voters, where the personal bond supersedes the one with the institution of the party. Another aspect of voting that could limit the *murid* from voting for their *pir* is a practical one. Whether or not one can cast a vote for a candidate depends on where one is registered to vote. Simply put, If one is registered in the same constituency from which the *pir*-politician is contesting office. In effect, this duty could practically be limited to the bounds of a constituency. How do *murid*-voters support their spiritual leaders through their vote if they cannot cast a direct vote for them? One *murid* explains the process in detail.

> We vote for whatever political party that the Sain tells us, but **normally** we just vote for the person that is part of the **list.** Take my example, I can't technically vote for Sain because I belong to Sindh [his pir was running from Punjab]. In this situation I just vote for the candidate who belongs to Sain's party in our area.
>
> *(Interview, Multan, November 2015)*

This strategy, to vote for candidates via a list provided, or in the absence of such a list, for the political party that the *pir*-politician belongs to, appears to be a general trend among *murids* across the congregations, whether they belong to the congregations of Syed Yousaf Raza Gillani, Makhdoom Shah Mehmood Querishi or the followers of Makhdoom Jamil-uz-Zaman. Voting is understood by *murid*-voters to be a religious duty, and is accommodated and adjusted according to the knowledge at hand – specific (lists) or general (voting for the political party).

No exit?

The second, and perhaps more important aspect that may hinder *murids'* exercise of choice is that one cannot change their *pir*. As elaborated earlier, when entering this religio–clientelistic bond, the *murid* takes an oath of allegiance – this entails exclusive submission to one spiritual leader (Ewing 1983). Furthermore, many times, the choice of *pir* is a matter of tradition, that is, swearing allegiance to the same *pir* that one's fathers and forefathers did. This aspect of tradition in combination with the oath of allegiance can make the idea of changing a *pir* seem implausible. When asked if one can change their *pir*, one *murid* was dumbstruck, and responded

> …this is a very strange question, it's like asking if I can change my religious sect – becoming Shia from Sunni, or vice versa. We cannot change our sect, can we? So, in the same way, no you cannot change your pir. This is a matter of one's beliefs.
>
> *(Interview, Multan, October 2015)*

This highlights a loyalty that exists between both actors. It prevents them from choosing a patron in accordance with the best offer. This is in contrast to the contemporary understanding of the client, where clients are assumed to be able to go 'patron shopping', where the vote is used as a bargaining chip by clients with potential patrons, which the patron needs in order to gain political office. Effectively clients exchange their vote for the best material inducement offered, or in the words of Herbert Kitschelt and Steven Wilkinson, a situation in which clients are "willing to surrender their vote for the right price" (2007: 2). This is not the case for the *murid*-voter.

Furthermore, because the religious linkage supersedes the political one, for *murids* the vote does not translate to a bargaining chip when dealing with their *pirs*. In fact, for the *murid* to switch patrons comes with extreme social costs because of the sworn allegiance to the *pir* as spiritual leader. To borrow Anna Grzymala-Busse's phrase, religion as an identity is not fungible, you cannot leave without incurring a disproportionate social cost and the psychological burden of damnation (2012). The fear of damnation is best illustrated through the interview extract, where a *murid* confronted his *pir* and challenged his ability to provide spiritual advice because he himself was not following the advice he gave his followers.

CLIENT: "Why should I listen to you? You yourself are not doing those things that you tell us to do. In fact, you are indulging in things that you yourself say are not permitted for us [the pir-politician is widely known to be an alcoholic]. How can you then be a spiritual advisor?"

PATRON: "Let us light a fire here." [They light a small bonfire. The pir tells the murid to bring some water, and as there is no fresh water around, he tells him to fetch some from the nearby open sewer and throw it on the fire. The client did as he was told; he threw the pail of sewage onto the fire, and the fire went out.] The pir turned to the client and said "You see what just happened here? No matter how dirty I am, at the end of the day, I am still the one that will save you from the fires of hell and provide you salvation in the afterlife."

(*Interview, Karachi, November 2015*)

The underlying role of this relationship as an inherent part of the *murid*'s social identity also begins to surface and provides better insight into why an exit from the relationship is more complicated than just opting out. The oath of allegiance, and tradition together with "this is part of who we are" (interview, Hala, November, 2015), makes for a layered relationship that serves not only one's religious inclinations but also social ones. It helps us understand how social sanctioning is part of the active considerations the client operates with.

Social sanctioning

The third aspect of the relationship that may potentially stymie the *murid*'s self-determination via the vote, is social sanctioning. As the above sections show the relationship itself is inherently a socio-religious identity that forms part of the *murid*'s day-to-day existence. The clients have a choice to vote or not to vote for the patron. If they vote – they are guaranteed to receive the non-material goods (the promise of salvation, religious guidance, social wellbeing). If they choose not to vote for the patron there is a high social cost to pay; they lose insurance of salvation, religious guidance but more so, their social wellbeing/reputation is affected in an adverse manner. Because of religious clientelism operating at the collective and individual levels at once, not to cast a vote in favour of one's *pir* can be viewed as betraying the entire congregation. In a conservative society like Pakistan, reputation and "face/honour" can be the highest thing an individual possesses; therefore, this plays an imperative role in how other members of society perceive and react to one. Social standing not only affects the day-to-day quality of life but also is a major aspect of how one operates in various aspects of society. Therefore, social sanctioning in the form of social ostracism can result in isolation of not only the individual but also the individual's family, revoking an imperative part of social identity and belonging. As such, the client is not only reacting to the goods provided to him by the patron but also reacting to the fellow *murids* of the congregation that are to be found in his surroundings.

The far-reaching effects of social sanctioning are best underscored by the example of exclusion of a well-to-do *murid*. He is a local landlord who belongs to the elite of the country, both asset- and access-rich (he obtained his post-graduate degree in the USA, and currently manages 5,000 acres of land of his own) but also has his own vast contact network across the country, with family members active politicians at the national level. His family was excluded from their congregation for displeasing the *pir* and had their "hands tied". In effect, he was ousted from the congregation and the status of *murid* revoked through public announcement. Within the community word quickly spread of a social boycott against not only the offending individual but also the members of their immediate family. Members of the community stopped communicating with them, refused to intervene to provide any form of help, and also removed themselves from any public association with the former *murid*. This resulted in a social boycott and ostracization, where any work the client tried to perform in this context was limited to their own devices. In close-knit communities, social boycotts can spell doom for an individual actor, where even the well-off client will be subjected to the same demands and expectations as any other client – that is, both implicit and explicit expectations between client and patron. As such, revoking this relationship, or going against one's *pir*, may come with extreme social costs, where at the collective level it functions as a collective identity that provides social standing, protection of the patron and an added layer of insurance – especially in the case of conflict (such as land squatting issues). As one former superintendent of police (SP) of Sindh detailed "this is especially so in areas in which the state is lacking in the provision of the public good of law enforcement, and where even the local superintendent police officer has been appointed through the consent of the local *pir*, whether or not they are active politicians" (interview, Karachi, April 2019).

Discussion and conclusion

The empirical analysis above clarifies two important points. First, it highlights the important role of non-material considerations in a *murid*-voter's decision-making process of casting a vote. These considerations are overwhelmingly tied in with social aspects of the relationship, where voting is not viewed as a bargaining chip in their exchanges with their *pir*-patron. Instead one's vote is part of the expectations between the two actors, where the vote is perceived as "it's just a vote" relative to other expectations from the relationship. The social embeddedness is underscored by the sanctioning that takes place by not only the patron, but also by community members.

The second point clarified is the need to make our models more reflective of how clientelism operates on the ground. So far, the literature has attempted to forward a parsimonious model of how voters operate, where the focus has heavily been on seeing and understanding clients through an economic lens, where the clients opt for the best material inducement. This reduces the lived reality of voters to simplistic models that are not reflective of the real world these citizens operate in. The above analysis, however, clarifies that we have to make space for non-economic considerations when attempting to further our understanding of clientelism in general, but client-voters specifically. Specifically, we must pay attention to the client's various identities and the social contexts they find themselves in, thus going beyond the quid pro quo of material goods. Put simply, the inclusion of long-term bonds into our analysis shows us how the murid-voter's political behaviour is not just a result of the material exchange relationship between himself and the pir-politician, instead it is a more complex and nuanced approach that accounts for the clientelistic bond as a whole, where non-material supernatural goods also feature.

Furthermore, it underscores how clients themselves monitor their own behaviour, and thus stop themselves from taking certain actions. This specific finding addresses the overall monitoring debate of clientelism, where a general assumption held is that patrons monitor clients' actions and sanction them if they renege on their end of the bargain, despite scant evidence in support of this assumption (Hicken and Nathan 2020). In this case, self-monitoring as portrayed by my empirical findings can help address this evidentiary gap.

Finally, the importance of this type of clientelism and its effect on a country's democratic trajectory is highlighted in developing contexts such as Pakistan, where political parties do not operate as programmatic ones; instead politics is personalized, where voters relate to politicians through personalized linkages provided by the myriad of power relationships that they find themselves in. The importance of these linkages, especially religo-political ones, is reinforced in how these can affect the democratization or autocratization of a nation. This type of clientelism has the potential to operate in either direction – towards democratic consolidation or autocratization. In the absence of programmatic parties, one way to use this relationship towards democratic consolidation of developing democracies is to follow examples of countries such as Ghana, where tribal chiefs are legally barred from running for office. In this case if the *pir*-politician were to refrain from participation in the political arena, and actively encourage his disciples not only to participate in elections but ensure that they go to cast their vote, then the relationship could be a step in the right direction, to reinforce democratization efforts. Nevertheless, this does not negate the potential risk posed by *pirs* acting as brokers between political parties and the voters, where their lack of direct participation can be geared towards indirect influence instead. For the success of such an initiative the *pir*-politician would have to remove themselves from the political process altogether, by not encouraging any affiliations or endorsements, but only to ensure their followers partake in the electoral process by casting their vote for whomever they please. If the relationship is used in the above manner, it would help reinforce democratic consolidation.

However, if this relationship operates and hinders the choice of *murid*-voters due to the above reasons discussed, not only will the presence of such a relationship continue to stagnate the one man, one vote concept, but such ties will continue to contribute to the autocratization of nations like Pakistan. This is especially in an environment where the voters' choice of candidate is not driven by their own understanding of the political sphere; instead their decision-making is driven by loyalty factors. That said, if *murids* vote for these *pir*-politicians because they believe them to be the most suitable actors able to represent their interests in the political arena, where a blend of material and non-material exchanges continue to be swapped, then at its core it will be an exercise in choice. For that to take place though, other factors available to citizens in democratic settings must also be present – such as freedom to express oneself without repercussions, insurance of one's personal safety in day-to-day life and access to hold one's politicians accountable. Until these other factors in Pakistani politics are assured, the *pir–murid* relationship will continue to be perceived by analysts at large as one that pulls Pakistan towards autocratization.

Bibliography

Ansari, S. (1992). *Sufi Saints and State Power: The Pirs of Sind, 1843–1947* (Cambridge South Asian Studies). Cambridge: Cambridge University Press. doi: 10.1017/CBO9780511563201

Boissevain, J. (1966). Patronage in Sicily. *Man*, 1(1), new series, 18–33. doi: 10.2307/2795898

Chandra, K. (2007). Counting heads: A theory of voter and elite behavior in patronage democracies. In H. Kitschelt & S. Wilkinson (Eds.), *Patrons, Clients and Policies: Patterns of Democratic Accountability and Political Competition* (pp. 84–109). Cambridge: Cambridge University Press. doi: 10.1017/CBO9780511585869.004

Ewing, K. (1983). The Politics of Sufism: Redefining the Saints of Pakistan. *Journal of Asian Studies*, 42(2): 251–268. doi: 10.2307/2055113

Gilmartin, D. (1979). Religious Leadership and the Pakistan Movement in the Punjab. *Modern Asian Studies*, 13(3): 485–517. doi: 10.1017/S0026749X00007228

Granovetter, M. S. (1973). The Strength of Weak Ties. *American Journal of Sociology*, Vol. 79, Number 6, May 1973.

Grzymala-Busse, A. (2012). Why Comparative Politics Should Take Religion (More) Seriously. *Annual Review of Political Science*, 15: 421–442. https://doi-org.ezproxy.ub.gu.se/10.1146/annurev-polisci-033110-130442

Hicken, A. (2011). Clientelism. *Annual Review of Political Science*, 14: 289–310. https://doi-org.ezproxy.ub.gu.se/10.1146/annurev.polisci.031908.220508

Hicken, A. and Nathan, N. L. (2020). Clientelism's Red Herrings: Dead Ends and New Directions in the Study of Nonprogrammatic Politics. *Annual Review of Political Science*, 23(1): 277–294.

Hosking, G. (2014). *Trust: A History*. Oxford: Oxford University Press.

Khan Mohmand, S. (2011). *Patrons, Brothers and Landlords: Competing for the Vote in Rural Pakistan*. Doctoral dissertation. Institute of Development Studies, University of Sussex.

Khan Mohmand, S. (2019). *Crafty Oligarchs, Savvy Voters: Democracy under Inequality in Rural Pakistan*. Cambridge: Cambridge University Press (South Asia in the Social Sciences). doi: 10.1017/9781108694247

Kitschelt, H. and Wilkinson, S. I. (eds) (2007). *Patrons, Clients and Policies: Patterns of Democratic Accountability and Political Competition*. Cambridge: Cambridge University Press. doi: 10.1017/CBO9780511585869

Malik, A. and Rinchan, Mirza. (2015). Religion, Land and Politics: Shrines and Literacy in Punjab. The Pakistan Strategy Support Programme (PSSP) Working Paper no. 030.

Malik, A. and Malik, Tahir. (2017). Pirs and Politics in Punjab, 1937–2013, *Modern Asian Studies*, 51(6): 1818–1861. doi: 10.1017/S0026749X16000949

Newton, K. (2007). Social and Political Trust. In R. J. Dalton and H. D. Klingemann (Eds.) *The Oxford Handbook of Political Behaviour*. Oxford: Oxford University Press. doi: 10.1093/oxfordhb/9780199270125.003.0018

Piliavsky, A. (Ed.) (2014). *Patronage as Politics in South Asia*. Cambridge: Cambridge University Press.

Scott, J. C. (1972). Patron-Client Politics and Political Change in Southeast Asia. *American Political Science Review*, 66(1): 91–113. doi: 10.2307/1959280

Stokes, S. C., Dunning, T., Nazareno, M. and Brusco, V. (2013). *Brokers, Voters, and Clientelism: The Puzzle of Distributive Politics*. Cambridge: Cambridge University Press (Cambridge Studies in Comparative Politics). doi: 10.1017/CBO9781107324909

Talbot, I. (2010). *Pakistan: A Modern History*. Second Edition, London: Palgrave MacMillan.

Wilder, A. (1997). *The Pakistani Voter, Electoral Politics and Voting Behaviour in the Punjab*. Oxford: Oxford University Press.

14

DIGITAL AUTOCRATIZATION OF PAKISTAN

Rizvan Saeed

Introduction

The recent digital revolution has brought a new form of social organization which has been referred to as the Network Society. In the network society technological, social and media networks define linkages of individuals, groups and organizations. Pakistan is no exception to this development. The growth spurt in Pakistani social media use over the past decade indicates a shift from traditional mass society to a (digital) network society, though the volume of network society in Pakistan is quite low compared to the total population. But the transition is there, and the digital space allows faster and more information transfer along with provisions of opportunities to develop larger networks to earn more social capital. However, it is important to see how this digital world is being governed by the State and what sort of treatment is being offered to its "citizens", especially the religious minorities. This chapter explores key laws related to cyberspace in Pakistan, and how religious minorities and dissident voices are being treated in the online space.

Laws regarding cyber space in Pakistan

This section encompasses main laws related to regulation of cyber space in Pakistan. It shows that the promulgation of cyber laws followed the technological advancements in the country regardless of type or form of government.

The Government of Pakistan has promulgated various laws since 2002 to monitor digital data. The first of its kind was the "Electronic Transactions Ordinance 2002". Under its section 36, any unauthorized access to any user's data was criminalized. This law also asked for the establishment of a Certification Council under the Ministry of Information Technology and Telecom (MOITT) within 60 days of the promulgation of Ordinance 2002. Key functions of the Certification Council included granting and renewing accreditation certificates, conducting research in cryptography and preparing legislative recommendations for the protection of data and privacy of electronic subscribers.

In 2010, the "Monitoring and Reconciliation of Telephony Traffic Regulation" was passed (Pakistan Telecommunication Authority, 2010). According to new legislation every long-distance and international service provider was bound to have real-time monitoring of the

DOI: 10.4324/9781003042211-17

origin and destination of the call along with the duration of the call. The service providers were bound to keep a record of the traffic for a certain period of time.

In 2013, "The Investigation for Fair Trial Act" was promulgated, allowing officials with a judicial warrant to access electronic data of any citizen. This law was intended to protect citizens against State oppression. Any officer of the relevant law-enforcement agency has to seek a judicial warrant to arrest an alleged culprit of cybercrime. However, the Act authorizes an Investigation Officer to request a warrant even on the basis of suspicion that any citizen is 'in the process of beginning to plan' a crime under Pakistani law.

In 2014, a massive terrorist attack took place in Peshawar where hundreds of students of the Army Public School were martyred by the terrorists. In response to this heinous attack, the State prepared a 20-point National Action Plan (NAP) to fight extremism and terrorism in the country. Point 14 of the NAP directly addressed the social media. It stated that measures should be taken against abuse of the internet and social media for terrorism (Ahmed, 2016). In pursuance of this plan, the parliament passed the Pakistan Electronic Crimes Act (PECA) 2016, which addresses cybercrimes including online hate speech and violent extremism. PECA 2016 was a sincere attempt to make digital spaces safer. However, this law has three problems. First, the reason quoted by the State to promulgate the law is to ensure national security, not the digital users' online safety. Second, the law gives powers to the State to monitor the online activities of any digital user in real time. This aspect becomes crucial for the digital rights of the users because there is not any law in the country that provides data protection and privacy rights to digital users. In the absence of any such constitutional protection, exploitation of personal data by the State institutions cannot be overlooked. In addition, the lack of privacy and data protection makes the users vulnerable and susceptible to data theft and misuse. Third, there is ambiguity in the definition of certain terms in the law. For instance, Section 10A of the PECA states, "Whoever prepares or disseminates information. through any information system or device that advances or is likely to advance inter-faith, sectarian or racial hatred, shall be punished with imprisonment for a term which may extend to seven years or with fine or with both." This section mentions the groups against which hate speech may be used, but it does not define what constitutes "hate speech"? This is the case with other terms like "public order" and "national security" used in the law. This ambiguity may put digital users at greater risk of State oppression, especially for the users who are human rights defenders and criticize State actions.

The control over citizens' online activities became stringent with the introduction of the "Removal and Blocking of Unlawful Online Content (Procedure, Oversight and Safeguards) Rules 2020". Again the focus of these rules was to control social media and increase the State's surveillance.

These rules were passed without consultation of relevant stakeholders. Moreover, these rules asked social media companies to share the data of any user, and to block and remove any content that the government of Pakistan asks to be removed. Under these rules the definition of "extremism" is vague and so broad that it could easily be misused by the State to suppress anyone's voice. The definition of extremism reads: " 'extremism' means the violent, vocal or active opposition to fundamental values of the State of Pakistan including the security, integrity or defence of Pakistan, public order, decency or morality, the rule of law, individual liberty and the mutual respect and tolerance of different faiths and beliefs" (Shahzad, 2020).

The presence of a nationwide monitoring system and vague definitions of national security, extremism and hate speech, coupled with the absence of public data and privacy protection laws, means the digital crimes regulatory laws are a tool in the hands of the government to silence dissenting voices and human rights defenders. Under the existing laws, the Federal Investigation

Agency has a dedicated cell to investigate electronic crimes and present a report to the parliament biannually. However, no report has been submitted to the parliament so far. Meanwhile many citizens have been arrested, vaguely accused of threatening national security and for acts described as "hate speech" (Jahangir, 2019). On the other hand, there are organized campaigns in online spaces against religious minorities, journalists and women's rights activists but no significant actions are taken against these organized troll groups. This selective implementation of the law (although the law itself is authoritarian in the absence of privacy protection to citizens) has given a message to social media users that anyone can get away with whatever he/she shares on social media as long as that user is in favour of the government.

Digital freedoms and restrictions in practice

In this section I will talk about the persecution of minorities, especially Ahmadis, in online space. Religious minorities, including Sikhs and Hindus, also faced abuse in online space, but Ahmadis are the ones who face the most abuse, hatred, threats and online harassment.

The Ahmadis

Followers of the Ahmadiya religion believe that Mirza Ghulam Ahmad was a "Subordinate Prophet" (Hashim, 2018) to the Muslims' last Prophet. They were considered Muslims until 1974 when then parliament enacted a constitutional amendment declaring them non-Muslims. Now they are non-Muslims as per the constitution of Pakistan. Their population is roughly 5 million in Pakistan and they are the most vulnerable religious minority. Ahmadis are a persecuted minority and generally considered to be socially undesirable. Dining and doing business with Ahmadis is opposed by the majority of Muslims. Their places of worship are attacked, their households are threatened and their social exclusion is a "norm". People who hate Ahmadis proclaim two main reasons to justify their hatred. They believe that Ahmadis are the apostates and as per their interpretation of Islamic teachings, an apostate should be punished with death. Secondly, the haters claim that Ahmadis are blasphemers as they do not believe in the finality of the prophethood of the Muslims' last Prophet, Muhammad (Peace Be Upon Him).

The persecution of Ahmadis in the digital sphere

Pakistani Twitter witnesses massive abuse against religious minorities, especially Ahmadis. The last two years' Twitter data was collected against hashtags that targeted Ahmadis and it showed a surge in hatred against them in online space. Generally, any hashtag on Pakistani Twitter against a particular group (whether political or religious) would remain on top trend for a few hours but when it is against Ahmadis it remains on the top trend panel for a day or two. Moreover, the number of users engaged in the propagation of the hashtag against Ahmadis also remains higher as compared to hashtags on political or any other social issues. On average, an organic hashtag on the Pakistani Twitter panel has 5,000 to 15,000 users participating, sending 5,000 to 20,000 tweets. But when it comes to the anti-Ahmadiya hashtag the number of tweets goes up to 78,000 with more than 10,000 users. This high number of users engaged in tweeting against Ahmadis indicates that general public sentiment is against Ahmadis and whenever a hashtag appears on Twitter, religiously motivated users contribute to its propagation. During the last two years, "Qadiani (the word used for Ahmadi) is the worst infidel" was propagated on Twitter multiple times with the total number of tweets exceeding 300,000. Four things were highlighted in the hashtags during the last two years: first, Ahmadis are the worst infidels and rejecting them is part of religion; second, Ahmadis are traitors; third, Ahmadis should be thrown out of government jobs; and fourth, Ahmadis should be murdered as they are blasphemers. No doubt, TLP remained on top in propagating violent hashtags against Ahmadis but supporters of other political parties and the general public also added their voices. In July 2020, an Ahmadi was murdered during his court hearing in Peshawar. His murderer, Khalid Khan, was glorified on social media and hashtags "The winner's message is 'death to blasphemer'" and "Salute to the winner Khalid's courage" were propagated on Pakistani Twitter and these hashtags remained on the top trend panel for more than two consecutive days with more than 200,000 tweets. These hashtags were not promoted solely by any single political party or religious group, but general users participated actively. This shows the level of public antipathy towards the Ahmadis. The cyber laws are meant to safeguard every citizen, but their poor or selective implementation gives space to social media users to threaten and propagate hate against minorities.

It is important to highlight that the Tehreek e Labbaik (TLP) emerged as the most prominent group who propagated the most hashtags (almost 70% of all anti-Ahmadiya hashtags) against Ahmadis. So to understand the modus operandi of online groups who promote violent extremism, I chose TLP to do further analysis.

The Tehreek e Labbaik (TLP)

The TLP Pakistan is a far-right Islamist political party that was founded by a cleric, Khadim Rizvi, in 2015. Khadim Rizvi belonged to the Barelvi sect of Islam. Traditionally this sect was considered more peaceful and polite. Its main representation was Sufism as compared to the Deobandi and Ahl e Hadith sects who aggressively propagated and were engaged in Jihad during the Afghan war in the 1980s and 1990s. After 9/11, the War on Terror started in Afghanistan and in Pakistan too. The State started "cleaning operations" against Talibans in Swat and tribal areas of Pakistan. This time the State started to patronize the Barelvi sect as its component of Sufism was effective to portray a soft image of Islam against the Taliban (Farooq, 2020). Khadim Rizvi was, however, an exception to the traditional Barelvism. He was a firebrand mullah who believed in using violence to push his agenda. He gained popularity on his support for Mumtaz Qadri who murdered the then Governor of Punjab, Salman Taseer on the charge of blasphemy. TLP built its political campaign on the blasphemy issue and got registered as a political party in 2015. They actively protested against the hanging of Mumtaz Qadri in 2016. Since then TLP has capitalized its popularity by pushing the agenda of blasphemy. In 2017, TLP staged a sit-in against PMLN on a slight change regarding declaration of finality of the prophethood in one of the annexes to Election Bill 2017 (the words "I solemnly swear" were replaced with "I believe"). The protesters had tacit support of the military establishment (Siddiqui, 2017). This support gave TLP a kind of legitimacy to push their agenda. The military establishment wanted to oust PMLN in the 2018 general elections, so to curtail the vote bank of PMLN, they supported TLP to gain visibility in public (Butt, 2017). Since TLP's sit-in in 2017, they aggressively campaigned against religious minorities, especially Ahmadis (Hashim, 2018). In 2018, they staged a huge protest against the acquittal of a Christian woman Asia Bibi who was falsely accused of blasphemy. But this time the military establishment stood with the civilian government of PTI and a crackdown was done against TLP on staging the sit-in.

Study methodology

Data against hashtags that were propagated by TLP during 2019 were collected. The Social Network Analysis (SNA) technique was used to analyze structural properties of online social networks of TLP. To analyze the text of the tweets, the content analysis technique was used. A total of 2,03,900 (figure rounded to nearest hundred) tweets from 17,200 Twitter users were collected. This data was analyzed by using SNA to see the structures of online social networks among TLP supporters.

Main findings in the social network analysis

SNA is a technique used to understand structures of networks and to see the position of a node in the given network. Node means a Twitter user. Tie means the connection a user establishes with another user by reply, mention, quote or retweet activity. For instance, if a user sends a tweet without mentioning anyone and this tweet is neither retweeted nor quoted/replied, no Tie will be established.

Network Density (ND) is another characteristic that helps to understand the pace of communication within the network. The higher the density, the faster the communication within the network. It also reflects how sparsely or densely the nodes are connected. If the density is one, it means all the users in the network are connected to every other user. A density close to one may reflect that users are working as a team and might know one another in offline space.

For the given dataset, the density of the whole network of 17,200 users was 0.001, which means that only 0.1% ties were formed out of all possible ties that could have been established in the given network. However, the analysis of the network of the top few hundred most active users revealed that there existed very strong connections. Two samples of 100 and 200 user-networks were taken to see if there existed any online relations among Twitter users. The results revealed that the network of top 100 Twitter users had a density of 0.90, meaning that 90% of all possible ties were established. This high percentage is reflective of very strong connections between the most active users. The graph density for the network of the top 200 users was 0.46, which means 46% of all possible ties were established.

Reciprocity is a measure of mutual ties. It shows a conversation or interaction is taking place between two users. For the TLP network the reciprocity was 0.039. It means roughly 4% mutual ties were established. Further analysis of edge ties shows that Retweet percentages is the highest (96%). It means out of all (100%) ties that could be "mention", "reply", "quote" or "retweet", the maximum proportion (96%) was retweets. It reflects that the users are not engaging in discussion, rather simply retweeting the exact tweet that was sent by someone. Such a high percentage (96%) of retweet shows that the hashtag is propagated inorganically by a group of people. Inorganic propagation means that organized groups in online space retweet a particular tweet multiple time. This phenomenon generates traffic on Twitter and its algorithms pick that particular tweet/hashtag and display it on the Top Trend panel. If a hashtag is propagated organically it means more people from diverse geographic locations are tweeting with that hashtag and it contains a good proportion of reply and quote tweets. It seems unnatural that 96 out of 100 users are retweeting something without even saying a word of their own. There is no exact rule what percentage of retweets makes a trend organic or inorganic; however, I have observed that on Pakistani Twitter organic trends had a less than 80% retweet ratio, generally.

There are certain characteristics of Twitter users that do not come under SNA but still can give important insights about users. For instance, Twitter issues a blue tick to users whose identities are confirmed by Twitter and they belong to categories of journalists, activists, or public figures. For the given dataset, out of 2,03,900 tweets, only three tweets were sent from a verified account. Most Twitter users from Pakistan do not have verified accounts but the absence of verified users for a whole year nevertheless hints that people with known social identities and social following did not endorse the messaging of TLP.

On Twitter, there is a common observation that most people with real accounts have more followers as compared to friends (Twitter friends are the users who are following each other). But for TLP users the number of friends was higher than the number of followers. The average number of "followers" of each user were 1,699 while the average number of "Friends" were 1,780. Most Twitter users have more followers than friends but the case was the reverse for TLP users. For a comparison, the data of users who tweeted about the women's march was looked into by the author. It was found that on average each user who tweeted with hashtag #AuratMarch had 6,222 followers and 868 friends. In Pakistan, the propagandists who work in groups, create multiple Twitter accounts and then mutually follow to increase outreach. TLP supporters used the same technique.

TLP's account opening pattern

In the given dataset, 266,261 and 755 accounts were opened in 2015, 2016 and 2017 respectively. The number of new accounts increased in 2018 where 1,927 new accounts were opened. But a massive increase occurred in 2019 when 4,478 new accounts were opened in the first three months. Out of 2,03,900 tweets that were sent in 2019 by TLP, two-thirds were sent by the accounts that were opened in 2019. This trend indicated that the latest accounts were opened with the intention of propagating TLP messages on Twitter through an organized effort.

The first massive wave of account openings occurred in January 2019. This was the time when the government did a crackdown on the TLP leadership in response to their agitation against the acquittal of Asia Bibi. The second was in August 2019. This might have been done to protest against the revocation of Article 370 in India, which concerned Kashmir's special status.

Qualitative analysis

Qualitative analysis of the collected tweets revealed that TLP supporters abused religious minorities, especially Ahmadis and the liberal voices. They labelled political opponents with titles that were reflective of their disconnect from Islam. Also, they glorified a convicted terrorists and threatened political opponents and minorities. TLP instigated violence among its followers and supporters by glorifying the terrorist acts of Mumtaz Qadri and Khalid Khan. The former murdered a governor while the latter murdered an Ahmadi in Peshawar Court where he was facing trial under blasphemy charges.

TLP propagated hashtags with words demanding the cleansing of Ahmadis. TLP followers expressed their views that Pakistan was created in the name of Islam so there was no place for blasphemers in the country. They incited violence with tweets containing messages like "any lover of the Prophet (PBUH) can get offended and kill the person who had been accused of blasphemy". "It is time to fulfil the promise made to the winner Mumtaz Qadri" (Mumtaz Qadri was convicted of the murder of Salman Taseer), "we will cut out your tongue", "Anyone with good faith should stand up and murder the blasphemer" and "expel them from the country". TLP introduced the slogan "There is only one punishment for the blasphemer, and it is beheading." Also, they propagated that if a blasphemer is apologizing, do not believe him/her. He/she is faking it. Similarly, they ran an online campaign against Sikhs claiming that TLP followers would take revenge on Sikhs. Khadim Rizvi, the leader of the TLP, said in his speech that it is time to take revenge for the Muslim women who were kidnapped by Sikhs at the time of Partition.

Modus operandi of TLP

A pattern was identified in running hashtags and mobilizing people by TLP. Based on social network analysis of the online networks along with content analysis, I identified the following three characteristics of TLP's Modus Operandi.

Everything is blasphemy

Using accusations of blasphemy remained a core strategy of TLP's campaigning, and they used it extensively in online space. A pattern can be seen in the accusations that TLP made against political opponents, especially Prime Minister Imran Khan, and the ideological opponents like liberals and supporters of non-violence. They termed every "non-desired" behaviour at the social and political level as blasphemy. For instance, Pakistan's leading English-language newspaper *Dawn* ran a story about a Pakistani-born British citizen who was involved in the London Bridge attack in 2019. The newspaper wrote that the attacker was of Pakistani origin (Rehman, 2019). This act of *Dawn* was labelled as blasphemy by TLP and a whole campaign was run on Twitter against the newspaper. TLP proclaimed that *Dawn* had digressed from the right path and should be punished for fighting against Allah and His Prophet. TLP instigated violence against the newspaper by propagating tweets like "If the State can't do [anything against *Dawn*], then send a message to Allah and the Prophet's (PBUH) personal security guards. Qadris [referring to Mumtaz Qadri who murdered Salman Taseer] would act upon it" (مُسلَّمُونَ, 2019). Similarly, on the issuing of a 50 rupee coin in the name of Sri Guru Nanak to mark his 550th birthday (Jamal, 2019), TLP declared the act as blasphemy and launched an online campaign against the government. TLP's social media supporters said "Isn't it dishonour (blasphemy) to Riasat e Madina [State of Medina]? No fear of God, no respect for the Prophet PBUH" (Adil, 2019). For them, issuing a coin in the name of any non-Muslim was equivalent to blasphemy and that should be punished. TLP turned every issue into blasphemy in an effort to keep themselves publicly relevant.

In 2019, university students organized a series of protests calling for an end to the ban on forming student unions. In 1984, the then dictator General Zia ul Haq imposed the ban. Apparently, the argument was to reduce on-campus violence, but this act damaged the very democratic fabric of society. Student unions were like nurseries where political and democratic ideas were introduced and cultivated in young minds. Decades later, students organized marches where they demanded the restoration of student unions. Women students actively took part in protests and the protesters chanted slogans citing liberal and democratic values. TLP found these student marches blasphemous and a threat to religious values. To counter student marches they propagated a hashtag – #WhenGreenWillSway (in Urdu). Under this hashtag thousands of tweets were sent, challenging and threatening the organizers and supporters of student marches. The wording of the hashtag was very symbolic. Some student protesters carried red flags, symbolizing the Left. In response, TLP threatened that when the green (symbolizing religion and TLP, as their flag colour is also green) will come to power, the Left will have no place in society. Liberal voices and human rights defenders who supported the student marches were also attacked by the TLP social media teams. Liberals, non-conservatives and leftists were labelled as "filth" that needed to be cleansed before it spreads to the whole country. Through Twitter hashtags, TLP spread a message that the cleansing of "filth" would only be possible when religion (Islam) comes into power in the country.

Creating false analogies: paving the way for blasphemy accusations

TLP created a false analogy that joining TLP is tantamount to love for the Last Prophet of Muslims and that anyone who claims to be a Muslim and lover of Muhammad (PBUH) should join TLP. Opposing TLP means the opposer hates the defenders of the honour of the Prophet Muhammad (PBUH). This messaging through social media won many supporters to TLP. Now whenever TLP runs a hashtag on blasphemy many non-TLP supporters also contribute to the hashtag, presumably because they are expressing their love for religion and the Prophet. Similarly, TLP changed the etymology of the word traitor (Ghaddar) that's in frequent use on Pakistani social media to silence dissenting voices. TLP interpreted this word as deviance from religious teachings. They said that a traitor is a person who betrays their religion by not fighting for the finality of the Last Prophet of Muslims. Summative analysis of data revealed that the word "traitor" was used 1,300 times for the person who betrays their religion and the Prophet (PBUH).

At times, the blasphemy accusations were not labelled overtly and at once. A case was built gradually by alienating the person from Muslims, first. Then leveled blasphemy accusations against the person. For the purpose, a series of religious titles were used to alienate a person. For instance, words like "Gumrah" (astray), "Zindeeq", "Murtad" (apostate), "Munafiq" (hypo-crite), "Kafir" (infidel), "Mulhid" (atheist) and "Dajjal" (Anti-Christ) were frequently paired with the name of a "potential blasphemer". In religious connotation and in local cultural settings it becomes easier to accuse a person of blasphemy if that person's reputation, outlook and ideology are not very religious. Therefore, assigning titles of "religious deviance" to lib-eral and apparently non-religious people and ideological opponents, makes it easier for TLP to accuse these people of blasphemy. Data revealed that the word blasphemer was used 7,000 times, followed by the word infidel (3,000 times), traitor (1,400 times) in the context of betrayal of religion (unlike the actual meaning of the word), hypocrite (1,200) and apostate (1,100). This reflects how frequently the political opponents are labelled with words that challenge the accused's allegiance to Islam. Consequently, it becomes easier to convince the general public that the accused is a blasphemer as he/she was never a good Muslim.

Maintaining a unique identity

TLP claims that their religious purpose is to protect the honour of the last Prophet of Muslims and their purpose is beyond mundane things. But their actions in online space reveal that they are no different from any other political party or pressure group who struggles to maintain its public presence. TLP propagates hashtags on Twitter in favour of blasphemy laws but when any other group propagates a hashtag with similar content TLP would not participate. This clearly shows that they talk about the issue when they alone get the credit. When it is a joint effort of multiple groups talking about blasphemy, TLP would disengage themselves in online space. The most active TLP supporters would never propagate a hashtag that had not been initiated by their own group. A visual representation of Twitter data explains this phenomenon. Figure 14.1 shows a relationship among online users and how they were aligned in different teams. There are four clusters of circles (each circle represents a Twitter user): three are placed on the top end of the figure and are connected to each other very tightly. However, the fourth one is at the bottom and has stronger intra-cluster connections (the lines connecting two circles represent online connection) but weaker inter-cluster connections. This figure is an actual represen-tation of Twitter users who were propagating two separate hashtags. The top three clusters represent TLP users who propagated a hashtag on blasphemy, while the lower cluster represents

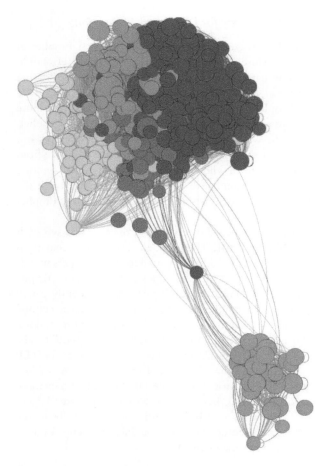

Figure 14.1 Same issue but divided they tweet.
Source: Twitter Data, compiled by the author (Rizvan Saeed)

another group who propagated hashtag #CyberGhustakhAzadKiun (translation: why cyber blasphemers are free). Now it is interesting to note that both groups tweeted against blasphemy but they ran separate hashtags. A few lines that are connecting the top and bottom clusters are of "mention" or "reply" ties. In simple terms, these lines appeared as a result when a member of one group tagged or replied to a few individuals of the other cluster. There were no lines (ties) that reflected retweeting of each other's tweets. Despite the fact that both the groups were tweeting against blasphemy, TLP did not join the other hashtag. And the very next day, TLP again ran its own hashtag against blasphemy and accused the Prime Minister Imran Khan.

TLP has aggressively promoted a convicted terrorist in online space along with propagating hate speech against minorities. They clearly instigated violence against Ahmadis. All these acts are criminalized under the law of the land. Section 9 of PECA 2016 clearly mentions that glorification of a terrorist, a terrorist offence and hate speech are liable to punishment. Section 503 of the Pakistan Penal Code, which criminalizes intimidation. Likewise the propagation of malicious hashtags targeting the integrity and honour of any individual is also a criminal offence. Section 20 of the PECA criminalizes displaying or transmitting information that a person knows to be false and that harms the reputation of a person.

Conclusion

Pakistan has witnessed consecutive democratic rule since 2008. The age of social media is also almost the same. Therefore, it is hard to make a comparison between the situation of social media control under a dictatorship and during democratic government. However, the situation worsened with each change of government since 2008.

During the autocratic rule of General Pervez Musharraf cyber laws were introduced to facilitate registration and accreditation of electronic subscribers and service providers. At that time, social media was not rampant in Pakistan. In the following years, the democratic government of Pakistan People's Party introduced the Investigation for Fair Trial Act with the intention to protect citizens' rights against unfair trials. However, the most important legislation regarding social media regulation was passed in Pakistan Muslim League Nawaz's tenure (2016), when laws were introduced to counter online violent extremism and hate speech. Later the PTI's current government added new regulations to PECA 2016 to control hate speech and violent extremism on social media. Regarding the implementation of the cyber laws, successive governments adopted a more selective approach. Despite visible evidence of hate speech against minorities and violent extremism by groups like TLP, the governments did not take effective actions under cyber laws. Pakistani Twitter remained inundated with hashtags that contained derogatory and violent content against minorities, especially Ahmadis. Although there have been democratic governments since social media expanded substantially in the country, they have failed to protect the democratic rights of minorities to take part freely in the digital world and to optimize their potential to contribute to the cyber world. Now be it poor or selective implementation of cyber laws, the most vulnerable victims are Ahmadis. This seems to continue, whether it is an autocratic regime or democracy, until the State takes concrete steps to effectively and impartially implement the cyber laws.

Bibliography

Ahmed, S. (2016). A Twenty-Point Recipe of Peace – The National Action Plan for Pakistan: Context, Analysis and Evaluation of Successes and Pitfalls, APSec2016 Conference.

Butt, T. (2017). TLP protest was aimed at curtailing PML-N vote bank. [online] Thenews.com.pk. Available at: <www.thenews.com.pk/print/250870-tlp-protest-was-aimed-at-curtailing-pml-n-vote-bank> (Accessed: 1 March 2021).

Farooq, U. (2020). Anti-Politics Dream Of Establishment And The Rise Of TLP. [online] Naya Daur. Available at: <https://nayadaur.tv/2020/11/anti-politics-dream-of-establishment-and-the-rise-of-tlp/> (Accessed: 14 March 2021).

Hashim, A. (2018). How will Pakistan's new far right perform in elections? Available at: www.aljazeera.com/features/2018/7/6/tehreek-e-labbaik-new-far-right-campaigns-against-blasphemy (Accessed: 3 September 2021).

Jahangir, R. (2019). Special report: The mechanics of silencing online dissent, DAWN.COM. Available at: www.dawn.com/news/1483248 (Accessed: 3 September 2021).

Jamal, S. (2019). Coins issued to mark Guru Nanak anniversary. Available at: https://gulfnews.com/world/asia/pakistan/coins-issued-to-mark-guru-nanak-anniversary-1.67494767 (Accessed: 3 September 2021).

Pakistan Telecommunication Authority. (2010). *Monitoring and Reconciliation of Telephony Traffic Regulations 2010*. Government of Pakistan.

Peoples Under Threat. (2020). Peoples Under Threat – An Annual Ranking of Countries According to the Risk of Mass Violence Faced by Communities. [online] Available at: <https://peoplesunderthreat.org> (Accessed 3 March 2021).

Rehman, A. (2019). *London Bridge Attacker Identified as Usman Khan, UK National of Pakistani Origin.* [online] DAWN.COM. Available at: <www.dawn.com/news/1519693> (Accessed 29 January 2021).

Saeed, R. (2020). [image] Available at: <https://twitter.com/SaeedRizvan/status/12472138424 86177803> (Accessed 5 March 2021).

Shahzad, A. (2020). New internet rules to give Pakistan blanket powers of censorship, *Reuters*, 19 November. Available at: www.reuters.com/article/pakistan-socialmedia-censorship-idUSL8N2I53OW (Accessed: 3 September 2021).

Siddiqui, N. (2017). Analysis | What's behind the Islamist protests in Pakistan?, *Washington Post*. Available at: www.washingtonpost.com/news/monkey-cage/wp/2017/12/08/whats-behind-the-islamist-protests-in-pakistan/ (Accessed: 3 September 2021).

15

A SUPREME COURT OR A CONSTITUTIONAL *JIRGA*?

Moeen Cheema

This chapter investigates the role that the Supreme Court has played in the context of an increasing democratic deficit and the emergence of what is being widely referred to as a civil-military 'hybrid' regime in Pakistan. It looks closely at high-profile constitutional cases decided before and after the 2018 parliamentary elections and the resulting transfer of power to the current Pakistan *Tehrik-e-Insaaf* (PTI) government led by Prime Minister Imran Khan. These include cases in which former Prime Minister Nawaz Sharif was disqualified from being a member of parliament for life, and from formally heading his political party, an outcome which significantly undermined his party's prospects in the 2018 elections. In another notable case, the Supreme Court heard a challenge to the extension of the incumbent Army Chief's tenure, but rather than laying out clear rules for such a scenario referred the matter to parliament, which inadvertently paved the way for greater military intervention in the political process. In a more recent case, the apex court reviewed the constitutionality of the proceedings for the removal of a Supreme Court judge known for stern critique of the military's involvement in politics. This case, which is still making headlines at the time of the writing of this chapter, has resulted in visible divisions within the court itself and tarnished the reputation of the judiciary, leaving it a less credible arbiter of constitutional controversies.

The chapter argues that in such cases involving matters of high constitutional law and politics, the apex court has developed a method to temporarily reduce the political and inter-institutional tensions by mediating between the various power centres and reaching intermediate outcomes, rather than principled peremptory decisions. As such, the court acts more like a proverbial *jirga* (council of elders in customary dispute resolution) seeking a negotiated settlement between the parties than a forum of legal adjudication. While such judicial intervention temporarily reduces the political strains, it ultimately enables the military-backed hybrid regime to assert its dominance under the cover of judicial oversight, contributing to autocratization in Pakistan. These cases and crises litigated before the Supreme Court are mere symptoms of a chronic ailment. The prospects of meaningful democracy in Pakistan are undermined by structural defects that no institution or political agent can remedy in the short term. At this stage it appears unlikely that the entire democratic set-up will be dispensed with through yet another military coup. Neither does it appear likely that mere continuity of the political dispensation will improve Pakistan's prospects of becoming a more democratic nation. The key

DOI: 10.4324/9781003042211-18

institutions – governments, opposition political parties, courts and the military – remain firmly entrenched in their positions and seem determined to guard their respective turfs rather than negotiating long-term solutions to the challenges of corruption, electoral malpractices, devolution and consensus-based policy-making on administrative and legal reform that might lead to a more stable and democratic Pakistan. The judiciary could play a significant role in such an environment in terms of setting firm constitutional rules for the game of politics. However, its strategy of mediating political crises and finding short-term compromises has exacerbated political divisions rather than improving the democratic process. Furthermore, the Supreme Court is increasingly looking like a divided house itself.

The Panama case and electoral engineering

Pakistan's previous government at the federal level was formed by the Pakistan Muslim League (PML-N) in 2013 and led by Prime Minister Nawaz Sharif for an expected five-year parliamentary term. The first two years of the party's rule were dogged by claims of large-scale electoral rigging by the most vocal opposition party, the PTI, led by cricketer-turned-politician Imran Khan (Cheema, M 2016, pp. 76–8). After a protracted political crisis, the controversy temporarily died down when both parties agreed to the formation of a judicial commission to investigate the allegations. While the judicial commission exonerated the ruling PML-N on the count of organized rigging, it nonetheless identified serious failings in the electoral process (Cheema, M 2016, pp. 78–9). A parliamentary committee formed as a result of the crisis failed to develop a consensus on electoral reforms and the issue was likely to reignite with a vengeance as the 2018 elections approached.

The PML-N government enjoyed barely a year of stability in the aftermath of the PTI protest movement when in April 2016 the International Consortium of Investigative Journalists released leaked documents of a Panama-based law firm. The 'Panama Papers' revealed several offshore companies owned by Prime Minister Nawaz Sharif's family and proved their ownership of high-end properties in London (Cheema, H 2016). The Sharif family has been in the business of politics and power either in the centre or Punjab, Pakistan's largest province, for much of the last three decades. There had been allegations of corruption, money-laundering and tax evasion during every term that the party has won elected office, especially during Nawaz Sharif's two terms as Prime Minister in the 1990s. However, the Sharifs and their party managed to avoid both political fallout and judicial scrutiny of corruption charges. In contrast to the PML-N, the Pakistan People's Party (PPP), which formed the government from 2008 to 2013, was dogged by high profile corruption scandals and intense judicial review by the Supreme Court. The PML-N had provided unwavering and visible public support to the court's accountability drive including the decision to disqualify former Prime Minister Gilani for failure to institute corruption charges against President Zardari, also dating back to the 1990s (Mahmood 2012). Unlike the PPP's judicial ordeal, however, the corruption and money-laundering allegations against the Sharifs appeared to have become past and closed transactions, a matter of history, until the release of the Panama Papers.

Despite the demands from the PTI for the formation of another judicial commission to investigate corruption and money-laundering allegations released in the Panama Papers, neither the government nor the court relented. In August 2016, Imran Khan, who has adopted an anti-corruption platform as the main charter of his party, decided to take the matter to the Supreme Court under Article 184(3) of the Constitution, which provides for the 'Original Jurisdiction' of the court. In such cases, the court can directly take up matters of "public importance with reference to the enforcement of any of the Fundamental Rights" including important questions of constitutional interpretation. After months of regular hearings which received almost daily coverage in the national media, the five-member bench issued its first judgment in April 2017 (*Imran Khan v. Nawaz Sharif*, PLD 265). All five members of the bench appeared to agree that Prime Minister Nawaz Sharif and his family had failed to satisfy the court regarding the source of their immense wealth, or to provide a satisfactory account of when and how the properties in London were purchased. The respondents' explanations seemed evasive and had shifted dramatically over the course of the proceedings. There was no proof of any bank transactions or any financial evidence of when and how the properties were purchased.

Nonetheless, the case raised challenging issues regarding the interpretation of the provisions on disqualification of members of parliament pursuant to which the removal of the Prime Minister was sought. Article 62(1)(f) of the Constitution states that a person "shall not be qualified to be elected or chosen as a member of Majlis-e-Shoora (Parliament) unless ... (f) he is sagacious, righteous, non-profligate, honest and ameen, there being no declaration to the contrary by a court of law." The question before the court was whether it could issue such a declaration under its Original Jurisdiction and disqualify the Prime Minister in the same proceedings based on the material on the record. The respondents argued that the court could only disqualify a member of parliament if there had been a prior conviction or judgment by a court of competent jurisdiction for tax evasion, money-laundering, possession of wealth beyond known means, or a judicially proven misdeclaration of assets in the nomination forms filed as a candidate at the time of the elections (Cheema, M 2018). It is on this crucial question that the bench split with only two judges holding that Nawaz Sharif was disqualified from being a member of parliament and hence the Prime Minister for lack of integrity and financial probity. Justice Khosa, who was scheduled to be the next Chief Justice, wrote a lengthy and scathing opinion arguing that there was *prima facie* evidence of corrupt practices by Prime Minister Nawaz Sharif (*Imran Khan v. Nawaz Sharif*, PLD 265). Since the Prime Minister and his family were the only people who held complete knowledge of the transactions the onus was on the respondents to provide such a 'money trail.'

The majority of the bench, however, took a different stance on the issue of jurisdiction under Article 184(3). While also noting the glaring gaps in the Sharif family's explanation of their financial dealings, nonetheless, they argued that the court could not disqualify a member of parliament in the absence of "admitted facts or indisputable documentary evidence" (Cheema, M 2018). Nonetheless, all three judges forming the majority in this phase of the case directed the creation of a Joint Investigation Team (JIT) to probe the allegations against the respondents and produce a report within sixty days after which the Supreme Court may again take up the matter. While the government initially expressed joyous relief at the Supreme Court's interim order, the composition and the conduct of the JIT caused anxiety amongst ministerial ranks. The JIT not only included senior officials from a range of civilian agencies chosen by the court but also representatives of the military's intelligence services. The majority justified the inclusion of the military intelligence officials on the grounds that all civilian investigation agencies appeared to be under the control or influence of the incumbent Prime Minister and had refused to investigate the allegations (Cheema, M 2018).

In July 2017, the JIT presented a voluminous report to the 'Implementation Bench' comprising the three judges who had directed the formation of the JIT (*Dawn*, 11 July 2017). The JIT's report unveiled extensive offshore holdings and businesses of the Sharif family well beyond what had surfaced in the Panama Papers. The JIT report also provided considerable evidence that the stance of the respondents on several issues and some of the documents furnished by them to the court were patently false and fabricated. The three judges who had directed the formation of the JIT focused almost exclusively on one piece of information in the dossier which was admitted by the Prime Minister. Nawaz Sharif had remained the chairman of the board of a UAE company named Capital FZE for six and a half years leading up to the 2013 elections and was entitled to receive a salary. This position was used to obtain a permit to work and live in the UAE. Nawaz Sharif's lawyer admitted before the bench that the salary had accrued to the respondent as chairman of the board, but he had not withdrawn it at any stage until the company was dissolved in early 2013. The bench used this admission, and relying on dictionary definitions, held that accrued receivables were assets which were required to be declared by a candidate for election. Since the Prime Minister had failed to disclose this asset in his nomination papers at the time of the 2013 elections, he was disqualified from being a member of parliament for life, and hence this deposed him from office (*Imran Khan v. Nawaz Sharif*, PLD 692).

Of the plethora of material included in the JIT report, the accrued but un-withdrawn salary from Capital FZE was arguably among the weakest evidence of financial impropriety against the disqualified Prime Minister. Even though the five-member bench ultimately reached a unanimous decision after a convoluted two-stage process, the majority's reliance on accrued salary as undeclared asset provided both sides of the political divide with a basis to strengthen their respective narratives. The PML-N criticized the court's decision as biased and legally incorrect, and several of its most vocal members were charged with and some were also convicted of contempt of court for such criticism. The Supreme Court's decision in the Panama case, and the resulting trial of Nawaz Sharif before an Accountability Court on corruption charges and possession of assets beyond known means, strengthened the opposition PTI's narrative as well as electoral prospects. The ruling PML-N as well as the PPP also claimed that pre-election rigging was also in play, whereby the military and its intelligence agency (ISI) were involved in the business of persuading 'electable' politicians and some minor parties to join the PTI.

There were again complaints of significant poll day rigging in the 2018 elections (Mir 2018). The elections resulted in a victory of sorts for the PTI as it emerged as the largest party in the National Assembly and in the provincial assembly of Punjab. However, it lacked a clear majority and needed the support of an array of minor parties and independently elected candidates to form governments at the federal level and in Punjab. There were also rumours that the formation of this seemingly fragile coalition had been facilitated by the military, providing the basis of the narrative that Imran Khan's elected government was merely the cover for what was in essence a civil–military hybrid regime. This accusation against the PTI-led elected governments at the federal and provincial levels has only been strengthened by subsequent controversies, some of which ended up before the Supreme Court for adjudication.

Extension of Army Chief's tenure and parliamentary complicity

Despite the complaints of the opposition and allegations of electoral manipulation, the PTI governments at the centre and in Punjab appeared to be relatively stable. The opposition by and large accepted the results and unlike in the aftermath of the 2013 elections grudgingly conceded the outcome of the 2018 elections. While there were progressively increasing concerns about the capacity of the PTI to institute effective governance as the party lacked previous experience of ruling, the opposition initially proclaimed that it would provide it with the space to rule for the maximum term of five years as stipulated in the Constitution. However, as the PTI began an increasingly assertive and relentless campaign of accountability for political corruption against major opposition figures, the working relationship between the government and opposition in the legislative assemblies began to visibly deteriorate (Rehman 2020). The public debate between the government and the opposition became increasingly personalized and vitriolic, and political fragmentation in the country appeared to be reaching heights not experienced since the 1990s.

In November 2019, the incumbent Army Chief's three-year term was due to expire. The retirement of the Chief of Army Staff (COAS) and the selection of his successor has historically been a politically sensitive moment. In August 2019, in order to pre-empt any speculation as to the matter, the PTI government attempted to grant General Qamar Javed Bajwa a three-year extension in his tenure as the COAS arguing that a difficult regional security situation required continuity in his command of the armed forces. A relatively unknown petitioner filed a challenge to the extension of tenure before the Supreme Court under its Original Jurisdiction (*Jurisdiction Foundation*, PLD 52). However, the petitioner refused to pursue the case but the court, nonetheless, continued the proceedings on the basis that a public law case brought under its Original Jurisdiction does not automatically cease if the petitioner seeks to withdraw it. Effectively, the court thus turned this petition into a *suo motu* case, that is, one initiated by the court itself. At issue in the initial proceedings of the case were the legality of the notification issued by the government purporting to grant an extension in the COAS' tenure. There were several irregularities in the issuance of the notification itself, which represented confusion on the part of the government as to the appropriate process. First Prime Minister Imran Khan had himself issued the initial notification of extension in tenure, then immediately realized that under Article 243 of the Constitution the power of appointment rests with the President so the Prime Minister's office sent a summary to him recommending the re-appointment of the COAS who instantly approved it. The very next day, the government recognized that the Prime Minister's recommendation needed prior approval by the Cabinet, which was sought *post hoc* through circulation of the draft summary rather than through a Cabinet meeting (*Jurist Foundation*, PLD 1).

As the court proceedings unfolded, a very peculiar legal problem began to crystallize. Although the tenures of Army Chiefs had been extended on several occasions in Pakistan's history, there was no legal framework governing the tenure and terms of service of the Army Chief. The Army Act, 1952 which had been framed by Pakistan's first Constituent Assembly pre-dated all three of Pakistan's constitutions (respectively framed in 1956, 1962 and 1973). After considerable vacillation, the government and the COAS' lawyers settled on the argument that in the absence of any relevant legal provisions in the Army Act, Article 243(3)(b) of the Constitution – which granted the President the power to appoint the Army Chief on the advice of the Prime Minister – was effectively a self-executing provision, that is, one which can be given effect to without the aid of legislation. The government also argued that there existed an unwritten convention that the tenure of the COAS was initially for three years and could be extended for another term of any duration under Article 243 (*Jurist Foundation*, PLD 1). The court had two clear legal options before it. It could have accepted the government's position that Article 243 was a self-executing position and the appointment, re-appointment, and extension of tenures of the COAS were completely the President's prerogative, subject to the advice of the Prime Minister and Cabinet. While this position would have assisted the government in the instant case and legalized the problematic practice of extending Army Chiefs' tenures, it would have juridically established the primacy of civilian governments in the appointments of the COAS, historically a matter fraught with tensions between civil and military leaderships. Alternatively, the court could have taken a categorical position against extensions of tenure of Army Chiefs and held that since Article 243 is not a self-executing constitutional provision, in the absence of any relevant provision in the Army Act enabling the extension of the COAS' tenure such a purported extension was illegal.

Instead, the court chose a middle ground that temporarily placated both sides. The court delved into the constitutional history of Article 243 and observed that Article 40 of the 1956 Constitution had stated that until "Parliament makes provision *by law* in that behalf, the President shall have the power ... to appoint Commanders-in-Chief of the Army." The court interpreted this provision as transitory, and given that the Army Act, 1952 was already in existence, an expression of the assertion that the Army Act needed to be substituted or amended to provide for more comprehensive regulation of the armed forces (*Jurist Foundation*, PLD 1). Similarly, the court analyzed comparable provisions in the 1962 and the original form of the 1973 constitutions, which provided for the command of the armed forces and the power to appoint services chiefs to be vested in the President "subject to law" and observed with some surprise and consternation that no such law had been passed since the promulgation of the 1973 Constitution. The court subtly glossed over the fact that contrary to its interpretation of Article 40 of the 1956 Constitution, the phrase "subject to law" could be interpreted to mean that the framers of the 1962 and 1973 constitutions proceeded upon the assumption that such law already existed in the form of the 1952 Army Act, evidenced further by the absence of any attempts to substitute or significantly amend it. Nonetheless, the court proceeded to interpret the requirement of raising and maintaining the armed services "subject to law" under Article 243 of the Constitution to hold that legislation governing the tenure, retirement age, and the process for the extension of service of the Army Chief needed to be passed by the parliament. In an exercise of "judicial restraint" and enabling a compromise between the government and the opposition, the court effectively granted an interim six-month extension to the COAS' tenure during which parliament may pass legislation to regulate the services chiefs' tenures on a permanent basis (*Jurist Foundation*, PLD 1).

Such legislation required the support of the opposition as the government lacked a majority in the Senate, the upper house of parliament. However, despite the challenging parliamentary equation, and despite mutterings of discontent from the opposition, the legislation was speedily passed in January 2020 validating the extension in the COAS' tenure. Contrary to the seemingly broader import of the Supreme Court's judgment, the Act focused exclusively on the President's power to appoint, reappoint and extend the tenures of the services chiefs. It clarified that the initial appointment of the COAS will be for a term of three years, which may be extended for an initial period of up to three years at the discretion of the President upon the advice of the Prime Minister (Pakistan Army (Amendment) Act, 2020). The Act also provided that the maximum retirement age of the COAS will be 64 years. The ease with which the Act was rushed through the parliament gave credence to rumours of backroom dealings between the military establishment and the two major opposition parties, the PML-N and the PPP. Such claims of accommodation between the military and the opposition gained further strength when prior to its enactment Nawaz Sharif was granted bail in the corruption cases against him on medical grounds and allowed by the government and the courts to travel abroad to seek treatment for an allegedly serious immune disorder.

Since his departure to the UK, no evidence has been forthcoming of Nawaz Sharif's continuing serious ailment or of any medical treatment he may have received in that regard. As such, while the Supreme Court's decision nominally resulted in upholding the parliament's right to legislate on military affairs, as a matter of political reality it only showed that not only the government but also major opposition parties are susceptible to the military's influence as and when the need for their complicity arises. Furthermore, protracted corruption investigations and trials against virtually all significant opposition leaders thus provide both the government and the military with considerable leverage over the opposition and have strengthened the narrative that the hybrid regime uses accountability processes for political manipulation.

Judicial accountability and a fractured Supreme Court

In May 2019, the President filed a reference against Justice Qazi Faez Isa, a sitting judge of the Supreme Court, before the Supreme Judicial Council alleging the ownership of undeclared and unaccounted-for foreign properties by his spouse and children. The Supreme Judicial Council (SJC) – comprising the Chief Justice, the two most senior judges of the Supreme Court, and the two most senior Chief Justices of the provincial High Courts – issued a show cause notice to Justice Isa commencing proceedings under Article 209 which provides the exclusive mechanism for the scrutiny and removal of a judge for misconduct. Justice Isa responded to the show cause notice, and also filed a petition challenging the reference under the Original Jurisdiction of the apex court arguing that the presidential reference to the SJC was *mala fide* (i.e., issued in bad faith) and had been initiated to discipline him for certain judgments in which he had criticized the involvement of the military in politics (*Justice Isa*, PLD 1). The case acquired additional significance because Justice Isa is scheduled to become the Chief Justice in September 2023, coinciding with the end of the current parliamentary term and the resulting elections if the presidential reference against him were quashed. There were a number of legal defects manifest in the record and the preparation of the reference. As such, the court could have simply quashed the reference and ended the matter at that point, of course leaving open the possibility for the government to prepare a more thorough reference if it wished to do so at some political cost. Conversely, the court could have held that since the SJC has already taken cognizance of the matter, that is the preferable forum.

Instead, once again, the court chose an intermediate form of action and proceeded with hearings in the case for approximately ten months before a ten-member full bench (*Justice Isa*, PLD 1). In the process, regular coverage of the proceedings in the media caused considerable damage to the court's standing for amongst other things Justice Isa objected to the original composition of the bench as it included two judges who would stand to benefit: one would become the Chief Justice of the Supreme Court for a short duration; the other would have his tenure extended if Justice Isa were to be removed from office. Both judges recused themselves from the bench under protest as their impartiality had been implicitly impugned by Justice Isa's request. The petitioners, which included not just Justice Isa but also an array of senior lawyers and representatives of bar associations, had argued that the presidential reference had been motivated by malice and was designed to undermine the independence of the judiciary. In June 2020, all ten members of the bench held the reference to be a nullity (*Justice Isa*, PLD 346). However, the majority judgment, in which seven members of the bench joined, declared the reference to be *mala fide* in law as there were several grave errors of law in the preparation of the reference which represented a blatant disregard of the law, but there was no malice in fact on the part of the President or the government.

The errors in the preparation of the reference included the fact that it was not the President who had initiated the investigation upon the advice of the Prime Minister as required by the Constitution, but instead the Law Minister had authorized the Asset Recovery Unit attached to the Prime Minister's office to conduct the investigation upon the supposed application of a relatively little known and dubious informant. The majority also observed that the basis of the reference was essentially a tax matter, but unsubstantiated allegations of money-laundering had been included in the reference. The President was required to act on the advice of the Prime Minister but in the present context was also required to seek independent advice and exercise his own judgment prior to forwarding the reference to the SJC, which he failed to do. As such, the presidential reference to the SJC, and consequently the SJC's show cause notice to Justice Isa, were quashed. However, at the same time, the seven-member majority of the bench sent the matter to the Federal Bureau of Revenue (FBR) to investigate the allegations contained in the reference and issue notices to Justice Isa's spouse and children under the relevant tax laws "to offer an explanation regarding the nature and source of the funds (*Justice Isa*, PLD 1)." The FBR was also directed to present a report to the SJC, leaving open the possibility that a new reference may be initiated by the SJC *suo motu* in case of adverse findings against Justice Isa in the FBR report. The court thus temporarily diffused the crisis, chastising the government for the manner in which the reference was filed, but also partially substantiated the allegation leaving the proverbial sword of Damocles hanging over the future Chief Justice.

Contrary to the three judges in the minority who insisted on the end of all proceedings against Justice Isa in the quashing of the reference, the majority insisted that a perception of the accountability of the judiciary also needed to be maintained (*Justice Isa*, PLD 1). Since the ownership of three properties in London by the spouse and children of Justice Isa, even though financially independent, had been admitted the source of the funds and the mode of their transfer needed to be investigated by the tax authorities. This was necessitated by the definition of 'misconduct' under Article 209 of the Constitution which, according to the seven-member majority, included both professional and private actions, and not just conduct related to the performance of official/judicial functions. Furthermore, the judicial code of conduct requires judges to "avoid litigation and to be diligent in their financial affairs to minimise the chance of any embarrassment in the performance of their functions (*Justice Isa*, PLD 1)." Given that the close family of a judge enjoy many of the incidental perks and privileges of their office, it is incumbent upon the family members to also demonstrate probity and discretion in their affairs. As such, it is also incumbent upon judges to be reasonably aware of their family's financial affairs and they cannot thus simply take the plea that their close family are financially independent. As noted above, although the majority of the bench sought to balance the need to protect judicial independence from interference by the executive with transparency in judicial accountability, the end result was a prolongation of the crisis which has left not only the public perception of the judiciary tarnished but has also led to deepening divisions in the Supreme Court.

In a review of the Supreme Court's decision, Justice Isa notably and in an unprecedented manner decided to argue his own case before his colleagues on the bench. In protracted proceedings, which are rare in review cases as the court is only empowered to reassess the legality of its original decision, Justice Isa not only levelled serious allegations of persecution by the government at the behest of the military command for criticizing the military's role in politics, but also criticized members of the apex court for failing to safeguard judicial independence. Such public criticism of the judiciary from an apex court judge arguing his own case has taken its toll on the Supreme Court's reputation, and divisions within the court over Justice Isa's case have also become manifest. Although the bench decided by a narrow majority of 6:4 judges to quash all proceedings against Justice Isa, the court will be the ultimate loser. As Justice Isa has been absolved of charges of misconduct against him without providing the 'money trail' or chain of transactions in the purchase of foreign properties by his family, parallels with Nawaz Sharif's case will be inevitable. The critics of the court will accuse the judiciary of setting a different standard of probity for judges than was set for elected politicians in Nawaz Sharif's disqualification case. This would also strengthen the PML-N's narrative that Nawaz Sharif's disqualification was in error of law. On the other hand, when Justice Isa ascends to the office of the Chief Justice, his impartiality on issues relating to the PTI and the current government will remain under a cloud.

Conclusion

As noted in the introduction, and highlighted in this chapter, the Supreme Court has become the arena for resolution of high profile and potentially destabilizing constitutional and political controversies. Instead of laying down clear constitutional principles and bright line rules governing the conduct of governance, politics, and institutional powers and parameters, the apex court has repeatedly sought to act as a mediator and found various devices to temporarily diffuse the underlying political tensions.

In the Panama case, the court failed to avail the opportunity to lay the ground rules on how corruption charges against ruling politicians and allegations of financial impropriety ought to be dealt with. Instead, the majority on the bench found an intermediate solution by creating a Joint Investigation Team (JIT) that may engage in fact-finding and enable the court to determine the probity of the allegations against former Prime Minister Nawaz Sharif. The outcome was a decision that was principally muddled and has given an extended lease of life to political fragmentation. In the Army Chief's tenure case, the court again diffused the tensions in the interim by referring the matter to the parliament rather than reaching a clear and precise legal formulation, resulting in the extension of the controversy and paving the way for the military's enhanced involvement in parliamentary politics. Finally, in Justice Isa's case, rather than deciding the matter on clear constitutional grounds by either completely quashing the reference or letting the Supreme Judicial Council (SJC) conduct its proceedings, the court reached a compromised interim solution of referring the matter to the tax authorities. This has only resulted in further controversy with protracted proceedings which have cast a shadow over the court's credibility as an independent and impartial arbiter of constitutional controversies.

In a constitutional scheme such as Pakistan's, given the contexts of increased polarization and the heightened role of the military in the political process, an independent and credible judiciary is needed to act as a check on increasing autocratization and reduce controversies that serve to destabilize the fragile democratic system. Not only has the court failed in that task, its mediatory approach has only served to enhance the dialectic of autocratization and destabilization, and the judiciary itself is now under strain as a result of that failure.

Bibliography

Cheema, Hasham, 2016, "How Pakistan's Panama Papers probe unfolded", *Dawn*, 3 April.

Cheema, Moeen, 2016, "'Election disputes' or disputed elections? Judicial (non-)review of the electoral process in Pakistan" in P J Yap (ed.), *Judicial Review of Elections in Asia*, London: Routledge.

Cheema, Moeen, 2018, "Pakistan: The state of liberal democracy", *International Journal of Constitutional Law*, vol. 16, no. 2, pp. 635–42.

Mahmood, Amjad, 2012, "Nawaz threatens 'all options' to unseat Gilani", *Dawn*, 27 April.

Mir, Asfandyar, 2018, "What just happened in Pakistan's election? And what happens next?", *Washington Post*, 26 July.

Pakistan Army (Amendment) Act, 2020. Government of Pakistan.

"Read full text of Panama Papers JIT report", *Dawn*, 11 July 2017.

Rehman, Abdul, 2020, "Pakistan: How 'Accountability' Became a Tool for Political Oppression", *The Diplomat*, 13 February.

Cases

16

AUTOCRATIZATION AND RELIGIOUS MINORITIES IN PAKISTAN

Ahmad Salim and Rizvan Saeed

As opposed to the findings of Fukuyama and others almost 30 years back, elucidating that a liberal democracy could last forever since it had maintained due dominance, today's democracies paint a picture of gradual decline (Lührmann and Lindberg, 2019). This view is furthered by ambiguity that subsists about the thrust and ferocity of the existing upsurge of autocratization in the world (ibid., 2019). To understand the framework of a liberal democracy, characteristics of the "illiberal democracy" (Zakaria, 2007) have to be explored further to understand various facets of its interaction with the rights of minorities in a modern-day democracy. According to Democracy Index 2020 by the Economist's Intelligence Unit, the average global score for democracy fell from 5.48 in 2018 to 5.37 in 2020 on a scale of 0–10 where 10 indicates full democracy and 0 means fully authoritarian states. In 2020, Pakistan secured 105th position in global ranking with 4.31 points. This score was a slight improvement over 2019, when it was 4.25 and Pakistan's global democracy ranking was 108th. However, Pakistan is still under the category of Hybrid Regime. The question is, are the liberal democratic rights that do exist distributed equally in society? An important undertaking is to see whether the situation of minorities did improve when Pakistan climbed on the democracy index. This chapter unpacks the history of minority rights in Pakistan parallel to government shifts between sporadic democratic moments to martial law. It is often assumed that minorities suffer more in times of autocratization. We argue that this is not always the case – at least not in Pakistan.

Minorities in Pakistan – the legal definition

The word "minority" is used twice in the Preamble of the Constitution of Pakistan while Article 36 of the Constitution is specifically about minorities to guarantee minorities' legitimate rights and interests including their due representation in the Federation and Provincial services. While in the Preamble, minorities and backward and depressed classes are discussed in the same breath. Besides these three references, there is no separate discussion of minorities in the Constitution. Articles 8 to 28 of the Constitution of Pakistan deal with fundamental human rights of citizens but they talk on a collective level, not mentioning minorities specifically.

DOI: 10.4324/9781003042211-19

There is no exact definition of "minority" given in the Constitution of Pakistan. However, the Ministry of Religious Affairs and Interfaith Harmony talks about minorities as religious minorities in its official documents and states that they work for inter-religious and inter-sectarian harmony (Government of Pakistan: Ministry of Religious Affairs and Interfaith Harmony, 2020). While highlighting the Ministry's role in improving the lives of minorities in Pakistan through special initiatives, the Ministry refers to religious minorities only. Since Shia Muslims are not considered a minority officially by the State of Pakistan, so they are not discussed as a religious minority, in this chapter. They formally enjoy the same rights as all Muslims in Pakistan. This, however, is no attempt to diminish the importance of atrocities and violence that Shias, especially Hazara Shias, are facing in Pakistan today.

A segment of Muslims known as Ahmadis was declared non-Muslim in 1974 through a Constitutional Amendment. In 1889, a then Muslim scholar Mirza Ghulam Ahmad from Qadian (a city in today's India) claimed to be the "messiah". Mainstream Islamic scholars of the time opposed his claim and declared him a heretic. However, he attracted a good following and they were called Ahmadis after his name Ahmad. They remained part of the Muslim community until 1974, when they were declared non-Muslim by the Parliament of Pakistan. According to the 1998 Census of Pakistan (Pbs.gov.pk, n.d.), Ahmadis constituted 0.2 percent of the total population. In numbers, this makes roughly 300,000 individuals. However, this figure is quite contested. Some sources estimate that there are more than half a million Ahmadis in Pakistan (UNHCR, 2017).

In the subcontinent, Christians started proselytization of Hindus, Sikhs and Muslims during the sixteenth century. In the area that is now Pakistan, the majority of converts were low-income, landless workers who were mostly Hindu Punjabis (Church of Pakistan, 1998). According to the 1998 census, 1.6 percent of the population were Christians. The population census was next conducted in 2017, recording Pakistan's total population as 220 million. However, the detailed results have not been published yet. A government body – the Council of Common Interest (CCI) – has to approve the results for publication. On December 22, 2020, the CCI approved for release the Census 2017 results but as of September 2021, the government had not published any details on the minority population. However, Ramesh Kumar – then a Member of the National Assembly – shared that there were 5 million Christians in Pakistan by 2019 (Tunio, 2019). Converting this number to a percentage share of Christians out of a total population as per Census 2017, it translates into 2.4 percent roughly.

At the time of independence of Pakistan, Hindus constituted about 15 percent of the population. During the initial years after independence, a large migration took place from Pakistan to India. Pakistan's first census of 1951 recorded the Hindu population as 13 percent and most of them were living in East Pakistan. Then in 1971, East Pakistan became Bangladesh and the Hindu population share in today's Pakistan declined substantially. According to the 1998 census, the share of Hindus was only about 1.6 percent excluding Scheduled Castes. The latter are Hindus but not considered part of four Varna groups of Hinduism. These were given the status of Scheduled Castes through a Presidential Order in 1957. Ramesh Kumar, who is a Member of the National Assembly on a minority seat and is Patron-in-Chief of the Pakistan Hindu Council, claims that the Hindu population is closer to 4 percent.

Evidently the religious minorities in Pakistan are so small in numbers that even if they acted together in politics as a united force, they would still represent less than 10 percent of the population. The small share of the population is most likely a reason that contributes to their exposed situation in the country.

Formative years and minority rights

The founder of Pakistan, Muhammad Ali Jinnah, laid the ideological foundation of the country in his speech on 11 August 1947. He said, "We are starting in the days where there is no discrimination, no distinction between one community and another, no discrimination between one caste or creed and another. We are starting with this fundamental principle: that we are all citizens, and equal citizens, of one State."

Unfortunately, Jinnah did not live long enough to ensure equal citizenship of all citizens. He passed away on September 11, 1948 and the very next year the then Prime Minister Liaquat Ali Khan presented a bill to the Constituent Assembly that asked for the inclusion of the Objectives Resolution as Preamble to the Constitution of Pakistan (that was yet to be formed). The Objectives Resolution stated that Pakistan's Constitution would be Islamic in nature and should be devised in the light of the sacred books of Muslims. The minority members of the Assembly expressed strong disagreement to the move. They feared that making Pakistan an Islamic State would affect the status of minorities of "equal citizens" and turn them into second-class citizens. However, the Objectives Resolution was passed on March 12, 1949. The 25-member Basic Principles Committee (BPC) subsequently sketched the layout of the Constitution, which then was formed under the chairmanship of Maulvi Tamizuddin Khan. The first report of the Committee was presented in 1950 but any fruitful deliberations could not be carried out due to the assassination of Liaqat Ali Khan in 1951. Finally, the report was presented before the Assembly on December 22, 1952 by the then Prime Minister Khwaja Nazimuddin. The foremost recommendation in the report was restricting eligibility for being the Head of the State to Muslims only. Naturally minority members opposed this recommendation as this would *de jure* and *de facto* make them second-class citizens. Another recommendation of the Basic Principles Committee was to set up Ulema Boards by the Governor General and the provincial governors. All the laws would be presented to these boards for a review in the light of the Quran and the Sunnah. This made it clear to the minorities that the proposed changes were not only about the head of the State. All laws were to be structured according to Islamic teachings. An influential Muslim scholar of the time, Maulana Maudodi, clearly mentioned the dichotomy of citizenship in an Islamic State. He believed that there should be a difference between Muslim citizens and the *dhimmies* (the protected subjects) – the non-Muslims living in a Muslim country (Nasr, 1996). His interpretation was popular at the time and it gave air to the fears that had been expressed by the minorities over Islamization of the newly formed State of Pakistan, unlike the vision of her founder.

During Pakistan's formative years (1947–1956) the issue of separate and joint electorates remained under discussion. Preceding the provincial elections in East Bengal (part of Pakistan until 1971) in 1953, to cater to certain political needs of the province a suggestion was surfaced to amend the Government of India Act 1935. This Act was used as the Interim Constitution for Pakistan till the formation of the first own Constitution in 1956. The suggestion was to provide for separate electorates for Caste Hindus and Scheduled Castes. But this recommendation was opposed by Hindu minority members. They felt that representation of Hindus can be ensured within a system of joint electorate so there was not any need of a separate electorate for Hindu minorities. However, they were in favour of reservation of seats for Christians, Buddhists and the Scheduled Castes. In 1952, a conference was held in Comilla, East Pakistan, by minorities where they objected to the suggestion of having separate electorates. In 1953, when the draft Constitution was being debated in the legislative assembly of Pakistan, the issue of a separate electorate was discussed again. The report of the Committee on Fundamental Rights that was formed in 1947 to safeguard rights of minorities, was presented. This report had dissenting notes by three non-Muslim members: B C Mandal, P H Burman and R K Chakravarty. They declared that a separate electorate would not be in the interest of minorities (Report of the Basic Principles Committee, 1954). However, the dissenting notes of the three minority leaders were not considered and a separate electorate was introduced. This was a major first blow to equal and effective representation of minorities in Pakistan's legislative assembly.

Muhammad Ayub Khan's Era – associating minorities with enemies

Pakistan saw its first military coup in 1958 – spearheaded by one of the generals of the Pakistan army, Ayub Khan, who overthrew the first President of Pakistan, Iskander Mirza. During Ayub Khan's reign, after recurring conflicts with India over the Kashmir region, the enemy in 1965 was branded as Hindu instead of Indian. This created hostilities towards Pakistan's Hindu communities too. Moreover, Christians were increasingly perceived and labelled as foreign agents Malik (2019). This naturally increased the insecurities of Christians in Pakistan. During severe tensions between Pakistan and India in 1965, there were also reports that many Christians were spies for India. The archives of the Special Police records in Lahore provide abundant evidence that cases of this nature were registered against Christians at that time.

Consequently, the situation for minorities was complicated from the start after Partition. However, the situation would soon become even worse.

Zulfiqar Ali Bhutto's democracy – legalizing exclusion

Succeeding the dictator Ayub Khan, the civilian leader Zulfiqar Ali Bhutto was received as a democratic leader. However, he proved worse for minorities than his predecessor. In 1974, under the leadership of Zulfiqar Ali Bhutto, the Ahmadis were declared non-Muslims through a Constitutional Amendment. It was a big blow to Ahmadis who were already vulnerable to societal discrimination. The legal framework gave legitimacy to existing violence and prejudices against them, and at the time there already existed a long history of anti-Ahmadi sentiments and discrimination against the community by the larger Muslim population.

In 1953, riots targeting Ahmadis broke out in Lahore; their shops in Lahore were set on fire and there were cases of mob violence directed specifically against them ('1953 Lahore riots', 2015). Ultimately, the then government had to impose Governor's Rule to control the situation. But there were no attempts at government level to declare Ahmadis as non-Muslims. It was two decades later, when Zulfiqar Ali Bhutto brought the debate on the faith of the Ahmadis to the floor of the National Assembly, when they were finally declared non-Muslims. Since the emergence of Pakistan, the minorities were facing discrimination at societal level with no state patronage explicitly. But in 1974, the then government joined the bandwagon and capitulated to pressure of religious political actors. This paved the way for long-term entanglement of religious-based political parties in the power game. After getting Ahmadis declared non-Muslims, these religious groups started to push the government to include Shias, Zikris and Ismailis on the list of minorities (2008, 109).

Surprisingly, however, a year later, Zulfiqar Ali Bhutto introduced a Constitutional Amendment in favour of minorities including the Ahmadis. It was to give them effective representation in the Parliament. Under the 4th Constitutional Amendment in 1975, minorities were given special seats in the National Assembly. The non-Muslims (including Ahmadis according to the Constitution) got the right to vote for non-Muslim candidates as well as for Muslim candidates. Bigger minorities including Hindus and Christians were given four seats each, while Sikhs, Parsi and Ahmadis were given one seat each. One seat was reserved for representatives of other religious minorities (Election Commission of Pakistan, 1990). This political move was meant to ensure equal rights of minorities for their political participation. However, this leverage could not last long and soon Zia ul-Haq – the then army chief with anti-liberal ideology – toppled the government and imposed martial law. Hence began another dark chapter for the minorities and liberal elements of society.

Muhammad Zia ul-Haq's Islamization – patronizing violence

Zia ul-Haq overthrew the elected government of Zulfiqar Ali Bhutto in 1977. After a year (in 1979) of his coup, the USSR invaded Afghanistan. This changed the geopolitical situation of the region. The US used Pakistan as a proxy and entered into the Afghan war to counter the USSR. From a Pakistani perspective this war was termed as Afghan Jihad. The label of Jihad helped the US and Pakistan governments to recruit fighters from Islamic countries, especially from Pakistan. To create more *mujahideen* (the fighter who fights in name of Islam), Zia ul-Haq used the Islamic religion as a tool to motivate the youth to join the Afghan Jihad (Stern, 2000). Simultaneously, Zia ul-Haq went the extra mile to impose Islamic laws in Pakistan.

Minorities' security and identity were threatened badly during Zia ul-Haq's regime. Zia ul-Haq reverted the part of the 4th Constitutional Amendment that gave representation to minorities in the legislature. The nullification of a separate electorate for minorities was a big blow to all minorities especially the Ahmadis who were under constant societal persecution. Eliminating the separate electorate at that moment of history meant causing more damage to Ahmadis. They had recently been declared non-Muslims (in 1974) in response to public hatred against them. Under a joint electorate they had no chance of having their fair representation in the National Assembly.

For Zia ul-Haq, there were two main factors that motivated him to withdraw rights for minorities: First, Zia ul-Haq wanted to counter the popularity of Zulfiqar Ali Bhutto's Islamic socialism and liberal views. Therefore, he introduced "real" Islamic values. In order to hinder alliances between Zulfiqar Ali Bhutto's "Pakistan People's Party" (PPP) and the religious majority, Zia ul-Haq pursued non-secular policies (Yasmeen, 1999). Secondly, the geopolitical situation of the region in the 1980s created a need for *mujahideen* to fight against the USSR in Afghanistan. Islamization was used by Zia ul-Haq to attract young men for Jihad. In sum, slogans of Islamization served his purpose to refute Zulfiqar Ali Bhutto's socialist ideology to one end and to garner emotional support and ideological grounds for war against socialism (USSR). Where counter-narratives were not available to subdue Zulfiqar Ali Bhutto's actions, Zia ul-Haq showed extremity. He inflicted severe punishments on allies of Zulfiqar Ali Bhutto. Many *jialas* (supporters of Zulfiqar Ali Bhutto) were arrested on fake charges and were imprisoned for years.

Zia ul-Haq did not stop at eliminating the separate electorate, his legislative proselytization continued. His legal initiatives of amending blasphemy laws put the minorities at further risk of isolation and discrimination. To gain popular support, he played havoc with the society by channelizing societal prejudices into legal courses of action against dissenting and unwanted voices. Sub-sections 295B and 295C were added to the Pakistan Penal Code. These sections criminalized the defiling of the Holy Quran with life imprisonment and defiling of the name of the Holy Prophet with the death sentence, respectively. Also, a new section of the Constitution, section 298A, was included in 1980 that criminalized defiling of any other personage revered in Islam with three-year imprisonment. The changes legitimized anti-minority sentiments and gave a legal tool to persecute the minorities.

Zia ul-Haq's amendments to legal instruments regarding religious offences created more advantages in favour of the majority Muslims. Ahmadis, who had been declared non-Muslims only a decade earlier underwent another legal persecution in 1984 where they were barred from reciting Azan (the religious call to prayer) and calling their prayer houses Masjid (the word for Muslims' prayer house). These legal amendments put the Ahmadis at an even further margin of society. The legal discrimination coupled with cultural violence gave a social legitimacy to the incidents of direct violence against Ahmadis in particular. Since the promulgation of blasphemy laws in the 1980s, the misuse of these laws against minorities and fellow Muslims began. Fake cases had been registered for economic gain and personal vendettas. The number of cases registered under the blasphemy laws show that minorities fell prey to these laws disproportionately. At the time in Pakistan, less than 4 percent of the population belonged to minorities; however they faced 45 percent of the blasphemy accusations (Curtis, 2016).

Zia ul-Haq's patronage of religious segments catalyzed the opening of new religious seminaries across the country. The number of religious seminaries (*madaris*) increased exponentially during the 1980s. These *madaris* were receiving foreign funding as well as they were supported by the State from the Zakat Fund (Zakat is a religious tax that every Muslim has to pay annually at the rate of 2.5 percent of his/her total wealth). Zakat was considered a private matter but Zia ul-Haq institutionalized its collection. All the banks were ordered to deduct Zakat from all Muslim account holders on the first day of the Islamic month of Ramaddan. Zia ul-Haq used these funds to finance religious seminaries to create more *mujahideen* for the Afghan war. Up to thirty-six percent of the costs of the madaris, especially of the Deobandi sect (one of two main branches of Sunni Islam in Pakistan), were met by the government (Yasmeen, 1999). The increased number of students boosted the street power of religious–cum–political parties including Jamiat Ulema e Islam (a political party which is derived from the Deobandi sect's philosophy). Jamat e Islami (JI), another religious based political party that was founded by a religious scholar Maulana Maudodi who believed in a dichotomy of citizenship between Muslims and non-Muslims, also played a key role in Zia ul-Haq's government. The Jamat eIslami remained an ally of Zia ul-Haq and occupied key ministries in Zia ul-Haq's cabinet including the education ministry where a curriculum was introduced that promoted the Jihad element of Islam. Extremist religious actors that had established their legitimacy during the Afghan Jihad era acquired space in mainstream media. Graduates of religious seminaries were awarded certificates equal to a Master's degree, and they were eligible to apply for any mainstream job that required a Master's degree. Zia ul-Haq's patronage of religious extremists brought them to the mainstream and they became a regular party in power games at the national level. The process of religious politicization can be compared to the militarization of politics which had not ended since martial law was first introduced by Ayub Khan.

Zulfiqar Ali Bhutto's declaration of Ahmadis as non-Muslims was followed by Zia ul-Haq's Islamization, and the backlash against democracy (especially in the 1980s) substantially ousted the non-Muslims from political life. In 1988, Zia ul-Haq was killed in an air-crash and democracy got a new chance. However, the democratic experiment lasted for just a decade.

The fragile democracy of the 1990s

When Pakistan saw a short spell of democracy after Zia ul-Haq's death, politicians in Pakistan then downplayed the opportunity to strengthen democracy by conspiring against elected governments. Benazir Bhutto, the daughter of former Prime Minister Zulfiqar Ali Bhutto, was elected as Prime Minister in 1988. Although she was more inclined towards liberal ideology but the democratic transition could not bring any significant change to minorities' rights. Her government was toppled on accusations of corruption. Then, Nawaz Sharif who remained Chief Minister of Punjab (the most populous province of Pakistan) under Zia ul-Haq's regime, became the Prime Minister. Sharif was more inclined towards right-wing Islamic ideology. And under his leadership, in 1998, the Parliament passed the 15th Constitutional Amendment that added Article 2-B to the Constitution. Under this law, the government got the authority to impose Sharia laws in the country. Additionally, it withdrew Parliament's power of laying down a Code of Ethics for official functionaries including judges and legislators. These powers were transferred to the government itself. This Amendment put minorities at further risk of State discrimination.

The tragedy of Shantinagar also took place during the tenure of an elected government in 1997. A village in the Khanewal district of Punjab was raided by a furious mob of Muslims who suspected that some of the residents of the village of Shantinagar had defiled the Holy Quran. In a series of incidents, Muslims destroyed 13 churches, 1,500 houses of Christians and numerous shops (Religious Extremism and its Impact on Non-Muslims, 2018). Ahmadis had long been facing mob violence but this was one of the first incidents where Christians also faced large-scale mob violence. Nevertheless, the situation would change, but for unexpected reasons.

Pervez Musharraf's enlightened moderation

By the end of the 1990s General Pervez Musharraf was the army chief. However, tension and distrust between Musharraf and Nawaz Sharif, the then Prime Minister, had started to build. In 1999, Nawaz Sharif tried to replace Pervez Musharraf with a new Chief of Army Staff. Instead, Pervez Musharraf toppled Nawaz Sharif's government through a coup and imprisoned leaders of the Pakistan Muslim League Nawaz, including Nawaz Sharif. A year after the coup, the 9/11 attacks in 2001 on the US changed the geopolitical situation again to something similar to the situation during Zia ul-Haq's initial years. The United States demanded Pakistan's support to fight terrorists in Afghanistan. General Pervez Musharraf agreed to support the US. However, unlike Zia-ul-Haq, domestically Musharraf promoted the idea of "Enlightened Moderation", which focused on promoting moderate Islam and discouraging the extremist interpretation of Islamic teachings. This turned extremist Muslims against Musharraf while minorities welcomed this idea. During his time in power, the government restored the reserved seats for religious minorities in 2002. The seat division was similar to that when there was a separate electorate, i.e. four seats each for Hindus and Christians, one each for Sikhs, Parsis and Ahmadis and one for Buddhists. However, in the following years, the number of reserved seats for the minorities remained the same despite a 32 percent increase in total seats for the National Assembly of Pakistan.

2008–2018: violence against minorities by non-State actors and the State's response

General Pervez Musharraf eventually allowed for a new transition attempt towards democracy. It started in the most terrible way when Benazir Bhutto was assassinated in December 2007 after just having returned from her exile. A democratic election was eventually held in February 2008, and then until 2018, the Pakistan People's Party (the left-inclined political party) and the Pakistan Muslim League Nawaz (the party inclined towards the Islamic right wing) once again had alternating terms in the government of five years each. Since Pakistan had become a US ally in the War on Terror, and was carrying out operations in the country to fight terrorists, the terrorists who claimed to be religious fundamentalists increased attacks targeting security forces, civilian populations and minorities. Terrorists equated Christians with supporters of the US and thus carried out deadly attacks on churches in Pakistan. To mention some of the attacks, in September 2013, a church in Peshawar was bombed by terrorists where nearly 85 people died (Boone, 2013) and the attackers claimed that the bomb blast was the response to the killing of Muslims in tribal areas of Pakistan by the US drone strikes. Two years later, in 2015, two churches were attacked in Lahore claiming 20 lives with several injured.

For Ahmadis, the situation was always bad, but it got worse during this decade when "democratization" was supposedly taking place. To mention a few of the incidents, in 2010, the Ahmadi prayer area was targeted, and hundreds were killed (CNN Wire Staff, 2010). In 2018, a 100-year-old prayer facility of the Ahmadiya community was destroyed in Sialkot (Sayeed, 2018). Along with these brutal attacks they were consistently harassed by the majority Muslims. The State machinery could not protect well the community and its worship places. Even non-Ahmadis who stood for religious minorities and civil liberties were targeted. For instance, Sabeen Mahmud – a progressive human rights activist, was murdered for speaking up for human rights. Another human rights defender, the lawyer Rashid Rehman, was also murdered because he was defending Junaid Hafeez (a lecturer at Baha uddinn Zakariya University Multan), who was accused of blasphemy. However, the State did conclude some high-profile anti-minority criminal cases. Also, the murderers of Sabeen Mahmud were arrested and sentenced to death.

Furthermore, through a landmark judgment in 2016, Mumtaz Qadri who murdered the Governor of Punjab province, was sentenced to death despite massive public pressure. Mumtaz Qadri was a police official who was on duty to provide security to the then Governor (Salman Taseer, a public opponent of anti-minority blasphemy laws). Qadri's action was celebrated by many lawyers who offered free legal support to him. He was declared a hero by many religious elements. Public rallies were organized in favour of his action. However, the government did not submit to the extremists' demands for Mumtaz Qadri's release. Eventually Qadri was hanged. Similarly, the culprits of 2010 attacks on the Ahmadi mosque were sentenced to death by the anti-terrorism courts. In another case, five individuals were booked under the charges of a mob attack that killed a Christian couple over blasphemy allegations in 2014 (Ghumman and Gabol, 2016).

However, even if it is evident that the state has tried to counter terrorism in the country targeting minorities, there are many more ways that suppression of minorities continues to be exercised in the country. Forced conversions of Christians and Hindus to Islam is another challenge faced by the minorities. At times, the conversions are voluntary, but many times non-Muslims are forced to convert by extremists. Hindu and Christian girls are kidnapped and to cover up the crime they are converted to Islam forcefully. Due to fear of forced conversions many parents marry off their young girls (Saeed, 2016). The issue of forced conversion has been prevalent for decades, but it certainly got worse after 2008 due to a general increase in criminality and religious extremism.

For the last two decades the successive governments have taken few concrete steps to soften the environment of tension between the Muslim and non-Muslim segments. To end discrimination against minorities, the Supreme Court of Pakistan gave a judgment in June 2014 that led the Federal Government towards developing a dynamic task force for the protection of religious minorities. The then Parliament passed a law titled "National Commission for Minorities Act 2015". This Act established a National Commission for Minorities with six official and eleven non-official members. Non-official members included representation from Hindu, Christian, Sikh, Bahai and Parsi communities. However, Ahmadis were not given any representation. The establishment of the National Commission for Minorities under the Ministry of Religious

Affairs was a concrete step forward for protecting minorities (Glendon and Swett, 2015). But the exclusion of Ahmadis showed the then government's poor stance on ensuring the rights of *all* minorities.

Recent developments relating to discrimination and the situation for minorities

In October 2018, Pakistan Tehreek e Insaf (Pakistan Justice Party) came into power. This popular party has managed to engage youth and brought a more positive image of Pakistan to the outside world. With regards to improvements to lives of minorities, this government has also taken some initiatives. First, the National Commission for Minorities formed in 2016 was renotified in May 2020 with an addition of a member from the Kalash community. Ahmadis were given representation initially, but the government changed the decision shortly after due to public pressure. The renotification of the Minority Commission expressed the government's intentions to safeguard minorities. However, the move was not welcomed by minority representatives. The Chairman of People's Commission for Minority Rights, Peter Jacob, criticized the process of formation of the Commission. He stated that the Supreme Court ordered to establish the Commission through an act of Parliament, but the government had created the commission through cabinet approval. This does not give the Commission the legal sustainability and administrative and financial autonomy that is required for independent working (Pakistan Today, 2020). In the same year, the government established an economic advisory committee that included a US-based Pakistani economist Atif Mian who happened to be an Ahmadi too. His nomination had to be withdrawn due to anti-Ahmadiya sentiments that gave rise to massive public pressure.

The situation for other minorities has seen some improvements. In 2019, the government established the Kartarpur Corridor to allow the Sikh community from within Pakistan and from India to visit their holy site Darbar Sahib, located in Pakistan at a distance of 4.5 kilometres from the Pakistan–India border. A special access package for the Indian Sikh community has been introduced allowing them to visit the Gurdwara inside Pakistan without a visa. Although this step facilitated the Indian Sikh community, it gave a message to minorities of Pakistan that the State is considerate of their religious rights.

In 2020, another positive step to ensure minorities' right to practice their religion was taken by the federal government by allocating land for construction of a Mandir (temple) for the Hindu community in Islamabad. However, the construction process had to be stopped for a while due to massive public outrage. The government engaged Muslim religious scholars and asked them to harmonize public sentiments in favour of construction of the temple. This strategy worked and the construction of the temple was resumed. Similarly, in another incident, the government took firm action against criminals who were involved in the desecration of a Hindu temple in the Karak district of Pakistan (Siddiqui, 2020).

The impression of how the situation for minorities has changed over time is to say the least chequered.

Conclusion

In Pakistan, steps have been and are being taken by the State to ensure rights of minorities. The successive State patronage in the past has nonetheless developed strong anti-minority sentiments among Muslim masses that will take long, consistent and concerted efforts by the successive governments to undo. The damage caused to the minorities is extensive. In Pakistan the evolution of minority rights did not remain linear; instead it evolved in a circular way with the change of governments and regimes, and not always following or being synchronized with autocratization and democratization movements. However, one constant component was the escalation of negative emotions among masses against minorities, although the hatred against each minority group is at a different level and because of different reasons. To reiterate the context, Hindus are hated because of animosity against India, while Christians are associated with the West and America. Ahmadis face the fiercest antipathy, caused by a religious interpretation that anyone who leaves Islam is punishable with death. Pakistan's history reflects that it does not simply struggles between military and civilian forces that put minorities at more risk. For instance, the decision of declaring a segment of community non-Muslim through a Constitutional Amendment was done by a democratically elected government (Zulfiqar Ali Bhutto's). Moreover, the representation of minorities in the Senate was raised by a dictator (Musharraf). To empower minorities, it will take concerted efforts by successive governments with a multi-pronged strategy to deflate anti-non-Muslim sentiments, along with stricter implementation of the existing laws related to protection of minorities in a more genuine democratic setting.

Bibliography

'1953 Lahore riots' (2021). Wikipedia. Available at: <https://en.wikipedia.org/w/index.php?title=1953_Lahore_riots&oldid=1029957349> [Accessed: 2 September 2021].

2018. *Religious Extremism and its Impact on non-Muslims*. Christian Study Centre, pp.140–41.

Boone, J., 2013. Pakistan church bomb: Christians mourn 85 killed in Peshawar suicide attack. *The Guardian*. [online] Available at: <www.theguardian.com/world/2013/sep/23/pakistan-church-bombings-christian-minority> [Accessed: 11 January 2021].

Church of Pakistan | Protestant denomination, 1998. *Encyclopedia Britannica*. Available at: <www.britannica.com/topic/Church-of-Pakistan> [Accessed: 2 September 2021].

CNN Wire Staff, 2010. Death toll rises to 98 after Lahore attacks – CNN.com. Available at: <www.cnn.com/2010/WORLD/asiapcf/05/28/pakistan.violence/index.html> [Accessed: 2 September 2021].

Curtis, L., 2016. Religious Freedom in Pakistan: Glimmers of Light on a Darkening Horizon. *The Review of Faith & International Affairs*, 14(2), pp.23–30.

Election Commission of Pakistan, 1990. Report on The General Elections 1988, Vol I. [online] pp.205–7. Available at: <www.ecp.gov.pk/ge/General%20Elections%201990%20Vol-I%20Report.pdf> [Accessed: 11 January 2021].

Glendon, M. and Swett, K., 2015. The National Interest – Where Your Religion Can Still Send You to Jail. [online] USCIRF.gov. Available at: <www.uscirf.gov/news-room/op-eds/national-interest-where-your-religion-can-still-send-you-jail> [Accessed: 11 January 2021].

Government of Pakistan: Ministry of Religious Affairs and Interfaith Harmony, 2020. *Year Book 2019–2020*.

Ghumman, T. and Gabol, I., 2016. ATC Sentences Five to Death over Burning Alive Christian Couple in Kot Radha Kishan in 2014 [WWW Document]. DAWN.COM. Available at: <www.dawn.com/news/1298157> [Accessed 13 October 21].

Lührmann, A. and Lindberg, S., 2019. A third wave of autocratization is here: what is new about it?. *Democratization*, 26(7), pp.1095–113, DOI: 10.1080/13510347.2019.1582029.

Malik, A., 2019. Narrating Christians in Pakistan through Times of War and Conflict. *South Asia: Journal of South Asian Studies*, 43(1), pp.68–83.

Nasr, S., 1996. *Mawdudi and the Making of Islamic Revivalism*. New York: Oxford University Press.

Pakistan Today, 2020. Suddle challenges reconstitution of 'toothless' commission for minorities. [online] Available at: <www.pakistantoday.com.pk/2020/05/07/suddle-approaches-supreme-court-minorities-commission/> [Accessed: 11 January 2021].

Pbs.gov.pk, n.d. DEMOGRAPHIC INDICATORS – 1998 CENSUS | Pakistan Bureau of Statistics | Pakistan Bureau of Statistics. [online] Available at: <www.pbs.gov.pk/content/demographic-indicators-1998-census> [Accessed: 11 January 2021].

Saeed, R., 2016. Construction and Manifestationof Masculinities among Hindu Communitiesof Mirpurkhas and Tharparkar, Sindh. [online] Islamabad. Available at: <https://rozan.org/a-formative-research/> [Accessed: 11 January 2021].

Sayeed, S., 2018. Pakistani mob destroys 100-year-old minority Ahmadi mosque. [online] www.reuters.com. Available at: <www.reuters.com/article/us-pakistan-ahmadis/pakistani-mob-destroys-100-year-old-minority-ahmadi-mosque-idUSKCN1IP20H> [Accessed: 11 January 2021].

Siddiqui, N., 2020. 14 arrested for destroying Hindu shrine in KP's Karak. [online] Dawn.COM. Available at: <www.dawn.com/news/1598867> [Accessed: 28 January 2021].

Statisticstimes.com, 2020. Democracy Index 2019 – StatisticsTimes.com. [online] Available at: <http://statisticstimes.com/ranking/democracy-index.php> [Accessed: 11 January 2021].

Stern, J., 2000. Pakistan's Jihad Culture. *Foreign Affairs*, 79(6), p.115.

Tunio, H., 2019. Census 2017: Two years on, govt mum on official minority count. *The Express Tribune*.

UNHCR, 2017. UNHCR Eligibility Guidelines for Assessing the International Protection Needs of Members of Religious Minorities from Pakistan, January 2017, HCR/EG/PAK/17/01. Available at: <www.refworld.org/docid/5857ed0e4.html> [Accessed: 3 September 2021].

Yasmeen, S., 1999. Islamisation and democratisation in Pakistan: Implications for women and religious minorities. *South Asia: Journal of South Asian Studies*, 22(sup001), pp.183–95.

Zakaria, F., 2007. *The Future of Freedom*. New York: W.W. Norton & Co.

17

CPEC, GOVERNANCE, AND CHINA'S BELT AND ROAD IN SOUTH ASIA

The path of most resistance?

Marc Lanteigne[1]

Introduction: CPEC and China's South Asian strategies

Although China's Belt and Road Initiative (*yidai yilu*一带一路) (BRI) trade policies have frequently been presented by Beijing as primarily an economic exercise, designed to more effectively link China with key cross-regional markets, both political and security concerns have never hovered far from the BRI in several ways. At the same time, Belt and Road agreements and investments have also had effects on various levels of local governance among BRI partners. Few examples of these effects have more effectively been demonstrated than in South Asia, where reactions to these emerging trade routes have been especially polarizing. While this region acts as a key land bridge to other parts of Asia, just as crucial for the BRI has been the Indian Ocean, which is by far the most important link in the '21st Century Maritime Silk Road' which Beijing wishes to create, since the waterway connects the Chinese economy to regions, especially Africa and the Middle East, with which Beijing is especially anxious to deepen engagement. Moreover, China is also seeking to expand its economic presence within the Indian Ocean area itself, raising questions about potential regional rivalries given India's traditional dominance of that region.

Several South Asian / Indian Ocean governments have engaged China in the wake of its BRI overtures. By far, however, the most prominent actor in the South Asian 'wing' of the Belt and Road has been Pakistan, a venerable Chinese ally and political partner since well before the government of Xi Jinping introduced the BRI in 2013. Islamabad has been the recipient of arguably the most formal and intricate element of the Initiative, namely the China–Pakistan Economic Corridor (*ZhongBa jingji zoulang*中巴经济走廊) or CPEC (Ministry of Planning – Pakistan 2021). This development blueprint was founded in 2013, a result of a proposal by Chinese Premier Li Keqiang, as a constellation of development and infrastructure projects designed to further develop the Pakistani economy and consolidate the country's bilateral economic ties with Beijing (Reuters/SCMP 23 May 2013). Central to the success of this enterprise was the development and expansion of the Pakistani port of Gwadar to act as a transit hub for Chinese maritime shipping and a nexus for Chinese trade further inland, to South and Central Asia. Both China and Pakistan frame CPEC as an exercise in mutual economic

DOI: 10.4324/9781003042211-20

development. Yet in many ways, CPEC is also a microcosm of the Belt and Road as a whole, reflecting the challenges of developing infrastructure and the relevant financing, in addition to having to integrate the economic aspects of the BRI with local and regional politics and strategies, effecting various levels of governance within Pakistan and creating a challenge to the already-fragile political structures which were created after the return to civilian government in the country in 2008.

At present, it remains too soon to judge the success of CPEC, as many of its components have been beset with delays, political pushback within various administrative levels in Pakistan and ongoing security challenges. The economic and health effects of the post-2020 global pandemic on the region and on Sino–Pakistan cooperation are yet to be determined. However, in addition to occasional strains on the Sino–Pakistan relationship since CPEC's creation, the plan's evolution has prompted concerns about domestic political directions in Pakistan. However, even at this (indeterminate) stage, it can be argued that the Corridor plan has greatly affected the economic relationship between China and Pakistan and as will be argued, has also added an additional layer to existing regional diplomacy and security concerns, especially in the case of Pakistan's main adversary, India.

CPEC can also be considered a difficult learning experience for Beijing, given that the BRI in Pakistan has also shone an uncomfortable spotlight on the limitations of the Belt and Road in separating developmental from governance and security concerns. However, CPEC's progress thus far should also be evaluated in regard to its potential effects on pluralism in Pakistan, and whether the Corridor may be exacerbating political and security stresses within the country which may open the door to greater risks of autocratization, defined in this sense as a process of regime change towards greater autocracy (Cassani and Tomini 2020). By placing such a great emphasis on the success of the CPEC process, Islamabad may be opening the door to greater risks of both political schisms and regional rivalries within Pakistan, as well as forcing questions about the internal security of the country as it continues to struggle with insurgencies and terrorism in the country's peripheries.

The inception, and uneven trajectory, of the BRI in South Asia

During the two initial speeches by President Xi which inaugurated China's Belt and Road projects, the first outlining the 'belt' as a series of land routes connecting Northeast Asia to Europe via Russia and Eurasia, and the second detailing the 21st Century Maritime Silk Road, South Asia was not directly mentioned, but it became obvious that the region was going to be affected very much in its early stages by the BRI. President Xi first described the 'belt', during his speech in Astana, Kazakhstan, as working its way through Central Asia, while the subsequent speech on the Maritime Silk Road was given in Jakarta and featured the Association of Southeast Asian Nations (ASEAN) as the main case example (Xi 2014).

Yet, since both Central and Southeast Asia are adjacent to South Asia, it was clear that for Beijing to be successful in the development of both facets of the BRI, the Indian Ocean region would be needed by China as a vital conduit to numerous overseas markets. Moreover, for the BRI in that part of the world to be successful, Beijing would not only need to develop many partnerships with countries in the region, but also multiple points of access for Chinese trade, especially given concerns about both rival sea powers India and the United States (Kaplan 2011, 277–93). Before turning to the specific case study of Pakistan, it is necessary to observe how the BRI has developed in the overall South Asia / Indian Ocean milieu, given that while Islamabad remains the anchor of the BRI in the region, the Belt and Road has been making regional gains elsewhere with the possibility Pakistan may evolve into a core of the initiative's expanded Indian Ocean network.

India, a strategic rival to China, is an ideal starting point as well as the antithesis to the Pakistani case. New Delhi, an avowed non-participant in the BRI, dominates South Asia not only geographically but also due to its economy and its military power. Sino–Indian trade has traditionally been robust, and the two states also participate in larger economic and strategic regimes, including the Group of Twenty, the 'BRICS' configuration (the economic cooperation between the large emerging economies of Brazil, China, India, Russia and South Africa), the Shanghai Cooperation Organisation (SCO), and the Beijing-led Asian Infrastructure Investment Bank (AIIB) (Cooper and Farooq 2016). China is also an observer in the South Asian Association for Regional Cooperation (SAARC), which counts India and Pakistan as its largest members. Politically, however, the Sino–Indian bilateral relationship has a far different shape, starting with the two powers being regional adversaries who fought a frontier conflict in 1962 which resulted in China's annexation of the Aksai Chin region. The two countries continue to maintain a tense watch over their disputed mutual border which has occasionally bubbled over into violence in the succeeding decades. China's close relations with Pakistan, starting with a friendship agreement in 1956 and continuing with closer economic and security cooperation (Khan 1961), further elevated Beijing as a security challenge in the eyes of the Indian government.

What has changed due to the BRI are emerging Indian concerns about Chinese economic encirclement via the various land and sea elements of the Belt and Road, as well as the possibility that the BRI in South Asia could evolve into a 'Trojan Horse' to reduce India's own power in the region. Thus, New Delhi has kept out of the Initiative, reflecting the ongoing disconnect between the economic and strategic dimensions of the Sino–Indian relationship, a situation which commentators have referred to as the 'four C' problem ('conflict, competition, cooperation and containment') (Sachdeva 2018; Joshi 2018). While both China and India are large economies with burgeoning markets, Prime Minister Narendra Modi has declined to sign a Belt and Road cooperation agreement with Beijing.

Decades of mistrust between Beijing and New Delhi, including over the status of their border and Beijing's robust, 'all-weather' (*quantianhou* 全天候) relationship with Pakistan (Mu 2018), have been more recently compounded by concerns in New Delhi about an increasing Chinese security presence throughout the region. This stance not only reflects worries about expanded Chinese economic diplomacy in many parts of South Asia and the Indian Ocean, including via the BRI, but also the enhancement of Chinese military land and sea-power which may challenge traditional Indian hegemony in these regions. In 2015, Beijing announced its intention to build a 'logistical support facility' (*baozhang sheshi* 保障设施) in Djibouti, the first such Chinese overseas base (Cabestan 2020). Although it has been described by Chinese authorities as required for resupply and support for multilateral missions, such as counter-piracy operations and peacekeeping, the placement of the facilities on the Red Sea and in a position to oversee North Africa, the Middle East and the Arabian Sea, has further underscored the importance of the Indian Ocean to Chinese security interests (including economic security via the BRI).

The most pressing concern for India *vis-à-vis* a China security threat has been their mutual disputed border. The Doklam Incident in mid-2017, when Chinese and Indian soldiers were involved in a tense faceoff on the tri-border area with Bhutan, starkly illustrated the fact that although there remains a cold peace on the Line of Actual Control (LAC), meaning the frontier between the two powers, an agreement on the demarcation of the boundary in the politically fragile Kashmir region remains elusive (Panda 2017).

A brief but violent skirmish in June 2020 between Chinese and Indian soldiers in the Galwan River Valley, in the Aksai Chin area resulted in at least twenty fatalities from the Indian side and an unspecified number of deaths and injuries of Chinese military personnel. Despite the fact that no firearms were present during the fighting, rocks, batons and other improvised mêlée weapons were used, while some deaths were reportedly caused by falls from great heights. This was the first time such an incident of such magnitude took place along the LAC since 1975. The political aftershocks, and Indian outcry after the incident, further degraded the diplomatic situation between the two governments (Peri et al. 2020; Goldman 2020; Singh 2021). The Modi administration has thus been forced to walk a fine line between moving to better check Chinese security interests in South Asia, and maintaining key Indian economic links with Chinese markets despite the souring political relationship, especially in the wake of Indian public outcry over the Doklam and Galwan incidents.

Elsewhere in the region, medium powers Bangladesh and Myanmar have been much more open to BRI engagement, and both countries have been central to Beijing's interests in developing a stronger presence on the Indian Ocean coast. The BRI has gained support in Bangladesh, not only because of Chinese economic power but also because the initiative opens the possibility of developing Beijing ties as a counterweight to India. China, in turn, has expressed interest in engaging Bangladesh through various development programmes including the Bangladesh–China–India–Myanmar (BCIM) corridor (Mardell 2020, Saimum 2020). China has retained its dominant role in Myanmar regional relations, with Yangon as a supporter of the BRI despite Myanmar's own security concerns with Beijing and local Myanmar concerns about the financial viability of the China-backed Kyaukphyu port project (Lanteigne 2019; Reed 2020; Ryack 2020). Small states Bhutan and Nepal have found themselves often caught between two giants, as China and India have accelerated their geopolitical rivalry in the Himalayas. The Doklam Incident, for example, underscored Bhutan's tenuous strategic situation, and that state has also eschewed participation in the BRI. Nepal, by contrast, has been more receptive to Chinese investments, especially since the 2015 earthquakes, as Beijing was a major provider of aid and support to the Nepalese government during that crisis (Parashar 2019; Vater and Siegel 2019).

To the south, Sri Lanka has been frequently presented in the West, especially the United States, as a Belt and Road cautionary tale about the dangers of a too-close embrace of the BRI in the form of Chinese 'debt traps'. However, in reality the island nation represented a (rare) case of an asset transfer to Beijing, in this case the port facilities at Hambantota, due to non-payment of debts. Despite being commonly cited as an example of alleged Chinese predatory loan practices, the Sri Lankan case in reality was a result of overall poor financial management of which China was only a minor player in Colombo's overall debt crises (Kratz et al. 2019; Jones and Hamieri 2020; Hundlani and Kannangara 2020). However, Chinese economic dominance in Sri Lanka continues to be a concern not only for detractors within the country but also for India. In December 2020, for example, it was announced that a Chinese firm would build a US$300 million tyre manufacturing plant near Hambantota, which would make the first major BRI Chinese investment in local manufacturing. Moreover, there remain concerns that Hambantota itself could in the future be used not only to service civilian ships but potentially Chinese naval vessels as well. This despite the fact that plans were announced in mid-2018 to use the port for the Sri Lankan navy, not Chinese military vessels (Agence France-Presse / South China Morning Post 2020; Reuters 2 January 2018).

Finally, the island economies of the Maldives, Mauritius and Seychelles have become the focus of Beijing's local 'small state' diplomacy within the Belt and Road frameworks (MacDougall and Taneja 2020; Robinson 2015, 88–93). Chinese debts in the Maldives related to the BRI, including the centrepiece Sinamale Bridge project completed in 2018, became the source of intense political concern in the latter's government. The situation is less confrontational in

Mauritius, however, as that state celebrated the activation of a bilateral free trade agreement (FTA), the first China has penned with an African state, in January 2021. China has expressed hopes that this deal will be a test for future agreements in Africa, as Chinese economic diplomacy on the continent continues to accelerate at a rapid pace (Ethirajan 2020; Mundy and Hille 2019; Nyabiage 2021). The government of the Seychelles has also been a supporter of the BRI, and the island state's willingness to foster closer economic cooperation with Beijing was further affirmed during a visit by Chinese Foreign Minister Wang Yi in the first month of 2021, with meetings which included pledges of further Chinese support in the areas of energy, tourism and transportation, as well as health in the wake of the global pandemic which began the previous year. Seychelles also received the distinction of being the first African state to distribute the China-made vaccine for the Covid-19 coronavirus (CGTN 2021; AFP / SCMP 10 January 2021).

Thus, Beijing has made significant gains in its 'ink spot' strategy in developing the BRI in South Asia, as well as addressing the potential for pushback by India. All of these regional successes, however, remain modest compared to the commitments which the Chinese government made to Pakistan via the CPEC process. The potential successes of CPEC would be seen by Beijing as a significant vote of confidence for the greater Belt and Road, which has now become the centrepiece of Chinese foreign policy and cross-regional diplomacy.

The fundamentals of CPEC and Pakistan's responses

The economic relationship between China and Pakistan, despite weathering numerous political storms, has remained robust since the Belt and Road was initiated, with total trade in 2019 measured at just under US$18 billion (down from a 2017 peak of US$20.1 billion). The two countries had signed a free trade agreement in 2006, following up that pact with a similar agreement of liberalization of services three years later and with an updated FTA in 2019. By 2011, China had become Pakistan's largest trading partner (MFA China 2021; Shah et al. 2020; Kundi 2020), and given the strength of bilateral cooperation, as well as Chinese strategic interests in the Indian Ocean, it was not surprising that Islamabad would be amongst the first, and the largest, of BRI-related initiatives.

As the name suggests, the core of CPEC was the planned creation of infrastructure which would connect the far western Chinese territory of Xinjiang with international markets via the southern Pakistan coast, and specifically that country's port city of Gwadar. However, in addition to communication and transportation (highways and railways), CPEC is also envisioned as a platform for bilateral cooperation with other sectors including agriculture, energy, finance, health, human development, information technology and tourism. Various China-backed Special Economic Zones (SEZs) were also established in various Pakistani provinces, including Balochistan, Punjab, and Sindh, as well as in the Federally Administered Tribal Areas (FATA), which in 2018 were incorporated into the province of Khyber Pakhtunkhwa, and Pakistan's holdings in Kashmir, referred to in Pakistan itself as Azad Jammu and Kashmir, but in India as Pakistan-occupied Kashmir (PoK). Economic security concerns were also incorporated into CPEC thinking, as illustrated by the additional focus on counter-poverty measures as well as maintaining border stability and associated human security and stability in the frontier regions, especially given the often-precarious situation in Kashmir (Government of Pakistan 2020; Syed 2020; Chen and Zhang 2016).

What made the CPEC idea distinct, however, was that its projects would loop together aspects of both the land based 'belt' and the maritime 'road', via what was referred to as a '1+4' planning structure, with the 'one' being the actual economic corridor, accompanied by four sets of projects: energy, industrial cooperation, infrastructure, and the Port of Gwadar development initiatives (Wing et al. 2020). As one Chinese academic paper argued, there were many 'early harvest' (*zaoqi shouhuo*早期收获) successes within CPEC projects, including the expansion of Gwadar, as specific energy and transportation infrastructure as well as in agriculture and services, but the Corridor is far from complete (Tao and Gu 2019). There have also been considerable problems faced by both Beijing and Islamabad which have slowed progress. These matters include internal political disputes within Pakistan, concerns about Pakistani debts in relation to the projects, and looming security concerns threatening the project, as well as whether the state of the global economy post-pandemic will adversely affect global trade patterns at least in the near-term.

The original budget for CPEC was estimated at US$45 billion after its original inception, but that figure was later raised upwards to over US$60 billion. Nonetheless, a September 2020 critique by Andrew Small suggested that the latter figure was over-optimistic given that many projects were scaled back between 2015–18, with pandemic-related effects seen as likely adversely affecting the Corridor's bottom line as well (Ul Hassan 2020, Small 2020). Beyond the potential developmental benefits for Pakistan, Islamabad also sees advantages to the Corridor in an improved counterbalance of diplomatic pressures from India, as well as the United States. Despite longstanding diplomatic ties between Islamabad and Washington, American influence in Pakistan relative to China was thought to be eroding, especially during the isolationist US presidency of Donald Trump and its interests in severely reducing financial support for the Pakistani military (Shah 2017; Chacko 2018). Thus, CPEC was also a product of a perceived window of opportunity for the Xi government to further improve its diplomatic and strategic standing in South Asia. In addition to the economic dimensions of CPEC, the Corridor also opened up opportunities for closer cooperation between the Chinese and Pakistani militaries, including reportedly in the areas of joint weapons development and satellite launches (Abi-Habib 2018). However, considering the still-strong role of the military within Pakistani politics, the domestic political effects of this partnership do carry risks involving power-sharing between Pakistan's civilian government and its armed forces.

All roads, figuratively and at times literally, within CPEC lead in some way to Gwadar, and it is this municipality which continues to be a barometer of CPEC's overall progress. Gwadar is a coastal town on the Arabian Sea with an estimated population of 85,000, but with ambitious government plans announced to increase that number to two million by 2050 (Aamir 2020). The area had been an area of interest for China that long-predated the inception of the Belt and Road, but once the BRI had begun to expand in South Asia, the region was to be incorporated into China's Maritime Silk Road interests in the Indian Ocean, as well as Beijing's strategy of developing friendly ports around the area in anticipation of increased Chinese sea traffic. This strategy has frequently been referred to as a 'string of pearls' (*zhenzhu lian*珍珠链) approach on Beijing's part, and many of China's BRI arrangements in and around the Indian Ocean could also have emerging strategic value, much to the chagrin of both India and the United States (MacDonald et al. 2004; Miller 2017, 167–8).

Gwadar and the surrounding areas were purchased by the Pakistani government in 1958 from the Sultanate of Oman, which had overseen the region for approximately two centuries. Islamabad had high expectations of developing an expanded port facility there, while Gwadar's location, not only close to Iran but also to the oil emirates and the fossil fuel-rich Persian Gulf and Strait of Hormuz, caught the attention of China by the late 1990s as Beijing was seeking to develop alternative energy routes to the Malacca Straits in Southeast Asia (Khetran 2014; Khan 2018; Chongyang Institute for Financial Studies of Renmin University 2016; Kalim and Syed 2020). At the turn of this century, the Chinese government was seeking to develop stronger maritime capabilities but was also concerned with the 'Malacca dilemma' (Lanteigne 2008), namely the strategic risks of having the Malacca Straits interdicted by an outside power. Even though importing fossil fuels and other goods via Gwadar was far less cost-effective than the traditional means of using the Strait and the South China Sea route, the former option was considered a vital option in case the latter was threatened. Plans by the Pakistani government to turn Gwadar into a maritime transport hub ran into logistical problems shortly after construction began in 2002, and five years later it was agreed that the contract to complete the work would be granted to the China Overseas Ports Holding Company (*Zhongguo haiwai gangkou konggu youxiangongsi*中国海外港口控股有限公司). The first substantial shipment of Chinese goods to pass through Gwadar was celebrated by both governments in November 2016 (Reuters 13 November 2016; Miller 2017, 175).

As one China-based analysis detailed, the most significant effects of CPEC thus far have been the improvement of 'all-weather strategic cooperation' between the two states and the development of economic 'growth points' within Pakistan thus improving overall economic performances. In addition, CPEC was described as an invaluable model of the advantages of Belt and Road Cooperation, and so Beijing has remained dedicated to ensuring the Corridor is successful (Zhang 2019). From the viewpoint of Pakistan, however, the results have been considerably more mixed, creating political stresses within the country and exacerbating many internal political and regime tensions. After the early harvest successes of CPEC, by 2017 the various processes were beginning to slow down, and concerns were raised that growing tensions between then-Prime Minister Nawaz Sharif, a strong supporter of deepening economic ties with China, and the Pakistani military might lead to a political crisis.

As the aforementioned 2020 study by Andrew Small argued, Mr Sharif's dedication to the CPEC idea resulted in raised suspicions amongst military leaders about a too-close geopolitical relationship with Beijing and the potential for corruption (Small 2020, 35–40). This uncertainty subsequently plagued any further CPEC-related progress until the controversial July 2018 elections, which saw the coming to power of Imran Khan of the Pakistan Movement for Justice (*Pakistan Tehrik-e-Insaf* – PTI) party with the new Prime Minister continuing to support the Corridor but taking on a more balanced stance and noting that Pakistan could also stand to learn from China's previous developmental successes (Al-Jazeera 2018). Prime Minister Khan's arrival in office signalled a more nuanced, smaller-scale 'CPEC 2.0' approach which better fitted the economic realities of both China and Pakistan, but despite the planned slower approach, many of the economic and strategic issues surrounding CPEC remained.

CPEC next: making the most of an uncertain future?

While the global economic trauma during 2020 contributed to reservations about CPEC's short-term agenda, obstacles to its development from various directions had begun to appear well before the pandemic. Among these have been direct political and security concerns for Pakistan which have been affected by CPEC, demonstrating the difficulties created by trying to separate the Corridor from the strategic challenges of the region but also problems of governance and risks of greater autocratization facing Islamabad should various internal power balances be upset by the ongoing development of CPEC plans. These have included the exacerbation of political cleavages within Pakistan, including between various provinces and regions, as well as between civilian actors and the still-politically powerful Armed Forces. After the military government of General Pervez Musharraf, which seized power in 1999, gave way to civilian administrations nine years later, the Pakistan Armed Forces never strayed far from the main levers of power in the country, and under the Khan government, the Army Chief of Staff,

General Qamar Javed Bajwa, exercises considerable influence over the country's foreign affairs, including relations with Beijing (Krishnan 2021, Shah 2020). Thus, CPEC will continue to act as a critical variable in questions of both pluralism and risks of autocratization in the country.

In analysing these concerns, it is efficacious to examine Pakistan's current strategic concerns. Various mechanisms within the CPEC process have found themselves entangled, and in many cases unwittingly, in security concerns plaguing both the north and the south of Pakistan. Chinese CPEC-related investment in Pakistani-held Kashmir has been a sore point for the Modi government since the development of the Corridor. The Line of Control (LoC), which separates Indian- and Pakistan-held Kashmir, routinely sees both sides accusing the other of ceasefire violations, with China, including local Chinese investments, being more frequently seen as an unstable additional element in Kashmir's security situation. Moreover, since the main links for CPEC's transportation projects run through Pakistan-held Kashmir, it remains in Beijing's interests to assure stability, especially with the restive Chinese territory of Xinjiang right across the border (Ramachandran 2018). The Xi government retains hopes that the successful set of CPEC economic and transportation links will also have a stabilizing effect on China's far west, but navigating Pakistan's internal politics and security risks remains a challenge for Beijing.

In keeping with traditional Chinese foreign policy views equating security with counter-poverty, the CPEC process has sought to include components in Pakistan's territory in Kashmir, including a planned SEZ at Moqpondass which would specialize in raw material processing, including metals and minerals (Ministry of Planning – Pakistan 2020; Bhat 2019). However, India's worries about the strategic impact of CPEC's investments in Kashmir, including the Moqpondass installations, were not assuaged when Prime Minister Khan began to moot suggestions in 2019 that Pakistan's territory in Kashmir, still claimed by India, could eventually be incorporated as a new province of Gilgit-Baltistan. Such a move, however, would be seen in New Delhi as not only an escalation of local tensions, but also serving Chinese economic interests, including the enhancing security of the main transport lines under CPEC (Hussein 2020; Kartha 2021; Shahid 2020b).

The security situation facing CPEC is just as precarious in southwestern Pakistan, especially in the case of Balochistan, the least developed province of the country despite being resource-rich and which includes Gwadar. Within the province, local militants and separatists, supported by *Daesh*/Islamic State, have staged attacks and kidnappings, with Chinese nationals also being targeted. This has prompted concerns in both Beijing and Islamabad about the potential for further attempts to destabilize CPEC projects, and these threats have served to create a rift between the country's civilian policymakers and the armed forces. In mid-2020 the Pakistani military began to push for additional legislation which would permit that body to have more direct control over CPEC projects, with the argument that military oversight would quicken the pace of the Corridor's development, given the dysfunction of the Khan administration, as well as assuring Beijing that their investments would be more secure (Findlay 2020; Shakil 2020). Critics of the move, including opposition parties in Pakistan, have expressed concerns that such a new law would considerably strengthen the overall policymaking and economic power of the military. Plans were mooted during 2020 to entirely fence in the Gwadar port facilities before local authorities reversed the decision in January of the following year under public pressure (Aamir 2021; Keegan 2021).

Local anger in Pakistan at China's economic presence in the region has not been aided by the global backlash against reports of re-education facilities in Xinjiang which have targeted the region's Uighur populations. Beijing is seeking to walk a fine line between ensuring the security of its CPEC investments, especially since the Corridor remains at the core of many of China's BRI plans, and avoiding perceptions of developing a hegemonic relationship with

Pakistan. One solution has been for closer, targeted security cooperation between the two governments designed to protect the integrity of the CPEC process, especially in the case of the tenuous security situation in Balochistan caused by the ongoing threat by local militants (Basit 2019). The Chinese and Pakistani governments are worried about direct attacks on CPEC facilities by the Balochistan Liberation Army (BLA), a radical organization which for the past two decades has sought independence from Pakistan, and affiliated groups. Since the CPEC processes began, the BLA has also considered Chinese interests to be legitimate targets (Beg et al. 2019; Washiyama 2020; Chaudhury 2020). Islamabad is concerned that these threats, coupled with the slowdown of the Chinese economy caused by the post-2018 Sino–American trade war and the global pandemic, may temper Beijing's enthusiasm for continuing CPEC at its previous pace, and therefore the Khan government has been interested in allaying Chinese fears over the Corridor's integrity. Improved Sino–Pakistani security cooperation may address issues related to the complications of completing CPEC's main plans in a timely and safe fashion, but it is clear that the problems facing the Corridor are starting to adversely affect civil–military relations within Pakistan, and could create further problems for South Asia's overall stability, especially as it relates to India but also the Indian Ocean as a whole, given regional concerns about China's economic and strategic expansion and whether Pakistan may further evolve as a platform for these ambitions.

Politically, China is also having to face an often-uncertain atmosphere in Islamabad, including concerns about divisions between political actors in Pakistan, communications between government actors and their Chinese counterparts, and managing public expectations of CPEC's goals. The latter became more complicated given the economic shocks, which had begun to weaken the Khan government, caused by the start of the 2020 pandemic and subsequent depressed global economic activity (Liu 2016; Kundi 2021; Findlay and Bokhari 2021). When the project began, the Pakistani political establishment was far from united on the benefits of the Corridor, and Chinese officials were wary of numerous areas of underdevelopment in Pakistan which would hamper CPEC goals, in addition to the difficult security situation in the country. Ensuring that the benefits of CPEC are distributed as evenly as possible throughout Pakistan has also been a considerable challenge for both governments, especially since regionalism, including in Balochistan, has been a longstanding problem for many Pakistani administrations.

Moreover, there has been the omnipresent problem of corruption in Pakistani political quarters, at times creating a backlash on the CPEC process, with one notorious example being an opposition campaign in 2020 to remove the Khan government's main official overseeing CPEC operations, Asim Saleem Bajwa, a retired Lieutenant-General in the Pakistan Army, on corruption and misappropriation of funds charges. In October of that year, Mr Bajwa agreed to step down as an advisor to Prime Minister Khan, but retained his post as CPEC head (You and Zhou 2019; Ahmad et al. 2020; Shahid 2020a; The Hindu / PTI 12 October 2020). The affair further illustrated the problems that the Xi government has had in trying to keep CPEC projects free of influence by internal Pakistani affairs, and underscored the fact that despite the ongoing potential of the Corridor, its eventual success will be greatly dependent on whether a sufficient degree of political (and governmental) stability in Pakistan is maintained. However, CPEC has also revealed another facet of the precarious political balance between the civilian government and the military within Pakistan, and with so much investment at stake, there is the question of whether the push to stabilize Pakistan's economic and security situation so that CPEC can conclude will throw open the door to more visible power struggles and threats to the current system of governance in the form of autocratization risks.

CPEC was crafted to be an economic conduit between China and Pakistan, as well as the 'jewel in the crown' amongst various Belt and Road projects in the South Asia / Indian Ocean regions. Yet, ultimately the Corridor could not escape the development of both a political and a strategic identity, and its building blocks have started to have significant effects on the Sino–Pakistani relationship as well as matters of governance, including effects on civilian–military relations, pluralism, and the integrity of the current system of civilian government, within Pakistan itself. The projects which comprise CPEC have experienced periods of both optimism and pessimism since 2013. The after-effects of the global pandemic, political instabilities within Pakistan, and the cooled relationship between Beijing and New Delhi are all variables which will now determine the near future of CPEC's evolution. The end point of this branch of the Belt and Road may not be easy to predict at present, but it can be argued that its progress has already had a significant effect on questions of governance, the questions of security and stability, and the risks of autocratization in Pakistan, as well as the political and security question throughout South Asia.

Note

1 The author would like to thank Lynn Gardinier, Francesca Rán Rositudóttir and Mingming Shi for their invaluable assistance in the preparation of this chapter.

Bibliography

Aamir, Adnan. (2020). 'Gwadar Port: New Dubai or Pie in the Sky?' *The Interpreter*, 1 May, <www.lowyinstitute.org/the-interpreter/gwadar-port-new-dubai-or-pie-sky>.

Aamir, Adnan. (2021). 'Deadly IS Attack Threatens China's Belt and Road in Pakistan,' *Nikkei Asia*, 10 January 2021, <https://asia.nikkei.com/Spotlight/Belt-and-Road/Deadly-IS-attack-threatens-China-s-Belt-and-Road-in-Pakistan>.

Abi-Habib, Maria. (2018). 'China's "Belt and Road" Plan in Pakistan Takes a Military Turn,' *New York Times*, 19 December 2018.

Agence France-Presse / South China Morning Post. (2020). 'Belt and Road Initiative: China Builds US$300m Factory Near Sri Lanka Port,' 8 December, <www.scmp.com/news/article/3113076/belt-and-road-initiative-china-builds-us300m-factory-near-sri-lanka-port>.

Agence France-Presse / South China Morning Post. (2021). 'Coronavirus: Seychelles Becomes First African Nation to Start Vaccinating Population, Using Chinese Drug,' 10 January, <www.scmp.com/news/world/africa/article/3117144/coronavirus-seychelles-becomes-first-african-nation-start>.

Ahmad, Riaz, Hong, Mi and Lloyd, W. Fernald. (2020). 'Revisiting the Potential Security Threats Linked with the China-Pakistan Economic Corridor (CPEC),' *Journal of the International Council for Small Business* 1(1): 64–80.

Al-Jazeera. (2018). 'Imran Khan's Speech in Full,' 26 July, <www.aljazeera.com/news/2018/7/26/imran-khans-speech-in-full>.

Basit, Saira H. (2019). 'Terrorizing the CPEC: Managing Transnational Militancy in China–Pakistan Relations,' *Pacific Review* 32(4): 694–724.

Beg, Saadia, Tasawar, Baig and Muqarrab, Akbar. (2019). 'Analysis of the Impact of China-Pakistan Economic Corridor (CPEC) on the Insurgency in Balochistan and Options for Conflict Resolution,' *Pakistan Journal of Social Sciences (PJSS)* 39(2): 459–71.

Bhat, Vinayak. (2019). 'Pakistan & China are Building an SEZ in PoK's Gilgit-Baltistan, Satellite Images Show,' *The Print* (India), 27 August, <https://theprint.in/world/pakistan-china-are-building-an-sez-in-poks-gilgit-baltistan-satellite-images-show/282413/>.

Cabestan, Jean-Pierre. (2020). 'China's Military Base in Djibouti: A Microcosm of China's Growing Competition with the United States and New Bipolarity,' *Journal of Contemporary China* 29(125): 731–47.

Cassani, Andrea and Luca, Tomini. (2020). 'Reversing Regimes and Concepts: from Democratization to Autocratization,' *European Political Science* 19: 272–87.

CGTN. (2021). 'China, Seychelles to Jointly Promote Belt and Road Construction,' 10 January, <https://newsaf.cgtn.com/news/2021-01-10/Chinese-FM-holds-talks-with-Seychellois-counterpart-WVaAX7bT1K/index.html>.

Chacko, Johann. (2018). 'The US-China Cold War is Now Playing Out in Pakistan,' *Quartz*, 3 September, <https://qz.com/india/1377225/the-us-china-cold-war-is-now-playing-out-in-pakistan/>.

Chaudhury, Dipanjan Roy. (2020). 'Balochistan & CPEC: China's Achilles' Heel,' *The Economic Times* (India), 31 December 2020, <https://economictimes.indiatimes.com/news/international/world-news/balochistan-cpec-chinas-achilles-heel/articleshow/80049872.cms>.

Chen, Jidong and Zhang, Jianquan. (2016). '中巴经济走廊在 "一带一路" 建设中的定位', ['The Location of Sino–Pakistan Economic Corridor in "One Belt and One Road" Construction,'] 《新疆师范大学学报（哲学社会科学版）》 [*Journal of Xinjiang Normal University (Philosophy and Social Sciences)*] 37(4)(July): 125–33.

China Pakistan Economic Corridor, Ministry of Planning, Development and Special Initiatives, Pakistan. (2021). <http:// cpec.gov.pk>.

Chongyang Institute for Financial Studies of Renmin University. (2016). *Pivot Cities on the Belt and Road* (Beijing: New World Press).

Cooper, Andrew F. and Asif, B. Farooq. (2016). 'The Role of China and India in the G20 and BRICS: Commonalities or Competitive Behaviour?' *Journal of Current Chinese Affairs*, 45(3): 73–106.

Ethirajan, Anbarasan. (2020). 'China Debt Dogs Maldives' "Bridge to Prosperity",' *BBC News*, 17 September, <www.bbc.com/news/world-asia-52743072>.

Findlay, Stephanie. (2020). 'Pakistan Army Muscles in on Belt and Road Project,' *Financial Times*, 28 August.

Findlay, Stephanie, and Farhan, Bokhari. (2021). 'Pakistan's Opposition Circles Floundering Khan,' *Financial Times*, 14 January.

Goldman, Russell. (2020). 'India-China Border Dispute: A Conflict Explained,' *The New York Times*, 17 June.

Government of Pakistan. (2020). 'CPEC Vision and Mission,' <http://cpec.gov.pk/vision-mission/3>.

The Hindu / PTI. (2020). 'Pakistan PM Imran Khan's Top Aide Steps Down Amid Corruption Allegations,' 12 October, <www.thehindu.com/news/international/pakistan-pm-imran-khans-top-aide-steps-down-amid-corruption-allegations/article32834854.ece>.

Hundlani, Divya and Pabasara, Kannangara. (2020). 'The Belt and Road in Sri Lanka: Beyond the Debt Trap Discussion,' *The Diplomat*, 7 May, <https://thediplomat.com/2020/05/the-belt-and-road-in-sri-lanka-beyond-the-debt-trap-discussion/>.

Hussein, Tom. (2020). 'Is China Behind Pakistan's Plan to Annex Kashmir's Gilgit-Baltistan?' *South China Morning Post*, 26 September, <www.scmp.com/week-asia/politics/article/3103109/china-behind-pakistans-plan-annex-kashmirs-gilgit-baltistan>.

Jones, Lee and Shahar, Hamieri. (2020). 'Debunking the Myth of "Debt-Trap Diplomacy",' *Chatham House*, 19 August, <www.chathamhouse.org/2020/08/debunking-myth-debt-trap-diplomacy/4-sri-lanka-and-bri>.

Joshi, Manoj. (2018). 'Fresh Overtures Hint at a Thaw in India-China Relations,' *Asia Times*, 9 March, <https://asiatimes.com/2018/03/fresh-overtures-hint-thaw-india-china-relations/>.

Kalim, Inayat and Areeja, Syed. (2020). 'Maritime Economy and Gwadar Port: A Growth Catalyst,' *Policy Perspectives* 17(1): 73–82.

Kaplan, Robert D. (2011). *Monsoon: The Indian Ocean and the Future of American Power* (New York: Random House).

Kartha, Tara. (2021). 'Pak Caught in Maze of Legality Over Gilgit,' *The Tribune* (India), 5 January 2021, <www.tribuneindia.com/news/comment/pak-caught-in-maze-of-legality-over-gilgit-193743>.

Keegan, Elmer. (2021). 'China-Pakistan Relations: Security Fence at Gwadar Port Creates New Tensions,' *South China Morning Post*, 2 January, <www.scmp.com/news/china/diplomacy/article/3116180/china-pakistan-relations-security-fence-gwadar-port-creates>.

Khan, Hafeez-ur-Rahman. (1961). 'Pakistan's Relations with the People's Republic of China,' *Pakistan Horizon* 14(3): 212–32.

Khan, Naimat. (2018). 'Arab Legacy Lingers as Pakistan's Gwadar Grows from Tiny Fishing Town into Port City,' *Arab News*, 29 April, <www.arabnews.com/node/1489531/world>.

Khetran, Mir Sherbaz. (2014). 'The Potential and Prospects of Gwadar Port,' *Strategic Studies* 34(4): 70–89.

Kratz, Agatha, Allen, Feng, and Logan, Wright. (2019). 'New Data on the "Debt Trap" Question,' Rhodium Group, 29 April, <https://rhg.com/research/new-data-on-the-debt-trap-question/>.

Krishnan, Ananth. (2021). 'China and Pakistan Sign Military Deal Amid Tensions with India,' *The Hindu*, <www.thehindu.com/news/international/china-and-pakistan-sign-military-deal-amid-tensions-with-india/article33219358.ece>.

Kundi, Imran Ali. (2020). 'Second Phase of Pakistan–China Free Trade Agreement Comes into Effect,' *The Nation* (Pakistan), 2 January, <https://nation.com.pk/02-Jan-2020/second-phase-of-pakistan-china-free-trade-agreement-comes-into-effect>.

Kundi, Imran Ali. (2021). 'Pak Economy to Witness Modest 1.5 Percent Growth in FY2021: Moody's,' *The Nation* (Pakistan), 14 January, <https://nation.com.pk/14-Jan-2021/pak-economy-to-witness-modest-1-5-per-cent-growth-in-fy2021-moody-s>.

Lanteigne, Marc. (2008). 'China's Maritime Security and the "Malacca Dilemma",' *Asian Security* 4(2): 143–61.

Lanteigne, Marc. (2019). '"The Rock that Can't be Moved": China's Revised Geostrategies in Myanmar,' *Pacific Review* 32(1): 37–55.

Liu, Zhongyi. (2016). '中巴经济走廊建设：进展与挑战,' ['Construction of the China-Pakistan Economic Corridor: Progress and Challenges'], 《国际问题研究》 [*International Studies*] 3: 122–38.

MacDonald, Juli A., Amy, Donahue and Bethany, Danyluk. (2004). *Energy Futures in Asia* (McLean, VA: Booz Allen Hamilton, 2004).

Mardell, Jacob. (2020). 'The BRI in Bangladesh: Walking the Tightrope between Beijing and Delhi,' *MERICS*, 11 August 2020, <https://merics.org/en/analysis/bri-bangladesh-walking-tightrope-between-beijing-and-delhi>.

McDougall, Derek and Pradeep, Taneja. (2020). 'Sino–Indian Competition in the Indian Ocean Island Countries: The Scope for Small State Agency,' *Journal of the Indian Ocean Region* 16(2): 124–45.

Miller, Tom. (2017). *China's Asian Dream* (London: Zed Books).

Ministry of Foreign Affairs of the People's Republic of China. (2021). '中国同巴基斯坦的关系 (最近更新时间：2020年4月),' [Relations between China and Pakistan (Last updated: April 2020)'], January, <www.fmprc.gov.cn/web/gjhdq_676201/gj_676203/yz_676205/1206_676308/sbgx_676312/>.

Ministry of Planning, Development and Special Initiatives – Government of Pakistan. (2021). 'CPEC China-Pakistan Economic Corridor,' <http://cpec.gov.pk>.

Ministry of Planning, Development and Special Initiatives – Government of Pakistan. (2020). 'Moqpondass SEZ Gilgit-Baltistan,' <http://cpec.gov.pk/project-details/67>.

Mu, Xuequan. (2018). 'China, Pakistan Vow to Push Forward All-Weather Strategic Cooperative Partnership to New High,' *Xinhua*, 9 August, <www.xinhuanet.com/english/2018-09/08/c_137454716.htm>.

Mundy, Simon and Kathrin, Hille. (2019). 'The Maldives Counts the Cost of its Debts to China,' *Financial Times*, 11 February.

Nyabiage, Jevans. (2021). 'China-Mauritius Free-Trade Deal Creates Model for Beijing's Trade with Africa, Observers Say,' *South China Morning Post*, 3 January, <www.scmp.com/news/china/diplomacy/article/3116198/china-mauritius-free-trade-deal-creates-model-beijings-trade>.

Panda, Ankit. (2017). 'The Political Geography of the India-China Crisis at Doklam,' *The Diplomat*, 13 July, <https://thediplomat.com/2017/07/the-political-geography-of-the-india-china-crisis-at-doklam/>.

Parashar, Sachin. (2019). 'After India, Bhutan Too Likely to Skip BRI Forum,' *Times of India*, 14 April, <https://timesofindia.indiatimes.com/world/china/after-india-bhutan-too-likely-to-skip-bri-forum/articleshow/68869308.cms>.

Peri, Dinakar, Suhasini, Haidar and Ananth, Krishnan. (2020). 'Indian Army Says 20 soldiers Killed in Clash with Chinese Troops in the Galwan Area,' *The Hindu*, 17 June 2020.

Reed, John. (2020). 'China and Myanmar Sign Off on Belt and Road Projects,' *Financial Times*, 18 January.

Reuters. (2016). 'Pakistani PM Welcomes First Large Chinese Shipment to Gwadar Port,' 13 November.

Reuters. (2018). 'Sri Lanka to Shift Naval Base to China-Controlled Port City,' 2 July.

Reuters / South China Morning Post. (2013). 'Li Keqiang Urges Development of "China-Pakistan Economic Corridor",' 23 May, <www.scmp.com/news/china/article/1244267/li-keqiang-urges-development-china-pakistan-economic-corridor>.

Robinson, J.J. (2015). *The Maldives: Islamic Republic, Tropical Autocracy* (London: Hurst, 2015), 88–93.

Ryack, Gene. (2020). 'A Hitch in the Belt and Road in Myanmar,' *The Diplomat*, 3 December, <https://thediplomat.com/2020/12/a-hitch-in-the-belt-and-road-in-myanmar/>.

Sachdeva, Gulshan. (2018). 'Indian Perceptions of the Chinese Belt and Road Initiative,' *International Studies* 55(4): 285–96.

Saimum, Rubiat. (2020). 'The Prospect of Belt and Road Initiative in the Context of Bangladesh,' *China Report* 56(4): 464–83.

Shah, Aqil. (2020). 'Will Pakistan's Military Lose Its Grip on Power?' *Foreign Affairs*, 22 December, <www.foreignaffairs.com/articles/pakistan/2020-12-22/will-pakistans-military-lose-its-grip-power>.

Shah, Saeed. (2017). 'China Pushes US Aside in Pakistan,' *Wall Street Journal*, 18 June.

Shah, Syed H., Muhammad, A. Kamal and Da L. Yu. (2020). 'Did China-Pakistan Free Trade Agreement Promote Trade and Development in Pakistan?' *International Journal of Finance and Economics* (20 November) <https://doi.org/10.1002/ijfe.2331>.

Shahid, Kunwar Khuldune. (2020a). 'Asim Bajwa Exposé Underlines the Corruption Linking the Pakistan Army and CPEC,' *The Diplomat*, 4 September, <https://thediplomat.com/2020/09/asim-bajwa-expose-underlines-the-corruption-linking-the-pakistan-army-and-cpec/>.

Shahid, Kunwar Khuldune. (2020b). 'The Unheard Voices of Kashmir,' *The Diplomat*, 24 December 2020, <https://thediplomat.com/2020/12/the-unheard-voices-of-kashmir/>.

Shakil, F.M. (2020). 'China Slowly Retreating from Pakistan's Belt and Road,' *Asia Times*, 26 December 2020, <https://asiatimes.com/2020/12/china-slowly-retreating-from-pakistans-belt-and-road/>.

Singh, Sushant. (2021). 'Why China Is Winning Against India,' *Foreign Policy*, 1 January, <https://foreignpolicy.com/2021/01/01/india-china-himalayas-ladakh-standoff/>.

Small, Andrew. (2020). 'Returning to the Shadows: China, Pakistan, and the Fate of CPEC,' *German Marshall Fund of the United States – Asia Programme* (16)(September).

Syed, Jawad. (2020). 'China's Belt and Road Initiative: A Pakistani Perspective,' *China's Belt and Road Initiative in a Global Context – Volume II: The China-Pakistan Economic Corridor and its Implications for Business*, ed. Jawad Syed and Yung-Hsiang Ying (Cham, Switzerland: Palgrave MacMillan, 2020), 13–40.

Tao, Jiyi and Gu, Heqiang. (2019). '中巴经济走廊 "早期收获" 阶段建设成效探析,' ['The "Early Harvest" Phase of the China-Pakistan Economic Corridor'], 《国际论坛》 [*International Forum*] 3: 3–21.

Ul Hassan, Yaqoob. (2020). 'China-Pakistan Economic Corridor (CPEC) and Questions on Pakistan's Economic Stability,' *Strategic Analysis* 44(2): 137–52.

Vater, Tom and Laure, Siegel. (2019). 'Belt and Road Reaches Nepal's Wild North, Winning China Influence,' *Nikkei Asia*, 9 March, <https://asia.nikkei.com/Spotlight/Belt-and-Road/Belt-and-Road-reaches-Nepal-s-wild-north-winning-China-influence>.

Veena, Ramachandran. (2018). China-Pakistan Economic Corridor: The Uyghur Challenge and the Chinese Security Model,' *The Diplomat*, 30 March, <https://thediplomat.com/2018/03/chinapakistan-economic-corridor-the-uyghur-challenge-and-the-chinese-security-model/>.

Washiyama, Yumi. (2020). 'Balochi Militants Take Aim at Chinese Interests,' *The Diplomat*, 24 July, <https://thediplomat.com/2020/07/balochi-militants-take-aim-at-chinese-interests/>.

Wing, Him Yeung, Yilisha, Pang, and Asad, Aman. (2020). 'South–South Cooperation in South and East Asia: An Event Study of the China–Pakistan Economic Corridor,' *Global Business Review* 21(1): 54–67.

Xi, Jinping. (2014). 'Work Together to Build the Silk Road Economic Belt,' / 'Work Together to Build a 21st Century Economic Silk Road,' *The Governance of China* (Beijing: Foreign Languages Press, 2014), 315–24.

You, Hongbing and Zhou, Zhenzhen. (2019). '中巴经济走廊：推动区域全面合作的新枢,' ['China-Pakistan Economic Corridor: A New Hub to Promote Regional Cooperation'], 《国际经济合作》 [*International Economic Cooperation*] 2: 60–9.

Zhang, Yaoming. (2019). '中巴经济走廊建设:成果、风险与对策,' ['Construction of the China-Pakistan Economic Corridor: Results, Risks and Countermeasures'], 《西北大学学报 (哲学社会科学版)》 [*Journal of Northwest University (Philosophy and Social Sciences Edition)*] 49(4): 14–22.

PART III

Bangladesh

Towards one-party rule

18

BANGLADESH

In pursuit of a one-party state?

Ali Riaz

With democratic backsliding unfolding in an incremental manner in Bangladesh for years, concerns have been expressed since 2016 whether the country will descend into a one-party state. The Strategic Forecast predicted in May 2016 that the country would shift toward single party authoritarianism (Strategic Forecast, 2016) and in early 2018 the Bertelsmann Foundation described Bangladesh as an 'autocracy' (BTI, 2018). In April 2018, a report of *Aljazeera* asked the question – "Is Bangladesh moving towards a one-party state?" (Aljazeera, 2018).

It is against this background that this chapter explores the political trajectory of Bangladesh and examines the likelihood of transformation of governance to a one-party state. The ongoing strategy of the government to neuter the opposition along with a rapid shrinking of space for dissent, and the country's previous history of experiencing a one-party state have contributed to the growing salience of this question. Bangladesh experienced a one-party system between January and August 1975 under the Bangladesh Awami League (AL) which is currently in power. The party had never acknowledged the introduction of the one-party system as a misstep, instead in the context of diminishing trust over the election Prime Minister Sheikh Hasina had suggested in 2019 that reviving the one-party system (Jugantor, 2019), introduced in 1975 by her father Sheikh Mujibur Rahman, offers a solution to the elections–without–voters problem.

One-party states: the nature and scope

In this chapter one-party states are defined as, "states in which, effectively, only one 'mass' political party had full legal existence and in which party membership was practically the *sine qua non* of political power" (Rothman, 1967, p. 675). In discussing the nature and scope of a one-party state, a distinction between *de jure* one-party state, and *de facto* one-party state must be made. *De jure* one-party states are those where the constitutional and legal framework allow only the ruling party to operate. In the 1950s and 1960s, *de jure* one-party states proliferated in various parts of the world, especially in the newly independent countries. The reasons for the emergence and survival of these states were variously explained; for example, a culturalist argument was advanced on the prevalence of one-party states on the African continent (Carter, 1962). Many of the 29 African states that became independent between 1956 and 1965 adopted the one-party system. It was argued that centralizing power was an essential element for stabilizing

DOI: 10.4324/9781003042211-22

the country, particularly where nationalist movements have taken place (Carter, 1962, p. 4). "The lack of social stratification and social classes in traditional African society was often cited as one causal factor" (Rothman, 1967). Elsewhere, it was viewed as a necessary effort for a nation to be educated "into becoming modern and national by enlightened state leadership" (Lamprou, 2017, p. 514). Ideological imperatives of socialism created a number of one-party states under the Communist parties, especially in Eastern Europe. In Asia and Latin America, a trend accompanied the growing intervention of the military in politics between the 1960s and 1980s. As such, various forms of *de jure* one-party states emerged – some with civilian leadership, others under military rule.

With the proliferation of democracy globally, described by Huntington as the "Third Wave of Democracy" (Huntington, 1993) beginning in 1974, the number of one-party states started to decline. The crisis of legitimacy, democracy promotion by Western states, and snowballing contributed to the decline (Huntington, 1991, p. 13). Consequently, a handful of ideological one-party states, such as China, North Korea and Cuba, remained as examples of one-party states. Many of these *de jure* one-party states, including many ideological one-party states in Eastern Europe, embarked on liberalization and democratization.

However, by the late 1990s, there were concerns about the future of the wave (Diamond, 1997) and by the early 2000s it became evident that the third wave, like the previous two waves, had not only stalled, but also begun to be reversed (Diamond, 2000). Stagnation, erosion and reversal of democracy among the transitional countries, particularly the third wave democracies, necessitated differentiating them from both democracy and authoritarianism. While many of them displayed some democratic attributes like regular elections, allowing opposition parties to exist and citizens to exercise some civil and political rights, there were serious concerns about the quality of elections, the limited space for dissent, and the absence of an independent judiciary. This emerging system was named variously, for example, illiberal democracy/liberal autocracy (Zakaria, 1997, pp. 22–23), feckless pluralism/dominant-power politics (Carothers, 2002, pp. 10–14), competitive authoritarianism (Levitsky and Way, 2002, p. 53), electoral authoritarianism (Schedler, 2002, pp. 41–46), and semi-authoritarianism (Ottaway, 2003, pp. 16–20). These concepts were brought under a broad term – hybrid regime – by Larry Diamond (Diamond, 2002). The defining characteristics of the hybrid regime according to the Economist Intelligence Unit (EIU) include, substantial irregularities in elections, flaws in functioning of government, restrictions of political participation, and harassment of and pressure on journalists, and the judiciary is not independent (EIU, 2015).

These developments increasingly diminish the scope for checks and balances of the executive branch, limit the space for opposition parties to operate and manipulate elections making it a tool for sustaining the regimes. These are the markers of a *de facto* one-party state. As for the opposition, it is "suffocated by the ruling party who accuse them of being traitors, disloyal, oligarchic etc. ... Deprived of any kind of means and platforms to express itself, the opposition succumbs into vegetarian life, as if it is a body still alive yet dysfunctional" (Dean, 2017). These "discontinuous series of incremental" developments have led, in some cases, to a *de jure* one-party state.

Bangladesh: erosion of democracy

The democratization process in Bangladesh began in 1991 and in the initial years it fulfilled five key indicators of electoral democracy – suffrage, elected officials, clean elections, freedom of association, and freedom of expression and alternative sources of information, as identified by Varieties of Democracy (V-Dem) (V-Dem, 2018, p. 71). Two parties – Bangladesh Nationalist

Party (BNP) and the Bangladesh Awami League (AL) – were elected to power alternately through relatively fair elections until 2008. However, democratic institutions remained fragile. The failure of both parties to build strong democratic institutions, create a democratic culture and their engaging in incessant acrimony added to the fragility and contributed to the gradual erosion of democracy. Both demonstrated a proclivity towards a dominant party system, "which refers to a category of parties or political organisations (sic) that have successively secured election victories and whose defeat is unlikely for the foreseeable future" (Laws, 2016). The constitutional amendment which reintroduced the parliamentary system in 1991 had also provided unbridled power to the Prime Minister. With the Prime Minister as the head of the party, the leader of the house and the leader of the parliamentary party, executive aggrandizement was a natural consequence.

The 13th Amendment of the Constitution ensured that free and fair elections are held upon completion of the term of the incumbent and provided safeguards against manipulation of elections. The amendment created the provision of the caretaker government (CTG) – a non-partisan government to oversee the election. The provision stipulated that an 11-member non-partisan cabinet will be appointed upon the completion of the term of the elected government. The cabinet will be headed by the immediate past Chief Justice of the Supreme Court. With no other accountability mechanism in place and increasing politicization of state institutions, election remained the only means for keeping the incumbent in check. In late 2006, ahead of the election scheduled in January 2007, law and order broke down as the opposition led by the AL launched street agitations to prevent the immediate-past Chief Justice from becoming the head of the CTG, while the incumbent BNP engaged in machination to influence the forthcoming election (Riaz, 2014). In the midst of the crisis, the military staged a promissory coup, a form of military intervention which "frame[s] the ouster of an elected government as a defense of democratic legality and make[s] a public promise to hold elections and restore democracy as soon as possible" (Bermeo, 2016, p. 8). After a failed attempt to reform the political system, banish two former Prime Ministers Khaleda Zia and Sheikh Hasina from politics, address corruption issues in combination with growing disillusionment with the government, the Asian economic crisis and external pressure, the caretaker government handed over power through a general election held in December 2008. The Awami League secured a landslide victory.

Four steps towards a *de facto* one-party state

With three-fourths majority in the parliament, the AL began to adopt measures since 2010 which were designed to incrementally weaken the opposition, make elections ineffective, muzzle the press and create a culture of fear. Four steps were pivotal in establishing the control of the AL over politics and the electoral process: the removal of the CTG provision from the Constitution, persecuting the opposition including Khaleda Zia and other BNP leaders with frivolous cases, adoption of legal and extra-legal measures to silence the critics, and curtailing the independence of the judiciary.

The first crucial step in the process of establishing complete control was the removal of the CTG system. The CTG provision, which allowed a non-partisan government to oversee the election, led to four free, fair, and inclusive elections, in 1991, 1996, 2001 and 2008. In June 2011 the incumbent scrapped the caretaker government provision from the Constitution through an amendment. The argument of the ruling AL was that a verdict of the Supreme Court had voided the system. The verdict in question had declared the 13th Amendment unconstitutional. However, the justices observed that the next two parliamentary elections could be "held under the provisions of the above-mentioned 13th Amendment," provided that the parliament chose to do so. The justices also agreed with senior lawyers' opinion that there would be anarchy should the ensuing election be held under a partisan government. A parliamentary committee comprised of AL members also favoured continuing the system, but Prime Minister Sheikh Hasina decided otherwise.

The new provision stipulated that an election must be held within 90 days of the completion of a parliament's tenure (or within 90 days of a dissolution of parliament before it completes its term). The BNP and all opposition parties threatened to boycott the election unless the CTG system was restored. The BNP and the opposition made good on their threat and boycotted the election held on 5 January 2014. Deletion of this provision enabled the incumbent to remain in power with all the tools at its disposal to manipulate the electoral processes. Without an independent electoral commission and growing politicization of civil administration, the provision created an uneven field for the opposition (Riaz, 2014; Riaz, 2016, pp. 88–102). With no opposition candidates, the result of the election was a foregone conclusion. More than half of the parliament members, 153 candidates of the ruling party and its allies were elected unopposed. It created a parliament with no opposition. In an unprecedented move, the incumbent designated one of its coalition members, the Jatiya Party (JP) led by the former dictator H M Ershad, the parliamentary opposition. It was intended to marginalize the legitimate opposition and render them ineffective. An election with the lowest voter turnout and lowest participation of parties became the most consequential election in the history of the nation.

The consequence was not only limited to the 2014 election, but also influenced the election five years later. In the December 2018 election, although the BNP and other opposition parties participated, the deck was stacked against them. Weakened by years of persecution and the entire administration, including the Election Commission and the law enforcing agencies, working in favour of the incumbent the election delivered an unprecedented victory to the AL. Of 300 seats of the parliament 288 seats were won by the ruling party and its allies. The election was described by the *New York Times* as "farcical" (The New York Times, 2019) and by the *Economist* as "transparently fraudulent" (Economist, 2019). As such, two consecutive parliamentary elections were manipulated to create parliaments with no opposition and the legislative body became subservient to the executive.

To weaken the opposition, especially the BNP and its allies, the ruling party began to file cases against its leaders from 2010. The Islamist party, Jaamat-i-Islami (JI), was the first to face the wrath. As the JI and many of its leaders were opposed to the independence of Bangladesh and sided with the Pakistani Army in its genocidal acts in 1971, they were charged with crimes against humanity in 2010 when the government established the International Crimes Tribunal (ICT). Although the trial process had some procedural flaws, it enjoyed enormous support from the Bangladeshis. The long overdue justice for those who became victims of the genocide was the primary reason for such overwhelming support, but over time it is alleged to have become a political tool of the incumbent. As the verdicts began to be delivered in February 2013, the JI unleashed unprecedented violence to stop the trial and further isolated itself from a large number of citizens.

The BNP, however, was on the receiving end of the heavy-handed measures for its movement for the restoration of the CTG system. From the beginning of AL rule, Khaleda Zia became a target of persecution. For example, during the military-backed caretaker government of 2007–2008, several graft cases were filed against both Sheikh Hasina and Khaleda Zia to banish them from politics. By May 2010, less than 18 months after the AL came to power, all 15 cases against Sheikh Hasina including those filed during the BNP government between 2001 and 2006, were dropped or quashed by courts (BBC, 2010), while cases against Khaleda Zia remained (The Daily Star, 2018). By 2019, 36 cases had been filed against her

(The Business Standard, 2020). She was convicted in two graft cases in 2018 and sentenced to 17 years in prison (Firstpost, 2018). At least 30 cases have been filed against the Secretary General of the BNP. The party alleged in October 2018, two months before the election, that 4,100 cases were filed against its activists involving more than 800,000 party members (The Daily Star, 2018a). The number grew exponentially in the following months prior to the election; activists, including opposition candidates, were charged and arrested. The failed attempt of the BNP to launch a mass movement against the government on the anniversary of the election and widespread violence around the country provided the government an excuse to adopt heavy-handed measures. The BNP's inability to involve a large populace and a lack of a concrete strategy backfired.

With the growing authoritarian bent of the incumbent since 2009, legal and extra-legal measures have been adopted to silence the critics. The amendment to the 2006 Information and Technology Act in 2013, particularly Section 57, with harsh punitive measures for the use of cyberspace for publishing "prejudicial to the image of the state" and providing power to law enforcement agencies to arrest someone without a warrant and to detain him/her for an indefinite period sent a chilling message. A human rights group reported that "between 2013 and April 2018, police submitted 1,271 charge sheets under the law, most under Section 57 of the Act" (Reuters, 2018). In 2017, 300 cases, including two dozen against the journalists, were filed (The Daily Star, 2017), and various websites were blocked. Other laws were used against the journalists and editors. Seventy-nine cases were filed against an editor (Sattar, 2016) after the PM had spoken harshly against the editor (Bdnews24, 2016), another editor was incarcerated for years (BBC, 2016), the government forced businesses to stop advertising in two newspapers to deprive them of revenue (DW, 2015), and a photojournalist was detained for months (Meixler, 2018). The relentless campaign against civil society organizations and leading members of the civil society, and vilification of them were encouraged by the ruling party. This was to ensure that no accountability mechanism could emerge. In October 2018, months before the election the government implemented a vaguely defined law with harsher punitive measures called the Digital Security Act of 2018 which practically criminalized dissent. These measures were accompanied by the growing number of extrajudicial killings and enforced disappearances. Between 2009 and 2018, at least 1,921 people became victims of extrajudicial killings and 109 were victims of enforced disappearances, according to a Human Rights group (Odhikar, 2020; Odhikar, 2020a). A combination of these permeated fear throughout society.

As in other new authoritarian systems, the judiciary in Bangladesh became an arena which came under the influence of the incumbent. When the High Court and the Supreme Court nullified the 16th Amendment of the Constitution, the ministers and the parliament members reacted furiously. The amendment empowered the parliament to impeach Supreme Court judges. In 2018, after the Supreme Court rejected the appeal of the government, the Chief Justice came under pressure. He left the country and later in a memoir claimed that he was forced to resign (Bergman, 2018). In a similar vein, the government also issued the rules which retain the power of appointment, administration and removal of lower court judges in the president's hands as opposed to the Supreme Court. The Bangladesh Judicial Service (Discipline) Rules 2017 contravene the spirit of the separation of the executive and the judiciary (The Daily Star, 2018b).

These four steps in the past decade demonstrate not only shrinking space for dissent and increasing draconian measures adopted by the government, but also show that the boundaries between the state, government and the ruling party have become blurred. They began acting in unison. This is a marker *de facto* one-party state. However, the question remains whether the façade of the democracy will remain in the future. The question has the theoretical aspect referred to previously.

Authoritarianism in the wake of Covid-19

The growing authoritarianism of the incumbent was laid bare in the wake of the Covid-19 global pandemic as the government intensified various coercive measures to silence the critics of the government through legal and extra-legal measures. Since the first case of coronavirus infection and death were reported in March 2020, the government adopted a three-pronged strategy to suppress any dissent. These include imposing a ban on government and semi-government officials including teachers of public educational institutions to talking to media or posting on social media, restrictions on mainstream media, and filing cases against journalists, social activists, and citizens at large.

Bangladesh, like many other countries, was ill prepared to handle the pandemic, although leaders of the ruling party underestimated the danger of Covid-19 and claimed that the country was ready. Denial, deliberately limiting the number of tests, uncoordinated responses and complacency marked the early responses. The public healthcare system began to fail after years of neglect and corruption. Patients were turned away from hospitals and health workers complained of lack of protective equipment. Members of poor and lower middle-class families, especially those who were in the informal sector, were badly hit. After much delay, the government began to offer relief, sold food at subsidized prices, and started a cash-transfer programme, but these efforts were marred by large-scale corruption perpetrated by the local level ruling party activists. Despite the number of deaths rising and the virus spreading, the government claimed successes and anything contrary to the government narrative was considered 'anti-government/anti-state activities.'

Examples of the government's restrictions abound. In March 2020, two college teachers were suspended (The Daily Star, 2020), a doctor was sent to jail (The Daily Star, 2020a). On 16 April, the government instructed the nurses of the public hospital not to speak about the lack of preparation; on 23 April, Health Minister Zahid Maleque ordered all health officials not to talk to the media; on 24 April, members of the civil service were told not to write in or talk to the media, including social media, without government permission; on 3 May, government-run hospital health workers were instructed not to engage with the media; and on 7 October, the government prohibited students and teachers from "writing, sharing, 'liking', or posting anything that "ruins the image of the government or the state", or "disrespects any important person, institution or profession" on social media (The Daily Star, 2020b).

Hundreds, including journalists, academics, opposition activists, a doctor and students, were arrested by the government for posting content on social media critical of the government under the controversial Digital Security Act (DSA) 2018. According to the British Rights Organization Article 19, at least 63 journalists have been attacked and assaulted between March and June of 2020, either by the members of the law-enforcement agencies or the supporters of the ruling party (Article 19, 2020). According to a Bangladeshi research organization, the Centre for Governance Studies (CGS), between 1 January 2020 and 25 February 2021, about 800 cases have been filed under the DSA. The organization gathered information of 402 cases, in which the total number accused was 873. A breakdown of the professions of the accused revealed that 13.68% of them are journalists (CGS, 2021). It is not only the journalists who are being persecuted; social activists, independent writers, bloggers, and cartoonists were arrested. An author and social activist Mushtaq Ahmed was arrested in May 2020 along with eleven others including a cartoonist; they were charged under the DSA and detained in a high security prison. On 25 February 2021 Mushtaq died inside the high security prison (The Daily Star, 2021). He was denied bail six times. Cartoonist Ahmed Kabir Kishore, who was later granted bail for six months, alleged that Mushtaq was tortured in police custody and he was tortured by unknown abductors (The Daily Star, 2021a). In June 2020, a 15-year-old was detained and sent to the juvenile correction centre for 'defaming' the Prime Minister on Facebook (Gulf News, 2020). Restrictions on media reportedly increased. On 26 March 2021 the government appointed 15 government officials to 'monitor' the 30 private television channels. The decision was withdrawn after severe criticism.

Situating Bangladesh in the global trend

Bangladesh's recent experience of democratic backsliding raises the question about the pathway of the third wave democracies. In the early days of the global wave of democratization, it was prophesied that these countries will follow a linear path – opening to transition to consolidation. But faced with the reality of stalled democracy and erosion, attention has now turned to the examination of pathways of the emergent democracies. According to Freedom House data: more countries which began the journey towards democratization after 1988 have experienced backsliding: "of the 23 countries that suffered a negative status change over the past 13 years [2006–2019] (moving from Free to Partly Free, or Partly Free to Not Free), almost two-thirds (61 percent) had earned a positive status change after 1988" (Freedom House, 2019). Equally notable are the findings of Mainwaring and Bizzarro, that "among the 91 new democracies that (by our count) emerged from 1974 to 2012, 34 experienced breakdowns, often in short order. In 28 cases, democracy stagnated after transition, usually at a fairly low level, and in two more it eroded. Democracy advanced relative to the starting point in only 23 cases. Few countries have succeeded in creating robust liberal democracies (Mainwaring and Bizzarro, 2019, p. 100)." These data show that Bangladesh's experience is not unique, although disturbing, particularly considering that the country was founded with the promise of liberal democracy.

The nature of these new autocracies is also different from previous forms of authoritarianism. Frantz and Kendall-Taylor have argued that newly emerging autocracies are distinctly different from classical autocracies as these are more individual centric, that is power is placed in a single leader. They show that "From 2000–10, 75% of authoritarianisation (sic) cases led to personalist (as opposed to other forms of) dictatorship." This has been made possible because "these leaders succeed in eliminating their potential opponents and autonomous centers of power" (Frantz and Kendall-Taylor, 2017, p. 62). They state, "Since the end of the Cold War, … highly personalised (sic) dictatorships have become the most common form of authoritarianism. In 1988, personalist regimes comprised just 23% of all dictatorships. Today, [2017] 40% of all autocracies are ruled by strongmen" (Frantz and Kendall-Taylor, 2017, p. 63).

These characteristics are worth bearing in mind while looking at the current system of governance and the rise of Sheikh Hasina at the helm of power in Bangladesh. Repeated insistence by the party leaders (Prothom Alo, 2016; The New Nation, 2019) and pro-government journalists (Rahman, 2019) that there is no alternative to Hasina shows the personalistic nature of her leadership. The demands for her intervention in solving any problems, from capital markets (Mia, 2020), to helping innocent children (Bangladesh Post, 2020), to school-level examinations (The Daily Sun, 2020), only reaffirm that there is no other power centre in the country.

Conclusion

Despite a propitious beginning towards democratization in 1991, Bangladesh experienced the gradual erosion of democracy through the subsequent 15 years. The promissory coup of 2007 accelerated the backsliding. Although there were hopes that this short-lived experience will help politicians, particularly the incumbent, to chart a new course of inclusive democracy and institution building, the journey has been in the opposite direction. The incumbent has led the country further away from a democratic path; institutions, such as legislative and judiciary, have been further weakened and the executive has seized more power with the PM at the helm. Executive aggrandizement, elimination of the vertical accountability mechanism, shrinking space for dissent, emasculation of the opposition and the blurring of state and party does not portend well. It validly raises the concerns that the country will descend into a one-party state.

Building on the insights about other third wave democracies and drawing on the developments of the past decade, further autocratization of the system of governance in Bangladesh is the most likely scenario and the strengthening of the emerging *de facto* one state is the most prospective situation in the coming years. However, unless the incumbent faces a serious challenge a *de jure* one-party state is unlikely, for several reasons. One of the key reasons is that the incumbent would like to keep the democratic façade as hybrid regimes tend to do. The apparent 'democratic' identity helps the regime garner international legitimacy on the one hand, while striving for domestic approval from its citizens, on the other. In the absence of moral legitimacy, thanks to two manipulated elections, the incumbent will show that it has constitutional legitimacy. The international environment of growing authoritarianism has created an enabling environment for the regime. However, various sporadic movements such as the road safety movement (BBC, 2018) in 2018, testify to simmering discontent.

Since 2014, especially since 2018, the international community has left the question of democracy behind for other considerations (Riaz, 2020). This has helped the incumbent pursue its agenda without any repercussions. The mutation of the hybrid regime into an authoritarian regime is also dependent on the role of the opposition, which thus far have failed to mount any effective resistance to the ruling party's agenda. The opposition, particularly, the BNP, is wrecked due to the absence of a bold leadership; its organizational capacity has weakened, and it is acting rudderless. Its ability to reshape itself will have a bearing on the nation's path forward.

Bibliography

Aljazeera. (2018) 'Is Bangladesh moving towards one-party state?', 4 April. Available at: www.aljazeera.com/indepth/features/sheikh-hasina-turning-bangladesh-party-state-180404082024893.html. (Accessed 15 March 2020).

Article 19. (2020) 'Highlights of the Data Sheet,' Press Release, 17 July, 2020.

Bangladesh Post. (2020) 'PM's intervention sought to protect innocent children,' 17 October. Available at: https://bangladeshpost.net/posts/pm-s-intervention-sought-to-protect-innocent-children-5087. (Accessed 18 October 2020).

BBC. (2010) 'Bangladesh drops leader Sheikh Hasina corruption case,' 30 May. Available at: www.bbc.com/news/10194392. (Accessed 16 March 2020).

BBC. (2016) 'Bangladesh opposition editor Mahmudur Rahman released,' 23 November. Available at: www.bbc.com/news/world-asia-38081334. (Accessed 16 March 2020).

BBC. (2018) 'Bangladesh protests: How a traffic accident stopped a city of 18 million,' 6 August. Available at: www.bbc.com/news/world-asia-45080129. (Accessed 16 March 2020).

Bdnews24. (2016) 'Prothom Alo, Daily Star lied to have me arrested, PM Hasina says,' 29 February. Available at: https://bdnews24.com/bangladesh/2016/02/29/prothom-alo-daily-star-lied-to-have-me-arrested-pm-hasina-says. (Accessed 18 March 2020).

Bermeo, Nancy. (2016) 'On Democratic Backsliding,' *Journal of Democracy*, 12(1), pp. 5–19.

Bergman, David. (2018) 'Bangladesh: Ex-chief justice alleges he was "forced" to resign,' *Aljazeera*, 28 September. Available at: www.aljazeera.com/news/2018/09/bangladesh-chief-justice-alleges-forced-resign-180927103453932.html. (Accessed 2 April 2020).

BTI. (2018) 'Infographic: BTI 2018 – The Bertelsmann Stiftung's Transformation Index.' Available at: www.slideshare.net/BertelsmannStiftung/infographic-bti-2018-the-bertelsmann-stiftungs-transformation-index. (Accessed 12 April 2020).

The Business Standard. (2020) 'Three dozen cases Khaleda Zia faces,' 8 February. Available at: https://tbsnews.net/bangladesh/corruption/three-dozen-cases-khaleda-zia-faces-42953. (Accessed 30 March 2020).

Carothers, Thomas. (2002) 'The End of the Transition Paradigm,' *Journal of Democracy*, 13(1), pp. 5–21.

Carter, Gwendolen M. (1962) *African One-Party States*. Ithaca: Cornell University Press [Toronto: Thomas Allen Limited].

Centre for Governance Studies. (2021) 'DSA Tracker'. Available at: https://freedominfo.net/. (Accessed 18 March 2021).

The Daily Star. (2017) 'Section 57: Over 300 cases filed this year,' 17 November. Available at: www.thedailystar.net/frontpage/section-57-over-300-cases-filed-year-1492531. (Accessed 30 March 2020).

The Daily Star. (2018) '34 Cases Against Khaleda,' 8 February. Available at: www.thedailystar.net/backpage/34-cases-against-khaleda-zia-bnp-chairperson-bangladesh-1531510. (Accessed 11 March 2020).

The Daily Star. (2018a) '4,100 cases filed to keep BNP off polls,' 7 October. Available at: www.thedailystar.net/politics/90340-cases-against-bnp-activists-lodged-mirza-fakhrul-islam-1643377. (Accessed 12 March 2020).

The Daily Star. (2018b) 'Lower courts' freedom undermined by 3 rules,' 2 January. Available at: www.thedailystar.net/frontpage/lower-courts-freedom-undermined-3-rules-1513600. (Accessed 11 March 2020).

The Daily Star. (2020) 'Coronavirus fears: 2 college teachers suspended for "critical" Facebook posts,' 27 March. Available at: www.thedailystar.net/coronavirus-fears-2-college-teachers-suspended-for-critical-facebook-posts-1886230. (Accessed 12 October 2020).

The Daily Star. (2020a) 'Spreading Rumours: Doctor put on 3-day remand,' 23 March. Available at: www.thedailystar.net/city/news/spreading-rumours-doctor-put-3-day-remand-1884649#:~:text=A%20Chattogram%20court%20yesterday%20granted,media%20through%20an%20audio%20clip. (Accessed 18 April 2020).

The Daily Star. (2020b) 'Posts on Govt, Military, Police: Govt slaps gag on social media,' 14 October. Available at: www.thedailystar.net/frontpage/news/posts-govt-military-police-govt-slaps-gag-social-media-1977489. (Accessed 21 October 2020).

The Daily Star. (2021) 'Death sets Mushtaq free from DSA, jail,' 26 February 2021. Available at www.thedailystar.net/frontpage/news/death-sets-mushtaq-free-dsa-jail-2051465. (Accessed 18 March 2021).

The Daily Star. (2021a) 'Kishore was tortured in custody,' 1 March 2021. Available at www.thedailystar.net/frontpage/news/kishore-was-tortured-custody-2052617. (Accessed 18 March 2021).

The Daily Sun. (2020) 'PM's intervention sought to cancel O, A-level exams,' 24 September. Available at: www.daily-sun.com/printversion/details/507479/PM%E2%80%99s-intervention-sought-to-cancelO-Alevel-exams. (Accessed 21 October 2020).

Dean, Damien. (2017) 'What we see in Venezuela is the faith of hybrid regimes,' *Foreign Policy News*, 28 August. Available at: https://foreignpolicynews.org/2017/08/28/see-venezuela-faith-hybrid-regimes/.(Accessed 24 March 2020).

Diamond, Larry. (1997) 'The End of the Third Wave and the Global Future of Democracy,' *Institut für Höhere Studien – Institute for Advanced Studies (IHS)*. Available at: https://irihs.ihs.ac.at/id/eprint/1000/1/pw_45.pdf. (Accessed 4 April 2020).

Diamond, Larry. (2000) 'Is Pakistan the (Reverse) Wave of the Future?', *Journal of Democracy*, 11(3), pp. 91–106.

Diamond, Larry. (2002) 'Elections Without Democracy: Thinking About Hybrid Regimes,' *Journal of Democracy*, 13(2), pp. 21–35.

DW. (2015) 'Bangladesh blocks media ads, curbs press freedom,' 30 October. Available at: www.dw.com/en/bangladesh-blocks-media-ads-curbs-press-freedom/a-18816842. (Accessed 19 March 2020).

Economist. (2019) 'Obituary of a Democracy: Bangladesh,' 30 January. Available at: https://espresso.economist.com/0390aff9c68eeb7b64fbebe21c878de3. (Accessed 6 April 2020).

EIU. (2015) *Democracy Index 2015: Democracy in an age of anxiety.* London: EIU. Available at: www.yabiladi.com/img/content/EIU-Democracy-Index-2015.pdf. (Accessed 26 March 2020).

Firstpost. (2018) 'Khaleda Zia suffers another setback as her 17-year prison term poses big hurdle for contesting in upcoming polls,' 30 October. Available at: www.firstpost.com/world/khaleda-zia-suffers-another-setback-as-her-17-year-prison-term-poses-big-hurdle-for-contesting-in-upcoming-polls-5473611.html. (Accessed 24 March 2020).

Frantz, Erica, and Kendall-Taylor, Andrea. (2017) 'The Evolution of Autocracy: Why Authoritarianism Is Becoming More Formidable,' *Survival*, 59(5), pp. 57–68.

Freedom House. (2019) *Freedom in the World 2019: Democracy in Retreat.* Washington D.C.: Freedom House. Available at: https://freedomhouse.org/report/freedom-world/2019/democracy-retreat. (Accessed 15 April 2020).

Gulf News. (2020) 'Bangladesh boy, 15, arrested for Facebook criticism of PM,' 24 June. Available at: https://gulfnews.com/world/asia/bangladesh-boy-15-arrested-for-facebook-criticism-of-pm-1.1593004320296. (Accessed 28 June 2020).

Huntington, Samuel. (1991) 'Democracy's Third Wave,' *Journal of Democracy*, 2(2), pp. 12–34.

Huntington, Samuel. (1993) *The Third Wave: Democratization in the Late Twentieth Century.* Norman: University of Oklahoma Press.

Jugantor. (2019) 'There wouldn't be a problem if the BKSAL was in place' (in Bengali), 19 March. shorturl.at/zFPXZ. (Accessed 4 April 2020).

Lamprou, Alexandros. (2017) 'Political Petitioning, Denunciation, and State–Society Relations during the Single-Party Period in Turkey,' *Turkish Studies*, 18(3), pp. 514–541.

Laws, Edward. (2016) 'Dominant party systems and development programming,' *GSDRC Helpdesk Research Report*, 19 October. Available at: https://gsdrc.org/wp-content/uploads/2016/12/K4D-report-4-Dominant-party-systems-and-development-programming.pdf. (Accessed 11 April 2020).

Levitsky, Steven, and Way, Lucan A. (2002) 'Elections Without Democracy: The Rise of Competitive Authoritarianism,' *Journal of Democracy*, 13(2), pp. 51–65.

Mainwaring, Scott, and Bizzarro, Fernando. (2019) 'The Fates of Third-Wave Democracies,' *Journal of Democracy*, 30(1), pp. 99–113.

Meixler, Eli. (2018) '"Journalism Is Under Threat." Inside a Bangladeshi Journalist's Dangerous Journey from Photographer to Prisoner,' *Time*, 30 December. Available at: https://time.com/5475494/shahidul-alam-bangladesh-journalist-person-of-the-year-2018/. (Accessed 21 April 2020).

Mia, Sujan. (2020) 'PM's intervention sought to save capital market,' *The Asian Age*, 16 January. Available at: https://dailyasianage.com/news/214361/pms-intervention-sought-to-save-capital-market. (Accessed 16 October 2020).

The New Nation. (2019) 'AL has no alternative to Hasina, says Quader,' 17 February. Available at: http://m.thedailynewnation.com/news/206607/al-has-no-alternative-to-hasina-says-quader. (Accessed 22 March 2020).

The New York Times. (2019) 'Bangladesh's Farcical Vote,' 14 January. Available at: www.nytimes.com/2019/01/14/opinion/editorials/bangladesh-election-sheikh-hasina.html. (Accessed 26 March 2020).

Odhikar. (2020) 'Total Extra-judicial killings from 2001 – 2019.' Available at: http://odhikar.org/wp-content/uploads/2020/02/Statistics_EJK_2001-2019.pdf. (Accessed 30 March 2020).

Odhikar. (2020a) 'Enforced Disappearances (2009 – 2019): State Agencies Responsible.' Available at: http://odhikar.org/wp-content/uploads/2020/02/Statistics_Disappearance_2009-2019.pdf. (Accessed 30 March 2020).

Ottaway, Marina. (2003) *Democracy Challenged: The Rise of Semi-Authoritarianism.* Washington D.C.: Carnegie Endowment for International Peace.

Prothom, Alo. (2016) 'No alternative to Hasina: Kamal,' 17 April. Available at: https://en.prothomalo.com/bangladesh/No-alternative-to-Hasina-Kamal. (Accessed 11 October 2020).

Rahman, Peer Habibur. (2019) 'No alternative to Hasina in running the country,' *The Daily Sun*, 21 November. Available at: www.daily-sun.com/printversion/details/440389/No-alternative-to-Hasina-in-running-the-country. (Accessed 12 October 2020).

Reuters. (2018) 'Factbox: Bangladesh's broad media laws,' 12 December. Available at: www.reuters.com/article/us-bangladesh-election-media-factbox/factbox-bangladeshs-broad-media-laws-idUSKBN1OC08S. (Accessed 29 March 2020).

Riaz, Ali. (2014) 'A Crisis of Democracy in Bangladesh,' *Current History*, 113(762), pp. 150–156.

Riaz, Ali. (2016) *Bangladesh: A Political History since Independence.* London: I B Tauris.

Riaz, Ali. (2020) 'Leaving Democracy Behind,' *Netra News*, 7 January. Available at: https://netra.news/2020/leaving-democracy-behind-623. (Accessed 19 March 2020).

Rothman, Stanley. (1967) 'One-Party Regimes: A Comparative Analysis,' *Social Research*, 34(4), pp. 675–702.

Sattar, Maher. (2016) 'Bangladesh Editor Faces 79 Court Cases After an Unusual Confession,' *The New York Times*, 27 March. Available at: www.nytimes.com/2016/03/28/world/asia/bangladesh-editor-faces-79-court-cases-after-saying-he-regrets-articles.html. (Accessed 30 March 2020).

Schedler, Andreas. (2002) 'Elections Without Democracy: The Menu of Manipulation,' *Journal of Democracy*, 13(2), pp. 36–50.

Strategic Forecast. (2016) 'Bangladesh's Descent into Authoritarianism,' 31 May. Available at: https://worldview.stratfor.com/article/bangladeshs-descent-authoritarianism. (Accessed 12 July 2018).

V-Dem. (2018) 'Democracy for All? V-Dem Annual Democracy Report 2018,' Department of Political Science, University of Gothenburg, Gothenburg. Available at: www.v-dem.net/media/filer_public/3f/19/3f19efc9-e25f-4356-b159-b5c0ec894115/v-dem_democracy_report_2018.pdf. (Accessed 21 March 2020).

Zakaria, Fareed. (1997) 'The Rise of Illiberal Democracy,' *Foreign Affairs*, 76(6), pp. 22–43.

19

THE DECLINE OF DEMOCRATIC GOVERNANCE

Protests at the Phulbari and Rampal coal mine

Shelley Feldman[1]

Introduction

Bangladesh has become an icon of dramatic economic growth and is also recognized for having made "the greatest progress in human development indicators in recent decades" (UNDP 2010). Moving up the development hierarchy of countries, from a low to a lower-middle income country, has often been associated with increasing democracy as a form of rule and participation. The promise of increasing democratization, accompanied by good governance, is assumed to help steer market-led development reforms. These twin goals of development and democracy have inspired Bangladeshi elite for many years, even as key indicators of their success highlight the neocolonial or dependent character of the country's political economy. These aspirations are fuelled by a desire for the country to continue on "its journey to upper middle-income status, in close cooperation with the government, stakeholders, and development partners," where development partners include continuing support and dependence on bi- and multilateral assistance that contributes to shaping development policy (e.g. World Bank 2020). Yet, governance in recent decades is characterized by a rise in autocratic practices which raises these critical questions: Can the country realize the promise of strengthened democratic rule while also achieving sustained economic growth with the support of donors and development partners? Or, with indications of democratic backsliding, is a rise in autocratic practices a more likely long-term consequence? The discussion below focuses on answering these critical questions.

Rounaq Jahan (2020) and Ali Riaz (2020), two eminent political scientists of Bangladesh, draw attention to old and new challenges to democracy, the rise of autocratic practices, and the making of one-party rule. Like other political scientists, they highlight the economic and institutional correlates of a process of democratic decline across world communities (Luhrmann et al. 2018, 2019; Lührmann and Lindberg 2019; Cassani and Tomini 2020). They focus on these correlates to explain failures in electoral politics and the rise of one-party rule, or on challenges to democratic rule, such as declines in the rule of law and freedom of individual expression and social media (Riaz 2019). While this approach reveals the processes entailed in the consolidation of executive power and the challenges this poses for parliament and the judiciary, it gives far less attention to practices of governance and everyday practices of rule, including securing rights to democratic engagement such as exercising demands

DOI: 10.4324/9781003042211-23

for recognition and for government accountability, including through protest and popular mobilization.

In this chapter, I draw attention to state practices involving large-scale infrastructural development as sites where challenges to demands for democratic participation expose the (re)making of state–society relations. Attention to the practices through which state–society relations are constituted thus offers a window on the declines in democracy and processes of legitimation that secure or enforce rule. I argue that current government interventions in the form of large-scale rural infrastructural development projects increasingly override or elide consideration of democratic participation, in particular, popular representation and demands for accountability. I focus, by way of example, on the protests that have risen in opposition to development projects promoting coal extraction, which are often elided in decisions about policy choices to expand opportunities for economic growth and where far too little attention is paid to how land will be acquired, compensation paid, and livelihoods ensured. I argue that by repressing popular mobilization and protest, the government has decentred civil society from its role as central to democratic practice. In highlighting protests at sites of investments in coal extraction, a central feature of the current government's development strategy, I expose the contradiction between the adoption of a neoliberal growth strategy and participatory democracy.

The discussion is organized as follows: I first situate decisions about the country's development trajectory in relation to its aspiration to move up the development hierarchy of countries. I follow with a brief comment on civil society and its contradictory relation to democratic practices before turning to a discussion of the energy sector and the construction at coal extraction sites. Here I emphasize issues raised by the protest movements, including environmental degradation, land grabbing, corruption, and transformations in everyday sociality. Finally, I turn attention to the government's response to these protests that has marked a decline in democratic participation and decision making. Available secondary evidence for this discussion comes from two resource extraction sites: Phulbari, Dinajpur and Rampal, Khulna, the latter adjacent to the Sundarbans (Gardner et al. 2012; Ahasan and Gardner 2016; Chowdhury 2016; Faruque 2018; Chowdhury 2016, 2017; Mahmud, Roth and Warner 2020; Misra and Mookerjea 2017). These sites are two among a number of coalfired power plants under construction which garner support from the government, often in concert with support from China and India (Gallagher et al. 2021) but, distinctive about the Phulbari and Rampal sites is the ongoing opposition they have faced, offering a window on contestation between local communities and the government.

Eclipsing democracy and the rise of autocratic rule

By the dawn of the twenty-first century, the fragility of the country's democracy had become increasingly evident, especially after the military-backed Caretaker Government that ruled Bangladesh from 2007 to 2008. Riaz (2020) views the period between 1990 and 2009 as one of semi-authoritarianism where democracy is being eroded and power is being concentrated in the hands of the executive. Such monopolization indicates that rather than a replacement of the executive, such as is common in coups, backsliding in Bangladesh is more akin to processes where there is a weakening of checks on executive power and a series of institutional changes that hamper the power of an opposition to challenge executive preferences. Under Sheikh Hasina, it has entailed a process that consolidated executive power by defying the procedural norms of liberal democracy. Under her rule, this was made especially evident when she removed the system of a caretaker government and the strategic manipulation of the electoral process in favour of incumbents. This change was accomplished by ignoring the "objections of the members of civil society and opposition political parties," effectively undermining the efficacy of elections and undercutting institutions of accountability, as well as opportunities for voice and representation (Riaz 2020: 9).

Mass mobilization against autocratic rule is not new in Bangladesh. Opposition politics has often been characterized by popular protest, including *hartals*, which could bring the country to a standstill, and also by the pro-democracy alliance that led to the ouster of the Ershad regime – the second military regime to hold power in the country since 1977 – and ushered in democratic elections. Such mobilization and resistance continued to characterize the conflict between the Awami League (AL) and the Bangladesh Nationalist Party (BNP) under electoral democracy, first through hartals, confrontation, and violence, and, subsequently, through house arrest and the crippling of parliament and other democratic institutions. As I suggest below, the BNP and the AL have fought for leadership since 1991 even as they broadly share policy priorities and, to some extent, policy practices.

Popular protest also marked the 2013 Shahbag movement seeking the death penalty for those sentenced and convicted of crimes committed during the independence-war in 1971. This initially peaceful struggle for justice for the events of 1971 has been recognized as a watershed moment representing grassroots mobilization against the country's continuing corruption and dysfunctional political culture, exposing the tension between recognition of Bangladesh as a secular state and a religious backlash that led to government repression of the unrest which ensued. Repression also framed the spontaneous protests of students in Dhaka that emerged following the death of two children by a speeding bus that brought Dhaka to a standstill. Not only was the protest met with tear gas and rubber bullets, with police injuring more than forty, and arresting mostly the young for protesting against institutional corruption, but the demand for accountability in how licences were issued or road safety insured was not addressed. A number of journalists, including the renowned photographer Shahidul Alam, were also charged or detained. Defined as an embarrassment, the government blocked internet services so as to inhibit further mobilization (BBC 2018). This led to an international response, including calls to stop the government's "violent crackdown" on "overwhelmingly peaceful student protesters" that signal the place of repressive tactics in securing rule, even under the guise of electoral democracy.

Moreover, Sheikh Hasina's reelection in both 2014 and 2018 was boycotted by the major opposition party, the BNP. Defining her "landslide victory" as neither free nor fair (Feldman 2015; Riaz 2020) further undercut trust in the electoral process and confirmed allegations of creeping authoritarianism, given the silencing of political rivals as an emblematic feature of democratic backsliding. Regrettably, what began in 1991 as a political environment which sought to uphold the five principles of democratic rule: electoral, liberal, participatory, deliberative, and egalitarian is, instead, characterized as an electoral autocracy (Jahan 2020; Mechova, Lührmann, and Lindberg 2017; Riaz 2020). Further, contributing to AL's loss of credibility and the institutionalization of one-party rule is the erosion of civil and political rights, including the failure to adjudicate crimes against civil rights activists, secular bloggers, and political protesters. She has, for example, negotiated with those who sought the death penalty for bloggers and wanted school textbooks to remove secular and Hindu references. In other instances, however, she has employed repressive measures such as directing security forces to detain opposition leaders without judicial due process, and, in still other instances, has failed to investigate and adjudicate those who murdered writers and bloggers who wrote on "controversial freethinking or atheistic topics," or on LGBT issues (BBC 2016; Hussain 2017; Saez 2018). In these cases, balancing democratic governance with her political interests and economic policies has led to a backsliding on democratic principles, with contradictory effects for her legitimacy.

Aspiring economic growth and inclusion in the global economy

While framing Bangladesh's economic growth in terms of its desire to continue its journey to upper middle-income status is relatively new, demands for improving the country's performance in the global economy have long been part of the conditionalities of the WB, the International Monetary Fund (IMF), the Asian Development Bank, and other International Financial Institutions (IFI). These demands have been accompanied by the promise of a neoliberal development strategy that offered both greater economic prosperity and the potential of a "third wave" of democracy. Accordingly, achieving the promises of development and democracy has entailed opening the economy to export-led growth supported by structural adjustment conditionalities set by the WB and the IMF, that would support new forms of participation in circuits of bi- and multilateral lending, capital investment strategies, and integration into the global economy.

New and expanded investments from China, however, have changed the aid landscape which increasingly showcases large-scale infrastructure development (Sarkar 2014). As Hussain (2019) argues, China's one-belt-one-road strategy resembles "a grandiose globalized version of the US Marshall Plan," and all that is implied by the influence sought by China's commitment in the region. While relations with China have long been a feature of South Asian engagement, especially regarding their interest in Chattogram, the location of Bangladesh's major port and the Bay of Bengal, current relations sustain interest in "Bangladesh's unique geo-political position" which bridges South and Southeast Asia via a modern Silk Road that is marked by trans-Asian highways and railways (Mannan 2019: 55). This commitment, coupled with the growing demand for energy, has led China, as well as India, to become leaders in a "new international energy order," each investing heavily in Bangladesh (Mannan 2019) where Chinese investments focus on large bridge and infrastructure projects, export processing zones (EPZs), special economic zones (SEZs), and coal extraction.

To be sure, since the mid-1970s, the World Bank has occupied a central position in the dissemination of development knowledge and practice and, along with the IMF, has been instrumental, not only in shaping the contours of the Bangladesh economy, but also in shaping relations with the NGO community. NGOs, for their part, began in rehabilitation efforts following the 1971 war and as a resource of rural mobilization. By the later 1970s, however, opportunities for NGO collaboration with bi- and multilateral aid agencies institutionalized their development role, thereby transforming a significant proportion of the sector from civil society institutions concerned with mobilization and conscientization, as well as processes of democratization, to institutions offering services and resources that acted increasingly as para-statals (World Bank 2013). This means, for example, that an increasing number of NGOs offer microcredit (Grameen Bank) and primary village education (BRAC) to support or contribute to government institutions already in operation in contrast to those which promote conscientization and advocate for justice and rights as a voice of civil society. Recognizing the multiple roles played by NGOs reveals how the institutionalization of NGOs alters state–civil society relations.

Such changing state–civil society relationships have created new subjectivities by reconstituting the liberal subject as primarily wage earners and small-scale entrepreneurs who are increasingly dependent on individualized credit, thereby transforming rural production relations that included wage labour, but, also, in-kind exchanges, sharecropping arrangements, and relations of subsistence production. In rural areas, this shift has been enabled by the dramatic expansion of NGOs that provide resources and services and are to be distinguished from those that work with and represent civil society and advocate for change. In urban areas, the dramatic increase in export production has similarly contributed to creating new subjectivities, particularly of women, by providing employment for millions, while contributing to the country's sustained growth rate through participation in the country's export regime.

An export-led development strategy has been embraced by both military and democratic regimes, including various forms of one-party, oligarchic rule. In the transition from import substitution to export-led growth, for example, the policies of both Zia Rahman (1977–1981) and Mohammad Ershad (1982–1990) responded similarly to the structural adjustment requirements of the Bretton Woods institutions, including Ershad's adoption of a New Industrial Policy (NIP) which attempted to "restore macroeconomic balance and improve prospects for the emerging private sector" (Quadir 2000: 208). As Naomi Hossain (2017) reminds us, international donors had been pressing the government to deregulate and privatize the economy for some time, and the military governments were receptive to this challenge. Between 1972 and 1982, such reforms largely responded to internal and short-term exogenous economic shocks. But, since that time, the reform process sought to "change the entire direction of the economy towards a private enterprise dominated market economy" (Sobhan 1993: 925). Each regime stabilized its military rule with large-scale rural development projects, decentralization strategies, and an increased role for NGOs that contributed to building a political network through the distribution of resources and patronage (Quadir 2000: 197). As Shamsul Haque (2002: 414) argues, each regime was able "to coopt and use large NGOs as substitutes for opposition political parties." Consequently, the country's NGO elite have operated as a distinct section of the national elite who, alongside bureaucratic and political elites and a network of industrial and corporate capital, intersect with international capital that is reputed to be characterized by widespread corruption and competitive clientelism (Lorch 2018).

Neoliberalism or democracy: a contradictory relation?

The deepening crisis of the Ershad regime was felt especially by intellectuals and students who were central to the 1990 mobilization which brought military rule to an end. The election which followed in 1991, under Justice Shahabuddin Ahmed, chief justice of the Supreme Court, was described as "free and fair" by local nongovernment and foreign observers alike. But this election result revealed the growing consolidation of the elite who, according to Talukdar Maniruzzaman (1992: 217–218), by benefiting from foreign aid during previous regimes secured its place as "a new class of beneficiaries, consisting of private intermediaries who acted as commission agents, both legally and illegally, for foreign suppliers of goods and services financed by the aid." As Maniruzzaman continues, aid helped

> industrialists who borrowed money from aid-financed DFIs or who ran their factories on foreign exchange provided as commodity or as program aid to finance recurring imports … . [and] helped construction contractors on aided projects and local consultants working under various aid-financed programs of technical assistance.

This class also benefited from a policy of patrimonialism and crony capitalism (Feldman and Geisler 2011) that included "the massive transfer of public wealth to private hands" (Maniruzzaman 1992: 218). These relations, coupled with relatively inexperienced political and administrative personnel, failed to provide the basis for long-term democratic rule, even as it held the promise of doing so.

Khaleda Zia's coming to power in 1991 had support from some segments of this emergent elite and further aided in promoting the neoliberal development agenda by simplifying the regulatory role of government agencies. In the words of Fahimul Quadir (2000: 206), Zia assumed "a promotional rather than regulatory role in facilitating the development of the private sector," a commitment that corresponded to pressure from the donor community. Moreover, the Policy Framework Paper (PFP) negotiated between the IMF and the Government of Bangladesh in 1990 continued through the first democratic BNP government of Prime Minister Khaleda Zia who made efforts to remove remaining "barriers to the development of a liberal-capital model" and further the programme of economic liberalization as a vehicle to consolidate the ruling elite. This was accomplished by allowing "business elites to use economic restructuring as the primary tool to attain their financial and economic objectives" (Quadir 2000: 208).

Sheik Hasina also endorsed the PFP and the Enhanced Structural Adjustment Facility (ESAF), acknowledging that there has been little difference between the economic policies of the Awami League (AL) and the Bangladesh National Party (BNP). Sheik Hasina, however, was "said to be concerned about their political image [and] ... reportedly told the Fund that advanced publicity about the negotiation of a possible ESAF arrangement would be politically damaging" (note 24, p. 225, note 35). Such ambivalence reveals that a political environment characterized by extreme polarization, requires balancing a program of economic liberalization with the challenges of democratic governance. While this balance has been a concern of prior governments, each has sought to create legitimacy differently. How did Sheikh Hasina balance economic liberalization, on the one hand, with governance, on the other hand? The balance she chose seems to have tipped in favour of economic growth over democracy in order to facilitate the country's shift from aid-focused policy to an investment-oriented strategy that largely corresponds to efforts to move the country up the development hierarchy. It is also a strategy that is best accomplished through public–private partnerships in infrastructure investment (Amin 2016). From a policy perspective, this has entailed support for free trade and limited government intervention and the development of infrastructure, including roads, highways, and transportation, as well as support for the energy sector and a dramatic increase in the number of SEZs to attract investment.

I now turn to examine Sheikh Hasina's relation to the energy sector in the resource extraction areas of Phulbari and Rampal, two sites of ongoing mobilization against the construction of open-pit coal mining. At these sites, protest against the siting and extension of these large-scale development projects has faced repression and other forms of state intervention that limit freedom of speech and assembly, including extra-legal practices that expose a governance strategy that is increasingly autocratic.

The energy sector

As the cases of the Phulbari and Rampal energy projects will show, development goals, along with increased domestic energy demands, led to prioritizing energy production over democratic participation in decisions made in the energy sector. Under military rule, the WB and the Asian Development Bank (ADB) began their support of the energy sector through production-sharing contracts (PSCs) with multinational oil companies (Muhammad 2014). During the first democratically elected BNP government PSCs were signed with gas companies that include Chevron, Santos, Cairn Energy, and Shell. These energy deals were struck when the country's need for electricity was evident and daily load-shedding had a direct effect on productivity that threatened the country's export sector, prompted an uproar among the urban middle classes, and challenged popular support for the government. In 1996, the National Energy Policy (NEP) recognized the urgency of ensuring proper exploration, production, distribution, and the rational use of energy sources. It also acknowledged the rapid changes in global, as well as domestic conditions. Since then, they have prioritized energy diversification of available indigenous commercial energy resources where coal is assumed to play an expanding role in providing the country's future energy needs. More recently, the International Trade Administration offered advice to US and international businesses indicating that the Bangladesh government plans to increase power generation beyond expected demand to propel growth in the export-oriented economy and meet the needs of a growing middle class. The plan calls for raising US $70 billion in total investments in the sector over the next 15 years (Bangladesh Trade Guide 2020).

Increased domestic demand for energy, coupled with pressure from the donor community, have thus helped to secure policy reforms adopted by the government via the PSCs (Muhammad 2006). Anu Muhammad (2006), in his detailed history of the sector, argues that Bangladesh was once able to meet its need for gas but, under PSCs, would eventually have to purchase its own gas using foreign currency. At this time, power generation came mostly from gas and oil, but the need for more energy turned attention to coal-based power stations which were central to new PSCs signed with multinational oil companies. These agreements were signed despite findings by scientists that extracting and burning the world's remaining coal reserves would be the world's single biggest contributor to global warming thus tipping the scale towards irreversible climate change.

Yet, as coal production in the global north has declined, often in response to concerns about climate change, investors have turned to sites in the global south. This put pressure to move ahead on the Phulbari project involving not only collusion between multinationals and Bangladesh in shaping the country's investment climate, but also aggressive efforts by the US which were not surprising "given that there was 60 percent of US ownership" in the project (Chowdhury 2016: 91; Muhammad 2014). For their part, the government continues to expand its plans to build coal-fired power plants to reduce the increasing gap between its energy demand and supply, with the goal of diversifying its energy mix (Kotikalapudi 2016). However, as Chaitanya Kumar Kotikalapudi (2016) points out, this strategy builds on a weak energy governance structure, violations of environmental norms, a refusal to engage the public through consultations, the cooptation of the development narrative, and a lack of transparency and accountability which, together, reveal a failure to maintain democratic norms.

Moreover, since much of the production will be for export, it is worth heeding Joseph Stiglitz's remark: "A country that sells off its natural resources, privatizes its oil company, and borrows against future revenues, may experience a consumption binge that raises GDP, but the accounting framework should show that the country has actually become poorer" (quoted in Muhammad 2014: 62; Kotikalapudi 2016: 161). Thus, whatever benefits the country may reap in its growth rate from such energy policy will be only short term with immediate concerns that include the relationship between energy resources and security that have exposed how corruption, poverty, inequality, and repression "go hand in hand with the exploitation of natural resources" thereby challenging the balance between development and democratic governance (Muhammad 2014: 59).

The cost to be paid for the relation between corruption and repression on the one hand, and natural resource exploitation, on the other hand, may be experienced most acutely by those living in resource-extractive communities who protest, collectively, to protect their rights, lives, and livelihoods. Most such opposition movements have identified land grabbing, displacement, the loss of rights to what they view as common property, and the environmental havoc that results from open-pit mining as their central concerns. Also significant is the importance dwellers at sites of extraction give to the loss of "sociality, dignity, and personhood" (Nuremowla 2016: 3). In Phulbari, for example, in only one mining community, 14,660 acres (23 square miles) will be destroyed, 80 percent of which is farmland, including ponds, fruit and timber trees, as well as businesses, homes, schools, health facilities, mosques, temples and churches, graveyards, and two archaeological sites (UN News 2012; Jahan 2014: 16). This will not only have serious environmental consequences, but will displace, by some estimates, 220,000 people, many of whom are indigenous and vulnerable. Such displacement is accompanied by the loss of employment, and, given a shortage of "empty" land, resettlement will be difficult, if not impossible, for those seeking to engage in agricultural production. Further, the project threatens the country's food security by transforming one of its most fertile agricultural regions into an open-pit mine with its attendant infrastructure (UN News 2012) and damaging the most massive aquifer in north-western Bangladesh resulting in the depletion of the groundwater in the immediate vicinity, as well as outside the mining zone (Muhammad 2014).

Faced with the impacts on their lives and the environment, rural dwellers attempted to signal opposition to these projects. But their efforts to engage government were met with intimidation and violence. Muhammad (2014) and others (Gardner et al. 2012; Chowdhury 2016; Faruque 2018) detail the bloody uprising in Phulbari in 2006 where 50,000 people had gathered to protest against the open-pit coal mine (Nuremowla 2016). Three people were killed at the site and hundreds more were injured when semi-military (BDR) forces, usually charged with guarding the border, fired on the crowd, exposing the government's deployment of forces that threatens the right to protest and portends continuing state intimidation and violence against protesters (Gain 2006).

Perhaps based on the need to balance development policy and an increasingly elusive democracy, the government agreed to three conditions for moving forward: Asia Energy, the PSC partner, would be forced to leave, there would be no open-pit mining anywhere in the country, and any future decisions regarding coal development would include community input. However, despite the apparent success of the protest, and the agreement signed between the government and the community, pressure to resume the project won out. But, as people's resistance continued, so did the government's repressive response. These government actions led a group of UN experts to question the transparency and legitimacy of project operations, noting concerns over the repression of human rights defenders who peacefully protested at the mine. As one UN rapporteur noted in support of the freedom of peaceful assembly and association, "People must be informed throughout, and must not be intimidated out of exercising their rights to express their opinions and peacefully assemble" (UN News 2012).

Again, in 2016, ten years after government agreements made with protesters, there was again a lack of transparency and accountability regarding the government's decision to move forward on the project. This time, Phulbari protesters joined with climate activists in London, during the annual general shareholders meeting of GCM, formerly Asia Energy, where they continued to press their demands to stop the project. In 2019, however, GCM Resources confirmed that it had entered into a bilateral agreement with China Nonferrous Metal Industry and Power Construction Corporation of China (PowerChina) to jointly manage the Phulbari Coal Mine project. And, in February 2020, they said they had secured a US$1.5 million increase to its existing loan facility of US$3 million with Polo Resources Ltd, raising the total loan amount to US$4.5 million (Global Energy Monitor). Still, as Ahasan and Gardner (2016) point out, activists continue to protest decisions that privilege partnerships with foreign companies who exploit the country's natural resources and the profits that are captured by multinationals and corrupt government officials.

While the government has moved ahead with the Phulbari project in spite of continued opposition to open-pit mining, opposition has also occurred in Rampal, an area 14 kilometers from the Sundarbans Reserve Forest, where the government is moving ahead with the development of another coal power plant without consideration being given to its impact on the environment or on people's lives. The Rampal plant is owned by the Bangladesh-India Friendship Power Company (BIFPCL) as a joint venture between the National Thermal Power Company (NTPC) of India and the Bangladesh Power Development Board (BPDB). The Indian company, Bharat Heavy Electricals (BHEL), will construct the plant in a financial agreement reached in 2017, with debt financing provided from the Indian Export-Import Bank. Covering 1,834 acres of mostly agricultural land, the coal plant will threaten the livelihoods of over two million inhabitants who depend upon the Sundarbans forest's resources to meet their daily needs. Its adverse effects will threaten agricultural and fisheries production as well as food security (Muhammad 2013).

The plant would also leach toxic substances from deposited coal burned ashes that contain many heavy metals including arsenic, lead, mercury, nickel, vanadium, beryllium, barium, cadmium, chromium, selenium and radium, which are dangerous if released into the environment (Chowdhury 2017). Discharging toxic water into the Passur River, and oil and chemical wastes from coal-carrying vessels will likely further contaminate the water, a worry that is already evident from the recent capsizing of a vessel carrying 350,000 litres of furnace oil that capsized in the Shela River in 2014, followed by another cargo vessel capsizing only a year later in the same river (Mookerjea and Misra 2017).

Residents at Rampal will also face greenhouse gas emissions and anticipated climate change that will increase the salinity of the water and contribute to drinking and irrigation water shortages in the coastal regions. Moving ahead on the Rampal project also threatens the rich biodiversity of the Sundarbans and, once operational, will permanently destroy the Sundarbans' ecosystem, a natural defence against extreme weather events. The eight million tons of CO_2 that it will emit each year will harm local residents and contribute to global warming (UNESCO n.d.; Sourcewatch 2015; Human Rights Watch 2020). In addition, it will leave the south-western coast of Bangladesh vulnerable to storms, cyclones, and other natural disasters. As noted by environmental scientists, including Abdullah Harun Chowdhury, who forcefully identifies the long-term effects of the Rampal plant: "most of the impacts of coal-fired power plants are negative and irreversible, [and cannot] be mitigated" (Chowdhury 2017: 85).

In response to these social, economic, and environmental concerns, and similar to protests mounted against the Phulbari project described above, from November 24 to 26, 2016, more than 10,000 people marched from Dhaka to Khulna to "Save the Sundarbans" and persuade the government to drop its backing for the construction of coal plants near the Sundarbans. Soon thereafter, a report by the United Nations World Heritage Centre and the International Union for the Conservation of Nature's World Heritage Programme recommended that the proposed coal plant be relocated to prevent harm to the Sundarbans. This was followed by an open letter from prominent Indian organizations to the prime minister of India urging him to withdraw support for the project in a context where a "similar proposal to build a thermal power plant in … West Bengal … was turned down … for being too proximate to the forest" (Misra and Mookerjea 2017: 5). According to Earthjustice, this growing pressure was met by forceful government pushback, including threats, harassment, and unlawful detention of protesters. Not only has the government portrayed activists opposing the plant as terrorists, but "prominent

opposition figures have even received anonymous death threats" (https://earthjustice.org/blog/
2016-november/environmental-defenders-are-under-threat-in-bangladesh). Such responses
have characterized the government's reaction to protest over the mine for some time. In August
2016, for example, a student activist was arrested for criticizing Sheikh Hasina's position on the
mine (Earthjustice 2016), and in October of the same year, police in Dhaka attacked peaceful
protesters with tear gas shells and water cannons, leaving about 30 people injured, some critically (Dhaka Tribune 2016). Protesters also demanded transparency and accountability and
opposed extra-legal forms of violence against their efforts. But, for its part, the government
held to its contention that the siting of coal plants "will have little to no impact on the forest,
saying they will use the latest technology to mitigate pollution" (The Guardian 2016).

Open-pit coal mining clearly offers the Government an opportunity to secure cheap electricity. However, supporting mines located either in Phulbari or Rampal fails to account for other
development goals that include ensuring the safety and livelihoods of its large population or a
commitment to food security and ecological sustainability. Moreover, the Government's decision leaves open to question whether coal production is the only way to secure cheap electricity
to sustain economic growth. And, crucial for this discussion, are the questions: How will legitimacy for the AL be maintained, if popular protest is suppressed, ignored, or responded to with
legal and extralegal violence? And, will autocratic rule increasingly shape not only the electoral
system but, also, other relations of governance? Stated differently, what we are witnessing in
Bangladesh is an increasingly fragile balance between development goals and autocratic rule
that seeks to achieve development goals at any cost.

Conclusion

To complement discussions of autocracy focused on the consolidation of executive power,
I have examined democratic backsliding at the grassroots level in the context of attempts by
various governments to balance the twin goals of economic ascendance and democracy. With
the adoption of a neoliberal development strategy, viewed as central to economic growth,
I have examined investments in two open-pit coal mines, one in Phulbari and a second in
Rampal. Such investments expose long-term contestation over the siting and construction
of these mines for reasons of ecological and social sustainability. Opposition by thousands of
local community members has highlighted the consequences of removing thousands of acres
of productive agricultural land and its people under circumstances which result in displacement, dispossession, insecurity, and the disruption and destruction that such loss portends for
community solidarities. Opposition also garnered the support of a national and international
community who, like community members, acknowledge the need for energy security, but are
concerned with the environmental costs of open-pit mining, including the costs to biodiversity, CO_2 emissions, pollution of waterways, and climate change. Yet, none of these concerns
have been adequately addressed with policies that would secure the lives of residents and the
sustainability of the environment. Instead, protests have been met with authoritarian responses
that include exclusion, intimidation, police fire, and, significantly, extra-legal forms of violence
without the possibility of adjudication.

The analysis of these sites reveals that investment in open-pit mining is one outcome of
bureaucratic and economic elite interests in moving up the development ladder by sustaining
short-term, if high, rates of economic growth. Evidence also suggests that the cost of open-
pit mining leads to long-term ecological devastation, despite claims to the contrary, and social
instability and loss. It has also come at the cost of the instantiation of democratic rule in
1991 and the failure to maintain the basic tenets of democracy and, instead, has given rise to

autocratic rule. Significantly, the failure to maintain these basic tenets of democratic rule is the result not of internal interests alone, but corresponds as well to pressures from the multi- and bilateral aid community and private sector to adopt policies that strengthen Bangladesh's integration into the global economy while maintaining its dependent status.

As I have shown, both class pressures and those of the international aid regime have shaped decisions regarding energy development for more than forty years, but, today, coal mining has come to hold a central place. This is the case even as a major investor in one open-pit mine rejected the opportunity to build a similar plant on the other side of the Bangladesh–Indian border, and when the global north has sought to find more sustainable forms of energy production. I conclude by acknowledging the challenges involved in balancing resource extractive growth policies while sustaining democratic norms and the promise of democratic governance. But, as the Phulbari and Rampal examples show, those who seek economic, social, and ecological security, when living under governments that apply autocratic rule to achieve partisan development interests, have neither rights nor voice in securing a sustainable future. Or, as this development contradiction exposes, when class and international pressures for economic growth prevail, democratic participation falls by the wayside and is relegated to the realm of the ideal.

Note

1 This work was supported by Horizon 2020 research and innovation program under the Marie Skłodowska-Curie grant agreement: grant number 665958.

Bibliography

Ahasan, A. & Gardner, K. 2016. Dispossession by "Development": Corporations, Elites and NGOs in Bangladesh. *South Asia Multidisciplinary Academic Journal* [Online], 13, 1–17.

Amin, M. R. 2016. From Aid to Investment: A Paradigm Shift in Sheikh Hasina's Development Policy. *The Daily Star*. 4 February. Accessed 7 December 2020.

Bangladesh Trade Guide. Bangladesh Country Commercial Guide, Power and Energy www.trade.gov/country-commercial-guides/bangladesh-power-and-energy. Accessed 7 December 2020.

BBC. 2016. Bangladesh LGBT editor hacked to death. www.bbc.com/news/world-asia-36128729. Accessed 17 January 2020.

BBC. 2018. Bangladesh protests: How a traffic accident stopped a city of 18 million. 6 August. www.bbc.com/news/world-asia-45080129. Accessed 7 December 2020.

Cassani, A. & Tomini, L. 2020. Trajectories and Modes of Autocratization in the Early 21st Century. Partecipazione e Conflitto, *The Open Journal of Sociopolitical Studies*, http://siba-ese.unisalento.it/index.php/paco/article/viewFile/23062/19316, 1539–1558.

Chowdhury, A. H. 2017. Environmental Impact of Coal-based Power Plant of Rampal on the Sundarbans (World's Largest Mangrove Forest) and Surrounding Areas. *MOJ Ecology & Environmental Science*, 2, 85–98.

Chowdhury, N. S. 2016. Mines and Signs: Resource and Political Futures in Bangladesh. *Journal of the Royal Anthropological Institute*, 22(1), 87–107.

Dhaka Tribune. 2016. Police foil Rampal protesters in march toward Indian High Commission. www.dhakatribune.com/bangladesh/2016/10/18/police-foil-rampal-protesters-march-towards-indian-high-commission/. Accessed 7 December 2020.

Earthjustice. 2016. Environmental defenders are under threat in Bangladesh. https://earthjustice.org/blog/2016-november/environmental-defenders-are-under-threat-in-bangladesh. Accessed 7 December 2020.

Faruque, M. O. 2018. Mining and Subaltern Politics – Political Struggle against Neoliberal Development in Bangladesh. *Asian Journal of Political Science,* 26, 65–86.

Feldman, S. 2015. Bangladesh in 2014: Illusive Democracy. *Asian Survey*, 55, 67–74.

Feldman, S. & Geisler, C. 2011. Land Grabbing in Bangladesh: In-Situ Displacement of Peasant Holdings. Future Agricultures Consortium, Institute of Development Studies, University of Sussex, UK.

Gain, P. 2006. 'Killings in Phulbari Ignite Unstoppable Protest: Local Communities Stand Strong against Open Cut Mining', Dhaka, Society for Environment and Human Development.

Gallagher, K. S., Bhandary, R., Narassimhan, E. & Nguyen, Q. T. 2021. Banking on Coal? Drivers of Demand for Chinese Overseas Investments in Coal in Bangladesh, India, Indonesia and Vietnam. *Energy Research & Social Science*, 71, 1–10.

Gardner, K., Ahmed, Z., Bashir, F. & Rana, M. 2012. Elusive Partnerships: Gas extraction and CSR in Bangladesh. *Resources Policy*, 37, 168–174.

Global Energy Monitor Wiki n.d. Rampal power station. www.gem.wiki/Rampal_power_station#cite_ref-bankt_11-0. Accessed 28 December 2020.

Hance, J. 2016. Thousands to march against coal plant threat to Bangladesh's Sundarbans forest, *The Guardian*. www.theguardian.com/environment/2016/mar/02/thousands-to-march-protest-coalplant-threat-bangladeshs-sundarbans-forest. Accessed 7 December 2020.

Haque, M. S. 2002. The Changing Balance of Power between the Government and NGOs in Bangladesh. *International Political Science Review*, 23, 411–435.

Hossain, N. 2017. *Bangladesh – The Aid Lab: Understanding Bangladesh's Unexpected Success*. Oxford: Oxford University Press.

Human Rights Watch. 2020. www.hrw.org/news/2020/06/18/bangladesh-coal-plants-threaten-worlds-largest-mangrove-forest. Accessed 8 December 2020.

Hussain, I. 2019. Encircling India: China Tightens South Asian Noose. In: Hussain, I. (ed.) *South Asia in Global Power Rivalry: Inside-out Appraisals from Bangladesh*. Singapore: Palgrave Macmillan, Springer Nature Singapore Pte Ltd., 101–123.

Hussain, M. 2017. Bangladesh Criticized for Slow Progress in Blogger Murders. www.voanews.com/east-asia-pacific/bangladesh-criticized-slow-progress-blogger-murders. Accessed 7 December 2020.

Jahan, F. 2014. Phulbari: Where Grassroots Gathered Against Global Capital. *BANKwatch*, XII, 16–18.

Jahan, R. 2020. Challenges to Democracy: Old and New. *The Daily Star*. 15 September. Accessed 17 September 2020.

Kotikalapudi, C. K. 2016. Corruption, crony capitalism and conflict: Rethinking the political economy of coal in Bangladesh and beyond. *Energy Research & Social Science*, 17, 160–164.

Lorch, J. 2018. Civil Society and Mirror Images of Weak States: Bangladesh and the Philippines, Creative Commons Attribution 4.0 International License (http://creativecommons.org/licenses/by/4.0/). London: Palgrave Macmillan.

Lührmann, A. & Lindberg, S. I. 2019. A Third Wave of Autocratization Is Here: What Is New about It? *Democratization*, 26, 1095–1113.

Lührmann, A., Mechkova, V., Dahlum, S., Maxwell, L., Olin, M., Petrarca, C. S., Sigman, R., Wilson M. C. & Lindberg, S. I. 2018. State of the World 2017: Autocratization and Exclusion? *Democratization*, 25(8), 1321–1340.

Mahmud, M. S., Roth, D. & Warner, J. 2020. Rethinking "Development": Land Dispossession for the Rampal Power Plant in Bangladesh. *Land Use Policy*, 94, 1–13.

Maniruzzaman, T. 1992. The Fall of the Military Dictator: 1991 Elections and the Prospect of Civilian Rule in Bangladesh, *Pacific Affairs*, 65, 203–224.

Mannan, M. 2019. "Shining" or "Suffering" South Asia? China's South Asian Footprints. In: Hussain, I. (ed.) *South Asia in Global Power Rivalry: Inside-out Appraisals from Bangladesh*. Singapore: Palgrave Macmillan, Springer Nature Singapore Pte Ltd., 49–80.

Mechkova, V., Lührmann, A. & Lindberg, S. I. 2017. How Much Democratic Backsliding? *Journal of Democracy*, 28, 162–169.

Misra, M. & Mookerjea, S. 2017. Why New Delhi must Withdraw from the Rampal. *Economic & Political Weekly*. 6 May.

Mookerjea, S. & Misra, M. 2017. Coal Power and the Sundarbans: Subaltern Resistance and Convergent Crises. In: Kapoor, D. (ed.) *Against Colonization and Rural Dispossession: Local Resistance in South/East Asia-Pacific and Africa*. London: forthcoming in Zed Books.

Muhammad, A. 2006. FDI in Bangladesh, People's Uprising in Phulbari and the Right Signal. *Countercurrents.org*, 22 September.

Muhammad, A. 2013. "Rampal power plant: A project of deception and mass destruction". Bdnews.24.com – The Opinion Pages. 19 September. https://opinion.bdnews24.com/2013/09/19/rampal-power-plant-a-project-of-deception-and-mass-destruction/ Accessed 7 December 2020.

Muhammad, A. 2014. Natural Resources and Energy Security-Challenging the "Resource-Curse" Model in Bangladesh. *Economic & Political Weekly*, XLIX, 59–67.

Nuremowla, S. 2016. Land, Place and Resistance to Displacement in Phulbari. *South Asia Multidisciplinary Academic Journal (SAMAJ)*, 13.

Primorac, Marina. 1998. *External Evaluation of the ESAF*. Washington, D.C.: International Monetary Fund.

Quadir, F. 2000. The Political Economy of Pro-market Reforms in Bangladesh: Regime Consolidation Through Economic Liberalization? *Contemporary South Asia*, 9, 197–212.

Riaz, A. 2019. How New Autocrats Curb Press Freedom. *The Daily Star*. Accessed 7 December 2020.

Riaz, A. 2020. The Pathway of Democratic Backsliding in Bangladesh. *Democratization*, 28(1), 179–197.

Saez, L. 2018. Bangladesh in 2017: Bloggers, Floods, and Refugees. *Asian Survey*, 58, 127–133.

Sarkar, N. M. 2014. Bangladesh-China Relationship at the Dawn of the Twenty-first Century. *Peace and Security Review*, 6, 72–96.

Sobhan, R. 1993. Structural Maladjustment Bangladesh's Experience with Market Reforms. *Economic & Political Weekly,* 28, 925–931.

Sourcewatch 2015. Bangladesh and Coal. www.sourcewatch.org/index.php/Bangladesh_and_coal. Accessed 7 December 2020.

UN Development Programme (UNDP). 2010. Human Development Report: Asian countries lead development progress over 40 years. http://hdr.undp.org/en/media/PR6-HDR10-RegRBAP-E-rev5-sm.pdf. Accessed 7 December.

UN News. 2012. Open-pit coal mine project in Bangladesh threatens human rights – UN experts. https://news.un.org/en/story/2012/02/404922-open-pit-coal-mine-project-bangladesh-threatens-human-rights-un-experts#.VIISzovF98E. Accessed 7 December 2020.

UNESCO. Decision: 39 COM 7B.8, The Sundarbans (Bangladesh) (N 798). http://whc.unesco.org/archive/advisory_body_evaluation/798.pdf. Accessed 8 December 2020.

World Bank. 2013. Strategic Framework for Mainstreaming Citizen Engagement in World Bank Group-Supported Operations (https://consultations.worldbank.org/consultation/engaging-citizensimproved-results) addressing the relationship between NGOs and their programming. Washington, DC: World Bank. Accessed 7 December 2020.

World Bank. 2020. Globally Bangladesh is a Model for Poverty Reduction: World Bank [Press release]. www.worldbank.org/en/news/press-release/2020/01/29/globally-bangladesh-is-a-model-for-poverty-reduction-world-bank. Accessed 7 December 2020.

20

DISASTER GOVERNANCE AND AUTOCRATIC LEGITIMATION IN BANGLADESH

Aiding autocratization?

Maren Aase

Introduction

Bangladesh is among the most disaster vulnerable countries in the world (Behlert et al., 2020). Yet, steady expansion of response capacity to recurrent hazards, including floods and cyclones, has impressed many. During the past 15 years, attainments such as a decline in recorded cyclone deaths, innovative warning systems, fine-tuned crisis policy frameworks, humanitarian engagement, and climate advocacy have earned Bangladesh an international reputation as a rising star within disaster risk reduction (DRR).

However, if Bangladesh ever did live up to this label, this is certainly not the case anymore, when accelerating autocratization prevents enlightened discussion of risks. In February 2021, Dhaka activists protested over the death in jail of writer Mushtaq Ahmed whom the police had arrested for criticizing pandemic preparedness (Mahmud, 2021). The government framed his and similar arrests as legitimate security measures for preventing corona virus 'rumours' that could compromise crisis management. This approach, criticized by human rights organizations for being repressive (AI, 2020; Article19, 2021; HRW, 2020a), displayed a textbook authoritarian disaster response, where autocrats use crises as opportunities to maintain a responsible façade while at the same time curbing dissent (Diamond, 2020).

In light of what therefore seems a dramatic shift in Bangladesh's approach to disasters, this chapter examines the under-explored and uncomfortable possibility that efforts ideally geared towards preventing and tackling disasters can, in fact, also enable autocratization. From a DRR perspective, such questions are critical because autocratization, this chapter demonstrates, intensifies and expands vulnerability and – by fear and by force – suppresses social warning systems, creating vicious circles for disaster risks. How could Bangladesh's disaster governance become so repressive so fast, and with so little criticism from partners home and abroad? Has disaster governance aided autocratization, and if so, how? What consequences does the country's authoritarian disaster response have for its capacity to tackle future risks?

The chapter first introduces relevant concepts and context for exploring the links between disaster governance and autocratization. After that, discussions of responses to cyclone risk, refugee crisis and a pandemic unpack the opportunities that disaster governance provides to

DOI: 10.4324/9781003042211-24

authoritarian forces, and show how they are seized. Thereafter, the extent to which increased crisis-focus in global development leaves democracy in Bangladesh behind is considered. Lastly, the conclusions summarize the bleak prospects for comprehensive risk reduction in a state that suppresses core disaster preventive mechanisms such as free speech and real elections.

Concepts and context: the risk-creating politics of disaster governance in Bangladesh

Research documenting Bangladesh's path to autocratic rule has concentrated on constitutional mechanisms and institutions (Riaz, 2019; Riaz and Parvez, 2021). The following focus on disaster governance opens for further discussion how additional processes and actors, including foreign aid, can also enable autocratization.

Disasters, risks and responses

Bangladesh is a hot spot for disaster risks. Disaster risks are inherently social products of vulnerability, exposure to hazards, and capacity to anticipate and tackle crises with disastrous potentials. Disasters (involving large-scale destruction or fatalities) only materialize when vulnerable people and places are exposed to human-made or natural hazards that states and societies lack the will or ability to protect them from (Wisner, 2016).

Bangladesh's capacity for disaster management has improved radically since Independence, which in part was catalyzed by West Pakistan's callous response to the historically fierce 1970 cyclone that washed away between 250,000 and 500,000 lives. Protective investments include direct (cyclone shelters, flood warning, earthquake drills) and indirect (public health, building codes, poverty reduction) measures. Bangladesh has also pursued a policy shift from single responses to comprehensive risk reduction. Many risks remain though, and new ones develop: The global textile industry has increased workplace risks (Hossain, 2019c). Donor-supported infrastructure development has negatively affected ecology. Unchecked global trade and regional crises have presented complex transboundary challenges such as climate change, refugee influx and health hazards.

Bangladesh's risk realities demonstrate the value of disaster governance, meaning actors, norms and practices concerned with processes that drive or protect against disasters (Forino et al., 2018). Because the crises later discussed are of the kinds that carry disastrous potentials, associated crisis management practices are conceptualized as sub-ventures of disaster governance.

The normative presentation of disaster governance can be worlds apart from its real effects (Barnett, 2013; Hilhorst, Boersma and Raju, 2020). Aid and government analyses rarely discuss unintended impacts. DRR receives far more attention than disaster risk creation (DRC) (Lewis and Kelman, 2012). Conventional disaster governance routinely fails to include disaster-affected people in planning and evaluation, while repressive governance actors actively keep people and practices that can compromise them at bay.

Domestic disaster politics

Disasters have shaped Bangladeshi politics ever since the dawn of Independence. The painful experiences of the 1970 cyclone Bhola and the 1974 famine, Hossain (2018, 2019a) has shown, stimulated a social contract through which elites would prioritize the basic welfare of people. Disaster management became a prioritized issue, and protection in situations of disaster a symbol of independence and citizenship.

Ability to make performance personal is key. After the Ershad military regime's 1990 fall, the two major political parties, Bangladesh National Party (BNP) (founded by its present leader's late husband; currently in opposition) and the Awami League (AL) (founded by its current leader's late father; presently in office) and their various blocks have (with some intermissions), competed in turbulent elections, and alternated in power. Because few political differences exist between the two, ideologies of nationhood (Hossain, 2019b) and each party's lineage to towering figures in Bangladesh's political history have become emotionally powerful resources. Political networks combine patronage and patriotism to mobilize supporters, and various governments install personalized mechanisms such as the Prime Minister's Relief Fund (Khan and Rahman, 2007).

Confrontational and patronage political realities have stimulated routine blame games and elite manipulation of disaster funds (Mahmud and Prowse, 2012), but also responsive public action. Demonstrating ability to deliver the goods in times of crisis is important for governments, members of Parliament and opposition parties alike, and the electorate values leadership traits such as swift and far-reaching networks (Ruud, 2011). Political competition, a relatively un-censored press, and committed local and international partners have mutually supported each other in advancing disaster management. While no single disaster has ever made a measurable impact on Bangladesh's elections (partly because everyday risks matter more to most than occasional hazards), political leaders nevertheless have reasons to believe that a scandalous disaster response could (Hossain, 2019a; Rubin, 2020).

With the gradual breakdown of electoral democracy, this system is undergoing a silent collapse. For autocrats, disaster response becomes a hybrid arena for keeping up a veneer of accountability, and at the same time a pretext for curbing criticism. Autocracy in a political culture that sees political criticism as personal offence moreover enables state mechanisms such as the 2018 Digital Security Act (DSA) that criminalizes defamation, with blurred or no boundaries between offences against the image of the state and offences against the ruling party. This way, authoritarian rulers can promote a disaster-responsive image while also using pseudo-legal means, corrupt police and packed courts to downplay and deter criticism.

Foreign influence

Apart from specialized state institutions, notable disaster governance actors in Bangladesh are donors, UN agencies, and local and international development and humanitarian organizations. Norms include UN frameworks for DRR, national regulatory frameworks (promoted by actors such as NGOs or the UNDP) and organizations' codes of conduct. Practices centre on specialized areas such as relief and rehabilitation, where also disaster-affected people, expatriate networks, companies, and social organizations are involved. Other factors include aid policy trends like blurring public–private boundaries, goal expansion associated with the global Sustainable Development Agenda (UNISDR, 2015) and increased results-focus. In theory, that focus can motivate positive effects, yet in practice also stimulate easily measurable (irrelevant, or even harmful) achievement rather than sustainable impact.

Interactions through which disaster governance can aid autocratization

How, then, does domestic disaster politics and increasingly managerialist foreign influence interact to enable autocratization? Changing aid realities stimulate pragmatism amongst all parties. Bangladesh's aid dependence has declined and its bargaining position has increased. Aid funding increasingly hinges on measurable theories of change that downplay political problems of accountability. Moreover, conventional disaster aid, Barnett (2011, p. 221) observes (for humanitarianism) is "hardly a paragon of democratic rule". Autocratic or semi-autocratic donors like China, Saudi Arabia and India are also on the market. When foreign project reports highlight measurable outputs such as numbers of people evacuated and relief packages distributed, domestic political networks can nurture an accountable façade.

Disasters provide opportunities for autocrats to repress political opposition. Yet, no regime can rule by coercion alone, and von Soest and Grauvogel (2017) have shown that autocrats also employ and combine multiple legitimation strategies. Closed regimes mobilize primarily around national identity (for example, saviour narratives) while hybrid regimes prefer procedures, and all stress performance. Below, this chapter will show that in Bangladesh, conventional disaster governance primarily aids autocratization through the supply of performance pointers that autocratic forces can link to, and therefore use to promote an image as a superior, future-oriented, renowned and compassionate liberator and protector.

Disaster governance and autocratic legitimation in practice

The following are examples from cyclone, refugee crisis and pandemic handling that intersect autocratic processes before and after democratic collapse (see Lührmann and Lindberg, 2019). The examples highlight how disaster governance's risky disaster reductionisms have paved the way for autocratization, produced boosting materials to autocrats and been slow to link disasters and human rights. Examples of authoritarian crisis management also demonstrate that although the present regime goes to lengths to demonstrate efficiency, autocracy is by nature a vicious risk accelerator.

Fifty years of fighting cyclones: power concentration and seizure of simplified success

In Bangladesh, every biannual 'cyclone season' brings intense storms from the Bay of Bengal that coastal people have to weather. On average, once per third year cyclones reach levels of intensity classified as 'severe'. A few times per decade, fierce cyclones and associated storm surges intersect low-lying delta lands, shallow rivers and funnel-shaped coastlines to trigger large-scale destruction if striking exposed lands and people, especially during high tide.

Forecast and warning systems have steadily improved, increased evacuation, and inspired UN officials and other disaster experts to deem Bangladesh a champion within DRR (Paul, 2009). The key indicator referred for this status is radical decline of recorded cyclone-related fatalities. While the lethal combination of extreme poverty, minimal preparation and record-high storm surges led past cyclones to claim hundreds of thousands of lives, fewer cyclone fatalities followed later. After 2007 Cyclone Sidr, with wind speeds up to 240 km/h, several analysts compared the death toll (between 4,000 and 10,000) to past catastrophes; the 1970 cyclone Bhola and 1991 cyclone Gorky (138,000 fatalities), and theorized that Bangladesh had become significantly better at saving lives in the face of cyclones. These appraisals marked the beginning of a success narrative premised on considering Cyclone Sidr in juxtaposition to past cyclones, thus emulating a natural experiment without controlling either for natural factors such as landfall timing (high tide can, for example, increase storm surges and more than double impact) or for root social factors apart from mitigation issues.

Despite Paul's (2009) methodological critique of these comparisons, the narrative travelled further, into authoritative texts such as the 2014 *Human Development Report*, which first signalled success and thereafter attributed it to formal disaster governance measures:

236

a severe cyclone in 1991 caused nearly 140,000 deaths, while a 2007 cyclone of similar magnitude killed 4,234 people. The reduction in cyclone-related deaths was achieved mainly by improving early warning systems, developing shelters and evacuation plans, constructing coastal embankments, maintaining and improving coastal forest cover and raising awareness at the community level.

(UNDP, 2014, p. 107)

Sustained use of questionable cyclone event comparisons as evidence for a trend is unsurprising because aid analyses are increasingly wired to emphasize inspiring results that enable the sector to renew engagements. Linking capability to tackle cyclones with growing concerns for extreme weather, for example, the state and aid partners used the policy window opened by Cyclone Sidr to establish climate-funding mechanisms.

Downplayed, however, are problems that affected people have to battle in the shadow of success, some of them fashioned by a disaster management system that looks better on paper than it works in practice. For example, many Sidr-affected people just barely survived with help from neighbours with slightly sturdier houses, because public shelters were too few, too far away, in too dangerous conditions or full. Invisible is also the supply of financial and technical means that (government, bureaucratic and NGO) elites can seize to manipulate post-cyclone relief and recovery (Aase, 2020; Nadiruzzaman and Wrathall, 2015). Lastly, development strategies that have concentrated political power on few hands (van Schendel, 2009) are shielded from review. Illustrative here is coastal land transformation for shrimp exports and associated embankment construction near the Sundarbans mangrove forest, in part framed as flood mitigation. These choices have incentivized saline water intrusion, corruption, displacement and exploitation of landless people, and other risk multipliers that also increase floods and cyclone danger. Yet, plans continuously present embankments as protective, and now promote them as climate adaptation (Dewan, 2020).

During the past decade, the idea of Bangladesh as a DRR champion took the shape of a never-ending story. With every new (and most of them weaker and with a less dangerous path and timing than, for example, the 1991 or the 2007) cyclone, the system has been presented by disaster governance actors and analysts as having passed a test, while it in reality has passed smaller-scale (but also important) preparedness challenges. Opportunities for constant gratification suit aid for reasons discussed. They also, however, suit autocrats.

Recently, the current regime seized the simplified success story: Ironically, Cyclone Sidr hit during the controversial reign of the (in part donor encouraged) military-backed 2006–2008 Caretaker government that coordinated the response. The same government also clumsily and unsuccessfully tried to 'clean' politics by jailing the two major political party leaders for corruption charges. In the election manifesto speech held prior to the 2018 rigged (Riaz and Parvez, 2021) elections, the ruling party made no reference to this period. Blaming the opposition for the 1991 cyclone fatalities was confrontational politics as usual, as was connecting disasters and shame, claiming that previous rulers had "turned Bangladesh into a dependent and beggar country" and a "symbol of flood, drought, cyclones" (BDAL, 2018). Later, however, the party in power – at a time when opposing its image was becoming increasingly dangerous – also seized the aid-created success narrative premised on decline in fatalities that can only be explained by many and much more complex and combined factors than political leadership, if at all. For example, answering the opposition's criticism of the 2020 coronavirus response, the Information Minister used the never-ending rationale discussed above to claim that "Hasina [the PM] handled all disasters" (TIB, 2020b), thus converting 'country performance' into personal and 'evidenced' delivery.

Bangladesh has now reached a dangerous situation where the stakes for upholding success are likely to lead to higher control over natural hazard narratives. It has also reached a situation where disaster death tolls of earlier magnitude appear unthinkable, which is untrue and no good news considering, for example, climate change or the state's recent relocation (discussed below) of thousands of refugees to a cyclone-exposed island. The disaster governance narrative that Bangladesh's aid partners have co-produced, in part to inspire more and better DRR action, has contributed to this situation.

The 2017 Rohingya refugee crises: maximizing humanitarian performance

In August 2017, crackdowns against Rohingya (predominantly Muslim) minorities that Myanmar had discriminated against and denied citizenship for decades escalated into attempted ethnic cleansing. Organized murder, rape and village burning forced more than 700,000 refugees to flee to Bangladesh. Bangladeshi society responded with solidarity and spontaneous help. The AL Government (whose 2014 victory manifested in part because the opposition distrusted the possibility of actual competition, and boycotted them) formalized the response, and displayed sympathy with victims whose story echoed Bangladesh's own struggle for Independence while underscoring that support would be temporary until refugees could return home. The state built camps, provided relief and organized collaborations with local and transnational aid actors (Lewis, 2019).

The responsibility that Bangladesh took to protect the Rohingyas – that few else, including the UN, had previously shown (Zarni, 2019) – received much acclaim. In September 2017, a British television report from a refugee camp called the PM the 'Mother of Humanity'. This label, which appeared tailor-made for the ruling party's political heritage story and complemented a determined daughter's narrative with motherly softness and care, soon appeared beneath the PM's images on roadside campaign posters. Shortly after, the Cabinet approved a Mother of Humanity Award (which the PM 'refused' to progress in her own name), where local government bodies could nominate persons committed to social causes all over the country and awardees would receive a gold medal and a Tk 200,000 cheque.

The crisis also enabled the (officially secular) Government to validate ordinary people's faith-based solidarity with the Rohingyas and protect Islam during a phase where it courted religious groups such as the radical Hefazat-i-Islami to broaden its support base. Meanwhile, the rapidly deteriorating human rights situation driven by the party machinery itself received limited attention. In December 2018, the PM's efforts for the Rohingya cause earned her the Inter Press Service's International Achievement Award and the Global Hope Coalition's Special Distinction Award for Leadership. These New York events took place only six weeks after the ruthless arrest of renowned photographer Shahidul Alam (for press coverage of the 2018 road safety protests) exposed the regime's hardline approach to critics globally (Ahmed, 2018; Hasan and Wadud, 2020), and made domestic headlines prior to the general elections in December the same year (The Daily Star, 2018).

After the AL had secured another electoral victory, the Government's approach changed, and borders were closed. About 1.2 million refugees in poor and packed refugee camp conditions had brought concerns such as public resource stress, employment tensions, and potential radicalization. After several futile (including forced) repatriation attempts, the Government took up its previously initiated plan to relocate 100,000 refugees to the remote and highly cyclone-exposed Bhasan Char island, which previously had been abandoned after criticism from human rights activists. Bhasan Char was 'developed' through contracts officially worth over US$ 300 million, resulting in concrete houses, cyclone shelters, energy infrastructures, livelihood facilities, and new state–business connections. Refugees have overall, however, refused to relocate. A study by Zaman et al. (2020) found that 90 per cent of Rohingya respondents opposed relocation, citing the unique vulnerability of the less than 20-year-old silt island to cyclones and tidal flooding as primary reasons. The UN and rights groups have insisted that independent experts assess the relocation's feasibility, but no unconditional access has been granted.

In 2020, the Government effected the relocation of some thousand refugees, and used the coronavirus as an argument to speed up the process. Overall, observers have refuted official claims that all resettled refugees have consented freely (DW, 2021). Some agreed to go due to uncertain pull factors such as hearing that the island would have more facilities than provided in camps. There are, however, reports of ruthless push factors such as having one's name appear on official relocation lists with no explanation, or being threatened, forced or bribed into "consent", and transportation, by public officials (McPherson and Paul, 2020).

Rights groups have claimed that life on Bhasan island involves dire living conditions, sexual harassment by the Navy and contractors, restricted freedom of movement and free speech, and violent retaliation for protest. Naval and government spokespersons have denied the allegations, saying that the Rohingyas are guests that are taken care of (Hossain, 2020). To justify the relocation, officials draw on Bangladeshi culture for resilience and gratitude. Ministers uphold that cyclones are part of ordinary coastal life, that solid structures are better than temporary tents, and that the island facilities are better than anything available to millions of impoverished Bangladeshis. This attitude is hard to distinguish from conventional disaster aid that routinely empowers privileged people to determine the acceptable risks of poor and unconsulted others.

The international community's failures to address Myanmar's brutality towards the Rohingyas along with its excessive praise of Bangladesh have aided identity-based autocratic legitimation and helped the Government into a position from where it now, through the relocations, can demonstrate its long-sought superiority of ends over means.

The Covid-19 pandemic: 'responsible' repression in the time of Corona

In March 2020, the coronavirus that triggered the Covid-19 pandemic was found in Bangladesh. After initial reluctance, the Government took diverse lockdown measures to control the spread of the virus. Narrative control soon followed. A private university's pressure against a researcher to withdraw his scientifically modelled Covid-19 predictions was the first sign that the response would be anything but open and informed. Along with China, Egypt and Venezuela, Bangladesh became a pioneer in curbing criticism, belittling expertise and criminalizing inconvenient facts or opinions, framed as 'covid rumours' (HRW, 2021a). The state means applied were wide-ranging:

> The Government issued a circular on May 7, banning all government employees from posting, "liking," sharing, or commenting on any content which might "tarnish the image of the state" or the Government's "important persons," warning that violation of this order would result in legal action. The authorities have increased surveillance of anyone who might spread "rumors," and has ramped up media censorship. The Rapid Action Battalion (RAB), the country's primary counterterrorism unit, recently formed a "cyber verification cell" to identify Covid-19 "rumors."
>
> *(HRW, 2020b)*

The regime never had to declare a state of emergency in order to control dissent, because the executive already had empowered itself by passing the deliberately vague 2018 Digital Security

Act (DSA) which enables the politically penetrated state to curb criticism. Through the DSA, online expressions 'found to' create instability or offend the state can be punished with up to 10 years in prison, or life sentence (for repeated "offences"). Its arbitrary and excessive use is inconsistent with human rights law requirements for legality, non-discrimination and proportionality (AI, 2018; Carmalt and Dale, 2012).

Efficient crisis response depends upon combining capacity and trust (Christensen et al., 2016). Pandemics are different from Bangladesh's 'usual' disasters because their management demands higher, and longer-term, score on both dimensions. Social distancing is particularly difficult for millions of people living in poverty who lack access to protective equipment, testing, treatment and crisis assistance and cannot afford to ignore subsistence. Knowing this, and knowing that starvation is more damaging to legitimacy than a quiet pandemic, the state relaxed public health restrictions in practice. A study by Ali, Hassan and Hossain (2021) found that ordinary people's non-compliance was widely tolerated, and that upholding protective legitimacy with citizens took priority over pandemic management. Due to low testing and generally unreliable data, the extent to which this approach cost or shielded lives is indiscernible.

Its hard line approach to state critics and lenient approach on the ground illustrate that the regime prioritized its own survival over public safety. In theory, concerns raised by persons arrested under the DSA could have improved relief, informed the 'war' against the virus, or supplied ideas for post-crisis economic restructuring. In practice, the risk that critics also could have exposed an underfunded and corrupt health system (where certificates can be bought and funding pocketed, see Al-Zaman, 2020) and compromised the interests of regime supporters, became too high.

Nine months after his arrest under the DSA for criticizing shortage of protective equipment for healthcare workers and for sharing a drawing from (also arrested and tortured) cartoonist Kishore's "Life in the time of corona" series on Facebook, Mushtaq Ahmed died in pre-trial custody (HRW, 2021b). The regime's excessive force against critics has long been an open secret. Yet, Ahmed's death and pandemic repression presented new trials for autocratic legitimacy because the global pandemic had high salience across the world and human rights watchdogs increasingly engage with disaster issues. The UN is now pressurizing Bangladesh on revising the DSA. Domestically, post-pandemic economic crisis may challenge the performance legitimacy that the Government prioritized in the first active phase of the pandemic. Large-scale and (due to supply via India) relatively early Covid-19 vaccinations can lower the challenge, and reductionist reports of 'impressive' disaster response efforts by an earlier developing country might be expected in the years to come.

Leaving democracy behind?

The following section lifts the gaze from specific crises discussed thus far, to reflect on the broader links between the merging of disaster and development taking place under the 2030 Sustainable Development Goals (SDG) agenda, and autocratization. Due to multiple risks associated with climate change, Bangladesh's strategic role for foreign improvement projects (Hossain, 2018) is under renewal. This happens while development-related problems increasingly are framed as crises. Calhoun (2004) has warned that this "emergency imaginary" stimulates symptoms treatment over systems change. In this context, free speech and political competition, it seems, can pragmatically be subordinated to urgent crisis action.

The present Government in Bangladesh often uses development jargon to prove crisis commitment abroad while also delivering the charisma needed to mobilize loyalty at home. In

2021, the government launched the *Mujib Climate Prosperity Plan*. The name 'Mujib' cultivates a political heritage line from the freedom fighter, first PM, 'father of the nation' or 'friend of Bengal' ('Bangabandhu') Sheikh Mujibur Rahman, to his daughter, the present PM. This imagery uplifts her capacity to lead for the future. Abroad, the plan was 'lauded' by ambassadors and UN personalities for its "transformative climate concept for sustainable economic growth through investing in nature and climate resilience" (TIB, 2020a), thus disconnecting civil rights from sustainability.

The development sector increasingly elevates personal crisis management traits of political leaders. In 2015, the PM was awarded the United Nations Champions of the Earth Award by the UN Environment Programme, for climate advocacy. In 2020, the Guardian's online development section provided a platform for the PM and a CEO for the Global Center on Adaptation, which is a multi-stakeholder advocacy group initiated by former UN General Secretary Ban Ki Moon. On this arena, and in this company, the regime could present its 'fights' with cyclones and the coronavirus, and display sympathetic future-oriented concerns and capacity writing for example that: "as countries we can learn from successes around the world and support each other. It's by pulling together that we will emerge stronger and more resilient" (Hasina and Verkooijen, 2020).

So far, the international scene has been a low-risk arena for the regime. When the Overseas Development Institute hosted the PM's talk on the country's development "policy, progress and prospects" (ODI, 2018), the presenter was shielded from human rights questions (Channel4news, 2018). On (the few) occasions where the government openly has been questioned and even confronted, it has used development success to gloss over the situation. In a TV interview on the state of democracy, the international affairs advisor eluded criticism of enforced disappearances (i.e. unlawful abductions or other liberty-depriving actions that are conducted, and concealed, with direct or indirect support by the state apparatus), with responses such as "that is not our policy" or by deflection by referring to empowerment initiatives (Al Jazeera, 2019). Meanwhile, at home, the ruling party's Centre for Research and Information (CRI) communicates that the PM's policy of "leaving no one behind" (i.e. the slogan of the SDG agenda) reflects the policy of Bangabandhu (bdnews24.com, 2020).

When risk and rights are subordinated to development, autocrats can thrive. However, playing the development card may be less efficient if donor interests are directly challenged. Recently, when an Al Jazeera documentary suggested high-level political association with a surveillance scandal that could jeopardize military interests at home and abroad, the Government accused the news medium of being part of a plot to destabilize "the secular democratic government of Bangladesh with a proven track record of extraordinary socio-economic development and progress" (The Daily Star, 2021). Domestic media in turn publicly conveyed that real journalism on the matter would imply economic or personal risks that could threaten their existence, and the UN initiated investigations.

With stronger international spotlight on its power abuse and a weakened opposition, the regime might opt for a softer approach. Other options include changing the means of oppression or altering the meaning of democracy altogether.

Conclusion

This chapter has shown that disaster governance has supplied boosting materials for autocratic legitimation in Bangladesh. Governance of disaster processes can concentrate power and misrepresent risk realities, and by combining the two, aid autocratization. Autocrats adapt the performance boosts that disaster governance supplies to support a politically powerful image of might and care, and to gloss over the fact that the politicized state apparatus also uses crises opportunities to curb opposition.

In Bangladesh, the vicious circles that autocratization creates for disaster risk need more attention. First, autocratization intensifies existing disaster vulnerabilities of people living in marginal economic and social conditions. When regime-loyal economic elites can elevate themselves above the country's rich environmental and social policies, more risks are also created in the dark. Second, autocratization creates new risks among people who are usually not on disaster governance actors' watch lists, and who, in situations of disaster, can press for efficient response. Bangladeshi writers, students, scholars, artists, activists, journalists, opposition leaders, bloggers, civil servants, public employees and others who call the will, capacity or legitimacy of the powerful into question are now at unprecedented risk of human rights violations ranging from subtle sanctions to arrests, torture and enforced disappearances. Third, self-censorship sweeps valuable information about system dysfunctionalities under the carpet, and increases the distance from the most vulnerable to decision-makers, and humanitarian organizations that operate in restrictive countries trade non-discrimination in exchange for access (Desportes, 2020). Lastly, in the culture of fear that autocratization instils, much-needed serious discussion (Jasanoff, 2010) about future risks becomes illusory. Imminent threats of magnitudes that could overwhelm Bangladesh's capacity – likely co-created by economic interests associated with politics – receive dangerously shallow attention. Imagine, for example, earthquakes in export-processing zones, food industry-driven antibiotics resistance or record-high storm surges from deforestation and carbon emissions. Another imminent risk is land-use change-driven transmission of zoonotic viruses such as Nipah – with death rates up to 75 per cent recorded in Bangladesh (Constable, 2021) when only the wealthiest, best connected and least exposed can expect high-quality care.

Bangladesh's disaster warning system is crumbling. At stake is the country's inherently imperfect (Wisner, 2016) yet all the same historically unique capacity to tackle recurrent natural hazards and other crises, progressed by affected peoples, various governments, and committed national and international partners over almost 50 years. At this point in history, when core disaster preventive mechanisms such as free speech and real elections have been stripped away, any assessment of the country as a champion within disaster risk reduction is invalid, hazardously ignorant or simply propaganda.

Bibliography

Aase, M. (2020) 'Listing for change? Exploring the politics of relief lists in Bangladesh after Cyclone Sidr', *Disasters*, 44(4), pp. 666–686.

Ahmed, Q. (2018) 'Why did Bangladesh arrest Shahidul Alam?' *Al Jazeera Opinion*, 9 August [Online]. Available at: www.aljazeera.com/opinions/2018/8/9/why-did-bangladesh-arrest-shahidul-alam (Accessed 10 March 2021).

AI (Amnesty International) (2018) 'Bangladesh: Muzzling dissent online', *report*, 12 November [Online]. Available at: www.amnesty.org/en/documents/asa13/9364/2018/en/ (Accessed 10 March 2021).

AI (2020) 'Bangladesh: Escalating attacks on the media must stop', *Article*, 8 October [Online], Available at: www.amnesty.org/en/latest/news/2020/10/bangladesh-escalating-attacks-on-the-media-must-stop/ (Accessed 10 March 2021).

Al Jazeera (2019) 'Is Bangladesh a one-party state?', *Head to Head, TV programme*, 1 March, [Online]. Available at: www.aljazeera.com/program/head-to-head/2019/3/1/is-bangladesh-a-one-party-state/

Al-Zaman, M. S. (2020) 'Healthcare Crisis in Bangladesh during the COVID-19 Pandemic', *The American Journal of Tropical Medicine and Hygiene*, 103 (4), pp. 1357–1359.

Ali, T.O., Hassan, M. and Hossain, N. (2021) 'The moral and political economy of the pandemic in Bangladesh: Weak states and strong societies during Covid-19', *World Development*, 137 [Online]. Available at: www.sciencedirect.com/science/article/pii/S0305750X20303430

Article 19 (2021) 'Bangladesh: Alarming crackdown on freedom of expression during coronavirus pandemic', *Article19.org*, 19 May [Online]. Available at: www.article19.org/resources/bangladesh-alarming-crackdown-on-freedom-of-expression-during-coronavirus-pandemic/ (Accessed 10 March 2021).

Barnett, M. (2011) *Empire of Humanity: A History of Humanitarianism*. Ithaca, NY: Cornell University Press.

Barnett, M. (2013) 'Humanitarian Governance', *Annual Review of Political Science*, 16, pp. 379–398.

BDAL (2018) [Bangladesh Awami League] 'Election Manifesto 2018, speech by Sheikh Hasina' [Online]. Available at: http://manifesto2018.albd.org/election-manifesto-2018-speech-by-sheikh-hasina/ (Accessed 10 March 2021).

Bdnews24.com (2020) 'Hasina adopted Bangabandhu's policy of leaving no one behind', 21 September [Online]. Available at: https://m.bdnews24.com/en/detail/bangladesh/1803326 (Accessed 10 March 2021)

Behlert, B., Diekjobst, R., Felgentreff, C., Manandhar, T., Mucke, P., Pries, L. Radtke, K., and Weller, D. (2020) *World Risk Report 2020*. Bündnis Entwicklung Hilft, Ruhr University Bochum: Institute for International Law of Peace and Conflict.

Calhoun, C. (2004) 'A world of emergencies: Fear, intervention, and the limits of cosmopolitan order', *Canadian Review of Sociology*, 41 (4), pp. 373–395.

Carmalt, J. and Dale, C. (2012), 'Human Rights and Disaster', In Wisner, B., Gaillard, J. C. and Kelman, I. (eds.), *Handbook of Hazards and Disaster Risk Reduction*, London: Routledge, pp. 55–64.

Channel4news (2018) 'Bangladesh PM refuses to answer questions on human rights record', *TV report*, 18 April, [Online]. Available at: www.channel4.com/news/bangladesh-pm-refuses-to-answer-questions-on-human-rights-record (Accessed 10 February 2021).

Christensen, T., Lægreid, P. and Rykkja, L. H. (2016) 'Organizing for Crisis Management: Building Governance Capacity and Legitimacy', *Public Administration Review*, 76, pp. 887–897.

Constable, H. (2021) 'The other virus that worries Asia', *BBC Future*, January 12 [Online]. Available at: www.bbc.com/future/article/20210106-nipah-virus-how-bats-could-cause-the-next-pandemic (Accessed 10 March 2021).

The Daily Star (2018) 'PM receives 2 int'l awards for hosting Rohingyas', 29 September [Online]. Available at: www.thedailystar.net/rohingya-crisis/news/bangladesh-pm-sheikh-hasina-receives-two-un-international-awards-hosting-rohingyas-1639951 (Accessed 10 March 2021).

The Daily Star (2021) 'Bangladesh govt terms Al Jazeera report 'false, defamatory and a politically motivated smear campaign', 2 February [Online], Available at: www.thedailystar.net/bangladesh/news/bangladesh-govt-terms-al-jazeera-report-false-defamatory-and-politically-motivated-smear-campaign-2037929 (Accessed 10 March 2021).

Desportes, I. (2020) *Repression Without Resistance: Disaster Responses in Authoritarian Low-Intensity Conflict Settings*. Erasmus University Rotterdam.

Dewan, C. (2020) '"Climate change as a spice": Brokering environmental knowledge in Bangladesh's development industry', *Ethnos*, pp. 1–22 [Online]. Available at: https://www.tandfonline.com/doi/full/10.1080/00141844.2020.1788109?scroll=top&needAccess=true

Diamond, L. (2020) 'Democracy Versus the Pandemic. The Coronavirus is Emboldening Autocrats the World Over', *Foreign Affairs*, 14 June [Online]. Available at: www.foreignaffairs.com/articles/world/2020-06-13/democracy-versus-pandemic (Accessed 10 March 2021).

DW (Deutsche Welle) (2021) 'Rohingya: Relocated refugees say life was better at Cox's Bazar', *news report*, 26 February [Online]. Available at: www.dw.com/en/rohingya-relocated-refugees-say-life-was-better-at-coxs-bazar/a-56717730 (Accessed 10 March 2021).

Forino, G., Bonati, S., & Calandra, L. M. (eds.) (2018) *Governance of Risk, Hazards and Disasters: Trends in Theory and Practice* (1st ed.). London: Routledge.

Hasan, M., and Wadud, M. (2020) 'Re-conceptualizing safety of journalists in Bangladesh', *Media and Communication*, 8 (1), pp. 27–36.

Hasina, S. and Verkooijen, P. (2020) 'Fighting cyclones and coronavirus: how we evacuated millions during a pandemic', *Op. ed*, *The Guardian*, 3 June [Online]. Available at: www.theguardian.com/global-development/2020/jun/03/fighting-cyclones-and-coronavirus-how-we-evacuated-millions-during-a-pandemic (Accessed 10 February 2021).

Hilhorst, D., Boersma, K. and Raju, E. (2020) 'Research on Politics of Disaster Risk Governance: Where Are We Headed?', *Politics and Governance*, 8 (4), pp. 214–219.

Hossain, A. (2020) 'Rohingya relocated to remote island against their will, rights groups say', *BBC news report*, 4 December [Online]. Available from: www.bbc.com/news/world-asia-55177688 (Accessed 10 March 2021).

Hossain, N. (2018) *The Aid Lab: Understanding Bangladesh's unexpected success*. Oxford: Oxford University Press.

Hossain, N. (2019a) 'The 1970 Bhola cyclone, nationalist politics, and the subsistence crisis contract in Bangladesh', *Disasters*, 42 (1), pp. 187–203.

Hossain, N. (2019b) 'Winner Takes All: Elite Power Struggles and Polarization in Bangladesh', In Carothers T. & O'Donohue A. (eds.), *Democracies Divided: The Global Challenge of Political Polarization* (pp. 177–198). Washington, DC: Brookings Institution Press.

Hossain, N. (2019c) 'Rana Plaza, disaster politics, and the empowerment of women garment workers in Bangladesh', *Contemporary South Asia*, 27 (4), pp. 516–530.

HRW (2020a) 'Bangladesh: End Wave of COVID-19 "Rumor Arrests"', *HRW news release*, 31 March [Online]. Available at: www.hrw.org/news/2020/03/31/bangladesh-end-wave-covid-19-rumor-arrests (Accessed 10 March 2021).

HRW (2020b) 'Bangladesh: Mass Arrests Over Cartoons', *HRW news release*, 7 May, [Online]. Available at: www.hrw.org/news/2020/05/07/bangladesh-mass-arrests-over-cartoons-posts (Accessed 10 March 2021).

HRW (2021a) 'Covid-19 Triggers Wave of Free Speech Abuse', *HRW report*, 11 February [Online]. Available at: www.hrw.org/news/2021/02/11/covid-19-triggers-wave-free-speech-abuse (Accessed 10 March 2021).

HRW (2021b) 'Bangladesh: Writer Dies After 9 Months in Custody', *HRW news release*, 26 February [Online]. Available at: www.hrw.org/news/2021/02/26/bangladesh-writer-dies-after-9-months-custody (Accessed 10 March 2021).

Jasanoff, S. (2010) 'Beyond Calculation: A Democratic Response to Risk', In Lakoff, A. (ed.) *Disaster and the Politics of Intervention*. New York: Columbia University Press, pp. 14–41.

Khan, M. R. and Rahman, M. A. (2007) 'Partnership approach to disaster management in Bangladesh: A critical policy assessment', *Natural Hazards*, 41 (2), pp. 359–378.

Lewis, D. (2019), 'Humanitarianism, civil society and the Rohingya refugee crisis in Bangladesh', *Third World Quarterly*, 40 (10), pp. 1884–1902.

Lewis, J. and Kelman, I. (2012), 'The good, the bad and the ugly: Disaster risk reduction (DRR) versus disaster risk creation (DRC)', *PLOS Currents Disasters* [Online]. Available at: http://currents.plos.org/disasters/index.html%3Fp=1829.htm (Accessed 10 March 2021).

Lührmann, A. and Lindberg, S. I. (2019) 'A third wave of autocratization is here: what is new about it?', *Democratization*, 26 (7), pp. 1095–1113.

Mahmud, F. (2021), 'Anger in Bangladesh over dissident writer's death in prison', *Al Jazeera* 26 February [Online]. Available at: www.aljazeera.com/news/2021/2/26/anger-in-bangladesh-over-prominent-writers-death-in-prison (Accessed 10 February).

Mahmud, T. and Prowse, M. (2012) 'Corruption in cyclone preparedness and relief efforts in coastal Bangladesh: lessons for climate adaptation?', *Global Environmental Change*, 22 (4), pp. 933–943.

McPherson, P and Paul, R. (2020) 'Rohingya coerced into going to remote island, refugees and aid workers say', *Reuters*, 3 December [Online]. Available at: www.reuters.com/article/us-bangladesh-rohingya-idUSKBN28D0RQ (Accessed: 10 March 2021).

Nadiruzzaman, M. and Wrathall, D. (2015) 'Participatory exclusion – cyclone Sidr and its aftermath', *Geoforum*, 64, pp. 196–204.

ODI (Overseas Development Institute) (2018) *Bangladesh's development story: policy, progress and prospects*, 17 April [Online seminar]. Available at: www.odi.org/events/4550-bangladesh-s-development-story-policy-progress-and-prospects.

Paul, B. K. (2009). 'Why relatively fewer people died? The case of Bangladesh's cyclone Sidr', *Natural Hazards*, 50 (2), pp. 289–304.

Riaz, A. (2019) *Voting in a Hybrid Regime: Explaining the 2018 Bangladeshi election*. Singapore: Springer.

Riaz, A. and S. Parvez (2021). 'Anatomy of a rigged election in a hybrid regime: the lessons from Bangladesh', *Democratization*, 28 (4), pp. 801–820.

Rubin, O. (2020) 'The political dynamics of voter retrospection and disaster responses', *Disasters*, 44(2), pp. 239–261.

Ruud, A. E. (2011) 'Democracy in Bangladesh: A village view', In Madsen, S. T., Nielsen, K. B. and Skoda, U. (eds.) *Trysts with Democracy: Political practice in south Asia*. London: Anthem Press, pp. 45–70.

TIB [*The Independent Bangladesh*] (2020a) 'Hasina's "Mujib Climate Prosperity Plan" lauded globally', 5 February [Online]. Available at: www.theindependentbd.com/post/259026 (Accessed 10 February 2021).

TIB (2020b) 'Sheikh Hasina aptly handled all disasters: Hasan', 23 July [Online]. Available at: www.theindependentbd.com/post/250669 (Accessed 10 March 2021).

UNDP (2014) *Human Development Report 2014: Sustaining Human Progress – Reducing Vulnerabilities and Building Resilience.* New York.

UNISDR (United Nations Office for Disaster Risk Reduction) (2015) *Disaster risk reduction and resilience in the 2030 agenda for sustainable development.* New York: UNHQ Liaison Office.

Van Schendel, W. (2009) *A History of Bangladesh.* Cambridge: Cambridge University Press.

Von Soest, C. and Grauvogel, J. (2017) 'Identity, procedures and performance: how authoritarian regimes legitimize their rule', *Contemporary Politics*, 23 (3), pp. 287–305.

Wisner, B. (2016) 'Vulnerability as concept, model, metric and tool', *The Oxford Research Encyclopedia of Natural Hazard Science* [Online]. Available at: https://oxfordre.com/naturalhazardscience/view/10.1093/acrefore/9780199389407.001.0001/acrefore-9780199389407-e-25. (Accessed 10 March 2021).

Zaman, S., Sammonds, P., Ahmed, B. and Rahman, T. (2020) 'Disaster risk reduction in conflict contexts: Lessons learned from the lived experiences of Rohingya refugees in Cox's Bazar, Bangladesh', *International Journal of Disaster Risk Reduction*, 50, pp. 1–17.

Zarni, M. (2019) 'The UN Has Failed the Rohingya in Myanmar. Now it Should Take Responsibility', *The Wire*, 30 June [Online]. Available at: https://thewire.in/south-asia/united-nations-rosenthal-report-rohingya-myanmar (Accessed 10 March 2021).

21

ISLAMIST EXTREMISM IN BANGLADESH

A pretext for autocratization

Asheque Haque

Introduction

Bangladesh is a land of contrast; this rather small country in terms of landmass with an incredibly large population, which makes it one of the most densely populated countries in the world, is home to many exceptions and expediencies, especially when it comes to politics. Yet, there is one experience that stands out in recent years, and that is the continuous increase of authoritarianism in the country. Riaz (2019) has labelled Bangladesh as a "Hybrid regime" – an authoritarian state that looks and acts like a democratic one while a study by the Bertelsmann Foundation (Croissant 2020) classified Bangladesh as relapsing into an autocratic state. In 2020 Freedom House (2020) gave Bangladesh a score of 39 out of 100 in its Freedom of the World Index and labelled the country as "Partly free" while Human Rights Watch in its World Report 2021 (Human Rights Watch 2021) stated that the Bangladeshi government had "doubled down on authoritarian crackdown on free speech, arresting critics, and censoring media".

Two of the most prominent laws used by the authorities in the past two decades to prop up increasing authoritarianism – the Information and Communication Technology (ICT) Act 2006 and the Digital Security Act (DSA) 2018 – were labelled as tools to counter violent extremism by the government. Bangladesh is a Muslim-majority country, and like many other countries around the world, jihadi ideology-based violent extremism spread among a small portion of the population over the past two decades. The ICT Act 2006, originally created to combat cybercrime, was amended in 2013 to address terrorism in the digital space. It was replaced by the DSA 2018, which was supposed to counter radicalization and the spread of jihad on the internet. The Prime Minister of Bangladesh, Sheikh Hasina, said that the DSA was enacted in order to provide the people with digital security to live in the "Digital Bangladesh" that her government built. She said, "It's our duty to prevent the youth from taking a wrong path or getting involved in militancy and terrorism; we must make sure that they do not do anything harmful to the country and the people." And she added, "This is why digital security is absolutely necessary" (bdnews24.com 2021).

However, in December 2019 Shariat Bayati, a Baul folk singer, was arrested and a case was filed under the same DSA 2018 (Abrar 2020). His values, ideologies and worldview could not be any further from that of a jihadist. How is it that a law, which is enacted to counter violent extremism, is also being used to suppress long-standing local cultural practices and performances?

DOI: 10.4324/9781003042211-25

Amnesty International claimed in 2020 (*The Daily Star* 2020) that since the law was passed, the DSA 2018 has been "wielded as a weapon to silence critics and suppress dissent".

In this chapter I discuss the origin of the DSA 2018 and the experience of violent Islamist extremism in the past decade leading to the search for a comprehensive legal remedy. The subsequent discussion focuses on the DSA 2018 and its various sections that curtail civil liberties and freedom as well as the section that covers terrorism-related offences. This is followed by the discussion on how these counter-terrorism laws were used to increase authoritarianism in the country and support the ruling regime. The discussions show that countering violent Islamist extremism has played a counter-intuitive, yet significant, role in Bangladesh's slide towards an autocratic system over the past two decades. 'Militancy', as violent Islamist extremism or terrorism has been termed in the local context, has provided a pretence for the incumbent regime to curtail the civil liberties and human rights of the population, weaken democratic institutions, but strengthen the capabilities of the state security apparatus. The chapter shows that the Bangladeshi government enacted the Digital Security Law 2018 claiming that it was a counter-terrorism tool, but in reality it was used to ensure the survival of the regime by prosecuting their opponents, and thus increasing the authoritarian control over the country.

It is worth noting that the DSA 2018 is not the only law that the government has in order to prosecute violent extremist organizations and their members. The Anti Terrorism Act 2009, the more generic Bangladesh Penal Code 1860, various Rules enacted over the years, and even Executive Orders by the President have had the effect of controlling or curtailing civil and political rights of the citizens if they commit such offences. But among them the DSA 2018 stands out in its scope, reach and the potential of abuse or arbitrary use. This chapter focuses on the DSA 2018 in order to analyze how a counter terrorism law for the digital spaces has become the widely abused mechanism for stifling intellectual pursuits in the country.

The democratic backsliding in Bangladesh

The political experience of Bangladesh as an independent nation is full of bold strides of democracy, frequent interventions by unelected forces, innovations to find a unique local governance method and rabid corruption fuelling massive economic disparity. In the 50 years of its history, the country has seen 11 national elections (Al Jazeera 2018), as well as ten military takeovers or attempts (Ali 2010 and *The Daily Star* 2012).

Bangladesh's slide from a democratic country towards an authoritarian, autocratic state has been discussed by many authors in the past few years. Riaz (2019) elaborated how Bangladesh went from "an electoral democracy to a hybrid regime" where he stated that the democratic process in the independent Bangladesh started in 1991, but within the next two decades the quality of democracy deteriorated and the governing polity became an "electoral authoritarianism". He argued that Bangladesh quickly transformed into a "hegemonic authoritarian regime" as was demonstrated by the national elections in 2014 and 2018 and the process continued to "institutionalize the hegemonic authoritarianism via an election" (Riaz and Parvez 2021). Riaz claimed that democracy in Bangladesh ended with the manipulation and blunt rigging of the 2018 national election by the incumbent political party. He identified that the manipulation included, among other means, the establishment of control over the media, which was predominantly carried out by the then newly enacted DSA 2018. The law, which was passed only two months prior to the election, was used to arrest 63 people including online and cultural activists and journalists between 8 October 2018 and 15 January 2019.

Mostafa and Subedi (2020) noted that three socio-political mechanisms – marginalization of political oppositions, institutionalization of authoritarian policies, and co-option of religious leaders – added to the election manipulation to increase authoritarianism in Bangladesh. As such, proponents of democracy and functioning institutions, as well as of progressive ideas and secular values, have all faced scrutiny and oppression under the DSA 2018 and other policies of the regime. Abrar (2020) blames "the rise of obscurantism, coupled with political expediency by the ruling elite" for the recurring violence against "artists, singers, art enthusiasts and cultural activists who stand for freedom, diversity and coexistence". In an interview with CIVICUS, Ferdows argues that self-censorship and fear are common among civil society members, human rights defenders, journalists, and citizens in general in Bangladesh. She lists several key challenges that relate to various sections of the ruling authority and create obstacles to freedom of expression and assembly in the country (CIVICUS 2019). Hossain, Billah and Islam (2020) argue that faced with the strict control by the Bangladeshi Government over civil society spaces, most civil society organizations and media entities are following a "see-no-evil" policy to continue operating in the country, while those who attempt to report violations of human rights face excessive pressure from the ruling authorities.

ICT Act 2006 and violent Islamist extremism in Bangladesh

The origin of the DSA 2018 can be traced back to the Information and Communications Technology Act 2006, abbreviated as the ICT Act 2006. This law created the groundwork for basic jurisdiction regarding computers and the internet and focused mostly on implications of computer and ICT usage in business and administration while providing rules for e-commerce and cyber-crimes (Ali 2011). There was one particular article in this law that still proved to be controversial; Article 57 of the ICT Act 2006 elaborated the "Punishment for publishing fake, obscene or defaming information in electronic form". The article describes that the use of computers or the internet deliberately to "prejudice the image of the State or person or causes to hurt or may hurt religious belief or instigate against any person or organization" will be an offence. The punishment for this offence was set to be imprisonment for up to ten years along with the possibility of a large monetary fine (Government of Bangladesh 2006). The Bangladesh Government amended the ICT Act 2006 in 2013 and increased the maximum punishment under Article 57 from ten years to 14 years. At the same time, the Bangladesh Police was given the authority to "file a case and arrest any person under the law" without prior permission or warrant (Adhikary 2017).

Even though the origin of DSA in the form of the ICT Act 2006 was in order to provide a legal structure and solutions to issues such as e-commerce and cyber-crimes, the necessity to include another category of offences soon emerged. With the proliferation of smartphones, increased access to the internet and relatively affordable internet data packages provided by multiple, competitive mobile phone operators, larger portions of the population started to be active online (Hasan 2020). The opening up of this digital space allowed various fringe groups who did not have access to the public space in real life to become vocal. Among them were Islamists and jihadists who used the opportunity to radicalize and recruit Bangladeshis.

Bangladesh's experience with violent extremism based on jihadism was a part of the global jihadi movement. In the post 9/11 world, the jihadi ideology started to spread further increasing the number of sympathizers in Bangladesh and leading to several jihadist attacks in the early 2000's. These included attacks on government officials such as the police or judges as well as public spaces such as cinemas, theatres or cultural events. Probably the most prominent of the attacks was the assassination attempt on current Prime Minister Sheikh Hasina in 2004, even though she had faced attempts before (International Crisis Group 2018). Still yet, radicalization, network growth and operational aspects of the jihadist groups remained traditional and used rudimentary communications methods without much online presence. With the spread of mobile phones in the county and the development of digital technologies, Bangladesh and Bangladeshi jihadists started to open up to the digital space. Hizbut Tahrir was one of the earliest Islamist groups in Bangladesh that organized its movement using both online and physical worlds. Heavily connected to their branch in the UK, the Bangladeshi chapter started using social media sites such as Facebook and maintained an active website for the Bangladeshi audience. But the main activities of this group remained in the physical world, especially around mosques and at different education institutions (Khan 2015).

Hizbut Tahrir was soon followed by the more violence-prone Ansarullah Bangla Team, who were spreading the ideology of Al Qaeda and global jihad in the Bangla language using the internet. Mufti Jashimuddin Rahmani was the spiritual leader of this terrorist group and was perhaps the first prolific ideologue to use information technology to spread one of the largest compilations of violent extremist materials in the Bangla language. His sermons during Friday prayers were laden with jihadi ideological and operational discussions and calls for action. These sermons would be uploaded on the internet within hours and spread around the world to his large number of online followers on various platforms. He is the first jihadist leader to successfully utilize the digital space for the Bangla-speaking audience. Along with preaching about jihad, his followers used the internet to actively recruit others and to raise funds (Haque 2016).

At this time, Bangladesh was in the middle of the International Crimes Tribunal proceedings, a judicial process established to prosecute the perpetrators who had committed war crimes, crimes against humanity and genocide during Bangladesh's War of Independence in 1971 (Samad 2016). Many of the accused were involved in Islamic politics, and several leaders of Bangladesh Jamat-e-Islami, a mainstream political party in the opposition, were among them. Following a verdict of a Jamat leader by the Tribunal, members of the general public started a popular movement in Shahbagh Square in the capital, giving it the moniker Shahbagh Movement. This was initially led by an online group of bloggers and freethinkers. Soon, this turned out to be a major popular uprising with people joining around the country. Islamists labelled these bloggers as "atheists and blasphemers" and started a counter-protest led by Hefazat-e-Islam, another Islamic movement (Sarker 2017). This ongoing political development gave Rahmani the perfect opportunity to increase his impact and make his followers carry out jihadist actions.

With the active promotion of jihadist violence in Bangladesh by Rahmani using the digital space, violent extremist attacks quickly increased in the country. Ansarullah Bangla Team, and their affiliate Ansar-al-Islam, killed a number of bloggers, rights activists, free thinkers, and progressive writers within a span of two years. They continued to maintain a heavy presence online and used the digital space to be constantly in touch with their supporters and sympathizers (International Crisis Group 2018). The experiences of 2013 with regards to both the growth of militancy in the country and the rise of mainstream political movements using digital means led to the amendment of the ICT Act in 2013 making it stronger in order to control this space. Riaz (2021) said that this amended law was used "against 'secularist' bloggers on the one hand while clamping down on Islamist websites on the other".

Bangladeshi jihadists started to show their support to the Islamic State (IS) soon after it was established in 2014. The sharing of various news from the IS and the subsequent discussions about this terrorist organization primarily took place online for the Bangladeshi supporters, and soon this resulted into radicalization and recruitment efforts (Roul 2015). IS also published articles concerning Bangladesh and produced other jihadist content in the Bangla language and shared it online for their Bangladeshi audience (Haque 2020). While initially the activities of IS in Bangladesh did not garner much notice, IS supporters staged perhaps one of the biggest terrorist attacks in the country at Holey Artisan Café in Dhaka on 1 July 2016. Twenty-two people, including 17 foreign nationals, were killed in that attack carried out by five Bangladeshi young men. The attackers were heavily armed, well-trained and were incredibly brutal in their tactics. They were only stopped when a combined force of military commandos stormed into the building. The shock from this attack reverberated around the country and abroad (*The Daily Star* 2016). From early on it was clear how the digital space enabled and amplified this attack and glorified jihadism. The IS had not only made threats about attacks; they provided live updates as well as published videos and statements claiming the attack – all using the digital space (Deutsche Welle 2016).

With this attack it was clear that Bangladeshi terrorists had become increasingly sophisticated with their use of the online spaces for their radicalization, recruitment, and operational activities. As the intensity of violence from terrorism increased, which was evidently connected with the online space, securing that space became a matter of utmost importance. In the physical world, the Bangladeshi security forces relied upon legal measures such as the Anti-Terrorism Act 2009 and also some extra-judicial methods, as have been detailed by various rights organizations (International Crisis Group 2018). But these measures were not possible to emulate in the digital space, and the need for a far reaching and controlling mechanism was apparent. Even though the Anti-Terrorism Act 2009 was further amended in 2013 for courts to accept evidence in the form of communication over social media or the internet, it did not ban such activities legally speaking (The Daily Star 2019). As such, a law that would curb the online space for radicalization and recruitment of these terrorists, as well as curb the conduit to violent actions, was desirable for the authorities for whom it was common to be heavy handed in dealing with terrorism. At the first glance, the DSA 2018 had the possibility to provide this kind of measure. As it happened, two developments in Bangladesh – the rise of Islamist extremism and the expansion of digital spaces – that happened simultaneously, were expected to be managed by one mechanism – the DSA 2018.

The Digital Security Act 2018

The Digital Security Act, 2018 is described as "An Act to make provisions for ensuring digital security and identification, prevention, suppression and trial of offences committed through [a]digital device ..." (Government of Bangladesh 2019b). This Act, with nine chapters and 58 sections, covers various topics related to the digital life of the Bangladeshi populace. The National Parliament passed this Act on 19 September 2018 through a voice vote, with a minuscule 11 Members of Parliament opposing it in writing. The bill was placed before the Parliament on 9 April with several discussions and approvals by various Parliamentary Committees taking place before the final vote. Immediately after the passing of the Act, journalists, media houses and rights activists raised concerns that "the act goes against the main spirit of the Constitution and will restrict free-thinking, freedom of speech and freedom of expression" (Hasan 2018).

Several sections of the DSA raised concerns from early on. Among them sections 21, 25, 28, 31, 32 and 43 were highlighted to go against the freedom of speech and independent journalism by journalists and media rights activists (Nazeer 2020). Sampadak Parishad, a platform of the country's newspaper editors, denounced eight sections – 8, 21, 25, 28, 29, 31, 32 and 43 – as posing serious threat to freedom of expression and media operation (Hasan 2018).

The following are short excerpts from the DSA 2018 of these sections (Government of Bangladesh 2019b). Section 8 gives the power to the Bangladesh Telecommunications and Regulatory Commission to remove or block any data-information that creates a threat to digital security. Section 21 outlines punishments for making any kind of "propaganda or campaign against liberation war, spirit of liberation war, father of the nation, national anthem or national flag". Section 25 punishes the transmission or publication of propaganda with "an intention to affect the image or reputation of the country". Section 28 punishes the "publication, broadcast, etc. of information in website or in any electronic format that hurts the religious values or sentiment". Section 29 penalizes the publication, transmission, etc. of defamatory information Section 31 penalizes offences that deteriorate law and order, and explains that anything "that creates enmity, hatred or hostility among different classes or communities of the society, or destroys communal harmony ... shall be an offence". Section 32 punishes the breach of secrecy of the Government under the Official Secrets Act, 1923 using digital means. Section 43 states that if any police officer has reasons to believe that an offence under this Act is likely to be committed, then the officer can conduct search, seizure and arrest without a warrant. Section 53 of the Act states that offences under section 21, 28, 31, 32 and a few others as well as a subsection of section 29 will be non-bailable offences. The Act also has extra-territoriality to cover offences committed outside of Bangladesh as described in section 4, which states that "if a person commits any offences under this Act beyond Bangladesh which would be punishable under this Act if committed in Bangladesh, the provisions of this Act shall be applicable in such manner as if he had committed such offence in Bangladesh". The punishments for many of these offences are very strict and harsh, as described in the Act.

In comparison to this long list of sections regarding various offences for expressing opinions, only section 27 of the DSA discusses the offences and punishment for committing cyber terrorism (Government of Bangladesh 2019b). There is no other section describing offences related to violent extremism, radicalization, or recruitment. There are several sections about cyber-crime, forgery, identity theft or violation, hacking or damages to information infrastructure, but they are not connected to violent extremism in the Act per se. When placing this Act before Parliament, the Telecom and ICT Minister argued that ensuring the country's security from digital crime and ensuring the security of people's lives and property were the main objectives of this law (The Daily Star 2018). Sajeeb Wazed Joy, the Prime Minister's son and her ICT Advisor, said in a statement that the DSA had been enacted to "stop spreading of falsehood and militant activities through social media to protect minority communities" (Prothom Alo 2018). The importance of the DSA 2018 in combating terrorism is evident in the Anti-Terrorism Unit Rules 2019 of Bangladesh Police where section 8 states that the unit will be able to investigate offences under the Anti-Terrorism Act 2009 and other listed Acts including the ICT Act 2006, amendments to it, and the DSA 2018 (Government of Bangladesh 2019a). Sayeed Ahamed termed online propaganda by global terrorist groups as cyber-crime and argued that traditional laws were not suitable for digital spaces, and as such these crimes provided the context for the DSA 2018 (Jamal, Mahtab, and Sajen 2016). Parvez (2019) commented that the DSA 2018 follows other laws to govern digital spaces which Bangladeshi violent extremists have been using for "psychological warfare, publicity, propaganda, data mining, recruitment, mobilization, networking, information sharing, planning, coordinating and training".

This discrepancy between the offences for which this was claimed to be enacted and the ones for which it was being implemented, also becomes evident when looking through the arrests made and cases filed under the DSA 2018. Zaman (2020) noted that between October 2018 and November 2020 there have been more than 1,000 cases filed under the DSA 2018 against "ordinary citizens, activists, academics and journalists for 'criticizing' the government policies or its political leadership". Between January and June 2020, a total of 208 people were booked under the DSA in 113 cases, and 114 persons were immediately taken under arrest. She argued that, "an astonishingly high number of enforced disappearances, crackdowns on any critics, jailing of political opponents and the routine treating of democracy advocates and citizens under the Digital Security Act show the abysmal state of civil and political rights in the country". The Centre for Governance Studies in Bangladesh found that between February 2020 and February 2021, 873 individuals under 402 cases were accused under the DSA 2018, out of which only 22 people received bail and three were released. Among the accused, 13% are journalists, another 13% are politicians, 5% are students and 2% are teachers (Jagonews24.com 2021).

On 26 February 2021, Mushtaq Ahmed died inside a prison while being denied bail for over nine months. He was a businessman and a writer who was arrested under the DSA 2018. Bangladeshi jurist Shahdeen Malik said that Mushtaq was a victim of the oppression by the Bangladeshi Government, and that this was a murder of freedom of expression itself. Bangladeshi authorities heavily cracked down on the civil society members protesting this death as well (*The Daily Star* 2021b). Ahmed Kabir Kishore, a cartoonist who was imprisoned around the same time with Mushtaq, was finally released on 4 March 2021, and described the horrific torture committed upon them by unidentified security officials of the regime while under custody (Islam 2021).

Compared to all these incidents, it has been surprisingly difficult to find a case where members of violent Islamist organizations have been arrested under the DSA 2018. Searching through multiple reports of arrests of militants in Bangladesh as published online by mainstream Bangladeshi media has not produced any result so far. Often the reports mention that a case has been filed under the Anti-Terrorism Act but on many occasions the media reports do not mention the Act under which the case has been filed at all. Even in the rather obvious incident where members of a known and officially banned terrorist group conducted activities with bitcoins online in order to raise funds for purchasing weapons, the media report does not provide this detail (Khan 2019). As such it cannot be confirmed whether or not any terrorists have been prosecuted under the DSA 2018 at this time.

From countering violent extremists to suppressing regime opponents

How did the DSA 2018, which was supposed to be a legal remedy to violent extremism in Bangladesh's digital space, end up being used for completely different purposes? The answer might not be very straightforward or easy to pinpoint. But it is clear from the discussion in the previous section that the DSA has been used regularly to suppress the freedom of expression in the country and crack down on perceived regime opponents. The DSA has aided the ruling regime to increase authoritarianism over the population on all three mechanisms as described by Mostafa and Subedi (2020) – marginalization of political oppositions, institutionalization of authoritarian policies and co-option of religious leaders that increases authoritarianism in Bangladesh.

Bangladeshi authorities have used the DSA 2018, and its predecessor the ICT Act 2006, in order to weaken and suppress the opposition political parties in the country. The ruling Awami League has consistently blamed the opposition parties, Bangladesh Nationalist Party (BNP) and Jamat-e-Islami (JI), as organizations that sympathize with, harbour and nurture militants in the country (Ramani 2016). This allowed the harassment of political opponents in the guise of anti-militancy operations. Ahmad and Kugelman (2018) argued that Bangladesh used a "counter terrorism pretext" in order to justify their crackdown on opposition members. They observed that while members of Jamat-e-Islami did not have any organizational connection with terrorists, many of their political actions included violence. This allowed Bangladeshi authorities to often term members of the political opposition as terrorists or extremists. This was evident in the language and tone used by the senior members of the ruling regime towards the leader of the opposition Khaleda Zia over several years. In March 2014, the then Information Minister of Bangladesh stated that Khaleda Zia was promoting militancy in the name of political movement

(Prothom Alo 2014). In February 2015, the then Finance Minister termed Zia as "the queen of terrorism" (Prothom Alo 2015b). In November 2015, the Information Minister stated that Zia was leading militant activities in the country with assistance from JI, and informed that the authorities were taking measures according to the law (Prothom Alo 2015a). In March 2017, the Information Minister termed Zia and her political party as the main supporters of militants in the country (Prothom Alo 2017). The fact that in 2015 approximately 125 people were killed by arson attacks during political protest and movement by the opposition parties only cements this sentiment among parts of the population (Firstpost 2018). In this context of violence and the increased rhetoric by the leaders in Government, the scope of the DSA was extended to use it against the opposition political parties.

Additionally, the Awami League promoted themselves as having an anti-militancy narrative which valued the sacrosanct "Spirit of the Liberation War" (Dhaka Tribune 2019). This, paired with the offence for tarnishing the image of the state under section 25 of the DSA, effectively led to the enforcement of the singular Awami League narrative that assisted in establishing a one-party state. Furthermore, there was no place for any doubters in this narrative. Civil society organizations that reported on the human rights violations or abuse of the judicial process fell at the crosshairs of the regime, and were labelled as disruptive to anti-militancy operations, hence committing anti-state activities which diminish the reputation of Bangladesh. Members of the media and civil society organizations were also acting as watchdog over the regime activities, as they do in most places of the world. But this meant that many uncomfortable questions, schemes of corruption, extravagances of the party officials, and abuses of power by regime officials were being raised about the current regime. In order to establish the regime narrative and provide the selected information, DSA was a convenient tool already present to suppress critics, just like it has been used to suppress regime opponents. Increasingly more of these crimes were booked under the DSA. Lacy and Mookherjee (2020) elaborated on the various ways in which journalists and rights activists self-censor themselves. As such the DSA played a part in the institutionalization of authoritarianism in Bangladesh.

Furthermore, Lacy and Mookherjee (2020) describe the aim of the Bangladeshi ruling regime to control the "virtual street" with the two laws regarding digital spaces. This stems from the intention of the ruling regime to preserve their political power. Bangladeshi politics found a new avenue in the past decade in the form of digital space. While the physical political space of the country was tightly controlled by the dominant political party in power, the new digital space was wide open and ushered in a new era of political discourse on social media and blogging forums. The DSA particularly attempts to control this space through its various sections curbing protest and dissent. Lacy and Mookherjee (2020) argue that the "criminal-isation of online speech highlights the vulnerability of the seemingly omniscient state". The ruling authorities were worried by this space and from the experiences of the Arab Spring they realized the capacity of this digital space in changing the political power of a country. As such the Shahbagh movement and the Hefazat-e-Islam movement that followed it were inherently considered a threat to the continuation of the regime. Lacy and Mookherjee claim that the "draconian amendment of the ICT law in 2013" was a response to the Shahbagh protests and the subsequent Hefazat-e-Islam protests in Dhaka.

Mostafa and Subedi (2020) argue that "the authoritarian regime in Bangladesh is less likely to survive without co-opting the religious leaders". This is because the authorities understand that Islam is a central organizing force and can provide massive support to the regime. Ramani (2016) argues that the rise of violent Islamist extremists was a response to the perceived secu-larization of the country by the ruling authorities. The Hefazat-e-Islam movement of 2013 was based on the premise that Islam was under threat in Bangladesh and the government was taking anti-Islamic actions. Aware of this outcome and intent on changing this, the regime subsequently placed emphasis on nurturing the relation with Islamic groups and leaders of the country to get a share of their popular support. Thus, the DSA 2018 was used in order to appease these Islamic groups by deliberately targeting bloggers, Bauls, rights activists and so on, who often express anti-regime opinions, along with taking a liberal and often anti-religion stance. The religious leaders, in return, co-opted with the regime and bestowed the Prime Minister with their recognition and approval by terming her as "the mother" of all them (Dhaka Tribune 2018).

In 2014 Alam maintained that "internet governance, that is, restricting or controlling access to certain information, cannot become a tool for muzzling of dissent, of the rights to air one's views …, and the rights to inform people of the facts". He worried that the Bangladeshi political culture was dysfunctional enough that the stipulations under one law could be extended over other groups who were not originally intended to be covered by that law. He added that, "it has happened before, and, if it does again, very likely would result in the kind of vicious political animosity that the country does not need" (Alam 2014). Unsurprisingly though, it appears that his warning has come true as we discuss the use of DSA 2018 and its predecessor the ICT Act to curb political dissent rather than to combat violent extremism, thus increasing authoritarianism in Bangladesh.

Conclusion

This chapter traces the development of legislative measures by the Bangladeshi authorities in order to govern digital spaces that grew in the first two decades of the twenty-first century. This development coincided with the growth of violent Islamist extremism or militancy in the country, which posed a security challenge to the authorities. The authorities claimed that the ICT Act 2006, then the 2013 amended version, and finally the Digital Security Act 2018 were legal remedies necessary for countering militancy, especially in the digital spaces. However, it has been evident from the discussions in this chapter that these laws were not used for their intended purposes most of the time for arresting and prosecuting terrorists.

On the contrary, it emerges that in the name of countering militancy, Bangladesh has empowered and enabled its security apparatus through enacting these strict laws. And this same apparatus, with these strengthened capacities, has systematically dismantled a political opposition, choked an independent media, suppressed a thriving civil society, and curtailed the civil and political rights of the populace in the physical and the digital spaces. While this has enabled the ruling regime to establish unquestioned, unchallenged control over state power, democracy has suffered significantly in the process along with political tolerance and pluralism. The country has further moved towards an autocratic regime, with a strict authoritarian rule but with some pretence of a democratic state.

The DSA 2018 is one of the most prominent tools in the hands of the regime authorities that enabled this autocratization. While it was claimed that this law would be used for countering violent extremism, from early on the multiple sections in the law that control and curtail various civil and political rights and liberties were pointed out by many journalists, legal experts and rights activists. The Editors' Council stated that this law will have a "chilling effect" on press freedom in the country (Mahmud 2018). Zaman (2020) claimed that the DSA reinforced punitive measures to curb freedom of expression and assisted in creating a digital authoritarianism in Bangladesh. Faisel, concerning Article 19 (The Daily Star 2021a), argued that the "act is not made to give security to common people rather to ensure security of a particular party". From the discussion in this chapter, it is also visible that the DSA 2018 provided political expediency and solidified political domination for the ruling party.

The DSA 2018 used the pretext of countering terrorism to achieve political gains, but in the process, it infiltrated into the lives of every citizen in the country to limit their rights. It has become so invasive and extensive that in 2020, a 15-year-old child was arrested by the Bangladesh Police under the DSA 2018 for defaming the Prime Minister and sent to a correction facility during the Covid-19 pandemic. Reporting about that incident Nazeer (2020) stated that the DSA was used to justify invasive forms of surveillance and to violate the rights of free speech of a minor. This incident exemplifies the necessity to reform the DSA 2018, but also to ensure that legal instruments that violate human rights that are enshrined by international norms and treaties are amended. Bangladesh may have been on the path of autocratization, but it is still possible to reverse the trend.

Bibliography

Abrar, Chowdhury R. "Shrinking Space for Cultural and Artistic Freedoms - *Twin Fangs of Bigotry and Intolerance of Dissent.*" *The Daily Star*, 2020.

Adhikary, Tuhin Shubhra. "The Trap of Section 57." *The Daily Star*, 7 July 2017, 2017.

Ahmad, Atif J. and Michael Kugelman. "The Death of Democracy in Bangladesh." The National Interest, 2018. Accessed 15 January 2021. https://nationalinterest.org/feature/death-democracy-bangladesh-36147.

Al Jazeera. "Bangladesh Elections 2018: What You Need to Know." Al Jazeera. Accessed 15 January 2021. www.aljazeera.com/news/2018/12/29/bangladesh-elections-2018-what-you-need-to-know.

Alam, Shahid. "Fathoming ICT (Amendment) Act, 2013." *The Daily Star*, 10 March 2014, 2014.

Ali, S. Mahmud. *Understanding Bangladesh.* London: Hurst & Company, 2010.

Ali, Rowshan, "Bits and Pieces of Cyber Law." *The Daily Star*, 15 June 2011.

bdnews24.com. "Hasina Explains Why Bangladesh Needs Digital Security Act." *Bdnews24.Com*, 2021.

CIVICUS. "Bangladesh: 'Out of Fear, People are being Silent'." CIVICUS, 2019. Accessed 15 January 2021. www.civicus.org/index.php/media-resources/news/interviews/4180-bangladesh-out-of-fear-people-are-being-silent.

Croissant, Aurel. *The Struggle for Democracy in Asia – Regression, Resilience, Revival.* Gütersloh, Germany: Bertelsmann Stiftung, 2020.

Deutsche Welle. "How 'IS' Terrorists used Social Media for 'Updates' on Dhaka Cafe Attack." Deutsche Welle, 2016. Accessed 15 January 2021. www.dw.com/en/how-is-terrorists-used-social-media-for-updates-on-dhaka-cafe-attack/a-19373763.

Dhaka Tribune. "PM Sheikh Hasina Branded as 'Mother of Qawmi'." *Dhaka Tribune*, 4 November 2018, 2018.

———. "PM: No Sympathy for those Involved in Graft, Terrorism." *Dhaka Tribune*, 23 November 2019, 2019.

Firstpost. "Bangladesh Court Orders Arrest of Khalida Zia for 2015 Arson Attack that Killed Eight People." *Firstpost*, 2 January 2018, 2018, sec. World.

Freedom House. *Freedom in the World 2020: Bangladesh.* Washington: Freedom House, 2020.

Government of Bangladesh. *Anti-Terrorism Unit Rules, 2019, Bangladesh Gazette,* 2019a.

Government of Bangladesh. *Digital Security Act, 2018,* Public Law 46, *Bangladesh Gazette,* 2019b.

Government of Bangladesh. *Information & Communication Technology Act, 2006*, Public Law 39, *Bangladesh Gazette*, 2006.

Haque, Asheque. "Understanding the Sermons of Mufti Mohammad Jashimuddin Rahmani, the Spiritual Leader of Ansarullah Bangla Team." Master of Arts in South Asia and Global Studies, King's College, London, 2016.

———. *. Violent Jihadist Ideology in South Asia: Socio-Political Implications.* Lund: Lund University, 2020.

Hasan, Mahmudul. "Bangladesh Adds 3.3cr Internet Users in a Decade - *Finds GSMA Study.*" *The Daily Star,* 9 November 2020, 2020.

Hasan, Rashidul. "Digital Security Bill Passed." *The Daily Star*, 20 September 2018, 2018.

Hossain, Zakir, S. M. Masum Billah, and Monjurul Islam. "Bangladesh: Civic Space and Minority Rights." In *South Asia State of Minorities Report 2020*, 29: The South Asia Collective, 2020.

Human Rights Watch. *World Report 2021: Bangladesh – Events of 2020.* New York: Human Rights Watch, 2021.

International Crisis Group. *Countering Jihadist Militancy in Bangladesh.* Brussels: International Crisis Group, 2018.

Islam, Zayma. "Scars of Torture all Over Him." *The Daily Star,* 5 March 2021, 2021.

Jagonews24.com. "1 Bochore Digital Nirapotta Aine 783 Mamla, Beshi Akranto Shangbadikra." *Jagonews24.Com,* 27 Feb 2021, 2021.

Jamal, Eresh Omar, Moyukh Mahtab, and Sahmsuddoza Sajen. "Digital Security Act, 2016 – how does it Affect Freedom of Expression and the Right to Dissent?" *The Daily Star,* 29 October 2016, 2016.

Khan, Mohammad Jamil. "ABT Converting Cash to Bitcoin to Buy Arms." *The Daily Star,* 27 September 2019, 2019.

———. "Banned Hizb Ut-Tahrir Now Prefers Direct Action." *Dhaka Tribune,* 3 July 2015, 2015.

Lacy, Mark and Nayanika Mookherjee. "'Firing Cannons to Kill Mosquitoes': Controlling 'virtual Streets' and the 'image of the State' in Bangladesh." *Contributions to Indian Sociology* 54, no. 2 (06/01; 2021/ 03, 2020): 280–305.

Mahmud, Faisal. "Bangladesh Editors Protest 'chilling' Digital Security Act." Al Jazeera, 2018. Accessed 15 January 2021. www.aljazeera.com/news/2018/10/16/bangladesh-editors-protest-chilling-digital-security-act.

Mostofa, Shafi M. D. and D. B. Subedi. "Rise of Competitive Authoritarianism in Bangladesh." *Politics and Religion* (2020): 1–29. doi: 10.1017/S1755048320000401.

Nazeer, Tasnim. "Bangladesh Silencing Teenage Dissent." *The Diplomat,* 29 Jun 2020, 2020, sec. Opinion.

Parvez, Saimum. "Bangladesh and India." In *Counterterrorism Yearbook 2019,* edited by Kfir, Isaac and Georgia Grice, 41. Australia: Australian Strategic Policy Institute, 2019.

Prothom Alo. "Jongi Kormokande Netritto Dichchen Khaleda Zia." *Prothom Alo,* 3 November 2015a, sec. Politics.

———. "Jongir Shongi BNP Ebong Khaleda Zia." *Prothom Alo,* 11 Mar 2017, 2017, sec. Politics.

———. "Joy for Immediate Passage of Digital Security Bill." *Prothom Alo,* 16 April 2018, 2018.

———. "Khaleda Zia Jongibadke Ushke Dichchen: Toththomontri." *Prothom Alo,* 4 March 2014, 2014, sec. Bangladesh.

———. "Khaleda Zia 'Shontrasher Rani'." *Prothom Alo,* 15 February 2015b, 2015, sec. Politics.

Ramani, Samuel. "Here's how the Bangladesh Government is Making Religious Violence More Likely." *The Washington Post,* 21 July 2016, 2016.

Riaz, Ali. "The Pathway of Democratic Backsliding in Bangladesh." 28, no. 1 (01/02, 2021): 179–197.

———. *Voting in a Hybrid Regime: Explaining the 2018 Bangladeshi Election.* London: Palgrave Macmillan, 2019. DOI: 10.1080/13510347.2020.1818069

Riaz, Ali and Saimum Parvez. "Anatomy of a Rigged Election in a Hybrid Regime: The Lessons from Bangladesh." (01/12, 2021): 1–20. Accessed 30 January 2021. https://doi.org/10.1080/13510347.2020.1867110.

Roul, Animesh. "Spreading Tentacles: The Islamic State in Bangladesh." *Terrorism Monitor* 13, no. 3 (2015).

Samad, Abdus. "The International Crimes Tribunal in Bangladesh and International Law." *Criminal Law Forum* 27 (29 April 2016, 2016): 257.

Sarker, Probir Kumar. "4 Years since the Shahbagh Movement." *Dhaka Tribune,* 5 February 2017, 2017, sec. Bangladesh.

The Daily Star. "Bid to Topple Government – Involvement of 'Parties' Under Probe." *The Daily Star,* 2012.

———. "Digital Security Act: Rise in use of the Law Alarming – *Says Amnesty.*" *The Daily Star,* 2020.

———. "Digital Security Bill Placed in JS Amid Concern." *The Daily Star,* 10 April 2018, 2018.

———. "DSA Enacted to Ensure Security for Select Few: Speakers." *The Daily Star,* 28 February 2021, 2021a, sec. City.

———. "Reflecting on the Anti-Terrorism Act 2009." *The Daily Star,* 3 December 2019, 2019.

———. "Terror Strikes Dhaka." *The Daily Star,* 1 July 2016, 2016.

———. "Unacceptable - Outrage all Over After Mushtaq's Death in Custody; Call for Scrapping DSA Gets Louder." *The Daily Star,* 27 February 2021, 2021b.

Zaman, Fahmida. "Digital Authoritarianism in Bangladesh: What You Need to Know." The National Interest, 2020. Accessed 15 January 2021. https://nationalinterest.org/blog/skeptics/digital-authoritarianism-bangladesh-what-you-need-know-172236.

22

SHEIKH HASINA OF BANGLADESH

The making of a strongman regime

Arild Engelsen Ruud[1]

Introduction: what is a 'strongman'?

Sheikh Hasina Wazed has been prime minister of Bangladesh since January 2009. Over these years, Bangladesh has seen a marked deterioration in its democratic status, with human rights bodies and international organisations voicing concern and objections over stage-managed elections, increasing surveillance, enforced disappearances and a legal regiment that stifles criticism (Human Rights Watch 2021). Sheikh Hasina and her party, Awami League, have slowly, meticulously and successfully built what in reality is a one-party state. Sheikh Hasina herself has become without question the most powerful leader in contemporary Bangladesh, in reality unchallenged by any political rival inside or outside of the political party she is leading. This chapter will employ the concept of strongman to investigate the case of Sheikh Hasina's prime ministership and ask how this change from electoral democracy to an authoritarian regime came to pass. What are the main elements in the construction not just of an authoritarian regime, but one in which there is an unquestioned leader?

The Introduction to this Handbook points out that there is a marked increase in forms of autocratic rule in South Asia, a development which is part of a wider trend. While authoritarian regimes exhibit some similar features, they are also different from one another. Efforts to analyze and understand this development and such regimes have over time given rise to a plethora of concepts, including authoritarian, autocratic, semi-democratic and sultanist. Derivatives such as 'sultanistic' have been tried out, as well as 'neo-sultanistic', 'authoritarian populist', 'illiberal populist', 'semi-authoritarian', 'electoral autocracy', 'constitutional autocracy' and others. The number of terms led an exasperated Collier and Levitsky (1997) to group all in the wide category of 'hybrid regime'.

The point of introducing yet another term, strongman, is to shift focus from regime type to regime construction. The tendency inherent in the effort to define regime types is to ignore the creation and formation of a regime (Young 1999). Observers look at the end product rather than the process by which such a regime is formed, its actual coming-into-being. But regimes are not simply there; they are constructions, coalitions of forces built over some time. This is all the more evident in the case of the current phase of transition, from functioning electoral democracies to hybrid regimes. While studies on an earlier form of transition could focus on

DOI: 10.4324/9781003042211-26

how elites let power slip, the current form of transition must focus on how disbursed power is increasingly centralised, how the many lose power to the few.

The argument here is that there is an active building process behind this transition, an active building of a regime. The term strongman also helps us shift focus to an observable fact, that much of the actual building process happens around one person. In the case of Bangladesh, this person is Sheikh Hasina. For the Philippines it is Rodrigo Duterte, for India Narendra Modi and for Cambodia Hun Sen. For Sri Lanka it seems to happen around the Rajapaksa family, or at least two of the brothers. There are many other similar cases.

There is reason to believe, and this chapter will make that suggestion, that this one person or family is of crucial importance to the regime changes. However, the challenge inherent in the term strongman is not to over-emphasise the role of the one leader. We need to keep eyes open for the other forces that engage with the leader, that support him (or her). Hence I shall prefer the term 'strongman regime'.

Strongman regimes are what Lai and Slater (2006) refer to as 'personalised regimes'. These are different from a 'junta' or a 'party machine' regime in which the leader is restricted by a larger group of people. This useful distinction should be modified to allow an understanding of the dynamics in which a regime moves from one type to another. The concept strongman regime encourages us to investigate the dynamics of the relationship between the strongman and the regime.

By drawing on the Bangladesh case, this chapter will focus on three aspects. First, a constitutional tweaking has facilitated the building of a coalition of state institutions and forces. Crucially, this coalition drew support away from Awami League's rival while also being a self-sustaining coalition in which different elements are mutually supportive. Secondly, the ideological construction of Sheikh Hasina and her family as exceptional and crucial to the country's identity, its very DNA, is important because it provides legitimacy to the regime. The narrative justifies the regime's focus on economic development rather than on maintenance of a liberal democracy. And, thirdly, the regime has implemented a legal framework that effectively stifles criticism and silences the opposition. Legal protection and tweaking is crucial to strongman regimes' maintenance (Morgenbesser 2020), and in the Bangladesh case it has proven to be an effective tool in the mutual support of the ruling coalition.

The 'strongman' term is justified because behind these developments and at crucial junctures, are politically savvy if risky choices. The leader is not just a figurehead but the core person. She has used what leverage she had with success although the challenges have been substantial. The transition from electoral democracy to an authoritarian regime was not a smooth, gliding process. It was a process characterised by conscious choices and determination as well as the ability to take advantage of opportunities as these arose. Hence the term strongman.

Constitutional tweaking and building a coalition

The Awami League government under Sheikh Hasina has successfully and with great dexterity shaped state institutions in a way that ensures their continued cooperation in maintaining its rule. Crucial in this were first its handling of a formidable rival state force, the military, and second two constitutional amendments.

When Sheikh Hasina became prime minister in January 2009, it was her second stint in office. She had been in power once previously, sitting a full term from 1996 until 2001 when her party lost the election. She returned to power after her party had won the December 2008 election with a convincing majority.

That election, however, was held two years late. Despite its nominally democratic constitution, the country had in 2007–2008 been ruled by an essentially unconstitutional government that had been backed by the military and implicitly supported by foreign governments and at least initially by substantial proportions of the middle classes. This government, known as the Caretaker Government, had pursued a 'minus two' agenda, seeking to send both Sheikh Hasina and her rival Khaleda Zia, the chairperson of Bangladesh Nationalist Party BNP, into permanent exile (Hagerty 2007). The Caretaker Government and its backers blamed the two political leaders for many of the country's ills, including corruption and violent political unrest. That this agenda did not succeed was largely due to intense political work, involving mobilisation and argumentation. One very clear lesson for Awami League and Sheikh Hasina when returning to government positions in January 2009, was that the rule of politicians was not a given. The armed forces constituted a real potential adversary.

The need to build bridges was made even clearer only a little more than a month later, when a mutiny erupted in the Pilkhana cantonment in Dhaka of the border security force Bangladesh Rifles (Momen 2010). The mutiny lasted two days and left about 80 people dead. It was probably caused by the overbearing attitude of army officers commanding the force. Army officers and their families living in the cantonment also bore the brunt of the mutiny. Sheikh Hasina had herself led the response, as minister of defence, and had emphasised the need to avoid further bloodshed. Although many army officers were enraged by the mutiny and the killing, the prime minister's calm and negotiated approach was appreciated by others.

After this, a conscious effort was made to bridge the gap of distrust and suspicion between Awami League and the armed forces. Relatives of the Pilkhana victims were given housing and government jobs. A number of transfers in the armed forces ensured promotion of Awami League sympathisers. Sheikh Hasina increased their budgets, attended ceremonies in person, and emphasised the army's contribution to the country's liberation. She took particular care of the 9th Infantry Division which is stationed in Savar and protects the main access route to the capital from any revolting army faction elsewhere in the country.

As she was building closer relationships with the armed forces, one serious challenge was that BNP had traditionally been seen as closer to the military than Awami League. BNP's leader Khaleda Zia was a rival for the military's affections being a former general's widow and had been living in a house in Dhaka cantonment since the 1970s. In 2011, Sheikh Hasina had her evicted from this house.

The Hasina government also expanded the role of the military. The 9th Infantry Division was in 2011 expanded to include special units in connection with the new bridge being built across the Padma. These new units included an engineering corps. This policy was replicated in several other cases and the military is increasingly involved in construction and contracting. One striking case is the Rohingya settlement built on the island Bhasan Char by the navy. The settlement has capacity for 100,000 refugees and is fitted with cyclone shelters and a solid protective embankment. The costs have not been disclosed. Companies hired by the military to execute such tasks are often manned and owned by retired officers and provide a welcome income in addition to the pension. The armed forces' welfare organisation (Sena Kalyan Sangstha) is successfully involved in a number of commercial and industrial ventures, including petrochemicals, cement-production, shopping centres and the Dhaka Radisson Hotel. The profit helps provide services to armed forces personnel, including retirees.

Sheikh Hasina has also ensured that the military can continue its attractive engagements in UN peacekeeping operations (Bangladesh is among the top three nations to provide troops for such operations). These not only allow welcome field experience for the military but also handsome salaries for the individual personnel.

A number of other perks have been instituted for bureaucrats and military officers above a certain rank (*Prothom Alo* 2018). In addition to the use of an official car, the perks include loans for buying a private car as well as generous maintenance costs for that car, and housing loans well below the going market interest rate. For bureaucrats there are several fellowship programmes for foreign degrees. In the words of one observer, these are 'benefits for allegiance' programmes.

In a different development, the Hasina government in 2011 abolished the Caretaker Government instrument arguing that Bangladesh was now a mature democracy (15th Amendment, June 2011). With this the government ensured political oversight over the election process. The Caretaker Government instrument had been introduced into the constitution in 1996 after massive street protests against the then BNP government's manipulation of the election process (Kochanek 1997). The Caretaker Government instrument was the instalment three months before an election of a neutral government headed by the last retired Supreme Court judge. The CTG as it is known ensured free and fair elections. It was in operation for the second election in 1996, which Awami League won, and in 2001, which Awami League lost and after which Sheikh Hasina resigned as prime minister. However, at the end of its period, in 2006, the BNP government again sought ways of manipulating the CTG by inter alia changing the retirement age for Supreme Court judges (Hagerty 2007). The unrest and street violence that followed justified the *de facto* military coup of January 2007. The lesson for Awami League was that in the 'toxic' political culture of the country (Islam 2013), even a constitutional provision would not ensure a level playing field. The amendment that abolished the Caretaker Government instrument was the logical outcome of this experience.

BNP protested against the abolition of the Caretaker Government instrument and engaged in violent and disruptive street protests. However, in the end they were ineffectual. Public opinion may also have swung against them. Moreover, the brutality of the protests provided the government with justification for dealing with the situation as a law and order problem rather than as legitimate political protest. But the police also pushed the boundaries of legitimate police action. It used with great effect what one senior police officer called 'the Khulna model', which was to put ten opposition leaders behind bars – 'and fifty others will go into hiding' (private communication; also Human Rights Watch 2018b). Because of BNP's boycott, 154 of the 300 members of parliament were 'elected' unopposed and without a vote. The voter turnout was extremely low (some put it at less than 25 percent). BNP, the former ruling party, ended up without representation and the role as official opposition went to Jatiya Party, a party closely aligned with Awami League (its founder-chairman was special advisor to the Prime Minister and members of the party served as cabinet ministers).

The point to underline is that none of this was strictly illegal or unconstitutional, however contrary to the spirit of democratic competition it may have seemed. In a sense, Awami League had successfully outmanoeuvred its main rival largely due to the rival's own tactical errors.

Another challenge turned opportunity was a very heated national debate and national mobilisation that took place in parallel to the election unrest. This development followed from Awami League's election promise to try the 1971 war criminals. This was a long-standing demand among many Awami League supporters and progressives. The vocal Ekattorer Ghatak Dalal Nirmul Committee had been established by leading intellectuals when Jamaat-e Islam leaders were introduced into government positions by Khaleda Zia in 1992 and had continued its pressure ever since. Jamaat leaders had opposed independence in 1971 and many had actively engaged in collaboration with Pakistani forces and committed atrocities against freedom fighters. In 2009 Awami League decided to act on its promise and set up the International Crimes Tribunal. The first indictments were issued in 2010 and the first verdicts passed in 2011. This started a period of intense cultural debate and conflict in the country. In February 2013 at least 100,000 progressives gathered at Shahbag in Dhaka because of fear that the government was too lenient towards the war criminals (De 2015). In May the same year the Islamist organisation Hefazat-e Islam mobilised several hundred thousand in what was widely seen as a counter-demonstration at Shapla Square in Dhaka to press for more Islamist policies, including laws against blasphemy and non-Islamic practices (Bouissou 2013). In the midst of all this, alleged atheist bloggers were targeted by violent jihadists and some were killed in bloody acts of violence.

During these months of heated debate and mobilisation, Sheikh Hasina and Awami League sought to strike a balanced agreement (Lorch 2018). The progressive Shahbag movement was partially co-opted and neutralised. More of a concern was the Islamist mobilisation. The Hefazat was a newcomer on the scene and represented the traditional (*qawmi*) Islamic clerics (*ulama*) and their many Islamic seminaries (*madrasa*). The Hefazat's capacity to mobilise had made a deep impression and the demands had resonated well even among Awami League supporters (Fair and Abdallah 2017). The Hefazat represents a theological tradition different from and often opposed to that of Jamaat. Sheikh Hasina seems to have acknowledged this with clarity and a degree of cynicism, and later that year she reached out to Hefazat leaders. Over the months and years that followed, her government implemented policies that were controversial among her core supporters because they reflected Hefazat demands. These include changes in the school textbooks (less progressive, less 'Hindu'), acceptance of qawmi madrasas as on par with government schools, the removal of a statue of a 'Greek goddess' (in fact, Lady Justitia) from the Supreme Court building, and a substantial increase in the salaries of madrasa teachers (Lorch 2018). She was later praised by Hefazat as 'Mother of Qawmi'. It is arguable that the government with some success has incorporated the qawmi ulama in the periphery of its grand coalition.

In another amendment to the constitution (16th Amendment, 2014), parliament was made superior to the Supreme Court and given the power to dismiss judges if allegations of incapability or misconduct against them are proved (*Dhaka Tribune* 2017). With this, judicial oversight over parliament was abolished and the judiciary made beholden to parliament and in reality to the ruling party. In connection with a judicial review of the amendment, the Chief Justice supported a view of the amendment as unconstitutional. A few months later he was forced to leave the country and subsequently dismissed (Riaz 2021). The next Chief Justice accepted the amendment as in line with the constitution. In the same amendment, a provision was introduced to the election law that made it mandatory for the court to hear the election commission's view first before issuing any judgment on an election complaint. The election commission is nominally independent of the executive, but in reality subservient to it.

These are the eye-catching developments. Quietly most major news outlets and television channels have been brought into the ambit and many owners or their family members made member of parliament or given other forms of preferential treatment (*Dhaka Courier* 2019; Riaz and Rahman 2021). Also important in the expanding coalition have been the law-enforcement agencies, of which the main ones are Rapid Action Battalion (RAB), the various branches of the police (Detective Branch, Special Branch, Criminal Investigation Branch), and Directorate General of Forces Intelligence (DGFI, the military intelligence). Members of these institutions plus the civil administration willingly employed double standards in dealing with opposition and government candidates during elections (Riaz 2019). There were instances of trumped-up charges against opposition candidates and their candidacy annulled by officials on flimsy grounds. Some 30,000 cases are alleged to have been filed against opposition activists and leaders and 8,000 allegedly arrested, causing each personal problems and inhibiting political space for the opposition. Officials in polling stations allowed activists to stuff ballot boxes and the police often turned a blind eye to acts of violence and intimidation by Awami League activists. The police was particularly visible during the 2018 election and many considered the police to have 'delivered' the outcome, including many in the police force. News outlets and organisations such as Transparency International Bangladesh documented extensive irregularities in almost all constituencies and the partisan role played by police or the administration in more than half of the constituencies (*The Daily Star* 2019).

Within the first few years in power, Awami League had in effect neutralised or co-opted major loci of power and authority in the country. The military, the bureaucracy and the judiciary had been significant alternative sources of authority and power in independent Bangladesh's early history. The traditions of the 'vice-regalism' (Shah 2014) ran deep in institutions that were partly rehabilitated after 1975 by the autocratic governments of Ziaur Rahman (1975–1981) and H.M. Ershad (1982–1990), who relied on the established classes to replace Awami League appointees (Baxter 1984). That these had remained formidable loci of power was proven by the 2007–2008 military-backed Caretaker Government, but by 2014 they had been co-opted into an Awami League coalition.

In addition, Awami League's rival BNP had committed tactical errors and marginalised itself from its constitutional rights while also proving to be dependent on the easily vilified Jamaat for its street presence. Crucially Sheikh Hasina had also ensured that Shahbag did not develop into an alternative locus of power on the progressive left.

Family and exceptionality

Central to ideological justification of her regime is that she is her father's daughter. Her father, Bangabandhu Sheikh Mujibur Rahman, was the independence movement's leader and the country's leader until he was murdered along with most members of his family in 1975. Sheikh Hasina was then abroad and returned to Bangladesh only in 1981. After a short debate which the *rokto* (blood) faction won, she has been the supreme and largely uncontested leader of her party – formally re-elected at regular intervals. She is now on her fourth general secretary. After the 2018 election, she surprised observers by easing out most senior party leaders from ministerial positions, including her own cousins and her daughter's father-in-law (Khalidi 2019). It was an exercise of supreme control.

That Sheikh Hasina is 'Bangabandhu's daughter' is deafening in a muted way. Her father's special place in the nation's history is emphasised and reinforced in numerous official and public acts. And yet in this there is no direct suggestion that her being Bangabandhu's daughter makes her genetically fit or dynastically endowed to be prime minister. Her exceptionality is reinforced more indirectly.

A clue can be had from the documentary film, 'Hasina: A Daughter's Tale'. This professionally made documentary directed by her nephew was released a month before the 2018 election in cinema halls all over the country. Here she is portrayed as an ordinary housewife, seen in her kitchen, making food for her family or talking happily with her grandchildren. These footages of contemporary happiness are contrasted by photographs and footage of her father and her reminiscences about him and what he meant for her both personally and politically. The soft approach of the documentary underlines the brutality of the assassination in 1975, the bloody attack on him that also killed her three brothers, her mother and several other members of her family.

This legacy of blood and loss is crucial to the creation of her political persona. She is an ordinary person with an extraordinary background, someone with strong leadership qualities but whose political outlook and aims have been shaped through terrible personal horror. She mentions her father in every speech and faithfully attends to his name and memory. Her undisputed and unquestionable loyalty makes her the nation's leader because it connects her personally and intimately to the father of the nation, its eternal leader (Ruud, forthcoming).

Shortly after her coming to power, his status of father of the nation (*jatir janak*) was given constitutional foundation, his portrait was to be found in all public offices and schools and he was given special legal protection against defamation. Over the years, an official cult has been constructed around him and his legacy. Several public holidays and national celebrations are directly or indirectly associated with him, such as his declaration of independence speech, his homecoming after the war and the assassination of him and his family – marked every year as the 'day of mourning'. His birth is celebrated as the national children's day but known as 'Mujibur's birthday'. His centenary is celebrated as 'Mujib year'. A range of government agencies, buildings, educational institutions, streets, tournaments and parks are named after him, mostly by Sheikh Hasina's governments. Generally the more prominent institution in any sector is named after him, such as the national football stadium, the country's largest conference centre, the country's first satellite, a heavily armed missile frigate and the prestigious Bangabandhu Sheikh Mujib Medical University. Major national investments include the Bangabandhu Bridge across the Jamuna and a large new international airport planned near Dhaka (to be called Bangabandhu International Airport).

Every Awami League poster has images of Sheikh Mujibur Rahman and Sheikh Hasina. And Awami League posters are everywhere, in every street and street corner, on every wall across the country. As Kuttig points out (2020), banners and posters are pervasive visual and material expressions in an environment where 'visibility means everything' (Blom Hansen 2004). The specialness of the family is part of the official cult, to a large extent reinforcing the sense of mourning and loss as legitimising strategy (Mookherjee 2007). Sheikh Hasina and her sister have special state protection as members of Bangabandhu's family (since 2009). Her son, known as Joy, is often included on the posters. Sheikh Hasina's mother is in some contexts referred to as Bangamata (the mother of Bengal). Her brothers are commemorated with ceremonies, and several sport clubs, tournaments and arenas are named after them. There is, for instance, a professional football club named after one brother, Sheikh Jamal, the name added to the original name in 2009, and an international football cup was set up and named after another brother, Sheikh Kamal, in 2015. The official crest of the cup bears his portrait.

It should be noted that many beyond Awami League share in the sentiment of Bangabandhu's specialness. It is not uncommon even for critics of Sheikh Hasina's government to refer to her father as 'the greatest Bangali of all times'. The phrase originated in 2004 in a BBC Bangla Service poll in which Mujibur Rahman came out ahead of Bengali Nobel laureate Rabindranath Tagore. Sometimes Mujibur is called 'the greatest Bangali of a thousand years'. Bangladesh was, of course, born in a terrible war of liberation that saw bloody violence and destruction as well as acts of daring resistance and sacrifice. Stories and memories of the war are to most Bangladeshis even fifty years on deeply emotional (Mookherjee 2015). To many of those who took part, Bangabandhu was a great source of inspiration.

The specialness of Bangabandhu and the specialness of Sheikh Hasina's family are complemented by another legitimising strategy: the assertion that Bangabandhu's vision was not just a great source of inspiration behind the independence movement, but *the* greatest; that the people were mobilised by his 'dream' for the country. The idea of Bangabandhu's 'dream' is important in the official narrative and he is often referred to as the 'dreamer of the Bengali nation'. The dream remains undefined but is generally thought to be a Sonar Bangla, a Golden Bengal, prosperous and free from hunger and poverty. Occasionally references are also made to his 'ideology', but historically Mujibur never formulated an ideology and what activists and supporters referred to as Mujibism was little more than a cult around his personality.

Nonetheless there is a strong emotive resonance in the way Bangabandhu's dream is understood today. In popular renderings, Bangabandhu as a person showed respect to high and low, ate simple food and treated all as his equals. These are values that are generally thought to have mobilised people to the suffering and sacrifice of the independence war. His daughter makes oblique reference to this aspect of the narrative when she claims that she is in politics to alleviate the suffering of the poor.

This 'dream' is central to how his daughter is exceptional. Sheikh Hasina and her party insist that they have come to power to fulfil the task he has started, to fulfil his 'dream', but that they have done so only 'after 30 years'. The great horror of the assassination is equal only to the bright future that was lost in that act. The sacrifice of the war was wasted in that atrocity, which makes it all the more imperative for the nation four or five decades later to strive to fulfil the promises embedded in that struggle. Bangabandhu's 'dream' and the emotive appeal of a country free from hunger and poverty are held up as the ultimate goal of the government and the country, and Sheikh Hasina's unquestioned loyalty to this 'dream' renders her uniquely appropriate to fulfil it. The connection is drawn in many contexts. One example is in the justification for the Digital Security Act (to which we shall return), as 'the revival of the Golden Bangladesh of the father of the nation Sheikh Mujibur Rahman [...] The great dreamer has given his own successor to fulfil the dream of Golden Bangladesh, Honourable Prime Minister Sheikh Hasina' (Bangladesh Government 2018).

There is also a practical side to this dream of a country free from poverty and hunger. Sheikh Hasina's government has seen economic development as central to its legitimacy and has worked towards this with not inconsiderable success (O'Neill 2018). On important social indicators, including life expectancy, food consumption and literacy rates, Bangladesh has moved up ahead of India. Economic growth has been substantial and in 2018 Bangladesh fulfilled all eligibility criteria for graduation from Least Developed Country to Middle Income Country. While the country is still characterised by mind-boggling economic differences between rich and poor, growth is visible in most parts of the country.

Infrastructural development and 'megaprojects' are very much part of the agenda: coal plants, a nuclear plant, and bridges, roads and a light railway in Dhaka (Mirza forthcoming). When in 2012 the World Bank pulled support for the Padma Bridge project after allegations of corruption in high circles, Sheikh Hasina angrily responded that Bangladesh would construct the bridge with its own funds. The decision to go ahead committed her political standing to a huge, daunting project in a striking mark of a strongman leader. The country would develop, she would pursue her father's 'dream', with or without the help of others.

Sheikh Hasina's place in the narrative as the successor who ensures the fulfilment of Bangabandhu's dreams is an obliging construction, committing her to the mast but also allowing her liberty to interpret his dream. She is a forceful politician in her own right, but it is her unique loyalty to her father's legacy – interpreted as the ambition of the nation – which ultimately legitimises her as the country's leader.

Violence and the law

However, a narrative is not sufficient to keep a regime afloat, and critics need to be silenced. It is possible to argue that politically, Bangladesh has always been a violent place (Jahan 2005, Tripathy 2014). There are many stories of politically motivated violence in the early years of the independent republic and even more from the years of military dictatorships. During the democratic years, up until 2006, violence had several forms. There were firearms in student hostels, bodies could be found floating in rivers or street gutters, Islamists in particular cut tendons of activists from rival camps, buses were burnt during street confrontations and general strikes (known as *hartal*) often included violent encounters and beating of anyone caught out.

From 2009 onwards and in particular after 2014, the forms have changed from vandalism and individual acts of violence to state orchestrated forms of repression (Suykens and Islam 2015). According to one report (Odhikar 2020a), the number of injured dropped from 24,000 in the year leading up to the 2014 election to 4,700 injured the year leading up to the 2018 election.

There are two significant developments behind this shift in political violence. One is the increased deployment of law-enforcement agencies against opponents rather than the deployment of party or student front activists. We will return to this in the next section. A second development is legal changes and in particular the introduction of laws effectively banning online criticism of the rulers. The legislation has permitted space for law-enforcement agencies to act with impunity and has created an atmosphere of apprehension that effectively does away with the need for street confrontations (Lacy and Mookherjee 2020).

The introduction of first the Information and Communication Technology Act (ICT act of 2006, amended 2013) and the Digital Security Act (Bangladesh Government 2018) has done much harm to the country's democratic credentials. In the EIC Democracy Index, a significant contribution to Bangladesh's fall between 2010 and 2020 is the drop in its score on 'civil liberties'. This was particularly due to the infamous Section 57, introduced to the ICT act in 2013. This section heralded 'significant' limitations on individual freedom of expression and serious challenges to democracy (Feldman 2015). It carried sentences of up to 14 years' imprisonment and 1 crore taka (approx. 100,000 euros) in fines, or both, for posting false, provocative or sensitive news however interpreted. The Digital Security Act (DSA) that replaced the ICT act has often been characterised as 'draconian'. It maintained the level of sentences but broadened the applicability of the law. The DSA gained much notoriety as a means of intimidation. According to one report, there were on average three cases a day, and in 2019 alone 1,135 persons were arrested in 732 cases under this act (*Prothom Alo* 2020a).

The DSA has commonly been applied to critics of government policies. Human Rights Watch (2018a) has held that the government made use of the DSA to detain political opponents and critics of its response to the ongoing pandemic. Under the law anyone in Bangladesh can be arrested for posts that are alleged to negatively affect the nation's image, including criticism of government policies (Committee to Protect Journalists 2020). The law has been widely criticised by international rights bodies including the UN High Commissioner for Human Rights, by Bangladeshi civil rights bodies and in newspaper editorials. They claim that the authorities 'increasingly used the DSA to harass and indefinitely detain activists, journalists and others critical of the government and its political leadership' (Human Rights Watch 2021). Lacy and Mookherjee (2020) have called the law 'a new technique of governmentality'.

Crucial here is that arrests have also been made for criticising the judiciary or other political leaders (Human Rights Watch 2018a). The case of Shafiqul Islam Kajol is illustrative. This editor of a lesser-known local newspaper was in 2020 picked up from a street in Dhaka and 'disappeared'. The police, as is common in these cases, claimed no knowledge of what had happened to him. While he was missing, a case was filed against him under the DSA, claiming that he had shared posts defamatory of certain Awami League leaders on Facebook. When he reappeared after 53 days he was immediately arrested (or rearrested) for his alleged crime under the DSA. He was released after seven months in jail.

A widely circulating interpretation is that he was picked up after the publication of an article on the arrest of an Awami League leader. The leader allegedly ran a secret escort agency where some senior Awami League leaders and members of parliament were said to have been clients. The case against Kajol was filed by a member of parliament. The case named others but Kajol was the only one arrested. It is alleged that he was singled out 'because some Awami League politicians suspected that he had incriminating information of the goings on in this escort agency and they feared exposure' (Netra News 2020).

This may or may not be true. The connection between Kajol's disappearance and his Facebook post is not established. The point is that it suffices to be rumoured to scare people away from criticising ruling party leaders and that the police and the judiciary seem happy to play along. Kajol's case is a good illustration of how the police, the judiciary and the ruling party together constitute a mutually protective coalition. The willingness of the police and the judiciary to protect leaders quite far down the political hierarchy is increasingly evident. In an illustrative case (*Prothom Alo* 2020b), the police arrested a 25-year-old village man 'on allegation of criticising leaders of ruling Bangladesh Awami League on Facebook'. The case had been filed by the local president of the Awami League volunteer front.

'Criticising leaders of ruling Bangladesh Awami League on Facebook' is the operative phrase. In an online survey of Bangladeshi journalists (Hasan 2019), almost all respondents claimed it was near impossible to pursue objective news reporting on certain issues because of the existence of a 'censorship machine'. Key actors in this censorship machine include a pro-government political apparatus, key government offices and certain leading politicians, the security agencies, and interestingly fellow journalists. Outside journalism, there are 'digital vigilantes' as well as 'the vast multitude of sycophants and attention seekers' motivated by personal rivalries or hoping for rewards (Lacy and Mookherjee 2020). The system shields itself from criticism in particular on certain 'no-no' topics (Riaz and Zaman forthcoming; Haq forthcoming). These include the prime minister and her family, the armed forces, and the official narrative about the war of 1971. But this political sensitivity and the DSA are opportunities widely exploited by individuals and by the system. While the prime minister earlier claimed that Bangladeshi journalists enjoy utmost freedom (*The Daily Star* 2020), she has also held that spreading false propaganda is not protected by freedom of speech (*The Daily Star* 2021).

Even more sinister than the DSA are the extrajudicial activities of law-enforcement agencies. 'Crossfires' or 'encounters' gained particular notoriety. The victims were often alleged criminals or radical opponents of the regime (such as Islamists and jihadists). A brief 'war on drugs' in 2018–2019 saw 395 alleged drug peddlers killed in 'crossfires' according to one report (*The Daily Star* 2020). Another report claims there were 225 extrajudicial killings in Bangladesh in 2020 (Odhikar 2020b). Another extrajudicial method is that of enforced disappearances ('*goom*'). Some have disappeared not to be seen again while others do reappear after a while, such as the journalist Kajol mentioned above. According to one report, there were 31 enforced disappearances in 2020 (Odhikar 2020b; Barua 2020).

The enforcement agencies and branches of the government seem to act on assumed directives rather than on direct orders, and they seem occasionally to operate in competition with one another. In an interesting development, the number of extrajudicial killings dropped drastically after July 2020 when a former army officer was shot and killed by police officers. This caused an uproar from the military side and the police officer and his accomplices were arrested. The sharp drop in extrajudicial killings after this indicates that the government could stop the practice when it wanted to but also that the police was largely operating independent of political directives.

The strongman leader

Sheikh Hasina is a strongman leader, but not necessarily of the same mould as other strongman leaders. The specialness of her family and her own unquestioned but constantly re-emphasised loyalty to her father and his dream constitute the central trope of an exceptionality and one that justifies her leadership as logical and necessary for the nation. Her specialness is not expressed in the same manner as Rodrigo Duterte (Curato 2015) or Donald Trump, for whom transgression into 'bad manners' of the boss mould was a trademark of their populist appeal and claim to represent 'ordinary' people (Moffitt 2016). But she does transgress, in ways that emphasise her personal rule. She on occasion disregards finer constitutional or moral niceties, and often (but not always) publicly so. A small but telling example found place in connection with allegations of corruption against the vice-chancellor of Jahangirnagar University in 2019. Both students and teachers staged demonstrations demanding a judicial inquiry, whereupon the prime minister warned them that if they were unable to prove their allegations they would be punished and government funding for public universities would be withdrawn (*Dhaka Tribune* 2019).

These transgressive acts are part of her masterfully brazen style that underlines her position as the strongest leader, the one whose control over the state machinery can threaten any action – possibly illegal, often transgressive, definitively doable. This is classic strongman ploy, as if saying 'I dare you to oppose me!'

Conclusion

A strongman regime centres on and depends on one person. It is a regime because it is a solid edifice, it has durability and resistance to external shock and pressure. It is unshaken by economic upheavals and unfazed by inept handling of disasters such as the Covid-19 pandemic. Such regimes often rely on ideological constructions such as the nationalistic cult the Bangladeshi regime has built around its father of the nation and his family, to which also the prime minister belongs, and on laws and agencies that protect against criticism. But the prime minister has also proven herself to be eminently pragmatic and this is perhaps one of her strongest points. She has forged solid bonds with forces that cold-shouldered her father, including the armed forces and the bureaucracy. She has neutralised the increasingly formidable challenge of Islamism. And she has harnessed the support of the somewhat sullen but ultimately cornered progressives.

The weakness of a strongman regime is its reliance on that one person – who not only provides legitimacy but also the political strength and prowess of the regime. Sheikh Hasina has been instrumental in building a regime that is self-protecting and mutually supportive. But the dangers are real. A rivalry between the police and the military and the ever-present need in Islamist quarters to assert themselves constitute potentially fundamental threats to the edifice. Threats such as an economic downturn that ruins elite privileges are still untested for the cohesion of the regime.

Currently the strongman regime appears solid, but because it is a strongman regime and not a junta or another form of authoritarian coalition regime, it relies on the continued presence of the steady hand of the prime minister and on her ability to legitimise the regime through her family association and her actions. Succession will be a huge challenge and the risk involved is considerable.

Note

1 I am grateful to Muhammad Mozahidul Islam, Niladri Chatterjee, Muhammad AbuBakar Siddique, Mubashar Hasan and the members of the Oslo South Asia Symposium for generous and helpful input.

Bibliography

Bangladesh Government. 2018. Digital Security Act 2018 (www.cirt.gov.bd, accessed March 20, 2020).

Barua, Jyotirmoy. 2020. A new trend in disappearance cases. *The Daily Star*, August 30, 2020 (thedailystar.net, accessed August 31, 2020).

Baxter, Craig. 1984. *Bangladesh: A New Nation in an Old Setting*. Boulder, CO: Westview Press.

Blom Hansen, Thomas. 2004. The production of political authority in the locality. In Zavos, John, Andrew Wyatt and Vernon Hewitt (Eds.), *The Politics of Cultural Mobilization in India*. New Delhi: Oxford University Press.

Bouissou, Julien. 2013. Bangladesh's radical Muslims uniting behind Hefazat-e-Islam. *The Guardian* 30 July (*theguardian.com*, accessed January 21, 2017).

Collier, David and Steven Levitsky. 1997. Democracy with adjectives: Conceptual innovation in comparative research. *World Politics* 49:3, 430–451.

Committee to Protect Journalists. 2020. Bangladeshi journalists face physical attacks, legal cases, and detention amid COVID-19 pandemic. At cpj.org, accessed February 21, 2021.

Curato, Nicole, ed. 2015. *The Duterte Reader: Critical Essays on Rodrigo Duterte's Early Presidency*. Ithaca, NY: Cornell University Press.

The Daily Star. 2019. Poll anomalies in 47 of 50 seats. 24 January (thedailystar.net, accessed January 21, 2021).

The Daily Star. 2020. 'Crossfires', 'Gunfights' in last 2 years. 22 August (thedailystar.net, accessed August 22, 2020).

The Daily Star. 2021. Know the facts, protest rumour. 3 March (thedailystar.net, accessed March 3, 2021).

De, Sanchari. 2015. Context, image and the case of the Shahbag movement. *Contemporary Social Science* 10:4, 364–374.

Dhaka Courier. 2019. Bangladesh TV: Ownership patterns and market crisis. 10 May (dhakacourier.com.bd, accessed March 30, 2021).

Dhaka Tribune. 2017. 16th Amendment debate. 18 August (dhakatribune.com, accessed November 12, 2019).

Dhaka Tribune. 2019. PM to JU protesters: Prove graft allegations or face action. 7 November (dhakatribune.com, accessed November 12, 2019).

Fair, Christine C. and Wahid, Abdallah. 2017. Islamist militancy in Bangladesh: Public awareness and attitudes. *Resolve Network Research Brief* 4, 1–18.

Feldman, Shelly. 2015. Bangladesh in 2014. *Asian Survey* 56:1, 204–209.

Hagerty, Devin T. 2007. Bangladesh in 2006. *Asian Survey* 47:1, 105–112.

Haq, Fahmidul. Forthcoming. Making cinema under authoritarian codes: the case of Bangladesh. In A.E. Ruud and M. Hasan (Eds.), *Masks of Authoritarianism*. Singapore: Palgrave Macmillan.

Hasan, Mubashar. 2019. Who suppresses free speech in Bangladesh: A typology of actors. In Elisabeth Eide, Kristin Skare Orgeret and Nil Mutluer (Eds.), *Transnational Othering – Global Diversities Media, Extremism and Free Expression*. Nordicom: Gothenburg, pp. 150–170.

HRW. 2020. Bangladesh: Mass arrests over cartoons, posts. (www.hrw.org, accessed February 21, 2021).

Human Rights Watch. 2018a. No Place for Criticism. (hrw.org, accessed February 22, 2020).

Human Rights Watch. 2018b. Creating panic. (hrw.org, accessed February 22, 2020).

Human Rights Watch. 2021. Bangladesh: Events of 2020. (hrw.org, accessed January 1, 2021).

Islam, Mohammad Mozahidul. 2013. The toxic politics of Bangladesh. *Asian Journal of Political Science*, 21:2, 148–168.

Jahan, Rounaq. 2005. *Bangladesh Politics: Problems and Issues*. Dhaka: UPL.

Khalidi, Toufique Imrose. 2019. The new cabinet: Full of surprises, and a first in Bangladesh. *Bdnews24.com* The Opinion Pages (opinion.bdnews24.com, accessed January 18, 2019).

Kochanek, Stanley A. 1997. Bangladesh in 1996. *Asian Survey*, 37:2, 136–142.

Kuttig, Julian. 2020. Posters, politics and power: Mediated materialisation of public authority in Bangladesh party politics, South Asia. *Journal of South Asian Studies* 43:4, 632–657. DOI: 10.1080/00856401.2020.1767901.

Lacy, Mark and Nayanika, Mookherjee. 2020. 'Firing cannons to kill mosquitoes': Controlling 'virtual streets' and the 'image of the state' in Bangladesh. In *Contributions to Indian Sociology* 54:2, 280–305 (special issue on Bangladesh edited by Mascha Schulz and Julian Kuttig).

Lai, Brian and Dan, Slater. 2006. Institutions of the offensive: domestic sources of dispute initiation in authoritarian regimes 1950–1992. *American Journal of Political Science* 50:1, January 2006, 113–126.

Lorch, Jasmin. 2018. Islamization by secular ruling parties: The case of Bangladesh. *Politics and Religion*, 1–27. https://doi.org/10.1017/S17550483180005731755-0483/18.

Mirza, Maha. Forthcoming. Are megaprojects inherently undemocratic? Field narratives from megaproject sites in Bangladesh. In A.E. Ruud and M. Hasan (Eds.), *Masks of Authoritarianism: Hegemony, Power and Public Life in Bangladesh*. Singapore: Palgrave Macmillan.

Moffitt, Benjamin. 2016. *The Global Rise of Populism: Performance, Political Style, and Representation*. Stanford: Stanford University Press.

Momen, Mehnaaz. 2010. Bangladesh in 2009: The peril within. *Asian Survey* 50:1, 157–163.

Mookherjee, Nayanika. 2007. The 'dead and their double duties': Mourning, melancholia, and the martyred intellectual memorials in Bangladesh. *Space and Culture* 10:2, 271–291.

Mookherjee, Nayanika. 2015. *The Spectral Wound: Sexual Violence, Public Memories, and the Bangladesh War of 1971*. Durham, NC: Duke University Press.

Morgenbesser, Lee. 2020. The menu of autocratic innovation. *Democratization*, 2–20. https://doi.org/10.1080/13510347.2020.1746275.

Netra News. 2020. A secret prisoner returns. 4 May (netra.news, accessed January 07, 2021).

O'Neill, Jim. 2018. The 'next eleven' and the world economy. *Hindustan Times* 28 April (hindustantimes.com, accessed March 12, 2021).

Odhikar. 2020a. Statistics on Political Violence. Political Violence from 2001–2020 (odhikar.org, accessed February 18, 2021).

Odhikar. 2020b. Bangladesh: Annual Human Rights Report 2020 (odhikar.org, accessed February 18, 2021).

Prothom Alo. 2018. Police, admin officials offered extra benefits ahead of polls. 30 November (en.prothomalo.com, accessed December 12, 2018).

Prothom Alo. 2020a. Three cases filed on average every day. *Prothom Alo*, 260720 (en.prothomalo.com, accessed August 26, 2020).

Prothom Alo. 2020b. Youth arrested under Digital Security Act for criticising AL leaders. 16 June (en.prothomalo.com, accessed June 17, 2020).

Reporters Without Borders (RSF). 2020. World Press Freedom Index (rsf.org, accessed January 15, 2021).

Riaz, Ali. 2019. *Voting in a Hybrid Regime: Explaining the 2018 Bangladeshi Election*. Singapore: Palgrave Macmillan.

Riaz, Ali. 2021. The pathway of democratic backsliding in Bangladesh. *Democratization* 28:1, 179–197.

Riaz, Ali and Mohammad, Sajjadur Rahman. 2021. *Who Owns the Media in Bangladesh?* Dhaka: Centre for Governance Studies.

Riaz, Ali and Fahmida, Zaman. Forthcoming. Working under the 'sword of Damocles': experiences of journalists in a hybrid regime. In A.E. Ruud and M. Hasan (Eds.), *Masks of Authoritarianism*. Singapore: Palgrave Macmillan.

Ruud, Arild Engelsen. Forthcoming. Bangabandhu as the Eternal Sovereign. *Religion*. Special issue on Political Deification edited by Moumita Sen and K.B. Nielsen.

Shah, Aqil. 2014. Constraining consolidation: military politics and democracy in Pakistan (2007–2013). *Democratization* 21:6, 1007–1033.

Suykens, Bert and Aynul, Islam. 2015. *The Distribution of Political Violence in Bangladesh (2002–2013)*. Ghent: Conflict Research Group.

Tripathy, Salil. 2014. *The Colonel Who Would not Repent: The Bangladesh War and Its Unquiet Legacy*. New Delhi: Aleph.

Young, M. Crawford. 1999. Resurrecting sultanism. Review of Sultanistic regimes, edited by H.E. Chehabi and Juan J. Linz. *Journal of Democracy* 10:3, 165–168.

23

LOCAL GOVERNMENT INSTITUTIONS UNDER AUTHORITARIAN RULE IN BANGLADESH

Serdar Yilmaz and Syed Khaled Ahsan

Bangladesh is a unitary state with national and local governments. Authoritarianism by the ruling party of the country has several attributes of the autocratization process: brutal party contestation, constrained space for exercising democratic rights, and absence of free and fair elections at the national and local levels (Lührmann and Lindberg 2019). The purpose of authoritarianism is to bring public administration structures at all levels under the control of the national government. The focus of this chapter is to provide a historical account of how the ruling party has constrained local democracy and hindered development of an institutional landscape that is favourable to the extension of political liberties and free and fair elections.

In Bangladesh, the local government system is organized around elected councils and administrative units reporting to the council. In the rural areas, there are three types of local governments: union *parishad* (UP), *upazila parishad* (a.k.a. sub-district local government) and *zila parishad* (a.k.a. district local government). In the urban areas, *pourashava* (a.k.a. municipality) and city corporation are the two administrative units of the local government system.

The Constitution (The Constitution of the People's Republic of Bangladesh 2019) has mandated an elected local government system without guarantees for autonomy. Articles 59 and 60 of the Constitution envisage locally elected political leadership managing local government administration and work of the public officials in the administrative units. Therefore, the concept of local government institutions (LGIs) refers to the locally elected political leadership and administrative units in the above-mentioned five types of local government. The responsibilities of LGIs include maintaining public order, preparing and implementing plans to deliver local public services and economic development, and imposing taxes to finance local budgets.

Parliament has been entrusted by the Constitution to enact laws to transfer and delegate power to the LGIs and enable them to plan and deliver services to the citizens. The LGIs are meant to provide all amenities to the citizens at the local level according to Articles 59 and 60 of the Constitution (Barakat *et al.* 2015). The Supreme Court of Bangladesh reiterated the features of the LGIs in a 1992 ruling as electoral accountability towards citizens and public sector accountability to the national government for the powers and responsibilities assigned

DOI: 10.4324/9781003042211-27

to them together with independent and substantial sources of income (Kudrat-E-Elahi Panir v Bangladesh 1992).

However, the Constitution gives the national government through parliament the power to change the regulatory framework for the local government system. Successive governments have exploited the provisions of the Constitution to dominate the LGIs to consolidate their powerbase. This is an ongoing process of democratic backsliding (Bormeo 2016). Like so many countries, Bangladesh has been experiencing a gradual process of autocratization under a legal façade (Lührmann and Lindberg 2019).

In Bangladesh, the autocratization process has affected the local democracy and LGIs alike. Hence, the LGIs have been facing an uphill struggle to assert their independence and roles in service provisions since independence of the country in 1971. This chapter provides a brief history and evolution of LGIs and local democracy since independence. It starts with a brief description of the process of the taming of local democracy and discusses the issues that impede the growth of the LGIs such as interference of the members of parliament (MPs) and civil servants, elimination of the opposition, uneven level playing field in the elections, monopolization, capacity challenge and financial insolvency.

Adoption of the Constitution and taming of local democracy

After independence, the Constitution was proclaimed in 1972 and general elections were held in 1973. Bangladesh Awami League (BAL) led by Sheikh Mujibur Rahman, the supreme leader of the independence movement, won the election. Until the assassination of Sheikh Mujibur Rahman by a group of junior army officers on August 15, 1975, the BAL governed the country with an absolute majority.

The first BAL government amended the Constitution on January 25, 1975 to introduce a one-party system. Articles 59 and 60 were rescinded and Article 11 was modified by dropping its last sentence reading, 'and in which effective participation by the people through their elected representatives in administration at all levels shall be ensured.' It was the first blow to the democratic local government system in Bangladesh. Later, the Constitution of the country became subordinated to the martial law proclamations from August 15, 1975.

After the assassination of Sheikh Mujibur Rahman, Bangladesh saw the rule of military dictators from 1975 to 1990. In 1976, Ziaur Rahman, a military ruler and founder of the Bangladesh Nationalist Party (BNP), promulgated the first local government ordinance in Bangladesh. The ordinance recognized three types of LGIs: UP at the union level, *thana parishad* at the sub-district (or *upazila*) level and *zila parishad* at the district level. Later, in 1980, a *swanirvar gram sarkar* or the self-reliant village government was introduced below the UP level by amending the local government ordinance of 1976. The amendment promoted unanimity to select the *gram prodhan* or head of the *gram sarkar* and other eleven members of the village government through consensus of villagers. The village government system was considered as an attempt to politicize the local government system. On May 30, 1981, Ziaur Rahman was assassinated by a group of army officers. After his death, the village government system was abolished by another martial law administrator in July 1982.

In 1982, the introduction of a new tier of LGI, *upazila parishad* at the *upazila* or sub-district level, triggered a strong reaction from political parties. The political parties, including the BNP led by Khaleda Zia, the widow of Ziaur Rahman, and BAL led by Sheikh Hasina, the daughter of Sheikh Mujibur Rahman, resisted the introduction of a new level of LGI by the military government headed by H. M. Ershad. They were concerned about the military government's efforts to consolidate its power at the local level to prolong its rule. The BNP and

BAL boycotted the first two *upazila parishad* elections held during the Ershad regime. In 1991, there was an attempt to start the democratization process in the country after the resignation of military dictator, H. M. Ershad and establishment of a non-partisan caretaker government in 1990. The BNP won the national election in 1991 and formed the government. The BNP-led government abolished the administrative tier at the *upazila* level altogether. The justification for the abolishment was that the *upazila parishads* were not economically viable for the country as they did not have the capacity to raise revenue from their own sources. In fact, the abolishment of *upazila parishads* was an attempt to strengthen the control of MPs in the LGIs (which was codified as a law in 1998). The judiciary reinstated the *upazila parishad* system in 1992. Nonetheless, the BNP government did not enact a legal framework for the *upazila parishad* during its term. In 1998, the BAL government formally reintroduced the *upazila parishad* level by enacting the *Upazila Parishad* Act, 1998. This back and forth of abolishing and reintroducing new tiers had a detrimental impact on the institutionalization of LGIs in Bangladesh.

After transitioning from the anti-democratic military regime to a civilian democratic system, the first general election was held in February 1996 under the BNP-led administration. However, this election was boycotted by the BAL and other opposition political groups. They demanded that the general election in the country be held under a non-party caretaker government. A genuine mistrust grew between the ruling BNP and the opposition political groups as the candidate of the then ruling BNP won in a controversial by-election for a parliamentary seat in March 1994. After that the opposition political groups did not participate in any elections held under the ruling BNP (Hossain 2021). Finally, the BNP succumbed to the demand of the opposition political groups and brought about the election-time caretaker government system. In June 4, 1996, just three months after the February 1996 election, a participatory general election was held under the caretaker government.

Election-time government practice was exercised during the 1996, 2001 and 2008 elections. As a result, transition of power through credible elections started maturing the foundation of the nascent democracy of the country. The BAL and BNP won the elections held under the caretaker governments in 1996 and 2001 respectively. However, the BNP-led government made attempts to manipulate the constitutional bodies to form a caretaker government to have election results in their favour in 2006. That triggered violent street protests organized by the BAL and other opposition political groups. The unrest in the country provoked the military to intervene to form a caretaker government. The general election was delayed until December 2008 and that was won by the BAL. Later, an electoral breakdown happened in 2014 as a consequence of 'a unilateral change in the rules of electoral administration (the elimination of the practice of a caretaker government before the election) that tilted the electoral playing field and triggered an opposition boycott' (Diamond 2015).

The practice of a caretaker government was instrumental to create a level playing field environment in which an election could be held in a free and fair manner without political influence by the outgoing government. We coined the term electoral breakdown in this discourse to describe the assault on the nature of free and fair elections providing *de jure* institutional guarantees for a level playing field. An uneven playing field is a common feature of contemporary authoritarianism (Way and Levitsky 2020). The departure from the election time caretaker government practice was a breakdown of an established electoral norm, which resulted in political polarization. Consequently, the polarization has exerted authority over all state and non-state institutions in the country and has prevented the consolidation of democracy. The political authoritarianism of both parties, BNP and BAL, has weakened the independence and growth of the LGIs and local democracy.

Interference in the LGIs

When the BAL-led government reintroduced the *upazila parishad* in 1998, they carved out an advisory role for the MPs. According to constitutional scholars, the advisory role of MPs, codified in section 25 of the *Upazila Parishad* Act, does not conform with Article 59 of the Constitution. The Article states that 'local government in every administrative unit of the Republic shall be entrusted to bodies, composed of persons elected in accordance with law.' The advisory role of the MPs in the *upazila parishads* disempowers the *upazila parishads* as an autonomous LGI (Sowdagar 2013). Both the BAL and BNP consider the *upazila parishad* as an impediment to sustaining their powerbase in the community. They perceive that the *upazila* system threatens the authority of their MPs. In 2008, the military-backed caretaker government promulgated a new *upazila parishad* ordinance and abolished the advisory role of the MPs. It is noteworthy that the military-backed caretaker government took the judicious measure to safeguard the local democracy, while successive civilian governments have used their authority (or legal façade) at the centre to choke the democratic system in the country. After the 2008 elections, the BAL-dominated parliament reinstated the role of the MPs in the *upazila parishad*. The opposition BNP did not oppose that. They expected that this provision would also benefit them when they return to power in the future. With the reinstatement of MPs in the *upazila parishads*, the elected representatives of the LGIs became hostage to the authority of the MPs and administrative apparatus of the national government. Party loyalty became the precondition for the selection of *upazila* level positions (Islam 2018).

The country's central bureaucracy is responsible for the civil servants' recruitments, placements, promotions and dismissals. The existing political culture requires the officials posted in the local governments to maintain relationship with the MPs and other leaders of the ruling party. Bureaucrats are often obliged to include beneficiaries recommended by an MP for various social safety net programmes of the government. According to Khan (2015), politicization of the administration has become the norm rather than an exception under highly authoritarian national governments in Bangladesh. As a result, the public administration has lost its edge in delivering public services to the citizens. The Bangladesh *Upazila Parishad* Association finds the *upazila nirbahi* (executive) officers as new rulers at the *upazila* level (Prothom Alo 2021). Their bureaucratic attitudes constrain the elected officials in performing their roles. Many consider neglecting the elected officials of the *upazila parishad* is a ploy to establish a feudal rule. The civil servants posted in the *upazilas* and districts are perceived to be more powerful than locally elected leadership. In fact, as the saying goes local bureaucrats do not serve under the LGIs, rather elected representatives of the LGIs are being made to serve under them. Overall, the interference of the civil servants in the LGIs has damaged the fabric between the citizens and LGIs.

Neither the ruling BAL nor the opposition BNP had a principled stand on the independence of the *upazila parishad*. The BNP did not oppose the advisory role of the MPs in the *upazila parishad* in the first place, expecting to use it for their advantage. Now they have voiced their concern of the section 25 of the *upazila parishad* act of 1998. The opposition political groups have had an insignificant representation in parliament during the last two terms, and the ruling BAL did not agree with their demand for dropping section 25. In 2019, an MP of the opposition BNP raised the issue of repealing section 25 in parliament. The government ruled out any possibility of removing the roles of the MPs in the *upazila parishad* from the *upazila parishad* act of 1998 (UNB News 2019). Parliament is unlikely to allow the LGIs to freely perform their constitutionally mandated roles, away from the control of a prevailing authoritarian environment. The administrative apparatus of the state remains loyal to the national govern-ment and political masters, and lacks respect for the elected officials of the LGIs. The Local Government Division's (LGD) holding of power to exercise control over the activities of the LGIs and mandatory advisory function MPs has further complicated the situation for the LGIs (As-Saber 2009). Thus, the LGIs have to remain heavily dependent on the national govern-ment. Their transparency and accountability to the citizens are compromised. They could not be self-governing institutions but an extension of the national government (Panday 2011).

The interference of any officials or an MP who are elected in the LGIs contradicts the ver-dict of the apex court of Bangladesh. The Chief Justice of the country described the situation in a full court judgment as local governments are '…meant for management of local affairs by the locally elected persons. If government officers or their henchmen are brought to run the local bodies, there is no sense in retaining them as Local Government bodies' (Kudrat-E-Elahi Panir v Bangladesh 1992).

Elimination of the opposition at the local level

The BNP and other opposition political groups paid a high price for the unprincipled com-promise with the ruling BAL in trying to dominate *upazila parishad* by granting the MPs an advisory role. Just a few months ahead of the 2014 national election under the BAL-led admin-istration, the victory of the opposition BNP-backed mayors in the city corporation elections in June–July 2013 rendered the BAL anxious. The opposition political groups started expounding the results of the city elections as an indication of citizens' support towards the demand for an election-time caretaker government to conduct the 2014 national election. The BNP and other opposition political groups declared boycotting the national election unless the election-time caretaker government system was reinstated. The elected officials of various LGIs from the opposition groups were active in the street protests demanding reinstatement of the caretaker government system to hold the national election in 2014. The BAL government accused them in many cases over their suspected involvement in the political violence like arson attacks, sabo-tage, vandalism, etc. Although, the government could not prove any allegations brought against them in court, they started targeting opposition-controlled local governments. The ruling BAL did not want to take chances and decided to abandon the election time caretaker government system. The targeting of the elected officials of the LGIs who had won from the opposition groups set a new precedent of autocratization by the BAL-led government in the country. As a result, the BAL had undermined the political opposition and extended its patronage roots further into the local communities to consolidate its position to cling to power (Lewis and Hossain 2019).

The interference of the government in the city corporations and other LGIs has jeopardized the connections between the citizens and LGIs and affected the service delivery to the citizens. The interference has become incremental and led to shrinking of the democratic space in the local governments and accountability of the LGIs to the citizens. In Khulna, Sylhet, Rajshahi, Gazipur and Barisal, for example, candidates from the opposition BNP won elections in the city corporations in the 2013 elections. However, the elected mayors in Sylhet, Rajshahi and Gazipur could hardly perform their mayoral roles. They were suspended on several occasions under section 12 of the Local Government (City Corporation) Act, 2009, which provides a legal basis for the suspension of a mayor or a councillor if he/she is convicted or charge-sheeted in a criminal case. While many councillors of different city corporations who belonged to the ruling BAL and were charge-sheeted in criminal cases were allowed to perform their duties, opposition parties faced harassment from the authorities. The government suspended twenty-four mayors of city corporations and municipalities, twenty-eight *upazila* chairmen, thirteen *upazila* vice chairmen and more than 150 union *parishad* chairmen and members between 2014 and 2015 (New Age 2017). They were charge-sheeted in different cases like arson and murder, but none was convicted by the courts in the end. The charges brought against the elected officials were apparently politically motivated. The Rajshahi mayor challenged the legality of the suspension order against him in 2017. The supreme court found an arbitrary exercise of discretionary power to suspend the mayor. Also, the court directed the LGD to inform the authorities concerned in the government and parliament to take steps to amend the provision on suspension of city mayors and councillors (*The Daily Star* 2017). The incidents of suspension of the elected officials have not stopped after the verdict nor has the government or parliament taken any measures to amend the act. The ruling party has been using the section of the act as means to control or diminish the power of the elected officials from the opposition political groups.

Elections on an uneven playing field

Amendments were made in all local government acts to introduce party-based local government elections in 2015. However, the party-based local government elections have so far failed to boost a constructive political climate. The UPs were the first LGI to go for party-based elections from March 3 to June 4, 2016. Incidents of selling of party nominations by the leaders of the BAL, BNP and others were rampant as the system created a scope for the local party leaders to get involved in corrupt practices (Panday 2019). In the UP elections, 145 people were killed, a record 214 were elected uncontested and 212 of them were from the ruling BAL (*The Daily Star* 2016).

In 2016, the first ever *zila parishad* elections were held in December. Since the *Zila Parishad* Act, 2000 does not have a provision for universal adult franchise, the 21-member body of the leadership of *zila parishads* was indirectly elected by the elected officials of other LGIs of the district. Although the voting in the *zila parishads* elections was held in a non-partisan manner (unlike the other elections for the LGIs), the candidates were aligned with political parties. Nearly all electorates for the *zila parishads* belong to the ruling BAL. Candidates who belonged to the ruling party won all positions in the *zila parishads*. The candidates from the opposition political groups hardly had any chance to be elected for any positions in the *zila parishads*. Hence, no opposition political groups dared to participate in the elections.

The elections of the LGIs are no more trustworthy, credible and competitive as a whole. Elections since 2016 have only deepened the feeling of despair among the general public and greatly weakened the country's democratic polity. The opposition BNP boycotted local elections in the first half of 2019, and the country saw an historically low turnout of voters on the polling day (Freedom House 2020). Since the eleventh parliamentary elections held on December 30, 2018, the voter turnout has been declining. The voter turnout for the Dhaka North City Corporation on February 28, 2019 was only 30%. It was 40% in the five-phase *upazila parishad* elections in 2019. On February 1, 2020, the voter turnouts were 25.85% and 29.07% for the Dhaka North City Corporation and Dhaka South City Corporation elections. The Daily Star reported an astonishingly low number of voters turned out at the centres in the city corporation elections in Dhaka. The poor voter turnout dampened the spirit common in elections in the country. Almost all the poll observers at the centres were for the mayoral and councillor candidates from the ruling BAL (*The Daily Star* 2020).

The poor voter turnout is a direct result of low levels of public trust in the election commission. The highly politicized election commission of the country failed in holding any impartial local government election. The commission is widely using the electronic voting machines (EVMs) in the elections. The EVM system in Bangladesh has no provision for a voter verifiable paper audit trail (VVPAT) or verified paper record (VPR) (Karim 2020). Introduction of the VVPAT could give confidence to the voters and the contesting parties against possible election fraud and malfunction. A majority of the opposition political parties and citizens' groups in Bangladesh are concerned by using the EVMs as the election officials lack credibility. However, the ruling BAL favours using the EVMs in the elections.

The government machinery controls each of the key stages of any contested election, such as campaigning, polling and declaring results. The end result is such that the elections are participatory, while their outcomes are not credible at all. The level playing field does not exist for the candidates in the local government elections. The election observers of an opposition candidate are not allowed to stay in the polling stations. The pattern has been common for the local government elections in Bangladesh.

The election preparation and campaign by opposition candidates are often obstructed by filing frivolous lawsuits against them. Candidates from the opposition political groups were prevented from contesting the municipal polls in 2015. About 3,000 activists of the opposition BNP were arrested in a single week before the elections (Mazumdar 2016). The trend has not changed as the municipal elections were taking place in January 2021. Violence and irregularities in the polling process made candidates from the BNP withdraw from the elections (New Age Online 2021).

Elections that were held in various LGIs of the country between December 2020 and January 2021 have made it clear that the election process has become one-sided and less competitive. The election commission, civil administration and law enforcing agencies have all worked in favour of the ruling party candidates in the municipalities and city corporation. All of which had a detrimental impact on citizens' participation in local democracy. To give one example, the voter turnout in the Chattogram City Corporation election held on January 27, 2021 was only 22.52%.

The BAL-backed mayoral candidate got all votes in 13 polling centres, while the BNP-backed candidates did not get any vote in 22 centres in the Chattogram City Corporation election. The ruling BAL-backed candidates and dissident BAL candidates won all the positions there. Elections in Chattogram, the second largest city of the country, mirrored what had happened in the elections in 83 municipalities on December 28, 2020 and January 16, 2021. The ruling BAL won 18 out of 23 and 40 out of 60 mayoral positions on December 28, 2020 and January 16, 2021 respectively. Intimidation of the opposition candidates and their election agents, obstruction of voters, capturing of polling stations, stuffing of ballot papers in ballot boxes and violence by the ruling BAL activists marred all the elections in the LGIs (Hossain 2021; New Age 2021).

In some instances, midway through the election day, the opposition candidates withdrew from the elections with allegations of irregularities in the polling process. According to Riaz (2019), the election commission in collusion with the civil administration, law enforcing agencies and ruling BAL party activists ensured victory to the ruling party.

Out of 40 candidates for the councillor positions nominated by the opposition BNP for the Chattogram City Corporation elections held on January 27, 2021, some 29 were accused in criminal offences. The number was only four for the candidates of the ruling BAL. The charges brought against the opposition political activists were '*gayebi*' or false according to the candidates from the BNP. Bringing charges against the political rivals serves as a strategy of the ruling party to obstruct them from election campaigning (Ghosh and Hasan 2020).

More recently, accusing the ruling party of winning the local elections by vote rigging and using muscle power and civil administration, the main opposition BNP decided to boycott the upcoming local elections in April 2021 (New Age 2021). It is very likely that the elections in 4,571 UPs scheduled to start in April 2021would be one-sided and candidates loyal to the ruling party would win in all the UPs.

The unfair and dubious elections have implications for democracy at the local level and service delivery to the citizens by the LGIs. The citizens' ability to hold the elected officials accountable for their service delivery is severely constrained. A nomination of the ruling party often guarantees a victory to a candidate in the election. The outcome is poor planning and implementation of development schemes and selection of beneficiaries for different services. As a result of these unfair and dubious elections, the local politicians have become more loyal to the ruling party than to the people they are supposed to be serving.

The Bangladesh country report of Freedom House has mentioned the concerns of the opposition political groups and international election observers of the lack of independence of the election commission and its biased attitudes. Unfair election practices favoured the ruling party in the country's general elections held in 2018 (Freedom House 2020). On December 14, 2020, a group of 42 distinguished citizens requested the President of the Republic form a Supreme Judicial Council to probe graft allegations against election commission officials. They requested they investigate 'irregularities in the 11th Parliamentary Election and elections in Dhaka (North and South) City Corporations, Khulna City Corporation, and Gazipur City Corporation' (Tithila 2020). The election commission and executive branch of the government will not be able to work independently and with integrity as long as they serve under an authoritarian government. Diamond (2015) observed that democracy would not return anytime soon to the country. The outcomes of the elections evidently strengthen the control of the ruling elites of the country over the LGIs at the cost of the independence and growth of the latter.

Monopolization of the LGIs

The LGIs are greatly politicized as a result of the confrontational politics and disrespect for democratic norms and institutions. Monopolization of the local government system and its resources has reduced the effectiveness of the LGIs in the country. This monopolization by a ruling party is termed *partyarchy* (Coppedge 1994). The *partyarchy* has adversely affected the service provisions in the LGIs and undermined democracy at the local level. As a result, service provisions by the LGIs are being marred by irregularities and corruption. A number of elected officials in different LGIs allegedly embezzled government cash aid and relief for the targeted beneficiaries during the ongoing coronavirus pandemic in the country (Dhaka Tribune 2020).

The monopolization of all state institutions and resources including the LGIs by the party in power has weakened the formal accountability mechanisms of the LGIs and put governance in crisis (Osman 2010). The ruling BAL has succeeded in capturing the majority of the LGIs of the country through coercive and undemocratic means. Coercion in the elections process ensured control of the ruling party over the LGIs at the expense of local democracy. The coercive force has also greatly undermined the legitimacy of the elected bodies of the LGIs in the country.

At present, over 90% of the municipal mayors and *upazila parishad* and UP chairmen are from the BAL. Out of 12 city corporations, only two have mayors from the main opposition party, BNP. The loyalty of the elected officials to their party bosses is damaging the checks and balances of democracy. The LGIs remain engaged in implementing the agenda set by the national government and defending the interests of the ruling BAL.

Two major problems to tackle in order to make local democracy work

In Bangladesh, the overriding problem for making local democracy work is the lack of capacity of LGIs, which is a function of autonomy. When local governments are assigned to perform certain functions, they should be given sufficient resources to fulfil their obligations together with freedom to design their own policies (Widmalm 2008). Otherwise, without autonomy to exercise discretion local governments will never develop capacity. According to Widmalm, '[t]he most central aspect of decentralization concerns the extent to which real power is moved downwards in the administrative or democratic structure' (Widmalm 2008: p. 44).

Although the LGIs in Bangladesh have been assigned to perform important responsibilities, they lack the means to independently perform those functions. This can be attributed to the failure of the national government to empower the elected officials with necessary authorities, resources and responsibilities to establish control over local bureaucracy and perform their duties. The LGIs remain merely a playground for the political parties in Bangladesh to exhibit their strengths every five years during the elections (Ahmed 2019). Configurations of the LGIs have often been changed for strengthening the powerbase of the ruling party of the country. The political dividends of changes in the LGIs to ruling parties are significant. Often the reasons for reconfiguration of the LGIs are to increase popularity in the voting population and create new spaces to accommodate more party leaders.

The UPs are one of the oldest democratic institutions in Bangladesh, predating the independence of the country, although, they are not well staffed and well resourced. The Local Government (Union *Parishad*) Act, 2009 provides a detailed organizational structure and lists positions to be filled. However, the national government controls the recruitment, salary and benefits, disciplinary measures etc. of the civil servants posted in the UPs. The UPs are allowed to appoint additional staff with prior approval of the government. They lack resources to finance the salary and allowances of any additional staff. In reality, therefore, no UP can afford to appoint any staff on their own. Until 2009, the secretary was the only full-time staff in UPs. The offices of the deputy commissioner at the district level have started recruiting the accounts assistants for the UPs in 2019. Out of 4,571 UPs, only a few now have two full-time staff.

According to the UP act, the government was required to specify the controlling power of UPs over the civil servants working at the union level through notifications. Yet no government has come forward to assign the civil servants working at the unions under the administrative control of the UPs to augment the staffing capacity. Thus, the UPs lack managerial capability and resources to provide service delivery to the citizens (Aminuzzaman 2010).

At the *zila parishad* level, the situation is more dire. Despite the elections that took place in the *zila parishads* for the first time in the country, the locally elected political leadership could not get a visible grasp of the local bureaucracy. The MPs and civil servants based in the district headquarters have been playing a major role in decision making since 2009 and they continue to do so (Ahmed 2016).

The second major hurdle in front of local democracy is the lack of financial resources for LGIs to perform their constitutionally assigned functions. The financial insolvency and politicization of financing prevent the LGIs developing the necessary capacities to be autonomous local government units in the service of their citizens. The ruling parties have done very little to improve the intergovernmental fiscal system. The share of local government expenditures in the national budget for the fiscal year 2020/21 is only 7% (Macroeconomic Wing 2020). As there are duplicative distributions of functional responsibility among the LGIs and between the LGIs and administrative apparatus, it is difficult to estimate the expenditure needs of the LGIs. The revenue fund and development fund are two sources of funds for the LGIs. They are surviving on budgetary support in the form of grant-in-aid from the national government and occasional assistance from the international donors. In the fiscal year, 2017/18, the UPs, *pourashavas* and city corporations spent USD 6.1, USD 18.0 and USD 44.2 per resident respectively (World Bank 2020). Although LGIs have an entitlement over the share of national resources, dependence on national government transfers has resulted in the losing of autonomy by the LGIs (Siddiqui 2014).

The grant-in-aid doesn't judiciously consider population, area, special needs and past performance of an LGI to allocate and disburse resources. At present, the World Bank-financed Local Governance Support Projects (LGSP) have been providing direct block grants to all UPs and a few municipalities. The LGSPs aimed at establishing an efficient and transparent intergovernmental fiscal system. Nonetheless, the LGSP model for intergovernmental transfer remained limited mainly to the UPs and dependent on external financing. The tax base of the LGIs could be strengthened by empowering them to take more control of the tax collection in their respective constituencies. Taxes on property transfer, land development and proceeds from markets, water estates, issuance of licences etc. are some potential sources of revenues for the LGIs. The distribution of authority among different LGIs on tax collection in some areas like leasing, issuing licences etc. lacks clarity too. The tax base of the LGIs remains insufficient to support service delivery to the citizens. The government could not give an enabling environment to the local government system to improve the prevailing situation.

Loyalty of the elected officials to the ruling party always put the LGIs in an advantageous position to receive financial support from the national government. In addition to accessing financial resources, the loyalty gives them impunity in case of irregularities too (Sabina, Khan and Badiuzzaman 2015). On the other hand, local jurisdictions managed by opposition parties are penalized. In the last five years, the mayors elected from the opposition BNP in thirty municipalities got less allocation for their projects than the mayors from the ruling BAL (Rahman 2021). Politicization of the financing deprived the citizens of municipal services who elected mayors from the opposition political groups.

The discriminatory behaviour of the government has ramifications for the future of local democracy. The ability of the local governments to respond to the preferences of its citizens is inseparably tied to the democratic system and its practice of a country. The opposition political groups would be inclined to mobilize their supporters for bigger protests if the authoritarianism is further entrenched in the country and the ruling BAL is not willing to give any of the levers of power. The protests by the opposition in Bangladesh often lead to political violence in the end. Ultimately, the LGIs will be losing their relevance in the local development and growth of democratic polity at large.

A future to look forward to?

The local governments are described in general terms in the Constitution of Bangladesh and they do not enjoy constitutional guarantees (Ahmed 2016). Although parliament is entrusted with the task of bringing the legal framework for the LGIs, there are questions about the independence of the legislative branch from the executive branch. The existing legal frameworks for the local governments have kept back most of the governing power with the national government, as the attributes of a unitary state are very dominant in the psyche of the ruling elites. Therefore, in order to safeguard the tenets of local democracy, the LGIs need some constitutional guarantees for autonomy and access to financial resources to deliver services to the citizens.

Few acts related to local government have provisions for the unelected officials to interfere in the LGIs. The *upazila parishad* act is one of the examples of abusing the legislative authority of the MPs. The act made it mandatory for the *upazila parishads* to accept their advice (Mazumdar 2010). The apex court of the country showed judicial activism in interpreting the constitutional principles of local-level democracy: 'Parliament is not free to legislate on local government ignoring Articles 59 and 60' (Kudrat-E-Elahi Panir v Bangladesh 1992).

Bangladesh has never witnessed any initiative of two major parties, BAL and BNP, to establish an effective self-governing local government system. The LGIs merely remain as extensions of the national government with limited citizens' engagement. The interference of the ruling party to capture the LGIs has increased manifold during the last decade. Yet, the introduction of the party-based local government system can potentially become a blessing in disguise. Hankala, Martinez-Vazquez and Rodriguez (2019) emphasized the need for balancing between democratic decentralization and party integration. Notwithstanding, democratic decentralization entails competitive local elections to generate accountability and incentivize local leaders to improve governance. On the other hand, integrated parties would pass down national preferences to the local level (Hankala, Martinez-Vazquez and Rodriguez 2019). The country would await an environment for the fair, honest and free elections for the LGIs.

One of the most destructive legacies of the authoritarian rule in Bangladesh would be numerous attempts to monopolize and weaken the local government system. Unqualified leaderships are brought in by the LGIs who are chosen for their political loyalty to the ruling party. Also, the influence and dominance of the self-serving bureaucrats over the LGIs have now increased manifold. Attempts to centralize roles and responsibilities of the LGIs have shrunk the democratic spaces and exposed the continuing autocratization trend in the country. A vibrant local government system in Bangladesh could thwart the ongoing autocratization process and pave the way for a transition to a liberal democratic rule.

Glossary

1. *Union* – The lowest tier of administration in Bangladesh
2. *Parishad* – Council
3. *Union Parishad* – Union Council, a local government institution
4. *Upazila* – Sub-district, the second tier of administration in Bangladesh
5. *Upazila Parishad* – Upazila Council, a local government institution
6. *Zila* – District, the administrative tier above sub-district in Bangladesh
7. *Zila Parishad* – District Council, a local government institution
8. *Pourashava* – Municipality, an urban local government institution
9. *City Corporation* – Local government institution in a large city
10. *Constitution* – Constitution of Bangladesh
11. *Swanirvar gram sarker* – Self-reliant village government
12. *Non-partisan caretaker government* – Election time government in Bangladesh
13. *Electoral breakdown* – a term describing assault on *de jure* safeguard mechanisms for free and fair elections
14. *Upazila nirbahi officers* – Upazila Executive Officer
15. *Local Government Division* – A national government agency under the Ministry of Local Government, Rural Development and Cooperatives
16. *Partyarchy* – Dominance over the various state and non-state institutions by the political parties
17. *Gayebi* – Unsubstantiated

Bibliography

Ahmed, Tofail (2016a). '*Zila Parishad in Bangladesh: Urgency for an election.*' The Daily Star, August 24. Available at: www.thedailystar.net/op-ed/politics/zila-parishad-bangladesh-1274479 (Accessed January 4, 2021).

Ahmed, Tofail (2016b). *Bangladesh: Reform Agenda for Local Governance.* Dhaka: Prothoma Prokashan.

Ahmed, Wasi (2019). '*Empowering local government institutions.*' Available at: www.thefinancialexpress.com.bd/views/empowering-local-government-institutions-1568732464 (Accessed February 1, 2021).

Aminuzzaman, Salahuddin M. (2010). *Local Government and Development in Bangladesh: Lessons Learned and Challenges for Improving Service Delivery of Union Parishad.* Bangladesh: Local Government Division.

As-Saber, Sharif N. & Rabbi, Md Fazle (2009). '*Democratisation of the Upazila Parishad and Its Impact on Responsiveness and Accountability: Myths versus Realities.*' JOAAG, 4 (2), pp. 53–71.

Barakat, Abul. et al. (eds.) (2015). *Local Governance and Decentralization in Bangladesh: Politics and Economics.* 1st edition. Dhaka: Pathak Shamabesh.

Bermeo, Nancy (2016). 'On Democratic Backsliding.' *Journal of Democracy*, 27 (1): pp. 5–19. 10.1353/jod.2016.0012.

The Constitution of the People's Republic of Bangladesh, 2019. Available at: http://bdlaws.minlaw.gov.bd/act-367.html (Accessed January 12, 2021).

Coppedge, Michael (1994). *Strong Parties and Lame Ducks: Presidential Partyarchy and Factionalism in Venezuela.* Stanford: Stanford University Press.

The Daily Star (2016). '145 killed in 'ghoulish' UP polls: Shujan,' *The Daily Star*, June 16, 2016. Available at: www.thedailystar.net/politics/145-killed-union-parishad-polls-shujan-1240543 (Accessed December 24, 2020).

The Daily Star (2017). '*Suspension, once again.*' The Daily Star, July 7, 2017. Available at: www.thedailystar.net/frontpage/gazipur-city-corporation-gcc

The Daily Star (2020). 'Voters keep off,' *The Daily Star*, February 2, 2020. Available at: www.thedailystar.net/frontpage/dhaka-city-elections-2020-voters-keep-1862272 (Accessed January 10, 2021).

Dhaka Tribune (2020). '*Relief embezzlement: 100 public representatives suspended till date.*' Dhaka Tribune, June 17. Available at: www.dhakatribune.com/bangladesh/2020/06/17/relief-embezzlement-100-public-representatives-suspended-till-date (Accessed December 23, 2020).

Diamond, Larry (2015). 'Facing Up to the Democratic Recession.' *Journal of Democracy* 26 (1): pp. 141–155.

Freedom House (2020). '*Freedom in the world.*' Available at: https://freedomhouse.org/country/bangladesh/freedom–world/2020 (Accessed January 11, 2021).

Ghosh, Sujon and Tasneem Hasan (2020). '*More cases against BNP candidates*' (in Bangla), *Prothom Alo*, April 12. Available at: https://bit.ly/3C0nRGa (Accessed January 3, 2021).

Hankala, Charles R., Jorge Martinez-Vazquez and Raul Alberto Ponce Rodriguez (2019). *Local Accountability and National Coordination in Fiscal Federalism: A Fine Balance.* UK: Edward Elgar Publishing Limited and USA: Edward Elgar Publishing, Inc.

Hossain, Akbar (2021). '*February 15 Election: The context and modality of the controversial and one-sided election in 1996 during the time of Khaleda Zia*' (in Bangla), BBC Bangla, Dhaka. February 15, 2021. Available at: www.bbc.com/bengali/news-56054285.amp (Accessed February 15, 2021).

Hossain, Md. Anwar and Pranab Kumar Baul (2021). 'AL didn't want voter turnout, BNP unable, EC silent.' Available at: https://en.prothomalo.com/bangladesh/politics/al-didnt-want-voter-turnout-bnp-unable-ec-silent (Accessed January 30, 2021).

Islam, Mohammad Tarikul (2018). '*Cooperation or interference: MP's role in local government.*' The Daily Star, December 11. Available at: www.thedailystar.net/opinion/news/cooperation-or-interference-mps-role-local-government-1671871 (Accessed December 13, 2010).

Karim, Riadul (2020). '*The BNP candidates lost security deposit in 12 municipalities*' (in Bangla). Prothom Alo, December 30. Available at: https://bit.ly/3E7Gavb (Accessed January 1, 2021).

Khan, Akbar Ali (2015). *Gresham's Law Syndrome and Beyond: An Analysis of the Bangladesh Bureaucracy.* Dhaka: University Press Limited.

Kudrat-E-Elahi Panir Vs. Bangladesh [1992] 44 DLR (AD) (1992) (Appellate Division (Civil) of the Supreme Court of Bangladesh), p.319.

Lewis, David & Hossain, Abul (2019). '*Local Political Consolidation in Bangladesh: Power, Informality and Patronage.*' Development and Change. 10.1111/dech.12534.

Local Government (Union Parishad) Act, 2009. Available at: http://chandanaish.chittagong.gov.bd/site/law_policy/b2e85554-2147-11e7-8f57-286ed488c766 (Accessed November 30, 2020).

The Local Government (City Corporation) Act (2009). Available at: www.clcbd.org/document/535.html (Accessed January 12, 2021).

Lührmann, Anna and Lindberg, Staffan I. (2019). 'A Third Wave of Autocratization Is Here: What Is New About It?' *Democratization*, 26 (7): pp. 1095–1113, DOI: 10.1080/13510347.2019.1582029.

Macroeconomic Wing (2020). '*Monthly Report on Fiscal Position.*' October 2020. Finance Division Ministry of Finance, Government of the People's Republic of Bangladesh.

Mazumdar, Badiul Alam (2010). *Local Governance and Political Reform: Keys to Poverty Reduction.* Dhaka: Agamee Prakashani, pp. 19–30.

Mazumdar, Badiul Alam (2016). '*How fair were the Paura Elections?*', *The Daily Star*, January 27. Available at: www.thedailystar.net/op-ed/politics/how-fair-were-the-paura-elections-207748 (Accessed January 10, 2021).

New Age (2017). '*Suspension of elected official is autocratic.*' *New Age*, April 4. Available at: www.newagebd.net/article/12672/articlelist/323/article/article/index.php (Accessed November 18, 2020).

New Age (2021). '*BNP to boycott upcoming UP elections.*' New Age, February 28. Available at: www.newagebd.net/article/131399/bnp-to-boycott-upcoming-up-elections (Accessed February 28, 2021).

New Age Online (2021). '*Municipality polls end amid violence, irregularities.*' New Age, January 16. Available at: www.newagebd.net/article/127342/municipality-polls-end-amid-violence-irregularities (Accessed January 16, 2021).

New Age Opinion (2021). '*Chattogram city elections betray failures of EC, govt.*' Available at: www.newagebd.net/article/128586/chattogram-city-elections-betray-failures-of-ec-govt (Accessed January 30, 2021).

Osman, Ferdous Arfina (2010). 'Bangladesh Politics: Confrontation, Monopoly and Crisis in Governance.' *Asian Journal of Political Science*, 18 (3): pp. 310–333.

Panday, Pranab Kumar. (2011). '*Local Government System in Bangladesh: How Far is it Decentralised?*', *LEX LOCALIS – Journal of Local Self-government*, 9 (3): pp. 205–230.

Panday, Pranab Kumar (2019). '*Party-based Local Government Election: Pains and Gains,*' *Daily Sun*, March 20. Available at: www.daily-sun.com/printversion/details/378876/Partybased-Local-Government-Election:-Pains-and-Gains (Accessed December 24, 2020).

Prothom Alo (2021). NOs are behaving like a ruler, said the public representatives' (in Bangla), Prothom Alo, January 2. Available at: https://bit.ly/3k6oeJf (Accessed January 3, 2021).

Rahman, Shamsur (2021). '*The BNP mayors are leaving behind*' (in Bangla). *Prothom Alo*, January 12. Available at: https://bit.ly/2VE9c44 (Accessed January 12, 2021).

Riaz, Ali (2019). *Voting in a Hybrid Regime: Explaining the 2018 Bangladeshi Election.* Singapore: Palgrave Macmillan.

Sabina, Nazme, Sayeedul H. Khan and M. Badiuzzaman (2015). 'Local Government by Whom,' in Barakat, Abul, et al., editors. *Local Governance and Decentralization in Bangladesh: Politics and Economics.* Dhaka: Pathak Shamabesh, pp. 61–75.

Siddiqui, Kamal (2014). *Local Government in Bangladesh.* Dhaka: The University Press Limited.

Sowdagar, Mezbah-Ul-Azam (2013). 'Challenges of Local Governance: A Study on New Upazila Administration in Bangladesh.' *Jagannath University Journal of Social Sciences*, 1 (1–2): pp. 56–73.

Tithila, Kohinur Khyum (2020). '42 citizens call for Supreme Judicial Council to probe graft allegations against EC,' Dhaka Tribune, December 19. Available at: www.dhakatribune.com/bangladesh/2020/12/19/42-citizens-call-for-supreme-judicial-council-to-probe-graft-allegations-against-ec (Accessed December 20, 2020).

UNB News (2019). '*No plan to drop section 25 from UZ Parishad Act.*' *UNB*, September 11. Available at: https://unb.com.bd/category/bangladesh/no-plan-to-drop-section-25-from-uz-parishad-act/27992 (Accessed December 26, 2020).

Upazila Parishad Act (1998). Available at: http://bdlaws.minlaw.gov.bd/act-827.html (Accessed February 2, 2021).

Way, Lucan Ahmad and Levitsky, Steven (2020). 'Why Democracy Needs a Level Playing Field.' *Journal of Democracy*, 21 (1): pp. 57–68.

Widmalm, Sten (2008). *Decentralization, Corruption and Social Capital from India to the West.* First Edition, New Delhi: Sage Publications.

World Bank (2020). 'Improving Local Governance and Service Delivery in Bangladesh: Role of Local Government Finance.' Available at: https://documents1.worldbank.org/curated/en/150821592287566995/pdf/Improving-Local-Governance-and-Service-Delivery-in-Bangladesh-The-Role-of-Local-Government-Finance.pdf

Zila Parishad Act (2000). Available at: http://bdlaws.minlaw.gov.bd/act-841.html (Accessed February 2, 2021).

PART IV

Sri Lanka

The resilience of the ethnic state

24

ETHNORELIGIOUS NATIONALISM AND AUTOCRATIZATION IN SRI LANKA

Neil DeVotta

Sri Lankans take pride in their island being Asia's oldest democracy—given that the country achieved universal suffrage in 1931, some seventeen years before independence and merely three years after Britain allowed the vote for all its citizens. Since independence in 1948, the island has evidenced competitive politicking, with parties/coalitions alternating in power at the national level multiple times and dozens of elections held at the local and provincial levels. Political participation has also been high, with turnout at the 2015 and 2019 presidential elections exceeding 80 percent. Yet this is also a country that has hardly gone a decade since independence without experiencing major violence in the form of ethnic riots and pogroms, left-wing insurgencies, and a grotesque civil war between majority Sinhalese and minority Tamils that lasted nearly thirty years (DeVotta 2019). In the past decade, since the ethnic conflict ended in 2009, Christian Evangelicals and especially Muslims have experienced episodic violence thanks to prominent politicians and Buddhist monks fanning communalism (DeVotta 2018).

Sri Lanka thus represents a democratic paradox: its citizens passionately value the franchise and the country holds relatively free and fair elections even while tolerating ethnoreligious violence. The added irony is that much of the ethnoreligious violence is promoted and justified in the name of Buddhism, given that the island is viewed as a sanctuary for Buddha's teachings and Sinhalese nationalists consequently insist on Buddhist superordination and minority subordination. Post-independence Sri Lanka initially looked like it was on the road to being a liberal democracy. However, the Sinhalese Buddhist majoritarianism that took root made the country into an ethnocracy, in that the Sinhalese Buddhist nationalist ideology undermines equal citizenship by dictating that minorities live in the island thanks to majority sufferance (Uyangoda 1994; DeVotta 2007).

The mainly state-sanctioned and -tolerated violence that continues to get perpetrated with impunity to promote majoritarianism disqualifies the island being branded a liberal democracy notwithstanding its competitive and inclusive politics. To rank as a liberal democracy, a country must go beyond merely holding competitive and inclusive elections; it must also uphold civil liberties for all citizens irrespective of ethnicity and religion, ensure an independent judiciary that fearlessly enforces the rule of law, tolerate civil society, minimize corruption, and balance against executive overreach (Diamond 2019a, 19). These are lofty criteria, and thus ensuring

DOI: 10.4324/9781003042211-29

liberal democracy in even democratically consolidated societies is a work in progress. This is because opportunistic leaders and populist movements can quickly undermine even robust democratic institutions. The specific causes promoting such destabilization in a particular country may vary, but some overarching reasons attributed for the ongoing global democratic regression include demo-sclerosis in the United States, the Iraq War and the attendant de-legitimation of democracy promotion, the proclivity among some Eastern European elites for soft-authoritarianism, illiberal populism in western democracies stemming from an aversion to globalization and immigration, and China's spectacular rise and support for authoritarian leaders (Diamond 2019b; *The Economist* 2014).

For much of the world's history people lived under authoritarian rule. Indeed, even today approximately 68 percent of the global population lives in autocratic states (Alizada et al. 2021, 7). The compromises and individual self-restraint required to ensure democracy, especially in ethnoreligious societies rife with crosscutting cleavages, are so daunting that it makes the quest for democracy appear foolhardy and arrogant. It is with good reason Rousseau noted that "If there were a people of Gods, it would govern itself democratically. Such a perfect government is not suited to men" (Quoted in Simon 2004, 433). Yet Rousseau himself and others urged societies to aspire towards democracy because it remains the political system most likely to promote peace and economic growth. If it is widely acknowledged that democracies tend not to wage war against fellow democracies (Russett 1993), it is also clear that people living in authoritarian states are more likely to suffer from famine, endure greater rates of poverty and mental illness, and also experience lower life expectancy (Kasparov and Halvorssen 2017).

If communism's demise as a dominant ideology seemed to suggest democracy was bound to be the only governance game in town, this was arguably because scholars and policymakers initially overlooked how elites in post-communist and post-authoritarian states with a proclivity to stay in power by hook or by crook were deft at manipulating societal cleavages to do so. Such elites and the hybrid regimes that consequently ensued have not only compromised these newly-democratized states (Carothers 2018), they have also goaded leaders in established democracies to embrace illiberal tactics to perpetuate power.

While the exact causes and extent of ongoing autocratization may be disputed (Levitsky and Ziblatt 2018; Mechkova, Luhrmann, and Lindberg 2017), we can agree that it "entails a deterioration of qualities associated with democratic governance" (Waldner and Lust 2018, 95). And while it is hard to pinpoint when precisely recent autocratization begins, the factors contributing to it are easily recognizable. These include corruption, executives seeking to operate extra-constitutionally and extra-judicially, and the state's inability to meet citizens' most basic needs (Diamond 2019a, 20). The manipulation of ethnoreligious cleavages and persecution of minorities for political gain and the absence of the rule of law, which prevents elites from being held to the same standards as everyone else, are other clear warning signs that the process of autocratization is in the works. As Larry Diamond notes, "No liberal democracy has ever just suddenly had a heart attack and died … . And it [does not] take the political scientist's version of a cholesterol test or an EKG to spot the emerging symptoms" (ibid). Consequently, while the world is yet to experience a full-blown third reverse wave leading to a large number of states ceasing to be democracies, there is no disputing that there has been a trend away from liberal democracy in the past fourteen years (Repucci 2020; Luhrmann and Lindberg 2019; Chu, Huang, Lagos, and Mattes 2020). Sri Lanka under especially the Rajapaksa family has contributed to this, although presidents who preceded the Rajapaksas laid the groundwork for autocratization.

Various exigencies can contribute to democratic backsliding. In Sri Lanka's case, ethnonationalism since the mid-1950s and the ensuing civil war that lasted nearly three decades led to security and sovereignty being privileged above individual rights and freedoms, and this cluster of factors especially compromised liberal aspects of democracy. Whatever the galvanizing reason at a given time, backsliding entails institutions that ensure transparency and horizontal accountability being weakened. It leads to checks on executive power being eroded, which typically gets done via new laws or referenda. The ensuing "executive aggrandizement" compromises good governance and promotes hybrid regimes (Bermeo 2016). In such instances, the pressure western democracies put on such regimes to counter their assault on civil society, civil liberties, and the rule of law could encourage opportunistic leaders to move closer to authoritarian states. Here too Sri Lanka stands out given how the Rajapaksas have gravitated towards China as part of a symbiotic relationship that has exacerbated corruption and autocratization.

That noted, democratic regression in Sri Lanka was baked at home and took shape in the 1950s, when Sinhalese Buddhist politicians eschewed consensus politics and instead pursued majoritarian politics that unleashed civil war. It is Sinhalese Buddhist majoritarianism combined with the civil war and authoritarian proclivities of certain leaders that compromised the island's democracy and pushed it in an autocratic direction (Tambiah 1986; Wilson 1988). In what follows, this essay briefly discusses how ethnonationalism contributed to democratic erosion in the island before critiquing the presidencies of Mahinda Rajapaksa (2005 to 2015) and Gotabaya Rajapaksa, brothers who together with their grasping family are most responsible for autocratization in Sri Lanka. The challenges stemming from the COVID-19 pandemic may have stymied Gotabaya Rajapaksa's majoritarian agenda, but the ensuing health and socioeconomic crises have allowed him to further militarize the island in ways that will make reversing autocratization extra difficult.

Ethnonationalism and democratic regression

As per Sri Lanka's most recent census, the Sinhalese comprise 74.9 percent of the population, while Sri Lankan Tamils, Indian Tamils, and Muslims are 11.2 percent, 4.1 percent, and 9.3 percent, respectively. In terms of religion, Buddhists are 70.1 percent, while Hindus, Christians, and Muslims are 12.6 percent, 7.6 percent, and 9.7 percent, respectively (Department of Census and Statistics Sri Lanka 2011). The island's demographics necessitated checks against majoritarianism. The absence of such structural constraints ensured it was only a matter of time before ambitious politicians played the Sinhalese Buddhist nationalist card to attain office. What ensued was a phenomenon of ethnic outbidding, which led to the main political parties— United National Party (UNP) and Sri Lanka Freedom Party (SLFP)—competing against each other on who could best provide for the majority community at the expense of especially the Tamil minority (DeVotta 2004).

Consequently, while Sri Lanka began its post-independence journey smacking of a liberal democracy, with one scholar noting that among the decolonized states the island had "the best chance of making a successful transition to modern statehood" (Wriggins 1961, 316), this promise was sundered within a decade. By the time the Sinhala language was instituted as the island's only official language in 1956, amidst riots against minority Tamils, the country was well on the way to becoming an ethnocracy, wherein belonging to the culturally dominant Sinhalese Buddhist nation trumps being a citizen of Sri Lanka (DeVotta 2018, 278; Smooha 2002). This is clear when one looks at the anti-minority and majoritarian policies that were instituted by the time the island celebrated a quarter century of independence in 1973: Tamil civil servants were forced to learn Sinhala to be promoted; Sinhalese civil servants were stationed in Tamil areas and Tamils forced to interact with them in Sinhala; Sinhala only was instituted into the courts system, including in the predominantly Tamil northeast region that Tamils consider part of their historic homeland; Tamil areas were provided little development assistance despite foreign aid earmarked for these regions; publications promoting Tamil culture from nearby Tamil Nadu state in India were banned; Tamil students were required to score higher than their Sinhalese peers to enter university; a quota system was developed to ensure that rural Sinhalese students got into the university more easily; and Sinhalese from the south were transplanted to the northeast to promote Sinhalese colonization and alter the region's demographics. Additionally, Buddhism was provided the foremost place within the 1972 constitution. Thus, illiberal populism rooted in ethnonationalism has long been a feature of Sri Lankan politics (DeVotta 2002).

Majoritarianism engenders sullen minorities, and it is hardly surprising that Tamil youth felt the urge to rebel. When a Lessons Learned and Reconciliation Commission was set up to analyze the civil war, its members baldly said that "The root cause of the ethnic conflict in Sri Lanka lies in the failure of successive Governments to address the genuine grievances of the Tamil people" (quoted in Minority Rights Group International 2014). As one author aptly noted when referring to the anti-Tamil policies that were instituted, "If the gods had wished to destroy, the madness of Sri Lanka's rulers gave them every opportunity" (Harris 1990, 222).

It is debatable if an ethnically tranquil Sri Lanka will have prevented certain leaders from acting in authoritarian vein, but it is indisputable that the ethnic conflict enabled authoritarianism. In this context, the semi-presidential constitution instituted in 1978 allowed President J. R. Jayewardene to act arrogantly, while the war and its triumphalist aftermath allowed Mahinda Rajapaksa to operate autocratically. Ultimately, while the actions of these two leaders especially nudged the country towards autocratization, the expanding militarization and majoritarianism under President Gotabaya Rajapaksa is ramping up autocratization in the island.

Constitutions designed for democratic societies ideally incorporate checks and balances as a way to institutionalize stability over the long term. Jayewardene's constitution, however, was partly designed to ensure the UNP stayed perpetually dominant (Oberst 1984). Jayewardene was wont to brag that the only thing he could not do under his constitution was change a man into a woman and vice versa. In this spirit, he amended the constitution 16 times between 1978 and 1988, often in partisan and whimsical fashion. In 1980 he vindictively stripped SLFP leader Mrs. Sirimavo Bandaranaike of her civic rights for seven years (in retaliation for her previous extension of SLFP rule by two years until 1977) and expelled her from parliament, thereby ensuring that his most effective opponent could not challenge him for reelection in 1982. He then refused to hold scheduled parliamentary elections that would most certainly have led to a loss of seats for the UNP and instead held a severely compromised referendum that extended the party's five-sixths majority for another term. He even forced all UNP ministers to turn in signed but undated resignation letters, which ensured that they followed his dictates. His attitude toward the democratic process was best captured when he boasted:

> We are contesting the election to win and at a time most favorable to us. We intend ... to demolish and completely destroy the opposition politically. After that I say to you, roll up the electoral map of Sri Lanka. You will not need it for another ten years.
>
> *(Samarakone 1984, 86)*

Jayewardene used his power to dominate and assault those who crossed him. For instance, he used hoodlums belonging to the UNP's labor union to suppress strikes, beat protesters, harass journalists and Supreme Court justices, and attack political opponents. These forces were also used to foment anti-Tamil riots in 1977 and 1983, with dire consequences for the island. All this took place amidst the escalating ethnic conflict, which helped justify executive overreach. Ranasinghe Premadasa, Dingiri Banda Wijetunga, and Chandrika Bandaranaike Kumaratunga followed Jayewardene as executive presidents between 1989 and 2005, with Wijetunga serving just 18 months to wrap up Premadasa's term after the separatist Liberation Tigers of Tamil Eelam (LTTE) assassinated him in May 1993. While Premadasa and Kumaratunga engaged in petty politicking and also abused their authority as president, their regimes were more illiberal than autocratic. That changed when Mahinda Rajapaksa succeeded Kumaratunga.

Autocratization under Mahinda Rajapaksa

No president undermined democratic governance as effectively and ruthlessly as Mahinda Rajapaksa. Sinhalese Buddhists had long overlooked spreading illiberalism, because the ethnocracy that came with this benefitted them materially and those who faced the consequences of illiberalism were mainly Tamils (DeVotta 2021b). However, the post-war illiberalism President Rajapaksa and his family instituted sought to create a Rajapaksa dynasty by undermining the state. As one of President Rajapaksa's younger brothers bragged in reference to family rule, "an era of 'ruler kings' has begun" (*The Economist* 2010, 49).

Rajapaksa became president in November 2005 and soon thereafter nearly 140 members of his immediate and extended family took over various government positions. Three Rajapaksa brothers, by virtue of controlling nearly 80 government portfolios, arrogated to themselves between 60 and 70 percent of the country's budget. For instance, Mahinda Rajapaksa, besides being president, was also the minister for defense, finance, highways, planning, and ports and aviation. These combined portfolios placed 78 government institutions directly under his control. While charming and politically savvy, the president brooked little dissent. His older brother, Chamal, was Speaker of Parliament. His younger brother, Basil, was the Minister of Economic Development, which included the Board of Investment and the Tourist Promotion Bureau. Gotabaya, another brother who is now the island's president, was the country's Defense Secretary. In addition to superintending the armed forces, police, and coast guard, Gotabaya Rajapaksa also oversaw immigration and emigration, the Land Reclamation and Development Corporation, and the Urban Development Authority. Mahinda Rajapaksa's son, Namal, was a member of parliament and was being groomed to succeed him. Namal and Basil routinely overrode decisions by ministers; and those seeking a government job typically had to have their approval. This led to a supine cabinet of ministers who dared not cross Rajapaksa lest they lost their positions and perks.

During the Rajapaksa years opposition politicians were harried, civil society was neutered, and thugs associated with the regime operated with impunity. Self-censorship was routine and those who criticized the regime or military were murdered or disappeared (Helf et al. 2015, 3–4). White vans operated by rouge units within the military were used for such purposes. Businesses, ranging from insurance companies to banks, were infiltrated via board membership and their policies influenced in ways that benefitted ruling politicians and hurt the regime's competitors. Such autocratic capture allowed the government to starve independent media and the opposition of resources. Instead of accommodating the defeated and broken Tamils in some fashion, the regime further humiliated them especially in Northern Province by resorting to militarization and tolerating predatory behavior among soldiers and regime supporters (DeVotta 2016).

The extent of the government's arrogance was evidenced when Rajapaksa targeted retired army commander Sarath Fonseka, who was responsible for the military strategy to defeat the LTTE but thereafter challenged Rajapaksa in the 2010 presidential election: he was forcibly dragged away from his office, court martialed for improper military procurements, divested of his civil rights and military honors, and sentenced to jail for three years.

The judiciary too was controlled, with telephone justice—whereby someone in the president's or attorney general's office called justices to tell them how to rule in certain cases—becoming common. The judiciary's weakened position and the government's authoritarian nature were especially highlighted when the country's first ever female Chief Justice was impeached in January 2013. Her sin was to rule that a government program designed to transfer funds to the Rajapaksas for patronage purposes was unconstitutional. An irate president set up a Parliamentary Select Committee (PSC) comprised of politicians from the ruling coalition that found her guilty of financial and official misconduct, which formed the basis for impeachment. This was done despite the Supreme Court ruling that the PSC had no right to investigate a senior judge and the Appeals Court ordering parliament to abandon the impeachment process. Civil society organizations, clergy members, foreign governments, and various international bodies likewise objected strenuously. President Rajapaksa disregarded their entreaties and summarily signed the order removing the Chief Justice, even as pro-government goons brandishing poles gathered outside her official residence to make sure she relinquished her post.

Rajapaksa's authoritarian proclivities were especially evident when he forced through the 18th Amendment to the constitution, which was incorporated in September 2010. The amendment abolished the 17th Amendment, which Sri Lanka's parliament passed unanimously in 2001 when Chandrika Kumaratunga was president. While it failed to achieve full enforcement, the amendment mandated the creation of a Constitutional Council with sole powers to appoint and dismiss commissioners overseeing elections, public service, police, finance, human rights, and bribery and corruption. The Constitutional Council was further empowered to appoint the chief justice and other justices in the Supreme Court, president and judges of the Court of Appeal, members of the Judicial Services Commission (excepting its chairman), attorney general, inspector general of police, auditor general, parliamentary commissioner for administration (or ombudsman), and secretary general of parliament. This was a belated attempt to halt political interference and promote independent, impartial, and professional operations among and within these institutions that were consistent with horizontal accountability (ibid).

The 18th Amendment did away with the Constitutional Council and empowered the president to appoint personnel to lead the institutions under its purview. The 18th Amendment also permitted the president to contest more than two terms, which President Rajapaksa utilized to run for a third term in January 2015. The president engineered crossovers from the opposition to ensure he commanded the requisite two-thirds majority to pass the amendment, and by some accounts some of these politicians were paid over half a million dollars to abandon the parties under whose banner they got elected.

Chauvinistic nationalists and their antisocial behavior can also play a major role in undermining democracy (Howe 2017), and Sri Lanka clearly has a fair share of these constituencies. The ethnoreligious strife in the island has been a boon for such elements, and politicians, businessmen, and religious bigots have eagerly used them for opportunistic purposes. Foremost among these in recent times is a Sinhalese Buddhist nationalist group called the Bodu Bala Sena (Buddhist Power Force, or BBS) that gained prominence by resorting to Islamophobia. The attacks against the Muslim community, which led to businesses, houses, and mosques being destroyed, were possible because the Mahinda Rajapaksa government tolerated the BBS and its ilk. Politics and cultural considerations rooted in Sinhalese Buddhist nationalism and economics have combined to unleash this Islamophobia (Haniffa 2017). But the ability of forces close to the government to operate with impunity was a big reason for the periodic, well-orchestrated postwar anti-Muslim rioting.

Under Mahinda Rajapaksa, the attempts to prevent institutions operating independently and fan anti-minority sentiment were deliberate. The civil war against the ruthless and terrorist LTTE made doing so easier. The literature on exceptionalism suggests that during "exceptional" periods of crisis or transformation institutionalized norms, rules, and laws can become irrelevant and countries can, consequently, veer toward authoritarianism. For crises provide opportunities to superimpose radical change that established social orders may otherwise oppose (Neal 2006). The exceptions can be instituted via extrajudicial and extraconstitutional means or by simply creating new laws that overturn extant laws (Ericson 2007). With the state mainly responsible for ensuring security and sovereignty, even new bad laws are easily legitimated and institutionalized. When this takes place in relatively democratized societies, the inevitable result is a move toward illiberalism and autocratization.

Exceptionalism is rooted in fear and insecurity and therefore predisposes people to violence (Huysmans 2006). During the ethnic conflict, ensuring security came at the expense of minorities' civil liberties and civil rights. A case in point is the draconian Prevention of Terrorism Act (PTA), which remains on the books. The Act allows the security forces to arrest, detain, and leave incommunicado for eighteen months anyone suspected of terrorist activities. Thousands of Tamils were dragooned using the PTA and recently dozens of Muslims have also been taken into custody using its statutes.

The illiberalism associated with exceptionalism enables untrammeled executive power in ways that undermine the rule of law (Huysmans 2008). In this regard, too, Sri Lanka stands out. Indeed, the exceptionalism that undergirded the island's ethnocentric and counter terror policies is part of the same narrative and logic that was used to legitimize autocratic politics since it easily justified extraconstitutional and extrajudicial practices to ensure security. Civil wars necessitate counter-terror practices, and the longer the conflict the more draconian these practices can become. The upshot is that ethnic conflicts end up compromising democracy and over the long term can lead to authoritarianism (Horowitz 1993).

Mahinda Rajapaksa's unexpected defeat in January 2015 was considered a win for democracy. Notwithstanding corruption scandals that tarnished the regime's reputation early on, the national unity government that succeeded Rajapaksa certainly enabled a freer society. And despite the serious anti-Muslim rioting that took place in a couple of instances, minorities felt more secure under this national unity government compared to the Rajapaksa years. This government also sought to institute ethnic reconciliation mechanisms in accordance with Sri Lanka's agreements with the United Nations Human Rights Council (UNHRC), although the progress made was halting and slow. It, however, bungled intelligence reports that might have averted the 2019 Easter Sunday suicide bombings by Islamist terrorists on Christian churches and hotels that killed nearly 270 people. This coupled with the inability of President Maithripala Sirisena and Prime Minister Ranil Wickremesinghe to get along allowed Gotabaya Rajapaksa, the former defense secretary and Mahinda Rajapaksa's brother, to win the presidential election in November 2019.

Autocratization under Gotabaya Rajapaksa

Gotabaya Rajapaksa capitalized on the Easter Sunday terrorist attacks and his leadership during the civil war and promised to institute effective government. Leading Buddhist monks and mainly Sinhalese Buddhist professionals fed up with the previous regime's directionless governance played a leading role in supporting his candidacy. Prominent serving and retired military personnel likewise supported him. Consequently, the vast majority of Sinhalese Buddhists voted for him while the vast majority of minorities voted against him.

Sri Lanka under Gotabaya Rajapaksa represents a militarized ethnocracy. This is reflected in how post-election spoils have been doled out. For instance, only three of 35 secretaries to ministries are ethnic minorities, while nearly all major appointees to leading state agencies are Buddhists. A number of military personnel accused of having perpetrated war crimes during the civil war were rewarded with prominent positions immediately after Gotabaya became president. Indeed, one former soldier who was court-martialed and whose death sentence, for killing eight Tamil civilians (including four children), was upheld by the Supreme Court was summarily pardoned by the new president. Some among such so-called *ranawiru* (war heroes) are now being encouraged to run for parliament (*The Island* 2020a) through the Rajapaksas' Sri Lanka Podujana Peramuna (Sri Lanka People's Front, or SLPP) even as the president has threatened to yank the country from international bodies that level war crimes charges against Sri Lankan military personnel (*The Island* 2020b). This was done after the government withdrew co-sponsorship of the UNHRC resolution, which the previous regime had initiated to pursue ethnic reconciliation and accountability for alleged war crimes during the civil war.

All this fits a pattern of disregarding minorities' concerns. For instance, when Sri Lanka celebrated its Independence Day in February 2020 and 2021, the Gotabaya Rajapaksa government prevented the national anthem being sung in Tamil, which the previous regime had reintroduced. Additionally, checkpoints were erected in some parts of Northern Province and surveillance of Tamil areas especially increased. On the one hand, military personnel and Sinhalese Buddhist nationalists have genuinely feared a recrudescence of Tamil separatism and the surveillance regime that was put in place in Tamil areas—partly using rehabilitated ex-LTTE cadre—is understandable. On the other hand, it is also clear that the surveillance system was used to keep Tamils marginalized and insecure even as avenues were created for Sinhalese Buddhist forces to colonize hitherto traditional Tamil (and Muslim) lands.

The Presidential Task Force for Archeological Heritage Management in the Eastern Province that the president created in June 2020 appears geared for this task. The Secretary to the Ministry of Defense, another retired military personnel alleged to have perpetrated war crimes, heads the task force, which initially comprised eleven members including two Buddhist monks. President Gotabaya Rajapaksa, who has set up a Buddhist Advisory Council comprising leading monks and meets with the group every month, subsequently added four more Buddhist monks to the task force. Over 75 percent of the population in Eastern Province are Tamils and Muslims, yet not one member from either community was included in the task force. The group's sinister agenda was made amply clear when a gazette authorizing the expansion of the task force stated that the archeological heritage in Eastern Province is influenced by Buddhism and hence "the guidance and patronage of the Venerable Maha Sangha is … needed" to identify and manage the relevant areas (The Gazette of the Democratic Socialist Republic of Sri Lanka 2020). Nationalists want all nine provinces to contain mainly Sinhalese Buddhists, and a policy of ethnic flooding à la that pursued in China's Tibet and Xinjiang regions could expeditiously achieve this result. In this regard, the expanding tentacles of China in the island not only stand to promote autocracy, they likely will also encourage ethnocracy.

The same day the task force pertaining to Eastern Province was created, Gotabaya Rajapaksa also created The Presidential Task Force to Build a Secure Country, Disciplined, Virtuous and Lawful Society. This body is comprised of military, intelligence, and police officials and its mandates appear designed to usurp the functions of civilian officials. Indeed, it is military personnel that President Gotabaya Rajapaksa has appointed to superintend the Sri Lanka Ports Authority, Telecommunication Regulatory Commission, Sri Lanka Customs, Consumer Affairs Authority, and Disaster Management Center. The president, who served in the military before emigrating to the United States seeking after greener pastures, has long held the police force in low esteem, and he has now placed the police and Criminal Investigation Division under the Defense Ministry.

The burgeoning autocratization amidst militarization does not bode well for civil society. For no sooner had Gotabaya Rajapaksa become president, NGOs began to be interrogated about personnel, funding sources, and individuals visiting them. And the defense ministry was also put in charge of registering NGOs. In the face of the COVID-19 crisis, numerous civil society groups have assisted the military to provide services, but this now leaves their personnel more exposed should the regime crack down on associational activities.

The task forces noted above were created amidst the COVID-19 pandemic, a clear indication that the economic crises stemming from the coronavirus hardly stopped the regime pursuing its autocratic and majoritarian trajectory. If anything, it has used the crisis to further militarize the country in ways that promote autocratization. Given that over 95 percent of the island's military forces are Sinhalese and Buddhist, this militarization conveniently combines an ethnonationalist agenda that threatens minorities and expands autocratization. For instance, the president picked the army commander (and not a public health official) to head the COVID-19 task force. The alleged war crimes committed by this officer were the basis for United States officials banning him and his family from visiting their country. And on January 1, 2021, the Gotabaya Rajapaksa government appointed a Major General in each of Sri Lanka's 25 districts to superintend coronavirus measures, thereby further expanding militarization.

In the early stages of the pandemic certain government personnel and pro-government media sought to blame Muslims for spreading COVID-19, and the government appeared to deliberately traumatize the community by insisting that Muslims who died of the coronavirus had to be cremated. The dictum was contrary to World Health Organization recommendations practiced throughout the world (Saroor 2020). The government, when seeking the support of predominantly Muslim countries like Pakistan and Bangladesh at the UNHRC, did change its policy in March 2021, which proved that the ban on COVID-19-related burials had less to do with science and more to do with humiliating and tormenting a Muslim community that voted overwhelmingly against both Mahinda Rajapaksa in 2015 and Gotabaya Rajapaksa in 2019.

Soon after Gotabaya Rajapaksa was elected, his brother and former president Mahinda was made prime minister. In March 2020, in accordance with the constitution, the president dissolved parliament six months before its term expired and called for elections the following month. The COVID-19 pandemic, however, forced the Elections Commission to postpone the polls twice. Article 70 of the country's constitution requires a new parliament to be in session within three months of the previous body being dissolved. Yet Gotabaya Rajapaksa refused to recall parliament, and during this period government expenditures and other business, including policies dealing with the coronavirus, were conducted without parliamentary oversight. Such autocratic governance could easily be repeated when the regime faces major crises and it may initially at least be tolerated among large portions of a public fed up with parliamentary anomie and malfeasance.

Notwithstanding the economic crises created by COVID-19 (Hewamanne 2021), Sri Lanka initially did well to curtail the spread of the virus. Sri Lankans across the ethnic divide appreciated the role the armed forces played in this regard. This, combined with the president's popularity among Sinhalese Buddhists and a weak opposition, allowed the SLPP to win 145 parliamentary seats and capture nearly 60 percent of the vote when elections were held in August 2020 (DeVotta 2021a).

Sri Lanka's parliament has 225 representatives and following the election the SLPP and its allies were easily able to form a supermajority. This allowed the Rajapaksas to pass the 20th Amendment to the constitution, which threw out the 19th Amendment or, otherwise put, reintroduced the 18th Amendment and most of its presidential prerogatives. If the 19th Amendment sought to limit presidential powers by empowering the prime minister, the 20th Amendment reverses this. Most Sinhalese Buddhists may associate a strong presidency and unitary state structure with sovereignty, but it is the executive presidential system that has enabled the tilt towards autocracy.

Amidst the ongoing COVID-19 crisis, the government set up a Presidential Commission of Inquiry into Political Victimization, which conveniently recommended the prosecution of lawyers associated with the Attorney General's Department, Bribery Commission, and Criminal Investigation Department who filed various charges against members of the Rajapaksa family, their cronies, and certain military personnel. President Gotabaya Rajapaksa and Prime Minister Mahinda Rajapaksa thereafter sought to use the commission's report to pass a resolution in parliament that summarily dismissed most charges, including cases undergoing trial. The charges in these cases range from murder and abduction, to money laundering and abusing state funds. This blatant attempt to promote impunity ensued even as the government flirted with stripping some opposition members of their civic rights, which would effectively marginalize them politically just as J. R. Jayewardene defanged Mrs. Bandaranaike by canceling her civic rights.

Today President Gotabaya Rajapaksa is also the Minister of Defense and Minister of Technology. Prime Minister Mahinda Rajapaksa is also the Minister of Finance; Economy and Policy Development; Buddhism and Cultural and Religious Affairs; and Urban Development, Water Supply and Housing Facilities. Chamal, another brother who was speaker of parliament during the previous Rajapaksa government, is Minister of Agriculture, Irrigation and Rural Development, Internal Trade, Food Security, and Consumer Welfare. A third brother, Basil, who is not a member of parliament, oversees two presidential task forces (Delivery of Essential Goods; and Economic Revival and Poverty Alleviation) and effectively uses the SLPP party network to channel COVID-19 aid. Mahinda Rajapaksa's son, Namal, is Minister of Youth and Sports. Altogether, the Rajapaksa clan controls around 140 of the 434 state institutions. Five years after being ousted from power, the family has recaptured the Sri Lankan state.

Conclusion

There can be no gainsaying that politicking rooted in ethnonationalism, the ensuing civil war, and the authoritarian predilections of leaders like Jayewardene and Mahinda Rajapaksa combined to undermine liberal democracy in Sri Lanka. None who worked closely with Gotabaya Rajapaksa associates him with pro-democracy either. Hitherto all Sri Lankan leaders matured politically within a parliamentary setting and the realization that parliament alone confers legitimacy forced them to seek the body's imprimatur even when enacting opportunistic legislation. Gotabaya Rajapaksa has little experience and regard for parliamentary procedures and niceties.

Prior to becoming president, Gotabaya Rajapaksa's service and career within government was military related; and while defense secretary he was known to disregard norms and rules associated with democratic governance. He promoted himself as a disciplinary nationalist technocrat while defense secretary, and it is that reputation that led Sinhalese Buddhists to vote for him. It is indeed instructive that a prominent Buddhist monk who pronounced blessings on Gotabaya Rajapaksa when he contemplated running for president said "Some people have described you as a Hitler. Be a Hitler. Go with the military and take the leadership of this country" (Sri Lanka Brief 2018). His decision-making since becoming president clearly indicates that he is likely to be more authoritarian than his predecessors. This will especially be the case once his brother Prime Minister Mahinda Rajapaksa leaves the political scene.

And the long-term challenges stemming from COVID-19 will provide sufficient "exceptional" justifications for ruling autocratically.

Countries that have experienced democracy are more likely to want to change the regime than change the system. Even where autocracies have come to power amidst popular support (Pakistan is a case in point), people quickly sour on the autocrats. Consequently, the clamor to appear democratic is arguably stronger than ever. This normative power associated with democracy is a big reason illiberal leaders prefer hybrid regimes to full-fledged autocracy (Mechkova, Luhrmann, and Lindberg 2017, 168; Luhrmann and Lindberg 2019).

Hybrid regimes can endure for lengthy periods (Ottaway 2003; Levitsky and Way 2010), but elections can dethrone autocratic leaders and reverse autocratization (Lindberg 2006; Carothers 2018). This is partly because autocratic populists like Gotabaya Rajapaksa are good at selling quick solutions to extant crises yet fail to solve problems upon gaining power. Thus, even flawed elections are better than no elections, because they provide a disgusted populace the chance to change leaders causing democratic erosion. In short, elections can produce autocrats, but elections also oust autocratic regimes. Sri Lanka did prove this when it ousted a seemingly unconquerable Mahinda Rajapaksa from power in 2015.

Furthermore, the longer a country has enjoyed the franchise, the harder it may be for a despot to get rid of it. As noted earlier, Sri Lankans have had universal franchise since 1931. While this combined with ethnoreligious nationalism undermined the potential for liberal democracy, it nevertheless created a culture that values the right to vote. As per the 2018 Values and Attitudes Survey, 74 percent of Sri Lankans prefer democracy over other forms of governance (Center for Policy Alternative 2019, 36). This figure is high, and it is way above the 66 percent threshold used to determine democratic consolidation status (Diamond 1999, 68–9). Only time will tell whether this appreciation will remain or if heightened ethnonationalism and the allure of strongman rule will cement autocratization.

Bibliography

Alizada, N., R. Cole, L. Gastaldi, S. Grahn, S. Hellmeier, P. Kolvani, J. Lachapelle, A. Lührmann, S. F. Maerz, S. Pillai, and S. I. Lindberg. (2021) *Autocratization turns viral. Democracy report 2021.* University of Gothenburg: V-Dem Institute.

Bermeo, N. (2016) "On democratic backsliding," *Journal of Democracy*, 27(1), pp. 5–19

Carothers, T. (2018) "The surprising instability of competitive authoritarianism," *Journal of Democracy*, 29(4), pp. 129–35.

Center for Policy Alternatives. (2019) *Values and attitudes survey on 70 years of independence in Sri Lanka.* Colombo: Center for Policy Alternatives.

Chu, Y., K. Huang, M. Lagos, and R. Mattes. (2020) "A lost decade for third wave democracies," *Journal of Democracy*, 31(2), pp. 166–81.

Department of Census and Statistics Sri Lanka. (2011) "Sri Lanka census of population and housing 2011." Available at: www.statistics.gov.lk/PopHouSat/CPH2011/index.php?fileName=pop43&gp= Activities&tpl=3.

DeVotta, N. (2021a) "Sri Lanka: The return to ethnocracy," *Journal of Democracy* 32(1), pp. 96–110.

DeVotta, N. (2021b) "The genesis, consolidation, and consequences of Sinhalese Buddhist nationalism,". In Rouhana N. N., and N. Shalhoub-Kevorkian (eds.) *When politics are sacralized: Comparative perspectives on religious claims and nationalism.* Cambridge: Cambridge University Press, pp. 187–212.

DeVotta, N. (2019) "Island of violence: Sinhalese Buddhist majoritarianism and ethno-religious conflict in Sri Lanka,". In Riaz A., Z. Nasreen, and F. Zaman (eds.) *Political violence in South Asia.* London/ New York: Routledge, pp. 167–81.

DeVotta, N. (2018) "Religious intolerance in post-civil war Sri Lanka," *Asian Affairs* 49(2), pp. 278–300.

DeVotta, N. (2016) "A win for democracy in Sri Lanka," *Journal of Democracy* 27(1), pp. 152–66.

DeVotta, N. (2007) *Sinhalese Buddhist nationalist ideology: Implications for politics and conflict resolution in Sri Lanka.* Policy Studies 40. Washington D.C.: East-West Center.

DeVotta, N. (2004) *Blowback: linguistic nationalism, institutional decay, and ethnic conflict in Sri Lanka.* Stanford: Stanford University Press.

DeVotta, N. (2002) "Illiberalism and ethnic conflict in Sri Lanka," *Journal of Democracy* 13(1), pp. 84–98.

Diamond, L. (2019a) *Ill winds: Saving democracy from Russian rage, Chinese ambition, and American complacency.* New York: Penguin Press.

Diamond, L. (2019b) "Democracy demotion: How the freedom agenda fell apart," *Foreign Affairs* 98(4), pp. 17–25.

Diamond, L. (1999) *Developing democracy: Toward consolidation.* Baltimore: Johns Hopkins University Press.

Ericson, V. E. (2007) *Crime in an insecure world.* London: Polity Press.

Haniffa, F. (2017) "Merit economies in neoliberal times: Halal troubles in contemporary Sri Lanka,". In Rudnyckyj, D. and Osella, F. (eds.) *Religion and the morality of the market.* Cambridge: Cambridge University Press, pp. 116–37.

Harris, N. (1990) *National liberation.* London: I. B. Taurus.

Helf, G., J. Aplon, S. Ludeman, M. Silva, J. Schaller, L. Carter and N. DeVotta. (2015) *Democracy, human rights and governance assessment of Sri Lanka—updated report.* Washington: United States Agency for International Development.

Hewamanne, S. (2021) "Pandemic, lockdown and modern slavery among Sri Lanka's global assembly line workers," *Journal of International Women's Studies* 22(1), pp. 54–69.

Horowitz, D. (1993) "Democracy in divided societies," *Journal of Democracy* 4(4), pp. 18–38.

Howe, P. (2017) "Eroding norms and democratic consolidation," *Journal of Democracy* 28(4), pp. 15–29.

Huysmans, J. (2008) "The jargon of exception—on Schmitt, Agamben and the absence of political society," *International Political Sociology* 2(2), pp. 165–83.

Huysmans, J. (2006) *The politics of insecurity: Fear, migration and asylum in the EU.* London: Routledge.

Kasparov, G. and T. Halvorssen. (2017) "Why the rise of authoritarianism is a global catastrophe," *The Washington Post* (February 13). Available at: at www.washingtonpost.com/news/democracy-post/wp/2017/02/13/why-the-rise-of-authoritarianism-is-a-global-catastrophe/

Levitsky, S. and D. Ziblatt. (2018) *How democracies die.* London: Penguin Books.

Levitsky, S. and L. Way. (2010) *Competitive authoritarianism: Hybrid regimes after the Cold War.* New York: Cambridge University Press.

Lindberg, S. I. (2006) *Democracy and elections in Africa.* Baltimore: Johns Hopkins University Press.

Luhrmann, A. and S. I. Lindberg. (2019) "A third wave of autocratization is here: What is new about it?' *Democratization* 26(7), pp. 1095–113.

Mechkova, V., A. Lührmann, and S. I. Lindberg. (2017) "How much democratic backsliding?" *Journal of Democracy* 28(4), pp. 162–69.

Minority Rights Group International. (2014) "State of the world's minorities and indigenous peoples 2014 – Sri Lanka." (July 3). Available at: www.refworld.org/docid/53ba8dd310.html

Neal, A. W. (2006) "Foucault in Guantanamo: Towards the archeology of the exception," *Security Dialogue* 37(1), pp. 31–46.

Oberst, R. (1984) "Proportional representation and electoral system change in Sri Lanka,". In Manor, J. (ed.) *Sri Lanka in change and crisis.* London: Croom Helm, pp. 118–33.

Ottaway, M. (2003) *Democracy challenged: The rise of semi-authoritarianism.* Washington, D.C.: Carnegie Endowment for International Peace.

Repucci, S. (2020) "The leaderless struggle for democracy," *Journal of Democracy* 31(2), pp. 137–51.

Russett, B. (1993) *Grasping the democratic peace: Principles for a post-Cold War world.* Princeton: Princeton University Press.

Samarakone, P. (1984) "The conduct of the referendum,". In Manor, J. (ed.) *Sri Lanka in change and crisis.* London: Croom Helm, pp. 84–117.

Saroor, S. (2020) "From Aluthgama and post-Easter Sunday to COVID-19: Muslims again at the margins," *Common Views* (April 27). Available at: www.commonviews.org/from-aluthgama-and-post-easter-sunday-to-covid-19-muslims-again-at-the-margins/

Smooha, S. (2002) "The model of ethnic democracy: Israel as a Jewish and democratic state," *Nations and Nationalism* 8(4), pp. 475–503.

Simon, J. (2004) "Singing democracy: Music and politics in Jean-Jacques Rousseau's thought," *Journal of the History of Ideas* 65(3), pp. 433–54.

Sri Lanka Brief. (2018) "Top monk asks Sri Lanka's ex-defence chief to return as 'Hitler'" (June 21). Available at: https://srilankabrief.org/2018/06/top-monk-asks-sri-lankas-ex-defence-chief-to-return-as-hitler/

Tambiah, S. J. (1986) *Sri Lanka: Ethnic fratricide and the dismantling of democracy*. Chicago: University of Chicago Press.

The Economist. (2014) "What's gone wrong with democracy." (March 1), pp. 47–52.

The Economist. (2010) "Beating the drum." (November 18), p. 49.

The Island. (2020a) "Members of armed forces, police will hold positions in SLPP govts. – PM." (May 19). Available at: www.island.lk/index.php?page_cat=article-details&page=article-details&code_title=222470

The Island (2020b) "President vows to quit international outfits attacking SL unfairly." (May 20). Available at: www.island.lk/index.php?page_cat=article-details&page=article-details&code_title=222512

The Gazette of the Democratic Socialist Republic of Sri Lanka (2020). Available at: http://documents.gov.lk/files/egz/2020/6/2178-17_E.pdf

Uyangoda, J. (1994) "Ethnicity, nation and state formation in Sri Lanka: Antinomies of nation-building," *Pravada* 3, pp. 11–17.

Waldner, D. and E. Lust. (2018) "Unwelcome change: Coming to terms with democratic backsliding," *Annual Review of Political Science* 21, pp. 93–113.

Wilson, A. J. (1988) *The breakup of Sri Lanka: The Sinhalese-Tamil conflict*. Honolulu: University of Hawaii Press.

Wriggins, H. W. (1961) "Impediments to unity in new nations: The case of Ceylon," *American Political Science Review* 55(2), pp. 313–20.

25

AUTOCRATIZATION, BUDDHIST NATIONALIST EXTREMISM AND THE MUSLIM MINORITY IN SRI LANKA

Farah Mihlar

On 16 November 2019, nearly seven million people, or 52 per cent of registered voters, elected Gotabaya Rajapaksa as President of Sri Lanka. Only five years prior to this his brother Mahinda Rajapaksa had been voted out, with the people rejecting nearly a decade of the Rajapaksa family's authoritarian rule, corrupt politics and nepotism (DeVotta, 2021). Gotabaya Rajapaksa was the defence minister at the time and largely responsible, in 2009, for ending three decades of armed conflict by destroying the leadership of the Liberation Tigers of Tamil Eelam (LTTE), who had been battling Sri Lankan armed forces for a separate state for the country's ethnic Tamils. The Sri Lankan military's handling of the last stages of war has drawn acute international criticism, including by two United Nations investigations which found credible evidence of war crimes and crimes against humanity (UN, 2011; OHCHR, 2015). In 2019, the majority of the country's population democratically elected the central person responsible for these crimes to the presidency, fundamentally on the basis that a strong, fearless leader was needed to guarantee security, primarily for the majority Sinhala Buddhist community.

There was little doubt that Gotabaya Rajapaksa's presidency would result in an autocratic turn, visible signs of which emerged quite early. A review of his first year shows an increased, centralised role for the military, especially in dealing with the Covid-19 pandemic; executive powers were used without parliamentary oversight (Keenan, 2020a; Keenan, 2020b); and as soon as his party won a majority in parliamentary elections, he proceeded to appoint his brother Mahinda Rajapaksa as prime minister and swiftly introduced constitutional amendments to increase powers of the presidency (ICJ, 2020; CPA, 2020). Democratic decline was also witnessed through the loss of civic space, evidenced in the rapid decrease in public protests and civil resistance movements, such as those by family members of victims of enforced disappearance, whilst many civil society activists and journalists have resigned themselves to self-censorship, fearing a return of the violent repression targeted at them during the previous rule of the Rajapaksas (Fernando, 2020; Satkunanathan, 2020).

The shift towards autocratization analyzed in this chapter is not unprecedented; Sri Lanka's post-independence history is marked by waves of serious democratic decline, the most recent periods being in the late 1980s to early 1990s under the rule of President Ranasinghe Premadasa and 2005–2015 during Mahinda Rajapaksa's presidency. Autocratization in both these cases was

DOI: 10.4324/9781003042211-30

enabled and necessitated as a response to a threat to the state and the arbitrary use of vast powers were sought, in the form of emergency and national security regulations, to deal with this threat (Coomaraswamy and de los Reyes, 2004). Both processes of autocratization associated the threat with an 'enemy' that had to be countered with the use of extreme violence and military prowess resulting in gross human rights violations. Premadasa's defeat of the Marxist insurgency by the Janatha Vimukthi Peramuna and Mahinda Rajapaksa's of the LTTE's secessionism were both violent projects. Enacting mass atrocities then must also be considered a primary feature of autocratization in Sri Lanka.

This chapter assesses the return to autocratization in Sri Lanka and its effect on minorities, with specific focus on the country's second largest minority group, its nine percent Muslim population. Insufficient consideration is paid to the role of identity politics in the conceptualisation of autocratization (Lührmann and Lindberg, 2019); where for instance change occurs not only because of the weakening of democratic indicators but also, as in the Sri Lankan case, as a result of ethnocracy (DeVotta, 2021). This article takes the position that religion rather than ethnicity is now the dominant identity of the ruling elite in Sri Lanka. Both Rajapaksa brothers have supported and thrived on Buddhist nationalist extremism, an off-shoot of Sinhala Buddhist nationalism, more than any other head of state in independent Sri Lanka. In this chapter I will argue that such religio-nationalist extremism is fundamentally attached to this phase of autocratization, aligned on the ideology of Buddhist nationalism, which has as its objective the reinforcing of a Buddhist nation-state and thereby subjugating the religious other who is framed as a threat to reaching their common goal. The construction of a threat is the nucleus of the development of autocratization in Sri Lanka. For Gotabaya Rajapaksa this has a dual nature, because of his association to Buddhist extremism; a threat to state security and Buddhist nationalism.

I will begin by defining Sinhala Buddhist nationalist extremism and explain its relationship to autocratization. Critically engaging with Lewis's (2020: 21) 'friend, enemy' framing, this chapter will analyze the association of this latest autocratization to minority relations in Sri Lanka, specifically to the Muslim population. It will explain how, for autocratization to survive and flourish, Muslims are repetitively identified as a threat and dealt with as an enemy. The chapter concludes with an exploration of the effects of autocratization on the Muslim minority population and their response to it.

Autocratization and Buddhist extremism: conjoined twins

Sinhala Buddhist nationalism has co-existed with, utilised and exploited democratic politics in Sri Lanka since independence (Tambiah, 1986; Holt, 2016; Ismail 2005). Premised on identifying nationhood on ethnic and religious lines, Sinhala Buddhist nationalist groups have, over decades, engaged in parliamentary politics, influenced the executive and military and at times supported violence and resisted peace negotiations aimed at ending the armed conflict (Holt, 2016; Schonthal, 2016). Rampton (2011) contends that irrespective of 'elite instrumentality' Buddhist nationalism is 'deeply hegemonic' in the majority population.

The origins of the ethnic conflict in Sri Lanka lay in competing Tamil and Sinhalese nationalisms that later led to militancy and civil war. Through most of the civil war the state aligned with Sinhala, Buddhist nationalist ideology and forces, and the triumphant defeat of Tamil militancy and nationalism was a victory for both Buddhist extremists and autocracy, which manifested in image, policy and practice of the post-war state (DeVotta, 2018; Minority Rights Group, 2010).

The post-war Buddhist nationalist state was one where ethnic and religious minorities were not only oppressed but dehumanised and subjugated. As victory celebrations were held in the capital city Colombo marking the end of the war, over 300,000 Tamil war survivors were held in internment camps, separated from their families, physically and emotionally injured and facing daily violations such as extra-judicial killings, abductions and sexual assault (Minority Rights Group, 2010; UN, 2011). When the survivors were eventually released many of them were prohibited from returning home, they faced abject economic difficulties in the areas where they were resettled and were acutely insecure in the presence of the Sri Lankan military whose numbers had risen threefold in comparison to the civilian population (ICG, 2017). Most notably the violations they suffered, including allegations of war crimes and crimes against humanity, were repetitively denied as was their quest for truth, justice and accountability (ICG, 2017). As Mahinda Rajapaksa grew in power, distinctly authoritarian in rule, the Tamil population in the north and east were left defeated, dejected and dehumanised, which he used to muster credibility and support among Buddhist nationalist forces (DeVotta, 2013; UN OHCHR, 2013; ICG, 2013).

Lewis (2020: 22) using the work of German Jurist Carl Schmitt, illustrates how Mahinda Rajapaksa constructed a 'political community through the constant articulation of distinctions between "them" and "us," between "friend" and "enemy".' He explains how the Rajapaksa regime since 2005 repeatedly differentiated between the LTTE and Tamil community singling out the former 'as the existential public enemy' and thereby denying its legitimacy and representation of the Tamil community. This in effect also negated legitimate Tamil grievances of political and cultural autonomy that stood at the heart of the ethnic conflict (Lewis, 2020: 22).

I find Lewis's 'friend-enemy' model of political society useful with the caveat that despite Rajapaksa's framing, from very early on, in practice and policy 'the enemy' included the Tamil population of the north. The speeches that Lewis references in his analysis were made by Mahinda Rajapaksa when the Sri Lankan government was facing international allegations of war crimes and to redeem his government, making such a distinction was crucial. Lewis recognises that as the construction of this political community was based on Sinhala nationalist discourse rather than 'civic nationalism' it 'repeatedly foundered' and 'the discursive framing always permits the widening of this identification to include a much wider spectrum of possible enemies, both contemporary and historical, internal and external' (Lewis, 2020: 22). Rajapaksa's early rhetorical distinction between Tamils and terrorists enabled him to present his government as 'saving' the former whilst legitimately destroying the latter. However, as previously explained his degrading treatment of Tamil war survivors in the north, blatantly different from the superiority given to Sinhala Buddhists, suggested ambiguity in the boundaries of enmity. This shared anti-minority sentiment is critical to both Buddhist nationalist extremists and autocratization, which within an 'enemy' framework extends to damaging and defeating these groups.

Buddhist nationalist extremism referred to in this chapter is a derivative of Sinhala Buddhist nationalism with higher levels of extremism, violent tendencies and with a greater focus on religion over ethnicity. Arguably this level of extremism and virulence always existed but has gained greater legitimacy and opportunity after the war. Ethnicity and religion were intertwined in nationalism, but without the threat of further ethnic militancy the new strand has taken on more religious fervour. Either way, since 2009, Buddhist nationalist groups with strong extremist tendencies such as the Bodu Bala Sena (BBS) and Mahasen Balakaya strengthened and began to structurally target Muslims and evangelical Christians (Schonthal, 2016; Imtiyaz and Saleem, 2015). Through well-executed, systematic hate campaigns in mainstream and social media both religious groups were attacked; the former accused of attempting to take over the country through population growth and economic strength and the latter for proselytisation (Holt, 2016). In subsequent hate campaigns, attacks and violence against Muslims superseded those against evangelical Christians.

Resultantly, as Lewis (2020: 25) states 'the lines of enmity were reproduced to target Muslims' constructing them as I have stated in my previous work as the 'new enemy' (Mihlar, 2018). Arson and violent attacks on Muslim business establishments started soon after the war and progressed into serious incidents of mob violence led by Buddhist extremist groups between 2013 and 2019 recorded in central and southern Sri Lanka (Mihlar, 2018). Attacks against Muslims were partly premised on accusations that the group enjoyed special legal status as they, together with other religious and caste groups, are governed by personal laws, and receive excessive freedom of religious practice leading to Islamic extremism. The call for prayer from mosques, celebration of religious festivals, public display of religious symbols, dress code for women, marriage and inheritance laws, halal stipulations and slaughter of cattle for religious sacrifice became subjects of virulent criticism on a daily basis in the mainstream and social media (Mihlar, 2018).

The autocratic Rajapaksa regime made minimal effort to limit the hate campaigns and attacks and Buddhist nationalist groups were largely unhindered and, at times, encouraged (DeVotta, 2018). Previously powerful Muslim cabinet ministers and Members of Parliament were unable to wield influence and eventually Muslim religious and political leaders compromised on a number of aspects publicly and privately (Mihlar, 2019). Notable in this relationship between the then government and Buddhist extremists was the lack of protection to minorities offered by other organs of the state. The military and police notoriously delayed their response or failed to offer protection to Muslims on a number of occasions during the violent attacks (Mihlar, 2018). Muslim lawyers and activists have also complained of the lack of judicial recourse in lower courts as well as the country's Supreme Court tasked with hearing cases of fundamental rights violations (Mihlar, 2018).

When Mahinda Rajapaksa was defeated in 2015, Buddhist nationalist extremist groups lowered their profiles for a couple of years but structurally and organisationally remained intact to return when the coalition government weakened and the return of the Rajapaksas was imminent. The 2019 Easter Sunday attacks, when nine ISIS-inspired Muslim suicide bombers attacked Christian churches and Colombo hotels killing 270 people, was the turning point. Within hours of the bombings, hate campaigns accelerated and overnight the Muslim community came under siege through increased surveillance enabled by new national security laws (Satkunanathan, 2020). Religious establishments, madrasas and Islamic pedagogical centres were the main source of tension, many having to close (Satkunanathan, 2020). In May, 2019, the country saw one of the worst religiously targeted incidents of violence as mobs, with police and army complicity, went on a rampage in the north-west of the country damaging, burning and vandalising mosques and Muslim neighbourhoods (Bastian, 2019; Mihlar, 2019). In the same month then-President Maithripala Sirisena pardoned and released from prison the leader of the BBS, Galagoda Aththe Gnanasara, a move criticised by international human rights organisations and one clearly meant to appease influential extremists in his majority Buddhist voter base (Bastian, 2019). Another consequence of the Easter Sunday attacks was the targeting of Muslim political leaders for their previous association with one of the bombers and a religious group linked to the attacks. A hunger strike initiated by a Buddhist monk, Athuraliye Rathana, in front of the historic Temple of the Tooth in Kandy, calling for the sacking of some Muslim ministers coupled with rising crowd mobilisation and public protests, led to the resignation of all nine Muslim ministers from their cabinet portfolios (Bastian and Marshal, 2019).

The Buddhist extremist violence which took place with some level of state complicity in 2019 presents a challenge to the thesis in this chapter as it occurred during the rule of a minority-friendly coalition government elected to reverse the democratic decline caused by their predecessors. Importantly, serious violations of minority rights and the minimal protection to Muslims were accorded during the rule of this coalition government, which was indeed incongruous given their reputation on this issue and their early policies in support of justice for war affected ethnic and religious groups. I would argue that there were two main reasons for this discrepancy. The first was that in the aftermath of the Easter Sunday attacks evidence pointed to an intelligence failure and a breakdown between the coalition as being responsible for failing to prevent the attack (ICG, 2019). Relations between President Sirisena and his Prime Minister Ranil Wickremasinghe were dysfunctional and Sirisena, aware of the threat to his rule and his increasing unpopularity, took these populist measures to attempt to win over the Buddhist majority voter base. The second argument I want to posit builds on the work of Singh (2014) who critiques most scholarly work for 'assumptions that central authority is definitive for authoritarian states.' Through research in Laos, Singh discusses 'ritual governance' where state-sponsored Buddhist rituals were used to maintain a coercive hierarchy. Though not through forms of religious rituals in previous research, I have found that power shifts that occurred in central government were not similarly reflected in the village structures (De Silva, Fonseka and Mihlar, 2019). In these peripheral political landscapes authoritarian power structures and what Glasius (2018) refers to as 'authoritarian practices' were difficult to dismantle and affiliation to autocrats continued to be periodically rekindled through patronage politics. A study in the villages bordering Sri Lanka's conflict zone found the structures, practices and relationships the Rajapaksas had in place remained and were latently active (De Silva, Fonseka and Mihlar, 2019).

The period of autocratization under the Rajapaksas was intimately associated with Buddhist nationalist extremism; governed by its ideology, supported by its forces and in turn fuelled by political and financial power from the centre (DeVotta, 2018). This was a symbiotic relationship as the protagonists were distinct but shared a common ideological basis of Buddhist nationalism and a mutually beneficial agenda, pursued where necessary through the use of violence. The Rajapaksas' politics taps into, thrives on and rekindles the 'deep hegemony' of Buddhist nationalism (Rampton, 2011) in the larger Buddhist population, most often together with, but when necessary independent of, Buddhist nationalist extremist groups. Both see Muslims as a threat to Buddhist nationalist objectives and have successfully constructed the minority group as an enemy of the Buddhist nation. Autocratization, however, requires a threat to the security of the state in addition to the commonly shared goal of Buddhist nationhood, which Muslims en masse were charged with following the Easter Sunday attacks.

Easter Sunday attacks – the aftermath

Buddhist extremist groups used the Easter Sunday bombings to validate their claims regarding Muslims and took the opportunity to galvanise and target Muslims more publicly. The threat of Islamic extremism, which was now seen as inseparable from Islam itself, was presented as a threat both to the security of the state and of the Buddhist nation and therefore had to be addressed. Meeting this purported new security threat and strengthening the Buddhist claim for nationhood required a different political leadership and when elections were called in late 2019 there was little doubt that the return of the Rajapaksas was imminent.

Gotabaya Rajapaksa and his party were elected on a majority Buddhist vote in the parliamentary elections of 2020 (DeVotta, 2021), significantly for the first time in the recent history of Sri

Lanka without the support of the minorities. Though some alliances with minority politicians were attempted in the run-up to both elections, both campaigns targeted and emerged victorious on the vote of the Buddhist majority. In a speech during his swearing in ceremony, President Gotabaya Rajapaksa acknowledged the lack of minority support for his victory, promised to provide state support to keep Sinhala and Buddhism at the helm of the country's culture but guaranteed the maintenance of religious and cultural identity of minority groups (Francis, 2019). Conspicuously he made this speech standing beside the statue of King Duttu Gemunu, considered to be one of Sri Lanka's greatest Buddhist monarchs for brutally defeating a South Indian Tamil ruler and under whose rule Buddhism flourished (Francis, 2019). A few months into his presidency, Gotabaya appointed a new committee to re-investigate the Easter Sunday bombings suggesting there was more evidence implicating Muslims with the terror threat.

Though this chapter classifies the autocratic tendencies of both Rajapaksa brothers as similar, as political rulers they have differences that need acknowledgement. Mahinda Rajapaksa has a far longer history of politics having served as a member of parliament since 1970. Even though his presidency was marked by a shift to autocracy and repression of political dissent and civil society during much of his own political career, particularly in opposition he was a left-wing campaigner for human rights, ironically one of the biggest critiques and opponents of Premadasa's authoritarianism. Gotabaya Rajapaksa on the other hand has a military background, spent part of his life in the United States and promotes capitalistic economic policies (DeVotta, 2021). Whilst Mahinda is considered more politically astute, works with and through networks of political actors at the local level and partakes in parliamentary politics; Gotabaya rules in a more centralised way with a small number of trusted individuals, in a regimental manner with the military enjoying more prominence. During his brother's presidency, Gotabaya Rajapaksa had a more significant role than Mahinda to play in the military onslaught that ended the war, in the gross violations of human rights and in supporting the ascendancy and dominance of Buddhist violent extremism (De Votta, 2021, 2018).

Forced cremation of Covid-19 dead

This chapter argues that the present shift to autocracy in Sri Lanka is conjoined with Buddhist nationalist extremism. In spite of differences between the autocratic regimes of Mahinda and Gotabaya Rajapaksa, they are both bound to Buddhist nationalist extremism with the current president seen to be more hard line (De Votta, 2018). Both autocratization and Buddhist nationalist extremism share the common agenda of consolidating Buddhist nationhood and the objective of giving Buddhism supremacy within the organs, culture and society of the nation-state. Consequentially, the autonomy and role within the state of other religious groups must be limited, especially when they are considered a threat to Buddhist nationhood.

To illustrate this point further, this chapter will analyze the case study of Gotabaya Rajapaksa's government's 2020 policy enabling only cremation as an option for disposal of Covid-19 dead bodies, which unexpectedly materialised through a change in regulation by the Ministry of Health when the first Muslim Covid-19 death was recorded on 1 April 2020 (Joint Civil Society Statement, 2021). The policy adversely affected Muslims for whom burial is a strict religious criteria (Saroor, 2021; Mihlar, 2021). Additionally, from April to December 2020, nearly half of the bodies cremated were those of Muslims, some of whom had not contracted the virus but were suspected of having done so (Saroor, 2021; Mihlar, 2021). World Health Organization guidelines stating that burial of Covid-19 dead poses no potential risk of spreading the virus were dismissed by government claims that Sri Lanka possesses a higher water table, increasing the risk of contamination. Pressure internationally from the likes of the

UN Resident Coordinator in Sri Lanka, the UN Special Rapporteur on Freedom of Religion or Belief and nationally from civil society and religious leaders calling for the policy to be revoked was disregarded (Joint Civil Society Statement, 2021). As Muslim victims rejected cremation, bodies were forcibly taken away from homes causing immense suffering to families and terrifying the rest of the community who feared the possibility of cremation (Saroor, 2021; Mihlar, 2021).

The forcible cremation policy is a pertinent and strong example of the return to autocracy. Not only was it pursued against international and national expert scientific advice, including from an 11-member task force of eminent virologists and microbiologists appointed by the Ministry of Health in December 2020, whose report was later denied (Mihlar, 2021), but Judicial and to a lesser extent legislative scrutiny of the policy was also limited. On 4 December 2020, the country's Supreme Court denied leave to proceed with a fundamental rights petition filed by 11 individuals claiming their constitutionally guaranteed right to freedom of religion was being violated by the policy. A civil resistance campaign of tying white cloths at crematoriums and public spaces following the forcible cremation of a 20-day-old baby, was disbanded by police and numerous civil society statements on the matter were ignored. Parliamentary scrutiny had some effect; repeated questioning of the procedure by a few opposition and minority members led to Prime Minister Mahinda Rajapaksa calling for the December expert review and eventually stating in parliament on 10 February 2021 that burial will be permitted. Gotabaya however remained silent on the matter, indicative of the dissimilar forms of autocratization pursued by the two brothers.

The eventual reversal of the policy came following a visit by Pakistan Prime Minister Imran Khan, whose visit was aimed at diverting Sri Lanka away from Indian influence towards that of China. Khan publicly invited Sri Lanka to join the China–Pakistan Economic Corridor (CPEC), whilst privately urging the Rajapaksas to do away with the forced cremation policy (newsin.asia, 2021). Khan's intervention came as international pressure on the Rajapaksas reached a critical point with Sri Lanka facing a new resolution at the United Nations Human Rights Council (UNHRC), following the expiry of the previous one calling for accountability for war time atrocities and reconciliation. Sri Lanka in 2015 supported this resolution but Gotabaya Rajapaksa had much earlier signalled he would withdraw support for it and the Rajapaksas needed to act swiftly to defuse rising anger by states belonging to the Organisation of Islamic Countries (OIC), most of whom have previously stood by Sri Lanka in the UNHRC. Irrespective of the external persuasion, the undermining of democratic structures and civil society in this particular case was palpable.

The initial resolve by the government to maintain a discriminatory policy, despite international pressure, was in line with its shared ideology and objective with Buddhist nationalist extremism (Mihlar, 2021). Campaigners working on this issue, interviewed by the author, have explained how representatives of Buddhist extremist groups have held that the policy of cremating Covid-19 dead aligned with their goal of one law for all Sri Lankans and in addition a few have claimed that Muslims could use Covid-19 dead bodies as biological weapons. Such comments and views originating from members and supporters of Buddhist extremist groups were also popularised on social media. Strikingly, however, towards the end of 2020, a few prominent monks, including the BBS leader, called on the government to reconsider their policy based on expert advice (lankanewsweb.net, 2020). This demonstrates that even though conjoined by a common aim as explained in this article, Buddhist nationalist extremism and autocracy can have auxiliary political interests that may diverge at different times, perhaps based on constituency demands. Such divergence is usually only temporary and often superficial. In this case too Prime Minister Rajapaksa, reportedly, only publicly announced the government's decision to allow burials after consulting Buddhist monks (newsinasia.com, 2021).

The policy of cremating all persons infected with and suspected of having Covid-19 provides an important case study in explaining the relationship between autocratization and Muslims. Gotabaya Rajapaksa was elected largely on the vote of the Buddhist majority to ensure the physical security of the Buddhist population and the protection of the Buddhist nation-state. Together with his Buddhist nationalist extremist allies he sees Muslims as an enemy, but for the purposes of strengthening autocratization he needs to additionally maintain a threat to the security of the state. The Easter Sunday attacks made this briefly possible, but in the absence of an organised enemy similar to the LTTE, Rajapaksa needed to maintain the perception of threat. The repeat investigations of the bombings in part were to achieve this and then the pandemic provided a new opportunity where Muslims, even in death, were construed as a threat to public health. The persistence of a threat calls for the defeat of the enemy through, for example, the vehement pursuit of the cremation policy which results in the intimidation of and damage to Muslims.

Gotabaya Rajapaksa's resolve even momentarily without the support of Buddhist extremists suggests not only that the goal of building a Buddhist nationalist state and supressing minorities is critical to autocracy, independent of its relationship to Buddhist violent extremism, but also that sustaining Muslims as the threat is vital for the survival of autocratization. Some have argued that rising frustration among Muslim youth over this policy may lead to extremism, validating claims of a threat and providing the autocrat with the credibility required to further oppress Muslims through more extreme measures (Economynext, 2021). This last factor augments the argument made in this chapter on autocratization using Muslims to maintain a sense of threat whilst simultaneously damaging them in order to be perceived as 'dealing with the enemy.'

The Muslim response

Forming conclusions of Muslims' response to this latest turn is difficult considering its full effects on the community are yet to be seen, hence this analysis is based on autocratization in Sri Lanka since 2009. Wachtel (2013) posits that marginalisation of minorities is more acute in democratic rather than authoritarian states in Central Asia; since authoritarian leaders are unelected they do not need to 'rally the majority population around ideas of the nation.' In the Sri Lankan case, as democratic processes were used to usher in the autocratic regime, the majority population was indeed rallied around the idea of electing a strong leader who can promote and protect the Buddhist nation. Autocratization in Sri Lanka closely resembles 'neopatrimonial authoritarianism' which uses systems of patronage to ensure and sustain loyalties through influential networks (Ilkhamov, 2007). This patronage politics sustained loyalty through the 2015–2020 change in government and manifests both at the central and local levels. The democratic process complicates this system of patronage which is accorded to both the head of government and the local MP; at times, especially in the case of minority politics, this can be competitive. The patronage that some stalwart Muslim MPs command exists irrespective of the MP's own political patronage; whichever political grouping the MP decides to align with. This results in the frequent creation and destruction of alliances based on disparate reasoning ranging from protection of the group to individual wealth accumulation.

Beyond using their vote to prevent autocratization, Muslims have publicly done little to challenge it. A few political and civil society activists and victim groups have been critical of the Rajapaksas' policies and practices, but often cautiously. During Mahinda Rajapaksa's rule some Muslim political and civil society representatives condemned the state's complicity with Buddhist nationalist extremism, especially when it resulted in violence. However, as I have previously discussed, Muslim community and religious leaders privately held that the community had not behaved as a minority group (Mihlar, 2019). These elites took deliberate measures to withdraw the externalisation of religious symbols and practices and hold back Muslim youth from retaliating to the religious violence. Their response was starkly submissive. On the issue of forced cremation there has been more public outcry by Muslim activists and commentators and few statements by political representatives, but here too their reaction can be described as subdued.

Fumagalli (2007) uses Gorenburg's (2003) definition of frames as 'interpretive schemes that condense and simplify a person's experience by selectively highlighting and encoding certain situations, objects, events and experiences' (2003:11) to explain the limited ethnic mobilisation in authoritarian regimes in Soviet-era central Asia. According to Fumagalli (2007: 568; 570) 'Frames do not emerge naturally, but are an essential tool used by political elites to mobilise or demobilise the broader community' and 'operate as the interface between background structural factors and the contingent choices of the elites.' Muslims in Sri Lanka as the second largest minority have always had to navigate between the two conflicting dominant ethnic groups – Tamils and Sinhalese. Muslim political elites have fought to establish an ethnic, religious identity distinct from these groups, but have also led the community to cooperate, particularly with the majority Sinhalese rulers. As Farzana Haniffa (2016) has stated, Muslims have held on to the reputation of being 'the good minority' unlike the Tamils who preferred secession. Muslim political and religious elites, in the face of religious violence, held fast onto this framing of shying away from resistance, avoiding confrontation and conflict. Following the Easter Sunday attacks violence and hate campaigns against Muslims increased, but Muslims were restrained, desperate to disown and isolate from the bombers and working with state forces, in spite of rising distrust due to the lack of protection, to cooperate and enable 'counter-extremism.' In my research in Kottarumulla, in the north-western province and Aluthgama in the south, Muslim youth have spoken in detail of their frustration and resentment with police and army who were complicit in the attacks stating that they were firmly restrained by community elders and religious leaders from responding.

The inhibited mobilisation of Muslims must be understood through this historical internal framing and the more recent external framing associating the group with extremism and terrorism. As the smaller minority Muslims have witnessed how extremism and terrorism among the larger minority, Tamils, was dealt with by the state, which will be avoided at all costs.

Conclusion

This chapter began by placing the current phase of autocratization in historical context and illustrated how such periods have emerged and developed based on elites leveraging a security threat to the state and mobilising popular sentiment to garner support so they can maintain their position. Previous autocratization, including the last which the current president was part of, was bolstered by dealing with such 'threats' with severity leading to mass atrocities. The chapter proceeds to argue that Sri Lanka's present shift to autocratization is conjoined with Buddhist nationalist extremism, sharing a common ideology and objective of congealing a Buddhist nation-state. This was also the case in the previous authoritarian turn, which Gotabaya Rajapaksa was integral to. Following the end of the armed conflict, Muslims were framed as the 'new enemy' posing a threat to both the physical security of the majority and the objective of achieving a Buddhist nation-state.

Utilising the case study of the government's April 2020 policy to permit only the cremation of Covid-19 dead, this article explains the relationship between Muslims and autocratization as one where the latter is maintained as a threat and attacked as an enemy. This subjugation of Muslims, which occurs even without the support of Buddhist nationalist extremism, indicates that consolidating the Buddhist nation-state and oppressing minorities is an independent goal of autocracy. The nature of relations between Muslims and this phase of autocratization will not remain static. As other challenges to the rule of the autocrat emerge, Muslim political elites may be wooed; such use and disposal, as previous patterns have shown, is part of dealing with the enemy. Muslims are necessary for this present form of autocratization, hence they cannot be annihilated but subjugating them is critical for the survival of autocratization. This can be achieved through the production of perceived and real physical threat to Buddhists and through working with Buddhist extremist groups on hate campaigns and violent means to eradicate the threat to the objective of Buddhist nationhood. The prevalence and progression of autocratization in Sri Lanka thereby threatens not only democratic, liberal values but also minority protection and rights, which in the post-war context have serious implications for conflict prevention and reconciliation.

Bibliography

Bastian, D. (2019). Sri Lanka declares curfew after mobs target Muslims. New York Times. Available at: nytimes.com (last accessed 1 February 2021).

Bastian, D. and Marshal, M. (2019). All 9 of Sri Lanka's Muslim Ministers Resign. New York Times. Available at: nytimes.com (last accessed 1 February 2021).

Centre for Policy Alternatives. (2020). Statement on the 20th Amendment. Available at: cpalanka.org (last accessed 1 February 2021).

Coomaraswamy, R. and de Los Reyes, C. (2004). Rule by emergency: Sri Lanka's postcolonial constitutional experience. *International Journal of Constitutional Law*, 2 (2), pp. 272–295.

De Silva, M., Fonseka, N. and Mihlar, F. (2019). *The Forgotten Victims of War: A Border Villages Study*. Colombo: NTT.

DeVotta, N. (2013). Sri Lanka's shift to authoritarianism. Asia Bulletin, East West Centre. Available at: eastwestcenter.org (last accessed 1 February 2021).

DeVotta, N. (2018). Religious intolerance in post-civil war Sri Lanka. *Asian Affairs*, 49 (2), pp. 278–300.

DeVotta, N. (2021). Sri Lanka: The return to ethnocracy. *Journal of Democracy*, 32 (1), pp. 96–110.

Holt, J. (2016). *Buddhist Extremists and Muslim Minorities: Religious Conflict in Contemporary Sri Lanka*. New York: Oxford University Press.

Economynext. (2021). Muslim leader accuses Govt. of attempt to radicalise youth by denying burial. Economynext online. Available at: https://economynext.com/muslim-leader-accuses-govt-of-attempt-to-radicalise-youth-by-denying-burial-77677/ (last accessed 1 February 2021).

Fernando, R. (2020). The Roller Coaster ride of rights activist in Sri Lanka. Groundviews. Available at: https://groundviews.org/2020/12/10/the-roller-coaster-ride-of-a-rights-activist-in-sri-lanka/ (last accessed 1 February 2021).

Francis, K. (2019). Gotabhaya Rajapaksa sworn in as President. Associated Press online. Available at apnews.com (last accessed 1 February 2021).

Fumagalli, M. (2007). Framing ethnic minority mobilisation in Central Asia: The cases of Uzbeks in Kyrgyzstan and Tajikistan. *Europe-Asia Studies*, 59 (4), pp. 567–590.

Glasius, M. (2018). What authoritarianism is... and is not: A practice perspective. *International Affairs*, 94 (3), pp. 515–533.

Gorenburg, D.P. (2003). *Minority Ethnic Mobilisation in the Russian Federation*. Cambridge: Cambridge University Press.

Haniffa, F. (2016). Stories in the aftermath of Aluthgama. In *Buddhist Extremists and Muslim Minorities: Religious Conflict in Contemporary Sri Lanka*, edited by J. Holt, New York: Oxford University Press, pp. 164–192.

Ilkhamov, A. (2007). Neopatrimonialism, interest groups and patronage networks: The impasses of the governance system in Uzbekistan. *Central Asian Survey*, 26 (1), pp. 65–84.

Imtiyaz, A.R.M. and Mohamed-Saleem, A. (2015). Muslims in post-war Sri Lanka: Understanding Sinhala-Buddhist mobilization against them. *Asian Ethnicity*, 16 (2), pp. 186–202.

International Commission of Jurists. (2020). Sri Lanka's newly adopted 20th amendment is a blow to the law. ICJ online. Available at: www.icj.org/sri-lanka-newly-adopted-20th-amendment-to-the-constitution-is-blow-to-the-rule-of-law/ (last accessed 1 February 2021).

International Crisis Group. (2013). *Sri Lanka Authoritarian Turn: The need for international action*. Asia report: 243. Available at: https://www.crisisgroup.org/asia/south-asia/sri-lanka/sri-lanka-s-authoritarian-turn-need-international-action (last accessed 1 February 2021).

International Crisis Group. (2017). *Sri Lanka's Conflict-Affected Women: Dealing with the Legacy of War*. Asia Report: 289. Available at: https://www.crisisgroup.org/asia/south-asia/sri-lanka/289-sri-lankas-conflict-affected-women-dealing-legacy-war | Crisis Group (last accessed 25 January 2021).

International Crisis Group. (2019). *After Sri Lanka's Easter Bombings: Reducing Risks of Future Violence*. Asia Report: 302. Available at: https://www.crisisgroup.org/asia/south-asia/sri-lanka/302-after-sri-lankas-easter-bombings-reducing-risks-future-violence (last accessed 25 January 2021).

Ismail, Q. (2005). *Abiding by Sri Lanka: On Peace, Place, and Postcolonality*. Minnesota: University of Minnesota Press.

Joint Civil Society Statement on Forced Cremation. (2021). Available at: www.cpalanka.org/statement-on-forced-cremations/ (last accessed 1 February 2021)

Keenan, A, (2020a). Sri Lanka's parliamentary election: Landslide win for the Rajapaksa puts democracy and pluralism at risk. LSE blogs. Available at: https://blogs.lse.ac.uk/southasia/2020/08/12/sri-lankas-parliamentary-election-landslide-win-for-the-rajapaksa-puts-democracy-and-pluralism-at-risk/ | South Asia@LSE (last accessed 25 January 2021).

Keenan, A. (2020b). Sri Lanka's Other COVID-19 Crisis: Is Parliamentary Democracy at Risk? *International Crisis Group*. Available at: https://www.crisisgroup.org/asia/south-asia/sri-lanka/sri-lankas-other-covid-19-crisis-parliamentary-democracy-risk (last accessed 25 January 2021).

Lankanewsweb.net (2020). Burial is part of Muslim culture. It is their religious right - Gnanasara. Available at: www.lankanewsweb.net/66-special-news/74949-Burial-is-a-part-of-the-Muslim-culture--It-is-their-religious-right---Gnanasara-Thera?fbclid=IwAR3gPe2IKzVJjz_FyHiIjmJ3uXFv3yyXJygo-rJ8ZMFMZmSIM4R9np-rpns (last accessed 8 March 2021).

Lewis, D.G. (2020). Sri Lanka's Schmittian peace: Sovereignty, enmity and illiberal order. *Conflict, Security & Development*, 20 (1), pp. 15–37.

Lührmann, A. and Lindberg, S. (2019). A third wave of autocratization is here: What is new about it? *Democratization*, 26 (7), pp. 1095–1113.

Mihlar, F. (2018). *Coming out of the Margins: Justice and Reconciliation for Conflict-affected Muslims in Sri Lanka*. Colombo: International Centre for Ethnic Studies.

Mihlar, F. (2019). Religious change in a minority context: Transforming Islam in Sri Lanka. *Third World Quarterly*, 40 (12), pp. 2153–2169.

Mihlar, F. (2021). Forcible cremation is not about public health, it is racial discrimination. Financial Times Online. Available at: www.ft.lk/columns/Forcible-cremation-is-not-about-public-health-it-is-racial-discrimination/4-711633 (last accessed 5 February 2021).

Minority Rights Group (MRG) International. (2010). No war no peace: the denial of minority rights and justice in Sri Lanka. London: MRG. Available at: www.minorityrights.org/10458/reports/no-war-no-peace-the-denial-of-minority-rights-and-justice-in-sri-lanka.html (last accessed 1 February 2021).

Newsin.asia. 2021. Imran Khan adds new dimension to ties with Sri Lanka. Available at: https://newsin.asia/imran-khan-adds-new-dimensions-to-ties-with-sri-lanka/ (last accessed 2 March 2021).

Rampton, D. (2011). 'Deeper hegemony': the politics of Sinhala nationalist authenticity and the failures of power-sharing in Sri Lanka. *Commonwealth & Comparative Politics*, 49 (2), pp. 245–273.

Saroor, S. (2021). Dead body politics and racism: a prayer for 2021. Groundviews. Available at: https://groundviews.org/2020/12/31/dead-body-politics-and-racism-a-prayer-for-2021 (last accessed 25 January 2021).

Sathkunandan, A. (2020). Sri Lanka: Minority Rights within Shrinking Civic Space. South Asia Collective. Available at: https://minorityrights.org/publications/sac-report-2020/ (last accessed 25 January 2021).

Schonthal, B. (2016). Configurations of Buddhist Nationalism in Modern Sri Lanka. In *Buddhist Extremists and Muslim Minorities: Religious Conflict in Contemporary Sri Lanka*, edited by J. Holt, New York: Oxford University Press, pp. 97–118.

Singh, S. (2014). Religious resurgence, authoritarianism, and "ritual governance": "Baci" rituals, village meetings, and the developmental state in rural Laos. *The Journal of Asian Studies*, 73 (4), pp. 1059–1079.

Tambiah, S. (1986). *Sri Lanka: Ethnic Fratricide and the Dismantling of Democracy*. Chicago: University of Chicago Press.

United Nations. (2011). *Report of the UN Secretary General's Panel of Experts on Accountability in Sri Lanka*. New York: United Nations.

UN Office of the High Commissioner for Human Rights (OHCHR). (2013). Opening remarks by UN High Commissioner for Human Rights Navi Pillay at a press conference during her mission to Sri Lanka Colombo, 31 August 2013. OHCHR.org. Available at: www.ohchr.org/EN/NewsEvents/Pages/DisplayNews.aspx?NewsID=13673 (last accessed 5 February 2021).

UN Office of the High Commissioner for Human Rights (OHCHR). (2015). *Report on the OHCHR Investigation on Sri Lanka*. Geneva: OHCHR.

Wachtel, A. B. (2013). Kyrgyzstan between democratization and ethnic intolerance. *Nationalities Papers*, 41 (6), pp. 971–986, http://dx.doi.org/10.1080/00905992.2013.771160

26

GLOBAL WORKER PROTESTS AND TOOLS OF AUTOCRATIZATION IN SRI LANKA

Rendering them silent

Sandya Hewamanne

In May 2011, global assembly line workers in and around the Katunayake Free Trade Zone (FTZ) staged a massive political protest against a new pension scheme that sought to curtail their financial independence. The then government responded by ordering a police crackdown that resulted in one death and serious injuries to hundreds of workers (BBC 2011; Samaraweera 2011) It thereafter resorted to varied underhanded ways to silence political protests demanding justice. This chapter analyzes the 2011 protest and, utilizing follow up research conducted among female global factory workers in 2016 and in 2020, assesses how suppression of this protest affected subsequent collective organizing among FTZ workers. It argues that the apathy resulting from such silencing damaged workers' political voice just as much as physical violence and property destruction and influences more consolidation of state power. With the recent state response to the Covid-19 pandemic in mind, this chapter further showcases how the 2011 scenario affected the global worker political organizing in particular ways, and highlights how the increasing autocratization and strong man politics in Sri Lanka has been accentuated today.

Autocratization and means of suppressing discontent

According to Cassani and Tomini (2018), autocratization is a process of regimes' change toward autocracy. Such processes make the exercise of political power more arbitrary and restrict the space for public contestation, and political participation. These processes can manifest in many forms that are peculiar to social, economic, and cultural contexts where they unfold. Sometimes the strategies, tactics and tools of suppression work well with the social and cultural fabric of a given society, so that it becomes difficult for people to see that their democratic rights are being curtailed via these means. With the relative absence of appropriate conceptual and empirical tools to diagnose and compare these subtle processes, it is difficult even for academics to

DOI: 10.4324/9781003042211-31

discern them (Luhrmann and Lindberg 2019). This difficulty is exacerbated by the context of the specific intermingling of liberal and illiberal elements that leads to ambiguity as to whether a regime is autocratic or not. The ambiguities are further complicated by liberal enclaves such as universities, or women and youth movements, which have been able to flourish under highly illiberal and autocratic governments. In this context it becomes crucial to closely study situations where already existing repressive measures, and new and craftier measures exist hand in hand to suppress political voices. This chapter will study such a case in Sri Lanka to show how the government and its agents used payments, threats, fractioning and co-option, to render the protesting groups silent.

Throughout history varied forms of autocracy came to prominence and declined. According to Luhrmann and Lindberg (2019), a third wave of autocratization has been unfolding for quite some time. Studying all autocratization episodes since 1900, they show the divergent ways autocratization unfolds, but also how it always entails the gradual regressing of democratic values within formally democratic parameters. Many countries today are experiencing subtypes of authoritarianism, such as hybrid regimes (Levitsky and Way 2010) or soft authoritarianism (DeVotta 2010; Kamaludeen and Turner 2013). Another concept that is often used in Asian contexts is competitive authoritarianism. Within this type, regimes retain formal features of democracy such as elections and party competition. However, in day to day politics they do not meet the standards of democracy (Levitsky and Way 2002, 2010). Croissant and Haynes (2020, p 4) note 'democratic decoupling,' whereby some aspects of democracy improve while others diminish. For example, some societies display highly improved elections, while civil and political rights diminish. Many of these concepts are easily applicable to South Asian countries in fluid combination of features. Sri Lanka, especially, had seen rapid ups and downs in democratic values during the last decade (DeVotta 2020) and displayed varied combinations of the features of the above subtypes. Paul Staniland (2020) contends that there is a marked ascendancy of the state within South Asian countries. Showing how by 2020 major insurgencies have been squashed or co-opted by South Asian regimes, Staniland notes the ingenious ways the governments have established greater control of previously contested territories. These creative ways include new technologies of surveillance, and new forms of state and non-state coercion, especially localized mob, militias and vigilante groups. Contesting voices have consistently been incorporated via state tools for controlling dissenting voices. However, Staniland still sees discontent emerging within these conventional and new forms of state power. In the last two decades Sri Lanka has seen similar co-option and creative use of surveillance and coercion increasing especially during the two previous Rajapaksha regimes. The Sirisena–Wickramasinghe coalition which came to power in 2015 promised to reinstate democratic values, but unfortunately, they have not been that successful in fulfilling these promises. The current Ghotabaya Rajapaksha regime confronted the global pandemic decisively with the use of the military in maintaining curfew and lockdown and managing quarantine centres. The heavy use of the military has accelerated the re-autocratization process even as contesting voices ebbed and flowed.

In fact, the Covid-19 pandemic is accelerating the autocratization in Asia. Leaders of many countries have used the pandemic as a pretext to increase their power. Writing about Southeast Asia, Lorch and Sombatpoonsiri (2020) identify five trends emerging as a result of the pandemic. These include tougher government restrictions on civil society organizations, contentious civil society action, new mutual aid initiatives, organized relief efforts, and repurposed advocacy groups. These five trends are in fact apparent in different combinations in many South Asian countries, including Sri Lanka.

As Youngs (2020) notes, although at the outset the virus responses seem to also have galvanized big government and autocratic politics, they also sharpened and intensified the importance of organized civil society action. He contends that if civil society is to be able to block autocratization, politically organized civic groups will need to form alliances with welfare-based groups, which have organically grown within local communities and are focused only on improving community welfare.

At this time of the specific dynamics created by the global pandemic, why is it important to re-visit a global garment worker protest that happened in 2011? Because, as I show below, the way the then government suppressed the protest and the subsequent collective organizing has a bearing on how global garment workers are now responding to the pandemic related infringements on their individual human rights, and labour rights (Hewamanne 2021). After a discussion of research methods, I will focus on the 2011 garment worker protest to show the means of suppression and the long-term effects of that suppression.

Researching gendered protests and responses

Research for this chapter was based on three field work seasons, 2011, 2016, and 2020. I was fortunate to be in Sri Lanka within three days of the May 2011 global factory worker protests and thus was able to conduct a group interview with 12 workers who took part in the pro-test, including two workers who were injured in the brutal police suppression. Interviews with NGO and trade union officials also informed the research, especially on some of the less obvious ways in which the protest and follow up actions were suppressed. Photos, and mobile phone audio and video recordings made by the participants, were useful as well. In addition, the newspaper and TV reports of the protest and aftermath were used to compare and contrast as well as to triangulate. I have also interviewed several former global factory workers, now residing in their villages, to get a more complete picture of the causes and consequences of the protest.

Five years later in 2016, I conducted follow-up research with the factory workers and NGO officials to see how the 2011 protest and the means of suppression have shaped the factory worker collective organizing, and NGO support and ideologies. In-depth interviews with workers who have participated in the protest in 2011 (3), new workers (10), and NGO officials (3) were used to collect data.

The pandemic-related restrictions on worker rights during the second wave of the pan-demic highlighted the need to extend the research to explore how global workers approached collective organizing in response to the arbitrary impingement on their freedom and mobility. This research utilized quite different methods for data collection than my earlier research. Just as livelihoods have been adversely affected by the pandemic, the research projects have also suffered setbacks. Universities have prohibited face to face research. Travelling for research, even on a private basis, has been next to impossible due to airport closures and quarantine requirements. As such the data was acquired via WhatsApp, Zoom, Skype, and phone interviews I conducted with six daily-hired workers, 11 home workers, three NGO officials, and one factory manager. Most of the crucial data was acquired through a Zoom focus group in which ten workers and two NGO staff members joined in from three locations.

During all three research seasons, I have considered the ethical issues carefully, and research questions were designed in association with NGO staff members and factory workers. Workers were informed of the research, and oral and written consent were obtained before the interviews and focus groups. Pseudonyms have been used in place of workers' names, and their village and factory names, to protect their privacy.

Protests, suppressions, and silences
"Don't kill our dowry"

On May 24 the global factory workers in and around the Katunayake FTZ stopped working, and got out of their factories to join the protest marches that spread outside their factory premises to the city streets. The protest was in opposition to the government's proposed private-sector pension scheme which sought to change the existing regulations regarding statutory welfare funds (BBC 2011). Under the existing labour law, FTZ workers can withdraw their Employees' Provident Fund (EPF) and Employees' Trust Fund (ETF) savings at the time they get married, provided they are able to produce a marriage certificate within three months of leaving the factory. The underlying idea was that the women would leave work to get married. Thus the EPF and ETF savings together with the factory gratuity payments as a lump sum would be what they would be taking to the new union; in other words their dowry. In fact, at the beginning of FTZs in Sri Lanka in 1978, and later when another government initiated the '500 global garment factories in 500 villages' programme, this stipulation was touted as 'young women earning their own dowry without being a burden to their poor parents.' Unsurprisingly, therefore, this lump sum came to be unofficially known as the FTZ dowry among the factory workers. Many rural women came to work in the FTZ with the hope of working for five years, and then obtaining these savings together with the factory gratuity payments when they left. Unlike in the beginning of the FTZ work in Sri Lanka, men are now welcome to join as machine operators due to the current labour shortages. Still, men are less than ten per cent of the total worker population and thus the savings are referred to as the dowry, especially when mentioned by or with regard to women workers.

The stipulation of having to present a marriage certificate within three months of leaving the factories to get the EPF/ETF savings galvanized the label of dowry. If the leaving workers missed this three-month window they could only withdraw these funds when they turned 55 years of age or in case of serious illness such as cancer, or as a housing loan. Thus many women hasten to somehow meet the requirement and obtain their savings and gratuity together at the time of leaving the factory. Many envisioned starting an income generating activity once they got married by using this lump sum. In fact research had shown that many have succeeded in utilizing the savings together with other micro- credit opportunities available in their villages to become successful local entrepreneurs (Hewamanne 2019; 2020). This success further strengthens the hopes of young village women waiting to work in the urban FTZs, and existing workers placed on obtaining the FTZ dowry.

The new bill proposed a pension scheme that would distribute these savings as a small monthly pension, after they turn 60. They will have to work ten years before they are to be entitled to this pension. As many women in the FTZs only work for five to six years they stand to lose their savings altogether. Moreover, the pension funds will be under the Central Bank and will charge 4 per cent (2 per cent from workers and 2 per cent from the employers) for maintenance. The monthly pension in fact is estimated to be only about 1,900 rupees ($US17.27) per month for the low-paid garment workers (Geekiyanage 2011).

Thus it was no surprise that one of the more prominent and passionate protest cries in 2011 was "don't kill our dowry" (*davaddata kellinepa*). Female workers, especially, were furious about the new scheme, which they found economically disadvantageous to them. Not only was the bill crafted without consultation with workers, its hasty introduction took even the unions by surprise. Workers who were interviewed by the BBC (2011), Samaraweera (2011) and Geekiyanage (2011), all mentioned how inflation would reduce the value of their savings by the time they turn 55. I arrived on the island on May 28 and was able to participate in a meeting at Dabindu (an NGO working among FTZ workers), where 12 workers, some still sporting bruises from the police beatings, met with NGO officials to discuss future actions. I interviewed three of the injured workers (two female, and one male) in addition to group interviews with workers and NGO officials. One worker I interviewed explained,

> what I can get today as FTZ dowry, will not be enough to even buy a vada and a cup of tea by the time I turn 55. According to this bill, even then we will only get small monthly payments. There's no way I will support a bill that takes away the one good thing about FTZ work.

These interviews as well as newspaper reports, TV footage, and photos showed that the marches were characterized by emotional outbursts, angry shouting as well as tears. A photo of a large group of workers at the closed FTZ gates wailing showed their frustration about the bill as well as other impingements on their rights. About 70 per cent of FTZ factories had to be shut down due to walkouts. The second day of protests, police brutality was used to break the marches. This resulted in the death of one worker and injuries to more than 100 other workers. The footage of the police brutality on mainstream media shocked the general public, and the next day the police were called back and confined to their barracks. Instead, the military was deployed to keep the peace. Now incensed by the sad loss of one of their comrades, the workers were even more emotional, angry and confrontational. Video footage and photos showed workers, mostly women, challenging military men who held heavy weaponry. They also evidenced that the soldiers showed remarkable patience by not reacting, yet holding the women off from restricted areas.

Although the walkout and loud marches seemed spontaneous, after the death of a worker, Roshane Shanaka, the protest shifted gear to focus on police brutality and the suppression of worker rights. Many trade unions, ones that have been working among the FTZ workers, as well as national unions, joined the marches. According to Chamila Thushari of Dabindu, the protest became much more organized and structured (Thushari 2011). Workers and unions were especially vocal in the days leading up to the funeral, and their banners loudly proclaimed, "Rest in Peace EPF/ETF and Gratuity." Specially designed black hats with EPF/ETF embossed on them were also distributed. Both of these underlined how important this lump sum payment was for the mostly female worker population, and that for the first time in the FTZs' history, the conventional unions were taking a gendered cause as a valid labour right concern. Workers were asked to come clad in white, the traditional mourning colours, and wearing the special black hats, to the funeral. The intention was to make the funeral a space for respectful protest. It was expected that the funeral procession would include shouting of slogans, and display of banners. The published time for the funeral was 4 p.m., and workers started lining up near the slain worker's house from 3 p.m. They were outraged to hear that at 2 p.m. the military took the coffin to the cemetery for burial, thus pulling the rug from under the union plans for an emotionally charged protest that was sure to receive much media exposure.

By this time, the government had already announced that they were retracting the bill for the pension scheme. In other words, the workers had won their demands. However, not many were feeling jubilant. They were stunned by what happened at the funeral and the sudden silence that overcame the topic of the death of a protesting worker. Many days after the death, minor rallies happened (100–200 and steadily declining) outside the FTZ gates to demand justice for Roshane Shanaka. His mother and family members were vocal participants of these gatherings. Family presence was a tremendous emotional boost to the gathered workers, as they held posters and pumped their fists while shouting slogans. A few days after the hijacked funeral, the mother and family members of the victim stopped coming to these rallies, and talking to NGO and union members. Around the same time the TV and newspapers published footage and photos of Shanaka's mother and brother visiting President Mahinda Rajapaksha in his official residence and receiving condolences and a compensation cheque. It was unclear how much money was given to them, but the popular belief among workers was that it was 25 million rupees (approximately US$ 227,000). Apparently, it had come with a gag order, as the family members completely cut themselves off from all activities related to the incident. The gatherings continued for a couple more weeks, but with the absence of the victim's mother, they lost their emotional anchor, and soon dwindled to just a few NGO and union protester(s).

The NGO activists I talked to were convinced that the Rajapaksha government, which was showing autocratic tendencies in several other political and judicial spheres, had deliberately undercut the burgeoning worker movement. Even though it started as a protest against the pension scheme, it evolved into a protest that was about many other important issues of worker rights and their livelihoods. Both the NGO activists and the workers I interviewed claimed that the unions had been bribed or threatened to undercut the movement. Their frustrations were mostly placed on one particular union. During the apex of the protest, workers showed animosity toward the leaders of this union for abandoning them when they most needed support. It stemmed from the last minute cancellation of a walkout called by a union collective just a day before workers defied the union and walked out on May 26 (Geekiyanage 2011). Within a week of the funeral, the national unions lost interest or deliberately cut ties with the FTZ worker protests.

An NGO official, whose name will be withheld to prevent any repercussions, said in an interview conducted in June 2011:

> This could have been the beginning of a very good movement, starting with the dowry, but then moving onto protesting against government corruption, high cost of living, and trampling on people's rights. But this government used bribery, threats, and military power to scare or buy off important stake holders. It is so cunningly done, that on one hand it seems like we won, but in the long run we have truly lost.

"This government had scared the hell out of union leaders, now there's nobody to look after the interests of the injured workers who cannot go back to work for months. And some of us have been arrested and we have court cases pending. No one is helping with lawyer costs either," a worker who was injured in the police beating lamented. One of her knees and a shoulder were injured and she needed at least two more months of recuperating, before she could go back to work. She had already been fired from her current FTZ factory by mid-June 2011.

Most of the interviewees expressed frustrations that were part of broader narratives of critique against the Rajapaksha government. These included the widespread corruption, skyrocketing cost of living and the general fear of speaking up against the current government. This fear was expressed as "we will be disappeared via a white van." This was a reference to the reports of white vans, supposedly manned by government friendly para-military men, abducting journalists and others who dared to criticise the government. These abducted people would then just disappear without a trace. The disappearance of the journalist Pradeep Eknaligoda was mentioned as one reason why the workers now felt that neither the workers nor the union leaders wanted to take the spontaneously galvanized worker movement forward (see Perera 2016 for more information on Eknaligoda and other disappearances).

NGO activists as well as some news reports (Geekiyanage 2011) noted that the neighbours and general public who they have spoken to supported the worker protest. In 2011 my research was mainly focused on former global garment workers in their villages, and the women I interviewed in June and July of 2011 were very vocal in their support for the FTZ worker protest in Katunayake. They too were shocked by how quickly the protests ended, and how they did not achieve anything beyond the retracting of the bill. Some of the former workers utilized notions of karma and fate to explain the helplessness that came over the worker population after the protest's short-lived climax. "At the end the workers will always end up under-foot, and defeated," one said.

We are still silent

In 2016, I revisited the protest by conducting follow up interviews with the NGO activists and workers who have participated in the protests and new workers. NGO activists talked passion-ately about how the government deployed nefarious means to break the back of a grassroots uprising that could have led to much transformative politics. They were especially surprised by the way the government denied them a locally meaningful emotional protest over the workers' funeral and how the government managed to buy the silence of the slain workers' family. However, they were also convinced to a certain extent that this protest was the beginning of the end for the then Rajapaksha government. In late 2014 many anti-government, anti-corruption forces joined hands to forward a common candidate, a defector from the existing government, Maithripala Sirisena, to run against the seemingly unstoppable President Mahinda Rajapaksha in the presidential election. This candidate unified many discontented elements of society leading to Rajapaksha's defeat in January 2015. The new government was formed around the concept of good governance and in 2016, the NGO activists were still hopeful that their demands for strong worker rights would be addressed soon.

The workers, however, had forgotten that successful protest which allowed them to still enjoy the FTZ dowry. Even the workers who had participated in the protest now reminisced about it in a defeatist tone. "Actually I have forgotten about that. Because it was just like a soda bottle. We thought we won, but as always, we did not win," one worker said. When I reminded her that they forced the government to retract the bill, and hence at a basic level they won, she smiled slightly and said,

> True. I am glad we did it. But you know what happened with the funeral and Roshane's mother refusing to talk to any of the unions or workers. They were bought by the government. Even the unions were bought, because they kept asking us to go back to work.

Another worker who participated in the protest said, "I was fine with the police beatings. That made us stronger. It's sad Roshane died, but we became more united because of it. It's all the underhanded stuff that made me feel hopeless about ever getting any justice." Samudra, a worker who still has a pending court case arising from the protest, said he feels utterly let down by the unions.

Workers who had joined factories after the 2011 protests initially seemed unaware of the reasons, details or the consequences of the protest. Only after I had given much information did they remember hearing about it or seeing TV footage. Although all of them were very keen to obtain their FTZ dowry at the time they leave work, they have not thought much about the protest that thwarted a hasty attempt to take this away from them. Although none claimed that they feared consequences if they talked about the protest, such fear could have been a reason why they were reluctant to celebrate a protest against government policies. They were, instead, very vocal about the hopelessness of protesting and asking for more rights from FTZ factories. As Ruvini, a worker, said,

> these factories belong to foreigners, and they don't care about our rights. The government has no powers over these owners. So what's the point in asking the government to enforce labour laws? That is a way to lose these factories to other countries, and lose our own jobs.

Ruvini in fact was referring to the cascading global subcontracting system that subjects local workers to 'just in time production,' demands of the contemporary global production networks (Mezzadri 2014; Barrientos 2013; Hewamanne 2020). Transnational production comes with the threat of factories moving to countries with lower manufacturing costs at a moment's notice. If workers are unwilling to work overtime and meet unreasonable production targets and ask for wage rises that cut into the profits of the buyers (companies in affluent countries, mostly located in the West), they shift their orders to lower-cost countries (Hewamanne 2008). A constructed myth of the disposability of global factory workers (Wright 2006), and the actual precarity of livelihoods associated with global assembly lines make workers reluctant to agitate for their rights. Thus even without government's autocratic tendencies, police brutality and underhanded tactics, the global workers have reasons to feel hopeless about fighting for labour rights.

Since unionization is prohibited within FTZ factories, young women who come from rural areas do not have easy and fast ways of developing class consciousness or engaging in collective organizing. By the Board of Investment (BOI) Sri Lanka stipulation, labour concerns within FTZ factories are dealt with by an outfit called the Joint Council of workers (JOC), which is comprised of management representatives and workers. Men dominated JOCs especially in the beginning. Factories now encourage women workers to join these councils as that makes factories look good in the buyers' eyes. Most workers I interviewed felt that the JOCs discouraged collective organizing more than they encourage, as it works as a problem-solving mechanism and gives the impression that workers and managers are trying to achieve the same ends. With all these barriers to their collective organizing, workers, at least at the outset, seem to be waiting for the government and factories to present their rights on a platter rather than collectively organizing to achieve rights. In-depth interviews and focus groups conducted in 2016, however, highlighted how the fears and helplessness created by the previous government's extrajudicial actions in suppressing working class movements made them reticent in voicing their discontent, and fighting for rights. Again, the 'white van disappearances' were frequently mentioned as a reason for this reticence. All the interviewees mentioned how the government bought Roshane's family and the unions to explain their current apathy. "No one wants to be disappeared via a white van," four of them said. Although in 2016 the government was led by the Sirisena–Wickremasinghe duo who came into power promising good governance (improved democratic values), it was obvious that the previous government's suppression of dissent created long lasting fears among the global factory workers.

Conclusion

As noted earlier, rural women who start work as young as 17 do not have opportunities to easily develop class consciousness and engage in collective organizing due to the prohibition of unionizing within FTZ factories. Nevertheless, this did not prevent them from agitating for change within their own factories in a piecemeal fashion. 2011 marked a crucial point in which the workers showed that they were able to collectively organize on a common platform. However, although it was a successful protest, the government's crafty means (in addition to the familiar police beatings) to prevent the protest leading to a broader workers' movement had significant impact on the FTZ workers. It led to feelings of hopelessness with regard to changes, and an overall sense of betrayal by general trade unions. Since 2011 there has not been such a broadly organized agitation for rights among the FTZ workers. Even during the 2015–19 period, when the Sirisena–Wickremasinghe good-governance regime was in power, there were no collective protests within the global production sector, although the interviews clearly showed that there were several conditions at workplaces and in society that could have motivated protests.

Fast forward to the new Rajapaksha regime, when workers are still presented with appalling working conditions, they are more silent than ever. As of now in Sri Lanka, the NGOs in the area are mostly engaging in distribution of charity/humanitarian aid to workers. Many workers I interviewed lamented that they have become charity recipients when the only thing they want to do is to work hard and earn enough for themselves and their families. However, there is no collective action to highlight their plight or to agitate for positive changes. The recently introduced pandemic-related laws and regulations and the heavy involvement of the military and the police in enforcing these rules seem to have further impacted a worker population that was already at a disadvantage when it comes to collective organizing. The new Rajapaksha government seems to revel in the conducive conditions of the pandemic anxieties to further consolidate their power via non-democratic means.

Throughout history governments have used violence against their own citizenry. This has taken many forms—physical, psychological, and cultural. This chapter highlights that psychological and cultural violence can in fact be even more effective in making gendered working-class groups silent. Psychological and cultural tools such as appeals to patriarchal values and loyalties, bribery, threat of disappearance, factioning and co-option have definitely made subsequent groups of FTZ workers wary of collective protest. Even as sporadic resistance emerges and submerges within different sections of society, this case study thus points toward a general declining of democratic values in Sri Lanka which began in 2011, only two years after the war ended.

Bibliography

Ada Derana News (2021) 'Wild elephant management.' [online] Available at: www.youtube.com/watch?v=sFzvlxgRJO0 (Accessed: 19 January 2021).

Barrientos, S. (2013) 'Labour chains: Analysing the role of labour contractors in global production networks,' *Journal of Development Studies*, 49 (8), p. 1058–71.

BBC Sinhala.com (2011) Garment workers dead after police crackdown [online] Available at: www.bbc.com/sinhala/news/story/2011/06/110601_protest (Accessed: 20 December 2020).

Cameron, M. A. (2018) Making sense of competitive authoritarianism: Lessons from the Andes, Latin American Politics and Society, [online] Available at: DOI 10.1017/lap.2018.3 (Accessed: 22 December 2020).

Cassini, A. and Tomini, L. (2018) 'What autocratization is,' in Cassini, A. and L. Tomini (eds.) *Autocratization in post-Cold War Political Regimes*. London: Springer, pp. 15–35. Available at: DOI: 10.1007/978-3-030-03125-1_2.

Croissant, A. and J. Haynes (2020) 'Democratic Regression in Asia,' *Democratization* [online] Available at: DOI: https://doi.org/10.1080/13510347.2020.1851203 (Accessed: 22 December 2020).

Dabindu Collective. (2020a) NEXT strike [online] Available at: www.facebook.com/chamila.thushari.18/videos/387335592729044 (Accessed: 22 December 2020).

Dabindu Collective. (2020b) Oppressed lives within Corona [online] Available at: www.facebook.com/dabinducollective/photos/a.726924291023570/1271108439938483/ (Accessed: 22 December 2020).

DeVotta, N. (2010) 'From civil war to soft authoritarianism: Sri Lanka in comparative perspective,' *Global Change, Peace & Security*, 22 (3), pp. 331–43. DOI: 10.1080/14781158.2010.510268

DeVotta, N. (2020) 'Knocked down, getting back up: Sri Lanka's battered democracy,' *Global Asia*, 15, pp. 42–7.

Geekiyanage, N. (2011) Sri Lankan Free Trade Zone workers demonstrate against pension bill. World Socialist Website (WSWS). [online] Available at: www.wsws.org/en/articles/2011/05/sril-m28.html (Accessed: 12 January 2021).

Hewamanne, S. (2008) *Stitching Identities in a Free Trade Zone: Gender and Politics in Sri Lanka*. Philadelphia: University of Pennsylvania Press.

Hewamanne, S. (2019) 'From global workers to local entrepreneurs: Former global factory workers in rural Sri Lanka,' *Third World Quarterly*, 41 (3), pp. 547–64.

Hewamanne, S. (2020) *Re-Stitching Identities in Rural Sri Lanka: Neoliberalism, Gender and Politics of Contentment*. Philadelphia: University of Pennsylvania Press.

Hewamanne, S. (2021) 'Pandemic, lockdown and modern slavery among Sri Lanka's global assembly line workers,' *Journal of International Women's Studies*, 22 (1), pp. 54–69.

Kamaludeen, M. N. and B. S. Turner. (2013) 'Governing as gardening: reflections on soft authoritarianism in Singapore,' *Citizenship Studies*, 17 (3) pp. 339–52. DOI: 10.1080/13621025.2012.707005

Levitsky, S. and L. A. Way. (2002) 'The rise of competitive authoritarianism,' *Journal of Democracy*, 13 (2), pp. 51–65.

Levitsky, S. and L. A. Way. (2010) *Competitive Authoritarianism: Hybrid Regimes After the Cold War*. Cambridge: Cambridge University Press.

Lorch, J. and J. Sombatpoonsiri. (2020) Southeast Asia Between Autocratization and Democratic Resurgence [online] Available at: https://carnegieeurope.eu/2020/12/07/southeast-asia-between-autocratization-and-democratic-resurgence-pub-83139 (Accessed: 22 December 2020).

Luhrmann, A. and Lindberg, S. (2019) A third wave of autocratization is here: What is new about it? *Democratization*, 26 (3), pp. 1–19. DOI: 10.1080/13510347.2019.1582029

Mezzadri, A. (2014) 'Industrial garment clusters and CSR norms: Incompatible agendas at the bottom of the garment commodity chain,' *Oxford Development Studies*, 42, pp. 238–58.

Perera, A. (2016) Sri Lanka's missing thousands: one woman's six-year fight to find her husband, *Guardian* [online] Available at: www.theguardian.com/world/2016/jan/29/sri-lankas-missing-thousands-one-womans-six-year-fight-to-find-her-husband (Accessed: 16 January 2021).

Perera, A. (2020). Government's extreme measures to contain the garment factory outbreak put workers at a great disadvantage. [online] Available at: https://adnasia.org/2020/11/09/in-tatters-sri-lankas-excessive-pandemic response/?fbclid=IwAR1L5VRWA62WDVZe9rvIjI5312yp4lihybIas-bwKbebM0TdEHuk-82KEjk (Accessed: 15 December 2020).

Samaraweera, D. (2011) 'Sri Lanka: Factory workers stage pension protests.' Just-Style [online] Available at: www.just-style.com/news/factory-workers-stage-pension-protests_id111177.aspx. (Accessed: 12 January 2021)

Staniland, P. (2020) Political violence in South Asia: The triumph of the state? [online] Available at: https://carnegieendowment.org/2020/09/03/political-violence-in-south-asia-triumph-of-state-pub-82641 (Accessed: 22 December 2020).

Thushari, C. (2011) Interviewed by the author on 3 June 2011 in Katunayake, Sri Lanka.

Thushari, C. (2020a) Condemn the uncivilized media. Youtube clip [online] Available at: www.youtube.com/watch?v=Tb7d4fDAC6E&fbclid=IwAR2pltIabAdHuF_uPtj2aNWUKM_MYJtdnCPKUfGyk3L-o8F02CyDWt8URPE (Accessed: 15 December 2020).

Thushari, C. (2020b) Workers are treated like criminals and lepers. Youtube clip [online] Available at: www.facebook.com/progressivewomensc/videos/2745646225692122 (Accessed: 15 December 2020).

Wright, Melissa. (2006). *Disposable Women and Other Myths of Global Capitalism*. London: Routledge.

Youngs, R. (2020) How the coronavirus tests European democracy [online] Available at: https://carnegieeurope.eu/2020/06/23/how-coronavirus-tests-european-democracy-pub-82109 (Accessed: 15 December 2020).

27

MILITARIZATION AND IMPUNITY IN SRI LANKA

Øivind Fuglerud

In this chapter, I will review some political developments unfolding in Sri Lanka since the presidential election in November 2019 that brought Gotabaya Rajapaksa to power. Focusing on the increasingly important role in public administration given to officers of the armed forces, I will review these developments against the backdrop of the country's long history of systematic human rights violations and a context of politically endorsed impunity for such violations. I argue that the 2019 presidential election represents a change towards autocracy in that military circles close to the president, supported by an ideology of ethnic majoritarianism, now openly assert control over civil government functions by way of presidential authority delegated to them. Let me begin with a brief contextualizing snapshot:

On 14 May 2020, the Sri Lankan secretary of defence and the two chiefs of the Sri Lankan army and navy paid an official visit to two archaeological sites, Muhudu Maha Vihara and Digavapi, both old Buddhist temples. Two of the three men, secretary of defence general (Rtd.) Kamal Gunaratne and commander of the army general Shavendra Silva, are widely known to the public as incarnations of the military might that in 2009 crushed the Liberation Tigers of Tamil Eelam (LTTE) and tens of thousands of Tamil civilians with it (see UN 2011: 41, also OHCHR 2015). By international human rights organizations, they are pointed to as war criminals (ITJP and JfD 2020; HRW 2021). In the words of the prominent Sri Lankan political commentator Dr. Dayan Jayatilleka who watched the news item on TV, the dignitaries arrived in a

> long convoy of glossy black four-wheel drives coming down a dusty road with a heat haze shimmering in the background. Elite guards in red berets and body-armor, sunshades and carrying Heckler-and-Koch MP6s dismount, escorting the Bosses, also in shades, one in civvies and tie, the others in uniform.
>
> *(Jayatilleka 2020a)*

Both Muhudu Maha Vihara and Digavapi are located in the southern part of the Eastern Province where the three major ethnic communities in Sri Lanka – the Sinhalese, the Tamils, and the Muslims – live in close proximity and compete for resources. Access to the two sites and the use of the land surrounding them have for more than 60 years been contested by local ethnic communities, as indeed has the surrounding area in a more general sense (Manogaran

DOI: 10.4324/9781003042211-32

1994; Nuhman 2016). The visit came about due to complaints of Muslim destruction of temple ruins considered sacred by Sinhalese Buddhists, presented to the president himself by the leaders of the Buddhist order, the Sangha. Having supported Gotabaya Rajapaksa's election campaign, they presented the complaint during the first monthly meeting of the Buddhist Advisory Council established by the new president. In the second meeting, following the military leadership's excursion, the president decided to entrust the survey and preservation of archaeological sites in the Eastern Province to a presidential task force headed by the defence secretary. Despite the complex demography of the Eastern Province, all members of the task force appointed by the president are Sinhalese (Gazette Extraordinary No. 2178/17). The president also decided to establish a separate naval military sub-unit to maintain the security in the environs of the Muhudu Maha Vihara (Balachandran 2020).

Spokespersons for the Tamil and Muslim communities in Sri Lanka claim that consecutive governments for decades have used archaeological findings as a pretext to mark locations as Buddhist sites in order to promote 'Sinhalization' of areas traditionally dominated by minority settlements (Tamil Guardian 2020a; see also Oakland Institute 2021). One connection between the visit on 14 May 2020 and the theme of this chapter lies in the fact that the visit and the establishment of the naval unit to protect the Muhudu Maha Vihara shows that the military now has become a 'first responder' in civic disputes between the ethnic communities in the country (Jayatilleka 2020a). The message to the public conveyed by the media coverage of the event, and by giving the leadership of the presidential archaeological task force to the defence secretary, is that complaints brought forward by the Buddhist Advisory Council may now be rectified by military means. As pointed out by Jayatilleka, where one in a democratic country would expect the police to investigate complaints, or civil state institutions to find balanced solutions or settle disputed claims by the rule of law, the 'current official discourse assumes that the matter is open-and-shut, and that the military arm of the state shall intervene on one side' (Jayatilleka 2020a). Jayatilleka, Sri Lanka's permanent representative to the United Nations in Geneva at the war's end in 2009, former ambassador to France and Russia, has repeatedly warned against the recently elected president's 'openly Sinhala-Buddhist supremacist line' (Jayatilleka 2020b) and the possibility of 'a fanatical Sinhala-Buddhist military rule' led by him (Jayatilleka 2018).

A new role for the armed forces

Providing a more prominent position to the military has been on top of the political agenda of the new president, who was secretary of defence between 2005 and 2015. In his election manifesto (Rajapaksa undated [2019]: 13), Gotabaya Rajapaksa pointed to the fact that under the previous government, in power between 2015 and 2019, 'personnel in our intelligence agencies, armed forces and the police have been subjected to humiliation, victimization, intimidation and imprisonment, which has resulted in a collapse of morale', a situation he promised to rectify if elected. Similarly, his brother, prime minister Mahinda Rajapaksa, president from 2005 until 2015, has argued that 'members of the intelligence services were persecuted, harassed, and jailed by the previous government on false charges' (Times online 2019). The 'false charges' referred to are allegations of war crimes brought forward in several reports by the UN, but also allegations of corruption, torture, kidnappings and extrajudicial murders not directly related to the war.

The human rights situation in Sri Lanka in general and the conduct of the Sri Lankan army during the last phase of the civil war in particular, has been an issue in the UN's Human Rights Council since the war ended in 2009. In March 2014 the Human Rights Council requested the High Commissioner for Human Rights to 'undertake a comprehensive investigation into alleged serious violations and abuses of human rights and related crimes by both parties in Sri Lanka', and 'to establish the facts and circumstances of such alleged violations and of the crimes perpetrated with a view to avoiding impunity and ensuring accountability' (Human Rights Council 2014: 4). This request mandated the investigation resulting in the report from the Office of the High Commissioner for Human Rights Investigation on Sri Lanka (OISL, see OHCHR 2015), which was tabled in the Human Rights Council in 2015 and was followed by Human Rights Council Resolution 30/1 (Human Rights Council 2015). Mahinda Rajapaksa saw the fact that the joint SLFP – UNP government that came to power after he lost the presidential election to Maithripala Sirisena in 2015 supported Resolution 30/1 as a direct affront to himself and his government as victors in the war against the LTTE. Consequently, this support was soon withdrawn after his brother Gotabya Rajapaksa was elected president and appointed Mahinda prime minister. One central proposal in Resolution 30/1 was the establishment of 'a judicial mechanism … to investigate allegations of violations and abuses of human rights and violations of international humanitarian law' in which members 'of Commonwealth and other foreign judges, defence lawyers and authorized prosecutors and investigators' were to participate (Human Rights Council 2015: 4). Resolution 30/1 is cast as a follow-up to the OISL-report, which among its many observations concluded that:

> … there are reasonable grounds to believe the Sri Lankan security forces and para-military groups associated with them were implicated in unlawful killings carried out in a widespread manner against civilians and other protected persons during the period covered by OISL's report.
>
> *(OHCHR 2015: 219, para 1116)*

This is a very different version of what happened during the last phase of the civil war from Mahinda Rajapaksa's, who in 2010 claimed that Sri Lanka's military had won the war 'carrying a gun in one hand and the Declaration of Human Rights in the other' (Rajapaksa 2010).

During the first six to seven months of his presidency, Gotabaya Rajapaksa and his brother and appointed prime minister took a number of steps to provide the armed forces a new role in the governance of the country. One of their first political decisions was to establish a special presidential commission mandated to inquire into and collect information on investigative agencies falsely accusing public officers of criminal activities (Gazette Extraordinary No. 2157/44 & No. 2159/16). This 'Commission of Inquiry to Investigate Allegations of Political Victimization During the Period Commencing 08th January 2015 and Ending 16th November 2019' was given broad powers, and immediately used its authority to order the attorney general's department not to proceed with several cases against politicians and security personnel pending in court. After the commission delivered its report in three volumes in early 2021, the president established another presidential commission to implement the recommendations of the former (Gazette Extraordinary No. 2212/53). This commission is authorized to recommend the imposition of civic disability on persons found guilty of political victimization, thereby bypassing established judicial institutions and mechanisms (CPA 2021a). According to Sri Lanka's Imposition of Civic Disabilities (Special Provisions) Act, 'civic disability' disqualifies a person from voting at elections; from being a candidate at elections; for membership of any local authority; for membership of Parliament; and for employment as a public servant. If subject to the imposition of civic disability, a person would therefore also need to vacate his or her Parliamentary seat, leave any public position, or terminate employment as a public servant.

One case the commission on political victimization tried but failed to close down was the legal proceedings against fourteen naval officers for the abduction, torture, extortion and conspiracy to murder of eleven persons in 2008 and 2009, among them one child and six students. Among the 14 accused were one former chief of defence staff and one former commander of the navy and advisor to the president on national security. The victims, none of them with any record of terrorist activity, were allegedly kidnapped in Colombo for ransom, after which they were taken to the Trincomalee naval base where they were later murdered (for a presentation of the case, see ITJP 2019b). In this particular case, the attorney general withstood the pressure from the presidential commission and scheduled new court hearings. However, in June 2020 proceedings were stayed by the court of appeal, raising doubts about the political independence of the judiciary. In April 2021, the prime minister tabled a resolution in Parliament seeking the acquittal of the accused and withdrawal of the indictment, as well as recommending that investigators and witnesses are charged under the Penal Code and Bribery Act for fabricating evidence. If accepted by Parliament such a Resolution would mean overriding the judicial process, in violation of the principles of the separation of powers and the rule of law in a constitutional democracy (CPA 2021b). On 4 August 2021, the Sri Lankan Attorney General's Department decided not to proceed with charges against former Navy commander Wasantha Karannagoda in the case (Amnesty International 2021).

Sensing which way the wind was blowing, Inspector Nishanthi Silva in the Criminal Investigation Department (CID), who in the 2015 – 2019 interregnum investigated a number of high-profile cases involving members of the Rajapakasa regime and security personnel associated with them, soon after the presidential election fled the country, seeking asylum in Switzerland (Colombo Telegraph 2019). One of the cases in his portfolio had been the murder in 2009 of Lasantha Wickrematunge, founding editor of *The Sunday Leader* and influential critic of the Mahinda Rajapaksa government. When murdered, Wickrematunge's newspaper was digging into a case of corruption involving the then defence secretary, and, reportedly, CID officer Silva had in an open court hearing pointed to Gotabaya Rajapaksa as the person responsible for the murder (Chandraprema 2018). Following Silva's escape, the government removed the director of the CID who had backed the investigations, and relegated him to a menial job in the southern part of the country. He was later imprisoned, accused of fabricating evidence against a police officer who had worked closely with Gotabaya Rajapaksa during his time as defence secretary. This police officer was in 2015 sentenced to death for murder. The will of the new president to uphold his campaign pledge 'to release war heroes languishing in prison over false charges and cases' (Rajapaksa undated [2019]) was proven by his pardoning in March 2020 of former staff sergeant Sunil Ratnayake who was convicted in 2015 for the murder of eight Tamil civilians, including three children, in Mirusuvil in April 2000. The conviction of Ratnayake, which was upheld by the Supreme Court only a few months before the pardon, is one of the very few exceptions to full impunity for military personnel in Sri Lanka for whatever crimes committed against members of the minorities.

In terms of public administration, a large number of civilian government services were soon after the instatement of the new president brought under the control of the Ministry of Defence, including the National Media Centre, the Secretariat for Non-Governmental Organizations, and the Telecommunication Regulatory Authority. This was part of a larger centralizing operation concentrating power in the hands of the president and the prime minister (News First 2019). Between 25 January and 2 June 2020, the president established seven different presidential task forces, several of them led by military officers. Common to all are their broad and vague powers, and the fact that they circumvent the accountability of Sri Lanka's Parliamentary democracy by operating outside government ministries' normal chain of command. Several of the task forces' fields of responsibility overlap with that of civilian agencies.

Especially worrying was the establishment in June 2020 of the 'Presidential Task Force to build a Secure Country, Disciplined, Virtuous and Lawful Society' (Gazette Extraordinary No. 2178/18). This, like the archaeological task force mentioned above, is led by the secretary of defence. It includes among its members the commanders of the Sri Lanka army, navy and air force, chief of the National Intelligence Service, director of State Intelligence Service, and the directors of the army-, navy- and air force intelligence units. The task force has sweeping powers and reports directly to the president. It is mandated to take 'necessary immediate steps to curb the illegal activities of social groups which are violating the law which is emerging as harmful to the free and peaceful existence of society at present', and 'to investigate and issue directions as may be necessary' on all matters within its broad and vague mandate. A number of civil society organizations in Sri Lanka have questioned the legality of the task forces within the constitution of Sri Lanka (e.g. CPA 2020) and have construed the powers given to them as a step in the direction of authoritarianism and military dictatorship (Sri Lanka Campaign for Peace and Justice 2020; Friday Forum 2020).

In installing his military-dominated regime, the new president was helped by the Covid-19 pandemic. When the pandemic struck in March 2020, the president's response was to give the overall responsibility for fighting the disease to general Shavendra Silva, commander of the Sri Lankan Army. In preparation for a general election in April, the president dissolved Parliament with effect from 2 March. However, due to the pandemic, the election was postponed until 5 August, and the Parliament remained dissolved for five months, two more months than the constitution allows. This made organized opposition to presidential rule difficult. A full two months nation-wide 'corona-curfew' dampened political debate further. News agencies reported the official number of arrested for breaking the curfew to be more than 60,000 (Xinhua 2020; Tamil Guardian 2020b), providing rich opportunity also to clamp down on criticism. Thirty-two trade unions, press freedom organizations and civil society groups in a joint statement noted in April 2020 that 'it appears, under the guise of the suppression of Covid-19 epidemic the government is suppressing the right of people to express their views and their right to protest' (Sri Lanka Brief 2020). In a joint statement published in late July 2020, ten international human- and civil-rights organizations, including Amnesty International, Human Rights Watch and the International Commission of Jurists, pointed out that since the presidential election a campaign of fear has intensified. 'Dissident voices and critics of the current government, including lawyers, journalists, human rights defenders and victims of past abuses, are being targeted by the police, intelligence agencies and pro-government media', the statement noted (Amnesty International 2020a).

With effect from January 2021, the president appointed 25 military officers, a majority with combat experience from the last phase of the war, as 'chief coordinating officers' to all districts to manage operations to control the spread of the coronavirus (ITJP and JfD 2021). While at the time of writing, the picture is not clear, according to one source the authority of the chief coordinating officers extends well beyond Covid-19 and includes coordinating economic revival, poverty alleviation, disaster management, and even overseeing police operations (Lanka e-News 2021).

Militarization and disappearances

The new role of the military in Sri Lanka's political landscape and the sabotaging of judicial investigations of security personnel and politicians are recent additions to a much larger picture emerging over time. I will briefly discuss two aspects of this picture here, militarization and human rights violations:

Sri Lanka's social fabric has since the late 1970s been gradually transformed by a process of militarization in the sense described by Cyntia Enloe (2000: 291) as a 'step-by-step process by which something becomes controlled by, dependent on, or derives its value from the military as an institution or militaristic criteria'. Militarization is a multi-stranded socio-political process through which certain assumptions, values, and beliefs are rooted in society. Among the core ideas of militarism are the conceptions that armed force is the ultimate resolver of tensions, and that hierarchical relations and lines of command produce the most effective action.

One dimension of militarization in Sri Lanka is the securitization of territories and communities. Throughout the civil war, the Tamil population in the conflict-affected areas were presented as a threat to the state that could be dealt with only through military means. The extended use of emergency powers and anti-terrorism legislation to govern during difficult times, has led to a state of exception remaining even after the state of emergency ceased to exist (Satkunanathan 2015: 374–375). Several reports by international human rights organizations have told of continued surveillance, arbitrary arrests, and torture in the former war-zone long after the threat to the state represented by the LTTE was eradicated in 2009 (e.g. ITJP 2015; HRW 2018). In 2017, one study found that in Mullaithivu, the district where the last phase of the war was fought, there was, eight years after the war ended, at least one army soldier for every two civilian residents (Adayalaam Centre for Policy Research & PEARL 2017).

Another dimension of militarization consists of what Venugopal (2011) calls 'military fiscalism', in which state expenditure through the security apparatus has established a lifeline to impoverished and otherwise neglected rural areas. By the 1990s, the Sri Lankan army had become the single largest employer in the country, and that with a salary level of almost double what salaried private sector jobs pay. In the five districts focused on in Venugopal's analysis, more than half of Sinhala Buddhist men between 18 and 30 in cash employment work in some branch of the military. In many of the poorest villages, almost every household has at least one member with either a salary, a pension, or some other financial bond to the military. The political support mobilized through these linkages is one probable reason for the counter-intuitive rise in the number of soldiers recruited after the end of the war in 2009. According to World Bank data, the number of Sri Lankan armed forces personnel grew from 223,100 in 2009 to 317,000 in 2017 (Macrotrends 2020). With this rise in numbers has come the encroachment of the military into almost every corner of civilian life from the production and retail of food to tourism, philanthropic undertakings, and leadership training for school principals and university students.

Impunity for human rights violations committed by the country's security forces has plagued Sri Lanka for many decades (for a discussion of legal provisions see International Commission of Jurists 2012). Since the 1970s, international and domestic human- and civil-rights organizations have continuously reported on abductions and unlawful killings committed by members of the country's security apparatus and militias associated with them. Many of the victims were never found. In its preliminary observations at the conclusion of its visit to Sri Lanka in 2015, the UN Working Group on Enforced or Involuntary Disappearances observed that enforced disappearances have been used in Sri Lanka in a massive and systematic way. It also noted that both 'during and after the war enforced disappearances were even used for purely economic extortion purposes by some State officials and affiliated paramilitaries' (WGEID 2015). In 2016 the leader of the government's Office on National Unity and Reconciliation, former president Chandrika Bandaranaike Kumaratunga, acknowledged that Sri Lankan governments had received at least 65,000 complaints of disappearances since 1994 (Reuters 2016). Amnesty

International observes that Sri Lanka has one of the world's highest number of disappearances, 'with between 60,000 and 100,000 people vanishing since the late 1980s' (Amnesty International 2020b).

Impunity and alliances

Enforced disappearances and military impunity in Sri Lanka are outcomes of irregular or non-institutional alliances between politicians, the military, and non-state armed groups. Such alliances became particularly noticeable during the suppression of the Sinhalese Maoist movement Janatha Vimukthi Peramuna ('People's Liberation Front'), JVP for short. This movement, which developed independently of the armed Tamil groups in the northern and eastern parts of the country, staged two rebellions against the Sri Lankan state, the first in 1971 and the second from 1987 onwards. By the end of 1988, Sri Lanka's South was close to anarchy; roads were blocked, supply of electricity sabotaged, telephone lines cut, public services closed down. Then, from 1989, the security forces changed their strategy and increasingly fought JVP with their own brutal methods. Death squads with pompous names became part of everyday life: 'Black Cats', 'Yellow Cats', 'Eagles of the Central Highlands', 'People's Revolutionary Red Army' (PRRA); masked men in civilian clothes, cars without number plates passing unhindered through security checkpoints, bodies with signs of torture burning on the roadside.

Central to these groups were networks of soldiers and intelligence officers operating apart from the formal chain of command, many of them personally marked by JVP's violence. The exact number of persons killed during the second uprising is unknown. Amnesty International suggests 'perhaps 30,000', and mentions in its report that the government at the time attributed to the JVP a total of 6,517 killings between 1987 and mid-March 1990 (Amnesty International 1990: 13). Politicians judging the brutal methods necessary backed those on the frontline, sometimes with private grudges thrown in. Inside sources have claimed that planned liquidations of JVP-members and their families were based on lists drawn up by powerful politicians and local dignitaries, some of them using the opportunity to solve private disagreements and animosities (Amnesty International 1990). After the war against the JVP was won, the methods developed were put to use in the war against the LTTE, prominent among them the use of irregular armed groups coordinated by military officers.

For understanding the present-day situation in Sri Lanka, it is significant that the current president himself and several of his close military associates cut their teeth in the fight against the JVP in the late 1980s. Current secretary of defence Kamal Gunaratna and army commander Shavendra Silva both served under president Gotabaya Rajapaksa during his time as commander of the Gajaba Regiment. The Gajaba regiment's place of posting in 1989 was Matale, where Gotabaya Rajapaksa was the security-coordinating officer until the end of the JVP insurrection. In Matale a mass grave with the remains of at least 154 people with signs of torture was discovered in 2013, believed by local forensic experts to be victims of the government's fight against the JVP. However, before conclusive evidence could be collected, the investigation was taken away from the judiciary and handed over to a commission established by Gotabaya Rajapaksa's president brother Mahinda Rajapaksa. In 2015, the commission concluded that the findings were not related to the JVP period (see ITJP 2019a). The two mentioned officers serving under Gotabaya Rajapaksa in the Gajaba Regiment went on to become among the most central military commanders during the end-fight against the LTTE, both of them subsequently pointed to as suspected war criminals by international human rights organizations (ITJP and JfD 2020; HRW 2021). Instead of being investigated, they were after the conclusion of the war generously rewarded with military promotions and diplomatic or political postings, as were many of their colleagues also mentioned in the reports.

After the election of Mahinda Rajapaksa for president and the appointment of Gotabaya Rajapaksa as secretary of defence in 2005, the collective trauma left by the death squads of the late 1980s was reactivated. The phenomenon of 'white van abductions', the kidnapping by unknown groups travelling in unmarked white vans, commonly assumed to consist of operators with links to the armed forces, soon reached new heights. By September 2006, the human rights group University Teachers for Human Rights (UTHR (J)) reported between three and eight killings per day in Jaffna. 'Killer units of the state go about in white vans and with masks on motorcycles and are by now unconcerned about hiding their affiliations', they noted (UTHR (J) 2006). A new trait now was that many abductions took place in areas controlled by the government, including Colombo. Many of those made to disappear from these areas had no discernible links to the LTTE (Jeyaraj 2016).

Unsurprisingly, the exact nature of who and what when it comes to disappearances and unlawful killings is shrouded in darkness. What is known is that the rise in numbers occurred at the same time as the security forces, under Gotabaya Rajapaksa's leadership, were increasingly making use of the services of Tamil militants at war with the LTTE. This relationship between the armed forces and Tamil militias was as such not new. In the North, the militia of Eelam People's Democratic Party (EPDP), at odds with the LTTE from the beginning of the civil war, had had a working relationship with the military for a long time. Now, after breaking away from the LTTE in 2004 the remaining forces of LTTE's former commander in the Eastern Province, Vinayagamoorthy Muralitharan aka 'colonel' Karuna Amman, operating under the name of Tamil Makkal Viduthalai Pulikal (TMVP), became the 'running dogs' of the military intelligence (Jeyaraj 2016). The two militias of EPDP and TMVP now competed for the delivery of irregular military services to the army in the government-controlled part of the country. While initially commissioned to undermine LTTE's networks and influence, their activity soon degenerated into profit-seeking crime. International Crisis Group points out that the reliance on paramilitaries to fight the government's war while refusing to pay them for it blurred the lines between political and criminal violence (ICG 2007: 11). They also point to the existence of 'hybrid groups', military intelligence cadres and Tamil paramilitaries operating together, resulting in a dissolving of institutional command structures and lack of accountability. The UN OISL report (OHCHR 2015: 81–94, see also HRW 2007) confirms this general picture.

Seen against this backdrop accusations made by field marshal Sarath Fonseka, former commander of the Sri Lankan Army, are interesting. In 2017, he claimed that the former defence secretary – the current president – personally supervised all security and intelligence operations in and around Colombo through a separate chain of command made up of loyalists, bypassing the normal organizational structures of the three -armed forces and the police. 'It is through this group', Fonseka stated on TV, that 'the Rajapaksas put together a faction to plan high profile assaults, abductions and murders of media personalities and others, under the auspices of the targets being a threat to national security' (Sri Lanka Brief 2017). After coming back to power in 2019, the president and prime minister have not forgotten their old Tamil paramilitary associates. Douglas Devananda, leader of EPDP, is a cabinet minister; the ex-LTTE commander Karuna Amman was in October 2020 appointed as district coordinator of prime minister Mahinda Rajapaksa for Batticaloa and Ampara in the Eastern Province (*The Island* 2020). His former deputy, Sivanesathurai Chandrakanthan aka 'Pillayan', was elected to Parliament in the 2020 election while in remand prison suspected of murder. As the sole elected representative of TMVP Chandrakanthan is currently part of the president's 2/3 majority in Parliament. In January 2021, the murder case against him was dropped (Adaderana 2021).

As indicated above, there is a continuity in human rights violations in Sri Lanka from the suppression of the second JVP rebellion of the late 1980s until today, both in terms of methods and in terms of individual organizers in the security apparatus (ITJP and JfD 2020). Currently, many of these organizers are filling political positions around the president and the prime minister.

Concluding discussion

What is unfolding in Sri Lanka after the presidential election in November 2019 is a qualitatively new development in the direction of autocratic rule. What appears is a democratically backsliding state in the shape of a hybrid between 'the garrison society' (Dibble 1966–67) and 'the oligarchic-corporate state' (Kapferer 2005). Dibble's concept 'garrison society' emphasizes the coalescence of different social spheres under the dominance of the military; that is the social embeddedness of military force, rationality, and knowledge. Characteristic of a garrison society is a situation where institutions and elites holding military, economic, and political power have become dependent upon one another; in which their goals and interests are complementary (Dibble ibid.: 106). In Sri Lanka, this development comes with a twist. Through their personalized control over state functions, and their alliances with business interests and the armed forces, the Rajapaksa clan between 2005 and 2015 provided the Sri Lankan state formation an increasingly 'oligarchic-corporate' character (Kapferer 2005). What this label denotes is rule by a body, a corporation, organized on the basis of personal association, patterns of patronal distribution, and loyalty to a leading family, coming together to pursue common interests, in this case power and profit. With the two Rajapaksa brothers back in power, this development has now entered a new and more militarized phase, consolidating a foundation of personal political–military alliances for dynastic rule.

Following the August 2020 Parliamentary election, which provided their party SLPP and its allies a comfortable 2/3 majority, allowing them to pass in Parliament amendments to the constitution considerably strengthening the executive branch of government, the new cabinet that was established included president Gotabaya and prime minister Mahinda Rajapaksa's elder brother Chamal and Mahinda's eldest son Namal Rajapaksa. In July 2021 the younger brother of the president and the prime minister, Basil Rajapaksa, often considered the family's main strategist, was added to the list of cabinet ministers. Between them, the five family members currently hold nine ministerial posts, including minister of defence and minister of finance. Basil Rajapaksa also chairs the powerful Presidential Task Force for Economic Revival and Poverty Alleviation, bringing together under his authority a broad range of actors drawn from the sectors of public security, government regulation, banking, and private enterprise. Again, this task force reports directly to the president.

With universal franchise being implemented in 1931, Sri Lanka (Ceylon) is considered Asia's oldest democracy. While bruised and battered by two Maoist uprisings and a long civil war the democratic structure still stands, if only barely. To what extent it will survive the structural changes in governance ushered in by the post-2019 regime remains to be seen.

Bibliography

Adaderana. 2021. 'AG to drop murder case against Pillayan'. News item posted 11 January 2021. www.adaderana.lk/news.php?nid=70671, last accessed 10 January 2021.

Adayaalam Centre for Policy Research & PEARL. 2017. *Normalising the Abnormal: The Militarisation of Mullaitivu*. Report from Adayaalam Centre for Policy Research and People for Equality and Relief in Lanka. http://adayaalam.org/wp-content/uploads/2018/01/Normalising-the-Abnormal-The-Militarisation-of-Mullaitivu.pdf, last accessed 15 March 2021.

Amnesty International. 1990. *Sri Lanka. Extrajudicial executions, 'disappearances' and torture, 1987 to 1990.* AI Index: ASA 37/21/90.

Amnesty International. 2020a. 'Sri Lanka: Human Rights Under Attack. Lawyers, Human Rights Defenders and Journalists Arrested, Threatened, Intimidated'. Joint press release. www.amnesty.org/download/Documents/ASA3728022020ENGLISH.pdf, last accessed 9 September 2020.

Amnesty International. 2020b. *Enforced Disappearances. Sri Lanka.* Amnesty International, What we do. www.amnesty.org/en/what-we-do/disappearances/, last accessed 9 September 2020.

Amnesty International. 2021. 'Sri Lanka: Authorities falter on accountability in 'Navy 11' case'. Press release 4 August 2021. amnesty.org/en/latest/news/2021/08/sri-lanka-authorities-falter-on-accountability-in-navy-11-case/, last accessed 3 September 2021

Balachandran, P.K. 2020. 'Why Rajapaksa Has Brought Archaeology Preservation Under His Defence Secretary', *The Citizen* 26 May 2020. www.thecitizen.in/index.php/en/NewsDetail/index/6/18792/Why-Rajapaksa-Has-Brought-Archaeology-Preservation-Under-His-Defence-Secretary-, last accessed 27 May 2020.

Chandraprema, C. A. 2018. 'Quest to implicate Gota in Lasantha's murder'. Lankaweb, posted 17 March 2018. www.lankaweb.com/news/items/2018/03/17/quest-to-implicate-gota-in-lasanthas-murder/, last accessed 5 October 2020.

Colombo Telegraph. 2019. 'CID Inspector of Police Nishantha Silva has fled the country after receiving death threats, Colombo Telegraph can reveal'. News item posted 24 November 2019. www.colombotelegraph.com/index.php/nishantha-flees-country/, last accessed 15 March 2021

CPA. 2020. *The Appointment of the two presidential task forces.* Discussion Paper, Centre for Policy Alternatives. www.cpalanka.org/wp-content/uploads/2020/06/Commentary-Two-Task-Forces-CPA-Final.pdf, last accessed 17 June 2020.

CPA. 2021a. 'Initial Concerns with the Report of the Commission of Inquiry to Investigate Allegations of Political Victimization and Subsequent Action'. Press release 12 March 2021. www.cpalanka.org/initial-concerns-with-the-report-of-the-commission-of-inquiry-to-investigate-allegations-of-political-victimization-and-subsequent-action/, last accessed 15 March 2021.

CPA. 2021b. 'Short Note on the Resolution Seeking Parliamentary Approval to Implement the Recommendations of the CoI on Political Victimization'. Press release 19 April 2021. www.cpalanka.org/short-note-on-the-resolution-seeking-Parliamentary-approval-to-implement-the-recommendations-of-the-coi-on-political-victimization/, last accessed 7 May 2021.

Dibble, Vernon K. 1966–67. 'The Garrison Society'. *New University Thought*, Vol. 5, No. 1 & 2, pp. 106–115.

Enloe, Cyntia. 2000. *Maneuvers: The International Politics of Militarizing Women's Lives.* Berkeley, Los Angeles and London: University of California Press.

Friday Forum. 2020. 'The Rule of Law and Democratic Governance'. Media Release, 11 June 2020. https://srilankabrief.org/2020/06/sri-lanka-friday-forum-calls-on-all-democratic-forces-to-urge-the-president-to-withdraw-the-military-task-force/, last accessed 17 June 2020.

HRW. 2007. *Complicit in Crime – State Collusion in Abductions and Child Recruitment by the Karuna Group, Human Rights Watch*, Vol. 19, No. 1 (c), 2007.

HRW. 2018. *Locked Up Without Evidence Abuses under Sri Lanka's Prevention of Terrorism Act.* Human Rights Watch. Report published January 2018.

HRW. 2021. 'Sri Lanka's UN Efforts to Stave Off Justice for War Crimes'. Human Rights Watch Commentary by Brad Adams, Asia Director 3 February. www.hrw.org/news/2021/02/03/sri-lankas-un-efforts-stave-justice-war-crimes

Human Rights Council. 2014. 25/1. *Promoting reconciliation, accountability and human rights in Sri Lanka.* Resolution adopted by the Human Rights Council on 26 March 2014.

Human Rights Council. 2015. 30/1. *Promoting reconciliation, accountability and human rights in Sri Lanka.* Resolution adopted by the Human Rights Council on 1 October 2015.

ICG. 2007. *Sri Lanka's Human Rights Crisis.* International Crisis Group Asia Report No. 135. ICG.

International Commission of Jurists. 2012. *Authority without accountability: The crisis of impunity in Sri Lanka.* Geneva: ICJ. www.icj.org/sri-lanka-new-icj-report-documents-crisis-of-impunity/, last accessed 12 January 2021.

ITJP. 2015. *A Still Unfinished War: Sri Lanka's Survivors of Torture and Sexual Violence 2009–2015.* International Truth and Justice Project. https://itjpsl.com/assets/stoptorture_report_v4_online.pdf#english, last accessed 15 March 2021.

ITJP. 2019a. *Shavendra Silva Chief of Army Staff Sri Lanka. Dossier*. International Truth and Justice Project, 29 January 2019. https://itjpsl.com/assets/shavendra-Silva_-final-dossier.pdf, last accessed 4 July 2020.

ITJP. 2019b. *The Sri Lankan Navy. A Collective Blind Eye*. International Truth and Justice Project October 2019. https://itjpsl.com/assets/press/ITJP_navy_reportfinal-2-SINGLES.pdf, last accessed 6 October 2020.

ITJP and JfD. 2020. 'Continuing Crimes – Matale to Mullivaikkal'. International Truth and Justice Project and Journalists for Democracy in Sri Lanka Joint Press Release 14 December 2020. https://itjpsl.com/assets/press/Final-OMP-Press-release-4-December-2020-copy.pdf, last accessed 07 January 2021.

ITJP and JfD. 2021. 'Sri Lanka's COVID Military Overlords'. International Truth and Justice Project and Journalists for Democracy in Sri Lanka Joint Press Release 6 January 2021. https://itjpsl.com/assets/press/Final-ITJP-JDS-press-release-6-January-2021.pdf, last accessed 07 January 2021.

Jayatilleka, Dayan. 2018. 'End of Civility, Barracks: Model of Politics and Millennium's Children'. *Daily Mirror*, 18 July 2018. www.dailymirror.lk/article/END-OF-CIVILITY-BARRACKS-MODEL-OF-POLITICS-AND-MILLENNIUM-S-CHILDREN-152839.html, last accessed 12 January 2021.

Jayatilleka, Dayan. 2020a. 'Defence re-defined: The military as first resort'. *FT Daily*, Lanka Guardian Column, Thursday May 21. www.ft.lk/columns/Defence-re-defined-The-military-as-first-resort/4-700510, last accessed 28 May 2020.

Jayatilleka, Dayan. 2020b. 'MR 2020: Elections and legacy'. FT Daily, Lanka Guardian Column, Thursday 4 June. www.ft.lk/columns/MR-2020-Elections-and-legacy/4-701137, last accessed 9 June 2020.

Jeyaraj, D.B.S. 2016. '"White-Vanning Culture" and the Lucrative Industry of Abducting Tamils for Ransom'. DBSJeyaraj.com, posted 26 August 2016. http://dbsjeyaraj.com/dbsj/archives/47804, last accessed 5 October 2020

Kapferer, Bruce. 2005. 'Introduction: Oligarchic Corporations and New State Formations', *Social Analysis: The International Journal of Anthropology*, Vol. 49, No. 1 (Spring 2005), pp. 163–176.

Lanka e-News. 2021. 'The country is reaching a turning point in militarization..! Colonels above Government Agents..!' News item posted 3 January 2021. www.lankaenews.com/news/3315/en, last accessed 06 January 2021

Macrotrends. 2020. 'Sri Lanka Military Size 1985–2020'. www.macrotrends.net/countries/LKA/sri-lanka/military-army-size, last accessed 02 November 2020.

Manogaran, Chelvadurai. 1994. 'Colonization as Politics: Political Use of Space in Sri Lanka's Ethnic Conflict'. In Chelvadurai Manogaran and Bryan Pfaffenberger (eds.), *The Sri Lankan Tamils. Ethnicity and Identity*, pp. 84–125. New York: Routledge.

News First. 2019. 'Defence Ministry vested with key institutions including TRCSL, DMC and CERT'. News item posted 11 December 2019. www.newsfirst.lk/2019/12/11/defence-ministry-vested-with-key-institutions-including-trcsl-dmc-and-cert/, last accessed 15 March 2021.

Nuhman, M.A. 2016. 'Sinhala Buddhist Nationalism and Muslim Identity in Sri Lanka: One Hundred Years of Conflict and Coexistence'. In John Clifford Holt (ed.), *Buddhist Extremists and Muslim Minorities: Religious Conflict in Contemporary Sri Lanka*, pp. 18–53. Oxford: Oxford University Press.

Oakland Institute. 2021. *Endless War. The Destroyed Land, Life, and Identity of the Tamil People in Sri Lanka*. www.oaklandinstitute.org/tamils-sri-lanka-endless-war, last accessed 15 March 2021.

OHCHR. 2015. *Report of the OHCHR Investigation on Sri Lanka (OISL)*, Advance Version. A/HRC/30/CRP.2, United Nations High Commissioner for Human Rights.

Rajapaksa, Gotabaya. Undated [2019]. *Gotabaya presents to you a Reconstructed Country with a Future. Vistas of Prosperity and Splendour*. Election manifesto, publisher not provided.

Rajapaksae, Mahinda. 2010. *Our Armed Forces Battled Carrying Gun in One Hand and the Declaration of Human Rights the Other*. Full Text of President Mahinda Rajapaksae's Address at the 'Victory Day' Celebrations at Galle Face, Colombo, 18 June 2010. Transcurrents. http://transcurrents.com/tc/2010/06/our_armed_forces_battled_carry.html, last accessed 12 November 2011.

Reuters. 2016. 'Sri Lanka admits 65,000 missing from war, insurrection'. News item posted 8 June 2016. https://in.reuters.com/article/sri-lanka-rights/sri-lanka-admits-65000-missing-from-war-insurrection-idINKCN0YU277, last accessed 7 October 2020.

Satkunanathan, Ambika. 2015. 'The Executive and the Shadow State in Sri Lanka'. In A. Welikala (ed.), *Reforming Sri Lankan Presidentialism: Provenance, Problems and Prospects*, pp. 371–398. Colombo: Centre for Policy Alternatives.

Sri Lanka Brief. 2017. 'Sri Lanka: Probe Into Lasantha's Murder Takes A Twist'. https://srilankabrief.org/2017/01/sri-lanka-probe-into-lasanthas-murder-takes-a-twist/, last accessed 4 October 2020.

Sri Lanka Brief. 2020. 'Sri Lanka Brief Up Date – 16 April 2020. Covid-19 Pandemic & Freedom of Expression Rights'. https://srilankabrief.org/2020/04/sri-lanka-brief-up-date-16-april-2020-covid-19-pandemic-freedom-of-expression-rights/, last accessed 9 September 2020.

Sri Lanka Campaign for Peace and Justice. 2020. 'Sri Lanka's slide into authoritarianism', press release 10 June 2020. www.srilankacampaign.org/sri-lankas-slide-into-authoritarianism/, last accessed 18 June 2020.

Tamil Guardian. 2020a. 'All Sinhala task force for Sri Lanka's 'archaeology' in East'. News item posted 03 June 2020. www.tamilguardian.com/content/all-sinhala-task-force-sri-lanka%E2%80%99s-%E2%80%98archaeology%E2%80%99-east, last accessed 15 March 2021.

Tamil Guardian. 2020b. 'Over 60,000 arrested in Sri Lanka for violating COVID-19 curfew'. News item posted 23 May 2020. www.tamilguardian.com/content/over-60000-arrested-sri-lanka-violating-covid-19-curfew, last accessed 15 March 2021.

The Island. 2020. 'Karuna Amman appointed district coordinator of Prime Minister'. News item posted 15 October 2020. https://island.lk/karuna-amman-appointed-district-coordinator-of-prime-minister/, last accessed 11 January 2021.

Times online. 2019. 'PM Rajapaksa pledges to rectify injustices suffered by Armed forces under previous Govt'. News item posted 13 December 2019. www.sundaytimes.lk/article/1112134/pm-rajapaksa-pledges-to-rectify-injustices-suffered-by-armed-forces-under-previous-govt, last accessed 10 June 2020.

UN. 2011. *Report of the Secretary-General's Panel of Experts on Accountability in Sri Lanka.* 31 March 2011. www.securitycouncilreport.org/un-documents/document/poc-rep-on-account-in-sri-lanka.php, last accessed 25 February 2021.

University Teachers for Human Rights (Jaffna). 2006. *The Wider Implications of the Human Rights and Humanitarian Crisis in Jaffna.* UTHR(J) Information Bulletin no. 41, 14 September 2006.

Venugopal, R. 2011. 'The Politics of Market Reform at a Time of Civil War: Military Fiscalism in Sri Lanka'. *Economic and Political Weekly* 46 (49): 67–75.

WGEID. 2015. *Preliminary observations of the Working Group on Enforced or Involuntary Disappearances at the conclusion of its visit to Sri Lanka (9–18 November 2015).* www.ohchr.org/EN/NewsEvents/Pages/DisplayNews.aspx?NewsID=16771&LangID=E, last accessed 10 July 2020.

Xinhua. 2020. 'Over 60,000 arrested in Sri Lanka for violating COVID-19 curfew'. News item posted 20 May 2020. www.xinhuanet.com/english/2020-05/20/c_139072700.htm, last accessed 9 September 2020.

PART V

How to comprehend autocratization in South Asia

Three broad perspectives

28

AUTOCRATIZATION AND REGIME CONVERGENCE IN SOUTH ASIA – AN UNDETERMINED PATH

Sten Widmalm

The contributions in this book have shown that South Asia is currently one of the world's regions where the level of democracy is declining sharply. Although the Indian subcontinent and its surrounding states are difficult to delimit in relation to the rest of Asia, the trend concerns India, Pakistan, Afghanistan, Bangladesh, Nepal, and Sri Lanka. Should we include Myanmar the impression would only deepen. Evidently, all states in this region either find it very hard to make significant gains in democratization, or have been caught in a seemingly unstoppable trend of autocratization. Are there more general explanations for the poor democratic performance of South Asia in addition to the country-specific chapters that have been presented here?

It is a truism that democracy means little if there is no economic growth. However, the regime trajectories described in the four countries in focus in this book, Pakistan, India, Bangladesh and Sri Lanka, provide further support for the claim that economic growth is not guaranteed to be accompanied by liberal democratic freedom. Instead, the familiar (Polanyi 2001) argument has been made here that when unchecked, economic expansion can rip through societies and leave gaps and conflicts behind, that may in turn support autocratization. To some extent non-governmental organization can mend immediate needs. Still, in the long run a well-governed state that respects universal rights is necessary to balance the needs of the citizens and to bridge gaps in society to make democracy work.

More is provided in the accounts here that tell us something about how *perspectives* on democracy have changed fairly recently. If the autocratization trend we see now was only about economic redistribution and sustainable development, party politics could have evolved where the fight for the support of the voters would have been played out along a left–right spectrum – by competing with different policy strategies and within a democratic framework. However, a substantial share of the political parties in this region has been caught in the wave of populism which increasingly defines politics in the world today. This region of the world has undoubtedly seen its share of this political phenomenon long before the most recent populist wave (Chatterjee 2020). However, the proliferation and intensity of populism is now unprecedented. The core feature is to declare political opposition in any shape and form as illegitimate (Müller 2016). But this standpoint is not only a *cause* of autocratization, it is a *symptom* of it. There is even more to be said about why the populist agenda is gaining so much appeal than

DOI: 10.4324/9781003042211-34

what is brought forward in this book. However, political leaders have understood that there is a strong support for populists as well as politically intolerant views among voters (Widmalm and Oskarsson 2013). Since autocratization occurs in countries where elections are held, can we not draw the conclusion that the political leaders are even without guilt if they mainly listen to the voices of the people? When we try to understand the present conditions in this region, as well as in other parts of the world, there is one line of thought that immediately presents itself which connects to this argument that will be discussed in this chapter. The focus will be on deterministic perspectives on the decline of democracy which claim, expressed in a simplified way, that although democracy was an interesting and commendable project for a while, history finally lost its patience with it. Sentiments and incentives more deeply rooted than ideologies – which evidently political leaders themselves find hard to believe in – were destined to make a comeback. Eventually, culture, history, and economic forces, which always have had the strongest impact on how the world changes, would resurface and adjust development trajectories – no matter what political dramas that had played out at the centre stages of politics.

There are arguments located in deterministic perspectives that need to be taken seriously. Overlooking them would be a mistake. However, there is also a dangerous side to placing all the explanatory power on, for example, culture or economy as natural or unstoppable forces. The arguments speaking for them may be more seductive than true. The fact that several countries may behave in a similar way at one point in time may have other explanations than, for example, shared underlying historical conditions. Concerted political behaviour may be caused by high costs for individual states breaking away from a regime-context. There may be reasons and options that may be dictated by factors taught in the discourse on collective action for example, which decide regime trends. And accepting a deterministic explanation may entail taking an analytical shortcut which entails disregarding in-depth studies of political processes. Doing that may eventually provide legitimacy for the powers that promote autocracy. These dilemmas and questions are the focus of this chapter which is a part of the final section of this book which discusses how to comprehend autocratization in South Asia. By employing broad overviews, the three chapters discuss the role of historical factors, ideological currents and how the geopolitical context is influenced by China. The ambition is not to provide one big final argument which unites the contributions in this book. The idea is to take one step back and see what becomes apparent when a wider lens is used and how that may complement the perspectives in the previous contributions.

We begin with a discussion in this chapter on historical factors and agency. Then Johan Lagerkvist gives his view on how China affects its neighbours in this part of the world. And finally, David Lewis provides an analysis for understanding autocratization in South Asia via the writings of the influential illiberal political theorist Carl Schmitt.

Authoritarian regime convergence in South Asia

The trends described in general in Chapter one, and more in detail in the country specific chapters, show how the states in South Asia converge in the way they are governed to a place which has been described as electoral authoritarian (Alizada et al. 2021), or worse (see Chapter 1 for definitions of autocratization and regime types). (Alizada et al. 2021), or worse (see Chapter 1 for definitions of autocratization and regime types). Therefore, the first question is, were they always on their way there? The trend since independence until 2020 is described in Figure 28.1 using V-Dem's Electoral Democracy Index which was presented in Chapter 1.

After independence and throughout the Cold War, authoritarian government was the rule in most states in South Asia. The exceptions in this regard, up until the early 1970s, were India

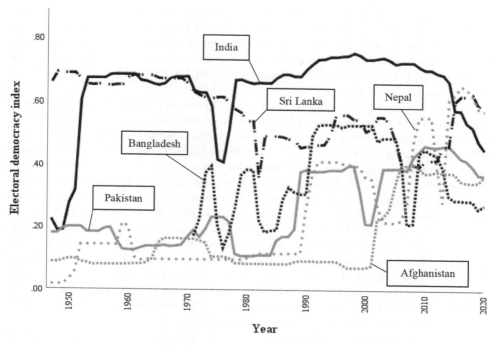

Figure 28.1 Electoral democracy (polyarchy) in South Asia, 1947–2020
Source: Varieties of democracy, version 11.1 (March 2021).

and Sri Lanka, which managed to hold elections and to protect several of the basic liberties essential for democracy. A decline then set in, where both India and Sri Lanka joined their neighbours on the autocratic path. In India in 1975, Prime Minister Indira Gandhi imposed the Emergency in an effort to put down violent protests and to suppress opposition parties. In Sri Lanka, the relatively open politics of the Bandaranaike era declined as communal conflicts grew in intensity. The democratic decline in India however proved to be temporary. The country saw 22 months of semi-authoritarian rule – and for a limited time its government declined into the authoritarian category. However, Gandhi ended the Emergency and India steered back to democracy, in a manner unique for countries that had been recently decolonized. The downward trend in Sri Lanka, on the other hand, led to civil war and ethnic purges. The time during which India's democracy was in rapid decline, around 1976, was the first time when all of the states of South Asia converged on non-democratic rule.

Then, for almost four decades, India stood out as an exception to the authoritarianism of its neighbours. It bears stressing that, inasmuch as India has such a large share of the population of South Asia (today almost 75 per cent), it can be misleading to give equal weight to all of the countries in the region when measuring democratic performance. Since independence, after all, a *majority* of the population in South Asia has lived under imperfect but nonetheless democratic rule – mainly thanks, of course, to India.

After the Cold War ended, moreover, there was a clear shift in the general pattern, as several countries in South Asia joined what has been called 'the third wave' of democratization (see Figures 1.1, 1.10 and 28.1). India seemed to be on a steady democratic path and democratization in Bangladesh was impressive. The general trend was greatly strengthened between 2004 and 2011. These years were when Afghanistan left the bottom of the scale, a more modern constitution was adopted under the leadership of Hamid Karzai and Nepal ditched its monarchy and became a secular state with democratic institutions. The civil war in Sri Lanka ended and even Pakistan seemed to prepare itself for a new and more democratic era after military rule ended in 2007. For a while, it certainly seemed that South Asia might converge on a fairly high level of democratic performance.

For several countries during this period, however, the situation can be described as volatile. And eventually there was the general downturn in democratic performance which has been the focus of this book. Sri Lanka made significant democratic improvements from 2014 to 2017, and it has even outperformed India since 2016. Nevertheless, the upward trend on the island seems to have been broken since 2018, mainly due to a worsening vulnerability of minorities and a shrinkage in the space for freedom of opinion and expression. It has also been claimed in contributions in this book that the foundation for democracy was never strongly established after the civil war to begin with. Nepal too, finally, has begun a slow descent on the democracy scale in the last few years (Nayak 2020). The gains in democratic performance seen not long ago have ceased or have even started to become undone by recent developments as South Asia joined the 'third wave of autocratization' (Lührmann and Lindberg 2019). The rapid decline of democracy in Bangladesh, a democratization process which was lost in Pakistan, a fragile democratization process in Sri Lanka, and Modi's authoritarian measure since 2014 led to the ongoing Episode of Autocratization (see Chapter 1) which means that South Asia has again, for the second time since independence, converged to authoritarian rule.

It is perplexing and surprising how fast the recent decline came about. And since the democratic decline has been so widespread it is tempting to see the current state of democracy as something created by some common denominator. After all, the Mughal Empire tied together what is now Pakistan, India, and Bangladesh. These three states share more history with each other than with other countries in South Asia. Most of the territories now within these states were also a part of the Maurya Empire (from the fourth to the second century BCE), the Gupta Empire (from the fourth to the fifth century CE), and the Maratha Empire (the eighteenth to the nineteenth century). Subsequently the British Empire took control over most parts of India, Sri Lanka, Myanmar, Pakistan and Bangladesh. And then the region decolonized in 1947 and 1948. Much more recently, moreover, Bangladesh was part of Pakistan – from independence in 1947 until 1971.

This shared history is one of the main reasons why making comparisons between these countries has been such an attractive research strategy for understanding regime development. It is difficult to find study objects in the field of regime studies which can so readily be argued to constitute a natural experiment. The favourite cases for comparison in South Asia are India and Pakistan. Or, in the words of Maya Tudor in her research on regime development:

> [T]he manifold structural similarities between India and Pakistan means that the comparison forms a rare social science approximation of a natural experiment in which many alternative explanations can be readily eliminated, thereby facilitating the task of drawing compelling causal inferences.
>
> *(Tudor 2013, p. 255)*

The comparative literature reveals a number of institutional factors important for explaining different outcomes of democratization from 1947 until recently. For example the State Reorganization Act in India in 1956, which allowed state borders to more logically coincide with linguistic borders which then defused separatist demands in several regions (Basu and Kohli 1998;

Kohli 2001). And this paved the way for democracy. Although feudal structures remain in India's North, land reforms have had some effect for lessening the deep inequalities that can destabilize democracies (Engelsen Ruud 1996; Bhattacharyya 1994). In Pakistan province borders still cut across ethnic communities and feudal orders have continued to dominate political alliances and systems of patronage (Tudor 2013; Shami 2012). At the time of partition, civilian leaders in India managed to shape the administrative systems and hierarchies so that the military was brought under the control of the defence minister. In Pakistan the military retained their control. All mattered for a relative success for democracy in India and hybrid regimes in Pakistan.

Most political historians also point to the importance of structures that were established before partition. The British Empire did not provide a uniform system of governance in South Asia as provinces were under direct rule and princely states were controlled indirectly. And even within these categories the style of governance and degree of autonomy varied greatly. Also, provinces varied greatly in size, and recruitment for the armed forces was carried out according to a system where groups were classified as different martial races which would distribute forces with different ethnic backgrounds unevenly in different areas. This also mattered for democracy later (Wilkinson 2014; Tudor 2013; Tan 2005). Furthermore, political elites in very different political parties grew increasingly important in the nineteenth century and until partition which certainly affected the capacity to establish civilian rule and democratic traditions in India and not in Pakistan (Tudor 2013; Jalal 1995). Natural, financial, and institutional resources were distributed in such a way that gave a great advantage to India to create a more stable development compared to the conditions that Pakistan provided (Jalal 1995). And, Pakistan was also affected by the refugee crisis in 1947 in ways that differed from India's experience (Talbot 2020). Consequently, India and Pakistan were not identical twins separated in 1947. Political and civil life developed differently because of legacies tracing roots much further back in time.

Nevertheless, even though there are no perfect natural experiments – and South Asia is no exception – research with comparative perspectives has undoubtedly been able to provide a more thorough and systematic understanding of the different paths that states in South Asia have trodden – in particular those leading to or from authoritarian rule. Institutions and resources do matter, political culture does too.

And yet, states in South Asia are now mostly heading in the same direction. The question then is, have the comparisons of states in this region led us to the wrong conclusions? If most of South Asia now has ended up in the authoritarian category, was not the post-colonial era just an interlude while waiting for the recent convergence? It is tempting to draw this conclusion. However, there is variation within all the countries that complicates the issue.

As Figure 28.1 shows, Bangladesh is the most authoritarian state in South Asia currently. This reflects how the Awami League and Prime Minister Sheikh Hasina have turned Bangladesh to what increasingly looks like a one-party state (Riaz 2019; Engelsen Ruud and Hasan Forthcoming 2021). The Awami League government has eliminated any free and effective political opposition. This includes the largest opposition party, the Bangladesh Nationalist Party, the leader of which, Khaleda Zia, has been imprisoned. In addition, the proceedings at the International War Crimes Tribunal, and the convictions recently handed down by it, have been used effectively to suppress political opposition. Autocratization here is deeply rooted in poverty, a 'soft state', and what happened at independence in 1971.

Pakistan takes second place from the bottom in Figure 1.1 and third place from the bottom in Figure 28.1. Pakistan has never managed to achieve a consolidated democracy. It never radically reformed its feudal economy or separated the military from the centres of power. This has always limited the scope for democratization. Furthermore, it has repeatedly become entangled with the fate of Afghanistan and conflicts beyond its influence in a way which is unique in

South Asia. However, after its return to civilian rule in 2007, no less than three elections took place in that country, resulting in relatively peaceful shifts of power without any subsequent reversion to military rule. For several years there were clear improvements in Pakistan's political life, signalling an unprecedented democratization process. The Pakistan Tehreek-e-Insaf (PTI) was clearly a part of this. Nonetheless, the past five years have seen a democratic setback, with restrictions on freedom of expression and freedom of association. Intimidation, torture, and the disappearance of journalists and civil-rights activists have substantially increased under the rule of Prime Minister Imran Khan and the PTI.

India shows the most important and dramatic change here, given its previous performance and its population of almost 1.4 billion. Sri Lanka thereby ranks higher than India currently – but its better democratic performance only benefits about 2 per cent of the population in the region. The decline in India in this regard has a profound effect on the whole region.

There was a slight downward trend in India's democratic performance beginning around 2013 – the final year of two consecutive Congress (I)-led governments. A much sharper downturn then got under way after the BJP came to power in 2014. Should the present trend continue, India's political system may reach the 'authoritarian' level – even lower than the level in 1975–1977 – within just a few years (Widmalm 2019a, b).

It is important to recall that the Congress (I), due to its penchant for dynastic principles of organization and its unwillingness or incapacity to keep checks on corruption, opened the door to a rival for power like the BJP. An even larger problem, from a democratic perspective, is what that rival did to democracy when it came to power. The steep decline from 2014 on is largely the result of a planned and sustained dismantling of democratic institutions pursued by the BJP government. And the BJP is a part of the Sangh Parivar which has roots going back a century. Since independence this movement has transformed and shaped India in a unique way. In spite of this, India long defied all predictions (Moore 1993) about the demise of its democracy.

Political scientist Rajni Kothari, however, provided perspective on the situation when he described India as supported by a steel frame consisting of a highly educated public sector, a fairly well-governed military, and the Congress Party – which together provided the stability needed for democratic consolidation (Kothari 1970). Nevertheless, the decline in the organizational structure of the Congress Party in the late 1960s, together with high levels of corruption, have since lessened India's capacity to absorb and channel the strong political engagement of its citizens and their demands for reform (Kohli 1990). Moreover, in more recent years parts of civil society with intolerant attitudes towards minorities have aligned themselves with like-minded forces at the level of India's constituent states, and even at the national level (Basu 2015; Widmalm 2016). The Hindutva movement is pursuing chauvinistic nationalist goals, while the Congress Party has withered dramatically. The BJP, by linking up effectively with actors in civil society, has acquired an unprecedented grip on the politics and political culture of India. Its outspoken ambition is to create a Hindu Rashtra – the Hindu version of an ethnic state. The contributions to this book provide detailed accounts of how the BJP government has pursued policies which differentiate civic rights along ethno-religious lines, and Hindutva-tied organizations on the ground have provided the muscle power – intimidating and even killing journalists, defenders of civil rights, and members of minority religious groups (Basu 2015). The strategy pursued by the government of Prime Minister Modi consists mainly of mimicking the leadership styles of the Pakistani and Chinese regimes. Until recently, it was hard to imagine how this could be done in South Asia, with its great diversity. For it was actually India's diversity, paradoxically enough, that was seen as the glue which kept it together, according to such scholars as Paul Brass (Brass 1990), Arend Lijphart (Lijphart 1996), and Yogendra Yadav, Juan Linz, and Alfred Stepan (Stepan, Linz, and Yadav 2011). Yet this diversity has not been enough, evidently, to stop the country's downward trajectory on the democratic scale. As some contributions to this book suggest, it may however be what brings India back on track to democracy. But such changes are not in sight now.

Sri Lanka, just like India, had a successful start for its democracy. At independence, universal suffrage had been in place for sixteen years since the introduction of the Donoughmore Constitution. Although the early history of Sri Lanka had differed greatly from India's, there were two decades after independence when the two countries seemed to travel on the same democratic path. Although they did separate themselves from each other, as India managed to keep its democracy alive while Sri Lanka did not, similarities remained. India experienced conflicts in Punjab and Kashmir, at the same time as Sri Lanka was increasingly plagued by a civil war. During these conflicts, in both countries, ethnic and chauvinistic nationalism took new forms which then shaped a new generation of political leaders which today are leading populist political campaigns in each respective country.

Evidently, even though comparative perspectives have shed light on different regime trajectories during the last 70 years, we have no coherent explanation for why South Asia has for a second time converged on authoritarianism. But there is a contender.

After the end of British colonial rule, and then after the end of the Cold War, the influence of the West and of Russia respectively in the region dramatically diminished. China has taken centre stage. Once the Cold War alliances broke down, was it not obvious that clashes of interest would be manifested in a pattern whereby different actors mainly aligned themselves on the basis of identities – identities which, while previously suppressed, were deeply rooted historically and culturally? In this region, the salient cultural, religious, and historically rooted identities can be labelled Hindu, Buddhist, Muslim, and Confucian. As Samuel Huntington claimed, moreover, the world can be seen as divided by borders delineating different regions with shared cultures, historical experiences, and above all religious traditions (Huntington 1993: 23–24). Huntington argued that, after the Cold War, *civilizations* would re-emerge as the highest order of organization (Huntington 1993). From this perspective, the Cold War served to suppress basic characteristics, thereby creating a false image of the world in which civilizational fault lines were hidden. As soon as the different civilizations re-emerged, moreover, they would clash with each other, largely due to their inherent contradictions with one another. Huntington described the civilizations of South Asia as non-secular, and as animated by values and beliefs that are far from democratic. In these respects he drew an explicit contrast with the West:

> Western ideas of individualism, liberalism, constitutionalism, human rights, equality, liberty, the rule of law, democracy, free markets, the separation of church and state, often have little resonance in Islamic, Confucian, Japanese, Hindu, Buddhist or Orthodox cultures.
>
> *(Huntington 1993: 40)*

It was thus expected that the West would lose its influence in South Asia eventually, and that states in the whole region would converge on a non-democratic political order – albeit perhaps in variable ways. Empirically, is that not what we see in Figure 28.1? Naturally, Huntington has been criticized for his generalizations and coarse categorizations, and for his penchant for portraying Western civilization as superior and morally most enviable. However, even if we steer clear of how Huntington ranked civilizations, we may find his controversial thesis troubling when we seek to understand South Asia. Already in 1993, Huntington made some highly prescient warnings regarding India's trajectory, and about the future role of Hindutva political forces and their project of building an ethnic state.

341

The historic clash been Muslim and Hindu in the subcontinent manifests itself now not only in the rivalry between Pakistan and India but also in intensifying religious strife within India between increasingly militant Hindu groups and India's substantial Muslim minority. The destruction of the Ayodhya mosque in December 1992 brought to the fore the issue of whether India will remain a secular democratic state or become a Hindu one.

(Huntington 1993: 33–34)

For all his faults, Huntington early espied a threat to India's democracy which scholars of South Asia too long underestimated. Moreover, it is striking how leaders all over Asia have taken increasingly to emphasizing cultural identity to provide legitimacy for non-democratic behaviour. The Hindutva movement in India is a clear example hereof, as it is openly promoting the creation of a 'Hindu state' – the Hindu Rashtra. Furthermore, China under Xi Jinping increasingly resembles the China of the 1960s, under Mao Zedong. In its efforts to achieve greater influence, moreover, China is increasingly relying on hard power (Nye 2000) and showing an open disdain for democratic values. There is one important difference, however, in how Xi Jinping portrays China's culture. Mao Zedong rejected Confucius, whereas the Chinese Communist Party today hails him as an important 'symbol of Chinese culture' (Dhull 2017). The West, on the other hand, is described in this context as 'decadent' (Stevens 2020). There are thus many current trends and political declarations that fit well with Huntington's idea of a Clash of Civilizations. The political rhetoric deployed by leaders in South Asia is in no way encouraging their countries to move upwards on the democracy scale. China sets the tone as it is feared in the region, but it has also long been admired for its ability to 'get things done'. Time and again, Xi Jinping is depicted as resolute and proud of his country's identity, and as someone who does not get stuck in all the squabbles and time-consuming diversions that democracy creates. The two final chapters of this book will provide an analysis which is very relevant to this.

Nor is it just political leaders in South Asia who regard China's regime culture as useful for providing legitimacy, and thus as worth mimicking. Populists in the West turn admiring eyes to China as 'democracy' and 'liberalism' seems to become something which is desired less among intellectuals both on the left and right, and among the young (Mounk 2018; Krastev and Holmes 2019). In practice, those in power who at least officially find the Huntingtonian way of thinking compelling are also drawn away from democracy. And it is fairly easy to point to all the conflicts within and between countries of South Asia – where mobilization has been predominantly along ethnic lines – as phenomena that can be termed civilizational.

Nevertheless, while we must acknowledge that central political actors are embracing Huntington's claims about how civilizations clash and that this appeals to electorates, there are several reasons not to accept Huntington's world view or the logic it sets out regarding conflicts and autocratization. With regard to South Asia, the most compelling reasons to be sceptical of the civilizational hypothesis are provided in the studies mentioned earlier which have treated South Asia as the scene of several political natural experiments. These studies have shown that, for more than seventy years, India managed to perform relatively well as a democracy in spite of its 'Hindutva' heritage. The political history of Sri Lanka, moreover, has exhibited variations which do not correlate with changes in its 'culture'. Furthermore, the fact that Nepal, and even Afghanistan have experienced dramatic changes in regime type, suggests that a deterministic approach here is problematic to say the least. In particular, the fact that democratic performance in Afghanistan could improve so quickly after 2001 was unexpected by many political scientists and political actors. And so was the speed of autocratization in 2021.

To this picture should be added the fact that Pakistan's strongest partner in the region is China. This relationship has thrived even though China is pursuing large-scale campaigns for the ethnic cleansing of religious minorities (including Muslims). China's concentration camps for Muslims are located very close to the Pakistan border – a fact which furnishes a natural (and of course horrible) experiment that speaks against Huntington's hypothesis. If Pakistan is supporting violent separatists crossing the Indian border into Kashmir mainly for cultural or civilizational reasons, then why is it not doing the same for Muslims in China's Xinjiang province? And if Hindus and Confucians see Muslims as a kind of 'civilizational enemy', how is it that India and China are not turning against Pakistan and Bangladesh together?

If we are to understand conflicts, we must indeed appreciate the importance of differences in values, culture, and views on history. It is another thing, however, to say that these are always the reason why conflicts arise or when democracy is failing. When Huntington formulated his Clash of Civilizations hypothesis, he did so on the basis of a very selective reading of history. In fact, his manner of proceeding – of making the civilizational explanation the overriding one simply by choice, rather than scientific support – resembles the arguments proffered by those who conduct nationalistic campaigns. Or, as the historian Eric Hobsbawm famously put it: 'History is to nationalism what poppy is to an opium addict'. This by no means implies, be it noted, that *all* conflicts where groups are mobilized on the basis of their identity are simply *constructed* by populists. Ethnic identities are built by wars, struggles for freedom, gains and losses, and other highly complicated events and phenomena; they are not simply inserted into people's minds as 'constructions'. They are also lived experiences, or parts of a living memory. Even so, this scarcely proves the world is divided into crude civilizational units doomed to collide. Culture is a core feature of people's identity, but it does not decree that everyone will clash – at least not by violent means. Kwame Ture thought overt conflict unavoidable, but Martin Luther King did not. And Nathuram Vinayak Godse did, but Mohandas Karamchand Gandhi did not. There is little proof ethnic identities are always the prime mover behind political outcomes. The Kashmir conflict in South Asia, for example, is commonly seen as an ethnic conflict in the sense that cultures clash in irreconcilable ways (Widmalm 2006). A deeper analysis shows that while ethnic mobilization has been important in the region, the conflicts over the years have roots in unresolved questions relating to autonomy since partition. It is evident, however, that political actors in South Asia, as in other parts of the world, find arguments relating to ethnicity, economics, culture and history serviceable not only for gaining support, but also for evading responsibility for having whipped up feelings that can escalate into violence. It becomes convenient in such cases to depict 'the power of the people' metaphorically as a 'natural force' which generates values and produces outcomes that leaders cannot control, or are 'forced' to follow (Gilmartin, Price, and Ruud 2020; Widmalm 2006). Rhetorical constructions of this kind – with the displacement of agency which they entail – are a part of politics.

When it comes to the Clash of Civilization-argument, Huntington's argument is a kind of 'just wait and see' argument; he gave no sell-by date for his predictions. Since politics involves processes of change, he will likely prove right at some time and in some place. Even a broken clock is right twice a day. The main counter-argument here is that conclusions about the authoritarian turn in South Asia relying on deterministic perspectives would deliberately have to overlook counter- cases and counter-arguments provided by a variety of trajectories since independence. The civilizational hypothesis is not always irrelevant. It is rather that it becomes deterministic, because of how it overlooks far-reaching regime variations, and how it disregards the large number of studies which have shown how such variations have come about.

What can reverse autocratization in South Asia?

Democracy's downward trajectory in South Asia is a disaster for human rights, minorities, free speech, media freedom, and academic freedom. For individuals on the ground, it means being attacked for belonging to the wrong religion, or being sent to prison for speaking truth to power. The Covid-19 crisis has added to the suffering immensely and also made it easier for populists to push through autocratic policy measures. The convergence described here, therefore, deserves an analysis far less simplified than one where not only history and culture but also economics become residual categories. What is needed more of is an analysis which takes underlying causes of conflict into account, but then also combines them with in-depth studies of the reasons why leaders choose non-democratic political paths. Political leaders and their strategies are shaped by outside forces as well. In South Asia in general the most important influence now is from China. Its sphere of influence is continuing to expand, and the regime model which it advocated is not only authoritarian. Since the cost of technology for making use of surveillance and control systems has gone down dramatically, a sustainable totalitarian model of governance is more than ever before a realistic plan for leaders in Asia, as well as in other parts of the world. The threat to democracy is that it has become so easy to replace it. Not that civilizations inevitably must clash.

The country-chapters in this book, and previous research, show that South Asia is not predetermined to stay in the authoritarian category. All the protest movements described here that have turned against the forces of autocratization attest to this. It is however evident that breaking free from the current situation is very costly for a single state that wants to do so on their own. Either concerted actions from political parties in several states in South Asia could lead to a push for democratization. Or a single state, a very strong and influential one, well experienced already in how democratic governance works, could lead the way. India is the main contender. However, nothing along these lines is likely to happen as long as Narendra Modi is leading the BJP and the country. And it will not happen as long as the political opposition is in such a poor state as it is in now. If the opposition cannot learn to adapt to the new situation and coordinate its efforts with other political parties, this episode of autocratization will continue. And the longer it does, the harder it will be to revive democracy.

Bibliography

Alizada, Nazifa, Rowan Cole, Lisa Gastaldi, Sandra Grahn, Sebastian Hellmeier, Palina Kolvani, Jean Lachapelle, Anna Lührmann, Seraphine F. Maerz, Shreeya Pillai, and Staffan I. Lindberg. 2021. *Autocratization Turns Viral – Democracy Report 2021.* Gothenburg: University of Gothenburg, V-Dem Institute.

Basu, Amrita. 2015. *Violent Conjunctures in Democratic India.* New York: Cambridge University Press.

Basu, Amrita, and Atul Kohli, eds. 1998. *Community Conflict and the States in India.* Delhi: Oxford University Press.

Bhattacharyya, Dwaipayan. 1994. "Limits to Legal Radicalism: Land Reforms and the Left Front in West Bengal." *The Calcutta Historical Review* 16 (1): 57–100.

Brass, Paul R. 1990. *The New Cambridge History of India.* Cambridge: Cambridge University Press.

Chatterjee, Partha. 2020. *I Am the People: Reflections on Popular Sovereignty Today, Ruth Benedict Book Series.* New York: Columbia University Press.

Coppedge, Michael, John Gerring, Carl Henrik Knutsen, Staffan I. Lindberg, Jan Teorell, Nazifa Alizada, David Altman, Michael Bernhard, Agnes Cornell, M. Steven Fish, Lisa Gastald, Haakon Gjerløw, Adam Glynn, Allen Hicken, Garry Hindle, Nina Ilchenko, Joshua Krusell, Anna Luhrmann, Seraphine F. Maerz, Kyle L. Marquardt, Kelly McMann, Valeriya Mechkova, Juraj Medzihorsky, Pamela Paxton, Daniel Pemstein, Josefine Pernes, Johannes von Römer, Brigitte Seim, Rachel Sigman, Svend-Erik Skaaning, Jeffrey Staton, Aksel Sundström, Ei-tan Tzelgov, Yi-ting Wang, Tore Wig, Steven Wilson, and Daniel Ziblatt. 2021. Dem [Country–Year/Country–Date] Dataset v11.1. Edited by Varieties of Democracy Project.

Dhull, Pardeep. 2017. "Once denounced by Mao, Confucius now being embraced by CPC." *The Tribune.* www.tribuneindia.com/news/archive/world/once-denounced-by-mao-confucius-now-being-embraced-by-cpc-470739.

Engelsen Ruud, Arild. 1996. "Land and Power." *Modern Asian Studies* 28: 2357–2380.

Engelsen Ruud, Arild, and Mubashar Hasan, eds. Forthcoming 2021. *Masks of Authoritarianism – Hegemony, Power and Public Life in Bangladesh.* Singapore: Palgrave Macmillan.

Gilmartin, David, Pamela G. Price, and Arild Engelsen Ruud. 2020. *South Asian Sovereignty: The Conundrum of Worldly Power.* Abingdon, Oxon; New York: Routledge.

Huntington, S. P. 1993. "The Clash of Civilizations." *Foreign Affairs* 72 (3): 22–49.

Jalal, Ayesha. 1995. *Democracy and Authoritarianism in South Asia.* Cambridge: Cambridge University Press.

Kohli, Atul. 1990. *Democracy and Discontent.* Cambridge: Cambridge University Press.

Kohli, Atul, ed. 2001. *The Success of India's Democracy.* Cambridge: Cambridge University Press.

Kothari, Rajni. 1970. *Politics in India.* Himayatnagar: Orient Longman.

Krastev, Ivan, and Stephen Holmes. 2019. *The Light that Failed: A Reckoning.* London: Allen Lane, an imprint of Penguin Books.

Lijphart, Arend. 1996. "The Puzzle of Indian Democracy: A Consociational Interpretation." *American Political Science Review* 90 (2): 258–268.

Lührmann, Anna, and Staffan I. Lindberg. 2019. "A Third Wave of Autocratization Is Here: What Is New About It?" *Democratization* 26 (7): 1095–1113.

Moore, Barrington. 1993. *Social Origins of Dictatorship and Democracy – Lord and Peasant in the Making of the Modern World.* Boston: Beacon Press.

Mounk, Yascha. 2018. *The People vs. Democracy: Why Our Freedom Is in Danger and How To Save It.* Cambridge, MA: Harvard University Press.

Müller, Jan-Werner. 2016. What *Is* Populism? Philadelphia: University of Pennsylvania Press.

Nayak, Ravi. 2020. "Democracy in Nepal Is under Threat." *South Asia Journal,* 9 May. http://southasiajournal.net/democracy-in-nepal-is-under-threat/.

Nye, Joseph S. 2000. *Understanding International Conflicts.* New York: Longman.

Polanyi, Karl. 2001. *The Great Transformation: The Political and Economic Origins of Our Time.* 2nd Beacon Paperback ed. Boston: Beacon Press.

Riaz, Ali, ed. 2019. *Voting in a Hybrid Regime – Explaining the 2018 Bangladeshi Election, Politics of South Asia.* London: Palgrave Macmillan.

Shami, Mahvish. 2012. "The Impact of Connectivity on Market Interlinkages: Evidence from Rural Punjab." *World Development* 40 (5): 999–1012.

Stepan, Alfred, Juan J. Linz, and Yogendra Yadav. 2011. *Crafting State-Nations – India and Other Multinational Democracies.* Baltimore: The Johns Hopkins University Press.

Stevens, Philip. 2020. "Democracy Faces Bigger Threats than Vladimir Putin or Xi Jinping." *Financial Times.*

Talbot, Ian. 2020. "Pakistan Refugee State." In *Refugee Crisis 1945–2000 – Political and Societal Responses in International Comparisons,* edited by Jan C. Janson and Simone Lassig, 83–104. Cambridge: Cambridge University Press.

Tan, Tai Yong. 2005. *The Garrison State: The Military, Government and Society in Colonial Punjab 1849–1947, Sage Series in Modern Indian History.* Thousand Oaks, CA: Sage.

Tudor, Maya. 2013. "Explaining Democracy's Origins: Lessons from South Asia." *Comparative Politics* 45 (3): 253–272.

Widmalm, Sten. 2006. *Kashmir in Comparative Perspective – Democracy and Violent Separatism in India.* Oxford: Oxford University Press.

Widmalm, Sten. 2016. *Political Tolerance in the Global South – Images from India, Pakistan and Uganda.* London: Routledge.

Widmalm, Sten. 2019a. Is India's Democracy Really in Decline? *The Wire.*

Widmalm, Sten. 2019b. Under Modi Govt, a Two-Pronged Attack on India's Democracy. *The Wire.*

Widmalm, Sten, and Sven Oskarsson. 2013. "Political Tolerance in India – Descriptions and Explanations from the Heartland." *Asian Survey* 53 (3): 533–558.

Wilkinson, Steven I. 2014. *Army and Nation – The Military and Indian Democracy since Independence.* Cambridge, MA: Harvard University Press.

29

GRAVITATIONAL PULL OF AUTHORITARIAN CHINA IN SOUTH ASIA?

Johan Lagerkvist

A strong and worldwide wave of autocratization has gained much scholarly attention in recent decades (Diamond and Plattner 2002, Lührmann and Lindberg 2019). In many parts of the world, liberal democracies have become less liberal, while authoritarian regimes have become more entrenched. For a long time, researchers related international economic linkages between the United States and other countries to openness to influence of American political norms, such as competitive elections, rule of law, human rights – and in turn, to democratization (Levitsky and Way 2010). The rise of the People's Republic of China (PRC), and other wealthy autocracies, as new economic power houses, however, has raised questions about the influence of authoritarian norms as a consequence of new economic partnerships and political engagements (Gat 2007). Since the early 2000s international linkages and norms also include non-Western alternatives – particularly China's authoritarian developmental model.

Against the backdrop of an emerging cold war between the United States and China, many countries in all world regions are finding themselves under increasing pressure to choose sides, or find ways to cleverly cooperate with both, between a liberal-democratic and free-market capitalist US camp, or a Leninist-authoritarian and state capitalist Chinese camp. We may thus find countries to oscillate between professed political ideals and economic needs and realities. In a climate of cold war rhetoric, American policymakers and analysts argue that China's government seeks to replace the US-led liberal and democratic world order with its own authoritarian model. In a speech in 2020, former US Secretary of State Mike Pompeo stated that "General Secretary Xi Jinping is a true believer in a bankrupt totalitarian ideology. It's this ideology, it's this ideology that informs his decades-long desire for global hegemony of Chinese communism" (Pompeo 2020). An already bankrupt ideology should not scare anyone, and there is no belief in China that "Chinese communism" will prevail globally, as Chinese analysts have noted the declining attraction of the PRC and its president Xi Jinping among populations around the world. Nevertheless, Pompeo's focus on ideology is important as it's a rallying cry for conservative Republicans and "China hawks" in the US Congress. Ideology can also be diffused in other ways than crude propaganda. More nuanced is the argument of Aaron Friedberg, who in *Foreign Affairs* argued that "Abandoning its past reluctance to be seen as an ideological challenge to the West, it now openly offers its mix of authoritarian politics and quasi-market economics as a model for nations that want to, in Xi's words 'speed up their development while preserving their independence'" (2020). The surfacing reality of constructed binary ideological opposites

DOI: 10.4324/9781003042211-35

and actually existing strategic security competition presents a challenge for small and medium-sized powers in all world regions. It is also troublesome for China, where analysts long have warned about turning geo-economic and geopolitical competition with the United States into an ideological battle, since this would mobilize diverse US interests against China. Arguably the Trump presidency managed to do just that, by labelling telecom firm Huawei as an agent of the Chinese party-state. For less affluent countries in Asia, the geographic proximity to rising China presents a particular set of opportunities and challenges. Regimes, ruling political parties, civil society, and opposition groups in neighbouring countries are affected, due to intensi-fied political and economic relations with China under the framework of the Belt and Road Initiative (BRI), which will connect countries across the vast Eurasian landmass. China, no doubt, pursues geopolitical and geo-economical strategies on regional and global levels, but is there an ideological component to these strategies – perhaps even autocracy promotion – akin to the logic of democracy promotion of the United States and its allies? This chapter seeks to tentatively answer this question by reviewing some of the theoretical and empirical literature on the subject, with a particular eye on developments in South Asia under the BRI-framework. Xi started to communicate his ideas of the BRI and his loose global plan for a "community of common destiny" immediately when taking office in March 2013, and he has since outlined the vision to global audiences at the United Nations headquarters in New York and at the World Economic Forum in Davos.

Autocracy diffusion and promotion

The worldwide turn towards authoritarianism has been conceptualized and studied as autocratization (Lührmann and Lindberg 2019; Skaaning 2020) and "democratic back-sliding", (Bermeo 2016). Most studies focus on domestic transformation and formal institutional set-ups, but some scholars have theorized international linkages of authoritarian rule as *autocracy diffusion* (Ambrosio 2010), *autocracy promotion* (Burnell 2010; Bader 2015), and *authoritarian policy transfer/learning* (Hall and Ambrosio 2017). The potential of creation and spread of non-Western norms has been scrutinized in international relations scholarship (Acharya 2004), and empirically studied in connection with Russian, Brazilian, and Chinese proposals to multi-lateral institutions. This literature suggests that cross-national ties in political, economic, and social dimensions contribute not only to the process of democratic diffusion and democratiza-tion of authoritarian regimes (Levitsky and Way 2010), but also to the autocratic diffusion and survival of incumbent autocratic leaders. International linkages may reduce the political space for democratic openings (Cameron and Orenstein 2012) but also protect and embolden auto-cratic elites (Vanderhill 2013). Autocratization oftentimes takes place as a gradual process, while keeping the facade of democratic institutions, such as elections for the legislative and executive branches (Cianetti and Hanley 2021). It is manifest in the practice of state power, using new and innovative techniques of repression (Morgenbesser 2020). Instead of banning NGOs, the ruling elites create government-organized NGOs (GONGOs) to generate the impression that civil society actors support government and muddle the political discourse by inserting moral relativity. Instead of imprisonment of political dissidents, for example, they raise the costs of being dissident by filing defamation lawsuits. Moreover, increasing linkages between autocratic regimes do not only diffuse innovative autocratic techniques internationally, they also provide the material basis for autocratic regimes – through increasing mutual reliance in the policy areas of trade, migration, and diplomacy (Tansey et al. 2017). The spread of ideas from major authori-tarian powers, on how to govern, is an important phenomenon since autocratization within a country seldom takes place in a context of insularity. One country's democratic regression, or autocratic consolidation, can be facilitated by other autocratic regimes. Such processes can be intended or unintended, directly or indirectly, actively or passively. In an important intervention, Oisin Tansey proposed that the concept of autocracy promotion should be used carefully to avoid conceptual overstretch. It is applicable when, and only when, there is "clear intent on the part of an external actor to bolster autocracy as a form of political regime as well as an underlying motivation that rests in significant part on an ideological commitment to autocracy itself" (2016: 142). This strict definition is useful as it disaggregates intentions, targets, and motives from the overburdened concept. He also leaves out the effects-side from the definition, as effects are hard to ascertain and lead to unsubstantiated claims, as in the literature on democracy promotion (Finkel et al. 2007). Policies without intention to spur autocratization can still have such effects, and policies with such clear intent can be ineffective. However, his key assertion about ideological commitment to a particular model of political regime as a "twentieth century phenomenon" of the fascist and communist past has echoes of Fukuyaman's "end of history". It neglects or underestimates the Chinese communist party's continuing adherence to the principles of Leninism, and pragmatic but firmly autocratic "Dengism" as is clear from former leader Deng Xiaoping's statements and speeches (Deng 2006). On the other end of the spectrum, as illustrated by remarks in the US foreign policy community there's overestimation and hyperbole regarding China's intent to export authoritarianism. China has certainly been active in denigrating liberal democracy, highlighting its failures, and preventing democracy promotion/diffusion in its regional neighbourhood (e.g. Hong Kong, Taiwan, South Korea). But there is little, if any, evidence of the PRC actively involved in *autocracy promotion* to other countries. An open question, however, is if "authoritarian learning/teaching" about China's developmental model and the central tenets of its mode of governance can be said to take place in bilateral and multilateral channels. These channels include preparation and negotiation of Chinese diplomatic proposals at the United Nations Human Rights Commission in Geneva, where China has forwarded "anti-universalist" human rights proposals in recent years (Richardson 2020), and suggestions to the International Telecommunications Union (ITU) that Western countries respect China's and other developing countries' "cyber sovereignty" and particularist conceptions of free speech (Segal 2020). But it can also take place on a bilateral basis. Thus, as a role model China can diffuse authoritarianism, but without having an explicit ideological content or intent, in line with Kneuer's and Demmelhuber's concept *authoritarian gravity centre* (2016), which lesser authoritarian states orbit around and learn from. For China it would be beneficial to see diffusion of its own norms and principles of governance to others. As Ambrosio has argued, authoritarian diffusion methods such as these serve to generally legitimate autocracy in the international system (2010: 377). Moreover, in concrete terms, the adoption of Chinese-made norms, technological standards and business practices could ease friction in multilateral and bilateral settings, serve to legitimate Chinese state capitalism, as well as increase economic opportunities for Chinese state-owned companies.

Authoritarian policy transfer/learning from China

Before Xi Jinping's ascent to power in the Chinese communist party, Yan Xuetong, a leading Chinese scholar of international relations, pondering China's increasing soft power, hoped that China would be able to "narrow the gap in these areas [sic!] within four to five years" (Yan and Xu 2008). Yet during the recent decade, and particularly after the failed containment of the Covid-19 virus in China, the attraction of the PRC among publics in the more affluent democracies has declined significantly (Silver et al. 2020). The advent of a strategically and diplomatically more assertive, and at times quite aggressive foreign policy is an obvious reason for this decline in public opinion worldwide. There is emerging scholarly consensus that the ascent to power of Xi Jinping has propelled a more assertive shift in Chinese foreign policy. In a time when Chinese efforts at soft power in the Global North are abandoned, there is a concerted push for advocating the successes of Beijing's developmental model in the Global South and at the United Nations (Liu 2018). Under the umbrella of the vision of Community of Common Destiny and the BRI, new forums of "South–South Cooperation" have also been created to better communicate China's developmental experience and policy successes (Peng 2017). Chinese state media, for example, has expanded globally and broadcast in many local languages. From around the world, journalists and educators, and GONGOs are invited to China to study the prerequisites of China's phenomenal economic growth. There are also new efforts at joint party-building exercises between the CCP and political parties in the Global South, as well as regular visits between parliaments and court systems. The Beijing-based Africanist He Wenping has argued that Africa is a "proving ground [sic!] for Beijing's community with a shared future doctrine" (2020: 40). Furthermore, she holds that: "African leaders are turning to Beijing for valuable lessons in not only traditional development issues like poverty reduction and economic growth but also government efficiency and ruling party building" (2020: 44). But not only African elites are impressed, as many citizens find China's developmental model attractive (Lekorwe 2016). The argument about party-building is in line with extant research, which argues that since Xi Jinping took office, the international department of the Chinese Communist Party has become more active, and is a "vehicle of authoritarian learning by sharing experiences of its modernization and authoritarian one-party regime" (Bader and Hackenesch 2019: 10). And as has been argued by Kneuer and Hemmelhuber, these kinds of "collaborative networks constitute the channels of communication (horizontal and vertical), which enhance the spread of ideas and institutional or policy innovations" (2016: 781). And Morgenbesser has likewise argued that "stransnational alliances between ruling parties are formal agreements to provide mutual support for the maintenance of autocratic rule", and that this "increasing cooperation between autocratic ruling parties around the world means opposition parties will suffer the consequences of innovation" (2020: 5). A case in point was the revelation that Chinese company Huawei's techniques of digital surveillance have aided governments to spy on opposition parties in African countries (Parkinson et al. 2019). This phenomenon warrants further study, as research by Bader showed that economic cooperation with China contributed to regime durability in those authoritarian countries that were party-based regimes (2015: 672). Political, economic, security and technological elites are arguably attracted to China's model of "technocratic developmentalism" with its focus on stability, order through digital surveillance techniques, and emerging standards and modes of data-driven algorithmic governance. More research focus on government-to-government authoritarian policy transfer/learning is needed as autocrats strengthen governance and party institutions through sharing experiences. The idea that authoritarian gravitation centres play "a role as an important pull factor for emulation, imitation or policy transfer" (Kneuer and Demmelhuber 2016: 777) – and influence institutional, policy, ideational, and administrative techniques in other countries – is gaining more importance.

Diluting democracy and redefining human rights

Over time China has moved from defence of the PRC's policies "with Chinese characteristics", to normative defence of states in the Global South and their right more generally to choose their own path of development, without interference of Western countries and their universalist teaching and preaching (Kinzelbach: 2012). With Xi Jinping's grand vision of a *Community of common destiny for mankind*, China has taken one more step. As elucidated in a key speech at the United Nations in 2017 (Hua 2017) and as outlined in a speech on a more active foreign policy at the 18th Party Congress, this vision showcases "Chinese solutions" to all the grave issues facing humanity, such as climate change and socioeconomic inequality. The PRC has since become more involved in authoritarian teaching of its developmental model and particularist values and norms. Thus, China has entered a new phase of more confidently transferring ideas of a specific Chinese model of development, and successfully made policy inroads in multilateral settings, such as the UN Human Rights Commission. I would argue that the fundamental tenets of this governance model consist of:

1) *socio-political stability* (including what in India is called "majoritarianism" and what some scholars have labelled "authoritarian peace" within a country)
2) *subnational experimentation to enhance economic growth and social stability*
3) *promoting the right to choose developmental alternatives according to cultural context*
4) *non-interference* in domestic sovereign politics
5) *defence of particularism* against what China's government frame as "so-called universal human rights".

Yet the overall modicum is still mostly defensive and related to China's core interests of sovereignty, territorial integrity, and non-interference. However, there is also a rising and troubling tendency in Western academia, especially among scholars trained at Chinese universities, to redefine the very meaning of democracy through describing China's autocracy as "vertical democracy" (Guo 2020). Similar academic tricks of moving goalposts are also used to overemphasize creativity and under-emphasize censorship in China's digital economy. It is probable that these efforts to reject (Western) universalism and instead offer "Chinese solutions" to global governance will increase in the post-pandemic phase, when score-cards over the failures of the largest Western democracies, the United States and the UK, are measured with China's health protection and sustained economic growth. It can be foreshadowed that in its vison of a "community of common destiny" China will advocate that collective safety and order and state sovereignty of states in the Global South must come before individual liberties.

In a world characterized by a declining United States, under conditions of mulitipolarity, China's normative arguments could propel the world into "ideational anarchy" where concepts of democratic human rights are diluted or even redefined. In the marketplace of ideologies and ideas, countries may freely choose developmental alternatives: liberal democracy or authoritarian "vertical democracy"; universal human rights or particularist rights that are culturally context-specific. On the one hand the results of China's governance have an impact by "speaking for themselves", on the other these objective results can be amplified by tailored information to target countries in the Global South.

China in South Asia

The existence of autocracy promotion by China in Southeast Asia has been investigated and refuted by Bader (2014) and Noesselt (2021). China's role in this regard as a force promoting autocratization has been studied by Vanderhill in Central Asia (2013) and Brautigam in Africa (2009) with similar results. On South Asian countries there is limited research on China's authoritarian influence. Discussion of China's relations with countries in this region mostly concerns China's economic and strategic influence and does not concern ideological components or Beijing as a prop for incumbent autocrats. According to Kneuer and Hemmelhuber, an authoritarian gravity centre "constitutes a pull factor in the regional environment: as a country that has the kind of leverage to promote autocratic elements or a country that is an attractive model for countries in geopolitical proximity, as it provides policy solutions that are perceived as suitable" (2016: 780). Whether China is seen as an attractive model in South Asia depends on what national setting, and which social group, a person belongs to. Since the announcement in 2013 of the BRI, the presence of activities fuelled by Chinese capital investment is keenly felt in the region. The initiative amounts to the Chinese state's monumental undertaking to connect countries via physical, digital and financial infrastructure across the Eurasian landmass and through the "Indo-Pacific region" to East Africa.

Among the South Asian countries, only Pakistan is a long time "all-weather friend" of China. However, not even this country has proven easy to cooperate with under the BRI-framework. For the success of the BRI, its flagship project the China–Pakistan Economic Corridor (CPEC) has been judged as crucial. However, there's been a heated debate in Pakistan and criticism of Chinese investments since 2017 (Dorsey 2019: 193). The foreign policy risks for Beijing and the vulnerabilities of rising China in connection with BRI (Cooley 2016), should not be underestimated as the tortuous progress of the CPEC has shown. Islamabad's arch-enemy India, on the other hand, has quite predictably remained suspicious of the BRI and China's long-term intentions. Partly because of Indian and American suspicion, Chinese analysts have also been prudent in their strategic assessments, not wishing through their writings to initiate a process that might shift the geopolitical and military balance in the Indian Ocean. Chinese caution is evident also in the limited military connections with other equally cautious small South Asian countries that avoid upsetting India's military (Samaranayake 2019: 8). It is one thing to provoke border skirmishes along the contested Sino-Indian border in the Himalayas, and quite another to patrol the sea around India with naval vessels and submarines. Instead, China has over the last decade sought to bolster good impressions through economic activities. Yet these attempts, and an ambition to increase Beijing's soft power, have been self-defeating, especially in the case of its longstanding adversary India (Jain 2017). And according to an informant in Ghiasy's study on Indian perceptions of China's geopolitical strategy under the BRI: "China is using micro-steps to encroach on and make advancements in South Asia's security realm: first through diplomacy, then through the economy, and then into security. Over time, in the aggregate, these micro-steps become major strides" (2021: 273). Yet, policy transfer and authoritarian learning from China can take place outside the realm of security strategy. In India's move towards "majoritarianism" (Sahoo 2020), for example, and its exclu-sionary practices regarding Muslim and other non-Hindu minorities, the ideational pull of China as an "authoritarian gravitational centre" on countries where democratic regression is ongoing should not be ruled out. Whereas Western democracies have condemned China's treatment of its Muslim minorities in the Xinjiang region, many states in the Global South have abstained from such criticism. The reasons may vary, but autocrats or elites in ethnic-ally diverse countries could ponder harsher minority policies to achieve political stability and economic development. In non-consolidated democracies such as Myanmar and Bangladesh, and in even more entrenched autocracies, such as Vietnam, leaders could follow the Chinese example of high-tech control in Xinjiang to enable a domestic "authoritarian peace". Jain notes that China's rise has afforded smaller nations in South Asia, such as Nepal, Bangladesh, Myanmar, Sri Lanka, and the Maldives, opportunities to swing out of India's sphere of interest. Aid and investments from China under BRI, as well as wishes to unhook from Indian tutelage, have propelled smaller South Asian countries to edge closer to China, to further their bargaining power vis-à-vis India (Ghiasy 2021: 272).

Yet, these economic and political motivations are offset by increasing Chinese assertiveness in the South China Sea and along the disputed border with India. It is especially the 99-year lease of Sri Lanka's Hambantota deep-sea port that has received attention in South Asian countries. Many observers have accused Beijing of conducting "debt trap diplomacy". The policies of China's state-owned policy banks do deserve scrutiny. Yet, as Sri Lanka's debt to China is only 5.9 per cent of all its foreign debt (Samaranayake 2019), such terminology lends itself to exaggeration. Nonetheless it is argued that concerns about the Hambantota affair in the region after 2017 "have not been eased by Chinese insistence that the investments are purely commercial in nature [and have] seriously damaged China's BRI soft power drive in South Asia" (Garlick 2018: 530).

China exerts significant influence in Dhaka due to its long-term support of Bangladesh's military. With Xi Jinping's visit to Bangladesh in 2016, this influence was expected to grow, as huge Chinese investments under the BRI agenda were promised. It was seen as evidence for China's expanded foothold in South Asian countries (Kumar 2019: 150). Yet, most of the projects and billions Xi earmarked for Bangladesh, worth USD 24 billion, have not materialized, as only three projects totalling USD 1.2 billion have been initiated. The overall impression is that initial grandiose ambitions and promises of the BRI have not materialized on the ground. Domestic backlashes against China's economic influence, as in Sri Lanka and Pakistan, as well as the Covid-19 pandemic, can explain some of the delays.

Uncertainty surrounding Beijing's long-term and far from transparent strategy should also be factored into the equation. Clouded in secrecy and contradictory as its diplomacy oscillates between assertiveness and prudence, Chinese foreign policy is notoriously hard to interpret. According to Pu Xiaoyu, China's diplomatic Janus face should be understood as China's leaders signalling to both domestic and international audiences, but also as a fundamental uncertainty about its changing role in world politics (Pu 2019). Several important empirical studies from around the world have refuted the Chinese party-state's direct involvement in autocracy promotion. However, more subtle diffusion of autocratic practices could be an outcome of China's growing influence as a role model. It can come as a by-product of economic leverage such as investment, trade, foreign aid, loans, technological standards, statecraft, and role-modelling in educational programmes and state visits. And as noted recently by Bader and Hackenesh (2019), the limited evidence of Chinese autocracy promotion is mainly manifest from the period *before* the 18th Communist Party Congress in 2017. At this important congress, Xi Jinping announced a strategic shift to actively communicate China's developmental experience. This has to date taken form, more as authoritarian learning than actual autocracy promotion. And as discussed above, China's vigorous defence of its authoritarian polity and attacks on universal human rights and re-defining of democracy are contributing to a global trend of ideational anarchy.

One avenue of future research in this field of communicating China's developmental experience concerns political relations, especially ties between the international department of the Chinese Communist party and political parties in South Asia. Chinese aid in party-to-party dialogues is underway with political parties in Pakistan and Bangladesh (Dawn Newspaper 2019). Notwithstanding nationalist resistance in South Asian countries against China's advance of geopolitical and geo-economical interests under the BRI, its mode of governance may still inspire, especially compared to recent perceptions of failings of Western democracies. This phenomenon especially warrants studies in countries such as Bangladesh, with a social memory of single-party rule, as described in the chapter by Ali Riaz in this volume.

Concluding remarks

Despite the transformation to a more assertive foreign policy under Xi Jinping, China's strategy remains relatively reactive, notwithstanding more vehement responses to statements about human rights abuses in the Xinjiang region. China is sensitive to arguments of not being a responsible stakeholder in the liberal world order and criticism of its human rights record. At the same time, China also responds to stimuli from states in the Global South to shoulder more responsibility to lead, and take political, not just geo-economic, initiatives. If governments, in Asia and Africa for example, express views that China act more decisively on the international stage, China may be nudged to act, and also should act as a role model, for states in the Global South. Thus, it is logical that Chinese foreign policy shift gears. China usually protest against democracy promotion by the United States and other liberal democracies, but do not actively have a programme to frustrate democracy promotion on the ground (Bader 2014, 2015; Noesselt 2021). Incremental changes have led to a more assertive China under Xi Jinping. Under Xi's rule China has initiated a process to move away from Deng Xiaoping's foreign policy tenet to "lie low and bide time" for ideas to "do some things" internationally (Yan 2008). As yet, however, this is not an ideologically assertive China, as US analysts and policymakers increasingly claim. One needs to distinguish between China's security-related, geo-economic, and political interests and influences. Nonetheless, the fundamental pillars underpinning Chinese technocratic and autocratic practices may come to inspire and exert attraction among autocrats elsewhere. Even in the absence of clear autocratic promotion, as no ideological "push factors" exist, it's still feasible that China's developmental technocracy and tenets on hierarchy, political stability, and minority policies may resonate with other countries' elites, civil servants, and technical experts. As a "pull factor" it could thus contribute to domestic processes of autocratization. The outcome of such processes is likely to differ across the spectrum of authoritarian settings, fragile democracies, and consolidated democracies. Autocrats in firm autocratic settings are emboldened by China, in less-than-consolidated democracies autocratic forces in society are energized. Autocrat-minded leaders even in Chinese-sceptical democracies such as India and Japan could perhaps be swayed by China-made norms and principles. Thus, the issue of a gravitational pull of authoritarian China is likely to grow in importance on the research agenda of autocratization in South Asia and beyond. However, autocratization can also come as a by-product of Chinese push-factors unrelated to its own governance model. If China would abandon strategic caution in the Indo-Pacific as it has done in the South China Sea, Premier Modi in India could as a response to Chinese assertiveness argue that civil liberties be curtailed to unify the country to withstand China. In light of persistent border skirmishes between India and China in recent years, and Modi's repeated attempts to reap electoral benefits by pointing to the military threat from Pakistan, such a scenario is not a foregone conclusion (Singh 2021).

Empirical research shows that China is not intentionally and actively exporting its particular political system overseas. Yet there are central tenets and principles of China's state-capitalist governance model that are taught to countries in the Global South, and forcefully defended in multilateral forums and argued as superior to Western democracy in diplomatic rhetoric and state-propaganda. These tenets are: *socio-political stability, subnational experimentation to enhance economic growth and social stability, promotion of the right to developmental choice according to cultural context, non-interference in domestic sovereign politics, defence of particularism* against what China's government frame as "so-called universal human rights". It would be negligent to believe that arguments about the logic and superiority of these tenets will fall on deaf ears, especially since China's concrete economic and social health scorecard in the post-pandemic Covid-19 phase speaks louder than words. According to Tansey's strict criteria and definition, these arguments hardly belong to active and intentional "autocracy promotion". Nevertheless, China's rhetoric in bilateral, regional, and multilateral settings and negotiations carries subtle ideological weight and erodes belief in the liberal and democratic principles of governance. Over time the gravitational pull of authoritarian China may propel autocratization, without it being the intended goal of autocracy promotion. Future empirical studies should, as argued by Kneuer and Hemmelhuber, explore "which mode of influence used by the authoritarian gravity centre (active intentional export or unintentional diffusion) is more effective in reality". Recent trends of authoritarian learning from, and teaching of, China's developmental model indicate that gravitational pull of China and intentional diffusion of governance practices are becoming real-world phenomena. This may not be overtly exporting world revolution from a Stalinist Soviet Union, which according to Oisin Tansey, amounts to real autocracy promotion having an explicit ideological commitment. Yet China's twenty-first century "authoritarian learning" and policy transfers may prove to be more effective precisely because they are so covert.

Bibliography

Acharya, Amitav. (2004) 'How Ideas Spread: Whose Norms Matter? Norm Localization and Institutional Change in Asian Regionalism,' *International Organisation*, 58(2), pp. 239–275.

Akhter, Majed. (2018) 'Geopolitics of the Belt and Road: Space, State, and Capital in China and Pakistan' in *Logistical Asia: The Labor of Making a World Region*, Neilson, B., Rossiter, N., Samaddar, R., (eds.) (Singapore: Palgrave Macmillan, pp. 221–241).

Ambrosio, Thomas. (2010) 'Constructing a Framework of Authoritarian Diffusion: Concepts, Dynamics, and Future Research,' *International Studies Perspectives*, 11, pp. 375–392.

Ambrosio, Thomas. (2012) 'The Rise of the 'China Model' and 'Beijing Consensus': Evidence of Authoritarian Diffusion?' *Contemporary Politics* 18(4), pp. 381–399.

Bader, Julia. (2014) *China's Foreign Relations and Autocratic Survival* (Abingdon: Routledge).

Bader, Julia. (2015a) 'Propping up Dictators? Economic Cooperation from China and its Impact on Authoritarian Persistence in Party and Non-party Regimes,' *European Journal of Political Research*, 54(4), pp. 655–672.

Bader, Julia. (2015b) 'China, Autocratic Patron? An Empirical Investigation of China as a Factor in Autocratic Survival,' *International Studies Quarterly*, 59(1), pp. 23–33.

Bader, Julia and Hackenesh, Christine. (2019) 'China: Same, Same, but Different?' *The Annals of Comparative Democratization*, 17(2), pp. 8–11.

BBC. (2021) 'Sikkim: Chinese and Indian troops 'in new border clash',' www.bbc.com/news/world-asia-55793112 (Accessed 7 March 2021).

Bermeo, Nancy. (2016) 'On Democratic Backsliding,' *Journal of Democracy*, 12(1), pp. 5–19.

Brautigam, Deborah, (2009). *The Dragon's Gift: The Real Story of China in Africa* (Oxford: Oxford University Press).

Bunce, Valerie, and Wolchik, Sharon. (2009) 'A Regional Tradition: The Diffusion of the Democratic Change under Communism and Postcommunism,' pp. 30–58, in *Democracy and Authoritarianism in the Postcommunist World*, Valerie Bunce, Michael McFaul, and Kathryn Stoner-Weiss (eds.) (Cambridge: Cambridge University Press).

Burnell, Peter. (2010) 'Is there a New Autocracy Promotion,' FRIDE Working Paper 96.

Cameron, David R. and Orenstein, Mitchell A. (2012) 'Post-Soviet Authoritarianism: The Influence of Russia in Its 'Near Abroad',' *Post-Soviet Affairs*, 28(1) pp. 1–44.

Cianetti, Licia, and Hanley, Sean. (2021) 'The End of the Backsliding Paradigm,' *Journal of Democracy*, 32(1), pp. 66–80.

Cooley, Alexander. (2016) *The Emerging Political Economy of OBOR: The Challenges of Promoting Connectivity in Central Asia and Beyond* (Washington DC: CSIS).

Dawn Newspaper. (2019) 'Chinese Communist Party, PTI Discuss Cooperation,' 28 November. Available at: www.dawn.com/news/1519224/chinese-communist-party-pti-discuss-cooperation (Accessed 7 March 2021).

Deng, Xiaoping. (2006) *Selected Works by Deng Xiaoping, Vol.1* (Beijing: People's University Press).

Diamond, Larry and Plattner, Marc (eds.). (2002) *Democracy after Communism* (Baltimore: Johns Hopkins University Press).

Dorsey, James M. (2019) *China and the Middle East: Venturing into the Maelstrom* (Cham, Switzerland: Palgrave Macmillan).

Finkel, Steven E., Perez Linan, Anibal S., and Seligson, Mitchell A. (2007) 'The Effects of U.S.Foreign Assistance on Democracy Building, 1990–2003,' *World Politics*, 59(3), pp. 404–439.

Friedberg, Aaron. (2020) 'The Way to Push Back Against Beijing,' *Foreign Affairs*, October/November.

Garlick, Jeremy. (2018) 'Deconstructing the China-Pakistan Economic Corridor: Pipe Dreams Versus Geopolitical Realities,' *Journal of Contemporary China*, 27(112), pp. 519–533.

Gat, Azar. (2007) 'The Return of Authoritarian Great Powers,' *Foreign Affairs*, July/August.

Ghiasy, Richard. (2021) 'The Belt and Road Initiative in South Asia: Regional Impact and the Evolution of Perceptions and Policy Responses,' pp. 265–290, in *Global Perspectives on China's Belt and Road Initiative: Asserting Agency through Regional Connectivity*, Schneider, Florian (ed.) (Amsterdam: Amsterdam University Press).

Guo, Baogang. (2020) 'A Partocracy with Chinese Characteristics: Governance System Reform under Xi Jinping,' *Journal of Contemporary China*, 29(126), pp. 809–823.

Hall, Stephen G.F. and Ambrosio, Thomas. (2017) 'Authoritarian Learning: A Conceptual Overview,' *East European Politics*, 33(2), pp. 143–161.

He, Wenping. (2020) 'A Community with a Shared Future: Beijing's Vision of China-Africa Relations,' *China Quarterly of International Strategic Studies*, 6(1), pp. 38–51.

Hua Xia. (2017) 'Backgrounder: 10 key quotes from Xi's speech at UN Office at Geneva,' www.xinhuanet.com/english/2017-01/19/c_135994782.htm (Accessed 21 March 2021).

Jain, B.M. (2017) *China's Soft Power Diplomacy in South Asia: Myth or Reality* (Lanham: Lexington Books).

Kapur, Ashok. (2015) 'Aftermath of the 1962 War,' www.indiandefencereview.com/spotlights/aftermath-of-the-1962-war/, 13 November (Accessed 7 March 2021).

Kenderdine, Tristan and Han, Ling. (2018) 'International Capacity Cooperation – Financing China's Export of Industrial Overcapacity,' *Global Policy*, 9(1), pp. 41–52.

Kinzelbach, Katrin. (2012) 'Will China's Rise Lead to a New Normative Order? An Analysis of China's Statements on Human Rights at the United Nations (2000–2010),' *Netherlands Quarterly of Human Rights*, 30(13), pp. 298–332.

Kumar, Sanjeev. (2019) 'China's South Asia Policy in the New Era,' *India Quarterly*, 75(2), pp. 137–154.

Kneuer, Marianne and Demmelhuber, Thomas. (2016) 'Gravity Centres of Authoritarian Rule: A Conceptual Approach,' *Democratization*, 23(5), pp. 775–796.

Lekorwe, Mogopodi et al. (2016) 'China's Growing Presence in Africa Wins Largely Positive Popular Reviews,' *Afrobarometer Dispatch*, pp. 1–31.

Levitsky, Stephen and Way, Lucian A. 2010 *Competitive Authoritarianism: Hybrid Regimes after the Cold War* (Cambridge: Cambridge University Press).

Liu, Huawen. (2018). 'China's new contribution to human rights,' *China Daily*, http://global.chinadaily.com.cn/a/201803/29/WS5abc2a4da3105cdcf6514f0b.html (Accessed 18 March 2021).

Lührmann, Anna and Lindberg, Staffan. (2019) 'A Third Wave of Autocratization Is Here: What Is New About It?' *Democratization*, 26(7), pp. 1095–1113.

Morgenbesser, Lee. (2020) 'The Menu of Autocratic Innovation,' *Democratization*, https://doi.org/10.1080/13510347.2020.1746275.

Noesselt, Nele. (2021) 'China's New Regional Responsiveness: Passive Agency and Counter-Agency in Processes of Democratic Transitions in Asia,' *Democratization* 28(1), pp. 219–236.

Parkinson, Joe, Bariyo, Nicholas and Chin, Josh. (2019) 'Huawei Technicians Helped African Governments Spy on Political Opponents,' *The Wall Street Journal*. www.wsj.com/articles/huawei-technicians-helped-african-governments-spy-on-political-opponents-11565793017?mod=breakingnews (Accessed 7 March 2021).

Peng, Ying (2017) 'Full text of Beijing Declaration adopted by the First South-South Human Rights Forum,' *Xinhua*, www.xinhuanet.com//english/2017-12/08/c_136811775.htm (Accessed 18 March 2021).

Pompeo, Mike. (2020) 'Secretary Michael R. Pompeo Remarks at the Richard Nixon Presidential Library and Museum: Communist China and the free world's future,' https://sv.usembassy.gov/secretary-michael-r-pompeo-remarks-at-the-richard-nixon-presidential-library-and-museum-communist-china-and-the-free-worlds-future/ (Accessed 16 February 2021).

Pu, Xiaoyu (2019) *Rebranding China: Contested Status Signaling in the Changing Global Order* (Stanford: Stanford University Press).

Richardson, Sophie. (2020) 'China's Influence on the Global Human Rights System: Assessing China's Growing Role in the World,' www.hrw.org/news/2020/09/14/chinas-influence-global-human-rights-system# (Accessed 7 March 2021).

Silver, Laura, Devlin, Kat, and Huang, Christine C. (2020) 'Unfavorable Views of China Reach Historic Highs in Many Countries: Majorities say China has handled COVID-19 outbreak poorly,' www.pewresearch.org/global/2020/10/06/unfavorable-views-of-china-reach-historic-highs-in-many-countries/ (Accessed 7 March 2021).

Samaranayake, Nilanthi. (2019) 'China's Engagement with Smaller South Asian countries,' *Special Report, United States Institute of Peace*, No. 446, April.

Sahoo, Niranjan. (2020) 'Mounting Majoritarianism and Political Polarization in India,' *Carnegie Endowment for Peace*, https: //carnegieendowment.org/2020/08/18/mounting-majoritarianism-and-political-polarization-in-india-pub-82434 (Accessed 7 March 2021).

Segal, Adam. (2020) 'China's Alternative Cyber Governance Regime,' Council on Foreign Relations, www.hrw.org/news/2020/09/14/chinas-influence-global-human-rights-system# (Accessed 7 March 2021).

Singh, Sushant. (2021) 'Why China Is Winning Against India,' *Foreign Policy*, https: //foreignpolicy.com/2021/01/01/india-china-himalayas-ladakh-standoff/ (Accessed 7 March 2021).

Skaaning, Svend-Erik. 2020 'Waves of Autocratization and Democratization: A Critical Note on Conceptualization and Measurement,' *Democratization*, 27(8), pp. 1533–1542.

Tansey, Oisin (2016) 'The Problem with Autocracy Promotion,' *Democratization*, 23, 141–163.

Tansey, Oisin, Koehler, Kevin, and Schmotz, Alexander. (2017) 'Ties to the Rest: Autocratic Linkages and Regime Survival,' *Comparative Political Studies* 50, pp. 1221–1254.

Vanderhill, Rachel. (2013) *Promoting Authoritarianism Abroad* (Boulder: Lynne Rienner Publishers).

Widmalm, Sten. (2019) 'A most dangerous interaction effect in India,' https: //theasiadialogue.com/2019/10/24/a-most-dangerous-interaction-effect-in-india/ (Accessed 6 March 2021).

Yan, Xuetong and Xu, Jin. (2008) 'Sino-US. Comparisons of Soft Power,' *Contemporary International Relations*, March/April, www.imir.tsinghua.edu.cn/publish/iis/7236/20120308004022054904369/2008-3Sino-U.S.ComparisonsofSoftPower.pdf (Accessed 7 March 2021).

30

AUTOCRATIZATION AS AN IDEOLOGICAL PROJECT

Carl Schmitt's anti-liberalism in South Asia

David G. Lewis

This volume provides evidence of a clear trend of autocratization in South Asian politics, which forms one strand of a much broader global process of 'democratic recession' since 2006 (Diamond 2021). In this chapter I argue that this process should not only be interpreted as a decline in the effectiveness of democratic institutions, as suggested by terms such as 'democratic backsliding' (Bermeo 2015). Autocratization should also be understood as the construction of a new form of governance, a political system that reasserts hierarchy and authority at the centre of political life while claiming to reflect the will of the people. In this chapter I use the work of the anti-liberal political theorist Carl Schmitt to demonstrate a theoretical coherence to this illiberal model of political governance that helps us to think comparatively about the ideational framework of autocratization, not only across South Asia, but on a global scale.

Attempts to explain the new wave of authoritarianism in Asia have largely overlooked the role of ideas and political theory. Croissant and Haynes (2021), for example, identify seven factors driving 'democratic regression' in Asia, but focus primarily on institutional weaknesses, such as the role of political parties and civil society and the extent to which power is concentrated in a presidency. Ding and Slater (2021) also explore the institutional aspects of autocratization, pointing to the structural tensions between electoral and rights institutions in democracy. Diamond highlights the agency of 'elected political leaders, greedy for power and wealth, who knock away various types of constraints on their power and enlarge and entrench it in undemocratic ways' (Diamond 2021: 30). Their success – or otherwise – is down to the resilience – or otherwise – of political institutions such as parties, civil society, and the judiciary.

These explanations tend to overlook ideational and normative aspects of autocratization, including those embedded in processes of globalisation. When the political impact of globalisation is discussed, scholars of comparative authoritarianism tend to focus on the disruptive effects of economic globalisation on communities. But it is also worth emphasising that liberal norms and liberal ideas – both those deliberately promoted by governments and non-governmental organisations (NGOs) and norms spread by contemporary culture, global travel and education – also provoke resistance and revanche in many communities. When authoritarian leaders weigh in against 'liberal elites' and their cosmopolitan ideas, this is not simply a populist device to mobilise populist support, but an ideological campaign informed by illiberal ideas. This 'global illiberalism' takes on country-specific forms, but has common roots in its rejection

DOI: 10.4324/9781003042211-36

of many aspects of post-Cold War international liberalism – a set of ideas that emphasised a pluralism of actors, the deconstruction of authority, a spaceless internationalism, and fluid and contingent identities (Bettiza and Lewis 2020). In opposition to liberal norms, autocratization in South Asia has been informed by a set of illiberal ideas, reasserting notions of authority, reifying boundaries of the political community, and seeking a new fixity of identity, defined by essentialised understandings of gender, sex, race, religion, and nation.

Carl Schmitt as a theoretician of autocratization

To explain the ideological framework of contemporary autocratization, I turn to the work of Carl Schmitt. Described as the 'twentieth century's foremost critic of liberalism' (McCormick 1998: 830), Schmitt achieved notoriety through his support for the Third Reich, his advocacy of Nazi expansionism, and his virulent anti-Semitism (Mehring 2014). Schmitt was a jurist by training; his work is at heart a foundational critique of liberalism and an argument in favour of authoritarian forms of political order as both more sustainable and – in Schmitt's particular understanding – as more democratic than the liberal, parliamentary state. Despite his reprehensible personal biography, Schmitt's critiques of liberalism and US foreign policy have inspired followers both among radical right-wing movements and on the European left (Müller 2003). In recent years his work has spread to other parts of the world, particularly Russia (Lewis 2020a) and China (Zheng 2015; Libin and Patapan 2020), where his anti-liberal thought has been hugely influential. In South Asia Schmitt's reach remains more limited, but his political theory has been deployed recently in discussions of the politics of Hindutva in India (Basu 2020) and the conflict in Sri Lanka (Lewis 2020b). Here I explore four of Schmitt's ideas that help us to interpret autocratization's third wave and to develop a comparative theoretical framework to identify and interpret many common and overlapping trends across very distinct political contexts.

Sovereign power

Schmitt's understanding of politics was informed by his experience of the Weimar republic, which he viewed as a weak polity fatally undermined by pluralist politics and liberal ideas. His response was a radical rejection of political pluralism and an assertion that political order is only possible when all decision-making power is concentrated in a fully sovereign political leader. Schmitt defines sovereignty not as 'the monopoly to coerce or to rule, but as the monopoly to decide' (Schmitt 1985a: 13). The true sovereign is an unconstrained political leader, who can take any necessary decisions to respond to existential threats to the state, without needing to consult parliament, follow laws or comply with constitutional constraints. The sovereign is defined by Schmitt as 'he who decides on the exception' (Schmitt 1985a: 5); the sovereign power is the leader who can declare an exceptional situation in which normal laws and rules do not apply and take any necessary decisions to address the emergency. In Schmitt's world, sovereigns are not despots – they do not act on a whim or take arbitrary decisions, nor do they monopolise decision-making on everyday issues, where norms and rules still apply. But in the extraordinary case, the sovereign can make any necessary decisions unconstrained by law or constitution.

The Schmittian sovereign is an ideal type, but the personalised dictatorship is a global trend, with the percentage of authoritarian states defined as personalist almost doubling to 40% between 1988 and 2017 (Kendall-Taylor, Frantz, and Wright 2017: 8). South Asia is no exception to this trend. In Sri Lanka President Gotabaya Rajapaksa has continued the drive of the wartime regime run by his brother and former president, Mahinda, to subordinate parliament and the judiciary to the regime's will and perpetuate strongman politics (Lewis 2020b; Mihlar, Chapter 25 of this volume). In Bangladesh, what was once a contested political system, in which political power was fought over by two major parties, has deteriorated into a *de facto* one party system, dominated since 2009 by the personalised political leadership of Awami League leader Prime Minister Sheikh Hasina (Riaz 2020; Ruud, Chapter 22 of this volume). As Riaz comments, 'The demands for her intervention in solving any problems, from capital market [...] to school-level examinations, only reaffirms that there is no other power center in the country' (Riaz: Chapter 18 of this volume). In India Narendra Modi has sought a similar monopoly of decision-making powers in the office of the Prime Minister, achieved through the marginalisation of other government agencies and ministries, parliament and the courts. Critics argue that the government pushes laws through parliament without proper scrutiny. After a controversial ten-day parliamentary session in September 2020, in which the government rushed through controversial new laws, Pratap Bhanu Mehta wrote that the parliament is moving 'from being the custodian of the dignity of legislation to being a site for the acclamation of authoritarianism' (Mehta P. B. 2020).

Schmitt's sovereign is defined by his or her ability to declare the exception, to define a particular situation as one in which the normal rules no longer apply. But there are no preconceived criteria to determine when this state of exception might be invoked: it is the sovereign who decides when there is an emergency and how to respond to it. A culture of exceptionalism has long been a familiar feature of South Asian politics, particularly in securitised environments and counter-insurgency campaigns. But the exception – declared in response to an emergency situation or an existential threat to the state – too easily becomes the norm, an everyday mechanism of governance, not a limited and time-bound aberration from the rules. In Sri Lanka emergency rule introduced temporarily in 1958 has continued in force for much of its modern history. Together with the provisions of the Prevention of Terrorism Act (PTA), these emergency regulations severely limit civil rights in sharp contradiction to international standards (Coomaraswamy and de Los Reyes 2004). In India the Armed Forces (Special Powers) Act (AFSPA) – also introduced in 1958 in the North-East – gives the government the right to declare that a particular area is 'disturbed' (in Schmittian terms, to declare it 'exceptional'). The declaration is not subject to judicial review, but the act effectively gives impunity to security forces to act as they see fit (HRW 2020).

But the Schmittian sovereign is not bound even by the very limited constraints of emergency regulations. The culture of exceptionalism extends even outside these limited legal frameworks. In Sri Lanka there is a long history of extrajudicial killings and disappearances, which was revived during the presidency of Mahinda Rajapaksa (DeVotta 2011). A series of notorious 'White Van' disappearances punctuated the war against the LTTE in 2006–2009 (Lewis 2020b). In Bangladesh, according to human rights defenders, between 2009 and 2018 at least 1,921 people became victims of extrajudicial killings and 109 were victims of enforced disappearances (Riaz, Chapter 18 of this volume). Indian policing demonstrates how easily the exception becomes the norm: critics argue that in everyday policing in India, poorer and marginalised social groups face police and security forces that suffer from an 'infamous record of systematic brutality, disappearances, systemic corruption and a chronic lack of investigative capacity' (Hansen 2019: 24). Extrajudicial killings have been commonplace historically, particularly in areas of conflict such as Assam and Kashmir. Police 'encounter' killings remain frequent against alleged criminals. In India's most populous state, Uttar Pradesh, police killed at least 119 suspects in such incidents in 2017–2020 (Mehta T. 2020). These extrajudicial killings are often celebrated by the public, rather than condemned, confirming Schmitt's instinct that the popular will always prefers a sovereign decision on justice rather than endless, liberal procedural wrangling in a flawed and corrupted court system. Schmittian decisionism becomes alluring to the populace when the alternative is a radical dispersal of power and authority in such a way that institutions become ineffectual.

Rule of law

An obvious corollary of the idea of sovereign power is that it excludes the possibility of the supremacy of law. Schmitt's understanding of law is diametrically opposed to the liberal concept of a rule of law, in which the judiciary stands aside and above the political fray. 'All law', argues Schmitt, 'is situational law': the law must be rooted in the concrete order, the cultural and political realities of the time, and not rely on universal norms promoted without regard to the political context. Schmitt rejects the idea of a positivist legality based on 'free-floating' norms: instead, '[l]ike every other order, the legal order rests on a decision and not on a norm' (Schmitt 1985a: 10). Schmitt opposes any idea that courts could be decision-making subjects in political affairs – for example, through processes of judicial review – because that line of reasoning produces an 'ersatz sovereign' which destabilises the political order (Meierhenrich and Simons 2016: 30). Schmitt contrasts what he views as the weak liberal idea of legality with political legitimacy. The danger, according to Schmitt, is that legality undermines the legitimacy of a sovereign leader, which is derived from the 'people's plebiscitarian will' (Schmitt 2004: 9). Ultimately, it is not for the judiciary to resolve or decide major political questions – these are the preserve of the sovereign. A normal, functioning judiciary must exist, but it cannot act as a counterbalance or constraint on sovereign power.

This assertion of political legitimacy over legality echoes across contemporary South Asian politics, where political leaders have often worked to undermine an already fragile independence of the judiciary. In Sri Lanka the impeachment of the Chief Justice Shirani Bandaranayake in 2013 was an important indicator of an illiberal turn in Sri Lankan democracy and interpreted at the time as 'the latest step in the gradual but systematic dismantling of the rule of law' (Crisis Group 2013). In Bangladesh in 2017 the Chief Justice of the Supreme Court retired and left the country, but he later claimed that he had been forced out after several rulings he had made against the government. The Awami League launched a campaign of politically motivated prosecutions against opposition leader Khaleda Zia and many of her associates: in 2018 she was sentenced to 17 years in prison. In India, human rights defenders accused the government of using the law for political ends. Human Rights Watch claimed that the government 'increasingly harassed, arrested, and prosecuted rights defenders, activists, journalists, students, academics, and others critical of the government or its policies' (HRW 2021). The government's critics claimed that the Indian Supreme Court no longer acted as an effective check on executive power. A.P. Shah, a former chief justice of the Delhi high court, warned of the decline of the Supreme Court as part of 'a larger, deliberately-crafted strategy on the part of the executive to seize control of the arms of the state, in ways that would benefit its own political agenda' (Shah 2020). This pattern of assaults on the rule of law across the region reflects the ascendancy of a generation of political leaders who view the judiciary not as an important mechanism of constraint on the executive, but as an obstacle to sovereign decision-making and a potential instrument of political power against their opponents.

Friend/Enemy

Schmitt makes a critical distinction between 'politics' – the everyday competition among parties and political leaders, which Schmitt treats with disdain – and 'the political', the foundational distinction between 'friend' and 'enemy' that in Schmitt's view defines the political community. In Schmitt's well-known aphorism: 'The specific political distinction to which political actions and motives can be reduced is that between friend and enemy' (Schmitt 2007a: 26). This apparently simple idea has far-reaching consequences. It defines the political community not on the basis of citizenship, or even ethnicity or nationality, but on something more elusive – a collective decision to define the enemy. This constructs an external boundary to the community that marks a constitutive dividing line between friend and enemy.

But the politics of enmity not only defines an external boundary to the community. It also effectively delegitimises pluralism within the community. Schmitt firmly rejects any suggestion that 'within one and the same political entity, instead of the decisive friend-and-enemy grouping, a pluralism could take its place without destroying the entity and the political itself' (Schmitt 2007: 45). The people must be united in their identification of the enemy, but it is inevitable that the search for an external enemy also identifies internal enemies. Schmitt's own bitter personal biography, haunted by his role in the rise of anti-Semitism in Nazi Germany, should be sufficient warning about the potential consequences of a politics defined by the friend/enemy distinction. The 'political enemy' is 'the other, the stranger; […] he is, in a specially intense way, existentially something different and alien, so that in the extreme case conflicts with him are possible' (Schmitt 2007: 27). But this leaves the identity of the enemy open to multiple interpretations and leaves the definition of the boundary line of the community (them/us) as open to contestation. The enemy can be anybody – a religious or sexual minority, a political party, a religious sect, a group of migrants or foreigners. It is the enmity line itself – not the identity of the enemy – that becomes politically relevant.

Across South Asia, attempts to forge identity through the identification of the enemy are not new. Indeed, many patterns in the modern politics of South Asia can be traced to an original, foundational division – the 1947 Partition between India and Pakistan. That dividing line continues to shape regional geopolitics and political identity in both countries. Nevertheless, across the region a process of contemporary autocratization has also been accompanied by an intensifying trend towards the construction of political communities through difference – the constant drawing of dividing lines between friend and enemy, between Sinhala and Tamil, Buddhist and Muslim, Hindu and Muslim, Indian and Pakistani. These historical cleavages have been compounded further by new divisions in society, evident in the campaigns against Pakistan's 'Aurat Azadi March' (Women's Freedom March), for example, or Islamist views of atheists and urban women in Bangladesh, which to varying degrees have been accommodated by national governments. The intensity of these campaigns to define enemies and to draw boundaries within and around communities surely reflects much wider anxieties about identity in an era of global change, in communities disrupted by mobility, economic upheavals and powerful new social trends. Schmitt understood only too well how defining the enemy could act as a powerful driver of identity formation. In his own phrase: 'Tell me who your enemy is and I will tell you who you are' (Schmitt 1991: 243).

The friend/enemy distinction is primarily invoked through discourse, but in India critics of the BJP government view new legislation as contributing to this divisive agenda. The 2019 Citizenship (Amendment) Act in India appears to be just such a boundary-producing mechanism, accelerating citizenship – membership of the political community – for non-Muslim immigrants from neighbouring states. Critics claim that the planned creation of a National Population Register (NPR) risks stripping citizenship from Muslims who do not have the required documentation (Basu, Chapter 3 of this volume). These legislative innovations were preceded by a sharp rise in sectarian violence, in which pro-BJP vigilante groups were given considerable leeway to threaten and attack Muslim citizens, mobilised by cow protection campaigns and other cultural issues (Ding and Slater 2021). In September 2019 the government imposed a lockdown in Kashmir and revoked the constitutional right of Kashmir to political autonomy. In so doing the government further evoked Kashmiri Muslims as a kind of representative other: Mrido Rai argues that 'Kashmiri Muslims are made to serve as contrapuntal symbols—of terrorist violence, illegitimate religious impulses, sedition—for contriving a mythical Hindu nation' (Rai 2019: 259).

Schmitt's search for the enemy always has this counterpoint: the construction of the united, homogeneous nation, a community defined by lines of difference. The image of this whole nation often refers back to an imagined, lost past. Anustup Basu argues that Hindu nationalism seeks a period of lost unity – an 'idealisation of the nation as a singular Samaj (society)', which 'takes the shape of an organismic Varna harmony rather than a contractual social order' (Basu 2020: 48). Hindu nationalists conjure up an idea of a 'spectral country in-essence', an imagined pure nation, which must 'be "taken back" from time to time, in extreme cases, from minorities, the bureaucratic government, or the legal and constitutional order itself' (Basu 2020: 13–14).

In the Sri Lankan context, David Rampton points to the ever-present frontier articulated in Sinhala nationalist discourse between the imagined nation and its external enemies. While the identity of enemies may change, the frontier 'remains a key element in fuelling a nationalist desire for [...] the reinvigoration of the lost glory of Buddhist kingdoms; of the ancient past through the reunification of the island as a Sinhala Buddhist state and society' (Rampton 2012: 379). There is little room for minorities to define their own identity within this anti-pluralist vision of unity. In a speech by President Rajapaksa in 2009, he claimed that 'We have removed the word minorities from our vocabulary. ... No longer are there Tamils, Muslims, Burghers, Malays and any other minorities'. Instead, claimed Rajapaksa, there were only two groups in the country: one was the 'people that love this country'; the other comprised people 'that have no love for the land of their birth' (Rajapaksa 2009). In articulating such a dividing line, political leaders seek to construct a new, united political community. But what emerges is not a new, inclusive unity, but a majoritarian polity, informed by the politics and culture of the majority group and too often characterised by violence against minorities. In the Sri Lankan case, after the war against the LTTE came to an end, there was an increase in violent attacks on the minority Muslim community (Mihlar 2019).

Democracy

Ding and Slater make the important point that indicators of autocratization do not all trend in the same direction. They point to a 'gap that has emerged between two core features of democracy: elections and rights' (Ding and Slater 2021: 65). Varieties of Democracy data demonstrates that 'electoral quality widely advanced on a global scale over the decade from 2007 to 2017, while rights and freedoms for individual citizens generally receded' (Ding and Slater 2021: 68). They identify cases in South Asia – notably India and Sri Lanka – as representative of this global trend. Ding and Slater use an institutionalist approach to interpret the divergent paths of electoral and rights institutions in a pattern which they term 'democratic decoupling', where 'a decline in rights may coexist with elections of consistent or even improving quality' (Ding and Slater 2021: 67). But much can also be learnt by applying Schmitt's theoretical approach to understand the potential tension between liberal rights and democratic elections.

Schmitt argued that the combination of liberalism with democracy was a fatal oxymoron: not merely a 'structural tension' as Ding and Slater phrase it, but an unsustainable contradiction that always threatens to undermine the political order. Schmitt, versed in the shortcomings of the Weimar republic, was highly critical of parliamentary democracy, of any attempts to mediate the popular will through representative institutions and constitutional norms. Schmitt complains that 'modern mass democracy rests on the confused combination of both [liberalism and democracy]' (Schmitt 1985b: 13). His aim is to split apart 'democracy' and 'parliamentarism', and to recover a version of democracy in which the popular will is no longer constrained by liberal norms, the rule of law and mediating institutions, but is united in its acclamation of support for a sovereign leader. In short, he argues that 'democracy can exist without what one today calls parliamentarism and parliamentarism without democracy; and dictatorship is just as little the definitive antithesis of democracy as democracy is of dictatorship' (Schmitt 1985b: 32).

This attempt to pull apart liberalism and democracy is at the heart of the majoritarian politics of autocratization in South Asia, in which elections have often enabled rather than constrained democratic regression. Despite the pressure on liberal norms and civil rights, the BJP further increased its parliamentary majority at the May 2019 election and Prime Minister Modi enjoyed high approval ratings of 74% in January 2021 – only 8% of those polled considered that he had done a bad job as prime minister (India Today 2021). In Sri Lanka, Gotabaya Rajapaksa enjoyed an easy victory at the polls in November 2019, winning 52% of the votes cast to his opponent's 41%, and garnering big majorities in the Sinhala heartland. In Bangladesh the opposition boycott of the 2014 election led to complete domination of the parliament by the Awami League (AL). In Pakistan Imran Khan's victory at the polls in July 2018 also represented a populist shift in the Pakistan establishment's search for support among a new, aspirant middle class (Akhtar 2021). Majoritarian democracy now represents the default political logic across South Asia.

Hansen explores how the political idea of representing majorities, as opposed to political parties that gained votes across different constituencies, became increasingly dominant in India after the 1990s. This was not merely electoral calculation, but something deeper, in which 'The notion of majority itself—*bahumat*—began to acquire a stronger affective and moral force' (Hansen 2019: 30). The emergence of majoritarianism in India has specific roots in post-colonial, linguistic and regional politics, but it also reflected a global trend, in which populist and authoritarian leaders frequently invoked the idea of a natural conservative majority stifled by the minority views of liberal elites (Lewis 2020a: 93–99). Liberalism, argued conservative thinkers, is not designed to represent the majority but to contain it. Schmitt's authoritarianism, by contrast, claims to liberate the voice of the majority in support of the sovereign leader and in denunciation of their enemies. Similar thinking is often evident in Sri Lanka, where Sinhala nationalists prioritised the democratic process as part of a wider legitimation strategy for a majoritarian politics and viewed democracy as a mechanism by which the voice of the Sinhala majority – too often stifled historically by minority groups or foreign powers – could finally be heard (Lewis 2020b).

While Schmittian authoritarianism claims to offer a way for the popular will to be articulated, Schmitt is also candid about how that popular will might be shaped and manipulated. On the one hand, Schmitt expects the state to reflect and channel some kind of submerged popular understanding about a people's place in the world. But at the same time, Schmitt is also clear that everything depends on 'who has control over the means with which the will of the people is to be constructed: military and political force, propaganda, control of public opinion through the press, party organisations, assemblies, popular education, and schools' (Schmitt 1985b: 29). Schmitt's thinking is summarised by the contradictory thought that 'only political power, which should come from the people's will, can form the people's will in the first place' (Schmitt 1985b: 29). Hansen echoes this thinking in his argument that 'the mightiest socio-political force in India today is neither the state nor the law but deeply embedded vernacular ideas of popular sovereignty', in which the category of 'the people' is not pre-given but 'needs to be continuously filled and performed in order to remain potent' (Hansen 2019: 35). In other words, governments and their allies must work hard to police discourse and undermine alternative views through new forms of censorship and control over freedom of speech. Autocratization in South Asian politics is most evident in the growing crackdown on dissent across the region, even in countries such as India, where freedom of speech and plurality of opinion have a long tradition. At the same time, governments work hard to develop and maintain a 'hegemonic discourse' – circulating ideas, tropes and narratives in society to promote the ruling elite's values and norms and to legitimise their hold on power (Lewis 2016).

Conclusion

Autocratization in South Asia is not divorced from global trends. Its specific contextual framework does little to disguise an underlying set of principles that reflects a wider, global backlash against liberalism. The democratic recession in the region is not simply the consequence of domestic institutional weaknesses or the decline of Western power, but reflects a global ideological challenge to the dominant norms and ideas of post-Cold War liberalism. The work of the anti-liberal thinker Carl Schmitt helps to interpret these trends and locate them in a coherent, ideological framework. Schmitt's authoritarian state is an abstracted, ideal type, and the reality of present-day autocratization is a messy reflection of his vision. South Asian states contain pluralistic societies which continue to contest many aspects of the current wave of autocratization. Yet states in the region are also experiencing profound challenges to liberal democracy that Schmitt would have recognised: the affective allure of majoritarian politics; the simplicity of a world divided into friends and enemies; the appeal of the leader who can cut through bureaucracy and special interests to make a decision. These are all powerful ideas that have remarkable emotional reach in a complex and threatening world. They reflect new ideological forces that are driving South Asia's autocratization and to which liberals in the region have yet to find a convincing answer.

Bibliography

Akhtar, Aasim Sajjad (2021) 'The war of terror in praetorian Pakistan: The emergence and struggle of the Pashtun Tahaffuz movement', *Journal of Contemporary Asia*, 51(3): 516–529.

Basu, Anustup (2020) *Hindutva as political monotheism* (Duke University Press).

Bermeo, Nancy (2015) 'On democratic backsliding', *Journal of Democracy*, 27(1), pp. 5–19.

Bettiza, Gregorio, and David Lewis (2020) 'Authoritarian powers and norm contestation in the liberal international order: Theorizing the power politics of ideas and identity', *Journal of Global Security Studies*, 5(4), pp. 559–577.

Coomaraswamy, R. and C. de Los Reyes (2004) 'Rule by emergency: Sri Lanka's postcolonial constitutional experience', *International Journal of Constitutional Law*, 2(2), pp. 272–295.

Crisis Group (2013) 'Impeachment of the Sri Lankan Chief Justice', *International Crisis Group*, 13 January 2013. Available at: www.crisisgroup.org/asia/south-asia/sri-lanka/impeachment-sri-lankan-chief-justice

Croissant, Aurel and Jeffrey Haynes (2021) 'Democratic regression in Asia: introduction', *Democratization*, 28(1), pp. 1–21.

DeVotta, Neil (2011) 'Sri Lanka: From turmoil to dynasty', *Journal of Democracy*, 22(2), pp. 130–144.

Diamond, Larry (2021) 'Democratic regression in comparative perspective: scope, methods, and causes', *Democratization*, 28(1), pp. 22–24.

Ding, Iza and Dan Slater (2021) 'Democratic decoupling', *Democratization*, 28(1), pp. 63–80.

Hansen, Thomas Blom (2019) 'Democracy against the law: reflections on India's illiberal democracy', in A. P. Chatterji, T. B. Hansen, and C. Jaffrelot (eds.) *Majoritarian state: How Hindu nationalism is changing India* (Oxford: Oxford University Press), pp. 19–40.

HRW (2020) 'India: New reports of extrajudicial killings in Kashmir', Human Rights Watch. 14 August 2020. Available at: www.hrw.org/news/2020/08/14/india-new-reports-extrajudicial-killings-kashmir

HRW (2021) 'World Report 2021 – India', Human Rights Watch. Available at: www.hrw.org/world-report/2021/country-chapters/india

India Today (2021) 'Mood of the Nation', India Today, January. Available at: www.indiatoday.in/mood-of-the-nation-survey-2021 (accessed 6 May 2021).

Kendall-Taylor, Andrea, Erica Frantz, and Joseph Wright (2017) 'The global rise of personalized politics: It's not just dictators anymore', *The Washington Quarterly*, 40(1), pp. 7–19.

Lewis, David (2016) 'Blogging Zhanaozen: hegemonic discourse and authoritarian resilience in Kazakhstan', *Central Asian Survey*, 35(3), pp. 421–438.

Lewis, David G. (2020a) *Russia's new authoritarianism: Putin and the politics of order* (Edinburgh: Edinburgh University Press).

Lewis, David G. (2020b) 'Sri Lanka's Schmittian peace: sovereignty, enmity and illiberal order', *Conflict, Security and Development*, 20(1), pp. 15–37.

Libin, Xie, and Haig Patapan (2020) 'Schmitt fever: The use and abuse of Carl Schmitt in contemporary China', *International Journal of Constitutional Law*, 18(1), pp. 130–146.

McCormick, J. (1998) 'Review: political theory and political theology – the second wave of Carl Schmitt', *Political Theory*, 26(6), pp. 830–854.

Mehring, R. (2014) *Carl Schmitt: A biography* (trans. by D. Steuer, Cambridge: Polity).

Mehta, P. B. (2020) 'Betrayal of procedure in Parliament is not just about technicalities. Deference to process builds trust', *The Indian Express*, 22 September. Available at: https://indianexpress.com/article/opinion/columns/parliament-monsoon-session-farm-bills-modi-govt-railroading-the-bill-6605281/

Mehta, T. (2020) 'Vikas Dubey and the problem of "encounter killings" in India', *The Diplomat*, 17 July. Available at: https://thediplomat.com/2020/07/vikas-dubey-and-the-problem-of-encounter-killings-in-india/

Meierhenrich, J. and O. Simons (2016) 'A fanatic of order in an epoch of confusing turmoil', in J. Meierhenrich and O. Simons (eds.) *The Oxford Handbook of Carl Schmitt* (Oxford: Oxford University Press), pp. 3–70.

Mihlar, Farah (2019) 'Religious change in a minority context: transforming Islam in Sri Lanka', *Third World Quarterly*, 40(12), 2153–2169.

Müller, Jan-Werner (2003) *A dangerous mind: Carl Schmitt in post-war European thought* (New Haven: Yale University Press).

Rai, Mridu (2019) 'Kashmiris in the Hindu Rashtra', in A. P. Chatterji, T. B. Hansen, and C. Jaffrelot (eds.) *Majoritarian state: How Hindu nationalism is changing India* (Oxford: Oxford University Press), pp. 259–280.

Rampton, D. (2012) 'A game of mirrors: Constitutionalism and exceptionalism in a context of nationalist hegemony', in A. Welikala (ed.) *The Sri Lanka Republic at 40: Reflections on constitutional history, theory, and practice* (Centre for Policy Alternatives, Colombo), pp. 364–401.

Rajapaksa, M. (2009) 'President Rajapaksa's Speech to Parliament on the Defeat of the LTTE, 19 May 2009. Available at: http://old.satp.org/satporgtp/countries/shrilanka/document/papers/president_speech_parliament_defeatofLTTE.htm (accessed 1 May 2021).

Riaz, Ali (2021). 'The pathway of democratic backsliding in Bangladesh', *Democratization*, 28(1), pp. 179–197.

Schmitt, C. (1985a [1934]) *Political theology: Four chapters on the concept of sovereignty* (trans. by G. Schwab, Cambridge, MA: MIT Press).

Schmitt, C. (1985b [1926]) *The crisis of parliamentary democracy* (trans. by E. Kennedy, Cambridge, MA: MIT Press).

Schmitt, C. (1991) *Glossarium: Aufzeichnungen der Jahre 1947–1951* (ed. by Eberhard Freiherr von Medem) (Berlin: Duncker and Humblot).

Schmitt, C. (2004 [1932]) *Legality and legitimacy* (Durham, NC: Duke University Press).

Schmitt, C. (2007) *Concept of the political* (Chicago: University of Chicago Press).

Shah, A. P. (2020) 'The only institution capable of stopping the death of democracy is aiding it', *The Wire*, 18 September. Available at: https://thewire.in/law/supreme-court-rights-uapa-bjp-nda-master-of-roster (accessed 6 May 2021).

Zheng, Q. (2015) *Carl Schmitt, Mao Zedong and the politics of transition* (Basingstoke: Palgrave Macmillan).

INDEX